TO PROTECT
THEIR INTERESTS

TO PROTECT
THEIR INTERESTS

*The Invention and Exploitation
of Corporate Bankruptcy*

STEPHEN J. LUBBEN

Columbia University Press
New York

Columbia University Press
Publishers Since 1893
New York   Chichester, West Sussex
cup.columbia.edu

Library of Congress Cataloging-in-Publication Data
Names: Lubben, Stephen J., 1971– author
Title: To protect their interests : the invention and exploitation
    of corporate bankruptcy / Stephen J. Lubben.
Description: New York : Columbia University Press, [2026] |
    Includes bibliographical references and index.
Identifiers: LCCN 2025027212 | ISBN 9780231213103 hardback |
    ISBN 9780231213110 trade paperback | ISBN 9780231559720 ebook
Subjects: LCSH: Bankruptcy—United States | Bankruptcy—History—
    United States | Business failures—United States | Corporate reorganizations—
    United States
Classification: LCC HG3761 .L83 2026 | DDC 332.7/5—dc23/eng/20250819
LC record available at https://lccn.loc.gov/2025027212

Printed in the United States of America

Cover design: Noah Arlow
Cover image: Shutterstock (train)

GPSR Authorized Representative: Easy Access System Europe, Mustamäe tee 50,
10621 Tallinn, Estonia, gpsr.requests@easproject.com

CONTENTS

Introduction   1

PART I. FOUNDATIONS

1. The Early Days of Corporate Reorganization and Texas Railroads   13

2. Jay Gould and the Texas and Pacific   47

3. The Start of Corporate Bankruptcy   73

PART II. REFINEMENTS

4. The Bankers Take Charge   111

5. The Statutes Arrive   139

6. The End of an Era   176

PART III. MODERNIZATION?

7. The Deregulation of Corporate Bankruptcy   209

8. The Always Evolving Chapter 11   227

PART IV. REFORM?

9. Modern Chapter 11 and the Ghosts of the Past   243

10. Chapter 11 Going Forward   261

Acknowledgments   273
Notes   275
Bibliography   353
Index   385

TO PROTECT
THEIR INTERESTS

INTRODUCTION

Reorganization, in its fundamental aspects, involves the thankless task of determining who should bear losses incurred by an unsuccessful business and how the assets of the estate should be apportioned among creditors and stockholders.

—Securities and Exchange Commission, 1977

This is a book about corporate bankruptcy. In particular, it is a historical account about how we developed the American corporate bankruptcy system that we have today. In the early days, all bankruptcy was business bankruptcy because bankruptcy was limited to "merchants," however defined.[1] But corporate bankruptcy (or "restructuring," or "reorganization") did not develop until corporations became widespread, outside of specific public projects: certainly no sooner than the 1840s.

The book is motivated by my prior glancing blows with business bankruptcy history. They revealed enough to make it clear that corporate reorganization did not begin with J. P. Morgan—despite the conventional wisdom to the contrary. Moreover, the parts of the story between J. P. Morgan in the 1890s and the enactment of the current Bankruptcy Code in 1978 always seemed to be told at high speed, with only a passing mention of the New Deal. While that approach draws out the connections between the 1890s and today—most evident regarding modern chapter 11—it assumes a strong, linear relationship that may not hold up to more thorough scrutiny. That is, there may not be a direct line between J. P. Morgan and leading modern bankruptcy attorneys like Harvey Miller or Corinne Ball.[2]

This book differs from previous corporate bankruptcy histories in two key respects. First, I place the "founding" of corporate bankruptcy at least a decade earlier than most prior authors. That is, rather than start with the "Morganizations" of the 1890s, I look to the work of Jay Gould in the 1880s. Particularly, as explained in early chapters of this book, I view the Texas and Pacific's 1885 receivership as a moment when several already-extant techniques came together to be used in the successful reorganization of a large railroad. This is less a genesis moment than simply a clear point of unity, in a context with economic significance. Gould did not invent any new reorganization tools in 1885—he simply used existing tools in a coherent way in the case of a large railroad (the Texas and Pacific) for the first time.

Second, the book spends limited time talking about legislation. Instead, I tell the story of the early development of corporate bankruptcy through the stories of key cases. Even when we get to more modern times, while I certainly note the changeover to statutes, my focus is on what actually happened in reorganization cases. In large part, this reflects my view that participants in the corporate bankruptcy system tend to adapt whatever statute might be available to fit their needs—regardless of what the drafters of that statute might have intended. Thus, I ultimately conclude that modern chapter 11 reflects much more Jay Gould than anything else that the 1978 drafters might have intended.

This is not to say that the controlling actors can do whatever they want when it comes to corporate bankruptcy. Rather, my argument is that "insiders"—those with sway over the corporate bankruptcy process—will flex a statute to meet their ends. When they are unable to do so—chapter X of the Chandler Act, which I discuss in connection with W. T. Grant in chapter 6, might be an example—these same insiders will simply avoid the specific corporate bankruptcy process in favor of something else whenever possible.

My thesis is that big corporate bankruptcy has been, since its inception, a flexible system that is dominated by large players focused on controlling debtor-corporations. Smaller actors, be they shareholders, employees, or creditors, are simply observers. Whether that is good or bad depends on the specific context, and often the specific interest of the outsider that we are considering. For example, in the nineteenth century, small trade creditors or nonemployee tort claimants were often treated pretty well, and indeed frequently were paid in full. Small shareholders, small bondholders, and employees with personal injury claims, on the other hand, frequently went unpaid.

Moreover, I argue that any corporate bankruptcy system involves trade-offs, always creating winners and losers. The current system might be better than

To the Honorable, the Judges of the United States
Circuit Court, in and for the Fifth Circuit and Eastern
District of Louisiana.

The Missouri Pacific Railway Company, a body corporate
under the laws of the State of Missouri, and a citizen and
resident of said State,- in its behalf, as well as of all
other corporations and persons similarly situated that
by intervention, bring themselves into this suit for
protection of their interests,- brings into this Honorable
Court its bill of complaint against The Texas and Pacific
Railway Company, a corporation existing under the laws of
citizenship and domicil the United States of America, and having properties and
rights in the States of Louisiana and Texas, under and by
virtue of the laws of both of said States, and having at
citizenship and domicil the same time offices and places of business in this District, and officers and agents herein, in the City of
New Orleans, on whom process may be served.

And thereupon your orator complains and says:

1. That the Congress of the United States of America,
by an act approved March the 3rd, 1871, created a corporation
under the name and style of The Texas and Pacific Railroad
Company and by an act approved the 2nd day of May, 1872,
supplementary to the said original act, changed the style
and title of the said The Texas and Pacific Railroad Company
to "The Texas and Pacific Railway Company;" and by said
acts, The Texas and Pacific Railway Company was authorized
and empowered to construct a line of railway from a point
at or near the eastern boundary line of the State of Texas,

1.1 The first page of the Texas and Pacific receivership petition, from the National Archives.
The document is dated December 15, 1885.

Missouri Pacific Railway Company v. the Texas and Pacific Railway Company, Box 683.

any alternative, but it is time to move away from the "everyone wins" stories that have dominated corporate bankruptcy policy discussions since at least the 1980s, if not earlier.

I also use this book to push against another Reagan Age chestnut: the confidence that regulatory systems work better when they solely rely on markets, rather than government, to address concerns. The current Bankruptcy Code, enacted in 1978, is steeped in this mentality. And certainly, the New Deal corporate bankruptcy system that it replaced sometimes did not work very well. But did the Bankruptcy Code, and its chapter 11, go too far in the deregulatory direction? That is, did the rush to trash the New Dealer's inelegant solutions reopen the door to the real problems that they had identified? I suggest that the answer is "yes."

• • •

But why is corporate bankruptcy important? Almost forty years ago, Elizabeth Warren (later to become a US senator) famously wrote that business bankruptcy is "an attempt to reckon with a debtor's multiple defaults and to distribute the consequences among a number of different actors. Bankruptcy encompasses a number of competing—and sometimes conflicting—values in this distribution . . . no one value dominates, so that bankruptcy policy becomes a composite of factors that bear on a better answer to the question, 'How shall the losses be distributed?'"[3] One easy solution might be to sell all of the debtor-company's stuff and divide the proceeds among the parties. This is commonly referred to as "liquidation of the debtor"; in modern times, it is conducted under chapter 7 of the 1978 Bankruptcy Code.[4]

Liquidation works reasonably well for whichever party is "first," however defined. If I have a $50 claim against a company and the right to get paid first, I am largely indifferent as to whether the sale of the company's stuff generates $100 or $100,000. If I am instead fourth to be paid, after three other $50 claims, I might care very much.

Liquidation remains a background option, but as we will see in this book, for more than 175 years it has been thought that there might be a better way. The resulting corporate bankruptcy—or corporate restructuring or corporate reorganization (in the United States, these terms are used interchangeably)— systems thus reflect our values, as Warren describes. To be sure, the liquidation priorities are not themselves the product of some sort of prelegal, free-market Eden; they reflect value judgments as well.

As discussed in this book, the real question is who should get to decide that there should be a deviation from the standard set of liquidation rules that applies to any situation where somebody (real or corporate) has run out of money. Corporate bankruptcy has long rejected the notion that paying the "first" creditor in full and quickly should be the predominate value, which is inherent in the rules of liquidation. While such liquidation rules prevailed in the early days, when businesses were comprised of individual owners or small partnerships, the senior creditors' interests have always given way in any of the systems that developed to address more complicated enterprises.

Since at least 1850 or so, the assumption has always been that keeping the debtor-company together—in some form—will be better than pulling the debtor apart in a liquidation.[5] Reorganization of the company in something like its current form preserves what is often called the "going concern" value of the debtor-company, which we might define as "the difference between the value of the company if it is sold and the proceeds distributed and the value if it is restructured and continues to trade."[6] That is, the increment of value between keeping the company going and liquidation is assumed to be something worth saving (when it exists).

Consistent with this assumption, the federal government has supported restructuring efforts through the court system and, starting in the Great Depression, statutory law and governmental participation.[7] *Whom* reorganization is better for is one key question that is threaded throughout this book, as is the closely related question of who gets to reallocate the extra value created by keeping the firm alive.

• • •

At this point, it might be useful to take a step back and consider how larger businesses are different from smaller businesses, and why it might make sense to have different bankruptcy rules for larger businesses. Indeed, the history told in this book is that of big business bankruptcy—we mention smaller businesses only when their history becomes hopelessly entangled with larger corporate debtors.

If I open a small ice cream shop, I have two basic choices about how to fund that business. I can put my own money into it or I could borrow money from somebody. In the first case, I have no obligation to pay back the money (to myself), but I might not have enough money now to both set up the business and pay for my other life expenses. So instead, I borrow the money, with a promise to pay it back out of the ice cream shop's future earnings.

If the ice cream shop is a bust—nobody likes the flavors that I like—the creditor who loaned me the money, be it a bank or a friend, gets paid back before I pay myself, and if I can't pay the creditor back, I file personal bankruptcy. The normal rules of liquidation work well. Nobody much misses my ice cream shop when it's gone.

Forming a business as a corporation opens the possibility of the business lasting long beyond its founder—just as Apple continues to thrive even after the death of Steve Jobs. Another attraction of the corporate form is that it facilitates investment by people who may not understand the details of the business but who are willing to risk comparatively small sums in exchange for potential high returns.[8] A corporation—as opposed to a partnership or a sole proprietorship—is responsible for its own debts, and investors are not.

A corporation is treated as a person under the law, even though it is quite inanimate—it is much more like a rock or a doorknob than a "person" in the normal sense of the word.[9] If this corporate person wants to put its own money into an ice cream business, it first has to get that money from somewhere. Unlike people, corporations do not get side jobs.

Starting in the early 1800s, that first slug of money put into a corporation was referred to as the company's "capital stock." That capital stock was divided into shares, which reflected the proportion of the total sum that each investor put in. These shares do not represent an entitlement to withdraw the specific money put in; rather, they give the holder a proportionate say in the running of the business, as well as a similar proportionate right to any extra money that the business might generate. When the business is ongoing, distributions of extra money are called "dividends," but we might also see a final dividend distribution to the holders of shares (or shareholders) upon a liquidation.[10]

In the early days of American corporations, each share of stock typically had a "par," or face value, of $100. Thus, a corporation with 1,000 shares outstanding was understood to have a capital stock of $100,000. That is, it was implied that the buyers of the shares had put at least that much into the company, which was not always true.[11]

Complaints about "watered stock" arose from a gap between the implied capitalization of a company and its actual funding. If a company with 1,000 shares received $10 per share when it sold its common stock, it would be said to have $90 per share of "water." In modern times, par value is set wherever a company wants to set it (often quite low). For example, Apple common shares have a par value of $0.00001 per share. In such a world, watered stock is rarely an issue.

Today, we tend to use the terms "stock" and "shares" interchangeably to represent bits of ownership in a corporation. Calling it "ownership" is a bit disingenuous, though, because ownership normally implies some control or dominion, whereas the holder of 100 shares in Apple has a minuscule fractional financial interest in the capital stock—or simply, the "capital" or "equity"—of a very, very large corporation chartered under the laws of California. The ability to exercise any control is quite attenuated. Rather than ownership, we might think of shares as representing rights in a collective enterprise. If you own enough of those rights, it begins to look like ownership, but unless you are Jay Gould or Elon Musk, most holders never approach that level of shareholding.

So one way that a corporation might start an ice cream business is by using the money it received from its shareholders. This has the advantage of flexibility: There is no specific promise to pay back the shareholders any specific amount, at any specific time. That is, for at least the past few centuries, the rule has been that shareholders provide permanent capital.[12]

But what if the shareholders have not put in enough money? Perhaps it will cost the corporation $1 million to get the ice cream business up and running, but the shareholders have put in only $100,000. Then the corporation could sell more shares.

But because a corporation is inanimate, it is a sock puppet to the whims of 51 percent of the shareholders. What if the existing shareholders do not want to dilute their current stake in the company, but they also do not want to (or simply cannot) put in more money?

The corporation might borrow the money. There are two main ways that companies can borrow money: from banks or by selling bonds on the bond market. A bank loan to a large corporation is often split among multiple banks in a syndication. A syndicated loan may have dozens or as many as two hundred lenders in a single transaction.

A corporate bond represents borrowing from individuals and other investors in $1,000 increments. Each bond represents $1,000 loaned, typically at a fixed interest rate. The interest payments are often referred to as "coupons" because in the old days, a bondholder actually had to detach and send in a paper coupon to get the interest payment. An example appears as figure 4.2 of this book.

So a 5 percent fixed-rate coupon will pay $50 per bond annually ($1,000 × 5%). Normally, the interest is paid semiannually, so the bondholder in this example would receive $25 every six months. The bond is a twin promise to repay $1,000 at some point in the future, with interest paid along the way, but the value of those paired promises might rise or fall over the life of the bond.

For example, in 1888 the Texas and Pacific Railroad promised to pay bondholders 5 percent until their bonds matured in the year 2000. Over the more than one hundred years that these bonds were supposed to be outstanding, that 5 percent interest rate might have looked more or less attractive, depending on market interest rates and the likelihood of actually receiving the coupon payments or the $1,000 back. As a result, the bond's price would have fluctuated above and below its par or face amount.

In the bond market, bond prices are quoted in terms of 100, which can be viewed as a percent of the bond's face value.[13] For example, if a bond is quoted at 95 in the market, the price is $950 for every $1,000 of face value and the bond is said to be trading at a "discount to par." If the bond is trading at 105, it costs $1,050 for every $1,000 of face value and the bond is trading "at a premium."

Lenders, be they a bondholder or a bank, might obtain a security interest in the form of a mortgage or a lien on some of or all the issuing company's property. By putting a lien on an asset, the lender gets the right to receive a priority distribution equal to the proceeds of the sale of that asset, to the exclusion of any other creditors.[14]

Large companies, like our ice cream firm, tend to issue a mix of stock and bonds—which we call the company's "capital structure"—over time, and the outcome is not always entirely coherent. For example, the ice cream company might have taken out a bank loan to build its first plant. Then it sold bonds to support the company generally. When it needed more money, maybe it sold secured bonds (which then jumped ahead of the existing bonds, but behind the bank loan with respect to the plant). When it wanted to build a new cone factory, maybe it put that new plant in a separate corporate box and had that company sell its own bonds.

At some point in time, our ice cream company finds that it has more debts than it can handle. Maybe the first round of bonds is coming due, and the company has no way to refinance them. And the cone plant is looking like a mistake because it turns out that the company could buy cones from another company (and slap the ice cream company's logo on them) for less than it costs to make its own cones.

On the other hand, liquidation might not make sense if the company has a popular product that consumers are eager to buy. The problem of complex capital and corporate structures is where corporate bankruptcy comes in. We need a tool to address these situations, but to recall Warren, that tool is going to determine who bears the costs of this company's past mistakes.

$\cdots$

Article I, section 8, of the US Constitution grants Congress the power to develop a uniform nationwide bankruptcy law.[15] Since 1978, the predominate corporate bankruptcy tool in the United States has been chapter 11 of the federal Bankruptcy Code. A debtor-company files a petition with a federal bankruptcy court, and all creditors are immediately stopped from collecting on their claims by an "automatic stay."[16] That includes unpaid bondholders, as well as tort claimants who might have been harmed by the company's products. In most cases, the debtor becomes a "debtor-in-possession"—a debtor that will keep possession and operational control of its assets in the ordinary course of business while continuing to manage the business, albeit supervised by the court during the proceedings. No receiver or trustee takes over for company management under modern chapter 11. Key parties negotiate a reorganization plan that becomes binding on everyone with a claim against the company, whether they vote for the plan or not.

Chapter 11 has become extremely economically important. The chapter 11 cases of Lehman Brothers, Washington Mutual, J. Crew, Sears, Enron, Owens Corning, Pan Am, General Motors, Chrysler, United Airlines, Texaco, Neiman Marcus, and Pacific Gas & Electric (twice) all attest to the central role of corporate bankruptcy in modern America.

The predominate explanation for corporate bankruptcy is that chapter 11 exists to promote the efficiency of the American economy. By providing an agreeable structure for addressing overindebted companies, chapter 11 reduces the finance costs of all companies. At its best, the common wisdom is to view chapter 11 as a government-provided framework for negotiation that protects the American economy from the failure of big firms. Chapter 11 is often painted as a kind of "win-win," in which everyone benefits from improved capital markets.

This understanding of business bankruptcy is also rooted in the prevailing history that designates J. Pierpont Morgan as the craftsman of the modern system, rehearsing that in the 1890s, the financier established the deal-based format that we still use today. The consensus view adopts Morgan's own framing of his firm's role as leading a noble effort to protect bondholders from the depravations of corporate insiders.[17] The acceptance of this account has the practical effect of dismissing the reform efforts of New Dealers, who moved to replace the nineteenth-century restructuring process with a new statute, while also legitimizing the current chapter 11 system (modeled on the nineteenth-century form), which features judicial deference to insider-negotiated deals.[18]

In this book, I instead argue that corporate restructuring has always been about buying consent from those who could stop you, and imposing your will on those who could not. That is, corporate bankruptcy is mostly about control. And while the New Dealers might have been misguided in their remedies, they correctly identified key problems with the roots of modern corporate restructuring that persist to this day. Only by understanding the history of corporate restructuring—stripped of the mythology of the magnanimous J. P. Morgan, putting down his cigar to rescue pitiful, oppressed English bondholders—can we understand the reasons for the defects of today's chapter 11, which recent commentators have deemed "lawless."[19]

Corporate restructuring indeed evolved from a lawless origin. It was designed by Jay Gould not as the efficient bondholder protection device of myth, but instead as a way for those in power to manipulate the legal system to retain power. Morgan embraced Gould's system and popularized it with good "spin." We see the same basic form at work in today's private equity-backed chapter 11 cases. Continuing to attribute the goals of chapter 11 to Morgan and his supposed good intentions represents little more than blind acceptance of his skillful public relations.

I thus offer a critical look at the DNA of a system of vital economic importance. This widely accepted story of corporate bankruptcy allows a sheen of "for the good of the people" to be applied to reorganization. In fact, the actual origin story exposes that it was developed as a way for power to maintain power. Only by acknowledging the true roots of the system can we understand its problems and how it might be fixed.

Too often, blind faith, an outgrowth of the Morgan myth, is weaponized to dispel criticism of the corporate bankruptcy system we have. When critical judgment raised against the current system is scorned as "populist," scholars and practitioners adopt a dangerous myopic stance. By understanding that today's embrace of "deals" has its roots in Gould's quest to retain control, we can see the need for more judicial skepticism about the deals that are presented to them—even those with marvelous ostensible support—and more understanding of what is really going on.

Indeed, one large policy question looming over the entire field is whether it makes sense to provide public support (through courts and the power of law) to maintain what amounts to a dueling ground. We may be largely indifferent to the question of "who wins" between Hedge Fund A and Private Equity Fund B, but why should taxpayers pay for the arena for such clashes? And who precisely gets hurt in these clashes? The historical approach that I adopt in this book helps make these questions—and their answers—plain.

PART I

FOUNDATIONS

CHAPTER 1

THE EARLY DAYS OF CORPORATE REORGANIZATION AND TEXAS RAILROADS

" . . . All we want is the success of the Texas Pacific and my uncle writes that Tom Scott is very confident, and working hard."

"But will he succeed?" Elvira asked.

"He has powerful enemies, but his cause is good. The construction of the Texas Pacific ought to be advocated by every honest man in the United States, for it is the thing that will help the exhausted South to get back its strength and vitality."

—María Amparo Ruiz de Burton, *The Squatter and the Don*

I n the United States after the Civil War (1861–1865), there were two distinct types of railroads. Railroads in the East provided a new form of transportation to existing customers who had previously been served by canals, plank roads, and turnpikes.[1] Railroads in the North connected communities to each other in a way that was less common in the South, where roads tended to run to ports, but in both cases, the roads largely had been established before the war.[2] Railroads in the far West, in contrast, mostly developed after the war and provided transportation through an area previously inhabited by people who were not always eager to become Americans.

As an initial matter, the Western transcontinental railroads were primarily designed to vault over the vast "uninhabited" area between the Mississippi or Missouri River regions and California.[3] And as a result, historian Richard White has argued that most of the North American transcontinentals were not actually necessary until at least the 1890s.[4] That is, they were built too soon, largely as a result of government subsidies.

As another historian has argued, in both Canada and the United States, the building of the

> trans-continental railways that would extend from coast to coast, constituted a major geopolitical reorientation in the western hemisphere. They consolidated two vast, land-based nations that were prodigiously endowed with agricultural potential and mineral resources, opening up the Midwest and the prairies to European markets, and increasing the American and British presence on the Pacific rim and the seas beyond. The American transcontinental railroad was completed in 1869 (and British Columbia only joined the Confederation on condition that an equivalent Canadian line would also be constructed); and in the same year, on the other side of the world, a similar geographical reorientation took place with the opening of the Suez Canal in Egypt, which dramatically shortened the sea route to India.[5]

Again, none of this was good news to those who long had inhabited the lands in question. But the consequences in all respects were substantial.

The South wanted its own transcontinental railroad line almost since the day there were railroads in this country.[6] Beyond the ordinary desires for economic development that accompanied all such continent-spanning plans, the South hoped to unite the Southern part of the United States in human slavery. The hope was that owning humans as property would be legal from Charleston to Santa Monica.[7] And indeed, early California, especially the southern half of the state, was heavily populated with what would later be called Confederate sympathizers.[8]

In 1857, Congress authorized the San Antonio & San Diego Mail (SA&SD) to develop an overland mail route to San Francisco.[9] The first SA&SD mail coach, departing from the company's offices in San Antonio in early July and pulled by a team of six mules, arrived in San Diego on August 31, 1857, launching the first transcontinental mail line.[10] From San Diego, mail could be taken by steamer or inland coach to San Francisco, the only important city on the American Pacific coast at the time. The South, and Texas in particular, wanted something more, and by the 1850s, the state legislature began handing out railroad charters with wild abandon.[11]

Two of those antebellum railroads are of interest to us. One was eventually given the grand name of the Southern Pacific Railroad Company, a designation that often confuses things, given both the subsequent, similarly named, but much better-known California railroad and the tendency of Southern pundits to use "Southern Pacific Railroad" as an all-purpose term to reference their dreamed-of transcontinental rail line to the West Coast.[12]

The Texas railroad was granted the right to build from "a suitable point on the eastern boundary line" to El Paso.[13] It got the right to take land by eminent domain to complete its course, and it was granted "eight sections of land, of six hundred and forty acres each, for every mile of railway actually completed," provided it had built at least twenty miles in six years.[14] In 1854, the state legislature sweetened the deal, offering any state-chartered railroad that within two years completed at least twenty-five miles an additional "grant of sixteen sections of land for every mile of road so constructed and put in running order."[15] And in 1856, the legislature decided that it would be a good idea to invest school funds in the new railroads as well.[16]

The aim was not simply to support the indistinct Southern goal of expanding slavery to the Pacific, but more particularly to develop a slave economy within the interior of Texas. As Professor Seth Shepard McKay recognized long ago:

> Slaves were confined to east and southeast Texas where cotton was grown; they were too expensive for use in growing grain or raising cattle. The absence of slavery in the regions away from the coast strip caused uneasiness among the pro-slavery leaders, and the fear that antislavery sentiment might take hold of northern and western Texas added a political demand to the economic motive in the agitation for a system of internal improvements which would bring these regions into reach of Gulf ports and would assimilate all districts of the state.[17]

Ultimately, the Southern Pacific built just twenty-five miles of railroad before the Civil War. The main line featured four stations: Marshall, Scottsville, Jonesville, and Waskom. Scottsville was named for the plantation of William T. Scott, one of the incorporators of the railroad and the largest slaveholder in Harrison County, which encompassed the entire line.[18] Another branch of the railroad left the main line at Jonesville and went north to Swanson's Landing on Caddo Lake, which provided access to the Red River.

Given Scott's involvement in the Southern Pacific and the pervasiveness of slavery in Harrison County at the time, it seems likely that enslaved people built at least part of the twenty-five miles of railroad in existence before the war.[19] As one historian has summarized, "Technology and modernity do not automatically bring freedom with them. In the case of the South, slaves built railroads which then facilitated their continued enslavement by helping sustain the cotton economy."[20]

During the early days of the war, the Southern Pacific advertised in New Orleans to rent or buy 1,000 slaves: "Families entire will be taken either by hire or purchase."[21] It made a special appeal to slaveholders in border states—including some that would never join the Confederacy—who wanted to move their human property away from the possible lines of fighting. It seems that the advertisement was largely fruitless: The railroad was built no farther until the Confederate army later used some two hundred enslaved people to rip up the Swanson's Landing branch, with the goal of using the rails to stretch the main line across the Louisiana border toward Shreveport, although the rails ran out before the road reached its destination.[22]

• • •

The other early Texas railroad of note, the Memphis, El Paso and Pacific Railroad Company (Memphis, El Paso), never actually built any railroad lines at all.[23] But it had influential friends—and a sordid history. This railroad was to run from northeastern Texas westward. At about Dallas, it was permitted to join up with the Southern Pacific, and the two railroads were allowed to build a single line to El Paso if they so desired, which was likely given the scant population in western Texas at the time. In short, it was another railroad designed to span the width of Texas, this one initially starting north of the other one. It too was to receive lavish land grants from Texas, amounting to more than 10,000 acres per mile, "with a reservation 16 miles wide, 8 miles on each side of its main line, as designated by surveys."[24]

Before the Civil War, the company had obtained subscriptions to $1 million of its stock, on which 2 percent was actually paid, and it did a lot of surveying. Purportedly, it had begun to grade about sixty-five miles to the north of the Southern Pacific's main line. No actual track was laid—in part because the Confederate army allegedly confiscated its supply of rails—but the state legislature extended its time for construction in light of the war.[25] And both Texas railroads were excused from their failure to meet the terms of the prewar school fund loans by an ever-generous legislature, which overrode the governor's veto.[26]

• • •

"There can be little doubt that, but for the war, the first [transcontinental] railway would have been on or near the thirty-second parallel," or the line that forms the southern boundary of New Mexico and the northern boundary of far western Texas.[27] But of course, the Civil War did happen, and the South lost its chance. Indeed, key Northern railroads received federal charters before the South would receive one, starting with the famed Union Pacific in 1862 and continuing with the Northern Pacific in 1864.[28]

After the war, the majority of the residents of Harrison County, Texas—as well as Marshall, where the Southern Pacific was headquartered—were newly freed African Americans, but the bulk of the land and wealth was still owned by the old white planter class.[29] In theory, the Southern Pacific or Memphis, El

Paso might have been an employer of the African American population look-ing to move out of agricultural work, but the local Freedmen's Bureau encour-aged them to sign contracts that tied them to the land.[30]

The Southern Pacific turned to a group of financiers from Louisville to com-plete the ten miles or so that would connect the railroad to Shreveport, Lou-isiana. R. B. Hall, a comparatively obscure businessman from Kentucky, and other members of his group took up the task of assembling the remaining bit.[31] By 1869, they had completed their work, but it seems that they might not have been paid.[32]

• • •

After the war, the Memphis, El Paso mostly operated from an office in New York City. From there, it proceeded to issue two sets of secured bonds—the first an issue of $5 million of bonds bearing 6 percent interest in gold, due in 1890; and the second "construction bonds" of $2.4 million. The right side of the company's balance sheet now showed more than $8 million of capitalization, which continued to grow as time passed—but the asset side was still a bit vague.

About the same time, former general John C. Frémont—explorer, former Republican presidential candidate, "hero" of the Bear Flag Revolt in California, early emancipator, and "the most romantic plunger of the Gilded Age"—was convinced to join the enterprise in exchange for promises of a large salary and other rewards.[33] He was essentially the celebrity pitchman of the Memphis, El Paso, but was also given nominal control of the "railroad."

The Memphis, El Paso was following a well-developed model. For example, a few decades before, English railroad developers had appointed members of the nobility to their boards to provide assurance of a railroad's investment poten-tial. It all came crashing down in a tremendous market flop in 1845, when it became clear that many of these English railroads would never build anything.[34]

Likewise, the Memphis, El Paso's bonds were not worth much to the com-pany unless somebody bought them, but in the United States, the road was well known for not actually doing any building. The company thus attempted to sell the bonds in Paris. It rented a swank office in the French capital and produced an array of prose about the glories of the railroad, all in the realm of fiction. A map showed the railroad extending from coastal Virginia to Southern Califor-nia, with large land grants indicated on either side of the line all the way across. According to some of these texts, the Memphis, El Paso's bonds were guar-anteed by the federal government under a special federal charter. Nearly $10 million in bonds were sold before the French press started to publish skeptical reports.[35] As one Supreme Court justice would write in 1872, "a more utterly fraudulent concern, a more empty bubble of speculation, is rarely to be met with in this highly speculating and fraudulent age."[36]

Frémont attempted to get congressional legislation to make at least some of the Memphis, El Paso's story true, at least retroactively. In this effort, he enlisted a variety of allies, one of which seems to have stolen his imagined railroad from him.

• • •

As a leading American legal historian has explained, "In 1800 corporation law was a torpid backwater of law, mostly a matter of municipalities, charities, and churches . . . By 1870, corporations had a commanding position in the economy. They never lost it."[37] Economist Hyman Minsky relatedly observed that "the corporation as the dominant means of organizing production is an outgrowth of the development and use of expensive and long-lived capital assets in production."[38] One of the prime early uses of corporations was in railroads. Railroad locomotives, tracks, and other related infrastructure are obvious examples of high-cost assets that could easily outlast the founders of a business, hence the need for something more than a partnership that ended with the founders.[39]

Once corporations began to be utilized, the question of what to do when they could not pay their bills soon became an issue.[40] Like other early corporations, such as banks, colleges, hospitals, and canals, railroads had a quasi-public nature that did not lend themselves to simple liquidation: somebody simply had to maintain and run the railroads, which were intensely vital to the communities along their lines, especially in the years before internal combustion.[41]

In the very early days, the familiar device of mortgage foreclosure worked well as an insolvency tool. The railroads of this period tended to be smaller, single-state operations, and many states enacted statutes to facilitate the process.[42] The net effect of such a foreclosure sale was to create a new company, operating the very same railroad, yet entirely free from claims and equity interests associated with the old (preforeclosure) railroad.[43] The old company—now stripped of its railroad assets—continued as a trust to pay off its remaining creditors.[44]

As Adrian H. Joline, a well-known reorganization lawyer (see figure 4.5), wryly wrote at the turn of the twentieth century:

> The procedure was simplicity itself. The trustee of the mortgage went into court, or resorted to the ordinary summary power of sale, and foreclosed the equity of redemption of the mortgagor. The stock, to use an expression more forcible and familiar than elegant, was "wiped out." That was the end of it. The unsecured creditor retired to his place of business, charged the debt to profit and loss account, and endeavored to make up his loss by over-charging the successor company. The stockholder went into the market to find some more bargains, hoping by a lucky stroke to "average."[45]

That, in theory, was how the process worked. But in some jurisdictions, it was not clear that the buyers at a foreclosure sale could count on obtaining a new corporate charter.

Before about 1870, most corporate charters were granted by state legislatures, originally for quasi-public functions, just as Parliament (and before that the Crown) was the source of incorporation in the British Empire.[46] A corporation was seen as a special grant of rights from the sovereign to conduct a specific enterprise.[47] Only after the Civil War did incorporation under statute become widespread in the United States.[48]

This presented a potential problem, as noted by one bondholder representative writing in 1858, who observed that "it seems doubtful, under the law of Ohio, if the franchise or corporate privileges of the road can be sold at all; at any rate it would have to be purchased by individuals who would have to work the line on their own account, and be liable for all expenses and debts as they accrue, as in an ordinary case of partnership with unlimited liability."[49] That is, the buyers at a foreclosure could not be certain that they would have a corporation to put the assets into, especially since getting a charter from the legislature might take a substantial amount of time in an era when legislatures often took long recesses, and the current legislature might be disinclined to grant a charter in any event. Only in states with specific statutes addressing the issue, like Texas or New York, would the process work reasonably smoothly.

The Southern Pacific in Texas underwent at least three foreclosure sales during its short life.[50] In the first two, the shareholders were invited to retain their interests in the railroad by paying an assessment—essentially buying back their shares. But in the final judicial sale, R. B. Hall purchased the railroad without making any offer to the unsecured creditors or shareholders.[51]

As a result, the shareholder list was transformed from many smaller local investors to a concentrated group of out-of-state financiers—not the last time we will see such an effect in a reorganization.[52] The widow of one such shareholder would write to the Texas and Pacific in 1890 inquiring about the shares, which she recalled her husband paid cash for at the kitchen table, while explaining to her that "it will help you when I am gone."[53] Other shareholders sued in Kentucky in 1873, and the case would drag on for a decade until the court finally ruled in favor of the Hall group.[54]

The Southern Pacific's next annual report, dated June 1, 1868, explains that the "company changed hands, having been sold out on the 5th day of May last. A new company has been organized." The 1870 annual report echoes and amplifies the point:

The present company bought and took possession of the road in May, 1868. While the sale might appear to have worked an injury to old stockholders, by causing them to lose their stock, yet, in point of fact, they lost nothing of value.

Some of the members of the present company were the largest owners in the old one, and they lost theirs also in common with the rest. The sales of the road were public, and after full notice to all and every person wanting to bid had the chance of doing so.

In the early 1870s, New York enacted a statute that allowed foreclosures to be used in conjunction with a reorganization plan that presented a new capital structure to investors.[55] This represented one of the earliest examples of statutory corporate reorganization. But well before then, the central players had grasped a key limitation of foreclosure sales: A state court could only foreclosure upon a mortgage within that state, sometimes only within a specific county. Indeed, in the 1868 Southern Pacific sale, the Hall group had to conduct separate sales in Texas and Louisiana, and then stitch the railroad back together again afterward.[56]

As railroads increasingly crossed state lines, this became a substantial problem. Two states might be manageable in some cases, but what if competing creditors ended up with different pieces of the railroad?[57] And what if several states were involved? The result might be something like if today's Acela rail line were operated by separate, competing companies in each state that it passed through. Already the key players were envisioning something better through an adaptation of the primordial law of receivership.

• • •

English law developed initially with two branches: the common law, which became increasingly rule bound, and equity, which was designed to address the inflexibility of the common law.[58] Equity itself eventually became wasteful as cases dragged out and various fees weighed down the process, such that it would earn the scorn of Charles Dickens and others.[59]

But equity developed a variety of important tools that softened the hard edges of the common law, among them the concept of the receiver, who is simply a person appointed to hold property for the court until it can figure out who is entitled to that property.[60] In many early railroad insolvencies, receivers were used for just this purpose—as a kind of holding pen or escrow before a foreclosure occurred.[61]

But soon investors realized that a receivership could be used to hold a multistate railroad together pending agreement on a reorganization plan. One of the earliest examples involved the Pittsburgh, Fort Wayne and Chicago Railway, which ran from Pittsburgh to Chicago and thus crossed several state lines.[62] It was formed in 1856 by the amalgamation of at least three predecessor railroads, each carrying its own capital structure (with multiple sets of outstanding bonds) to the combined enterprise. As the reorganization managers later explained:

There were nine kinds of bonds secured upon the road, eight of which were upon separate portions, including the one upon the Allegany bridge; two kinds of bonds secured upon real estate of the company; and several kinds of bonds issued to fund the various classes of coupons. On all of these bonds, except the bridge bonds, default had been made; the arrears of interest amounted to several millions; and the principal of the earliest in the series would become due in a few years, and the others at short intervals thereafter. The floating debt amounted to nearly two millions; the road was in an extremely bad condition, and an outlay of several millions of new capital was necessary to enable it to take the position to which it was entitled by its great natural advantages.[63]

When it got into financial trouble, separate receivers were appointed in Pennsylvania state court and the federal courts of the other states in which it operated.[64]

The parties soon realized that this situation was unworkable, and in 1860 they united around a plan to support the appointment of a single individual as receiver in all the cases. Meanwhile various investor groups got together and negotiated a new capital structure for the railroad, which was finally implemented in 1862. Herein lie the seeds for the receivership practice that followed.

Most railroads in the 1860s were still single-state operations, and the traditional foreclosure process worked just fine for them when needed. But in the 1870s, we begin to see a mix of receivership cases: In some cases, the receiver was performing the traditional receiver function of holding the company in stasis for the court, but in others, the receiver was plainly operating and restoring the company pending the implementation of a reorganization plan.[65]

Moreover, a process was developing in which the filing would be prearranged such that the same person (or persons) would be appointed receiver in all jurisdictions where the railroad operated. That is, the filings were organized to avoid the need of creditor agreement to achieve a united proceeding after the fact, as in the Pittsburgh, Fort Wayne and Chicago case. At the same time, the planners increasingly sought and obtained the appointment of senior management as at least one of the receivers, with the idea that such receivers could best operate the railroad pending the outcome of negotiations among investors.

Special masters would be appointed to hearing routine matters that need not take up the time of the judge, who was increasingly a federal judge, often a federal circuit judge. In the late nineteenth century, a federal circuit judge essentially became a kind of roving trial court judge who could sit in any of the districts within one of the federal judicial circuits, thus excusing the Supreme Court justices from their prior duty of "riding circuit." These circuit judges were increasingly willing to sign receivership orders for each district where they might have jurisdiction; thus bringing receivership petitions in front of a circuit judge allowed the simultaneous opening of proceedings in several contiguous jurisdictions at once.

A receivership was almost always instituted in response to a suit by an unsecured (or undersecured) creditor, coupled with the debtor's admission that the debt was due and the railroad was unable to pay.[66] That is, it was under a "creditors' bill" by an unsecured creditor rather than a foreclosure by a secured creditor. This allowed the quick appointment of a receiver before others could act, and the debtor-railroad's consent overcame the traditional rule that receiverships were a remedy available only to unpaid secured and judgment creditors.[67]

The need for the debtor to consent allowed the debtor, as well as its advisors, to control the entire process.[68] Moreover, a receiver appointed under a creditors' bill could be put in charge of all the debtor-corporation's assets, not just the ones that were subject to the mortgage (as would have been the case in a foreclosure or when a receiver was appointed at the request of a secured creditor).[69]

By the time the Philadelphia and Reading Railroad Company filed its own receivership, the "smooth manner in which counsel handled this series of procedural steps was a clear indication of the maturity attained by railroad reorganization procedure by 1880. While a substantial body of precedent did not yet exist in the law books, the proper procedures had been clearly articulated in the law offices of New York and Philadelphia."[70] The goal was to place the railroad's assets under court control, out of the reach of individual creditors.[71] Foreclosure and other collection activities were halted while the creditors negotiated a revised capital structure for the railroad. Or at least that was the public description of the process—as we will see, plans most often were dictated by insiders who then presented them as products of creditors' committees, even when they were drafted long before any committee existed.

Once a plan was ready, foreclosure suits commenced, typically combined with the original creditors' bill. The railroad was purchased in exchange for the various defaulted bonds under the committee's control, and the assets were placed in a new, corporate shell.[72] Often the new company would adopt a similar, although subtly different name. For example, the Reading *Railroad* might become the Reading *Railway*, or vice versa.

Shareholders typically retained their interest in the reorganized railroad only if they paid an assessment, which helped fund the new railroad's operating cash requirements. In some cases, shareholders also received subordinated debt or preferred shares upon payment of the assessment, which protected them in the case of a future receivership. Modern commentators often assume that the use of an assessment reflected the shallow capital markets of the time, which left railroads reliant on old investors, but the story is actually more complicated than that.

In many cases, the assessment was so large that smaller shareholders could not afford to pay it, and they instead sold their shares in the market for whatever they could get.[73] Writing in 1920, a leading corporate finance professor similarly argued that if "a stockholder has confidence in the future prosperity of the company he will probably find it to his advantage, if the assessment is over $10 a share, to surrender his old stock and buy the new stock on the open market soon after the reorganization has been consummated."[74] That is, even an optimistic shareholder was well advised to sell rather than pay a large assessment. This rush of selling in turn allowed insiders the opportunity to buy large stakes in the reorganized debtors at a discount, which might be enhanced by some negative news leaked to the press—this was an age before securities laws, after all.[75]

Shareholders and creditors who did not participate in the reorganization (or sell out) were left with claims against the old corporation, which now lacked operating assets. The corporate shell would be left with a token amount of cash, which was paid along with the old bonds at the sale, which might provide a small payment to nonparticipating senior creditors. Everyone else would be out of luck. In some cases, smaller creditors had no option to participate in the plan; they were simply left behind.

The process "in effect converted old equity forms originally intended to transform the debtor's property into cash for distribution among creditors into a procedure which achieved the opposite result, namely, preserving the properties intact while adjusting the debts."[76] As John Ayer has written, the receivership process "damages two groups. One is the unsecured trade creditors. The other group is the noninsider bondholders, not part of the management ring, who don't hold stock and who don't have the inducement of the managers to trade away their bond interest."[77] Arguably, we should add the small shareholders to the list as well, given that they were compelled to sell by overlarge assessments.

Thus, between 1860 and 1880, the shape of modern corporate reorganization began to take form in a series of smaller railroad cases because the railroads in question were initially smaller. As the century progressed, these tools would be utilized in bigger and bigger settings, as we will see in chapters 3 and 4. Moreover, "this practice spread to other industries, was approved by state courts, and became increasingly prevalent as each recession in the business cycle brought with it a new crop of major business failures. The formula became: No hope, bankruptcy [liquidation]; some hope of rehabilitation, equity receivership."[78]

But the receiverships were already acquiring a bad reputation. Figure 1.1, a cartoon from 1882, depicts the receivership of an insurance company. The company is a sinking ship that lawyers and court officials are taking bags of cash from, each labeled "Fees," while the policyholders and their beneficiaries struggle not to drown in the surf. A darkened lighthouse labeled "Trust" and "Justice" is nearby. Standing near the lighthouse is a man labeled "Referee," who is holding a pan labeled "False Beacon" that gives off smoke labeled "By Order

1.1 An 1882 take on receiverships.

Library of Congress, Prints & Photographs Division, Keppler, Joseph Ferdinand, Artist. Licensed wreckers—in the hands of the receivers, 1882. LC-DIG-ppmsca-28458.

of the Court," and in the pan, he burns papers labeled "Waste," "Outrageous Extravagance," "Extortion," and "Cost."

• • •

Despite limited labor and capital, the Southern Pacific and its new postsale owners resumed building the railroad, and the 1870–1871 edition of Henry Poor's *Manual of the Railroads of the United States* shows it having just over fifty-five miles of track in operation, from Shreveport, Louisiana, to the newly founded Hallsville, Texas, about sixteen miles west of Marshall.[79] R. B. Hall himself had died in 1869, and big changes were afoot, as Northern financiers began to take an interest in the Texas railroads.[80] Marshall Owen Roberts, a resident of New York City who had made his fortune in steamboats, was now the railroad's largest shareholder.[81]

Roberts bought into the Southern Pacific in December 1870 under a deal with W. C. Hall (presumably a relation of R. B. Hall; he was his executor and had been among the incorporators named by R. B. when he formed the new, postsale Southern Pacific in 1868), under which the company nearly doubled its outstanding stock.[82] Roberts agreed to pay for this new stock in an installment plan, while also committing to pay dividends to shareholders and refinance the company's debt.

Marshall Roberts was also a significant shareholder, along with Frémont, in the newly chartered Southern Trans-Continental Railway Company, which was authorized by the Texas state legislature to purchase the assets and franchise of the old Memphis, El Paso.[83] It was to build "beginning at a point on the eastern boundary of the State of Texas, bordering on the State of Arkansas, at or near Texarkana," which fixed the starting point of the railroad somewhat more plainly than under the Memphis, El Paso charter. It was also instructed to construct a branch line from Jefferson, Texas (about twenty miles north of Marshall) up to the main line. Why the branch did not simply start at Marshall is a mystery, but here we see the beginnings of what I shall call the "wonky rectangle." The charter also provided that the railroad "shall not intersect with the Southern Pacific Railroad east of the twenty-third degree of longitude west from Washington," so that at least in Northeastern Texas there would be two east-west lines.

The incorporators met in October 1870 and set the stock value at $1 million—of which $50,000 was actually paid.[84] The elected board included several New York City worthies, including John Jacob Astor, W. R. Stewart, and Edwards Pierrepont. Frémont was nominated as president, but he graciously declined in favor of Roberts.[85]

Roberts was also one of dozens of investors—including Frémont—who were lobbying Congress at the same time to charter a federal transcontinental railroad along a Southern route.[86] In buying into the two Texas railroads, he was apparently "frontrunning" that legislation, just as a developer might buy up land in a part of town that was going to receive a new subway, especially if it could be done before the subway was announced.

Frémont's own efforts to obtain a federal charter were increasingly hindered by the French scandal, which had crossed the Atlantic.[87] In March 1870, a French bondholder filed suit in New York against Frémont and others, seeking some recovery for the $116,430 in bonds that he had purchased.[88] The suit detailed how the railroad had received more than $4.5 million in bond proceeds, but most of that money ended up with brokers or the company's directors, including Frémont. The American press picked up the story, and Frémont was forced to publish denials in several New York papers.[89]

At the same time, more than half a dozen bills for a Southern transcontinental railroad were pending before Congress.[90] One featured leading incorporators Frémont, Roberts, and others associated with the Southern Trans-Continental, which had no more actual track than its predecessor. Another was backed by a group headed by Thomas A. Scott, then vice president of the Pennsylvania Railroad, and soon to be president of the Union Pacific (for a year).[91]

Scott and J. Edgar Thomson, the president of the Pennsylvania Railroad, had become enormously wealthy in the process of building the Pennsylvania

Railroad (PRR) into the largest American corporation of its day.[92] "Only two nations in the world, Britain and France, possessed more track than the Pennsylvania's 6,000 miles."[93] Scott and Thomson were the first controlling managers of corporate America, and they used the day-to-day demands of the Civil War to transform the Pennsylvania Railroad's board from a managerial role to the oversight role that we recognize in corporate boards today.[94]

In 1870, Scott had spearheaded the creation of the Pennsylvania Company, which controlled a group of railroads that extended the PRR lines west to Chicago and St. Louis—including the now reorganized Pittsburgh, Fort Wayne and Chicago Railway. The following year, Scott formed the Southern Railway Security Company to buy up small railroads in the South, some of them owned by financially distressed state governments, to provide feeder lines for the PRR's terminal at Washington, D.C.[95] In Danville, Virginia, one newspaper complained about the "giant corporation which seems to be extending its iron arms all over the United States; and whose purse is apparently deep as the sea."[96]

Scott personally owned $800,000 of the Southern Railway Security Company's $2.5 million in shares, which initially paid substantial dividends from its stable of southern railroads.[97] Scott and Thomson also were active in the new transcontinental lines, which

> provided Thomson, Scott, and their associates considerable opportunity for personal profit, through speculative transactions, access to government aid, and lucrative construction contracts. Even before dignitaries drove the golden spike at Promontory Point, Utah, on May 10, 1869, Thomson, Scott, and other railway executives hoped to capture a substantial portion of the California traffic that was certain to flow along the new transcontinental railroad. If that route would connect to the western end of the Pennsylvania Railroad system, then so much the better. If it funneled additional profits into the pockets of Thomson and Scott, then better still.[98]

What we would today call conflicts of interest were rife in corporate law and corporate reorganization until at least the Great Depression. Many corporate managers were paid comparatively less than today in salary, but they realized massive total compensation packages by taking on a host of side deals, some of which seemed to go against their primary company's interests.

For example, the young Andrew Carnegie "had an ironclad rule that he would never undertake an investment without inside information—and his connections to the PRR provided some of the best insider information available." He thus owned 20 percent of the company that became the chief supplier of metal bridges to the railroad, his nominal employer.[99] Two other investors in the bridge company were the railroad's bridge supervisor and chief mechanic.[100]

Another investment was in a sleeping car company, jointly owned with Scott and Thomson, which of course sold its cars to the PRR.[101]

As Maury Klein has noted, law was lagging far behind finance in this area:

> In the emerging corporate economy the close identity between a man and his firm was beginning to dissolve. A corporation could be looted in ways undreamed of in a proprietorship or partnership. What were the personal responsibilities of those who owned and/or managed large, publicly held enterprises? When did self-interest conflict with corporate duty? Clear rules had not yet emerged because the revolutionary role of the corporation in economic life was not yet understood.[102]

Bankers, attorneys, and other professionals likewise wore multiple hats, collecting fees from everyone along the way, without much thought that it might impair their judgment—indeed, anyone who had the temerity to suggest that was met with disdain.[103] In the nineteenth century, this same lack of sensitivity extended to many judges and legislators as well. In a culture of widespread faithlessness, it is perhaps not surprising that legal structures, like corporate bankruptcy, might develop with more focus on utility than equity, as equity took a backseat to personal connections in any event.

. . .

Meanwhile, the Memphis, El Paso still had valuable potential in the land grants from Texas, but creditors were demanding payment, and the French bondholders were up in arms. One of Frémont's associates suggested a receivership to solve this dilemma, but the receivership raised more than a few eyebrows.

John A. C. Gray, the Frémont associate in question, had been a sometime advisor to the general.[104] He assembled a motley crew of creditors and shareholders to support the petition, and he somehow managed to get Frémont himself to consent to the receivership and the appointment of Gray as lead receiver.[105] In July 1870, Gray went to Newark, New Jersey, to have the proceedings commenced before Joseph P. Bradley. In March, Bradley, himself a former railroad lawyer and investor, had been appointed to the US Supreme Court by President Ulysses S. Grant and was assigned, as a traveling circuit justice, to the Fifth (Southern) Circuit, so he had formal jurisdiction in Texas, even if he perchance had not been there yet. Justice Bradley "did not question the legality of the petition, the authority of the lawyer, or the signature of Frémont as president of the road when in fact he was chairman of the executive committee only."[106]

For the next eight years, Gray would report to Bradley in Washington, D.C., as receiver of the Memphis, El Paso, and Gray even sometimes told the French bondholders that he had been appointed by the Supreme Court.[107] Upon taking over the railroad, Gray let it be known that it had some $40 million in stock and $13 million in bonds outstanding, despite not having any actual track laid anywhere, and just $300,000 in its bank account.[108] Gray's control of the Memphis, El Paso give him an ability to tar Frémont with stories about its scandalous past, and it soon became clear that Gray was no longer operating in Frémont's interests.[109] Frémont had lost the Memphis, El Paso, and soon Roberts was running the Southern Trans-Continental Railway without the general's assistance as well.

Congress ultimately passed a comprise federal Texas and Pacific bill that listed more than one hundred incorporators, including several sitting members of Congress. Frémont (first on the list), Roberts, and Scott were all named, along with "and all such persons as shall or may be associated with them." In essence, Congress left it to the parties to work it out.

Under the terms of the Act of March 3, 1871, the Texas and Pacific Railway Company was incorporated under federal law and given large land grants, like the Union Pacific and Northern Pacific before it.[110] Specifically, the new railroad was to receive 25,600 acres per mile built in the territories (Arizona and New Mexico) and 12,800 acres per mile in California.[111] This new railroad was to run from Marshall, Texas, to San Diego, giving the South its long-sought connection with the Pacific.[112]

In what would turn out to be a fateful provision, Congress authorized California's Southern Pacific, then in the process of building down the length of the Golden State, to connect with the Texas and Pacific at the Colorado River—on the Arizona border with California—"for the purpose of connecting the Texas Pacific railroad with the city of San Francisco."[113] Thus, the Southern Pacific would provide connections to San Francisco and Los Angeles, while the Texas and Pacific itself would go "by the most direct and eligible route to San Diego, California, to ship's channel, in the bay of San Diego, in the State of California."[114] The planned route can be seen on the left side of figure 1.2, which also shows the anticipated connection with the Southern Pacific.

A key omitted provision of the Texas and Pacific federal charter was any requirement that the railroad address its customers and employees with equality. In the waning days of Reconstruction, with the threat of "redeemer" governments and the Ku Klux Klan (KKK) looming, such a provision would have been timely and appropriate.[115] Nevertheless, "white lawmakers had refused to link financial support of the lines to racial justice, and the injustice festered in Republican ranks."[116]

Lurking in the background of all the corporate restructuring discussed in the first four chapters of this book is the transformation of the Republican Party from one of abolition to one of big business. And then there was the broader issue of the land grants themselves: given quite freely to the Texas and Pacific, and earlier railroads, but not to newly freed African Americans.[117]

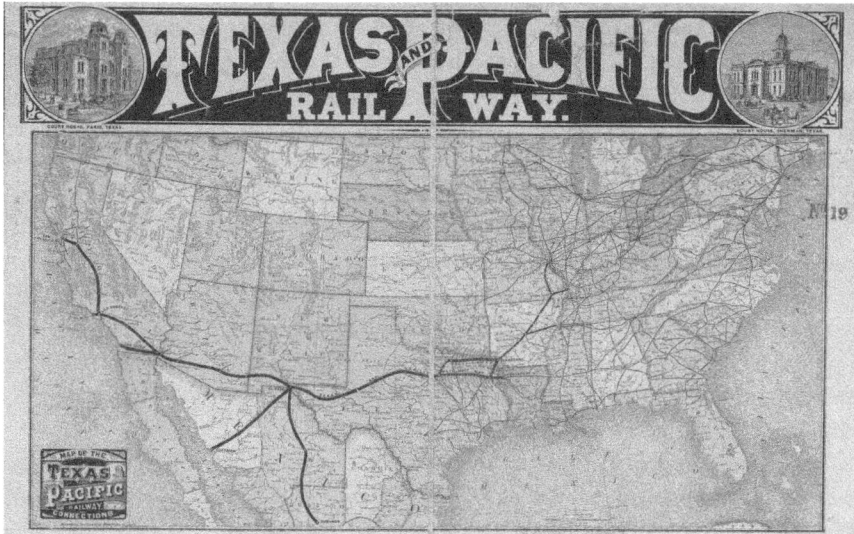

1.2 The planned route of the Texas and Pacific (with expected connecting lines in Mexico and California, and the Iron Mountain connection to St. Louis).

Texas & Pacific Railway, "Texas and Pacific Rail Way." Map. St. Louis: Texas & Pacific Railway Company, 1876. Norman B. Leventhal Map & Education Center at the Boston Public Library, https://collections .leventhalmap.org/search/commonwealth:4m90f705c (accessed June 19, 2023).

Lest we think that Congress at that time was otherwise reluctant to mix private and public functions in corporate legislation or to supersede state legislation, section 19 of the charter did provide that the Texas and Pacific "shall be and it is hereby declared to be a military and post road," with obligations associated therewith, including obligations to follow the federal instructions in this regard, despite contrary laws of "any State or Territory."

Shortly after Congress acted, the Texas legislature supplemented the federal act with more state land grant legislation. The federal legislation could not offer any land within Texas because Texas had kept all its land upon statehood, but recall that the state had been big-hearted in passing out state lands to all the railroads that it had chartered previously.[118] The state legislature agreed to transfer all these grants to the Texas and Pacific.[119]

In doing so, the state government brashly set out an explicit route for the federal railroad in northeastern Texas: from Marshall to Texarkana, from Texarkana to Paris and Sherman, and then down to Fort Worth. Thus the Texas and Pacific was required to trace a 500-mile wonky rectangle—or trapezoid—in the top-right corner of Texas (visible in figure 1.2). The railroad would spend precious time during the early 1870s building this section to secure its Texas land grants—time that may have cost it access to its federal land grants.

It turned out that Texas had promised more land than it could or would ever actually deliver. In an 1892 affidavit, a Texas and Pacific official explained that in various charters, Texas had offered railroads land "aggregating according to estimates about 128,000,000 of acres, or more than four times the amount of public domain the State had authority to dispose of." Ultimately, the Texas and Pacific would have been entitled "to 12,995,840 acres of land; all that it did succeed in obtaining, however, was . . . 5,175,040 acres."[120]

But importantly for the future, while "the Central Pacific/Union Pacific received money; the Texas & Pacific was given only land."[121] It would be hard to build a railroad without funding, and most of the land provided by both the federal and state governments was largely of future (speculative) value, dependent on the railroad's completion and settlers arriving.[122]

At an organizational meeting in New York on Saturday, April 15, 1871, the new Texas and Pacific shares were divided among the would-be buyers, and Marshall O. Roberts was appointed as chair. The press reported Roberts taking about half of the shares, with Frémont obtaining about another quarter, and those numbers have been repeated by several historians since.[123] Those numbers do not track the actual vote for the board one month later, which shows Thomas Scott holding the largest single stake, but Roberts exercising voting power for both himself and Richard C. Powers, which when combined exceeded that of Scott.

The meetings were held at the Southern Trans-Continental offices, which the press referred to as "Roberts's offices," on the northeast corner of Warren and West Streets in New York.[124] The location was then near the Hudson (today, Battery Park City is between West Street and the river), perhaps reflecting Roberts's nautical roots. The April 15 meeting was attended by a host of current and former congressmen, including Lionel A. Sheldon, a former Union Army officer from Ohio, now serving as a House member from Louisiana.[125] What these politicians intended by partaking in the meeting is unclear, but some commentators later speculated that they hoped to receive cheap (or free) shares in the Texas and Pacific—something that apparently did not happen.

The following Monday, the new shareholders met again at the Trans-Continental offices, apparently to elect the board. But one participant moved to delay naming a board, stating that it was important to give shareholders some time to think about who should manage the new railroad, and Thomas Scott quickly seconded the motion, noting that the chair could survey the field in the meantime.[126] One Southern paper reported that both Roberts and Scott denied any contest between them, which of course raised as many questions as it answered.[127]

TABLE 1.1 Texas and Pacific shareholder vote

Thomas A. Scott	5,535
Richard C. Parsons	5,135
Marshall O. Roberts	3,780

In mid-May, Roberts sent out notice of a new meeting of the stockholders to elect a board.[128] At the meeting, only three shareholders voted more than 1,000 shares (table 1.1).

Roberts voted the Parsons shares as proxy, and 17,737 votes were cast in total, of which the 14,450 held by these three individuals were clearly paramount.[129] Parsons was at the time serving as the marshal of the US Supreme Court, and he would later be elected to the House from Ohio, serving from 1873 to 1875. He was a named incorporator in the Texas and Pacific bill and was said to have lobbied on Frémont's behalf regarding earlier federal transcontinental bills. As such, perhaps we should view his shares, which Roberts voted, as really representing Frémont's holdings, as Frémont does not appear on the voting tally at all. On the other hand, there are no other indications (beyond the initial press reports) that Frémont actually owned Texas and Pacific shares. Some later correspondence stated that his shares were held by a nominee, but that person does not appear on the voting list either—although perhaps some shares were not voted, as the railroad was supposed to have 20,000 shares initially, about 2,300 more than were voted at the meeting.

More than a decade later, another Texas and Pacific incorporator made wild claims about the passage of the Texas and Pacific bill, and Parsons's role in the legislation:

> I returned to Washington on the 8th day of December, A. D. 1870. . . . About this time it was claimed that the bill could not pass the House without an outlay of a large sum of money. At this time R. C. Parsons, the acting agent and attorney of General Frémont, went to New York City and made a contract with M. O. Roberts, he (Parsons) agreeing first to pass said bill through the House, and afterwards to place said Roberts at the head of the organization, and for this he (Roberts) did agree to place in his (Parsons) hands for distribution $1,000,000 in the first-mortgage land bonds on said road lands. This agreement was finally made between said Parsons and Roberts as each Roberts, Parsons, and Frémont informed me at various conversations. R. C. Parsons does claim that he had contracted to pay out to different members of Congress the entire amount of $1,000,000 in said bonds, less 10 per cent., which he claimed for doing the business.[130]

The allegations never really went anywhere, despite getting some initial press attention, as there was little proof beyond the allegation itself.[131] Frémont denied the charges.[132] But even if only partially true, that may explain Parsons's large stock holdings and subsequent delegation of his vote to Roberts.

The true forces at work become clear by examining the board elected at this meeting, as it was split almost evenly between members associated with Roberts and members associated with Scott or the Pennsylvania Railroad.[133] Roberts was named president of the Texas and Pacific, but he would not hold that position for long.

...

By the second half of 1871, there were four railroads in the mix to build a Southern transcontinental, but only one actually ran any trains. Marshall O. Roberts had nominal control of three of them, and John A. C. Gray, as receiver, had control of the other. The new Texas and Pacific had the authority to acquire the state-chartered railroads, but first it had to get its own act together.

Initially, it seems that the Southern Trans-Continental was the most active, although perhaps it was just more careful about preserving its records. In June 1871, the railroad appointed a "committee of three," headed by Edwards Pierrepont, to negotiate a sale to the Texas and Pacific, but the committee reported in October that the Texas and Pacific had "as yet been in no condition to treat with them."[134] Roberts (as head of the Southern Trans-Continental) was pulled in yet another direction when the board formed another committee to meet with Roberts (as president of the Southern Pacific) to negotiate the purchase of that road.[135] In the meantime, the Southern Trans-Continental collected some $700,000 in bond donations and several acres in land donations from local communities along the projected route of the railroad, each hoping that stations and other facilities would be located therein.[136]

The Texas and Pacific itself seems to have done little during the second half of 1871, save for considering a somewhat quixotic report from its engineer that recommended building a narrow-gauge (rather than standard-gauge) railroad, which would have limited the possibilities for easy connection with the East.[137] Other press reports rather blandly indicated that "a proposition from the Southern Transcontinental and Southern Pacific Railway companies, in reference to the sale of the two roads, was favorably received" at an executive committee meeting in July.[138]

By the end of the year, rumors started surfacing that Roberts was going to sell out to Scott.[139] And in January 1872, a story appeared in a Chicago paper, which others picked up, that Roberts was having health problems and was ready to do just that.[140] During a deposition three years later, Roberts confirmed the story: "I was out of health at the time, and wanted to go to Europe,

1.3 Thomas A. Scott.

Author's collection, unknown artist.

where I remained nearly two years."[141] In the same deposition, he indicated that he took Scott's personal notes for his stock in all three railroads, but he did not indicate how much he was ultimately paid. Roberts would rejoin the Texas and Pacific board after his trip to Europe and stay on the board until his death in 1880—which tends to undercut the frequent suggestion that Scott had forced Roberts out.

By combining Roberts's large stake in all three companies with his already sizable stake in the Texas and Pacific, Scott was now free to fuse the enterprise. He moved fast: in mid-February, Roberts's resignation from the Texas and Pacific and Scott's elevation were announced.[142] The board was revamped—gone were the original political figures from around the nation, and in their place was an eight-member board, five members of which were employees of the Pennsylvania Railroad.[143]

Later that same month, at a special board meeting of the Southern Pacific held in Philadelphia, the shareholders agreed to call another meeting the following month to consider Scott's proposal to acquire the railroad.[144] He offered to give the railroad some $3 million in Texas and Pacific land grant bonds—that is, bonds that would be backed by the Texas real estate that the railroad would be entitled to—in exchange for all the Southern Pacific's assets. He also agreed to assume up to $700,000 of the railroad's debts, plus the $250,000 owed to the Texas school fund, and to buy out any shareholder who did not want to take the bonds at $100 per share in cash.[145] In modern terms, the deal looks something like an asset sale, with bonds as the purchase currency, backstopped with a tender offer (or put option) for the shares.

Recall that Roberts, and now Scott, owned a majority of the Southern Pacific's shares, so this was a deal that would give him personally a large block of Texas and Pacific bonds. That same month, he also entered a similar if less lucrative deal with the Southern Trans-Continental.[146] Scott signed for all the railroads in both deals.[147]

That left only the Memphis, El Paso, which was still under the control of Gray's receivership. Acquiring its assets—including its prodigious land reservation, which the Supreme Court confirmed it still held despite the palpable construction delays, blaming Texas's decision to join the rebellion for the delays—took a bit longer, but by June 1873 (or a year after he acquired the rest of the company), the Memphis, El Paso was in the fold too.[148] In exchange for the assets and many of the French bonds, the receiver obtained $150,000 in cash and a sizable chunk of Texas.[149] It was later estimated that the French bondholders received a return of about eight cents on the dollar.[150] Gray was doubtless the primary beneficiary of the receivership.

The railroad at this point ran from Shreveport to Longview, Texas, about sixty-five miles.[151] The remainder, stretching 1,500 miles to San Diego, was simply an intention.

But Scott was eager to get working.[152] In June 1872, utilizing a Pennsylvania company called the Domain Land Company, which had been given a charter by the state legislature the year before (among other things, Domain Land's charter gave it all the powers of the Pennsylvania Company), he launched the renamed California & Texas Railway Construction Company.[153]

On August 6, this company signed an agreement with the Texas and Pacific to build its entire rail line in exchange for "first-mortgage construction bonds at the rate of $35,000 per mile of road, and land-grant bonds amounting to $12,000,000."[154] Note the obfuscation in presenting one form of bond by mile, and the other as a total—the construction company was to receive $50,000 in bonds per mile it built, plus an additional $25,000 in Texas and Pacific stock per mile.

The California & Texas Railway Construction Company became a kind of holding company for the Texas and Pacific, as most of the railroad's stockholders agreed to put their shares into a trust controlled by the construction company in exchange for receiving shares in the construction company.[155] But there were other ways to get construction company shares: Texas and Pacific corporate records contain a receipt from Thomas Scott's exchange of more than 6,250 Southern Pacific shares into construction company shares.[156] Other similar receipts are in the same file, suggesting that some Southern Pacific shareholders converted directly to Construction Company shares, rather than land grant bonds. The Construction Company's *1874 Annual Report* likewise indicates that old Southern Pacific shareholders were allowed to exchange their Texas and Pacific bonds for Construction Company shares.[157]

In short, some shareholders of the Construction Company, including Scott apparently, had a bigger stake in that company than they did in the Texas and Pacific. That could have easily influenced their judgment in interactions between the two companies.

Scott had plans to float the Construction Company's Texas and Pacific securities in London.[158] And in April 1873, he signed a contract agreeing to pay a broker in Liverpool a commission on the sale of the Texas and Pacific construction bonds—with a small part of the commission going to another broker in Paris.[159] The construction bonds themselves were payable in either New York or London, reflecting the hopes for foreign sales.[160]

Scott may have latched on to the wonders of construction companies during his brief stint as head of the Union Pacific, where a select group of insiders had formed a company called Crédit Mobilier of America to undertake construction of the road at inflated prices, with the real work being subcontracted out to others. As Dolores Greenberg has explained:

> Such companies had nothing at all to do with actual building, but rather served as financial intermediaries between building contractors and railroad corporations. Formed almost always by the directors of the parent railroad, the subsidiary company, operating as a separate corporate entity, took financial responsibility for construction, issued its own stock, and when track was completed resold it to the parent line, sometimes for exorbitant sums greatly exceeding actual building costs.[161]

● ● ●

In August 1872, Scott took his private Pennsylvania Railroad car all the way to Oakland, California.[162] At a public meeting in San Francisco, he told the crowd that "within the last two months I have traveled over Texas about 1,360 miles in a wagon, and have been amazed."[163] One might wonder whether it would be possible to travel 1,360 miles in a wagon in two months, or why the senior executive of two major corporations would want to do such a thing, but the crowd was apparently delighted.[164] After his speech, Scott took a steamer south along the California coast, stopping in Santa Barbara, Los Angeles, and finally San Diego, where he negotiated the purchase of a land grant that had previously been given to the never-built San Diego & Gila, Southern Pacific & Atlantic Railroad Company.[165]

Town boosters were certain that the arrival of the Texas and Pacific would be just what San Diego needed to develop into a world-class city. Other towns in Southern California were anxious to participate, and some, including Los Angeles, offered to subsidize branch lines of the Texas and Pacific into their towns.

A twelve-page pamphlet apparently produced for the visit, complete with ads about purchasing property in San Diego, had the cumbersome title of "The Rising City of the West—San Diego, Southern California—The Pacific Terminus of the Texas Pacific Railroad."[166] Among other things, the opportunity for trade with the "Orient" from San Diego was highlighted, along with helpful information about the Southern California climate. A stirring train illustration from the back page of the pamphlet is reproduced in figure 1.4.

• • •

Scott hired former Union general Grenville Dodge to oversee building the new railroad, reportedly at the eye-popping salary of $20,000 per year (more than $500,000 today).[167] Dodge was also entitled to buy $250,000 of the Construction Company's shares, and the contract credited him with $100,000 toward the purchase price of those shares as additional salary.[168]

It is often said that Dodge built the Union Pacific—apparently with one hand, while using the other to fight off hostile Native Americans—but it might be more apt to say that he oversaw and supervised the building while also acting as the company's key lobbyist.[169] The fighting with Native peoples was largely left to the US army. With those provisos, he played a vital role in the foundation of that railroad, and indeed, he was one of the two men shaking hands at Promontory Point, Utah, in the center of a famous photograph.[170]

Like many in his time, Dodge was a man of elastic ethics: He acted as chief engineer (and lobbyist) for the Union Pacific, a Crédit Mobilier shareholder, and a congressman from Iowa all at one time.[171] Later, he would purchase land for the Texas and Pacific in his own name.[172] And he used Texas and Pacific supplies to build a subsequent (unrelated) railroad.[173] Further, throughout his long association with the Texas and Pacific, he served as a member of the Union Pacific board, despite the Texas railroad's intended role as a competitor of the Union Pacific.[174]

By May 1873, the Construction Company was already distributing Texas and Pacific land grant bonds to shareholders who had paid the seventh installment of the purchase price for their shares.[175] At that point, the shareholder had paid

1.4 San Diego (and its real estate industry) touts the planned Texas and Pacific.

Back cover of *The Rising City of the West* (1872).

$70 per share (of the $100 par value), for which the shareholder now received $65 in bonds. But these bonds were expressly nontransferable until the railroad was completed.

Under Dodge, the railroad pushed from Longview west to Dallas, from Marshall north to Texarkana, and from Texarkana west toward Sherman.[176] The 1873 report to shareholders suggested that all these routes were completed, but the report to the US Department of the Interior that same year indicated that just under 110 miles of railroad had been completed, which would scarcely cover the Longview to Dallas bit, let alone the rest.[177] The construction crew included African Americans, and according to press reports, at least one member of the crew was tortured and murdered by the local population during this time.[178]

In its 1874 report to the Interior Department, the railroad said that it had 320 miles in operation.[179] But the 1875 report showed just 326 miles in operation, a meager six-mile gain that was still not enough to complete the wonky rectangle.[180] The railroad was working slowly to complete that part, and hesitating to advance farther west than Fort Worth. What happened?

In short, it was the Panic of 1873: "The depression of 1873 so tightened the money market that the 35 miles from Dallas to Fort Worth could not be built and opened until July 19, 1876."[181] And for years thereafter, the railroad simply stopped at Fort Worth—the city's slogan ("Where the West Begins") was then quite literal.

Two years after it chartered the Union Pacific, Congress granted a charter, along with up to 60 million acres in land grants, to the Northern Pacific Railway Company to connect Minneapolis to Seattle.[182] Essentially, this line would run north of the original Union Pacific–Central Pacific line, while the Texas and Pacific would run south, providing three parallel, government-supported East-West transcontinental lines. In addition, the Canadian government was supporting a fourth East-West line even farther north, the Canadian Pacific.[183]

Following his success selling Union war debt, banker Jay Cooke took on the project of funding the Northern Pacific.[184] He underwrote a great mass of bonds, which he soon found nobody wanted to buy.[185] Cooke and Company closed its doors on September 18, 1873, a banking panic ensued, and the United States entered a depression that lingered until the end of the decade.[186] The partially built Northern Pacific would enter a receivership in 1875, its first of many.[187] On September 23, 1873, five days after Cooke's failure, the large broker Henry Clews & Co. suspended trading, further swelling angst.[188]

The effects of the panic were widespread, and even the mighty Pennsylvania Railroad was wounded: It temporarily paid dividends in scrip redeemable in 1875, and it was not until 1880 that its revenues exceeded those of 1873.[189] Shareholders demanded that Thomas Scott unwind his extraneous investments, and over the coming years, the Southern Railway Security Company would slowly liquidate its holdings throughout the Southeast.[190] Railroad construction across the country ground to a halt.[191]

The Panic put a quick end to Scott's plans to sell the Construction Company bonds, in London or elsewhere.[192] He turned to Congress to subsidize the Texas and Pacific, but he faced an image problem: The Union Pacific's relationship with the Crédit Mobilier had come to light.

As the Supreme Court would later remark, "When the [Union Pacific] was in a condition to be run, its bonds and stocks represented vastly more than the actual cost of the labor and material which went into its construction."[193] That is, there were clear indications that the construction company (Crédit Mobilier) had overcharged the railroad, with the insider-shareholders benefiting from the upcharges.[194] The fact that several politicians had received construction company stock as "gifts" (including one who was also a Union Pacific executive at the time) made the whole thing even more lurid.[195]

In November 1873, the *New York Tribune* reported that the "main cause of the depression in the stock market and on the street was the publication of the statement that the California and Texas was embarrassed. This company, it will be observed, bears practically the same relation to the Texas and Pacific Railway that the Crédit Mobilier did to the Union Pacific Railroad."[196] As Richard White has written: "It was astonishing that in the very year of the Crédit Mobilier, Scott, dragging the corpse of a similar construction company, persuaded creditors that he could induce Congress to offer him essentially the same arrangement that had plunged the Union Pacific and Congress into scandal. It was vintage Scott."[197]

In its 1874 annual report, the Construction Company reported that an agreement to sell its Texas and Pacific bonds was almost signed: "The papers were drawn and ready for signature on the 18th of September, when news of the financial crisis and panic that occurred in New York on that day, was telegraphed to London, which closed the negotiations."[198] This story offers a tidy explanation for subsequent events, but it does not stand up to much scrutiny.

If the Texas and Pacific loan fell apart on September 18, why did J. S. Morgan & Co. lend Thomson and Scott, along with three other men, £100,000 (worth approximately $1 million) on September 22, secured by $1.25 million in Texas and Pacific construction bonds?[199] Responsibility for the loan was shared among three parts of the Drexel-Morgan empire that had been established in the 1871: J. S. Morgan & Co. (London, overseen by Junius Spencer Morgan); Drexel, Morgan & Co. (New York, overseen by J. Pierpont, still the junior partner relative to his father and Drexel at this point); and Drexel & Co. (Philadelphia, overseen by Anthony Drexel).[200]

By October, it appears that Drexel-Morgan realized that the loan was a mistake, with Scott cabling J. S. Morgan from Paris "Please instruct Drexel to be modest in demand for security . . . all you want is safety."[201] In short, Drexel had made a margin call because the Texas and Pacific bonds were no longer sufficient to backstop the loan, especially given the broader economic collapse. And ultimately, J. S. Morgan had to agree to a kind of "workout" with the Pennsylvania Railroad officials, but it hardly seems that in September, they would have lent such a sizable amount of money against Texas and Pacific bonds if the same company were unable to borrow itself.[202] A skeptic might also note that the time that Scott spent negotiating this personal loan was time *not* spent obtaining a loan for the Texas and Pacific itself—although we should add the proviso that because the lines between Scott's interests, the Pennsylvania Railroad's interests, and the Texas and Pacific's interests were so rarely respected, it is possible that the latter railroad received some benefit from the loan.

The Construction Company attempted to collect $2.5 million in unpaid share subscriptions, but given the nation's economic conditions, the shareholders could not come up with the cash, and the company stopped paying its creditors in early November. The company reported more than $6.7 million in net debts, plus a need for more than $2.4 million to complete the wonky rectangle as required under Texas law.[203]

In late 1873, the company proposed a deal to its creditors to extend its obligations, with interest, but it did not get enough creditors to sign on.[204] By 1874, creditors were starting to have sheriffs attach construction materials.[205] Scott attempted to interest the Morgans in buying some bonds, at a reduced capitalization, but apparently nothing came of it.[206]

Then in March 1875, the Texas and Pacific and the Construction Company entered into a contract that essentially folded the latter back into the former.[207] The Texas and Pacific's *Third Annual Report* contained a regular annual report, dated August 1874, and a supplemental report, dated March 1875. The supplemental report explained the deal with the Construction Company, although unfortunately it did not indicate who negotiated for each party. The *Fourth Annual Report* then provided the details of the agreement, and the agreement itself was read into the record in litigation in Pennsylvania in the early 1880s.[208]

In short, the construction contract was cancelled and the shares of the Construction Company swapped for shares of the Texas and Pacific.[209] Interestingly, the trust remained in place for several additional years, leaving voting control of the railroad in the hands of Scott and his allies. Presumably, those who received Construction Company shares outside the original exchange for Texas and Pacific shares—like Thomas Scott—now had larger stakes in the Texas and Pacific than before.

The old land grant bonds were exchanged for new land grant bonds—more good news for the Construction Company insiders—and $4.1 million of new first-lien debt was issued to complete the wonky rectangle. Scott again attempted to interest J. S. Morgan in these bonds, writing him a long letter in May 1875 in which he argued that if he could sell these bonds for at least 80 percent of their face value, he could complete the railroad "in time for the Fall crop." He noted that thus constructed, the Texas and Pacific would become the dominant local railroad in the most settled part of Texas.[210]

A large majority of Construction Company creditors agreed to take new Texas and Pacific second-lien debt in exchange for their claims, and these new second-lien bonds would thus become known as the "consolidated" or Consol bonds, since they swept up a variety of prior debt. Both the first- and second-lien bonds were to mature in 1905, and they were secured by the railroad between Shreveport and Fort Worth—essentially the wonky rectangle and its immediate appendages. Together, these bonds totaled just over $13.1 million. As the first-lien debt was retired under its sinking fund provisions, the Texas and Pacific was permitted to issue new second-lien debt to take its place, maintaining the same total amount of outstanding first- and second-lien debt.[211]

Moreover, as the size of the first-lien debt pool shrank, the second-lien or Consol bonds became more secure.

The new land grant bonds were secured by the Texas state land grants and a third lien on the railroad as it then existed (the rectangle). These amounted to a kind of income bond, where scrip could be paid if cash were not available to meet the coupons (interest payments), and that scrip could be used to buy land from the Texas and Pacific. Indeed, in many years, the vast bulk of Texas and Pacific's land sales took the form of bond and scrip exchanges.[212]

The Texas and Pacific third annual report made much of the fact that this restructuring was taking place without a receivership or foreclosure sale. And it was this 1875 restructuring that would set in place the bulk of the capital structure of the central part of the Texas and Pacific for the coming years. The first- and second-lien notes carried sizable interest obligations for a rail line of just over 500 miles—for example, the annual report of August 1878 (which reflected the early stages of the American economic recovery) showed the railroad making net revenue of about $729,000, before interest expenses of just under $680,000. Not much margin for error there—and that was in a good year.[213]

And thus Scott went to work trying to get a congressional subsidy to complete the western leg of the railroad (the line to San Diego from Fort Worth). That task would consume the rest of his life.

• • •

Scott faced at least three problems in obtaining a congressional subsidy for the Texas and Pacific. First, the Democratic Party, whether in the North or South, had long opposed spending on "internal improvements"—going back to the days of the Hamilton-Jefferson conflicts.[214] Most famously, during the 1840s, the Democratically controlled Congress had refused to pay Samuel F. B. Morse $100,000 for the telegraph, which Morse wanted to sell to the Post Office.[215] While the Southern wing of the party was only just coming back to life in the early 1870s, the Northern wing had not changed its position on that issue.

Second, the Crédit Mobilier and other scandals of President Ulysses S. Grant's administration had splintered the Republican Party, with a "reform" wing—often called the "Half Breeds"—that saw government patronage and Reconstruction as the root of all (or most) evil and wanted to end government involvement with both.[216] As *The Nation* put it in May 1877:

> If the country wants the Whigs back it will have them, just as it will have the
> Federalist party if it wants that; but as long as it sees that Whig principles mean
> the Texas-Pacific job, and that the leading "Old Whig" is no other than "Tom
> Scott," we doubt if it will take much interest in the movement.[217]

Third, and most important, the mere existence of the Texas and Pacific represented a threat to Collis Potter Huntington and his associates, Mark Hopkins, Leland Stanford, and Charles Crocker (the "Big Four," as they were often called). They had built the Central Pacific to connect San Francisco with the Union Pacific in Utah, and they were now in the process of building the Southern Pacific from Northern to Southern California. They had no desire to see any other railroad enter California—"their" territory.[218]

In the early days of the 1873 crisis, Huntington offered Scott a compromise: Stop the Texas and Pacific at the Arizona-California border, and the Southern Pacific would support the subsidy bill in Congress.[219] Scott rejected the offer out of hand, telling Huntington that he need not have bothered to suggest changes to his bill, as "we expect to build our road to San Diego as already pledged to the public to do." He further wrote that the Southern Pacific's suggestions were "totally inadmissible."[220]

In the summer of 1873, the Southern Pacific apparently reached an agreement to sell itself to the Texas and Pacific.[221] If the agreement had been implemented, the Texas and Pacific would have run not only to San Diego, but to Los Angeles and San Francisco as well. But Huntington reported that "the failure of the Texas Pacific to meet the required payments prevented its passing into their hands." No doubt, this was the result of the 1873 Panic once again.

For the remainder of the decade, Scott spent most of his time asking for a subsidy. Since Dodge was doing little building, he spent vast amounts of time lobbying as well.[222] In 1875, Scott hired John Calvin Brown (figure 1.5), fresh off two terms as governor of Tennessee, as vice president of the Texas and Pacific, and Brown also spent most of his time lobbying Congress for a subsidy.[223]

Brown was a former Confederate general who "was with General Bragg on his Kentucky campaign; participated in the battles of Chickamauga; Missionary Ridge; Kenesaw Mountain; in the battles near Atlanta, Georgia; at Jonesboro, Georgia; and at Franklin, Tennessee."[224] He received one of the now-infamous pardons from President Andrew Johnson.[225] Brown's biographer reports that he was undoubtedly a member of the KKK, the first version of which got its start in Brown's hometown (Pulaski), and perhaps he was among the leadership of the KKK in Tennessee in the years before he became governor.[226]

Brown's election as governor marked the return of white supremacist or "redeemer" rule in Tennessee, and eventually the entire South.[227] Scott probably met Brown during his Southern Railway Security Company days, and apparently was not troubled by such things, and this put Brown front and center as a "true" Southern representative of the Texas and Pacific.[228]

Indeed, Brown was simply the most prominent of many ex-Confederates who were enlisted to support the Texas and Pacific, a group that included former Confederate president Jefferson Davis himself and his vice president,

1.5 John C. Brown.

Library of Congress, Prints & Photographs Division, Liljenquist Family Collection of Civil War Photographs, LC-DIG-ppmsca-77913.

Alexander H. Stephens, today mostly known for his infamous "Cornerstone Speech."[229] As Scott Reynolds Nelson has observed, "The Republicans of the Southern Railway Security Company clasped hands. . . . with white southern conservatives, and banished black Americans from the frame."[230] The same held for the Texas and Pacific.

One of Scott's primary arguments for the subsidy was parity: The North had received its subsidized transcontinental, so why not the South?[231] He also improbably cast himself as the people's champion against monopoly—the eastern monopolist vowing to free California from the clutches of "The Octopus," as the Southern Pacific would later be called.[232]

Both arguments were emphasized by María Amparo Ruiz de Burton, who made Thomas Scott the offstage tragic hero of her best-known novel, 1885's *The Squatter and the Don*. In it, the entire San Diego region suffers, and "through his opposition to the Texas Pacific, Huntington brings physical as well as financial misery into the world."[233]

Ultimately, none of Scott's many attempts to get a subsidy in the 1870s worked:

> In 1874 Scott had petitioned the federal government for a $60,000,000 subsidy over and above the land grants. This was later changed to a request for a guarantee of 5 percent interest annually for 50 years on $38,000,000 to cover estimated costs of $25,000 per mile on easier construction and $40,000 for the more difficult portions. In the end, the company proposed a straight $27,368 per mile and offered to mortgage to the government a portion of its future earnings and the line west of Fort Worth. The Texas and Pacific bill was reported favorably out of committee in both the House and Senate in early 1878 . . . On June 4, 1878 the Texas and Pacific bill was laid aside until the next session, and in the end it was never picked up.[234]

In short, Scott continually shrunk his requested subsidy but nevertheless failed to obtain any government support, despite an extensive (and undoubtedly expensive) lobbying effort.[235]

Meanwhile, the fight between Scott and Huntington became increasingly personal: On several occasions, Huntington wrote his associate, David Colton in San Francisco, that he looked forward to seeing the grass grow over Scott.[236] In 1876, Huntington reported on an encounter with Scott in which the tension seems palpable: "He told me this week that he is sure to pass his bill. He said he would give us enough to do to take care of what we had, without meddling with his. I said to him, with a smile, that I hoped that he would do nothing that would interfere with my helping him on his Texas and Pacific."[237] Huntington's letter continued with a report of the agents whom he sent to the South, to "set some back fires on Scott." In 1878, they both appeared before a congressional committee, and Huntington wrote that Scott "dumped a lot of stuff to the . . . Committee, and in my reply I went for him."[238]

By 1877, when the Southern Pacific reached Yuma, where the roads were to meet under the terms of the federal charter, the Texas and Pacific "was still more than 1,200 miles away," in central Texas.[239] Huntington used every financial resource at his disposal to push the Southern Pacific eastward, while Scott dithered, unwilling to take the risks that Huntington took.[240]

From the project's inception, Huntington realized the importance of pushing the Southern Pacific into Arizona, and he made a point of broadcasting the railroad's steady march toward El Paso. While Scott presided over a regional railroad in northeastern Texas, Huntington was stretching his resources to the limits to cross Arizona and New Mexico—building under charters obtained from the territorial legislatures—until it soon became apparent that the Southern Pacific might well get to El Paso before the Texas and Pacific did.

In late 1878, Huntington told his associates to make their intention to build to the Rio Grande public because "it will help us with the Southern members in the next Congress."[241] At that point, the Southern Pacific was still organizing its New Mexico subsidiary and had hardly built much in Arizona, but it was announcing its goals quite plainly, while the Texas and Pacific still stalled in Fort Worth, 600 miles away from El Paso, with no obvious plan to move forward.[242] Scott, quite frankly, was loath to cross the vast, hot, and lightly populated expanse of western Texas that faced him without assurances that doing so would not bankrupt him.

The part of the Texas and Pacific that he had already built had cost him dearly by 1875, nearly putting him into personal bankruptcy as a result of his backing of Construction Company notes, and he seemed hesitant to face such a risk again. So he looked to the government purse for reassurance. But the combined weight of Republican "reform" elements in Congress, along with Northern antisubsidy Democrats reacting to the backlash from the Credit Mobilier scandal and Huntington's lobbying efforts, was simply too much to overcome.[243]

Meanwhile, the Southern Pacific connected Los Angeles to the national rail network, while San Diego still waited.[244]

• • •

Toward the end of *The Squatter and the Don*, one character asks former California governor Leland Stanford, one of the Big Four, when San Diego will get its railroad. He responds:

"I don't see how I can help you San Diego people. If Mr. Huntington effects some compromise with Mr. Scott, we will then build a branch road, as I said."

"And if what there is no compromise?"

"Then, of course, there will be no road for you—that is to say, no Texas Pacific in California."

"Why not, Governor? Live and let live," Don Mariano said.

"You don't seem to think of business principles. You forget that in business every one is for himself. If it is to our interest to prevent the construction of the Texas Pacific, do you suppose we will stop to consider that we might inconvenience the San Diego people?"

"It is not a matter of inconvenience it is ruin, it is poverty, suffering, distress; perhaps despair and death," said Mr. Mechlin. "Our merchants, our farmers, all, the entire county will suffer great distress or ruin, for they have embarked their all in the hope of immediate prosperity, in the hope that emigration would come to us, should our town be the western terminus."

"You should have been more cautious; not so rash."

"How could we have foreseen that you would prevent the construction of the Texas Pacific?"

"Easily. By studying business principles; by perceiving it would be to our interest to prevent it."[245]

CHAPTER 2

JAY GOULD AND THE TEXAS AND PACIFIC

The Panic of 1873 devastated the American economy; "some 400 banks collapsed and more than 47,000 businesses failed."[1] From 1873 to 1875, corporate bond defaults totaled 36 percent, the worst default rate of any period in US history, including the 1930s.[2] Railroad construction came to a halt until the end of the decade.[3]

At the same time, Southern California was hardly established at all: Los Angeles, the largest city in the area, had about five thousand residents in 1870, when Omaha had more than sixteen thousand.[4] Los Angeles was still known mostly for its sheep and wool.[5] Only with the arrival of the Southern Pacific in the late 1870s, the introduction of navel and Valencia oranges, and the invention of refrigerated rail cars would Los Angeles begin to grow into something like the city we know today, becoming by 1920 the largest city in California.[6]

Thomas Scott thus faced a serious challenge in building the Texas and Pacific beyond Fort Worth. The railroad was to run through the meagerly populated regions of West Texas, New Mexico, and Arizona, only to arrive at San Diego, home to 2,500 people at most.[7] Indeed, once Los Angeles was connected to the national railroad network by the Southern Pacific, San Diego's population actually shrunk to about 1,500.[8] The Texas and Pacific intended to develop these areas, but until that happened, the railroad would want for customers. This hardly seemed like a sensible investment, particularly in times of economic stress.

As such, it is not wholly surprising that Scott sought a government subsidy for a railroad whose touted short-term benefits—such as national unity and development—were not appreciably commercial. What is more puzzling is Collis Potter Huntington's persistent opposition; indeed, his Central–Southern Pacific colleagues often questioned the decision to build past the California–Arizona border.[9]

Even after his congressional defeat in June 1878, it was widely assumed that Scott would continue to seek governmental support, and the topic remained the subject of spirited debate in the newspapers. However, it was perhaps telling that Scott gave the name of his California engineer to the Japanese government as somebody who could help organize their new railroad system, and indeed the engineer took a position as a consultant in Japan later that same year.[10]

That said, even in October 1878, *The New York Times* was still editorializing against Scott's request for a subsidy.[11] The *Louisville Courier-Journal* retorted that it was the policy of *The New York Times* that "the South has no right to be even indirectly the recipient of any Governmental aid for internal improvements, and should get along the best way it can, repenting of rebellion, etc."[12] *The New York Times* was indeed antisubsidy, while papers like the *San Francisco Chronicle* stressed the need for an alternative to the Big Four's monopoly in California.[13] "Reformers sided with the Texas Pacific in legislative attacks on the Central Pacific's monopoly, but they sided with the Central Pacific against the Texas Pacific in attacks on new subsidies."[14]

And then sometime in late October, Scott had a stroke.[15]

On October 31, *The Philadelphia Inquirer* reported that Scott had been confined to his house for several days with a "severe cold," and four days later, he left unexpectedly for Europe.[16] Shortly thereafter, the New York papers reported that the trip was ordered by his doctors, and a few days later, *The New York Times* reported that he had suffered a stroke and was partially paralyzed.[17] However, one Cincinnati correspondent disputed this, and remarkably reported seeing him striding through a New York hotel lobby days before he left for Europe (from Philadelphia).[18]

Scott would spend almost a year away, touring the Nile and visiting various cities in Europe.[19] He received a formal leave of absence from the Pennsylvania Railroad board, where he had taken over as president, but there was little mention of his equivalent role with the Texas and Pacific.

• • •

In early 1879, former Confederate vice president Alexander H. Stephens, now representing Georgia in the House of Representatives, gave a long interview—which at times reads more like a prepared speech—regarding his continued support for the Texas and Pacific.[20] And the *San Francisco Chronicle* wondered why there was so much opposition to the railroad, arguing that it was "for the interest of every State and Territory on this coast and of every farmer and merchant that there should be a transcontinental line of railway to compete with the existing monopoly."[21]

Cutting in the other direction, about two weeks after Stephens's interview, Congressman Henry W. Blair, a New Hampshire "half breed," gave a lengthy speech in Congress in which he argued that "the claim that something must be given to the south in the way of industrial improvements to balance the favor shown to northern interests, is simply preposterous."[22] He argued that the Southern Pacific was building without any governmental assistance—not even the land grants that the Texas and Pacific was entitled to—and saw no reason for taxpayer money to be used to support a private enterprise.

But by and large, activity surrounding the railroad was quiet until Scott neared his return that fall.[23] The 1879 edition of Henry Poor's *Manual of the Railroads of the United States* put the railroad at 443.86 miles, essentially the "wonky rectangle" with small nubs to Fort Worth on the left and Louisiana on the right, and forty-nine locomotives and twenty-eight passenger cars, equally split between first and second class—and nine officer's cars.[24] The special perks of senior management have a long heritage.

At the August annual meeting in Philadelphia, the board and shareholders approved a new bond issue of more than $24 million to complete construction from Fort Worth to the Pacific.[25] One board member, on his way home from the meeting, told reporters that the company had given up on getting government aid and was sending an agent over to Europe to meet Scott in an attempt to place the new loan there.[26] On the same day as the Texas and Pacific meeting, the voting trust held a meeting to consider if it should be disbanded.[27] The press did not follow up on the latter meeting, and no decision was reached at that time, but the combination of these moves suggests that something was afoot, just as the American economy finally was starting to come out of the doldrums.

In September, Scott was back in the United States, and in early November, he traveled to Louisville as part of a Pennsylvania Railroad trip, ostensibly in good health.[28] Somewhat less reassuringly, a report from Indianapolis on the same trip noted that "except unsteadiness on his legs, and increased apoplectic appearance, there is nothing to indicate his late stroke of paralysis."[29]

Later that same month, it was related that the Texas and Pacific had been in negotiations for weeks regarding renewed construction of the line, at least to El Paso.[30] But what precisely was going to happen, and who would be involved in the new deal, were the subject of much speculation and little insight. An improbable Scott-Huntington alliance was often suggested. At one point, it was proposed that the Texas and Pacific and the Pennsylvania would be combined to form a colossal, cross-country railroad to be headed by former president Ulysses S. Grant.[31]

Then, in December, it all started to come together. Texas and Pacific vice president Frank Bond gave an interview in which he acknowledged that the railroad was close to signing a new construction contract; according to him, growing European demand for American railroad bonds meant that the work would be privately financed.[32] He made plain that the contract would provide for building the railroad to El Paso, after which it would be built only so far as needed to meet up with the Southern Pacific—which at that point was well into Arizona and moving rapidly eastward.[33] That is, building to San Diego was no longer on the table, a point that the *Louisville Courier-Journal* later bemoaned as "a confession that the battle waged for the last five or six years . . . has ended in defeat."[34]

San Diego soon joined a lawsuit against the Texas and Pacific seeking to get the city's land back, with the aim of giving it to either the Southern Pacific (if they would connect their Los Angeles line to San Diego) or the new Atchison, Topeka and Santa Fe, then aiming to build into Southern California as well.[35] A few years earlier, Scott had telegrammed the city in response to complaints about the slow pace of construction: "Have used my utmost efforts to secure San Diego a railroad line on such route as can best effect the object; and if you can effect it any better shape than I can, I should be very glad to have you take it up and adjust it with any party, or on any terms that you may think best. But in taking these steps, I shall expect you to relieve me of any possible obligation."[36] The litigation lingered into 1880, when the railroad signed a settlement with the city.[37]

The Texas and Pacific board and the trustees of the share trust met again in Philadelphia to discuss the plans.[38] The next day, it was widely reported that the Texas and Pacific was going to give the construction contract to a newly formed construction company, headed by Jay Gould (figure 2.1) and Tom Scott.[39] While the latter's involvement was consistent with the insider tinge of most construction companies, the press was stumped by Gould's reported interest in the southern transcontinental, especially given that, as controller of the Union Pacific, he had only recently teamed up with Huntington to thwart Scott's subsidy bills.[40]

Jay Gould first became widely known when he joined Daniel Drew and James Fisk in a struggle with Cornelius Vanderbilt over the Erie Railroad that abused the still-adolescent corporate jurisprudence and discredited the judiciary.[41] And in 1869, he was part of the attempted cornering of the American gold market that resulted in the September "Black Friday" panic.[42] Both incidents left him with the reputation as the worst of the "robber barons," which he still enjoys today, as well as a notable fortune.[43] In the wake of the 1873 Panic, Gould began buying shares in the Union Pacific. Then, over the course of the next five years, "Gould astonished his critics by giving the Union Pacific the strong, unified leadership it had always lacked."[44]

2.1 Jay Gould.

Author's collection, unknown photographer.

Ironically, it was Eugene Debs who perhaps gave the fairest account of Gould among all of his contemporaries:

We do not believe that Jay Gould is a sinner above all the rest of his class. As a matador he has slain a good many bulls and bears and taken their hides. As a trapper he has been a success. He spreads out amazingly, but is no where very thin. He may lack conscience and soul because he can't buy such things nor trap them. He has gold, brass, water, and steam, an iron will and a sharply defined purpose. In such things he is neither worse nor better than the Vanderbilts, the Sages, Scotts, Garretts, Corbins, et at., to the end of the list. He is credited with a clean home. He is said to be an affectionate husband and a doting father. In such things he is human, if not a Christian. If he prefers gold to God as an object of worship he can play pagan to his heart's content.[45]

In 1881, in the midst of building his railroad empire, Gould also bought control of Western Union, which handled most of the nation's high-speed communications, and part-ownership of the Manhattan Elevated Railroad (he obtained full control in 1886).[46] The latter was the prime form of New York City public transit in an age before the subways. Both the Manhattan Elevated and Western Union investments were the result of careful planning that dated well back, to the 1870s.[47] As a result, Gould had important and substantial stakes in several key parts of the American economy throughout the 1880s.

• • •

The key to understanding Gould's Texas and Pacific moves during the early 1880s is to appreciate that at almost the same time that he agreed to build the line to El Paso, he acquired control over three railroads to the north and south of the Texas and Pacific. All of this was simply the southern portion of a strategy that focused on the Missouri Pacific, based in St. Louis, which Gould had purchased in late 1879.[48]

To unpack this, recall figure 1.2 and the wonky rectangle. At the top-right corner of the rectangle, the Texas and Pacific touched Texarkana. A short railroad, the St. Louis, Iron Mountain and Southern Railway, ran diagonally across Arkansas, connecting Texarkana to St. Louis. For years, it had been rumored that Tom Scott would buy the Iron Mountain to provide a needed bridge between the Texas and Pacific and the Pennsylvania Railroad at St. Louis. Jay Gould eventually bought the Iron Mountain, but for the purpose of providing a connection with the Missouri Pacific—it was surely only incidental that this provided his new partner with some benefit too.[49] The top-left corner of the wonky rectangle bent at Sherman, Texas. In 1879, Gould had bought control of the Missouri, Kansas & Texas Railway—commonly known as the MKT or the "Katy"—which was already in the neighborhood of Sherman, running south from its first two named states.[50]

And then, on the bottom of the rectangle, was the International & Great Northern Railroad, connecting at the southeastern corner, running southwest to Austin and San Antonio; later, it was extended all the way down to Laredo, Texas, on the Mexican border. Another spur went directly south from Palestine, Texas, to Houston and Galveston. A final spur connected the line to the southwestern corner of the wonky rectangle, creating an elongated "y" shape. Gould had purchased control of the International and Great Northern in December 1880 and leased it to the MKT.[51]

In short, the Texas and Pacific was simply a middle part of a large swath of railroads—from the Texas coast up to the Midwest—that quickly came under Gould's control.[52] At the head of it all was the Missouri Pacific, providing a link between Gould's southern railroads, the Union Pacific, and Gould's eastern projects like the Wabash, which stretched from St. Louis to Toledo; and then the Lackawanna, which ran from Buffalo to Hoboken, with Gould planning a link between Toledo and Buffalo.[53]

In total, by 1881, Gould controlled more than 13,000 miles of railroad throughout the United States, representing assets of nearly $600 million, beyond his control of Western Union and growing control of the New York City elevated train network.[54] His railroad investments included a large stake and role in the Union Pacific, but he was now slowly backing out of that in favor of this new Missouri-Pacific-focused system, which he could control more directly—the Union Pacific was heavily codependent on the Central–Southern Pacific and the Big Four.[55]

While the press flailed about trying to figure out who was actually involved in the new Texas and Pacific construction company, and under what terms, with the benefit of hindsight, we can see that the Pacific Railway Improvement Company was formed on December 31, 1879, in New London, Connecticut, although the articles for the company were first signed on December 18.[56] One might suggest that forming a corporation in bustling New London on New Year's Eve is not a move designed to foster transparency.[57]

The company had $1 million in shares—of the traditional $100 par value each—but the incorporators initially paid in $100,000, or 10 percent—if all shares were issued, but the list shown in table 2.1 totals to only 8,500, leaving

TABLE 2.1 First shareholders of the Pacific Railway Improvement Company

	City	Shares
G. P Morosini	New York	1,000
G. M. Dodge	New York	1,000
Sidney Dillon	New York	500
J. Schalle	New York	250
C. F. Woerishoffer	New York	2,000
J. J. Slocum	New York	500
Solon Humphreys	New York	500
William Bond	New York	250
John P. Green	Philadelphia	1,000
John P. Green	Philadelphia	500
Geo. M. Pullman	Chicago	500
Ex. Norton	New York	250
E. B. Hart	New York	250

1,500 somewhat vague. The initial shareholders as reflected in the Connecticut documents are shown in the table.

Green was an assistant to Scott at this time, and his shares are certainly Scott's, although the second batch might belong to somebody like Frank Bond, the Texas and Pacific vice president living in Philadelphia, who was increasingly associated with the Gould railroads.[58] Most of the other investors, including Pullman, were directly and solely associated with Gould. Morosini's shares are undoubtedly Gould's, as he often stood in as a proxy for him while serving as his secretary and bodyguard.[59]

Sidney Dillon, then-president of the Union Pacific, was a long associate of Gould's, whose nephew, former federal circuit judge John F. Dillon, served as in-house legal counsel to Gould (while also a tenured professor at Columbia).[60] Another Gould comrade, Russell Sage, is likely the real name behind his brother-in-law, Joseph J. Slocum.[61] Solon Humphreys was then president of the Wabash Railroad, a Gould property, as well as a board member of the Union Pacific, and William Bond was another Gould associate. And, of course, Dodge was already chief engineer of the Texas and Pacific and a Union Pacific board member, and was thus familiar to both Gould and Scott. Dodge, Sage, Dillon, and Frank Bond were also members of the MKT board.[62]

The press articles of the time describe Woerishoffer as a representative of German investors, and Professor Grodinsky describes him as "a stockbroker and active trader in New York," which is not inconsistent with representation of German investors.[63] He had earned foreign investors' trust in defeating Gould and Sage in a Union Pacific transaction a few years before, but apparently there were no hard feelings, and indeed he would participate in other Gould ventures in the coming years.[64]

The last name on the list—E. B. Hart—is perhaps the most entertaining. He also signed and accepted most of the corporate documents as "Commissioner for Connecticut," residing in Manhattan.[65] That is, the founders of the Pacific Railway Improvement Company never made the trip to New London, and perhaps the 250 shares were Hart's commission for handling the matter with discretion. He would later become secretary of the new construction company.

Dodge was named the president of the new company, Dillon the vice president, and Woerishoffer the treasurer.[66] The company had the power to build railroads anywhere in the United States or Mexico and could increase its capital stock to $10 million if it so desired. Annual meetings were to be held in New London unless the board preferred to meet in New York City. One wonders.

The newspapers indicated that the construction contract was signed in late December or early January—it was undoubtedly negotiated by then, but later evidence states that it was signed January 16.[67] The Pacific Railway Improvement Company was to receive $20,000 in 6 percent first-lien bonds—secured by the new Rio Grande Division to be built between Fort Worth and El Paso—which would be due in 1930, fifty years from the date of issuance, and $20,000 (or 200 shares) in Texas and Pacific common shares per mile built.[68] As a result, at the start of 1880, Gould's control of the Texas and Pacific was contingent but entirely foreseeable, given that he would receive something like 120,000 shares in the deal.[69] Shortly after the contract was approved by the Texas and Pacific board, Gould, Sage, and Frederick L. Ames (another frequent Gould coadventurer) joined that board.[70]

The Pacific Railway Improvement Company was funded by a variety of sources, starting with the money that it received from its shareholders.[71] Unlike many companies of the era, the shareholders were eventually called on to pay for their shares in full, but in exchange, they received large dividends—one estimate stated that shareholders received nearly a 700 percent return on their investment—in the form of both cash and securities.[72]

The latter took the form of not only Texas and Pacific securities, of which the construction company soon had plenty, but also shares in other Gould-controlled railroads, like the Missouri Pacific and the MKT.[73] For example, following payment of a call for 30 percent of the construction company's capital, on top of the half already paid at that point, shareholders were entitled to receive $50 in Texas and Pacific common stock, an equal amount of MKT stock, and $150 in Rio Grande Division bonds for each share of the construction company.[74] That is, shareholders were paying $30 per construction company share in exchange for a package of securities with a face value of $250, although the market value of the latter was undoubtedly lower.

A 1930s Interstate Commerce Commission (ICC) report indicates that the Missouri Pacific issued 852,250 common shares to Jay Gould "without consideration on account of his subscription to the capital stock of the Pacific Railway Improvement Company."[75] The most apt interpretation of this is that Gould used shares in these other railroads to pay for shares in the construction company, either his original batch (via Morosini) or to purchase some of the remaining unallocated shares. The Missouri Pacific Reorganization (MoPac) shares then formed the basis for a dividend to Pacific Railway Improvement Company shareholders, some large part of which were Gould and his friends. And if we take the ICC's "without consideration" literally—that is, as an indication that the shares were given to Gould for free—this means that the Missouri Pacific and MKT were subsidizing Texas and Pacific's construction with free shares given to Pacific Railway Improvement Company shareholders in exchange for their cash contributions to the construction effort. Some number of these shares presumably cycled back to Gould himself because of his holdings in the construction company.

The construction company also raised money by issuing subscription certificates to outside investors.[76] An investor would promise to pay $900 to the Pacific Railway Improvement Company in ten installments of $90 each, as the construction company called for funds (with ten days' notice).[77] Upon completion of the subscription payment, the certificate holder would be entitled to a $1,000 Texas and Pacific Rio Grande Division bond and 500 shares of Texas and Pacific company stock. Essentially, the certificate purchaser got a 10 percent discount on the bond, for a better potential yield, and some stock too, while the construction company locked in a stable price for part of its pool of Texas and Pacific securities. Whether the certificate investors would have been better off buying the securities in the market rather than through this complex forward-contract arrangement is an open question.

So Dodge, the chief engineer of the Texas and Pacific and before that the head of the California & Texas Railway Construction Company, gave way to Dodge, the president of the Pacific Railway Improvement Company, and construction of the Rio Grande Division to El Paso finally commenced in earnest. Recall that the construction contract paid a fixed package of securities per mile upon acceptance of the work by the Texas and Pacific.

But since the people ultimately in charge of the Texas and Pacific had large stakes in the construction company, there was little chance that the railroad would be too demanding in its oversight. And while a certain amount of speed was clearly required, given Huntington's rapid approach from the west, the suspicion would endure that the Texas and Pacific overpaid for what it received from the Pacific Railway Improvement Company.

In 1881, for example, the Galveston paper reported the arrival in port of an order of more than 512 tons of railway iron for the Pacific Railway Improvement Company.[78] By the 1880s, iron rails were being replaced with steel on American railroads, although the trend did not really take off until after the tariff on imported British steel rails was removed in 1883. But the decision to construct a new main line in iron in the 1880s would certainly have been unusual, and the fact that Texas and Pacific's Rio Grande Division was so constructed would be the subject of much future criticism, while the construction company had little motivation to use the more expensive steel if the contract (or Texas and Pacific's conflicted board) did not require it.[79]

By 1883, the Texas and Pacific, with only 15 percent steel rails, was far behind even the other railroads in Gould's Southwestern system, where steel rails ranged from 45 percent (International and Great Northern) to 73 percent (Missouri Pacific) of the total.[80] This issue illustrates the basic difficulty with construction companies, as it could hardly be expected that Dodge, Scott, and Gould could meet their obligations to the Texas and Pacific while at the same time being heavily invested in the Pacific Railway Improvement Company. The large percentage of steel rails at the Missouri Pacific also gives us a hint about where Gould's focus really was.

· · ·

The Pacific Railway Improvement Company built west while the Southern Pacific built east, each racing toward each other. The Southern Pacific construction team was predominantly Chinese, along with a small number of Native Americans, and all indications are that it built a better-quality railroad—probably because the Southern Pacific was owned by a small group of investors who would fully bear the cost of future problems.[81] Gould, on the other hand, was already dispersing his Texas and Pacific shares to certificate holders and other construction company investors.

The Texas and Pacific construction crew was described by contemporaries as a mix of white and Mexican.[82] The first category apparently included both American-born and Irish workers, while the latter might have included workers of Mexican heritage from either side of the border.[83] Some number of African Americans also worked in the Texas and Pacific construction crews, as they had before.[84]

The entire operation was protected from Native Americans by the 10th Cavalry—a unit of the famed Buffalo Soldiers.[85] The Native population apparently kept an eye on the progress but did not interfere; the buffalo

2.2 A Texas and Pacific locomotive built in 1881 rolls through Arlington, Texas (in the mid-1890s).

T&P Passenger Train, No. 1, 2:35 pm, Arlington, Texas, 1896. Collection of The Grace Museum, Museum Purchase, Texas & Pacific Railway Collection, H. D. Donner Collection.

population had already been decimated in West Texas by 1880, so the number of Native Americans in the area was probably also small.[86] On some level, the presence of the army represented just one more governmental subsidy to the Texas and Pacific.

It took a while for the Pacific Railway Improvement Company to ramp up to a pace comparable to that of the Southern Pacific, which had been steadily moving across Arizona and then New Mexico, by one estimate building about a mile per day.[87] Indeed, in less than five years, the Southern Pacific built all the way from San Francisco to the Texas border.[88]

On the Texas and Pacific side, as one engineer later wrote, "the first one hundred miles was laid in 190 days, the second in 159 days, the third in 102 days, and the fourth in 67 days; while the balance of the distance, one hundred and twenty miles . . . was laid in 97 days."[89] As noted, the quality of the work on the Rio Grande Division was often quite poor.

One journalist who rode the line between Toyah and Big Spring, Texas, shortly after it opened reported that the ties had been laid on top of the ground—"this section of the road can hardly be said to be ballasted"—much like a model train set on a kitchen table. When the dirt below settled, the ties were often left floating above the ground—"a rapid drive over such a road, on a freight train, is like being in a storm at sea."[90] In essence, the Texas and Pacific team was slapping down a provisional rail line to claim as much of its land grant as possible, but the Pacific Railway Improvement Company was getting paid as if it were constructing a lasting railroad.[91]

While workers were laying iron across western Texas, Scott and Gould hatched a plan to extend the Texas and Pacific southeast from Shreveport to New Orleans. Enter the American Railway Improvement Company, this time formed in Colorado, perhaps because Connecticut was found to be too close to the national press in New York.[92] Dodge, James P. Scott (son of Tom), Sidney Dillon, and G. P. Morosini, among others, were the founders.[93] A total of $2 million in shares were authorized, with an ability to increase that to $5 million, and it was given the power to build railroads anywhere in the United States or the "Republic of New Mexico" (sic).[94]

Dodge had the incorporation papers drawn up in New York and, in sending them to his Colorado counsel, instructed him, "I desire you to procure a sign, not necessarily very large, or expensive, bearing the words 'The American Railway Improvement Co.' and if convenient your own name as Secretary and have it placed where you are generally to be found."[95] Dodge was named president, James Scott vice president, and (once again) Woerishoffer treasurer.[96]

But the machinations regarding this construction company were even more complex than those of the prior company because the Texas and Pacific itself had no rights to any land grants within the state of Louisiana. Congress, in the original Texas and Pacific charter, had provided such a grant to the New

Orleans, Baton Rouge and Vicksburg Railroad Company, a company very much in the Frémont tradition, in that it had built no tracks while issuing millions of dollars in bond debt.[97] It was supposed to have been built along the east side of the Mississippi River. Allegedly, it had received its land grant and charter as the result of abundant gifts to state and federal legislators.[98]

But that was all in the early 1870s, and by 1877, the Louisiana legislature, under the control of the Democratic Party for the first time since the Civil War, after President Rutherford B. Hayes withdrew federal troops, had passed an act repealing the railroad's charter.[99] A nonexistent railroad would have a hard time claiming a land grant. Moreover, Gould and Scott much preferred the route of a competitor railroad, the ambitiously named New Orleans Pacific Railway Company, which was to run up the west side of the Mississippi from New Orleans.[100] Alas, this railroad had no congressional land grants.

Fortunately for all involved, a bondholder sued soon after the passage of the New Orleans, Baton Rouge and Vicksburg repeal legislation, arguing that his bonds became due and payable upon the railroad's loss of its charter. The railroad responded that the law in question was unconstitutional, and thus the bonds had not been accelerated after all. The court agreed and dismissed the bondholder's action. It is not clear that anyone bothered to tell the state of Louisiana about these proceedings, which were likely contrived by the investors, but the result was a federal court judgment that the law repealing the charter was unenforceable. This was not part of some grand, Gould-inspired plan, as the press would latter suggest, inasmuch as the litigation in question was filed in 1877, well before Gould became part of the Texas and Pacific.

Gould and Scott nonetheless faced the challenge that one Louisiana company had land grants, the other had an attractive charter, and neither was currently under the control of the Texas and Pacific. In April 1880, about two months before the American Railway Improvement Company was formed in Colorado, Scott and Gould jointly wrote the president of the New Orleans Pacific with a proposal to revamp that company's capital structure and replace its existing board with one acceptable to Scott and Gould, in exchange for building its rail line by March 1882.

In exchange for building, the New Orleans Pacific would give the American Railway Improvement Company $20,000 per mile in stock and $20,000 per mile in bonds. These bonds were newly issued, with a lien on the entire railroad, including the land of the New Orleans, Baton Rouge and Vicksburg, should that come into the New Orleans Pacific's possession.[101] All existing shareholders of the New Orleans Pacific were to swap into $350,000 of the new shares, just a slight reduction from the $355,600 then outstanding. Existing creditors of the New Orleans Pacific agreed to take $218,000 of the new bonds as payment in full, which *The New York Times* estimated represented fifty cents on the dollar of their actual claims.[102]

Dodge advised President Edward B. Wheelock of the New Orleans Pacific that the "principal subscribers [of the American Railway Improvement Company] are Messrs. Gould, Sage, Dillon, Perkins, Wicks, Woodward, Baldwin, Davis, Felsenheld and Woerishoffer of New York. Messrs. Thomas A. Scott and George F. Tyler of Philadelphia and Mr. W.T. Walters of Baltimore, most of them being parties intimately connected with the Union Pacific and Texas and Pacific enterprises. The subscription has not been offered except privately to such parties as we desire connected with the company."[103] Indeed, most were invested in the Pacific Railway Improvement Company as well. In the same letter, Dodge advised that he was setting aside $150,000 of shares of the construction company for Wheelock "to place in New Orleans if you see proper to do so." The sentence is quite suggestive, if oblique.

The American Railway Improvement Company also received Missouri Pacific shares through Gould and sold the requisite subscription certificates to outside investors, including Dodge's old friends from Iowa.[104] And in late July, the company actually signed the construction contract with the New Orleans Pacific, which it proceeded to build in the same general fashion as the Pacific construction was then building the Rio Grande Division.[105] That is, quickly and cheaply, once again laying iron rails all the way—Scott arranged to buy the rails in England, paying half cash and half New Orleans Pacific construction bonds.[106] The Texas and Pacific's chartering act required the use of American "iron or steel" rails, but there was an exception for "such as may have heretofore been contracted for by any railroad company which may be purchased or consolidated with" the Texas and Pacific.[107] Arguably, that applied only to contracts signed before the creation of the Texas and Pacific, but nobody seemed to press the issue.

But what about the land grant? Under the original Texas and Pacific chartering legislation, the land grant was given to the Vicksburg railroad or its "successors or assigns." The last is a bit of legalese that makes clear that the rights in question can be exercised by someone other than the original recipient. So, at a special meeting of the directors of the New Orleans, Baton Rouge and Vicksburg Railroad Company, held on December 29, 1880, a resolution was adopted authorizing the president and the secretary of the company to transfer all the interest of the company in the land grant to the New Orleans Pacific.[108] On January 5, 1881, the two men did just that.[109]

The president was former Connecticut senator Barnum, and his son, William Milo Barnum, a New York City attorney who would form a Wall Street law firm a few years later with his friends John Woodruff Simpson and Thomas Thacher, was the secretary. At the board meeting, the president was not there, and the minutes report that "Mr. Simpson" took the chair.[110] And we should note that Barnum the younger is listed as owning just over 35,000 of the 45,000 shares in the New Orleans, Baton Rouge and Vicksburg.[111]

At the end of 1881, the shareholders of the Vicksburg met to approve their board's actions. Barnum and other shareholders representing 42,775 shares in total gave Wheelock, the president of the New Orleans Pacific, their proxies at what then turned into a lightly attended meeting.[112] Not surprisingly, Wheelock voted to ratify the transfer to his railroad. Something was clearly afoot, and later authors have attributed the plan to Gould.[113]

An anonymous, undated memorandum in the Dodge papers provides insight into the deal.[114] First, the New Orleans Pacific was not to assume any of the Vicksburg's debts. That ruled out any direct merger of the two railroads, lest the Pacific get stuck with all the bonds that the Vicksburg had issued. Next, the New Orleans Pacific was to issue land grant bonds backed by the land rights that it had received from the Vicksburg, much like those issued by the Texas and Pacific. One-quarter of the bonds were to be reserved to settle claims against the Vicksburg, and the remainder split between the two railroads. Presumably, the Vickburg's share went to the railroad's shareholders—mostly the Barnums. The New Orleans Pacific's share of the land grant bonds was in turn to go to the American Railway Improvement Company.

About six months after the transfer of the land grant, most of the New Orleans Pacific shareholders (including the American Railway Improvement Company) swapped their shares for Texas and Pacific shares, giving that railroad control over the line from Shreveport to New Orleans.[115] The New Orleans Pacific effectively became a subsidiary of the Texas and Pacific.

Once again, the shareholders of the construction company did pretty well. In early 1882, it was reported that the shareholders had paid in $1.6 million (of the $2 million in shares) and received $1 million in Texas and Pacific shares and $600,000 in New Orleans Pacific bonds.[116] In 1885, the construction company announced that a resolution had been adopted declaring a final dividend of 60 percent, payable in the certificates of the New Orleans Pacific Railway Company, for the delivery of land-grant and first-lien bonds of that company, as well as 40 percent in bonds secured by mortgages in lands already delivered to the railroad. Upon the delivery of these bonds and certificates to the stockholders, they were to give the board proxies to authorize the dissolution of the company.[117] Some shareholders sued Dodge and others in Colorado to enjoin the winding-up until they received a fair share of the land-grant bonds, which suggests that the insiders were not distributing all the bonds that they had received.[118]

• • •

In May 1880, Tom Scott stepped down as president of the Pennsylvania Railroad to focus on his health.[119] He remained president of the Texas and Pacific and was reelected in August of that year.[120] At the same time, the board was revamped—Gould wanted more representation, and Frank Bond suggested that this could be achieved by dropping the San Diego representative and three other members.[121] The possibility of getting to the West Coast, particularly San Diego, while still sometimes mentioned, was becoming increasingly remote.[122]

In November, a high-powered group of railroad executives, including Scott, Gould, Sage, and Frank Bond, among others, headed out from Philadelphia in several private cars on a three-week tour of the Texas and Pacific.[123] They held a board meeting in Marshall, where John C. Brown met up with them, and then Scott and Brown, along with a large party of dignitaries, headed to the end of the line near Eastland (about 100 miles west of Fort Worth).[124] Later in the same trip, there was a subtle hint that Scott's health was not fully reestablished: in New Orleans, Brown delivered a speech written by Scott.[125]

Indeed, shortly after returning to Philadelphia, Scott apparently relocated to Florida for the remainder of the winter. In a March 1881 interview, David Felsenheld, who in the 1870s had been San Diego's chief lobbyist in Washington supporting a Texas and Pacific subsidy[126] and more recently an investor in the American Railway Improvement Company, told a San Francisco paper that Scott was doing much better, and he "only suffers from slight lameness in the left leg."[127] However, he also indicated that day-to-day management of the Texas and Pacific was now in the hands of Scott's son.

In late March, Scott returned to Philadelphia and indulged in a bout of philanthropy, donating large sums to several area hospitals and establishing an endowed chair in mathematics at the University of Pennsylvania that still exists today.[128] In early April, one paper reported that he intended to return to Florida, while another said that he would not, "as his Florida trip did not benefit him."[129] The latter article noted that he was largely paralyzed on his left side and had trouble speaking, a description confirmed by other newspapers. It seems likely that he had had another stroke.

Then, in mid-April, he called Jay Gould down to Philadelphia for a summit. Presumably, Gould already had had some inkling of the topic, as they met for less than an hour.[130] When they emerged, Gould had purchased Scott's equity stake in the Texas and Pacific for $4 million, writing what was reportedly the biggest single check to that point.[131] A board meeting was held where Scott's resignation as president and board member was accepted and Gould was elected president in his place. Shortly thereafter, Texas and Pacific moved their offices to the Western Union building in New York.[132] By May, Scott was dead. He was fifty-seven.[133]

Gould no longer had to wait until he completed construction to El Paso; he had control. He quickly suggested a merger of the Texas and Pacific with the Iron Mountain. When the Texas and Pacific bondholders resisted, he made the

Iron Mountain a subsidiary of the Missouri Pacific instead. There was a new controlling shareholder, with different interests than the prior one.

But there remained the threat of the Southern Pacific, which had arrived in Texas.[134]

* * *

On the same day that Gould took over Scott's stake and position in the Texas and Pacific, the board adopted a resolution expressing its Renaultian "shock" at learning—allegedly for the first time—that the Southern Pacific was building through land in New Mexico that had been reserved for the Texas and Pacific, and the Southern Pacific "might" be under the control of the "Big Four."[135] Since Huntington had met with Gould and Scott the year before to discuss some sort of merger of the two rail lines, and those discussions continued through late 1880, this all seems a bit much.[136]

The board then authorized the railroad's president—the newly installed Gould—to take action to rectify this situation. Shortly thereafter, Gould sent Charles Crocker a letter claiming ownership of "all the improvements, fixtures and structures, railroad and railroad material, equipment, etc. thus placed on [the Texas and Pacific's] land grant."[137] One month after the initial board meeting, the Texas and Pacific sued the Southern Pacific in New Mexico. Given that Gould's letter to Crocker had to go all the way to San Francisco, the Southern Pacific crowd probably had little notice of what was coming.

The complaint argued that the Southern Pacific was violating congressional intent by constructing a line that was controlled by the same parities that controlled the Central Pacific. As Judge Dillon (figure 2.3) colorfully put it, "It is obviously against the purpose of Congress to allow the Southern Pacific of California, to get a land grant subsidy for the purpose specially named in Section 23, and then put the knife to the main line of the Texas and Pacific, and defeat the ends which Congress had in view, to wit; an independent line to the Pacific, and a road under government control, and to impair the value of the capital already invested on the faith of Congressional charter in the Texas and Pacific road."[138]

In short, like Scott before him, Gould was casting himself in the improbable role of antimonopolist. The Texas and Pacific offered to buy the Southern Pacific's New Mexico line at cost, but otherwise they sought an injunction and other relief against Huntington's operation.[139] The Southern Pacific responded with a corresponding lawsuit in Arizona.[140] And Huntington made an offer to buy the Texas and Pacific's rights in Arizona for "Twelve thousand dollars in United States gold coin."[141]

JOHN FORREST DILLON

CIRCUIT JUDGE 8TH U. S. JUDICIAL CIRCUIT (1869-79)
JURIST AND AUTHOR. COUNSEL MANHATTAN EL. R. R.

FIGURE 2.3 John F. Dillon, Jay Gould's counsel.

Notable New Yorkers Of 1896–1899: A Companion Volume to King's Handbook of New York City (New York, 1898). https://lccn.loc.gov/99000945.

And the battle commenced. In his lectures at Yale about a decade later, Judge Dillon waxed poetic about the scene:

> On the one side lawyers from New York and elsewhere went in a special car twenty-five hundred miles to Santa Fé, the place of trial. I had arranged a telegraphic circuit, and had sent over the wire to the local counsel the text of the entire bill of complaint. On arriving there our car, which contained a parlor, dining-room, sleeping apartments, and a kitchen, was placed upon the side track of our railroad and served as a hotel, and immediately opposite to us, on another railroad, we saw a like car containing the opposing counsel who had journeyed nearly two thousand miles from the West. There, in the heart and centre of the continent, in the shadow of the Rocky Mountains, in the

old historic city of Santa Fé, which was founded more than two generations before the "Mayflower" landed at Plymouth, and more than one hundred years before the first English colony sailed into the Ashley River, were these two movable habitations, one of which had come from the Atlantic and the other from the Pacific, drawn up, as it were, in battle array. In an adobe building, one story high, with walls six feet thick, which had been the governor's palace under the Mexican régime, and which our government had converted into a court-house, with the old Baldy Mountain, scalped and uncovered, standing in silent majesty and stately grandeur, looking down upon us, we fought for six long midsummer days our legal battle.[142]

But what was the point of it all? The Texas and Pacific had already conceded that it was not aiming to build to San Diego anymore; taking over the New Mexico line would entitle the Texas and Pacific to a large swath of land across that territory, but like its lands in West Texas, it was scarcely inhabited. And both parties accepted that the line had cost more than it was presently worth.

Crocker's affidavit in the case gives us some insight into both parties' motivations. He notes that the Southern Pacific had expended great effort to build over the Tehachapi Pass and across the desert from Colton, California, to Yuma, Arizona, only to find that the Texas and Pacific had not even made it to Fort Worth. As such, the Southern Pacific faced the certainty that it had just built a four-hundred-mile railroad through nowhere, to nowhere, and it then decided to build a connection between Yuma and New Orleans through southern Texas. This was almost thirty-five years before the Panama Canal would open, and the ability to connect to shipping at New Orleans offered real economic potential to the Southern Pacific that otherwise simply represented a roundabout way to get to San Francisco.[143]

Of course, Crocker's affidavit conveniently neglects the monopolistic reasons for keeping the Texas and Pacific out of California, but the reasoning also provides insights into Gould's motivations. Building a railroad between Fort Worth and El Paso in the early 1880s was interesting but hardly gainful. Only by ensuring a reliable connection to California would the Texas and Pacific extension ever be worth anything. That left Gould with two basic choices: build the Texas and Pacific as planned to San Diego, an idea that the railroad had already rejected, or negotiate a deal with the Southern Pacific. The litigation looks like an attempt to obtain leverage for the latter course.

Meanwhile, the two railroads continued to build. The Southern Pacific passed through El Paso in early June 1881 and kept building southeast along the Mexican border. The Texas and Pacific was more than 100 miles from El Paso, although its grading crews soon passed alongside the Southern Pacific construction crews.[144] And then it all stopped.

In an 1893 deposition, Huntington told the story thusly:

> We had our road completed from El Paso out to Sierra Blanca, and Mr. Gould had got pretty well towards there with his track, and I met him in the street one day, and I said to him, "We have got a road there, and it seems to me that your interest and mine lie in the same direction, of both using it, as the road can probably do ten times as much business as we both have to do, and we will have the double capital to invest and double the expense of keeping up when one track will do it just as well," and Mr. Gould, said as I remember, and I think I do remember that very well—said, "I think you are right, Mr. Huntington," and he said, "We will see if we can get on on that basis."[145]

These well-heeled pedestrians met at Huntington's home on Park Avenue several more times until they reached a deal.[146]

Under the Gould-Huntington agreement, signed in November, the two railroads would join at Sierra Blanca, about eighty-eight miles outside of El Paso. East of Sierra Blanca, the Texas and Pacific line would swing slightly northward, roughly following the line of today's Interstate 20 toward Fort Worth, while the Southern Pacific's rails would swing toward the south, generally following the line of today's Route 90, running south of Interstate 10 into San Antonio.[147]

The Texas and Pacific would have track rights to come into El Paso, and it agreed not to build any further.[148] The Southern Pacific promised to accept trains bound for California on its tracks—the line to be operated "as one through continuous line"—and the agreement purported to transfer the Texas and Pacific land grants west of El Paso to the Southern Pacific. Nobody consulted Congress on that point, and legislation would eventually repeal the federal land grants altogether.[149]

There was a new transcontinental route, but the dreams of a southern transcontinental railroad had resulted in a railroad that ran in just two states, albeit for more than a thousand miles. After the Southern Pacific completed its own line to New Orleans through southern Texas, the Texas and Pacific would often complain that this violated the spirt, if not the text, of the Gould-Huntington agreement.[150] "The idea was that all of the business of the Southern Pacific would be poured over the Texas Pacific, and so over the Gould southwestern system to St. Louis and thence north over the Wabash."[151]

For obvious reasons, the Southern Pacific favored its own route to New Orleans, even if it was longer.[152] The Texas and Pacific's bitterness toward the Southern Pacific would linger—even in the 1930s, it was still arguing that the "Southern Pacific Company unlawfully preempted the located line of the Texas and Pacific, leaving this carrier but two alternatives: either (1) to construct a parallel line of railroad through barren territory, or (2) to enter into an agreement by which it secured to itself all the advantages which it would have obtained by constructing a parallel line of its own."[153]

But it is hard to give much weight to the Texas and Pacific's complaints, given that Crocker had pretty clearly stated the Southern Pacific's intentions in his affidavit months before the agreement was signed: "That defendant [Crocker] and his associates are now engaged in constructing a line of railroad . . . to the City of San Antonio, in the State of Texas, so as to form one continuous line of railroad from San Francisco to the Gulf of Mexico."[154]

To be sure, he could have been referring to Galveston, not New Orleans, but the effect would have been the same—diverting traffic to a line fully controlled by the Southern Pacific that connected to a significant port. And indeed, in October 1880, when Gould and Scott were jointly operating the Texas and Pacific, the front page of *The Philadelphia Inquirer* reported that a group from the Southern Pacific was in New Orleans, as "Mr. Crocker is looking for an out-let to the Gulf for his road, which he states will certainly be completed within two years, possibly earlier."[155]

Article VIII of the Gould-Huntington agreement did contain a vague pro-hibition on building parallel or duplicative lines, but only an extremely and perhaps unreasonably broad reading would pick up the Southern Pacific's tracks hundreds of miles to the south. Moreover, that part of the agreement was contingent on the parties pooling revenues, something the federal govern-ment would outlaw in 1887. The Texas and Pacific argument seems to rest on the notion that Gould was duped, something that his contemporaries would have found implausible—Huntington himself said that "Jay Gould was the very ablest man."[156] And as we shall see in chapter 3, Gould himself was quite attuned to the subtleties of language. The Gould-Huntington agreement seems like Gould's attempt to make the most of the Texas and Pacific's feeble position, given years of hesitation and failed attempts at obtaining a government subsidy, without having to actually build any more railroad through nearly vacant lands.

• • •

As 1882 dawned, the Texas and Pacific was finally complete, totaling more than 1,450 miles between New Orleans and El Paso, but existing as an auxiliary part of the larger Gould empire.[157] Moreover, the shoddy construction would soon become indisputable, especially as the American economy increasingly showed signs of reverting to its 1870s torpor.

The basic problem was that the Texas and Pacific was in essence two rail-roads. One, represented by the wonky rectangle and now known as the "Eastern Division," connected developed lands in northeastern Texas to the important hubs of St. Louis and New Orleans.[158] But this independently viable railroad had a very long tail—the "Rio Grande Division" between Fort Worth and El

Paso—that was badly built and lightly populated.[159] And long-haul business was increasingly bypassing this line in favor of the Southern Pacific's "Sunset Route" from Los Angeles to New Orleans via southern Texas.[160]

Indeed, the Rio Grande Division was considered so desolate that the railroad had trouble retaining employees.[161] It eventually staffed the division with Chinese labor—perhaps former Southern Pacific workers—who received the same wages as other Texas and Pacific employees, which was notable inasmuch as railroads habitually paid Chinese immigrants far less than other workers. Paying the same wages implicitly acknowledged the special situation in western Texas.

Nevertheless, the Texas and Pacific continued to underperform. In mid-1883, the road showed a modest profit of $59,000, while in 1884, it was already reporting a $113,000 loss.[162] And this in an area of extremely flexible accounting standards.

As one Gould official wrote in 1883, "there is none of our Roads which has the more constant care, attention and thought of the management, and which produces more unsatisfactory results."[163] And while these sentiments were not generally publicly aired, the market was beginning to take notice. As the *Baltimore Sun* summarized in 1883, the Rio Grande Division bonds "used to be above par, but they sold yesterday at $75^{1/4}$, and today were so freely offered that the quotation broke before noon to 70, some $200,000 changing hands. The incomes have been taking their fall gradually all week, sales making as low as $48^{3/8}$, against over 90, at which they once sold. The stock, which one time commanded over 70, fell yesterday to $21^{3/8}$, and today is not much better."[164]

At the same time, Gould himself was coming under personal financial strain. He had changed his role from speculator to owner, and thus became the subject of the kinds of market attacks that he would have previously launched on others.[165] And he was highly leveraged: for example, the J. S. Morgan records show Gould repeatedly borrowing £200,000 (about $1 million) on a short-term basis, secured by a large block of Missouri Pacific bonds, throughout 1882.[166] Rumors in the press suggest that this was just one of many such loans that Gould had outstanding during these years.

Thus, when Grant and Ward collapsed in May 1884, bankrupting the former president along with his son's firm and putting the economy right back to where it had been in the 1870s, both Gould and his key railroads were quite fragile.[167] Gould's Wabash would be the first major railroad to default on its debts—providing more pain for Grant, who had invested in Wabash bonds—but the Texas and Pacific followed soon thereafter, with its share price dropping to about $12 per share.[168]

As early as July 1882, the Texas and Pacific neglected to pay interest on its Income and Land Grant bonds.[169] In 1884, a bondholder, represented by John R. Dos Passos (figure 2.4), brought suit against the railroad for two years of missed coupons.[170] John Randolph Dos Passos—father of the author, John

JOHN R. DOS PASSOS
DOS PASSOS BROTHERS & MITCHELL, LAWYERS
AUTHOR TREATISE ON LAW OF STOCK BROKERS

2.4 John R. Dos Passos, corporate attorney.

Notable New Yorkers of 1896–1899. https://lccn.loc.gov/99000945.

Roderigo—was a well-known New York City attorney who had first come to prominence by defending Edward Stiles Stokes, who was charged with gunning down Jay Gould's business partner, Jim Fisk, in the lobby of the Grand Central Hotel.[171] He eventually became better known for corporate law work, including the establishment of the "Sugar Trust" in the 1890s.[172]

As noted earlier, the land grant indenture gave the road the option of paying interest in the form of script, which could be used to purchase land, but the railroad made the puzzling choice to argue that the bonds were pure "income bonds," where payment was contingent on sufficient earnings—as Adrian Joline said in 1910, "an income bond is so called because it seldom if ever pays any income."[173] That is, the railroad was arguing that it did not even have to pay in paper.

The New York federal courts would eventually reject this argument, and several years later, that decision was upheld by the US Supreme Court.[174] Notably, after a meeting between Dos Passos and Judge Dillon, the railroad attempted to retroactively pay script, but Dos Passos rejected it on behalf of his clients.[175] And upon the appeal to the Supreme Court, Jay Gould and Russel Sage both personally cosigned with the Texas and Pacific to pay the lower court's judgment, should it be upheld on appeal (as it was).[176] Less publicity was given to Gould's causing the Texas and Pacific to place $60,000 of its own Consol bonds in trust for Gould and Sage, should they be required to pay on the appeal bond.[177]

At about the same time that this litigation was ongoing, the Texas and Pacific stopped paying into the sinking fund to retire the 1875 first-lien bonds on the Eastern Division and skipped a coupon on its Consol bonds—the second-lien bonds that had been issued as part of the 1875 workout of the first construction company's financial problems. But the Missouri Pacific bought up all the coupons it could at face value, meaning that the Texas and Pacific bondholders had no cause for complaint.[178] Notably, this move also made the Missouri Pacific a creditor of the Texas and Pacific, and speculation soon began that a receivership was near.[179] Gould dismissed it all as a "trifle."[180]

Basically, Gould had come to agree that the Texas and Pacific needed work, and paying for that work while also making interest payments on the debt was not possible.[181] Of course, the shareholders, including Gould, could have put in new capital, but Gould would rather the bondholders pay for the repairs while at the same time permitting him to keep control of the company. While as a matter of corporate law theory, this could be dismissed out of hand—shareholders lose their stake when creditors go unpaid—in the real world Gould's position was quite viable, as it would be today.

Indeed, while it is mostly speculative since stock ownership records are nonexistent, it seems likely that Gould was retaining control of the Texas and Pacific with a minority stake at this point.[182] We have already noted his distribution of many shares to construction company investors. And Professor Grodinsky states that Gould sold most of the securities that he received from Scott at the peak of the market in the early 1880s.[183] If so, it only emphasized the point that Gould's real financial interests lay with the Missouri Pacific, and control of the Texas and Pacific would be made to serve that end.[184]

The company put forth a circular to bondholders based on an investigation of a subcommittee of the board.[185] The subcommittee was appointed the month before, and the "investigation" appeared to consist mostly of extracts from accounting records, although the report did note that the Texas and Pacific had much higher maintenance expenses than other comparable railroads.[186] All the bondholders were asked to skip some coupons—Rio Grande and New Orleans bondholders would get half in cash and half in new debt for more than four years, and the consolidated bondholders would get half cash for about two years, reflecting the relative strength of the divisions (and those that needed the most work).[187]

The creditors blanched. *The New York Times*, never a fan of Gould's, summarized the basic issue thusly:

Here is a road built only three years ago, bonded at the rate of $20,000 per mile on one division of 336 miles, and at the rate of $30,000 per mile on the other division of 1,151 miles, and with stock on the top of this aggregating $32,000,000, which never yet had traffic enough to earn the interest on its bonds, and yet, after this short time, is declared to need virtual rebuilding throughout its entire length. Total bonded debt about $42,000,000, and stock of $32,000,000 in addition, is represented by a road in such wretched condition that the cost of working it is 76 per cent. of the gross earnings; its rails are of the cheapest and commonest iron, and have worn out; and the roadbed is in so ruinous a state that the circular says the net revenue this year cannot be as much as it was last year. If this condition of things does not indicate a clean steal in the construction of the road what does it indicate? . . . They will probably do it, as Mr. Gould has got them where he usually gets his investors, namely, in a tight place.[188]

A bondholders committee formed, made up of Consol bondholders from the Philadelphia area, where Tom Scott had distributed most of this debt back in 1875.[189] The committee hired John C. Bullitt, a leading attorney of that city known for representing banker Anthony Drexel, among others, and engaged with Gould.[190] Bullitt and his longtime partner, Samuel Dickson, would play key roles in the coming events.

The committee was initially chaired by John C. Wright, but it also included Isaac Wistar, whom Gould soon found he could work with. Wistar was a former Union army general, lawyer, investor, and member of a prominent Pennsylvania family, who sat on the board of several Philadelphia financial institutions and likely represented those interests as much as his own in the Texas and Pacific.[191]

Not surprisingly, as the committee was made up only of Eastern Division bondholders, those bonds received better treatment in the renegotiated deal.[192] Their coupons were paid in cash, while all the other bonds received essentially the same treatment that Gould had originally proposed—half payment in new debt.[193]

Gould also agreed to put some of the Eastern Division bondholders, including Wistar and Bullitt, on the board, with the board meeting on a monthly basis, and to support a new investigation of the Texas and Pacific's maintenance needs.[194] In addition, Gould agreed to seek an independent report on the allocation of revenues among the Missouri Pacific system railroads—many critics felt that MoPac was being favored at the expense of the Texas and Pacific—but the resulting report ultimately just provided for minor adjustments in payments.[195]

Meanwhile, attorney Dos Passos was bringing further suits on behalf of the Income and Land Grant bondholders, and he was even seeking attachments against the railroad's assets to pay the judgments in these suits.[196] This pressure, small but undoubtedly annoying, combined with a realization that the Texas and Pacific needed far more work than could be achieved through skipping a few coupons, led Gould to consider using the restructuring techniques that had already developed in connection with smaller railroads as tools to force a recapitalization of his railroads, while still maintaining his control. As we will see, he tried this out on the Wabash, with mixed success, and it would be the Texas and Pacific that would first successfully utilize the receivership process on a grand scale.[197]

When Wistar and others left Philadelphia in their private railroad car in November 1885 to investigate the state of the Texas and Pacific and its needs for new capital, it would be in furtherance of these plans.[198]

CHAPTER 3

THE START OF CORPORATE BANKRUPTCY

Question: *It was stated yesterday . . . the reason why there was as much friction between railroads and their employés was in the fact that railroads issued stock largely in excess of the money actually invested. And he gave this character of explanation, that in evading the law upon that subject, men who organized a railroad company would also organize a construction company—composed of themselves—the same men, in other words, controlling both companies, and in that way the railroad corporation would pay to the construction company immense sums in stocks and bonds and other securities. Have you any knowledge of such construction companies?*

Jay Gould: *I never have . . . I have had no opportunity of knowing of any such transaction.*

—U.S. House Select Committee on Existing Labor Troubles, April 22, 1886

Right in the middle of the 1880s, Jay Gould faced the loss of key parts of his southwestern rail system. The Missouri Pacific remained solvent, but practically every other piece was on the ropes. Some would have to be let go, but others he desperately wanted to save, most notably the Wabash and the Texas and Pacific. "While Gould considered the Wabash as an indispensable eastern outlet for his southwestern system, he believed it equally essential to retain the Texas & Pacific as an important feeder of eastbound traffic."[1]

Gould adapted the corporate reorganization system as it existed in the 1880s, extending that system to address his much larger railroads to maintain his control over both railroads.[2] He had much prior experience with receiverships in his fights for corporate control—indeed, during the Erie contest in the late 1860s, he had been twice named receiver of that railroad.[3] Since that time, receiverships had become more commonly associated with financial distress, or insolvency, but control still loomed large in these contests.

The Wabash went first, in many ways acting as a kind of first draft for Gould's efforts to save his interests in the southwestern system. The Wabash reorganization has distracted scholars and commentators from the importance of the Texas and Pacific reorganization, not only because the Wabash was first, but also because Gould attempted to create a debtor-led reorganization process that looks a lot like modern chapter 11. As such, commentators tend to assume a direct line from the Wabash to today.[4]

But the Wabash reorganization was a failed attempt: It got bogged down in litigation and ultimately was reorganized a year after the Texas and Pacific, despite starting its proceedings the year before.[5] Moreover, Gould's attempt to create a debtor-initiated procedure flopped—in the late 1940s, prominent restructuring attorney Robert Swaine referred to Wabash as "the principal case, *of very few*, where a debtor itself was the plaintiff in the action in which its reorganization was effected."[6] The same decade, the Securities and Exchange Commission (SEC) would write that "the procedure failed to crystallize along these lines; instead, there was increasing resort to another, and less novel, form of legal action. This was the general creditor's bill, out of which the standard procedure was even then being fashioned in other cases."[7]

The Wabash-style procedure was unattractive, as it would not support a filing in federal court—most receiverships were instead started by creditors from a different state than where the railroad was incorporated, which provided the "hook" for federal jurisdiction because of the "diversity" of citizenship between the railroad and the creditor.[8] The frequent failure to distinguish among the many highly planned receiverships started by friendly creditors—under a "creditors bill"—and an atypical case like Wabash, started by the debtor-railroad itself, made the Wabash case seem far more important that it was.[9]

· · ·

Gould's Wabash, St. Louis, & Pacific Railroad Co. linked St. Louis with Toledo and the midwestern states in between. It was the key eastern arm of the Gould system, which otherwise stopped at the Mississippi. It had been formed from more than two dozen prior companies, each of which came with its own set of mortgage bonds. Gould had placed a distinct capital structure on top of the entire amalgamation, including one set of secured bonds that had been sold for the purpose of consolidating all the old, small mortgage bonds. But the consolidation never happened, and thus the new bonds simply added more debt to the convoluted capital structure.[10]

The road had been limping along for at least a year with the benefit of short-term notes signed by Gould, Russell Sage, Sidney Dillon, and Solon Humphreys, who had been president of the road in the early 1880s. Gould was now president of the railroad, while the others were all board members. The Wabash was leased to the Iron Mountain, which was part of the Missouri Pacific system, making the Wabash something like a second-tier subsidiary of MoPac (or MOP, as it was called in earlier days). Gould, Sage, and Dillon were involved in the management of all three, and of course Gould controlled the Missouri Pacific.

In 1884, the short-term notes were about to mature, at the very moment that the guarantors were short on cash themselves.[11] Thus Gould responded with "a stroke worthy of his reputation: ingenious, strikingly original, unexpected, and technically legal, and ethically dubious."[12] In short, the railroad filed its own receivership petition, asking that Humphreys and Thomas E. Tutt, a former judge, be appointed receivers. The receivers then issued a large batch of receivers' certificates—first-priority debt designed to facilitate reorganization—to pay off the short-term notes.[13] Basically, Humphreys the receiver paid off Humphreys and friends as the creditors, with new debt that moved the other existing debt further from getting repaid.[14]

The bondholders were shocked. "Journalists in the United States and abroad, especially in London, where some major investors lived, blasted the 'Wabash swindle.' "[15] In a profile of Gould, *The Washington Post* called Wabash the "stench in the nostrils of the financial world."[16] The creditors moved to replace the receivers, and succeeded for that part of the road that was east of the Mississippi, taking a large chunk of the road out of Gould's control.[17] Gould's "failure was not due to his own lack of shrewdness or foresight or trading ability, but rather the forthright independence of an able judge who had unhesitantly condemned the passive acquiescence of a brother member of the judiciary."[18] As we will see, rare stuff indeed.

The Wabash was temporarily split in two, and the lease to the Iron Mountain terminated, but it finally reorganized as a single railroad in 1889.[19] By then, the Texas and Pacific had already completed its own reorganization.

• • •

In December 1884, *The Sun* sent a reporter from New York City to Midland, Texas, to investigate the town that the Texas and Pacific had been advertising in posters and pamphlets in immigrant neighborhoods on the East Coast. The reporter's train arrived fourteen hours late, and the reporter found that Midland was somewhat less than the agricultural paradise that had been suggested:

> There is not a tree to be seen. The only approach to one is a palm, that is carefully nursed by a German who keeps a hotel across from the depot. The prairie is called fertile. There is not a drop of surface water, and the soil breaks up easily into alkali dust that chaps the lips and makes the eyelids sore. . . . The seventeen-room hotel which "for beauty and convenience is not exceeded in the State," according to the prospectus, can furnish the worst meal for the money to be found anywhere with hardest bed thrown in. The rooms are divided by a board partition.[20]

Midland, unimaginatively named for its location on the Rio Grande Division of the Texas and Pacific, was reflective of the railroad's operations throughout the state in those years. In early 1885, management's report to the board of directors noted that only some three hundred miles of the track (of nearly fifteen hundred) were laid with steel rails. The "entire New Orleans division from Cheneyville to New Orleans is subject to overflow from high waters of the Mississippi," and the company was carrying about $83 million in debt, with net income of less than $800,000.[21] One newspaper observed that the railroad earned less in 1884 than it did when Thomas Scott had owned it, and "its stockholders have been compelled to admit that they own one of the worst roads in the country."[22]

As one anonymous commentator later observed that "Mr. Gould and his friends . . . as Directors of the Texas and Pacific, agreed with Mr. Gould and his friends, as Directors of the Pacific Improvement Company, upon modifications in the contract by which the improvement company was saved a great deal of expense, and the railroad company made to accept inferior work, as it has since turned out to the serious injury of the deceived bondholders." The writer went on to note that the railroad's Rio Grande Division was poorly built to begin with, and then abused by the construction company in its race with the Southern Pacific, so it "was practically an old road when delivered to the transportation department of the company."[23] Similar observations could and would be made about the New Orleans Division.

The distribution of the debt among the three parts of the Texas and Pacific is shown in figure 3.1. In addition to what is shown in the chart, the railroad had about $2 million in various operational or "floating" debt and a further $2.7 million in script given to the Income and Land Grant bondholders in place of actual coupon payments. The biggest single issue was the bonds issued to Gould's construction company for the Rio Grande Division, but their lien was against the weakest part of the railroad. As we will soon see, a large amount of

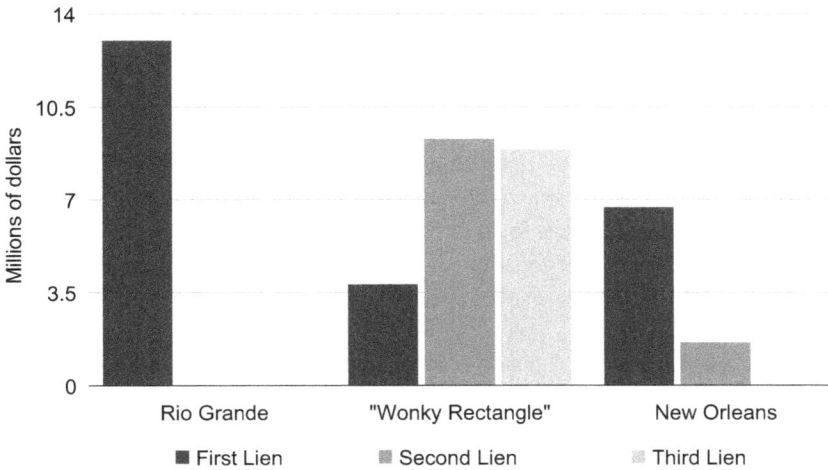

3.1 Texas and Pacific debt.

Figures taken from report to board.

this debt was owned in Europe—the result of sales by the controlling parties in the construction company.

The "Consol bonds," the 1875 second-lien debt against the wonky rectangle, were the most secure of the larger issues based on the current income of the railroad, and those were the ones that Isaac Wistar and his Philadelphia friends represented. The first lien on the New Orleans division was from its construction, while the second-lien debt was the new Terminal Bonds—ostensibly issued in place of part of the coupons on the Rio Grande and New Orleans bonds, although most ultimately ended up with MoPac—which represented a first lien on the terminal facilities at New Orleans and a junior lien on the remainder of the railroad. As a result, they also constituted a fourth lien after the Income and Land Grant bonds on the rectangle, and second-lien debt on the Rio Grande Division, but I show them in just the one location in the figure.

In sum, the four biggest bond issues shown in figure 3.1 come from construction companies: those on the "wings" of the railroad, the Rio Grande and New Orleans divisions, Gould construction companies, and those on the core (the wonky rectangle) from Scott's company and the reorganization of that company after the 1873 panic.

In March 1885, Gould cut workers' pay, and they went on strike at both the Missouri Pacific and Texas Pacific until Gould uncharacteristically agreed to meet the Knights of Labor's demands to restore wages.[24] In April, General

Wistar and his party met General John Calvin Brown, then serving as vice president and general counsel (or "general solicitor," as they called it) of both the Missouri Pacific and Texas Pacific, in St. Louis to commence a tour of the Texas railroad, only to have their private train crash into another on the Iron Mountain line, killing Wistar's nephew, who was riding in the engine.[25] The inspection tour never made it to Texas and Pacific territory, and it was put off for several months while everyone recovered—with Brown nursing a broken arm.[26]

Wistar's eventual report—from Philadelphia, dated December 8—was blunt, stating that the physical condition of the Texas and Pacific was "bad."[27] The committee identified three causes:

- First, From the modification, by the Construction Company, of the original plans of construction;
- Second, From the inferior construction and inferior material used by the Construction Company;
- Third, From the inadequate maintenance of the ties, rails and other perishable material, in the effort to pay interest on an aggregate indebtedness, which, including all classes, now exceeds $30,000 per mile of track owned.[28]

Bold stuff to present to a board that still contained members—most notably Gould and Sage—who had been closely associated with the construction company. But Gould clearly was thick skinned, being little worried about what today we would call his "public image."

And while the first two points are somewhat specific to the nineteenth century, the last is one that persists to this day—many a leveraged buyout target has alienated customers in an anxious attempt to make bond payments. The report concluded with an estimate that at least $4 million in new money was needed to get the railroad into proper shape.

By December 12, there were rumors that the report—which had still not been made public—would lead to a receivership.[29] On the 16th, the board met and adopted two resolutions: one approving the report and another stating that the company should not borrow any more money to pay interest on existing debt.[30]

The second resolution was the closest that the Texas and Pacific board would ever get to (retroactively) approving its receivership.[31] The day before, the Missouri Pacific had filed a petition—the first page of which is reproduced in the introduction of this book as figure I.1—in New Orleans:

The Missouri Pacific Railway company, a body corporate under the laws of the State of Missouri, and a citizen and resident of said State,—in its behalf, as well as of all other corporations and persons similarly situated that, by intervention, bring themselves into this suit for protection of their interests,—brings into this Honorable Court its bill of complaint against The Texas and Pacific Railway

Company, a corporation existing under the law of the United States, of America, and having citizenship and domicile, properties and rights in the States of Louisiana and Texas, under and by virtue of the laws of both of said States, and having at the same time citizenship and domicile, offices and places of business in this District, and officers and agents herein, in the City of New Orleans, on whom process may be served.[32]

The twenty-some-page petition recounted the corporate history of the railroad, beginning with its various acquisitions under Tom Scott and its complex capital structure, and concluded that "said Texas and Pacific Railway Company is an insolvent corporation, owning 1,487 miles of road, with mortgages thereupon to the amount of $43,340,000, the interest whereupon it is unable to meet; that the line of road is out of repair and in so dangerous a condition that the said company can not perform its duties as carrier, with safety, expedition and convenience to the public; that judgments have been obtained against said corporation under which the assets are liable to levy and sale." And thus MoPac requested the appointment of a receiver "for protection of their interests."

The petition was quickly followed by an answer from the Texas and Pacific admitting the bulk of the charges, and expressly stating:

In answer to paragraph 21 of complainant's bill, defendant admits its roadbed is not in such condition as to enable it to discharge its duties to the public as promptly and faithfully as is its duty to do; and admits that its present condition results from its earnings not being sufficient to pay its fixed charges and maintain its track in proper condition. It also admits that it has applied its earnings, after paying operating expenses, to the pay of its fixed charges, to the neglect of a proper maintenance of its roadbed as well as to the payment of the advances noted by complainant.[33]

Who had authorized the Texas and Pacific's answer and, more importantly, whether that person (most likely Gould) had authority as a matter of (federal) corporate law to do so in the apparent absence of board action were never addressed.[34]

From inception, the press viewed the receivership as a Gould plot for control at the expense of investors.[35] As one London magazine wrote about the Texas and Pacific shortly after the case commenced:

Even with honest management, it would require years of growth to be able to meet its fixed charges, let alone past deficits. Nevertheless, during the recent boom, Mr. Gould is believed to have succeeded in relieving himself of a large amount of Texas and Pacific Stock at 25 cents on the dollar. Should he succeed in maintaining his receivership, he will very probably be able to buy the bulk of the bonds for the price at which he sold his Stock. If so, Mr. Gould will have made both a clever and profitable exchange, while his friends will have been once more subjected to the operation which they jocularly call "freezing out."[36]

Another paper drolly headlined the news of the receivership with "Gould Rescues Another Railroad."[37] Even New York's staid *Christian Union* warned investors about "selfish, grasping schemes put forth by Gould and the Missouri Pacific to rob them of their security."[38]

The petition was submitted to Judge Don Pardee, a circuit judge in the Fifth Circuit. On the next day (the same day that the board met in New York), Pardee accepted the petition and appointed Brown and Lionel A. Sheldon coreceivers.[39] An ancillary case was quickly filed in federal court in Texas, where the same receivers were appointed by Judge Pardee, thus ensuring that the entire length of the railroad was under court protection.[40]

Even if most of the railroad's board did not know about the filing until after it happened, there are several indications that receivership was organized well in advance.[41] We can see a small but insightful indication of the extent of the planning in the Texas and Pacific corporate files, where a copy of the court's order commencing the receivership was date-stamped on December 16, the very day that the court entered the order, with "Office Receivers—Tex. & Pac. Ry., Dallas, Tx." on it.[42] Somebody had thought to have the rubber stamps ready for the big day and already knew of Brown's plans to operate out of Dallas (rather than Marshall, its Texas headquarters).[43]

The petitions and answer were drafted in Philadelphia—by John C. Bullitt, the Wistar committee's counsel (and a Texas and Pacific board member), at the Texas and Pacific's expense, despite MoPac being the supposed petitioner— and brought to New Orleans in advance of the filing, perhaps even in advance of the completion of Wistar's report on December 8.[44] Throughout the case, Bullitt (who would represent the prime committee in the case) and his partner, Dickson (who represented several of the bond trustees), would draw on key railroad cases from the greater Philadelphia area—like the receiverships of the Central of New Jersey and the Reading—to inform the process by which the Texas and Pacific case, the first successful large-scale receivership, should proceed.[45]

And with the filing, we see the definite establishment of the key form that receiverships would take for as long as they were utilized: a lawsuit commenced by a friendly unsecured-creditor-plaintiff, acting under the instruction of the debtor-railroad and its advisors. That is, the plaintiff-creditor was not really a plaintiff in the customary sense; rather, the entire "lawsuit" was for the protection and advancement of insider interests. In this case, Gould controlled both parties, but going forward, any malleable plaintiff-creditor would do, so long as they were headquartered in a different state from the debtor.[46]

Not only was counsel for MoPac and the Texas and Pacific present for the filing, but also counsel for the bond trustees (Dickson, who likely also had a hand
in drafting the petition), as well as John Dos Passos, counsel for the Income and
Land Grant bondholders who had sued the railroad in New York. The latter
had been adverse to the Texas and Pacific (and Gould), and he would continue
to flash about the edges of Gould's plans for a while longer, but his invitation to
New Orleans suggests he was already coming within Gould's circle—if Gould
had viewed him as truly adverse, he could have simply filed the case before Dos
Passos made it to New Orleans.

Brown was the company representative among the receivers, and indeed he
was present in New Orleans on December 16 and immediately took his oath.[47]
He nonetheless remained counsel to the Missouri Pacific for several months
after his appointment.[48] And he remained vice president of the Texas and
Pacific throughout the case. For example, his signature in that role appears on
a document, executed during the receivership, providing for the sale of more
than 6,000 acres of railroad land in Howard County, Texas, to Gould's sidekick
and fellow Texas and Pacific board member, Russell Sage, at $2 per acre, below
the value that the railroad had placed on the land.[49] Squaring the role of vice
president answering to the president (Gould) with the role of receiver, holding
the railroad's assets in trust, is difficult—likely impossible.

Brown's position as receiver represented the very American notion—present
in today's chapter 11—that having somebody who "knows the company" in
charge of the reorganization is more efficient and less disruptive than having a disinterested trustee or receiver. As Jay Gould later told Congress, "It
was because of [Brown's] familiarity with [the railroad] that the bondholders selected him as receiver. The judge added Governor Sheldon of his own
motion."[50] Given that Brown would later claim that Gould made him various
promises to encourage him to take the position, we might wonder whether it
was the bondholders who chose him.

On the other hand, Lionel A. Sheldon (figure 3.2) is a little-known figure today, who before 1885 had served several terms in the House of Representatives from Louisiana's 2nd Congressional District—recall that he was
among the political figures who attended the founding of the Texas and Pacific
in New York City in the early 1870s—and one term as territorial governor of
New Mexico.[51] Most important for present purposes, during the Civil War, he
and Don Pardee served as senior officers in the 42nd Ohio Volunteer Infantry,
under the command of future president James A. Garfield.[52]

After the Civil War, Sheldon and Pardee practiced law together in Louisiana
for three years, until Pardee became a state court judge. Sheldon then entered
politics, serving in the House from 1869–1875 before losing to a former Confederate in the Democratic congressional wave that followed the 1873 financial
collapse and brought the decline of Reconstruction. By 1879, he had returned to

3.2 Lionel Sheldon.

Library of Congress, Prints & Photographs Division. Brady-Handy photograph collection. LC-BH83-76 [P&P].

Ohio, where he was selected as a delegate to the Republican convention the following year, at which his former commanding officer received the Republican nomination for president.[53]

Following Garfield's inauguration in March 1881, Sheldon and his wife spent two months living in the White House—a considerable portion of Garfield's abridged administration.[54] During this time, Pardee was appointed to the federal court in New Orleans, and Sheldon to the governorship in New Mexico.[55] His four-year term as governor had ended, and he was three months into a newly established law practice in Socorro, New Mexico, when word came that he had been appointed receiver.[56] It seems that Sheldon and Pardee remained close—during the receivership, Sheldon's wife, Mary, took Judge Pardee's daughter on a trip to Pasadena as a guest of the railroad.[57]

Brown and Sheldon would each receive $10,000 per year (more than $300,000 today) plus expenses for their efforts.[58] As noted, Brown based himself in Dallas, while Sheldon largely worked out of New Orleans.[59]

· · ·

While Brown and Sheldon began to evaluate the railroad now in their charge, Gould negotiated a reorganization plan.[60] Precisely when this work commenced is impossible to know for sure, but it seems that sometime in December, Gould presented Wistar with a term sheet, which led Wistar to counter, and term sheets and telegrams went back and forth between New York and Philadelphia.[61] The fact that Wistar withheld his report for more than a week after its completion, allowing Gould to commence the receivership before the report was made public, might suggest that Wistar and Gould were already in discussions before the receivership.

Sometime around the start of 1886, Gould had a plan typed up. It began, "The Committee of reorganization appointed by the bondholders, propose the following plan . . .," although there was no such committee in existence yet.

The plan called for the replacement of all existing debt with a new fifty-year first-mortgage bond, subdivided into "series A" and "series B" bonds. The series A bonds would operate as traditional debt, while the series B would be income bonds, with coupons payable only if the railroad generated sufficient income in the year the payment was due.

Gould proposed giving the Consol bonds their full-face amount in series A bonds, and an additional 10 percent in series B bonds, to compensate for the extended maturity and the reduction in the coupon rate from 6 percent to 5 percent. Indeed, these changes were the only losses that Wistar's group would face under the proposed plan, and in exchange the bondholders were receiving securities with a face amount 10 percent greater than the old bonds.

Wistar used Gould's plan as the basis for his counterproposal, for which he agreed to seek support among the Philadelphia consolidated bondholders. He changed Gould's suggestion that the Rio Grande bondholders get paid half in new first-lien bonds and half in income bonds, to instead pay these bondholders mostly in income bonds (the two then settled on a 30/70 split). Wistar added a line about the scant rain in West Texas to help justify this treatment. He also made a subtle change to the plan, requiring MoPac to pay "at least" $15 for its shares in the reorganized company. Wistar also demanded that bonds and shares in the railroad's treasury could be sold only upon a two-thirds vote of the board at two successive meetings, suggesting some concern among the bondholders with a future under MoPac (and Gould's) control.[62] Gould accepted Wistar's proposed allocation of the series A and B bonds in a telegram to Wistar (written in Gould's own hand) dated January 5, 1886.

Shareholders would exchange their shares on a three-for-one basis, reducing the existing shares outstanding from just over 300,000 to 100,000.[63] The old shareholders were also given the right to buy one additional share at $15 per three old shares they owned, an option that (in the unlikely event every shareholder exercised it) would result in old shareholders retaining two-thirds of the reorganized railroad's shares. The Missouri Pacific would receive 100,000 new shares in exchange for its claims, or about one-third of the new shares. In short, Wistar's plan gave Gould a nice head start toward regaining his majority stake in the reorganized Texas and Pacific, and perhaps even represented effective control of the company, provided nobody else obtained a larger stake.

The losers were those who had invested in either of the two newer wings of the Texas and Pacific: the Rio Grande and New Orleans divisions. General Grenville Dodge and those back home in Iowa who took his investment advice are prime examples of this sort of investor. Indeed, Dodge would spend much of the receivership arguing that the Rio Grande Division was more valuable in the long term than the Eastern Division, clearly somewhat stung that Gould had left him behind regarding his plans for the railroad.[64]

Investors in the common stock were also in for a shock, facing a two-thirds reduction in their stake unless they stumped up $15 per share and a realization that Gould had slipped out the back door while they were not looking.[65] Now he was proposing to come right back in: "Again Gould had taken advantage of a small debt, created under questionable conditions, in order to dominate a property with a small investment."[66]

The basis of MoPac's claims against the Texas and Pacific would remain vague throughout the proceedings, even though they were apparently central to the viability of the receivership petition. The petition stated that "since 1881 [when Gould took over] The Texas and Pacific Railway Company, by an arrangement made between it and The Missouri Pacific Railway Company, by which the lines of The Texas and Pacific Company were to be, and in fact have been operated, in conjunction with The Missouri Pacific . . . [which] advanced in the payment of operating expenses and interest on account of The Texas and Pacific Railway Company, the sum of $1,688,015.79."[67]

About $1.1 million of the debt was collateralized with $2 million of the Terminal Bonds (of $3 million outstanding), which must have happened just before the receivership, as the Terminal Bonds were issued only as part of the negotiations with Wistar's Philadelphia bondholders.[68] Various other securities—including Texas and Pacific stock, New Orleans Pacific stock, and bonds given to the railroad by various Texas localities—provided collateral for other parts of the debt.[69]

Wistar, other than being a member of the Texas and Pacific board, had no formal role in the receivership at this point. Nevertheless, he and Gould continued to exchange drafts, and discussed plans for establishing a bondholder committee in the case, to be chaired by Wistar and populated by people of their choosing. The negotiations were kept from the public, with Wistar complaining to Gould's Texas and Pacific representative in New York—the steadfast C. E. Satterlee; Marshall O. Roberts had appointed him secretary of the railroad in 1875, and he would serve well into the twentieth century—when the press began to publish stores about the anticipated plan.[70] Indeed, he urged Satterlee to "give bad points to the papers" about the railroad, to tamp down what he viewed as excessive speculation in the Rio Grande bonds.[71]

• • •

Gould and Wistar came to an agreement on the form of a reorganization plan just in time for Judge Pardee's first scheduled hearing in the case. Attorney Dos Passos was there, filing an objection on behalf of his Land Grant bond-holders and arguing for the appointment of a third receiver—former Texas and Pacific vice president Frank Bond was mentioned.[72] Dos Passos also filed three motions: two on behalf of bondholders complaining that their indenture trustee was not actively protecting their interests, and one from shareholders making a similar complaint about the Texas and Pacific board.[73]

Most of these filings were on behalf of William T. Walters, a wealthy Bal-timore resident with Confederate sympathies who had spent most of the Civil War abroad to avoid arrest. Walters had been part of a Baltimore con-tingent investing in Tom Scott's Southern Railway Security Company, and a member of the original board of the Texas and Pacific in 1871, who traveled with Scott to San Diego.[74] He had also been an investor in the American Rail-way Improvement Company, according to Dodge. The Dos Passos pleadings actually requested very little beyond a voice in the case, but Judge Pardee brushed them aside, suggesting that an investor's committee could better address such concerns.[75]

While Dos Passos publicly acted as the fly, bothering Gould's plans in New Orleans without really stopping them, he also furthered them, cosigning the receivers' $50,000 surety bond, along with Gould and Sage.[76] His ultimate goals remained unclear, and perhaps he did not even have a specific plan, but at the very least he was signaling his continued consequence to Gould.

About the same time, Gould sent a long telegram to Satterlee from South Car-olina (he was yachting in the South during the winter) stating that Dos Passos should be kept off of Wistar's committee, when formed, as Gould hoped to work "with and through" him in connection with the reorganization. Perhaps he felt Dos Passos would lose flexibility upon becoming a member of the committee?

In the telegram, he also stated that "the plan you and I agreed to with Genl. Wistar is perfectly just to all interests and I hope the board will adopt it unanimously—a long and expensive receivership should be avoided." He concluded by telling Satterlee that "you may use this dispatch in your discretion," which seems like an invitation to leak it to the press, notwithstanding Wistar's prior complaints.[77]

In mid-January, the Texas and Pacific board resolved that Wistar, with Satterlee as secretary, should form a reorganization committee.[78] In future reorganizations, debtor-companies would be far more subtle about their role in launching friendly committees, but here we see the basis of the idea.

The terms of the Wistar-Gould plan were widely known and discussed in the business press, even though the plan had not been formally presented by anyone to anyone.[79] The *Commercial and Financial Chronicle* almost immediately denounced it as a scheme to put the Texas and Pacific into Gould's hands.[80] The article suggested that the Philadelphia involvement in the railroad were nothing more than a fig leaf to disguise Gould's aims.

It would not be until early March that the committee was actually appointed, and while the committee purported to represent all classes of investors, the initial members—Wistar, John Markoe, Winsor, Welsh, John N. Hutchinson, and Benjamin F. Newcomer—were the Philadelphia bondholders that the Texas and Pacific board had named earlier.[81] Two members from New York, one of which was Satterlee (whose stake as investor was never clarified), were added to the committee a few weeks later.[82] *The New York Times* reported that these additional members were added after consultation with Gould, which did nothing to improve the Wistar committee's reputation for objectivity.[83]

But as it turned out, this group was not unvaryingly fond of the plan that Wistar and Gould had previously negotiated.[84] When the committee stalled on approving the plan, Wistar suggested calling a meeting of just the Eastern Division bondholders, so that they might instead take up an offer to swap the consolidated bonds for Iron Mountain bonds.[85] So much for representing all the investors.[86]

This proposed swap, which was quickly forgotten, seems like a bit of Gould exasperation leaking through, as the result would have simply been a new Missouri Pacific interest at play in the reorganization, given that Iron Mountain was openly controlled by Gould's favorite railroad. Eventually, a slight redistribution of the bonds was agreed upon, whereby the consolidated bondholders would get 20 percent of their claim in series B bonds (as opposed to 10 percent) and the Rio Grande holders would get slightly better treatment as well, receiving 35 percent in series A and 65 percent in series B.[87] Nevertheless, the Rio holders viewed this as effectively a 65 percent haircut—inasmuch as they were dubious the series B bonds would ever pay anything.

The New Orleans Pacific bondholders would get half series A and half series B, while the Land Grant bondholders would be given the land outright. Wistar apparently contacted Drexel & Co. in Philadelphia to provide underwriting for the deal, but nothing much came of it.[88]

The final plan obscured the treatment of MoPac's claims, but that cat was already out of the bag. Even the dullest bondholder knew that this plan was Gould's.[89] As such, it was not well received.

. . .

Shortly after the receivership commenced, Brown and Sheldon filed a report on the Texas and Pacific's condition with the court.[90] They broadly observed that "the entire lines of the Texas & Pacific Railway are greatly in need of renewals in the shape of steel rails and new ties . . . All the tracks were laid originally with iron rails, many of which were of inferior quality, and have now become so worn as to render traffic and travel on many portions of its lines slow and dangerous."

They predictably spotted that the Rio Grande was in hideous shape, but also reported that the New Orleans line was "fearfully bad." They observed that Texas and Pacific passenger trains took ten hours longer than Southern Pacific trains to run from El Paso to New Orleans, despite the Texas Pacific having the shorter route. Alarmingly, they also noted that to achieve even this miserable performance, trains were running "at a higher rate of speed than is deemed safe on some part of the lines," given the condition of the railroad.

Sheldon later testified that "very little of the entire track is ballasted." He further noted that "the rolling stock is in bad condition."[91]

. . .

In the meantime, the Texas and Pacific was hit by a Knights of Labor strike that in the long run would absurdly harm the union more than Gould. The Knights had developed in the 1870s to become unlike any union before or since: "It offered workers of all races, skills, and sexes an alternative to the reigning exploitative culture. The Knights formally opposed the wage system and called for land reform, the eight-hour work day, monetary reform, an end to child and convict labor, and equal rights for women. Unable to move the mainstream parties on their issues, the Knights organized third party efforts in 189 towns and 34 states in the mid 1880s, with significant success."[92]

In March 1885, the Knights had facilitated the agreement with the Gould railroads that, among other things, rescinded recent wage cuts.[93] "Attended by wide publicity and speculation as to the supposed awesome power of the Knights, the triumph over Gould was followed by a surge in labor organization."[94]

Both Sheldon and Brown took the position that they were not bound by this agreement, even though the Texas and Pacific was arguably party to it.[95] Receivers did have the power to disavow unwanted contracts—just as modern chapter 11 debtors can "reject" such contracts—but in this case the receivers never terminated the agreement. Instead, they argued that to the extent the agreement was binding on the Texas and Pacific, it was not binding on them because it would work an unwarranted restriction on their powers as receivers.[96]

The immediate spark for the strike was the firing in late February 1886 of Charles Hall, an employee in Marshall, Texas, who was a member of the Knights.[97] Hall was a carpenter by trade, and he served as foreman of the Texas and Pacific shop that made and repaired boxcars. According to Hall's testimony, he asked his supervisor to be out for parts of three days to attend a local Knights of Labor meeting, but when he did so, he was terminated for being absent. As Ruth Allen has argued, even if Hall had misunderstood his supervisor's consent, "his discharge under the conditions and while the district assembly was in session can be explained only as crass ineptitude or as the expression of a desire to affront the workers with the serious possibility of forcing them to revolt."[98]

For the Knights, hooking their larger concerns to the specific issues associated with Hall proved to be a tactical error, as it allowed Gould, Brown, and Sheldon to paint the strike as an overreaction by the union to normal employer action at one railroad. Brown would repeatedly quip that Hall had been given a leave for three hours and stayed away three days, and the others would often argue that Hall was incompetent—all of this was probably untrue, but it distracted from the broader concerns that the Knights had with the operation of the Gould railroads.[99]

Once the strike began at Marshall in early March, the Knights of Labor put out a proclamation that is worth reprinting in full, as it gives us a sense of what the Knights felt the strike was about:

Laboring Men of All Classes!

Whereas the Missouri Pacific, leased and operated lines, and the Texas and Pacific Railway are now employing convict and Chinese labor on their different railways in Texas to the determent of honest labor; and

Whereas the said railways are continually violating their contract of March 15, 1885, and in fact have never complied with its provisions; and

Whereas we have resolved to come to the rescue of our downtrodden brethren, known as unskilled laborers: Therefore,

Be it resolved, that we call upon all laborers, track-men, engine-wipers, coach-cleaners, baggage and freight hands, etc. to lend us their aid in driving convict and Chinese labor from our different roads, and that all laborers receive just and fair renumeration for their services. Track-men, get clear out of sight of the track until we gain your victory.

Knights of Labor[100]

And thus began a strike that eventually expanded to the broader Gould system, from end to end.[101] Notably, Hall features nowhere in the proclamation, but the Knights were swiftly outmessaged by both Gould and the receivers. Without a clear explanation from the Knights of their motivations, the press adopted the cartoonish version of Hall's dismissal as the reason for it all.[102]

The Knights of Labor entered the strike internally divided. Their top leader, Terrance Powderly, seemed to view the Knights as a kind of social organization that would foster economic literacy among workers, as well as arbitration of grievances among labor and capital, while those closer to the "front lines" focused on more tangible issues like wages and hours.[103] The latter group was represented by the suitably named Martin Irons, who led the Knights organization in the southwest. He handled the Hall matter and would become the scapegoat for all that followed.[104] It was Irons that started the strike, while Powderly, the putative leader, would learn about it only from the press.

Before the strike commenced, Irons attempted to contact the receivers about Hall's firing, but quickly ran up against a railroad policy, which the receivers had continued, of refusing to speak with any representative of the Knights who was not also a railroad employee. It is unclear whether the receivers' continuation of this policy represented coordinated action with the nonbankrupt Gould railroads or simply a shared mindset, and in Brown's case, he was both receiver and corporate executive; but in either event, the notion that employment negotiations might be conducted through the employee's agent was apparently inconceivable.[105]

This despite the fact that the receivers and railroad executives were themselves agents and conducted business through innumerable agents. Even Sheldon, who was no fan of financiers like Gould, found the Knights hard to comprehend: "This is supposed to be a land of freedom. The American people have battled politically and in protracted and bloody war to install the principle of free labor over the whole land. Is there not danger that it will be stricken down by these Knights of Labor themselves? Appearances indicate that they are more absolutely under control of their leaders, than soldiers of the regular Army are under their officers."[106]

This led to several missed opportunities to head off the strike, which in turn fed suspicions that Gould had commenced the receivership to attack labor. Brown's central role in the receivership reinforced this idea.[107]

For example, when Irons sent the railroad two telegrams in late February warning that a strike would result if the Hall situation was not addressed, his messages were ignored. As the Texas and Pacific manager who handled the matter later testified: "I made inquiry as to who Martin Irons was—whether he was an employé of the company or not—and was told that he was not an employé of our company, and that he lived in Sedalia, Mo.; I therefore paid no attention to his message."[108]

A similarly peculiar encounter occurred when Sheldon's private car passed through Marshall shortly after Hall's firing. A group of three Knights, led by Irons, entered the car to speak with the receiver about the matter. Sheldon testified: "I told him that I could not settle that question with him or with any other stranger, and said that I should see Mr. Hall. He answered that Mr. Hall was out on the platform and that I could see him. I told him that I was in great haste to get to Dallas on some very important business, and to investigate this matter I had to hear both sides, and that I had then no time."[109]

A similar attitude also cropped up in one of the better-known episodes of the strike, when Gould appeared to agree to arbitration, only to take it back the very next day. Powderly met with Gould at the latter's home on Fifth Avenue, and the meeting resulted in a Gould telegram to the Missouri Pacific vice president in St. Louis, H. M. Hoxie, which ended with the line, "We see no objection to arbitrating any differences between the employés and the company, past or future."[110] The strange plural drafting reflects Gould's convenient rediscovery of corporate governance, and his instance that he could act only on behalf of the board.[111]

Powderly took this sentence to mean that Gould had agreed to arbitration, and he thus announced the strike would be ended.[112] Gould called him back to his house the next day and stated that all he had meant by that sentence was that Hoxie would receive no objection from the board if he decided to arbitrate. That is, the ball was in Hoxie's court.

The language could support such an interpretation, but it is hardly what a normal English speaker (i.e., a nonlawyer) would have made of it. Professor Klein suggests that it was a misunderstanding, since Gould always gave operational managers lots of discretion, but it is unclear why Powderly should have or could have known about the railroads' internal operations, and why such practices should have any bearing on Powderly's sensible interpretation of the language that Gould used.[113] But Klein aptly notes the fundamental absurdity of the situation: "Powderly negotiated as if he had control of the strike, which he did not, while Gould disclaimed having charge of developments when in fact Hoxie had done his bidding to perfection."[114]

Hoxie, of course, promptly announced that he would engage in arbitration only with actual railroad employees, which did not include any of the senior leadership of the Knights.[115] It seems entirely possible that Gould and Hoxie were doing a "good cop, bad cop" number on the Knights of Labor that got a bit confused. At the very least, Gould was being very slippery with language that he must have known would be understood in a way that conflicted with his own private meaning. Throughout the entire affair, Gould and the receivers seemed in little hurry to bring the strike to an end, perhaps correctly anticipating that the longer it went, the worse the Knights would look to the broader public.

In late 1885, the Knights had had some success in resolving their grievances against the Wabash by threatening the broader Gould interests at MoPac.[116]

The fact that the Wabash was in a receivership did not seem to come up, but in the Texas and Pacific case, the difference was made to matter.

Now the Texas and Pacific receivers gave the strikers notice that if they did not return to work, they would be terminated. And when the terminated employees continued to obstruct the operations of the railroad, the receivers went to court in mid-March, seeking court orders in both Texas and Louisiana to protect the operation of the railroad.[117] Writs issued by the district court judges along the railroad ordered the U.S. marshals in the districts to facilitate safe operations of the railroad.[118] In many cases, the marshals hired new deputies, and these often included Texas and Pacific employees.[119] In Louisiana, the marshal deputized men provided by a New Orleans detective agency, an expense that he would ultimately pass to the receivership estate.[120]

Handbills blanketed the two states, warning the striking employees that they were in contempt of court because the railroad was under the protection of a federal receivership.[121] Figure 3.3 shows an example of one of the more than two hundred handbills that the U.S. marshal in Louisiana posted around Gretna, where the Texas and Pacific operated a ferry terminal to connect with downtown New Orleans across the river.[122]

The U.S. marshal for the Northern District of Texas filed a ten-page affidavit detailing twenty-four arrests made under the court's writ, along with stories of burned bridges, disabled locomotives, and stones being thrown at him and the railroad employees.[123] Indeed, the increasing violence of the strikes undoubtedly led to the decline in community support that the Knights experienced in April 1886.[124]

In the end, Judge Pardee finished it all off with a mighty blast of reactionary rhetoric, garnished with anti-Asian bias:

> The Texas & Pacific Railway property is in the hands of a recognized constitutional court of the United States, fully able and willing to enforce its lawful authority, and to protect its officers; and that court cannot listen to demands of any secret organization, whether alleged to be social, political, or economical in character . . .
>
> the investigation made under direction of this court, and the development of affairs since the strike was ordered, satisfy me that such alleged reason was a mere scheme and pretense, and that the real motive for the order to strike was to compel a recognition of a certain secret labor organization (which, by evidence, has been shown to be about as arbitrary and autocratic in dealing with labor as the famous six companies of China) as an existing power, so that its officers shall be consulted in the operation and management of railroads in which they do not own any interest, and of which they do not even pretend to be employees.[125]

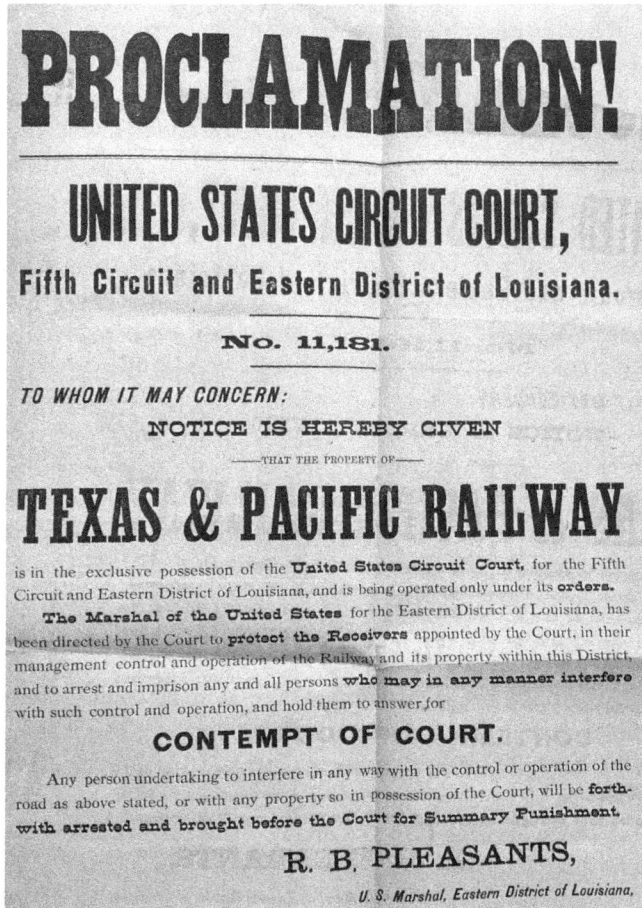

3.3 U.S. marshal's handbill.

Missouri Pacific Railway Company v. the Texas and Pacific Railway Company, Box 682.

He sentenced various strikers to the Dallas jail and received strong support from most of the nationwide press.[126] "The Knights suffered a total defeat. Not only did the union receive no concessions, but many strikers never got their jobs back."[127]

But Judge Pardee's odd connection of the Knights of Labor to the Six Companies—a San Francisco social organization that was often smeared as a furtive controller of Chinese immigrants in the United States—brings us back to the Knights' original complaints regarding the Texas and Pacific's use of Chinese and convict labor.[128] At heart, the Knights' argument was that labor provided through both channels served to depress the wages of unskilled workers.[129]

The Texas and Pacific receivers testified before Congress that they used Chinese labor only on the Rio Grande Division, where the railroad had long found it impossible to employ American labor—of any race. Indeed, Brown said that he could not even get African Americans or Irish people to work there for any length of time, suggesting that both groups demanded more entertainment that could be provided by the Staked Plains.

The receivers reported that just over one hundred Chinese laborers were employed on the division. If this number was accurate, then fully half these men were shortly thereafter subjected to a brutal racial attack in which they were tortured and robbed, with no apparent response by law enforcement.[130] It does not seem that anyone at the time drew any connections between this event and lingering tensions from the earlier strike, perhaps because by then, most had absorbed the understanding that the strike was about Hall's firing and Martin Iron's rogue attempt to achieve recognition for the Knights.

As noted in chapter 2, the railroad's unwillingness to pay workers more for service on remote parts of the line was the obvious reason for the Texas and Pacific's inability to retain employees for the Rio Grande Division. To solve this problem, press accounts indicate that the railroad entered into a contract with Sam Hing, an El Paso–based entrepreneur, under which he agreed to provide up to three hundred Chinese laborers to work on the division.[131] That number is notably higher than the one that Brown gave before Congress.

Press stories also indicate that Hing provided Mexican labor to work on other parts of the railroad—the receivers did not volunteer that information, and neither the congressmen nor the Knights seem to have been aware of the importation of non-Asian workers.[132] The Chinese were the subject of special animus at this time, the Exclusion Act having been passed just a few years before, and that might have blinded the parties to the broader issue.[133]

Before Congress, Brown likewise suggested that the Texas and Pacific had not used convict labor since the 1870s—press accounts indicate such use as recently as 1884—and he was cagey about whether the railroad might not use such labor again in the future.[134] Convict labor, especially given the strong racial element of penal labor in the former Confederacy, frequently replaced slave labor on railroads in the South, and it would be remarkable if the Texas and Pacific deviated from that pattern.

At heart, the unskilled workers represented by the Knights were just like the Chinese and convict laborers, in that they were being buffeted about by a corporate bankruptcy system that they did not understand and that gave them little voice. The strike's interaction with the receivership left most workers worse off, but Gould's entire railroad empire, in and out of bankruptcy, benefited from the thrashing that the Knights took in the receivership.

• • •

3.4 Charles McClung McGhee.

Used under license from the McClung Historical Collection, Knox County Public Library.

While the receivers and Jay Gould were snuffing out organized labor, the investors were standing up alternative committees. Domestically, one of the most active figures was Charles McClung McGhee (figure 3.4), formerly of Knoxville, Tennessee, but by 1886 largely residing in Manhattan.[135]

On the eve of the Civil War, McGhee had owned a thousand-plus acres—and sixty of his fellow humans—outside Knoxville.[136] East Tennessee was not a place of large-scale plantations, so McGhee was easily one of the largest slaveowners in the area. During the war, he operated a pork processing factory in Knoxville and acquired the title "colonel" for working with the Confederate commissary.[137]

He was apparently astute enough not to invest much of his meatpacking profits into either Confederate bonds or currency, as shortly after the war, he had the means to charter a bank in Knoxville.[138] That in turn led to investments in several small local railroads, which he consolidated under the banner of the East Tennessee, Virginia and Georgia Railroad.[139] McGhee and his fellow investors then sold out to Tom Scott and the Southern Railway Security Company. A term in the state legislature brought him in touch with Brown, who was then the governor.

After the 1873 Panic, Scott disbanded the Southern Railway Security Company, and McGhee got his railroad back. He ran it for the next decade with an array of financial partners—indeed, throughout his long career, he seemed to be able to adapt to a variety of styles, perhaps by operating largely out of the public eye—the last of which brought him into the world of New York high finance by listing the East Tennessee railroad on Wall Street. Consistent with the times, his New York friends also loaded up the railroad with an abundance of bond debt to fund several acquisitions of neighboring railroads. Throughout this period, McGhee enhanced his wealth with securities manipulations that would have been quite familiar to Gould and other better-known financiers of the age. For example, he shorted Tennessee state debt shortly before beginning a press campaign to foment rumors of a default.

The heavy load of debt got the East Tennessee in trouble during the Grant and Ward panic of 1884, and a receivership commenced. McGhee and his partners controlled a sizable amount of the bonds, and as a result, McGhee went on the committee. During the receivership, he met a variety of key players from the New York financial community, including Frederick Olcott, of the Central Trust Company, and even more important, Jacob Schiff and Robert Fleming, of whom more will be told later in this chapter.[140] In May 1886, the East Tennessee, Virginia and Georgia *Railroad* was sold to the East Tennessee, Virginia and Georgia *Railway*, and McGhee decided to stay in New York full time, among other things to represent the reorganized railroad on Wall Street.[141]

Somewhere along the way, McGhee had made a substantial investment in Texas and Pacific debt.[142] Part of this was in Consol bonds, but an even greater part was in the other bonds and the common stock that Gould and Wistar were eviscerating under their proposed plan. By the latter days of the restructuring, he held 530,000 shares of common stock, $237,000 in New Orleans Pacific debt, $230,000 of the Rio bonds, and $179,000 of the Consols. Interestingly, he also owned 100,000 shares of Missouri Pacific.[143]

In April, a meeting of the Rio Grande division bondholders was called at the offices of A. M. Kidder Co., McGhee's main brokers. Press stories after the meeting stated that McGhee had joined the new Rio Grande committee that was formed, and a notice to that effect was sent to Satterlee, but it appears that McGhee decided not to serve, as his was not among the names that were included on later committee publications.[144] Charles M. Fry, president of the Bank of New York, chaired the committee, and Mayer Lehman, one of the original Lehman brothers, acted as secretary.[145]

The committee quickly put out a circular to bondholders, asking them to pay $5 per bond toward expenses, along with an argument that the Wistar committee was allowing the Rio Grande Division to remain in disrepair, in order to strong-arm bondholders into depositing into Gould's favored plan.[146]

• • •

In receiverships, investors deposited their securities with trust companies that were working with specific committees. The three-way arrangement was subject to a deposit agreement:

> The deposit agreements are one-sided contracts. They are not negotiated by the parties dealing at arm's length. They are prepared solely by the committee, or more realistically, its counsel. In fact, seldom does the depositor see the completed agreement . . . Accompanying circulars may advise the security holders of particular provisions which the committee desires to emphasize as showing its honesty of purpose or as making deposit seem not unattractive. But ordinarily the security holders are not advised of the fact that the agreements confer upon the committees powers that are as broad as the ingenuity of counsel can design, and that give the committee almost unlimited control and dominion over the securities.[147]

The investors would receive a "certificate of deposit" in exchange for their securities, and often these certificates were themselves listed on the major stock exchanges for trading. Depositing a bond or other security with a specific committee meant that the depositor was supporting that committee's plan.[148]

As such, depositing served the same function that voting does in modern chapter 11 cases. Securities could be withdrawn only after a plan was announced and a deadline for withdrawals set, and only upon payment of a charge for the investor's proportionate share of committee expenses, including attorneys' and bankers' fees, which were quite large. This tended to discourage withdrawal since the investor would have to pay the expenses in cash. Depositors who remained until the plan was implemented paid expenses indirectly, through reduced payouts under the plan.

The deposit agreements also gave the committee full use of the deposited securities, which sometimes meant that there was effectively no way to withdraw since the committee might no longer have the securities, or might have pledged them in exchange for a loan.[149] The agreements thoroughly renounced any possible liability of committee members, and the courts adopted an indifferent approach to the deposit agreements generally, which they viewed as a contract among consenting adults.[150]

• • •

In May, the Rio Grande committee moved that Brown and Sheldon issue receivers' certificates to repair the division.[151] The committee reported that it represented more than $5 million in bonds (of about $13 million outstanding), including those held by "B. Neugas & Co., of London, a very large holder of the Rio Grande Securities."[152] Wistar and the railroad objected, arguing that the Eastern Division bondholders should not have to pay for repairing the Rio Grande Division.

Shortly thereafter, a committee of Income and Land Grant bondholders was established.[153] Among the members was W. C. Hall, apparently still representing the Louisville interests that had sold the Southern Pacific to Tom Scott more than a decade before. A stockholders committee followed, and then a committee of the New Orleans Pacific bondholders.[154]

The opposition was becoming increasingly active, although Gould and Wistar still had the advantage of controlling the direction of the reorganization, especially so long as the various committees remained distinct. Indeed, most of the committees proceeded to produce reorganization plans, further confusing matters.[155]

Gould swung Dos Passos over to his side by promising to get the reorganized Texas and Pacific to pay him $50,000 in cash for providing Wistar with guidance on the Land Grant Bonds.[156] The attorney also picked up some side work threatening to sue members of the equity committee who badmouthed Missouri Pacific employees and that company's treatment of the Texas and Pacific before the receivership.[157]

An international committee entered the mix in early June, after a group of Rio Grande Division bondholders met in London, at the headquarters of the English Association of American Bond and Share Holders on Great Winchester Street (not too far from J. S. Morgan's offices). The chair opened the meeting by noting that it had been called by members who held somewhere between $2 million and $3 million of the Rio Grande bonds. He then proceeded to summarize the proposed Wistar plan, concluding that "the essence of the whole thing . . . they proposed to get the control of a railway 1,480 miles long for £360,000; for that was really what the scheme amounted to. He fancied that the English holders of bonds were likely to coincide with the *Financial Chronicle* in thinking 'that such an arrangement was about the boldest plan to "squeeze" [investors] that had ever been conceived.' ('Hear, hear.')"[158]

The meeting then proceeded to appoint a committee to represent Rio Grande bondholder interests in the case, which included McGhee's friend Robert Fleming (grandfather of Ian).[159]

Robert Fleming was interested in bonds, American railroad bonds in particular.[160] He founded one of the first Scottish investment trusts (essentially what Americans would call a "mutual fund") to invest in American railroad securities.[161] The success of that and subsequent trusts resulted in frequent trips to the United States, particularly when the bond issuers needed to be reorganized. Among other restructurings, he was involved in the post-Gould receivership of the Erie railroad, the still-incomplete Rio Grande, and the East Tennessee, Virginia and Georgia, which as noted, had just completed its course when the Texas and Pacific came along.[162]

The London committee immediately sent him to New York to meet the relevant parties and attempt to work out an agreement that was fair to all investors. Whether such a thing is possible is something that we should keep in mind throughout our tour through corporate bankruptcy history, but at the very least, Fleming was tasked with seeing that the London Rio Grande bondholders had a voice in the discussion. He cabled McGhee that they should try to form a new "first class" committee and asked if McGhee's "Baltimore friends" had deposited their securities with Wistar.[163]

One of McGhee's Baltimore friends was undoubtedly Walters, who in the Dos Passos pleadings was identified as owning a large block of common stock and some $250,000 in New Orleans Pacific bonds.[164] Walters was one of many large investors that McGhee was in active correspondence with during the case.[165]

Fleming arrived in New York on July 11 and immediately went to work.[166] He met with the Rio Grande committee and accepted an offer to visit with the Wistar committee in mid-July. Before that meeting, he entered into an oral agreement with Kuhn, Loeb & Co.—the most prestigious American investment bank in the 1880s, and in later years the sole rival of J. P. Morgan & Co. (formed in 1895)—to backstop a little surprise that he intended to spring on Wistar.[167]

Under the agreement, Kuhn, Loeb agreed to backstop any offer for the Consol bonds that Fleming might make. That is, they agreed to buy the bonds on Fleming's behalf. To spread the risks of this deal—recall that there were more than $9 million of these bonds outstanding—they put together a syndicate of investors that agreed to join in buying the bonds. Kuhn, Loeb first brought in the Drexel-Morgan organization to take up one-third (or $3.1 million), which was in turn parceled out to the Drexel-Morgan offices in Philadelphia, New York, and London, as well as other brokers and investors.[168] For example, Robert Fleming himself took $200,000 of the Drexel-Morgan subsyndicate.[169]

Kuhn, Loeb likewise sold bits of their $6.2 million stake in the syndicate. McGhee took $165,000 and Walters took $160,000, but the latter soon sold his stake to McGhee, who thus ended up with $325,000 in total.[170] To collateralize this obligation, McGhee deposited his own block of Texas and Pacific Consols with Kuhn, Loeb.

Upon arriving in Philadelphia, Fleming offered to buy all the Wistar's committee's consolidated bonds for 95 plus accrued interest.[171] This was a bold move, designed to change the dynamics of the reorganization by shunting the Philadelphia contingent to the sidelines. The price undoubtedly tempted the committee members—the Consols had been trading at about 90—but Wistar (and more important, Gould) were not ready to quit just yet, and thus the committee turned down the offer.[172]

McGhee worried that Gould would now force through the original Wistar plan, using the Wistar committee's commanding position in the Consols to force the Rio Grande and New Orleans bondholders to join. Indeed, in mid-July, the Wistar committee was undoubtedly behind press articles reporting that "so great were the deposits of the Texas and Pacific Railway securities under the reorganization plan at the Fidelity Trust and Safe Deposit Company to-day that the regular business of the institution was retarded."[173] Fleming urged McGhee not to "give up the battle without putting on our armour," and stressed the need to undertake "joint and undivided action."[174]

At about the same time, Fleming was pushing Jacob Schiff, lead partner of Kuhn, Loeb, to actively participate in the reorganization.[175] "Jacob Schiff was to

JACOB HENRY SCHIFF
KUHN, LOEB & CO.
BANKERS

3.5 Jacob H. Schiff of Kuhn, Loeb & Co.

Notable New Yorkers of 1896–1899. https://lccn.loc.gov/99000945.

Kuhn, Loeb what . . . J. P. Morgan was to his firm."[176] He joined Kuhn, Loeb in 1875, and led it to becoming the leading railroad investment bank of the 1880s—muscling out Drexel from its prized position as lead banker to the Pennsylvania Railroad.[177] After 1890, Kuhn, Loeb and J. P. Morgan and Co. would be the topmost American investment banks until the Great Depression.[178]

McGhee eventually agreed to join the "first class" committee that Fleming was putting together with Schiff.[179] Fry and Lehman would join from the prior Rio Grande committee, but Olcott, of the Central Trust Company, would become chair of the new committee, a position that he had held in many other reorganizations (including that of the East Tennessee). Fleming, McGhee, and Schiff would be joined by Walters and J. Kennedy Todd, a Scottish-American banker who often represented European investors in restructuring cases in the 1880s and 1890s.[180]

The new Olcott-Fleming committee, as the press would call it, was open to every class of Texas and Pacific investor except for the Consol bondholders. On August 3, the new committee released an outline of its proposed reorganization plan and urged investors to deposit with the Central Trust Company in support of the plan.[181] Notices in the London papers encouraged overseas investors to do the same, and the English Association offered to help transmit the securities to New York.[182] The new committee put out their own stories about their overwhelmed trust company, and papers worldwide proclaimed the Wistar plan "completely defeated."[183] Some papers even reported that Newcomber had withdrawn from the Wistar committee to instead support his old Baltimore friends backing the Olcott-Fleming committee.[184]

The committee announced that the new plan would be based on three key principles:

1. A reduction of the fixed mortgage interest charge to a limit of absolute safety.
2. The reinstatement in the new company of all the present securities in equitable order and proportions.
3. Provision for putting the property in, such condition as to enable it to be operated with efficiency and economy.[185]

The plan called for replacing all the existing bonds—except a small morsel of Texas school loan debt still lingering from the old Southern Pacific—with new first- and second-lien debt.[186] These new bonds would pay 5 percent interest and become due in 2000—more than one hundred years in the future.

The new bonds would be redistributed as shown in table 3.1.

Notably, the plan basically ignored the Terminal bonds that had been given to MoPac to secure its purported claims against the Texas and Pacific.

The second-lien debt coupon payments would be payable "out of the net income of the company, and shall be non-cumulative."[187] That is, the company

TABLE 3.1 Olcott-Fleming proposed plan

	Old amount	New first lien	New second lien
First lien	3,784,000	3,784,000	0
Consol (wonky rectangle)	9,316,000	10,433,920	0
Rio Grande	13,028,000	5,211,200	10,422,400
New Orleans Pacific	6,720,000	4,032,000	4,032,000
Income and Land Grant	8,123,000	0	3,249,200
Terminal	750,000	187,500	0
Common shares ($32,164,600 par value)		0	3,216,460
Total	**41,721,000**	**23,648,620**	**20,920,060**

would pay interest on these bonds only if it could, and failure to pay one year would not carry over to the next.

But after 1892, the second-lien debtholders could appoint a committee to take over management of the railroad if coupons had not been paid. This provision addressed an important weakness in the Wistar plan, where many bondholders thought that Gould would manipulate the earnings of the Texas and Pacific to keep the series B bonds from ever receiving payments. Under the new plan—J. P. Morgan termed it the "Fleming scheme" in a telegram to J. S. Morgan—the Rio Grande bondholders, as the largest recipients of the new second liens, would get control if Gould attempted such a move.[188]

The first-lien debt was tied to the plan's first stated principle—namely, fixed charges should be reduced to a level that the railroad actually could afford to pay. The $23.6 million in first-lien bonds would result in coupon payments of about $1.2 million per year, and the committee estimated that even on a conservative basis, the railroad should be able to generate at least $2.4 million in net income. The total debt load actually went up a bit under this plan (about $44 million versus $42 million), but the maturity date was pushed out to the faraway land of the twenty-first century and just under half the coupons became elective.

The shareholders would keep their shares in full but pay a $10 per share assessment, which also entitled them to the second-lien debt shown in the table, in a face amount equal to the assessment.[189] It bears noting that $10 at the time is about equivalent to $330 today, so the assessment under any of the proposed plans represented a substantial burden for a shareholder who might own 100 shares.

This money, plus the next two years' earnings of the Texas and Pacific, were to be dedicated to fixing up the railroad, and paying MoPac's claim *in cash*. That last provision was sure to get Gould's attention. The committee was in some sense calling his bluff by treating the MoPac claim as if it were an actual claim, not a tool for control.

The old first-lien bonds would remain in place until they matured, with new bonds first, then the refinanced ones. The Land Grants would receive the land associated with the bonds, while the second-lien bonds were given in exchange for their release of their other liens on the railroad's property.

In a practical sense, what did this plan mean for an average bondholder? If we imagine a Rio Grande bondholder who received their bond by buying a certificate from the construction company, they paid $900 for the right to receive $1,000 in the 1930s, with semiannual interest at 6 percent. They never received most of those interest payments, and some came in the form of the Terminal bonds.

Now the promise to receive $1,000 in the 1930s was being replaced with a promise to receive $400 on the first mortgage bonds and $800 on the second mortgage bonds, but not until the year 2000, when this bondholder could never expect to be alive. Nearly all the value in the new bonds then was in the coupon payments, but only the first mortgage bonds actually *promised* interest payments, and both bonds offered payments at a slightly lower interest rate: 5 percent. That was certainly below market with regard to the second-lien debt, given the risk that interest might never be earned.

In some sense, the second-lien bonds were performing the same function as the common shares in the original certificate transaction: a kind of "lottery ticket" add-on to the primary security. Of course, our certificate holder might keep those old shares too, but they would have to pay $50 for the privilege of doing so, so we might consider that a bit of a wash.

The original bond, which cost $900, was now chiefly replaced with a bond that was worth at most $400, and when they were finally issued, they tended to trade below par. In December 1888, *The New York Times* had them at 90—suggesting that our investor's new first-lien bond was really worth $360.[190] The second-lien notes were trading at just under 40, so we might add those back in and conclude that our investor got a total package of securities worth $680 in exchange for her original investment. We might also note that two years later, the first liens were trading at 86 and the seconds at 30.5.[191]

· · ·

The Olcott committee immediately took up the syndicate agreement that Fleming had negotiated and adapted it to support the proposed plan.[192] Kuhn, Loeb and Drexel launched a public offer for the Consol bonds at 97.5 and accrued interest, in an attempt to sweep up the bonds that did not want to participate in the new plan.[193] But J. S. Morgan's records indicate that by then, the bonds were trading above par, probably in reaction to the newly proposed plan, so it is doubtful that the offer got many takers.[194]

The Olcott-Fleming and Wistar committees met, and Wistar hotly denied charges that he was advocating for Gould's interests.[195] He made a similar denial in his autobiography years later, instead presenting himself as the righteous defender of Philadelphia bondholders and mentioning nothing of his negotiation of a plan with Gould before his committee was even formed.[196] Brown wrote to McGhee in early August 1886 that he too knew nothing of relations between Gould and Wistar, and "if they have any, or are working together I know nothing of it."[197]

After the failed meeting with Wistar, the Olcott-Fleming committee appointed Schiff and Fleming as its agents to approach Gould about a possible deal. The three met and quickly reached an agreement, only part of which would be made public (or disclosed to Judge Pardee). The Olcott-Fleming committee approved the deal, with Olcott dissenting, and Gould telegraphed Wistar at 5 p.m.:[198] "I send you results of action of Fleming's committee today. Also the memorandum as initialed by Mr. Schiff and myself. I hope it will be satisfactory to you, as it is to me."[199] The next day, it was publicly announced that the two committees had agreed to a plan and would merge.[200]

The public terms of the deal were that the Wistar committee would remain the lead committee and the Wistar plan would remain the reorganization plan for the railroad. But the Wistar committee would drop three members, including Satterlee, and take on Fleming, McGhee, and Schiff. Thus New York had three members and Philadelphia had three general members, but Wistar gave Philadelphia the advantage. Moreover, the original Wistar plan would be amended to match the Fleming plan, with one significant change, noted next. In short, Wistar got to call Fleming's plan his plan.

The reorganized railroad would give the Missouri Pacific about $6 million (par value) in common stock in exchange for its claim, but the railroad would also issue $50 million in new stock under the plan. That is, MoPac would get more stock than under the original Wistar plan, but in a bigger pool of stock outstanding, and subject to the second-lien bondholders' right to take control of the company starting in 1892. MoPac would get about 12 percent of the common shares under this plan, as opposed to a third under the original Gould-Wistar plan.

The investment banking syndicate would buy any Consols owned by either committee, would agree to purchase up to $500,000 in receivers' certificates, and would also purchase any shares that went unsold because the old shareholder neglected to pay the assessment. The syndicate would also agree to give the "friends of the Philadelphia committee" a 10 percent stake in the syndicate.[201]

The private parts of the deal included a promise by the new committee to pay the legal fees and expenses of all prior committees, including the London committee. Satterlee would be secretary of the new committee, and Bullitt the general counsel. Isaac G. Rice, the secretary of the Olcott-Fleming committee, and Dos Passos would become associate counsel to the committee.[202] It is unclear if either of these latter two actually did any work in these positions, but they were paid.[203]

Also, in the private form of the deal, it was made plain that the "friends of the Philadelphia committee" meant Jay Gould, and that of the $2.5 million of Consols that the syndicate was obligated to buy from the "committee," $1.3 million belonged to Gould—the original Wistar plan would have benefited Gould coming and going.[204] The Wistar committee's rejection of Fleming's offer to buy them out also becomes more understandable—more than half of their bonds were owned by Gould, whose interests were not those of a typical bondholder. The reorganized railroad also would be bound to pay the syndicate for the difference between 97.5 (the amount at which the syndicate was publicly offering to buy bonds) and the amount that the syndicate had to pay the committee.

The New York members were to have a veto over the composition of the new board of directors.[205] The final typed version of the deal, which Gould, Schiff, and Fleming initialed, gave Fleming the right to name six board positions, to which he suggested he would name a mix of investors like himself, Schiff, McGhee, and Walters. He also suggested J. P. Morgan, but neither Morgan nor Schiff would ever sit on the Texas and Pacific board. Gould suggested himself, the Wistar committee members, Brown, and George Gould (Jay's son, about twenty-four years old at the time) for his slots. Satterlee was to be secretary and treasurer of the reorganized company.

The plan was acceptable to most, but not to the Land Grant bondholders or the stockholders, or at least the stockholders' committee. Gould viewed the latter mostly as annoying holdouts, and he would eventually agree to pay their "expenses" to make them go away.[206]

The Land Grant bondholders' committee proved more challenging, and it represented some $7.8 million of the $8.1 million of outstanding bonds, so it needed to be reckoned with.[207] But eventually a settlement was reached between the new Wistar-Fleming committee and the Drake committee (as the Land Grant bondholders committee was called then) to provide for a larger recovery in the new second-lien bonds (now 60 percent instead of the original 40 percent) and $75,000 of the latter committee's expenses.[208] Even then, Wistar doubted their reliability and asked Satterlee to mention to "Fleming & McGhee the great propriety of getting at least a proportional quantity of income bonds deposited by the Drake Committee" with the trust company, in advance of paying the Land Grant's expenses, because "our influence upon the Drake Committee for the complete execution by them of their part of the agreement, will be reduced" after payment.[209]

As a result of this settlement, the railroad's land grants (about 3.5 million acres in all) eventually went into an entity called the Texas Pacific Land Trust, a publicly traded entity that exists to this day, for the benefit of the Land Grant bondholders.[210] As of 2024, its web page proclaims it to be "one of the largest landowners in the State of Texas."[211] And at the end of 2024, the company was added to the S&P 500.[212]

Interestingly, this settlement was once again negotiated in New York by Gould, three New York committee members (Schiff, Fleming, and McGhee), and the members of the Land Grant committee, and was presented to Wistar thereafter, further undercutting Wistar's claims of independence from Gould.[213]

A governance dispute then broke out between Gould and the New York bondholders. In particular, the bondholders wanted Gould (still the president of the railroad) to step down in favor of an independent president. Brown was most often mentioned—and Brown felt that Gould had promised him such when he was named receiver—but his appointment was called into question when Gould turned on him, suggesting that he was "extravagant" in his management of the railroad.[214] Frequent trips to New York in the railroad's private car, as well as stays at the swank Fifth Avenue Hotel (located on the southwest corner of Madison Square), tended to support this argument. And indeed Fleming found some truth in it, despite his otherwise steadfast opposition to Gould—Brown and Fleming had a testy relationship throughout the receivership.[215]

Absent agreement on management, the New York bondholders wanted to keep the railroad in the receivership for as long as possible, or at least until the next shareholders' meeting could be held.[216] As McGhee wrote to Wistar in April 1888: "The presidency of the Company should be secured to Gov. Brown and we can not afford to surrender our control of the property until this is done. The commitments we have made to Governor Brown, as well as, the interests of the security holders are such that we can not afford to make any mistake in this regard, and upon this I think you and I fully agree."[217] But the bondholders were undercut by their conflicting desires to keep the Texas and Pacific's federal charter.[218]

On Friday, November 4, 1887, *The Philadelphia Inquirer* carried a short story on page 7: "The committee of the Texas and Pacific reorganization committee appointed to purchase the railroad at foreclosure sale started last evening for Texas. The committee consists of General I. J. Wistar, John N Hutchinson and John Markoe, of this city; Robert Fleming, of Scotland; . . . McGhee of Knoxville, Tenn., and C.E. Satterlee, of New York, and they were accompanied by Samuel Dickson, Esq, of this city, as counsel."

Four distinct foreclosure sales happened in late 1887—two in Texas and two in Louisiana; the Santa Fe even made a rare competing bid for the railroad.[219]

In addition to various bonds tendered, the committee paid a total of $27,500 in cash (in the form of certificates of deposit) and $190,000 in receivers' certificates.[220] The $27,500 would be the total pool of assets available to any creditors who did not participate in the plan, as everything else would be transferred over to the new corporate entity.

Of the thirty-one railroad foreclosure sales that year, the Texas and Pacific was by far the largest, measured by the length of track or bond debt outstanding. And of the receiverships commenced that year, only the Chesapeake and Ohio (C&O), with $33 million in bond debt (compared with $44 million for the Texas and Pacific) approached it in size.[221] Sheldon resigned shortly after the sales, assuming that the receivership would soon be over, and he looked forward to his new life in Southern California.[222] He would remain in Pasadena until his death in 1917.

The foreclosure sales were a prelude to the transfer of the railroad to a new operating entity, but the new entity would necessarily have to be a state-chartered corporation, there being no federal law that allowed for purchasers of railroads to plunk the assets into a new federal corporate shell.[223] Presumably, the new corporation would be more susceptible to Texas state railroad regulation, which was increasing in vigor as the 1880s progressed.[224]

Once all the major parties had agreed to the Wistar-Fleming plan, the committee began discussing the possibility of reorganization on a purely contractual basis, without the need for a sale that would destroy the federal charter. As a result, they held off from having Judge Pardee confirm the foreclosure sales, but this increased the risk that Gould might go to court and ask for the receivership case to be dismissed. After all, what exactly was the point of keeping the railroad in receivership if the foreclosure sales had been abandoned?

Letters flew back and forth between the parties, accusing Brown of mismanagement and Wistar of doing Gould's bidding. As Schiff bluntly put it in a letter to Wistar: "I think you are mistaken if you assume that the holders of the new securities will want to get out of the Receiver's hands quickly without inquiring closely into details; I think to the contrary, that these holders will expect from us to give them a chance to first say who shall manage their property hereafter, before we again deliver it into the hands of those who have ruined it, and I shall be very sorry to see you weakening in the position which I thought you had firmly taken."[225]

All the while, the public and the court was being told that the receivership was approaching its end.[226] The shareholders had paid their last installment of the assessment back in May 1887, and in early 1888, they approved the new mortgage bonds and the bonds were quoted in the market, although they were not yet issued.[227]

The parties finally came to an agreement in early April.[228] In June, the new securities were distributed to investors in exchange for their deposit certificates—including the estate of Thomas Scott, which received $346,050 of the new first-lien bonds.[229] The railroad would pay Dos Passos's original clients just under $28,000 to settle their lawsuits regarding the Land Grant bonds, and the Wistar committee paid itself just over $147,000 for "compensation and expenses."[230] The members of the Kuhn, Loeb and Drexel Morgan syndicate shared $524,000 of the new first mortgage bonds, and Jay Gould received a little over $1,500 in interest on a previously undisclosed loan of $211,000 to the committee.

Brown was appointed president—even while he still served as receiver (indeed, he addressed a Democratic election rally in El Paso while holding both positions)—and a new board was elected that included Fleming and McGhee, but was otherwise dominated by Gould people (or Philadelphia people recently affiliated with Gould).[231] Then, on October 31, the railroad received all its assets back from the receiver, and the case was dismissed.[232] The receivers ultimately reported spending more than $5.1 million on rehabilitating the railroad, about half of which went toward new steel rails.[233] This was paid for out of the railroad's earnings during the case and with the proceeds of more than $2.4 million in receivers' certificates, which were repaid with interest of just over $17,000, from the proceeds of the shareholder assessment.[234]

Brown's subsequent eye-watering salary—$25,000 according to Texas and Pacific corporate records—probably did little to improve his relationship with Gould.[235] No other Texas and Pacific president would earn as much, even on a nominal basis, until well into the twentieth century.[236]

The committee reported that, as of the end of 1888, the securities listed in table 3.2 were not deposited under the plan.[237]

The lack of a foreclosure sale did mean that the holders of these leftover securities could try to cause trouble because the securities were still good against the operating company.[238] One group of bondholders sought to institute a new receivership, arguing that the new mortgages unfairly usurped their

TABLE 3.2 Leftover securities

Consol bonds	$8,000
New Orleans Pacific bonds	$11,000
Rio Grande bonds	$40,000
Land Grant bonds	$91,000
Script on same (convertible to Terminal bonds)	$16,245
Unpaid coupons	$11,160
Common shares	693 shares

prior interests.[239] Another attorney simply advised Satterlee that it would be best to pay his clients' bonds in full, lest they raise a stink.

And some simply did not know what had happened. One of Bullitt's partners wrote to the company on behalf of "Anastasia Murphy, an Irishwoman, who in March 1883 purchased bond No. 2889 of the Texas & Pacific Railway Company for $1,000, secured by the mortgage to the Fidelity Company on the Rio Grande Division. She is an Irish servant woman, who knows nothing about business, and knew nothing of the proceedings for the reorganization of the Texas & Pacific Railway. Consequently she did not deposit her bond with the reorganization committee."[240] Corporate reorganization then, as now, was a game played by insiders. Small investors were often left out in the cold.

The following year, Gould flexed his power as controlling shareholder and took over the presidency. Brown went home to Tennessee, where he briefly became president of a coal company before passing away in late 1889. Fleming was voted off the board at the same time, but McGhee would remain for the rest of the century—long after Gould himself had died of tuberculosis.[241]

MoPac bought most of the new second-lien bonds in the open market, ensuring that the Texas and Pacific never came under bondholder control, despite its frequent inability to pay the coupons on the bonds. The Texas and Pacific would go through another receivership during World War I, but once again, the desire to avoid losing the rare federal charter meant that there was no foreclosure sale.[242] The Texas and Pacific would remain one of the few (nonbank) federal corporations until it merged with the Missouri Pacific in the 1970s.[243]

• • •

Just as the Texas and Pacific was undergoing its reorganization, San Diego finally obtained its connection to the wider world. In 1885, the Atchison, Topeka and Santa Fe Railway entered Southern California, ending the Southern Pacific monopoly in the state and ultimately connecting San Diego to Chicago.[244] But the Santa Fe's premier passenger trains—like the *California Limited*, commenced in November 1892—would go to Los Angeles, with but a connection offered to San Diego.

As late as 1899, leading San Diego citizens were still urging George Gould to finish the original railroad: "Tom Scott originally intended to come to San Diego with his Texas Pacific. Is not now the proper time to carry out that idea—make trackage arrangements with the Southern Pacific from El Paso or Sierra Blanca to Yuma—Build from Yuma to San Deigo 175 miles in distance. This road could be built for $3,000,000. San Diego would give you a subsidy of $350,000 to $500,000."[245]

It never happened.

PART II

REFINEMENTS

CHAPTER 4

THE BANKERS TAKE CHARGE

This field of reorganizations is an important field in corporate finance. They have in the past involved, and will continue in the future to involve, millions on millions of values, the fortunes of the rich, the savings of the poor, the prosperity of thousands, and even the welfare of communities. To the solution of their problems, some of the greatest men in politics, in finance, at the bar and on the bench, have given the most arduous labor, the highest forces of their intellects, and in some instances their very lives.

—Adrian Joline, 1910

While Charles McGhee was playing a central role in the restructuring of the Texas and Pacific, he was also wondering what to do with his reorganized East Tennessee, Virginia and Georgia. The railroad industry was consolidating, and the East Tennessee was going to be part of that consolidation.

McGhee controlled the railroad with Calvin S. Brice and Samuel Thomas, the two leading members of the prereceivership consortium that had brought the East Tennessee to the attention of Wall Street. Brice and Thomas were both former Union army officers from Ohio who had gained huge fortunes through steel, coal, and railroad investments, most notably the Nickel Plate Road— more formally the New York, Chicago and St. Louis Railroad—which they sold to William Vanderbilt of the New York Central in 1882 for $7.2 million.[1] Despite residing in New York City, Brice would be elected to the US Senate from Ohio in 1890.

McGhee was eager to combine the East Tennessee with the Norfolk and Western Railway, which the East Tennessee already worked with and which was overseen by, among others, old friends Robert Fleming and Jacob Schiff.[2] Brice and Thomas, on the other hand, were more interested in a union with the Richmond and West Point Terminal Railway and Warehouse Company, a holding company that already controlled the Richmond and Danville Railroad—like the East Tennessee, a former Southern Railway Security Company project—and the Baltimore, Chesapeake and Richmond Steamboat Company, connecting West Point, Virginia to Baltimore.[3]

The Richmond and Danville competed with the East Tennessee in several parts of the Southeast (see figure 4.1). As such, joint control would not clearly benefit either railroad, given that there was no prospect of shutting down overlapping lines in this era. Nevertheless, the Richmond Terminal, which operated

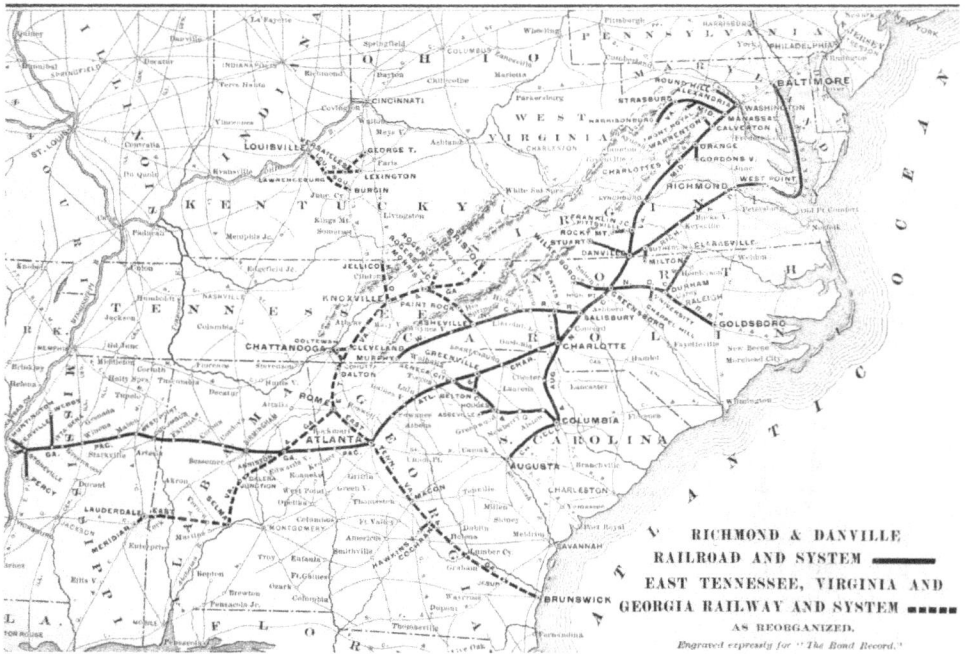

4.1 The Richmond Terminal system. The dashed line shows the East Tennessee, the solid the Richmond and Danville, including the ferry to Baltimore.

The Bond Record, Supplement, May 1, 1894, 98

no railroads itself, had been a plaything for speculators from the moment it was formed in 1880, and Brice and Thomas may have wanted to join in on the fun.[4] *The Financial Times* observed that Brice and Thomas "by no means represent the most savoury elements in Southern Railroads, being manipulators pure and simple."[5]

And while McGhee was certainly not disinclined to speculation—indeed, he had been involved with the Richmond Terminal in the early 1880s—he and his extended family had extensive business interests around Knoxville that would benefit from a reliable rail network.[6]

Under the 1886 reorganization plan, control of the East Tennessee was vested in the first preferred shareholders until they had received dividends for two years in a row. McGhee held a bit more than 9,000 of the 110,000 shares outstanding, but Brice and Thomas together held 60,000. In early 1887, Brice and Thomas agreed to sell their first preferred shares to the Richmond Terminal in exchange for a sizable pile of cash and $1.6 million in Richmond Terminal common shares.[7]

Richmond Terminal now had control over the East Tennessee, although in a strangely contingent form, which could be lost if the railroad performed well enough to pay the preferred dividends. By early 1888, McGhee was hedging his bets: He still held his block of East Tennessee preferred shares, but he also had 100,000 Richmond Terminal common shares.[8]

He continued to urge the Norfolk and Western to buy the railroad, but in August 1888, Frederick J. Kimball, that railroad's president, advised McGhee that "I have always agreed with you that the East Tennessee property was a very valuable one and capable of as much development as has been the case with the Norfolk & Western, but it will require large expenditures of money from year to year for improvements and equipment and the construction of spurs and feeders, and as additional equipment is provided it will necessitate increased sidings and other facilities all of which will require a considerable amount of money, and before doing anything it will be necessary to see that reasonable provision is made for future requirements."[9]

In short, the Norfolk and Western was proceeding with caution before purchasing what it feared could be a money pit. In September, McGhee wrote Fleming that he had "tried to bring about the sale of the East Tennessee stock to Kimball but did not succeed. I think the probabilities are that the East Tennessee System will be leased to the Richmond and Danville."[10] Less than a month later, that lease was signed.[11]

Under the lease, the Richmond and Danville would pay the East Tennessee an escalating amount of the latter's *gross* revenues as rent over ninety-nine years—which would have put the lease well into President Ronald Reagan's administration. Even more important, under another clause, the Richmond and Danville promised that rental payments would be sufficient to cover both the fixed charges of the East Tennessee and a 5 percent dividend on its preferred shares.

Thus, a ninety-nine-year lease was obtained using the control that would be lost by the very terms of the lease. The second preferred and common shareholders, of course, would get nothing out of this deal since no funds were provided for their dividends. McGhee swapped about half of his first preferred shares for more Richmond Terminal shares shortly thereafter.[12]

But less than a month later, a Tennessee court enjoined the lease, and the East Tennessee resumed normal operations.[13] The Richmond Terminal people thought the lawsuit was the work of the Norfolk and Western, and yet the East Tennessee remained in the Terminal's orbit despite the feeble strands that now bound them together—namely, contingent control through the preferred shares and the Terminal's small stake in the common shares, which even by 1892 constituted less than one-quarter of the shares.[14] In reality, control depended on Brice, Thomas, and, to a lesser extent, McGhee agreeing to maintain the relationship.

Just to make things even more interesting, at the same time the Richmond Terminal absorbed another major subsidiary, the intriguingly named Central Railroad and Banking Company of Georgia.[15] To avoid Georgia state laws that prohibited a railroad from owning a competitor, the Richmond Terminal purchased control of the Georgia Company—chartered in North Carolina, of course—which in turn held the shares of the Georgia Central.[16]

The Richmond Terminal was now among the largest railroads in the United States, encompassing more 8,500 miles of track.[17] But it was a strange sort of edifice, in that in some sense, it resembled the United States under the Articles of Confederation. As one commentator observed, "Their separate managements gave rise to clashes, and, as in many cases they run through the same territory, the singular spectacle was presented of two roads both owned by the same controlling company engaged in a vigorous rate war."[18]

The holding company was the weakest member of the group, rather than the leader. For example, while McGhee had a sizable block of Richmond Terminal common stock, he held an even larger stake ($256,000) in the East Tennessee's consolidated bonds.[19] Any dividend payments to the Richmond Terminal could undermine the value of those bonds, and yet the Terminal was entirely dependent on subsidiary dividends to pay its own obligations.

Governance of the Richmond Terminal became even more elaborate when Jay Gould took advantage of a dip in the share price to bump his stake in the railroad up to 15 percent.[20] He joined the board with his usual gaggle of friends—young George Gould, who had already been on the board, and the not-so-young Russell Sage and Sidney Dillon—leaving the board split at least three ways, if not more.[21]

Then, just six months later, the Richmond Terminal's share price began to sink for no apparent reason, and rumors surfaced that Gould had sold his shares and left the board.[22] If so, his timing would have been impeccable, as the entire Richmond Terminal edifice was about to collapse. The threat of failure was plain to most observers and the subject of frequent press comment, with *The Economist* noting in late 1891 that the Terminal "is a loosely joined system of railroads, aggregating 8,619 miles of track, whose financial position is decidedly precarious."[23]

But all indications are that Gould stayed on the board through early 1892.[24] However, he and his entourage played little role in the eventual reorganization, unquestionably due to Gould's declining health, which led to his death in December 1892.[25] In the coming decade, J. P. Morgan and Schiff and their respective banks, along with new figures like Edward Henry Harriman, would dominate corporate reorganization.[26]

• • •

The Richmond Terminal itself had 700,000 common shares, along with $5 million worth of 5 percent cumulative preferred shares.[27] The latter were a strange creature, at least by modern standards, in that they benefited from a pledge of $2.5 million in Richmond and Danville common stock, making them look a bit more like a subordinated secured bond than stock.[28] The holding company had also issued two rounds of bond debt: in 1887, about $5.5 million of 6 percent debt, and then in 1889, some $11.1 million in 5 percent debt. An example of the latter, with its unpaid coupons still attached, can be seen in figure 4.2.

Each of the two holding company bonds were secured by a distinct pool of securities issued by railroads ostensibly controlled by the Richmond Terminal. In many cases, the securities in question were common or preferred shares, so the holding company bonds were both structurally and actually subordinated in the overall capital structure, as foreclosure on the collateral would mean simply taking over the equity stake in an operating subsidiary. The 5 percent bonds from 1889 also had a second lien on the older bond's collateral pool.

Each of the three main subsidiaries—the East Tennessee, Richmond and Danville, and the Georgia Central—also had their own securities outstanding, and in some cases those railroads' subsidiaries also had outstanding debt. That is, the operating subsidiaries were themselves holding companies for many of the small railroads that they had collected, making the Richmond Terminal system a layer cake of corporations and capital structures.

For example, the East Tennessee, in addition to common stock and two layers of preferred stock, had $12.8 million of Consolidated Bonds, $4.7 million of First Extension Bonds, $6 million of Equipment and Improvement Bonds, and $6 million of Cincinnati Extension Bonds outstanding. The latter were issued jointly with the Richmond and Danville and guaranteed by the Richmond Terminal, and thus represented the only true group bonds in the Terminal's

4.2 Richmond Terminal bond (a) with unpaid $25 coupons attached (b). The bond is signed by Inman, and the first six coupons (through March 1892) are detached.

Author's collection.

intricate financial structure. The Richmond and Danville had $6 million of its 6 percent consolidated mortgage bonds, $4 million of the 6 percent debenture bonds, $11.2 million of 5 percent consolidated mortgage bonds, and $2.5 million of the 5 percent equipment mortgage bonds outstanding.[29]

In 1890, the East Tennessee had leased the Louisville Southern for ninety-nine years, and the leased railroad had $4.3 million of its own first mortgage bonds outstanding.[30] The East Tennessee also had a lease on the Knoxville and Ohio, which had $2 million of bonds. The list went on and on. By 1890, the entire Richmond Terminal system had more than $10 million a year in fixed charges, and despite gross earnings of more than $41 million, it had net income, when all was said and done, of just $2 million—mostly the result of the East Tennessee's contributions.[31]

And even these figures might have been overly enthusiastic, to put it politely. In July 1891, *The Philadelphia Inquirer* wrote that "for years the Richmond Terminal Company has been financiering on a false basis, or rather the entire conception of the company in its late career was a false one." In particular, the paper argued that the hodgepodge of railroads under a single holding company would never work and the slump in its stock suggested that the market was realizing the truth.[32]

Then on Saturday, August 8, 1891, the *New York Herald* devoted more than three full columns to a story headlined "A Big Deficit, But Dividends All The Same," and subtitled "Interesting and Curious Results Obtained from a Study of the Richmond Terminal Company's Bookkeeping."[33] As the titles implied, the article noted that the Richmond Terminal's subsidiaries had to keep paying dividends to allow the holding company to meet its obligations, but in many cases, those dividends exceeded what the operating companies actually earned. That reality was buried in confusing financial statements. As a subsequent company president would explain, "the financial jugglery which was necessary to carry out the plans of the Richmond Terminal Company during this period made conservative accounting and disposition of earnings from operation impossible."[34]

The *Herald* article by no means brought about an immediate collapse of the Richmond Terminal, but it did begin a period in which the press and investors began to question management's good faith; the health of the massive system was no longer taken for granted. Indeed, McGhee had to reassure William Walters that his East Tennessee consolidated bonds were "a long way from any trouble."[35]

• • •

John H. Inman had served as president of the Richmond Terminal since 1888. Inman, Thomas, and McGhee, as well as several other Richmond Terminal directors, operated out of offices at 80 Broadway in Manhattan—right near Alexander Hamilton's final resting place.[36]

Inman was from a prominent Georgia family, had been one of the original promotors of the Georgia Company and its Georgia Central, and indeed received a $25,000 bonus from the Richmond Terminal board for facilitating the sale.[37] On the other hand, in 1890 and 1891, Inman also personally guaranteed Georgia Central loans from J. S. Morgan in London.[38] In short, he had the same incompatible interests as everyone else at the top of Richmond Terminal.

In response to the *Herald* article and the controversy that followed, Inman issued an evasive statement suggesting that all would be made right once the new financial reports were published.[39] In November, he obtained the board's permission to send a letter to shareholders, which I reprint in full:

To the Stockholders of the Richmond & West Point Terminal Railway & Warehouse Co.

In view of the attacks which have recently been made on the management and credit of this Company, the following named gentlemen (who will have power to substitute others or add to their number),

Ex. Norton,
William Salomon, of Speyer &Co.,
Jacob H. Schfif, of Kuhn, Loeb &Co.,
Fred. P. Olcott, President of the Central Trust Co.,
Charles S. Fairchild, President of the New York Security and Trust Co.
Louis Fitzgerald, President of the Mercantile Trust Co.,

Having consented to carefully inquire into and examine the condition of your properties, and to aid your Company in perfecting the best plan for the permanent adjustment of its affairs, the enclosed proxy, if signed and returned me, will be voted at the annual meeting so as to secure the action of the above-named gentlemen, in the manner indicated, and for the re-election of the present President and Board of Directors.

The present Directors, desiring to cooperate in an adjustment of the Company's affairs, have consented to serve if re-elected, pending the formulating of a plan by the Committee.

Whenever the plan shall have been adopted, the stockholders will be requested to approve and ratify the same, and to hold an election for a permanent management.

Respectfully,
John H. Inman,
President.[40]

The letter both conceded the problem and attempted to maintain the status quo. As Professor Klein has noted, the composition of the committee was odd.[41] Ex. (Eckstein) Norton had recently served as president of the Louisville and Nashville, a Richmond Terminal competitor.[42] Schiff was of course affiliated with another competitor, the Norfolk and Western, and William Salomon, of Speyer, frequently worked side by side with Schiff, both having strong connections to German investors. And then there were the various trust company officials: Olcott ultimately declined to serve on this committee, and the others had no apparent connection to the Richmond Terminal. Indeed, none of the committee members had a clear interest in the success of the Terminal, and some would benefit from its failure.

The committee did manage to surface the lingering tension between the Richmond faction and the East Tennessee faction.[43] And when Thomas and Brice refused to cooperate, the committee gave up.[44]

That in turn led to the formation of a second committee, this time headed by Olcott.[45] This committee was expressly asked to come up with a reorganization plan. George Gould was reportedly asked to serve but declined.[46] The final members, besides Olcott, were Oliver H. Payne, Frederick D. Tappen, William H. Perkins, and Henry Budge.

Tappen and Perkins represented banks, and Budge, a former Schiff partner who was now a partner with a different investment bank, Hallgarten and Company, was known for his restructuring work. Oliver H. Payne was, among other things, a member of the board of Standard Oil. Years later, that company's stockbroker would disclose that Standard Oil had suffered big losses in Richmond Terminal shares—buying at $70 a share and selling at $30.[47] Olcott, Budge, and Perkins quickly formed a subcommittee to draft a plan.[48]

Less than two weeks later, the outlines of that plan began to appear in the press, perhaps floated as a trial balloon by the committee members.[49] The plan was formally released on March 1, with the admonishment that "receiverships, bankruptcy, disintegration of the properties and ruinous sacrifice of securities are inevitable, unless a remedy be applied without delay."[50] The plan proposed recapitalizing the entire organization on a voluntary basis, with no receivership whatsoever. As such, it was probably doomed from the start: A railroad riven by internal dissent was very unlikely to suddenly find unity at the point of reorganization.

The Danville and East Tennessee, along with the Terminal, would be folded into a new entity, "The Southern Railway Company."[51] The Georgia Central was excluded because it was already the subject of a receivership in Georgia, and litigation therein alleged that the Richmond Terminal should never have been allowed to buy it in the first place.[52]

Harris C. Fahnestock, vice president of the First National Bank, and J. Kennedy Tod were invited to join the committee, and the committee would select the board of the new entity. All investors would exchange their securities for new securities, but there would be no assessment of shareholders.[53] Stuart Daggett subsequently observed that "the principle which determined the various ratios of exchange is . . . difficult to discover."[54] By May, the plain had failed.[55]

By this point, Inman had resigned the presidency, to be replaced by Walter Oakman, who, like Fahnestock, was connected to the First National Bank.[56] Senior management of the bank reportedly held most of the Richmond Terminal's preferred shares, which gave them an interest in the survival of the holding company that was not necessarily shared with Brice, Thomas, and McGhee.

Following the collapse of the Olcott plan, yet another committee was announced, with Thomas, representing the East Tennessee interests; William Clyde, a wealthy speculator who had been in and out of the Terminal and the Danville almost since day one; and William E. Strong, who also held a stake in the Danville.[57] Thomas went first and proposed a plan that would have reorganized the Danville and the Terminal distinct from the East Tennessee: "The Richmond Terminal Company, he said, should be wound up and be succeeded by a new company with $43,000,000 of preferred stock and $70,000,000 of common. The present 6 per cent bonds should be given 170 in new preferred stock; the present 5 per cent bonds and preferred stock par in new preferred stock; and the present common should receive par in new common and be compelled to subscribe for $8,000,000 collateral trust two-year 6 per cent notes at 92½. This amounted to an assessment of 10 per cent upon the common."[58]

The First National group was displeased and asked Drexel Morgan to save them, arguing that "we have selected you to act in this matter because we feel that the necessities of the situation require that public confidence be at once re-established, and that your freedom from any bias arising from previous connection with the company's affairs will enable you to proceed with impartiality, and in the interests of all classes of securities."[59]

Drexel Morgan might have had no prior connection with the Richmond Terminal, but Drexel Morgan and First National were close allies, frequently coinvesting on deals.[60] First National's founder, George F. Baker, was one of the richest men in the United States—he endowed the Harvard Business School—and a close friend of J. P. Morgan.[61]

· · ·

By 1892, Drexel Morgan was increasingly centered on J. P. Morgan himself. J. S. Morgan, his father, had died in 1890, and Anthony Drexel would pass away in mid-1893.[62] Nevertheless, the New York office would remain Drexel, Morgan & Co. until 1895.

J. P. Morgan had played a secondary role in the Texas and Pacific receivership to both Jacob Schiff and his elders within Drexel Morgan. But in the late 1880s, he began to take the lead in the firm's finance operations, which increasingly focused on American corporations.[63] During the same years, he had also gained real exposure to corporate reorganization working on the Reading receivership with John Bullitt and Morgan's new partner, Charles Coster (figure 4.3).[64] It was in this case and others in the late 1880s that Morgan-led reorganizations began to use voting trusts, which, as we will see, would become a defining feature of the reorganizations of the 1890s.[65]

Like all Morgan partners of this era, Coster was of comparatively ancient American (and Protestant) stock, with roots going back to New Amsterdam

CHARLES HENRY COSTER
J. P. MORGAN & CO.
BANKERS

4.3 Charles H. Coster, J. P. Morgan's reorganization expert.

Notable New Yorkers of 1896–1899: A Companion Volume to King's Handbook of New York City (New York, 1898). https://lccn.loc.gov/99000945.

days.[66] His grandparents on both sides were millionaires in an age when millionaires were rare. He was also a prolific author of books on stamp collecting.[67]

John Moody and George Kibbe Turner described Coster as "a white-faced, nervous figure, hurrying from directors' meeting to directors' meeting; at evening carrying home his portfolios of corporation problems for the night. He went traveling across thousands of miles of country, watching railroad road-beds from the back platforms of trains. The accountant of the old-time South Street shipping firm with a genius for figures had reached the center of business pressure where no man's strength could last."[68] The last bit smacks of determinism—and at least shows the influence of the authors' knowledge of Coster's early death, at just forty-eight. As indicated, he had a knack for close examination of accounting statements, rationalizing financial structures, and would be the drafter of most of the "Morganization" plans of the 1890s, the first of which was the Richmond Terminal.[69]

As an important historian of corporate reorganization has explained:

> The Morgan reorganizations during the nineties followed the same general pattern manifesting three especially important characteristics. The immediate problem which had precipitated trouble—the finances of the road—were put on a sound basis. Secondly, Morgan was reluctant to surrender control of the roads after the reorganizations had been completed; by means of voting trusts his control was perpetuated and even after the trusts had been terminated, his representatives were usually found among the directors the companies. The third feature of Morgan's railroad activities in the late nineties was the establishment of the Community Interest idea, both theory and fact.[70]

We will see all these elements in the case of the Richmond Terminal.

In the Texas and Pacific receivership, Gould had been the driving force behind the reorganization. But by the 1890s, bankers like Morgan and Schiff took over the lead role, in large part because they could become involved in far more cases than a single, wealthy shareholder. Gould was only really interested in reorganizing railroads where he already had an interest or wanted to obtain an interest. Direct control was the important factor for him and others like him.

What were the bankers' motivations? As noted in the introduction to this book, the common view adopts Morgan's own framing of his firm's role: leading a noble effort to protect bondholders, especially foreign bondholders, from the depravations of corporate insiders.[71] As described by David Skeel, "Since the bankers were the ones who underwrote the bonds, they had a vested interest in protecting bondholders as much as possible. Otherwise, investors would be less anxious to participate in the bank's next bond offering. This reputational stake was magnified by the fact that such a large percentage of U.S. railroad bonds were owned by investors in England and other European nations. If J. P. Morgan and its peers expected to continue selling bonds to foreign investors, it was essential that they show that the U.S. markets were safe and dependable."[72] But as we will see in the remainder of this chapter, ultimately Morgan just embraced Gould's system and clothed it with good "spin."

The notion of the gallant J. P. Morgan rescuing mistreated foreign bondholders finds little support in the actual facts of the Richmond Terminal reorganization, or many other cases of the 1890s, but is instead consistent with the Morgan firm's wide-ranging effort to project a public image based around the notion that "the bank and its founder had always been guided by a desire to greater the public good."[73] As the SEC would observe some fifty years after the Richmond Terminal reorganization, "It would be error to conclude that when the bankers become active in a reorganization they are motivated solely and exclusively by the desire or obligation to protect the security holders. . . . As a matter of fact, it frequently is so far submerged as to appear at best as an excuse for being active in the situation. And it is the common situation to find houses of issue seeking and obtaining compensation for performance of this 'moral obligation.'"[74] Moreover, foreign bondholders were increasingly replaced by their domestic counterparts by the second half of the 1890s, and in general the degree of foreign investment in the United States dramatically declined as the country entered the ranks of developed nations, and returns began to decline congruently.[75] Writing in 1911, Harvard finance professor William Z. Ripley observed that "within a comparatively few years, a large proportion of our American Railway securities were repurchased from abroad. So abruptly in fact was this effect in 1899–1900 that the foreign markets were all but drained dry."[76] Further, the foreign investment that remained increasingly turned away from railroads.[77]

Morgan and other leading bankers were surely aware of these trends, which would have lessened their need to bow to offshore bondholders in reorganizations. Indeed, foreign railroad investment had peaked in the late 1880s, just before Morgan came to the forefront of reorganization practices. Morgan sold lots of railroad debt in England in the 1880s, but these railroads were not the ones that he reorganized in the 1890s.[78]

Further, recall that Drexel Morgan was first inserted into the Richmond Terminal reorganization by preferred shareholders rather than bondholders, foreign or domestic. The Terminal was controlled by competing groups of shareholders, while the bondholders, "though possessing a substantial aggregate of the outstanding securities, lacked either cohesion or the influence to voice their protest within the councils of power."[79]

It is notable that Professor Klein's masterful and comprehensive exposition of the creation and restructuring of the Richmond Terminal—which one railroad authority has called "the best job of explaining the ins and outs of a major reorganization of a railroad system"—contains no mention of foreign bondholders.[80] And indeed the notion of J. P. Morgan as the guardian of foreign bondholders in restructurings was little mentioned in the press at the time of the Terminal's receivership—rather, the focus was on the contending domestic shareholder interests that Morgan eventually mediated. Finally, from my review of the J. S. Morgan papers in London, it is clear that the London office, which we might expect to be especially involved in protecting English bondholders, played a largely passive role in the Richmond Terminal reorganization, chiefly focused on the syndicate, and otherwise passing on terms to clients that New York had dictated.

Moreover, Morgan played no role in underwriting any of the Richmond Terminal's outstanding debt and indeed had been expressly recruited on the basis that the bank had no prior relationship with the railroad. Thus, there was little reason to rush to the bondholders' aid. Instead, bankers like Morgan and Kuhn, Loeb & Co. were primarily motivated to conduct restructurings by the same basic control that inspired Gould, it just took a different outward appearance when exercised by a bank rather than an investor.

In this context, bondholder protection was little more than a noble-sounding smokescreen. As the future US Supreme Court justice Louis Brandeis observed, investment banks

> were not content merely to deal in securities. They desired to manufacture them also. They became promoters, or allied themselves with promoters. Thus it was that J. P. Morgan & Company formed the Steel Trust. . . . And, adding the duties of undertaker to those of midwife, the investment bankers became, in times of corporate disaster, members of security-holders' "Protective Committees"; then they participated as "Reorganization Managers" in the reincarnation of the unsuccessful corporations and ultimately became directors. It was in this way that the Morgan Associated acquired their hold upon the [Richmond Terminal and its successors] . . . It was in this way also that Kuhn, Loeb & Co. became potent in the Union Pacific and in the Baltimore & Ohio.[81]

Even in the 1920s, the final decade of the equity receivership, Kuhn, Loeb was making the "bondholder protection" argument, while at the same time thwarting efforts by those same bondholders to independently protect their interests.[82] That makes it palpable where the banks' true interests really were.

In sum, the SEC observed that "the evidence would seem to indicate that this professed moral obligation has frequently been assumed by the bankers, not with any genuine intention of properly discharging it, but rather as a justification of their dominant position in the reorganization process."[83]

· · ·

On May 25, 1892, the three-person Richmond Terminal committee met with a broader group of investors and agreed to send a letter to Drexel Morgan requesting that it also "take up" the issue.[84] On May 27, the firm wrote back to Strong, noting both his letter and the other earlier communication on the topic, and agreeing to begin an investigation into the Richmond Terminal group of companies.[85] Samuel Spencer (figure 4.4), Drexel Morgan's in-house railroad operations expert, was dispatched to tour the Richmond Terminal system with Oakman.[86]

Meanwhile, Clyde learned of a plot by the Georgia Central receivers to file a receivership petition against the Danville. As he later wrote to Drexel Morgan, "I sent to your office to ascertain if you were taking any steps to protect the system from this calamity and learned that you were not only

SAMUEL SPENCER
PRESIDENT SOUTHERN RAILWAY COMPANY
PRESIDENT AND DIRECTOR TRANSPORTATION COMPANIES

4.4 Samuel Spencer, the first president of the Southern Railway.

Notable New Yorkers of 1896–1899. https://lccn.loc.gov/99000945.

taking no steps, but did not regard yourselves in a position to do so, and that after receiving such information from you and similar information from the First National Bank, we took the steps which resulted in the appointment of friendly Receivers."[87]

On June 15, Clyde and two others told the federal court in Richmond that if a receiver were not quickly appointed, there would be a "race of diligence" among the creditors that would dismember the Danville.[88] The circuit judge entered an order appointing as receivers "Frederic W. Huidekoper, of Washington, and Reuben Roster, of Baltimore."[89] Ancillary receiverships were entered that day and the following day in "the circuit courts of the United States for the western district of North Carolina, the district of South Carolina, the northern district of Georgia, the northern district of Alabama and the northern district of Mississippi."[90]

Now the entire house of cards fell. On June 22, in the Southern District of New York, President Oakman became Receiver Oakman of the Richmond Terminal.[91] And then, on June 24, under a petition filed in the Eastern District of Tennessee by Thomas, who alleged that he was a large unsecured creditor, Henry Fink (a vice president and former receiver in the 1880s case) and McGhee were appointed receivers by none other than Judge Don Pardee.[92]

This was corporate reorganization 1860s style, showing none of the advanced planning and coordination that had developed by the 1880s. Of course, the Richmond Terminal's lack of integration was also old-fashioned compared to the Western systems or the bigger Eastern systems like the Pennsylvania or New York Central.

On June 28, Drexel Morgan resurfaced, with a letter to all the stakeholders announcing that "we have reached the conclusion that a reorganization is feasible on a basis of equity to all concerned, one that we should be prepared to undertake, and one which, in our opinion, would place your property on a sound financial basis."[93] But the good news was followed by the bad, as the letter went on to reveal that Drexel Morgan would not actually undertake the work, explaining that

> upon learning of the appointment of Receivers of the Richmond & Danville property by the U.S. Court, we applied to W. P. Clyde to know whether, in case we undertook the reorganization, the suit under his control would be transferred to us, and the present Receivers resign in favor of Mr. Spencer, stating to him that, in our opinion, such a course was essential. He declines to give us any such assurance, and our conversation with him leads us to doubt his loyalty to any reorganization plan whatever, although he, as one of your Committee, signed the request to us to undertake the same.

Indeed, correspondence had been going back and forth between Clyde and Drexel Morgan for several days, up to and including June 28. On June 24, the firm had sent a short note to say that it was still awaiting a response—and Clyde then met in person with J. P. Morgan, Spencer, and others. Clyde initially responded that

> I beg to say that agreeably to the request of your Mr. Pierpont Morgan, I have laid before such of the principal security holders of the Danville System as I have been able to reach in personal conference your proposition, to-wit: that as a preliminary to your forming or promulgating any plan of reorganization you would require that the securities chiefly affected should be deposited with your house, and that the Receiverships should be turned over to your Mr. Spencer in order to render impracticable any effective opposition to any plan which, after such preliminary deposit of securities and transfer of Receiverships, you

might see fit to bring out. I am compelled to report that the security holders so far seen have, without an exception, regarded these conditions as extremely undesirable, and, in fact, impracticable.

Drexel Morgan wanted all the securities irrevocably deposited and to get full control of the receivership before it would release a plan. Nothing short of absolute power would do. Clyde's group declined to participate on that basis.

Drexel Morgan then responded that Clyde had misunderstood and control of the receivership was the only issue at present, the question of deposits being one that "we will take up with the holders." Morgan clearly intended to go around Clyde when the time came. Clyde responded with a long letter that, at heart, rejected the idea that his group should uncritically bind themselves to a plan, "even under the leadership of a house enjoying your world-wide eminence in financial matters."

In short, there was a stalemate.[94] Drexel Morgan was willing to undertake the reorganization only if it had full control over the proceedings, while at least one group of investors wanted to see what their plan was before committing to it. *The New York Times* quoted Clyde as saying, "I know this property thoroughly. I have twice been in control of it, and know how valuable it is. If necessary we can take care of it without Mr. Morgan."[95]

And there things stood for seven months. McGhee, writing to his coreceiver, astutely observed that "it is now evident that a reorganization is necessary. It is also evident that several years may in all probability elapse before that can be accomplished. In the meantime a panic may occur."[96]

Various committees and proposed plans came and went without gaining any traction.[97] Shareholders of the Richmond Terminal attempted to elect a new board.[98] The various receivers issued massive amounts of receivers' certificates to fund operating expenses, but it remained unclear if the different parts of the Terminal would choose to walk or stay.

Finally, in early 1893, Clyde gave way, with only slight concessions from Drexel Morgan, and joined a letter asking the bank to restart work.[99] The bank agreed to reexamine the situation, and it announced that it would formulate a plan and create a syndicate to support that plan, and securities of all classes "have been deposited in an amount sufficient to demonstrate that the holders of such securities generally join in your desire that we shall undertake the work."[100]

The plan must have been at least sketched out already, because a few days later, Drexel Morgan sent the syndicate agreement, which referenced key provisions of the plan.[101] The syndicate totaled $15 million, which covered not only taking over stockholders' unpaid assessments, but also $8 million worth of bonds (offered at 85) and $33 million worth of common stock (offered at $15) that investors might purchase under the plan. Syndicate members would receive a 5 percent cash commission upon completion of the reorganization.

In addition, the syndicate agreed to provide a loan during the reorganization if needed. Here was a direct predecessor to the modern "DIP loans" given to chapter 11 debtors.

About half of the syndicate was taken up by the three main Drexel Morgan offices. Samuel Thomas took $1 million himself. He and Samuel Spencer—who took $250,000—were among the few individuals in the syndicate, which was largely dominated by institutional investors, in contrast to the syndicates of the 1880s. For example, the First National Bank, who had first brought Drexel Morgan into the reorganization, committed to $1.5 million. London sold parts of its piece to the Rothschilds and other institutional investors.[102]

The plan was dated May 1 but did not actually become public until May 23.[103] The circular released that day announced the formation of a reorganization committee headed by Coster, who was joined by Anthony J. Thomas (a frequent Drexel Morgan collaborator) and George Sherman, Olcott's vice president at the Central Trust Company.[104] This committee did not even pretend to be comprised of bondholders, bond trustees, or investors generally—a trend that would continue throughout the receivership era.[105]

The circular announced that the bank was happy with the level of deposits, but it would give investors until the end of the month to withdraw if they did not like the plan. Describing the Terminal's various railroads, the document pronounced that "a crisis in their affairs has been reached, and their general disintegration is imminent."[106] It described the system as running a $2 million deficit and said that large amounts of funds were needed to get the railroads into proper shape.

The plan itself tracked the Olcott plan in providing for the holding company and its two main operating companies to be folded into a single, consolidated corporation. Indeed, as we will see, that corporation would be named the Southern Railway Company, just as Olcott had suggested, but that was the main point of similarity between the plans.

The Drexel Morgan plan called for a simple, if somewhat distended capital structure: $140 million of first-lien bonds (second lien on those properties that had outstanding debt that would remain in place, but becoming first lien when that debt matured), paying 5 percent and maturing in one hundred years, $75 million worth of noncumulative preferred stock, and $160 million worth of common stock.[107] At least equity predominated, thus reducing the risks of future defaults. Both types of stock would be held in a voting trust for up to five years.[108]

The cuts at the Terminal level were severe, reflecting the structurally subordinate status of the securities. The plan frankly stated that "the $16,000,000 Richmond Terminal bonds are secured by collateral of importance, but of very small earning power, and, consequently, they must mostly be reduced to the rank of stocks."[109]

The 6 percent bonds would be swapped for 35 percent of new bonds and 70 percent of preferred shares. The 5 percent bonds, like that shown in figure 4.2, only got shares: 70 percent preferred and 30 percent common. The old preferred shares got 35 percent new preferred shares and 65 percent common, while the old common would receive an equal exchange into new common and 12.5 percent in new preferred, upon payment of a $12.50 per share assessment—their preferred thus represented the amount of the assessment.[110]

And so it went through the capital structure. Senior debt of the subsidiaries did pretty well—almost $70 million would remain in place to be paid according to the original terms, while junior debt and equity were largely converted to a mix of preferred and common stock. For example, four of the East Tennessee's most senior bonds would remain in place until maturity—that is, they were untouched by the plan. But its Cincinnati extension bonds would be converted to 125 percent preferred shares.[111]

"Compared with previous fixed charges the plan proposed noteworthy reductions; compared with the earnings of the lines involved it did not go far enough."[112] Indeed, given the massive capital structure proposed, it was somewhat disquieting to see projections that the net income of the reorganized railroad would be measured in mere hundreds of thousands of dollars for the next few years.

And Drexel Morgan attempted to push this plan forward in the face of an increasingly frightful economic situation.[113] "A mere three weeks before Grover Cleveland's second inauguration, three major American railroads went under, and before long some five hundred banks and fifteen thousand companies would fail."[114] The Panic of 1893 was one of the most severe financial crises in the history of the United States to that point.[115]

The heap of failed railroads, of course, already included the Richmond Terminal, but soon also many other major systems, including the Baltimore and Ohio, Union Pacific, the Santa Fe, and the Northern Pacific (again).[116] Schiff and Harriman would reorganize the Union Pacific, Schiff the Baltimore and Ohio, with Harriman joining its board, while Morgan and Coster would handle the Santa Fe and the Northern Pacific, along with the Richmond Terminal.[117] Handling three of the largest reorganizations in the decade certainly contributed to the myth that J. P. Morgan invented modern corporate reorganization.

But in the meantime, "the reorganization of Richmond Terminal appeared as driftwood in the stream of events."[118] Responding to an apparent inquiry for news, Drexel Morgan wrote to the London office in August that

> The financial depression has tended . . . to check the prompt payment of assessments to a very considerable degree, and, as this is a fundamental feature, it of course necessitates our holding somewhat in abeyance for the moment.

> In answering inquiries from the Public, we have not made any statements about the assessments, as yet, and we would ask you to follow a like course, treating the information in this report as for your use only.[119]

Reports about unpaid assessments nonetheless appeared in the American press in November, based on anonymous sources, but Drexel Morgan made no formal statement.[120] Late in the year, a *Wall Street Journal* article tersely stated that "Richmond Terminal properties are doing nothing and modifications of the reorganization plan must come before long."[121]

In January, J. S. Morgan received a draft of a revised plan from New York that dropped a few floundering subsidiaries from the deal, including the East Tennessee's Cincinnati extension.[122] It offered a new deadline—but the date was left blank in the draft—for payment of tardy assessments. The bonds to be issued were now listed as $125 million (versus $140 million prior), the preferred shares as $65 million (versus $75 million), and the common as $125 million (versus $160 million). The draft stated that the syndicate would no longer take the place of shareholders who did not pay assessments—hence the marked decrease in common shares. An accompanying letter from New York noted the need to amend the syndicate agreement as well.

An early February draft of the plan had further revisions.[123] The amount of the assessments was reduced and the securities paid in exchange were improved. For example, the Richmond Terminal and East Tennessee common would now receive one-quarter of the assessment in bonds, with interest payments staring January 1, 1896, and three-fourths in preferred stock, whereas under the original plan, the return was only in preferred stock. Certain near-term bond coupons would be paid in additional securities.

Consider, for example, the East Tennessee "Improvement and Equipment 5s," which were the most senior bonds of that railroad that were modified by the plan. Under the original 1893 plan, these bonds were to be exchanged for 60 percent of their face value in new 5 percent Southern Railway bonds, and 70 percent of the face value in new preferred shares, with the overdue coupons on the bonds to be paid in cash.[124]

At some point before the 1894 revised plans, that treatment changed, as both drafts of the revised 1894 plan refer to these bonds receiving 75 percent of face value in a special stepped coupon East Tennessee Reorganization Mortgage Bond, and 50 percent in preferred shares. The Reorganization bonds paid 4 percent interest for five years, and then 5 percent thereafter. And under the revised 1894 plans, all coupons from March 1893 through March 1895 would be paid in the form of Southern Railway bonds that would begin paying 5 percent interest in March 1895.[125]

A telegram sent on February 9 from Drexel Morgan in New York to London advised that the final version of the new plan was on its way by steamer, and the syndicate agreement would be amended to provide for the commission to be paid in securities rather than cash.[126] The telegram blithely reported that "we have consulted with large depositors and syndicate members here and all [are] delighted." No deep concern for foreign bondholders was in evidence.

On the contrary, J. S. Morgan received a letter from one London broker, who had also purchased a stake in the syndicate, asking it "very strongly, to protest in New York against any alteration whatever in the terms already accepted by, practically, every bondholder."[127] The letter went on to state that the broker would "not countenance any alterations such as you have foreshadowed," and that to do so would go against "the interest of those who look to us for protection." Dutch bondholders likewise felt left out of the plan negotiations. They formed a committee, representing more than $1 million in East Tennessee bonds, but still felt ignored by Drexel Morgan, who would not engage with them.[128]

Coster and Morgan pushed ahead, untroubled by these matters.[129] Indeed, their real goal was to overcome the clashing shareholder interests in the Terminal and consolidate all the pieces into a coherent whole—bondholders were of secondary practical importance.[130] The final revised plan was dated February 20, but only insiders like McGhee got to see it in February.[131] It would be released to the public in March.[132]

It was prefaced by a paragraph explaining the need for revisions:

> Owing to the financial events of the last eight months, and their especially disastrous effect on the railway interests of the South, it is impossible to carry out the Richmond Terminal plan as heretofore proposed. It is believed, however, that with some concessions, mostly temporary in effect, but necessary to bridge over the present situation, the plan can be carried out nearly on its original theory, with promptness, and with the ultimate advantages which were expected from its accomplishment. Deeming such a course conducive to the best interests of all security holders, your Committee submits such changes as it considers essential for further progress. With these changes accepted, the Committee is ready to press the work of reorganization.

Also on February 20, the Virginia state legislature passed "an Act authorizing the purchasers of the Richmond and Danville Railroad, their assigns and successors, to become and be a corporation, to adopt a name therefor, and to possess and exercise general powers; and authorizing the leasing to or by, and the consolidation therewith of, other corporations."

Then, on February 23, a revised syndicate agreement was signed, which provided for the payment of the commission in new securities instead of cash, the elimination of the obligation (or opportunity) to take over for nonpaying shareholders, and the reduction in the amount of common shares purchased by the syndicate to $25 million (from $33 million).[133] The syndicate was thus reduced in size from $15 million to $10.6 million.

The conversion of the commission into additional securities allowed the syndicate members to obtain a better return on the securities they were buying under the plan. For example, while the plan still listed the syndicate as buying the bonds at 85, the real price was effectively 75, once all the bonds the committee received were accounted for.[134]

• • •

It was soon announced that the new company would be called the Southern Railway Company, and it would be headed by Spencer.[135] He was also added to all the pending receiverships as an additional receiver.[136]

The naming of Spencer was widely heralded as putting a "true southerner" in charge of the railroad, rather than a "carpetbagger."[137] Commentators noted that Spencer had been born in Georgia on a plantation and had ridden with Nathan Bedford Forrest during the war.[138] Forrest was a Confederate general—likely also a war criminal—and the first Grand Wizard of the KKK. Hence, Spencer, the "true southerner," represented the Redeemer or "Lost Cause" South, but it is rare to find any such clarification in either the railroad, finance, or history literature.[139] For example, the leading history of the Southern Railway (published in 1985) speaks of Spencer's childhood in Georgia, "tended by servants."[140]

As with the Texas and Pacific's (and likely the East Tennessee's) predecessors, the Richmond and Danville was heavily associated with slavery.[141] Indeed, it assigned enslaved women as maids on passenger trains before the Civil War.[142] And during the war, "the Richmond & Danville was perhaps the most essential line of [the] Confederate system."[143]

After the war, much of its construction and maintenance were conducted with convict labor under slaverylike conditions—for example, its western extension purchased a coal mine along with the convict laborers who worked therein.[144] Such workers were mostly "jailed for petty larceny, with food so poor and conditions so abominable that they died by the dozens every year. Scurvy, dropsy, dysentery, and the ominous, all-encompassing "consumption" where the ills that killed the New South's early victims of railway-sponsored extractive industry."[145]

In this context, it is noteworthy that race comes up so little in any of the materials regarding the Richmond Terminal, a Southern railroad, built by slaves, reorganizing just before the Supreme Court would bless railroad segregation in the infamous *Plessy v. Ferguson* case.[146] Even before that decision, segregation was law in most of the area that the Richmond Terminal served.[147]

Nevertheless, the only direct mention of race in Richmond Terminal's reorganization comes in John Moody's 1919 book, *The Railroad Builders*.[148] He states that J. P. Morgan was initially reluctant to get involved with the Richmond Terminal because "he was much opposed to taking hold of this disintegrated and broken-down system of railroads operating largely in poor and unprogressive sections, populated for the most part by negroes."[149] He follows that sentence with a purported J. P. Morgan quote that includes a racial slur.[150]

Race was undoubtedly something that the Richmond Terminal's customers and employees thought about.[151] But since women and nonwhite men were largely excluded from the realm of finance, subsequent writers were permitted to adopt a narrow focus and act as if race (or gender) were irrelevant.[152]

• • •

A series of foreclosure sales then brought the new Southern Railway into existence.[153] In July 1894, the new Southern took charge of the assets of the Richmond and Danville.[154] That same month, the reorganization committee transferred $4.9 million of the East Tennessee Improvement and Equipment 5s that had been deposited with it (of the $5 million outstanding) to the new Southern Railway. In exchange, the committee received $4.5 million worth of the new East Tennessee Reorganization Mortgage Bonds from the Southern for distribution to bondholders under the plan.

On July 7, in Knoxville, the Southern used the old bonds as its bid for the assets of the East Tennessee, of which it officially took control in August. The Southern took the assets subject to several layers of bonds that were senior to the Improvement and Equipment 5s in the capital structure.

Those who received mostly bonds in the reorganization were likely reasonably content with the outcome of the case, as they were paid without incident. The equity was another story. The preferred soon paid a dividend, but not enough to get out of the voting trust and payments were erratic, while the common shares would not receive any dividend whatsoever until the 1920s.[155] Not unexpectedly, both dividends stopped again in the 1930s.[156]

The voting trust was established with three trustees: J. P. Morgan himself, George F. Baker of First National Bank, and Charles Lanier (from Winslow, Lanier & Co.), another of Morgan's friends. As trustees, the three exercised full voting power over all the stock.[157]

Originally, the trust was to last five years, but later it was extended indefinitely.[158] Those who voted against this extension discovered that their unstamped trust certificates were no longer admitted for trading on the stock exchange—a powerful way of obtaining overwhelming "consent."[159]

The extension papers were also printed in Dutch, suggesting the continued presence of those investors even after their disagreeable experience in the reorganization. They likely had little choice while the trust remained in place: There could not have been much of a market for large blocks of shares that came with no income, no voting rights, and scant opportunities for capital gains.[160] In 1913, a reader wrote the *Wall Street Journal* asking about investing in Southern common stock, to which the *Journal* replied:

> The common stock at current prices can be considered only as a speculation, but it should prove profitable for one who can afford to buy outright and lay it away for a long pull. The early opening of the Panama Canal should give impetus to the road's traffic, and this, added to the local growth and development of the South which should come during the next few years, makes the common stock look attractive. Common dividends are not in sight, and it is not likely that this question will be considered by the directors for a year or two yet.[161]

The last bit was optimistic by about a decade—dividends started in 1924—as the *Journal* (understandably) did not foresee the coming world war. When the voting trust was eventually terminated, the railroad's management reported that about one-third of the shareholders were foreign, primarily English and Dutch.[162]

In 1913, J. P. Morgan was asked about the long-enduring trust when he testified before Congress regarding the influence of investment bankers in the American economy, an issue that would come to be called the "Money Trust":

Mr. Morgan (interposing). You asked me about the voting trusts?

Mr. Untermyer. Yes.

Mr. Morgan. My idea is that in the infancy of a corporation, or in its incipiency, a voting trust is necessary for the protection of the property.

Mr. Untermyer. Now, then, you would not call 15 years the incipiency of the Southern Railway?

Mr. Morgan. Yes; the Southern Railway was created at that time.

Mr. Untermyer. When does it ever get out of swaddling clothes?

Mr. Morgan. We have been trying to get rid of it, but they will not take it.

Mr. Untermyer. You mean the stockholders will not take it?

Mr. Morgan. Yes; the stockholders.

Mr. Untermyer. All the trustees have got to do, under the agreement, is to distribute the stock, is it not?

Mr. Morgan. Yes; but we have made it a rule always to ask the stockholders whether they wished us to give it up.

Mr. Untermyer. That is the point. Do you not realize that these voting trusts, putting into the hands of one or a few men these great systems, tends to enormous concentration and control?

Mr. Morgan. No, sir.

Mr. Untermyer. You do not think it does?

Mr. Morgan. No, sir.[163]

The trust ultimately outlasted J. P. Morgan himself and was not dissolved until after World War I began in late 1914.[164] As noted, the prewar buyer of Southern shares, particularly common shares, got no dividends and no voting rights. About all they got was the hope that J. P. Morgan might someday grant their shares some economic significance.[165]

The Southern lived a precarious early life, growing in miles while often reporting very slender amounts of net income except in boom years.[166] For example, between 1912 and 1914, it reported net income of between $7 and $4.8 million, on earnings of between $69.5 and 63.5 million.[167] To even achieve those profits, it ran a threadbare operation.

Writing in 1908, Professor Daggett observed that "equipment appears to be still inadequate. Signals are imperfect, and speed and promptness seemingly impossible to attain. The late tragic death of Mr. Spencer was a forcible illustration of the deficiencies of the road which he had done so much to improve."[168] Spencer was killed in 1906 when his private railcar was rear-ended by a Southern train.[169] The railroad put up a statue in his honor, which was located at various places around Atlanta until recently, when it was decided that the former Forrest associate was perhaps a less-than-ideal symbol of the modern railroad.[170] The inscription on the plinth reads: "A Georgian, A Confederate Soldier, The First President Of The Southern Railway Company. Erected By The Employees Of That Company." In 2023, the statue was relocated to the Atlanta History Center, whose webpage questions the extent of Spencer's actual wartime service.[171]

Coster joined the Southern board, giving up his spot on the reorganization committee in favor of well-known restructuring attorney Adrian Joline (figure 4.5).[172] In 1907, the committee sold the shares that they received in the Georgia Central reorganization—it had become the Central of Georgia Railway—to E. H. Harriman.[173] Finally, the committee could disband.[174]

The Southern would buy back the Georgia Central in 1963.[175] And then, in 1982, the Southern merged with its old rival, the Norfolk and Western, to form today's Norfolk Southern.[176] The first mortgage bonds issued under the reorganization plan were reflected on the Norfolk Southern's SEC reports until they finally matured on July 1, 1994.[177]

• • •

As Professor Klein has observed, "While few if any of the principles contained in the Terminal reorganization were new in themselves, the pattern of the overall plan and its successful implementation furnished a working model for the torrent of reorganizations occurring after the Panic of 1893. In this respect the Terminal reorganization became a landmark in Morgan's railroad activities."[178] J. P. Morgan and Company was the central party in this reorganization, just as

ADRIAN HOFFMAN JOLINE
BUTLER, NOTMAN, JOLINE & MYNDERSE
LAWYERS

4.5 Adrian Joline, reorganization lawyer.

Notable New Yorkers of 1896–1899.

Jay Gould was the central actor in the Texas and Pacific reorganization. In both cases, the aim was control. Gould's desired control was direct: control of the debtor-railroad, for the benefit of his larger, Missouri Pacific focused empire.

In the case of the Richmond Terminal, Morgan equally benefited from control. The Congressional Money Trust committee recognized as much, explaining that "our archaic, extravagant, and utterly indefensible procedure for the reorganization of insolvent railroads has furnished these banking groups the opportunities of which they have not been slow to avail themselves, of securing the dominating relation that they now hold to many of our leading railroad systems."[179] J. P. Morgan received substantial fees for conducting the reorganization.[180] For example, the Southern granted the bank 50,000 common shares "as part compensation for acting as depositaries and for cooperation and supervision incident to the reorganization." That was in addition to the more than

$750,000 that the new railroad paid for "commissions, legal and other services" in connection with the reorganization, and whatever the committee (headed by a Morgan partner, Coster) paid to the bank before it turned over its remaining funds to the railroad.[181]

But far more important was the long-term relationship that J. P. Morgan locked in with the Southern Railway. This was the control that the bankers sought in reorganizations.[182] At least until the New Deal, J. P. Morgan was the sole banker for the Southern Railway.[183] Not only did it earn fees on every securities offering the railroad made during that time, but it also earned fees in connection with every new railroad that the Southern acquired as it grew.[184]

Morgan also obtained the benefits of control from having the Southern Railway within its larger "community of interests." By the end of the nineteenth century, J. P. Morgan and Co. had effective control over about a quarter of the nation's railroads; the steel industry, which was both customer and vendor to the railroads; and a sizable number of insurance and trust companies.[185] As controller of this broad network, Morgan could pick and choose winners and losers in transactions within the group.

We can see a small example of the effects of the "community of interests" in the J. P. Morgan records: on August 20, 1902, the Southern sold Morgan $1.5 million of the railroad's bonds; the bank resold the bonds the same day to the New York Life Insurance Co., a company whose investment committee included a bank partner. J. P. Morgan booked a profit of just over $38,000 (about $1.4 million today) on the deal, which seemingly involved no risk to the bank.[186] Indeed, in modern terms, this would be called a "riskless principal" trade. Repeated daily over many decades, such transactions amounted to real money.

This incident also provides an example of the way in which supposedly protecting Morgan's client-bondholders (the insurance company) could also mean protecting and advancing Morgan's self-interest. Corporate reorganization had become respectable, clothed in the notion that the banks who ran them acted in the public interest.[187] But reorganization had not fundamentally changed from its initial, Jay Gould form. A friendly creditor got the process started, while some controlling party dictated the terms. Courts, employees, customers, and similar stakeholders, along with smaller investors, were relegated to a passive role.

Bankers often reorganized companies where they had underwritten securities, and they often proclaimed that they did so to protect investors, but as we have seen, the real story was far more complex. Longtime investor Frederick Lisman—who provided the analysis behind the 1895 Richmond Terminal exposé "Millions in Deficits—Dividends Just the Same"—observed in the 1930s that a banker "presumably and generally does want to do the best he can for the security holders, but at the same time he may be looking out for his own personal advancement and thinking of possible future financing with accompanying profits, thorough information about the property which may enable him to trade in the securities to advantage, and possible committee fees. Vanity also plays a part . . . He may also in some cases be thinking about shielding some friends, or even himself, from the consequences of bad judgment or misdeeds."[188] As we shall see in later chapters, these words could just as easily have been written by a modern-day private equity sponsor.

More broadly, corporate restructuring has always been about buying consent from those who could stop you and imposing your will on those who could not. In the Richmond Terminal reorganization, Samuel Thomas ended up on the board of the new Southern Railway (literally hand-picked by J. P. Morgan, the trustee), while the complaining foreign bondholders were ignored. Thomas's position was large enough to thwart J. P. Morgan's control; the foreign bondholders could accept their fate in the reorganization or sell for whatever the market might give them.

CHAPTER 5

THE STATUTES ARRIVE

"By 1900, the nation's railroads were consolidated into six huge systems controlled by Wall Street bankers, principally J. P. Morgan and Company and Kuhn, Loeb."[1] As we have seen, these same banks were deeply invested in the corporate reorganization apparatus, centered around receiverships. Indeed, in many cases, the big railroad systems were assembled through the receivership process, as we have just seen with the Southern Railway.

The practice of seeking receiverships in the federal courts, granted upon the suit of a friendly (out-of-state) unsecured creditor, was seemingly approved by the 1908 decision of the US Supreme Court in *In re Metropolitan Railway Receivership*.[2] As such, the receivership mechanism saw widespread use with regard to both railroads and to other, growing industries of the age.[3]

Those railroads that did not reorganize in the 1890s were among the first to reorganize during the economic downturn that came with the onset of war in late 1914.[4] Kuhn, Loeb & Co. made about $200,000 in fees reorganizing the Texas and Pacific during this time, and a stunning $1.3 million for reorganizing its parent, the Missouri Pacific.[5] MoPac called for its new common stock to held in a voting trust for five years:

> The voting trustees, by the terms of the plan, were to be persons approved by the reorganization managers (Kuhn, Loeb & Co.), by the 5 percent bond-holders' committee (on which Kuhn, Loeb & Co. was represented), and by

the 4 percent bondholders' committee (on which Kuhn, Loeb & Co. was also represented).

The voting trustees approved by these groups were Mr. Otto H. Kahn, senior partner of Kuhn, Loeb & Co., and two other bankers.[6]

As with J. P. Morgan and the Southern Railway, Kuhn, Loeb's control of the railroad after the receivership was just as important as the fees that it earned during it, resulting in commissions through the 1920s of about $3.4 million.[7]

After the receiverships were over, Missouri Pacific controlled about 337,000 (or 54 percent) of the 624,000 votes in Texas and Pacific.[8] Most of this came from swapping the second-lien bonds issued in the 1885 receivership, which MoPac had gobbled up in the secondary market, for new voting preferred stock.[9] "But its board, almost with a collector's passion, went out to buy more of the Texas & Pacific common stock."[10]

In 1925, MoPac also purchased a group of railroads headed by the New Orleans, Texas and Mexico Railway, collectively known as the Gulf Coast Lines, which operated in Louisiana and eastern Texas. The Gulf Coast Lines also owned the International–Great Northern—the former Gould line running from the bottom of the Texas and Pacific's wonky rectangle to Laredo and Galveston, Texas—so in many respects, MoPac was busy putting the old Gould-Southwestern system back together again in these years.[11]

But MoPac itself was far more extensive than it had been the 1880s, with a main line that stretched all the way from St. Louis to Pueblo, Colorado. As described by the railroad itself in the early 1930s, "Missouri Pacific, bounded on the east by St. Louis, Memphis and New Orleans; by Omaha, Neb. on the north; Pueblo, Col. on the west, and by Brownsville, Texas on the south, serves the great grain belt of the Middle West and the oil and cotton producing areas of Oklahoma, Arkansas and Texas."[12]

In connection with its interests in Colorado, MoPac purchased a sizable chunk of securities in the receivership of the Denver and Rio Grande, so MoPac ended up owning half of the Rio Grande. Missouri Pacific operated a passenger train—which it named the "Colorado Eagle" beginning in the early 1940s, but it existed well before then—that ran from St. Louis to Denver, operating on Rio Grande tracks after Pueblo.

The other half of the Rio Grande was owned by the Western Pacific, a railroad built by George Gould to satiate his inherited transcontinental impulses. The Western Pacific connected with the Rio Grande at Salt Lake City and then ran through the mountains to Oakland, California.[13] The three linked railroads thus offered a connection from St. Louis (where, like Chicago, many of the eastern lines, such as the Pennsylvania and New York Central, terminated) and Northern California. Of course, MoPac's connection with the Texas and Pacific at Texarkana offered a way to Southern California as well.

Figure 5.1 shows the full extent of the Missouri Pacific system, including the Texas and Pacific. Near the center of the map, MoPac used the Texas and Pacific wonky rectangle to connect to Laredo via Texarkana and Marshall. Taken as a whole, the system comprised something like 12,000 miles of track. While the Texas and Pacific, with about 1,500 miles, was a large system in the 1880s, and

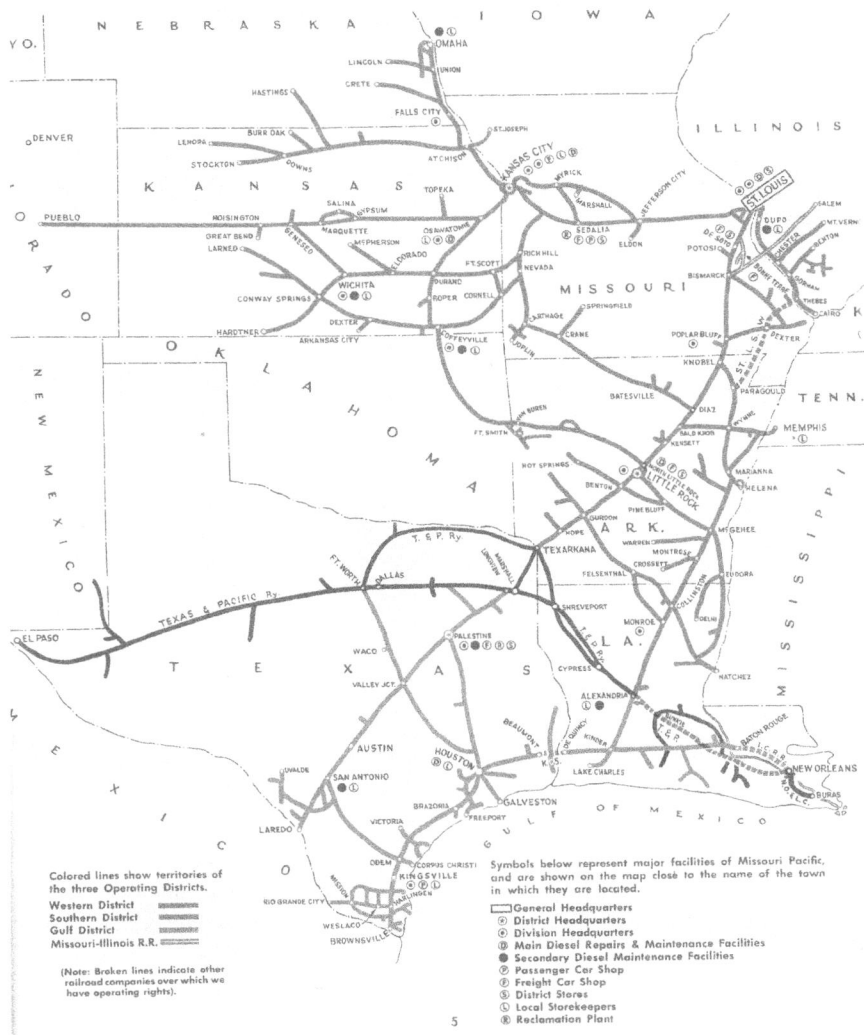

5.1 The Missouri Pacific system, including the Texas and Pacific.

A Few Facts About the Reorganized Missouri Pacific Railroad Company, 1956.

the 8,500-mile-long Richmond Terminal a large one for the 1890s, the consolidation trend continued apace in American rail systems.

By the time that the 1920s got roaring, MoPac had undone most of the work of its prior receivership and was once again heavily laden with debt—by 1932, it was carrying long-term debt of over $400 million, compared with $227 million when it exited its receivership in mid-1917.[14] This increase was a function both of its acquisitions spree and the fact that the receivership plan had not provided any real margin for upkeep of the railroad—all available cash flow had to go to servicing the bonds created by the receivership.[15]

MoPac was not alone in its capital structure choices. Back in the 1880s, most railroads were financed with 55 percent bonds and the remainder equity (stock). By the World War I era, that had shifted, and most long-term financing was coming in the form of bonds. By the 1920s, about 70 percent of railroad finance was taking the form of bonds. This heavy leverage was tolerable when the economy was booming and borrowed money easy to find, but the "experience of the 1930's disclosed the dangers of so heavy a burden of fixed charges," especially in an industry that was increasingly subject to competition from new forms of transportation, like automobiles, trucking, and airplanes.[16] By many measures, the railroad industry was in decline beginning from the end of World War I, and railroad bonds were similarly seen as less desirable investments.[17] At the same time, the continued viability of the equity receivership was coming into doubt.

• • •

The basic problem went back to the historic roots of the corporate reorganization: The receivership was never intended to facilitate reorganization; instead, it was adapted to serve that purpose. As such, it might be modified again, particularly if the courts felt that the system was being abused.

The origins of the retrenchment can be found in the US Supreme Court's 1913, 5–4 decision in *Northern Pacific Railway Co. v. Boyd*.[18] Under Charles Coster and Morgan's reorganization of the Northern Pacific, the assets of the Northern Pacific *Railroad* were sold to the Northern Pacific *Railway*. Common shareholders got new shares if they paid an assessment of $15 per share.

Boyd held a judgment against a subsidiary railroad that the Northern Pacific had bought the shares of by having the subsidiary issue a chunk of bonds—essentially an early leveraged buyout. He alleged that this new debt rendered the subsidiary insolvent, and the Northern Pacific was labile for the diversion of assets that could have otherwise paid him.

The Northern Pacific said, "Maybe, but your claim is against the old *Railroad*, and we are the new *Railway*. Please go away." Under the reorganization plan, bondholders received new bonds and stockholders received new stock upon paying an assessment. But the plan made no provision for unsecured creditors such as Boyd.

The majority of the Supreme Court held that "if the value of the road justified the issuance of stock in exchange for old shares, the creditors were entitled to the benefit of that value, whether it was present or prospective, for dividends or only for purposes of control." In short, if the shareholders are getting to keep their interest (even for a price), the creditors must not be frozen out.[19] The Court went on to suggest that the plan could offer such creditors cash, income bonds, or preferred shares. The four dissenting justices called the holding "alarming." Reorganization lawyers agreed.[20]

The Court did not yet state that a receivership had to follow the "absolute" or liquidation priority rule; instead, it simply prohibited the freezing-out of intermediate creditors. The courts would protect intermediate creditors when a reorganization plan "left the unsecured creditors inadequately provided for, while it made a considerable provision for the stockholders."[21] For a court to approve a plan that altered the rights of creditors, the affected creditors had to be included in the plan process, but what that precisely entitled was not always clear.[22] Eventually, especially during the 1930s, this concept would indeed be read to require compliance with the absolute priority rule: A reorganization could be deemed fair only if it followed liquidation priority, at least concerning dissenters.[23]

Then in the 1920s, the Supreme Court began to cast doubt on the continued viability of the friendly receivership generally, especially outside the specific context of railroads, beginning with a case called *Harkin v. Brundage*.[24] Chief Justice William Howard Taft wrote that "we do not wish what we have said to be taken as a general approval of the appointment of a receiver under the prayer of a bill brought by a simple contract creditor simply because it is consented to at the time by a defendant corporation."[25] Henry Friendly, later a federal judge, would write that while "earlier reorganizers had regarded the *Boyd* case as 'a veritable demon incarnate', reorganizers of the 1920's had far greater justification for considering the dictum in *Harkin v. Brundage* in a similar light. . . . The suggestion of 'irregularity' in the procedure regularly followed by the most eminent practitioners and consistently approved by the courts, came as a bolt from the blue."[26]

Then, in the case of *Shapiro v. Wilgus*, Justice Benjamin Cardozo instructed that

> receivers have at times been appointed even by federal courts at the suit of simple contract creditors if the defendant was willing to waive the irregularity and to consent to the decree. This is done not infrequently where the defendant is a public service corporation and the unbroken performance of its services is in furtherance of the public good. In re Metropolitan Railway Receivership, 208

U.S. 109, 111, 28 S.Ct. 219, 52 L.Ed. 403. It has been done at times, though the public good was not involved, where legitimate private interests might otherwise have suffered harm . . . We have given warning more than once, however, that the remedy in such circumstances is not to be granted loosely, but is to be watched with jealous eyes.[27]

Then the same justice, in *State of Michigan v. Michigan Trust Co.*, similarly advised that "receiverships for conservation have at times a legitimate function, but they are to be watched with jealous eyes lest their function be perverted."[28]

And in *First Nat. Bank v. Flershem*, Justice Louis Brandeis stated in a footnote that "all the cases in which this Court appears to have exercised this power [of appointment of receivers and judicial sale] in aid of reorganization . . . dealt with railroads or other public utilities where continued operation of the property and preservation of its unity seemed to be required in the public interest," further calling into question the use of receiverships to reorganize any business other than a railroad.[29]

The judicial pushback against receiverships reached a crescendo when a Montana district court held local counsel in contempt for attempting to commence an ancillary receivership for a five-and-dime chain that had filed in New York. The judge also denied the application for ancillary receivership, stating: "The suit is friendly, without real controversy, strategic, fictitious, presumptuous to put it mildly, and of the too common—yes, in plain English, collusion, if not conspiracy between embarrassed corporations and amiable courts to hinder and delay the former's creditors, quasi a crime."

The court's clipped diction continued in its rant against the filing and local counsels' role, noting the "messenger boy nature of their participation, mere instrument of New York counsel, and 'leaders of the bar according to Who's Who', regularity assumed, casual perusal and no analysis of pleading."[30] The court concluded with a long harangue:

New York counsel are leaders and of Who's Who is of course. The experience, skill, finesse, effrontery, prestige, and impressive personality of counsel of that rank were necessary to devise the plan and program and to impose it upon courts. Unethical practice is by no means limited to the lesser of the bar. It is ventured that the most subtle and effective ambulance chasers operate on golf links, in the club, at the poker table, behind a smoke screen of claim agents, and in collusion with banks and trust companies who are the ostensible advertisers for business the profit of which is divided.

Moreover, like Western Chinamen, all counsel should look alike, in court at least.

It may be true that, on the rare occasions when they failed, like sham and collusive suits have been merely dismissed and no penalty as for contempt imposed. The more reason for a precedent. These abuses, even as all violations of law, are encouraged, increased, and perpetuated by toleration and leniency. They have become a system or even a racket. No doubt counsel intended no personal disrespect to the court, no doubt they are surprised, if not shocked, disgusted, if not horrified, that this court did not accept the usual role, play the part or game, assume blindness, and like others permit its use to carry out this sinister plan or program . . . None the less they knew the facts, the system, the abuse, intended to invoke the aid of the court as they did; and in that is the disrespect and all the intent necessary to contempt, or to most crime for that matter.

The district court judge's decision was overturned by the appeals court a year later, and that court doubted the offensiveness of the receivership, but by then the damage was done.

The United States would enter the Great Depression with its corporate reorganization system in disarray.

· · ·

Meanwhile, MoPac's time in the Kuhn, Loeb universe and "as master collector of bones from the reorganization abattoirs came to a close in 1929."[31] The Van Sweringen brothers had arrived.

Oris Paxton Van Sweringen and Mantis James Van Sweringen (see figure 5.2) were Cleveland real estate developers who became railroad barons on the sly. Their first railroad was the Nickel Plate, which Calvin S. Brice and Samuel Thomas had sold to the New York Central (then controlled by the Vanderbilts), which in turn sold it to the Van Sweringens when the passage of the Clayton Antitrust Act in 1914 made the holding problematic.

Like most real estate developers, then and since, the Van Sweringens loaded their acquisitions with lots of debt and controlled them through complex corporate structures.[32] Multiple corporate layers not only increased the chances to add more debt (leverage—or "gearing," as the British say) to the capital structure, as debt could be nested at each level, but also obscured their control of the railroads from the ICC, which had gained new powers over rail mergers and acquisitions starting in 1920.[33]

In 1922, the brothers purchased 73,000 common shares of the C&O, a major coal hauler, from Henry E. Huntington and Arabella Huntington.[34] Arabella was Henry's wife and previously had been married to Henry's uncle, Collis Potter Huntington, of Big Four fame, who was the founder of the C&O. Together, the two reunited Collis's fortune and combined it with Henry's wealth from the Pacific Electric Railway.[35] The Huntingtons were moving out of railroads and into art collecting, the results of which can be seen today at the Huntington Library.

5.2 Standing (from left) are Oris Van Sweringen, J. P. Morgan, Jr., and Mantis Van Sweringen. Seated at bottom right is Ferdinand Pecora, speaking to three unidentified US senators. June 5, 1933.

AP Photo, used under license.

The Huntingtons' stake in the C&O was the largest available, but still only a small percentage of the common stock, and therefore,

over the next year and a half, the Nickel Plate spent another $6.5 million to buy enough additional C&O stock on the open market to give it a more comfortable 19.9 percent ownership. (The figure was intentionally held to less than 20 percent to forestall possible problems with the ICC.) The average cost per share for all this was $76—$24 less than the Huntington price. At the same time, the Vaness Company—the brothers' "personal basket"—spent $16.2 million for another 23 percent of the stock, for which it paid $93 a share. Those purchases, financed by loans from the Morgan bank and brokers Hayden, Stone and Paine, Webber, were made secretly and were not even recorded on Vaness's books for two and a half years. In all, the brothers got firm control of the C&O—about 43 percent of its stock—while keeping out of the ICC's reach for the time being.[36]

In the following years, the Van Sweringens also purchased stakes in the Erie Railroad and the Pere Marquette Railway as well.[37] Some of these railroads controlled other, smaller railroads. As with the C&O, much of the financing came from their stockbroker, Paine Webber, and from the Van Sweringens' bankers, J. P. Morgan and Co.[38] Morgan in turn syndicated many of the loans to other leading New York financial institutions, particularly the Chase National Bank, First National Bank, Bankers Trust Company, Guaranty Trust Company, and National City Bank. Bankers Trust, Guaranty Trust, and First National Bank were affiliated with J. P. Morgan.[39] Many of the brothers' holding companies issued bonds that were sold through these financial institutions as well.[40]

In the late 1920s, the Van Sweringens created a new holding company, the Alleghany Corporation, under Maryland law.[41] J. P. Morgan and its lawyers from Davis, Polk, Wardwell, Gardiner and Reed helped establish the company. Alleghany issued $35 million of secured convertible debt and $25 million of cumulative preferred stock, both underwritten by Morgan and the affiliated Guaranty Trust Co.

J. P. Morgan & Company received 1.25 million Alleghany common shares for $20 per share.[42] Of the common stock, 500,000 were sold to the Guaranty Company, 175,000 kept by Morgan, and the remainder was sold by Morgan to people on its "preferred list."[43] The worthies on the list obtained the shares at J. P. Morgan's cost, a sizable discount of the market price.[44] To the public, when they learned of it, the list seemed like "a form of polite bribery, a way of providing certain favored individuals and banking firms with a convenient way to make some money without much risk."[45]

Alleghany was listed on the New York Stock Exchange in early 1929, with the vague explanation that it would acquire various other corporations that the Van Sweringens or their holding companies already owned or might purchase in the future.[46] It promptly bought various securities, including shares in the C&O, from the Van Sweringens and exchanged its shares for shares owned by other Van Sweringen–controlled companies. Alleghany then proceeded to invest about $100 million, including new borrowing from New York bankers, into buying MoPac in late 1929 and early 1930.[47]

Voting control of the Missouri Pacific was accomplished by the end of March 1930. The purchases were made through two nominees—one, Kugler & Co., was named after a senior clerk working for Guaranty Trust—and kept in these names to avoid any association with the Van Sweringens or Alleghany until the takeover was made public.[48]

Otis and several of his associates joined the MoPac board in May 1930, and Otis was elected chair. Lewis W. Baldwin remained as president and ran the railroad's day-to-day operations.[49] In one fell swoop, the Van Sweringens doubled the size of their railroad empire.

MoPac already had about $348 million in bonds outstanding in late 1929, and now it was owned by a highly leveraged holding company, just in time for the worst years of the Great Depression. Alleghany, like the Richmond Terminal before it, was a pure holding company that depended on dividends from its operating companies, such as MoPac, to meet its own obligations.[50] "Under Alleghany—and ultimately Morgan control—the Missouri Pacific had become an open scandal. The railroad was milked for dividends while management fired thousands of workers, abandoned improvements, and made no provision for an emergency."[51]

In 1929, Alleghany had also acquired a package of terminal facilities and switching railroads that moved boxcars from railroad to railroad around the greater Kansas City area.[52] These companies were owned by Swift & Company and Armour, who were under pressure from antitrust authorities to sell. Alleghany paid top dollar for these properties—collectively housed in a company called Terminal Shares—despite the meatpackers' strong incentives to sell, and the suspicion was that the deal represented a clandestine kickback, as the Van Sweringens' Nickel Plate railroad was eager to get the Swift and Armour business.

While the Van Sweringens paid full price for these properties in early 1929, they then proceeded to sell them to MoPac for the exact same price (plus interest) postcrash, which MoPac would have to pay over time.[53] The Van Sweringens did a similar move with the Fort Worth Belt Railway.[54] In both cases, it seemed that MoPac was paying far more than it would have in an arm's-length transaction. And MoPac increased its debt load in the process.

To similar effect was the use of $4 million of MoPac's own money to repurchase shares of itself and its key subsidiaries—securities that by 1934 would have a market value of $200,000.[55] These purchases helped to solidify the Van Sweringens' control over MoPac by reducing the number of outstanding shares of the company while the Van Sweringens' stake remained constant.

All this occurred just in time for the Great Depression. The railroad industry, being closely tied to the health of the broader economy, was particularly hard hit. The stock market crash famously happened in October 1929, but the decline in share prices actually began the month before and continued until "reaching its nadir in June 1932 when it had fallen 80 percent (in real terms) below its 1929 peak."[56] And "by the end of 1932, railroad operating revenues generally had declined 50 per cent from their average of the preceding four years; and the avalanche of disaster was well under way."[57] The Missouri Pacific was in particular distress, with a good bit of its territory, particularly in eastern Colorado and western Kansas, within the "dust bowl" that saw the complete obliteration of all agriculture in the early 1930s.[58]

"Demand loans from a J. P. Morgan & Co.–led consortium (the other participants were Guaranty Trust and Kuhn, Loeb & Co.) to the Missouri Pacific were employed to conceal this unpalatable truth."[59] Morgan also underwrote the sale of $61 million worth of new MoPac hundred-year bonds to the public, which resulted in proceeds to the railroad of about $56 million, $10 million of which was used to pay off some of the aforementioned loans from Morgan.[60] Nevertheless, there were still more than $5 million of short-term Morgan notes outstanding in late 1932.[61] The railroad's common stock, which in 1929 had traded as high as $94 a share, was down to $4 by the end of 1932.[62]

As the broader financial crisis continued, banks and life insurance companies, the largest bond investors of the day, increasingly moved out of railroad bonds, selling at big losses, and into federal government debt.[63] As such, railroads and other corporations found it increasingly difficult to access the bond markets. "Despite all efforts, the ability of the Missouri Pacific to continue to obtain funds from the investing public finally came to an end. There was still, of course, the possibility of leaning on the taxpayers of the entire country, and borrowing from the national government."[64]

President Herbert Hoover signed the Reconstruction Finance Corporation Act on January 22, 1932, establishing the Reconstruction Finance Corporation (RFC). Under the law, the RFC was authorized to provide up to $2 billion in emergency loans to financial institutions and railroads.[65] As Oris himself later testified, MoPac was "sitting on their doorstep waiting for them to open."[66] Soon most of the Van Sweringen railroads except the C&O, which still had strong coal revenues, were receiving RFC loans.[67]

MoPac was a repeat customer, eventually borrowing more than $23 million from the RFC, about $7 million of which flowed back to J. P. Morgan to partially pay off loans from the bank.[68] At the same time, Missouri Pacific was paying Allegany $400,000 per quarter under the Terminal Shares installment plan, using borrowing from the RFC to make those payments.[69]

The RFC's standards emphasized loaning funds to solvent companies whose assets appeared to have sufficient long-term value to pay creditors, but which faced short-term liquidity problems. It was essentially a discount window for railroads.

It is not clear that MoPac met that standard, or as one author has put it: "In the process of applying for the various loans, there were some selective lapses in corporate memory to help assure the RFC that these were deserving cases. The Missouri Pacific neglected to mention that it had committed itself to the malodorous $19 million Terminal Shares purchase and had already paid out $3.2 million."[70] Although it seemed politically bizarre to bail out the Van Sweringen railroads, the Hoover administration designed short-term RFC loans "to prevent defaults on the railroad bonds held by so many banks, savings banks, and insurance companies. Stability in the money markets . . . rested to a large extent on the railroad bond market."[71]

But while the Hoover administration felt that the railroads were facing short-term liquidity problems, and hence it repeatedly extended six-month loans to the railroads, this conception (or hope) did not reflect the understanding of investors or industry insiders, who believed that the Depression had simply cleared away the smoke hiding the reality of the industry's long-declining revenues and increasing debt. A committee appointed in 1932, headed by former president Calvin Coolidge, concluded that "as long as the major railways were trapped in a revenue-debt squeeze, railroad bonds would remain depressed, and the investment position of banks, insurance companies, savings banks, and endowed universities would remain compromised."[72]

Eventually, the potential misuse of government funds, combined with the alleged evasion of ICC ownership regulations through the use of holding companies and dummy shareholders, led to the call for congressional investigation.[73] Initially, it was supposed that these hearings would produce the drama of the "Money Trust" hearings from the Progressive Era—where Samuel Untermyer had forcefully questioned J. P. Morgan and Jacob Schiff—or the more recent Pecora hearings, where the Senate Banking Committee's lead counsel, Ferdinand Pecora, had revealed how the country's leading financial institutions misled investors as to the attractiveness of certain securities and favored insiders over retail investors.[74]

The Committee on Interstate Commerce appointed a subcommittee to investigate "Railroads, Holding Companies, and Affiliated Companies." Initially, the subcommittee's chair, Burton K. Wheeler of Montana, played to a packed (and hot, and smoke-filled) room.[75] But soon his interests strayed to thoughts of war and court packing, and he handed off much of the work to his colleague, the junior senator from Missouri, Harry S. Truman, who had a particular interest in the fate of the Missouri Pacific.[76]

Truman had been elected in 1934, so he was truly new to Washington when he joined the "Subcommittee Pursuant to S. Res. 71," as it was inelegantly named. As a result, he often leaned heavily on committee counsel, Max Lowenthal (see figure 5.3).[77] Lowenthal was a 1913 graduate of Harvard Law School, who had previously worked for Cadwalader, Wickersham & Taft, a leading Wall Street law firm, before working at his own firm for several years, focusing primarily on labor law.[78] He remained close friends with Professor Felix Frankfurter of the law school, who was well connected to the New Deal. Lowenthal was also a frequent guest at the home of Supreme Court Justice Brandeis, whom he would introduce to Truman.

Lowenthal had served as assistant counsel to the Pecora Committee and published a popular book—*The Investor Pays*—on the receivership of the Chicago, Milwaukee, and St. Paul (or the "Milwaukee Road," as it was later called), the biggest reorganization of the 1920s.[79] As one commentator observed a decade later, "This infamous case played a highly prominent part in fanning the demand for a reorganization method not subject to such flagrant abuse as the equity proceeding, and resulted eventually in the enactment of [a statutory corporate bankruptcy system]."[80]

5.3 Senator Harry S. Truman (foreground) and committee counsel Max Lowenthal, October 28, 1937.

Library of Congress, Prints & Photographs Division, photograph by Harris & Ewing, LC-H22-D-2543.

In the book, Lowenthal recounted Kuhn, Loeb's efforts to find a cooperative judge—they interviewed the judge in advance of filing the case—and even a plaintiff (the petition was drafted with blanks, with the details of the plaintiff to be added later).[81] As one reviewer summarized:

> As Mr. Lowenthal sees it (and his views are shared by the present reviewer) the essential vice of the accepted machinery of reorganization is that all the posts are manned in advance by whose who precipitate the receivership—the management and their banker-allies. The legal machinery not only favors this result, but actually assists in carrying it out. The entire point of the book is that the committees, the counsel, the receivers, even the court itself, were selected in this instance by the bankers—to say nothing of the reorganization managers, for which the bankers nominated themselves. It is not surprising, therefore, that the plan . . . underwent only slight modification, despite scrutiny by the courts and attacks by independent committees.[82]

He was a natural choice for the new committee.[83]

Together, Lowenthal and Truman would continue turning out reports on the connections between Wall Street and the railroads right up until the US entry into World War II.[84] They would make few friends, with members of J. P. Morgan targeting Lowenthal with a variety of anti-Semitic remarks in their internal communications and Truman facing the ire of several MoPac executives.[85]

• • •

The codification of corporate reorganization, beginning with railroad bankruptcy, was the result of the combination of the extreme need of the early 1930s with the widespread belief that the receivership system no longer worked, or at least it did not work well. The codification of general bankruptcy law had a long and tortured history in the United States despite the Constitution's express inclusion of the Bankruptcy Clause in article I, section 8. At the time of the Constitution, bankruptcy was considered a reinforcement of the broader collection machinery that creditors used against a "trader," and the Bankruptcy Act of 1800 followed English practice in this regard.[86] The only eligible debtors were traders, and the statute could be invoked only by creditors—discharges were rare, at least by modern standards. The act was nevertheless repealed three years later, along with much other federal legislation, as part of the larger Jeffersonian takeover of the national government.

The first truly American bankruptcy law was not enacted until 1841.[87] It was open to all debtors, allowed debtors to voluntarily seek protection, and provided for easier discharges. It was widely used.[88] Nonetheless, it lasted only eighteen months.

The country again muddled along with no bankruptcy law until one was passed in 1867.[89] This lasted the longest of the early laws, but it was substantially revised in 1874—indeed, the revision was so considerable that it could be argued that it was a new law. The 1867 law was the first to accept corporations as debtors.[90] But corporate bankruptcy here meant liquidation, which was fine for smaller companies but seemed destructive when applied to larger businesses.

The revision in 1874 allowed for the first statutory form of reorganization— simple compositions (basically negotiated deals) between the debtor and its unsecured creditors.[91] The provisions in question were modeled on provisions contained in the English Bankruptcy Act of 1869. Using bankruptcy, instead of contract law, simply provided the ability to bind the minority creditors to the deal agreed to by the majority.

Again, this might have been useful for a small business, but for a more complex business, like a railroad, with a complicated capital structure and lots of secured debt, receiverships were much more attractive. The 1867/1874 law was repealed in full in 1878.[92]

The 1898 Bankruptcy Act, enacted after meandering debate following the 1893 panic, was the nation's first long-lasting bankruptcy statute, with parts enduring until 1978, but it too would be extensively remodeled, as we shall see in this chapter and chapter 6.[93] In its initial form, the 1898 act once again allowed for corporate liquidations, as well as 1874-style compositions under section 12, but it expressly excluded railroads in all respects.[94] Large nonrail corporations continued to reorganize in receiverships.

In 1929, federal judge Thomas Day Thacher and a committee of attorneys headed by William J. Donovan investigated alleged bankruptcy fraud in New York City.[95] Thacher was appointed solicitor general in the Hoover administration soon afterward, and he then expanded his study of bankruptcy nationwide.[96] The resulting report makes clear that business bankruptcy of this era was a world apart from corporate reorganization as conducted in receiverships. The average merchant bankruptcy case in 1930 was quite small: "89.92 per cent had assets of less than $5,000; 5.5 per cent had assets of from $5,001 to $10,000; 3.92 per cent had assets of from $10,001 to $50,000; 0.66 per cent had assets of over $50,000."[97] The largest business bankruptcy cases involved manufacturers, but even these cases represented only *total* assets (across more than 1,300 cases) of just over $22 million. The Texas and Pacific of the 1880s, with reported assets of more than $95 million, seems like a colossus compared to the business bankruptcy cases of the 1930s.[98]

Thacher proposed a comprehensive revision of the 1898 Bankruptcy Act that would have included a corporation reorganization provision, albeit only for nonrail corporations. His proposed "section 76" would have placed corporate debtors under the supervision of a trustee until a reorganization plan was approved by two-thirds of creditors, with an elaborate cram-down provision for imposition of a plan on dissenting classes.[99] The broader revision legislation, including the corporate reorganization provision, was introduced in Congress in early 1932 as the Hastings-Michener Bill, but it was never enacted.[100] Perhaps appropriately, statutory corporate reorganization would instead begin with the railroads.

• • •

For receivership insiders, like bankers and restructuring attorneys, Supreme Court caselaw provided the primary reason for abandoning receiverships. In addition, many insiders complained that the caselaw had facilitated the growth of holdouts, who could manipulate the system to demand payment in full. Of course, as we saw with the equity committee in the Texas and Pacific case, the notion of paying objectors to "go away" long predated the unfavorable Supreme Court caselaw.

The receivership system was also under attack from another group, which we might broadly term "reformers."[101] Lowenthal was clearly in that category, but it included others like ICC commissioner Joseph Eastman, Professor Frank-furter, Congressman Fiorello La Guardia, and several others connected to the soon-to-arrive New Deal.[102] As a presidential candidate, Franklin D. Roosevelt complained that receiverships were mostly "arranged so that every member of the bar can get his fair share of the assets."[103]

In a similar vein, Lowenthal noted that in the Milwaukee Road receivership, "six trust companies, and three individual trustees . . . employed sixteen law firms to act for them," all of which were paid out of the estate.[104] Kuhn, Loeb received more than $1 million for its work on the case,[105] and its counsel (Cravath) about $450,000.[106]

Sherman and Sterling, counsel for the bondholder's committee (and counsel for City Bank, which sat on the committee despite holding no bonds), may have received as much as $300,000 (more than $5 million today) in the case. The chair of the committee, a vice president of Met Life who had chaired two other prior Kuhn, Loeb–sponsored committees in recent years, said that he retained Sherman because he believed that the reorganization should be based on "the utmost economy."[107] Lowenthal concluded that "select circles shared in largesse drawn from the purse of the security-holders, and dispensed by those whose money it was not."[108]

Both sides accordingly desired reform of the railroad receivership process, but for different reasons.[109] Efforts initially began in late 1932, when Senator Hastings introduced a bill that was at least partially drafted by members of Cravath, Swaine & Moore.[110] That firm was representing MoPac at the same time "in connection with steps to be taken to protect the properties and assets of said Railroad Company from seizure and the rights and interests of its stockholders and creditors in the event said Railroad Company should default under any of its mortgages or indentures."[111]

While the bill was pending, Robert Swaine, the head of the firm, published a law review article supporting codification of corporate bankruptcy, based on four key faults that he identified with the receivership system:

1) The present necessity for obtaining the appointment of a receiver;
2) The present necessity, if the properties extend beyond one federal judicial district in the case of the ordinary industrial, or beyond one federal judicial circuit in the case of a railroad, of an expensive multiplicity of receivership proceedings;
3) The present necessity for judicial sales of the property of the debtor, involving cumbersome procedure, delay, expense, and opportunities for unconscionable extortion by dishonest minorities and their counsel; and
4) The present necessity for providing, in the reorganization, cash for the fair value of the claims of all creditors (and possibly stockholders) who have not affirmatively assented to the plan at the date of its consummation even though they may not have affirmatively dissented.[112]

In the House, La Guardia introduced a bill that would have given the key role to the ICC. As the American economy continued to unspool after the November 1932 election, there was pressure on Congress to pass some sort of bankruptcy legislation in the lame duck session before Roosevelt was inaugurated in early March, when he would have plenty else on his plate—most notably, the rapidly accelerating collapse of the banking system.

Finally, Congress blended the bills and passed what would become section 77 of the Bankruptcy Act, providing a tool for railroad reorganization.[113] Initially, the bill contained a general corporate reorganization provision as well, but this was dropped at the last second.[114] Perhaps indicative of the times, *The New York Times* published the full text.[115] President Hoover signed the law on March 3, 1933, the day before he left office.[116]

Section 77 of the Bankruptcy Act was the first federal corporate reorganization statute in the United States.[117] As the Supreme Court explained, the provision "manifests the intention of Congress to place reorganization under the leadership of the Commission, subject to a degree of participation by the court."[118]

A bankruptcy petition was filed with the federal district court where the railroad was headquartered, with no need for any ancillary proceedings. The ICC was instructed to hold a public hearing at which the debtor, any committee, or any group of investors holding at least 10 percent of the securities in a class could propose a plan. The ICC was then to recommend a specific plan to the court.[119]

If the court approved the plan, it would be sent out to the investors for voting. A class could approve the plan by a two-thirds vote, meaning that the plan could bind up to a third of the class without having to deal with their holdup power. After the ICC certified the results of the vote, the court would confirm the plan if satisfied that "such acceptances have not been made or procured any means forbidden by law."

There were provisions that allowed for the approval of a plan over the dissent of a class—that is, even when two-thirds did not approve—but they were fairly complex, in that they required either a sale or appraisal of the debtor-railroad. The latter apparently envisioned something like the appraisal of dissenting shares under state corporate law.[120]

A 1935 amendment to the statute provided that if a class failed to vote for a plan, the plan could nevertheless be approved by the court if the court found that it "makes adequate provision for fair and equitable treatment for the interests or claims of those rejecting it; that such rejection is not reasonably justified in the light of the respective rights those rejecting it and all the relevant facts."[121] As commentators explained, "Where the dissenters have refused to accept a plan found to meet the requirements of substantive law determinative of their interest, the court is empowered to inquire into the reasonableness of their rejection and to overrule it if it shall find that the rejection is not reasonably justified."[122]

• • •

On March 31, 1933, the Missouri Pacific and its two principal operating subsidiaries commenced the very first case under section 77, filing their petitions in St. Louis.[123] Interestingly, only three members of the board were at the Cleveland meeting to authorize the filing, so there may not have been a quorum.[124] Nobody seemed to notice. Eventually more than twenty distinct railroad-debtors made up the MoPac case.

It was front-page news for the *St. Louis Post-Dispatch*, although the other stories on that page—including a bank failure and the Nazi expulsion of Jewish judges from German courts—provide a reminder of the broader happenings at the time.[125] In December 1934, *Time* would observe that "one fifth of all U.S. railroad mileage is in the hands of the courts, and nearly one-third of that stricken mileage is accounted for by Missouri Pacific Railroad."[126]

Several other major railroads soon followed: The Southern Railway only barely avoided its own bankruptcy thanks to substantial RFC loans that kept it afloat until the war.[127] The RFC ended up managing the finances of the Baltimore and Ohio for thirteen years, and by 1935, the RFC had loaned more than $500 million to railroads, of which more than $140 million was in default. Even the mighty New York Central required $27 million in RFC loans, as it saw its bonds plummet from 256 in 1929 to 9 in 1932.[128]

Corporate reorganization had entered the statutory era, where it has remained ever since. Initially it was thought that section 77 proceedings would be speedy; subsequent events proved otherwise.[129] As the trustee's counsel would observe at a hearing in 1954, still two years from the end of the case, "the purpose of the Act was to bring about speedy reorganization; in this instance speed has been largely distinguished by its absence from the situation."[130]

Originally, there was no trustee in the MoPac case, and the railroad pioneered the "debtor in possession" concept, with company management leading the bankruptcy—recall that Swaine had identified receivers as the first of the faults of the old receivership system—but the RFC soon learned about the Terminal Shares transaction and demanded one.[131] The debtors responded confusingly that "there is no sufficient showing to require the appointment of a trustee or trustees, yet the Debtor interposes no objection to such appointment if and when the Court shall deem it necessary or desirable to make the same."[132]

Probably influenced by past receivership practices, the court appointed two trustees: Lewis Baldwin, the longtime president of MoPac (he signed the bankruptcy petitions), and Guy A. Thompson (figure 5.4), a local attorney and former president of the American Bar Association.[133] Baldwin was granted $3,000

5.4 Guy A. Thompson, MoPac's bankruptcy trustee for twenty-three years, waiting to speak before the SEC in 1938.

Library of Congress, Prints & Photographs Division, photograph by Harris & Ewing, LC-H22-D-3505. Thompson is erroneously identified as the trustee of the Union Pacific.

per month (in addition to his existing MoPac salary), and Thompson $1,500.[134] Starting in September, Thompson got a slight raise, to $2,000 per month.[135]

The salary probably reflected the initial reality of the roles, as Thompson would testify a few years later: "When I walked into the property I was very much at sea for quite a time because of my inexperience in rail road matters, and it took me some little while to get my bearings; but the atmosphere, so far as Mr. Baldwin was concerned, was all that I could have wished, I would say."[136] Baldwin's appointment would be highly controversial, given that he was president at the time of the Terminal Shares deal and the share repurchases; he would eventually resign (although he remained as chief operating officer and a board member until his death).[137] Section 77 was later amended to preclude the appointment of an insider, and trustees became mandatory.[138]

The railroad obtained court approval to honor paychecks and pay management salaries (including Baldwin, at $40,000 per year).[139] Employee pensions also continued to be paid.[140] And eventually, an action was brought to challenge the validity of the Terminal Shares agreements.[141]

Its common shareholder list—137 pages long, from Stephen Abbot, of Salt Lake City, to Revella Zychick, of Cleveland, and including the Boston Symphony Orchestra—makes clear that while Alleghany had a commanding stake in Missouri Pacific, there were myriad retail investors who were ensnared by the bankruptcy as well.[142] The bondholder lists were similar, with insurance companies like Northwestern Mutual, with tens of millions of dollars of bonds across various bonds, contrasted with Christina Sulgrove of Choteau, Montana, with one $1,000 bond.[143] Numerous universities—such as Yale, Harvard, and the Massachusetts Institute of Technology—along with charitable institutions like the 92nd Street Y (then called the Young Men's Hebrew Association)— appear on the lists of security holders.

The preferred shareholder list includes Fritz van Calker, a well-known Munich criminal law professor who was about to begin openly collaborating with the Nazi Party.[144] Also on the list is "Monsieur Pol Roger, Epernay, France."[145]

And then there were the personal injury claims from employees and passengers.[146] Other pending litigation against the railroad included an intriguing suit by Ernest and Eliza Anderson, who were seeking $100,000 in damages for false arrest.[147] The same attorneys were representing Virginia Anderson in a $25,000 suit against the railroad for trespassing.

As shown in table 5.1, MoPac's bonds were arrayed in a fairly complex capital structure, but the most immediately important was the Iron Mountain, 4 percent bonds due May 1933, secured by first lien on old Iron Mountain lines (shown at the top of the table).[148] These bonds made the bankruptcy filing particularly essential, as there was no way for MoPac to refinance $34.5 million in debt in the middle of a banking crisis.[149] That, along with various coupon and tax payments due, meant that the railroad faced coming up with more than $40 million before May 1.[150] Both key subsidiaries (the Gulf Coast Lines and the International–Great Northern) had their own bonds as well.[151]

The aforementioned Iron Mountain bonds were soon caught up in the broader monetary policies of the New Deal, as they contained a "gold clause," which Congress had outlawed as part of the effort to diminish the value of the dollar and thus stimulate the economy.[152] Why the bonds contained a gold clause was debatable, but the district court suggested that perhaps it was "because the term 'payable in gold coin of the United States of the present standard of weight and fineness' is a sonorous and mouth-filling phrase and indubitably it adds a dignity and a glamour of richness to all bonds, particularly to those which the maker had not and never had the remotest intention of ever paying in anything."[153]

TABLE 5.1 Missouri Pacific's debt

	Amount outstanding	Maturity	Coupon (%)	Annual interest
River & Gulf Div.— ST.L.I.M.&S. Ry. First Mtg.	$34,548,000	May 1-33	4	$1,581,920
Second Mortgage Pacific R.R. of Missouri	2,573,000	July 1-38	5	128,650
Third Mortgage Pacific R.R. of Missouri	3,828,000	July 1-38	4	155,120
First Mortgage Pacific R.R. of Missouri	6,996,000	August 1-38	4	279,840
First Mortgage Pacific R.R. of Missouri (Carondelet Bch.)	237,500	October 1-38	4-1/2	10,688
First Mortgage Little Rock & Hot Springs Wn. R.R.	1,140,000	July 1-39	4	45,600
First & Refunding Mortgage Series A	17,840,000	February 1-65	5	892,025
General Mortgage	51,550,000	March 1-75	4	2,054,000
First & Refunding Mortgage				
Series F	95,000,000	March 1-77	5	4,750,000
Series G	25,000,000	November 1-78	5	1,250,000
Series H	25,000,000	April 1-80	5	1,250,000
Series I	61,200,000	February 1-81	5	3,060,000
Texarkana Union Station Trust Certificate Series A	450,000	December 1-57	5	22,500
Secured Serial Gold Bonds	12,140,000	December 31– December 56	5-1/4	655,154
Equipment Trust Obligations	20,528,200			918,643
20 Yr. 5-1/2% Convertible Gold Bonds Series A	46,392,000	May 1-49	5-1/2	2,551,560
Real Estate Security Mortgage Pacific R.R. of Missouri	799,000	May 1-38	5	59,950
First Mortgage 6% Gold Bonds, Plaza Olive Building	809,000	October-40	6	48,203
Notes to Reconstruction Finance Corp.	6,950,000			599,768
Total	**$412,781,200**			**$19,871,619**

The judge ultimately ruled that Congress's declaration that gold clauses were against public policy was lawful, and thus the bonds in question could be paid in regular dollars—a decision ultimately upheld by the Supreme Court after Bankers' Trust, the indenture trustee, appealed.[154] If the ruling had been otherwise, these creditors would have had a swollen claim in the bankruptcy for the "gold value" of the bonds.[155]

Meanwhile, committees began to form, once again utilizing the old forms. John Stedman, a vice president at Prudential Insurance in Newark, had frequently formed committees in receiverships and was serving as chair of the "prior lien" bondholders committee in the pending "Frisco" receivership in St. Louis.[156] His notes indicate that he took an analogous approach to the MoPac committee that he would ultimately head:

Following the appointment of Mr. L. W. Baldwin as the agent of Judge Faris of U. S. District Court of St. Louis, resulting from the filing of a petition in bankruptcy by the Missouri Pacific on March 31,1933, I made a trip to St. Louis for the purpose of discussing the situation with both Mr. Baldwin and Judge Faris.

Judge Faris, whom I found at Cape Girardeau, stated that he would be in favor of a formal committee of insurance company holders of Missouri Pacific first mortgage bonds.

Upon my return, a meeting of large holders was called for April 19, at which there were present financial and legal officers of nine insurance companies . . .

A second meeting was held on May 3, at which were present, in addition to officers of nine insurance companies, two members of the firm of J. P. Morgan & Company and two members of the firm of Kuhn, Loeb & Company. The purpose of the meeting was to discuss with the bankers the advisability of a general committee representing all security issues, both bond and stock. As a result of this conference the insurance company representatives decided to organize a sub-committee of five to represent solely the First and Refunding 5s and to discuss with the bankers the possibility of finding common ground upon which the group and the representatives of other issues of securities could agree.[157]

The Stedman committee had the largest single pool of bonds in the case, and the most senior bonds (namely, the First and Refunding Mortgage 5 Percent Gold Bonds) that had been issued in several series.[158] The committee solicited deposits under the typical ironclad deposit agreement and offered depositors tradable certificates of deposits in exchange for their shares.[159]

As shown in table 5.2, the committee was comprised of five insurance company executives, in addition to Stedman himself, along with the president of Dime Savings Bank, the president of the Bank of New York, and a banker from Kuhn, Loeb.[160] Initially, a Morgan partner was also on the committee, but he

TABLE 5.2 John Stedman's protective committee for Missouri Pacific Railroad first and refunding mortgage 5% gold bonds

John W. Stedman, Chairman; Prudential Ins. Co. of America, Newark.
Philip A. Benson, Dime Savings Bank, Brooklyn, N.Y.
George W. Bovenizer, Kuhn, Loeb & Co., New York, N.Y.
Frederick W. Ecker, Metropolitan Life Ins. Co., New York, N.Y.
Robert A. Franks, The Carnegie Corp. of N.Y.
S. Parker Gilbert, J. P. Morgan & Co., New York, N.Y.
Frederick P. Hayward, John Hancock Mut. Life Ins. Co., Boston.
Harold Palagano, New York Life Ins. Co., New York, N.Y.
Sterling Pierson, Equitable Life Assur. Soc. of the United States, New York, N.Y.
John C. Traphagen, Bank of New York & Trust Co., New York, N.Y.
Frederick W. Walker, Northwestern Mut. Life Ins. Co., Milwaukee.

ultimately resigned. Truman and Lowenthal later revealed that many of the insurance company executives on the Stedman committee, or other senior management of those companies, had received below-market shares in Allegany as part of J. P. Morgan's special customer list.[161]

A committee of independent bondholders—headed by historian Charles Beard—formed to counter the efforts of the insurance companies and banks.[162] Other committees formed to represent specific bonds or the securities of specific subsidiaries.

Max Lowenthal noted that the Iron Mountain bondholders committee was "headed by an officer of the Bankers Trust Company of New York, a bank that rendered services and received fees on many occasions in Missouri Pacific history. It is now, as it was in the 1917 reorganization, trustee for holders of [MoPac] bonds and depositary for a protective committee. This bank does not have a dollar of its own money in any of the bonds it offers to protect. Its financial interest is directly opposed to that of the bondholders represented by the committee."[163]

Specifically, Bankers Trust had loaned large sums to the Van Sweringens, so while the MoPac bondholders might want to challenge the Terminal Shares transaction and other interactions with the brothers, doing so would undermine Bankers Trust's Van Sweringen loans. An officer of Bankers Trust also served on another committee, representing Gulf Coast bondholders.

That committee was chaired by the banker who arranged the sale of Gulf Coast to MoPac.

Lowenthal's deep understanding of the countless pieces of headwear that Bankers Trust was sporting was likely a result of passage of the Securities Act of 1933 in May, as section 2 of that law defined the securities subject to the registration requirements thereunder to include a "certificate of deposit for a security." When the Bankers Trust Company wanted to form its committee, it had to file a registration statement with the Federal Trade Commission—the SEC was not formed until 1934.[164] That registration statement is an awkward document, providing disclosures about the Iron Mountain, formally the issuer of the bonds, but noting that most of its officers and directors were no longer alive—in 1916, the railroad had sold all its assets to the Missouri Pacific (which had assumed responsibility for the bonds) as part of its own receivership.

The registration statement notes that Bankers Trust owned 7.5 percent participation in a $22 million J. P. Morgan loan to various Van Sweringen entities ("now in default") and a 6.7 percent interest in another similar $18 million Morgan loan, also indicated as being in default. Bankers Trust was also the trustee on two other outstanding MoPac bonds—this was all before the 1939 Trust Indenture Act (TIA) regulated bond trustees, although railroads would be exempt from the TIA until 1976 in any event.[165] The registration statement does contain a refreshing discussion of the broad powers given the committee under the deposit agreement, including the ability to use the deposited bonds as collateral for committee loans and the waiver of almost any possible Bankers Trust liability.

. . .

Into this stew of clashing interests went the ICC. Five plans were submitted initially—"two by the debtors, two by the Missouri Pacific first and refunding mortgage [Stedman's] protective committee, and one by the Missouri Pacific common stockholders protective committee."[166] The ICC held hearings beginning in February 1936, which were not concluded until September 1937. In February 1938, the various parties filed briefs on the plan. In October, the ICC examiner published a preliminary report. Exceptions to the report were due in early January 1939, with replies to the exceptions due in late January. In March, the ICC heard arguments on the proposed report and plan.

On January 10, 1940, the ICC issued its report and order approving a plan of reorganization. Thereafter, it issued a supplemental report and a supplemental order approving a modified plan of reorganization, all 350-odd pages of which was filed with the court.[167] Various parties, including the Stedman committee and the debtor itself (through its counsel), filed objections to the plan.[168]

The district court approved the plan in an opinion dated June 20, 1941.[169] Myriad disgruntled parties took appeals to the Circuit Court of Appeals for the Eighth Circuit.[170] Meanwhile, the ICC sent the plan for a vote, with notice of the same published in seventeen newspapers from Baltimore to San Francisco.[171] On March 28, 1942, the commission certified the results of the balloting, showing that six of the sixteen participating classes voted against the plan.[172] Ironically, that would not turn out to be the main difficulty with the 1940 plan.

At the Eighth Circuit, briefs were submitted and oral arguments held, but no decision was rendered before the aforementioned votes came in. Indeed, the parties were still waiting for a decision from the Eighth Circuit when in 1943, the Supreme Court rendered its opinion in *Group of Institutional Investors v. Chicago, Milwaukee, St. Paul & Pacific Railroad Company*, involving the 1935 section 77 case of the same railroad whose prior receivership (completed in 1928) had been the subject of Lowenthal's *The Investor Pays*.[173] Perceiving that the new decision had some relevance to the Missouri Pacific case, the Eighth Circuit sent the case back to the district court, still not having decided the appeal in front of it.

The district court agreed that the Supreme Court's decision would necessitate revisions to the plan.[174] But far more important, the district court observed that the world had changed, especially for those in the United States—the attack on Pearl Harbor happened while voting was underway. The nation, and thus MoPac, were in a vastly different place in 1943 than it was in June 1941, when the district court had approved the plan. Among other things, MoPac's earnings had gone from $7 million in 1939 to $50 million in 1942. The ICC had to start over.

Here, we see the essential problem with section 77: It was colossally slow.[175] "The Western Pacific and the Chicago & North Western reorganizations each took nine years; the Milwaukee-St. Paul reorganization, ten years; the Denver, the New Haven, and the Frisco reorganizations, eleven, twelve, and fourteen years, respectively; the Rock Island, fourteen."[176] MoPac easily beat them all for total length.

In particular, the ICC approached each step in the plan process with a tenured academic's sense of urgency. All hearings were quite formal, after full briefing, and ICC reports came out only months later. As previously noted, there were preliminary and final reports, and even the final reports might be revised upon consideration of written objections.

And then the process moved to the courts. Once the district court approved a plan, voting was to happen next. But the district court's ruling could be appealed to the Court of Appeals, and then even the Supreme Court. The Eighth Circuit's approach to the 1940 plan could hardly be called breakneck; likewise, the plan at issue in the Supreme Court's 1943 decision in *Group of Institutional Investors* had been approved by the ICC in 1940. And once the vote happened, the district court had to confirm the plan, and that confirmation order could also be appealed up the same chain.

• • •

The rapidly changing world combined with the slow section 77 process to keep MoPac in bankruptcy for twenty-three years. During this time, the trustee increasingly separated MoPac from its controlling shareholders at Alleghany. He stopped paying the managers located in Cleveland.[177] Upon the death of his counsel—MoPac's Alleghany-allied general counsel had been hired by Baldwin—he took the opportunity to appoint Russell L. Dearmont (figure 5.5).[178]

Dearmont was a former Missouri state senator who had lost the 1932 Democratic gubernatorial primary to the candidate favored by the Pendergast

5.5 Russell L. Dearmont, counsel to the trustee and later president and chief executive officer of MoPac, c.1958.

Author's collection, unknown photographer (MoPac press photograph).

machine of Kansas City.[179] His law firm, based in Cape Girardeau, represented the railroad in southeast Missouri. As such, he was unaffiliated with the St. Louis corporate offices and had not come under the sway of the Van Sweringens. It was later said that Thompson told him that the new position would last eighteen months to two years, and thus he obtained special permission from the ICC to keep his law firm in operation.[180]

Thompson remained aloof from the plan process, just like receivers before him, by instruction of the district court.[181] He operated the railroad, and everyone else would figure out the terms of the reorganization.[182]

New plans were put forth in 1944 and 1949. The 1944 plan was sent back to the ICC in 1947 because the railroad had accumulated so much cash during the war.[183] In the meantime, the Stedman committee disbanded and Stedman himself retired. Several other committees were formed in its place, including a group of institutional investors that included most of the insurance companies originally on the Stedman committee.[184]

The 1949 plan was the first to allow some return to equity—but only to the preferred shareholders. The common shareholders were still to be eliminated, as they had been in all the earlier plans, based on the ICC's finding that there was insufficient value in the railroad.[185] The court of appeals affirmed the district court's approval of this plan in 1951.[186]

An appeal to the Supreme Court was denied in 1952, but former professor, now justice Frankfurter issued a long concurrence commenting on "the long-drawn-out Missouri Pacific reorganization," in which he noted that the last three plans had called for the elimination of common shares based on ICC valuations of the company that turned out in retrospect to be quite wrong. Regarding the bondholders, he also observed that "the rights which the Commission has thrice deemed valueless, it has proposed to substitute securities less valuable than what bondholders at present own."[187]

Justice Frankfurter noted as well that the ICC's valuation errors were systematically in one direction: He charged the commission with a "uniformity of erroneous guessing." In short, it was continuing to value the railroad based on an anticipated return to the 1930s, when World War II, the Korean War, the Cold War, and the generally robust postwar economy had made such estimates inappropriate. He concluded by noting that the executive and Congress were rightly skeptical about the courts' and the ICC's competence in terms of reorganization.

The day after Justice Frankfurter's opinion was published, Lucian Hilmer forwarded it to the Truman White House, with "reference to the President's Interest in the Missouri Pacific situation."[188] Hilmer was an attorney that had previously worked under Lowenthal with then-senator Truman on the railroad investigation, and by the early 1950s, he was representing the independent (non-Alleghany) directors on the MoPac board in the bankruptcy.[189] In his cover letter, he noted that the "Commission's outstanding exponent of the kind of economic pessimism berated by the Justice" was awaiting reappointment.[190]

• • •

The onset of the war—or more aptly, active US involvement in it—changed MoPac's fortunes, to say the least. For the first half of 1941, the railroad's net income was $818,000; the figure for the first half of 1942 was $15 million.[191]

Soon the cash was piling up, and Thompson did not know what to do with it all.[192] A normal corporation might have paid dividends, but that hardly seemed appropriate with millions of unpaid bonds lying about. Large investments in government bonds followed, but he also began calling smaller pieces of outstanding debt, rationalizing the company's capital structure.[193] In 1945, he paid off the Iron Mountain bonds that had occasioned the bankruptcy filing.[194] He reached an agreement to pay off the RFC loans, the bank loans from J. P. Morgan, and eventually even settled the Terminal Shares matter.[195] In total, some $94.7 million of debt was paid off during the war.[196]

The railroad fully converted to diesel engines during its bankruptcy.[197] A substantial amount of new equipment was also purchased.[198] For example, in 1948 the trustee placed a large order for new, streamlined passenger cars, including thirty-eight new sleeping cars. In the order were coach car numbers 863 to 869, which were "divided chair cars," designed to meet the requirements of Jim Crow laws.[199] T. C. Davis, the chairman of the board—reflecting more Alleghany than operational mindset—complained that the trustee was creating a "gold-plated" railroad, a conspicuously American development, when railroads in the rest of the world where largely being demolished during this time.[200]

Exactly what the railroad's board did during these years, other than duplicate arguments made by Alleghany, is more than unclear, given that the trustee had control of all the debtors' assets.[201] Alleghany paid $229,750 to the board to resist reorganization plans. Alleghany also paid Davis $16,000 "to cover his expenses in opposing plans of reorganization which would have wiped out [Alleghany's] investment in the common stock of Missouri Pacific."[202]

"Following the death of O. P. Van Sweringen in 1936, control of Alleghany was passed along from George A. Ball, an Indiana glass-jar maker . . . then to a Wall Street syndicate headed by Robert R. Young."[203] Young's goal throughout the case would be to avoid confirmation of a plan that eliminated the shareholders (i.e., Alleghany), and unquestionably the everlasting section 77 process helped his quest.[204] And frankly the threat of elimination encouraged shareholders to make any conceivable argument they might have in order to keep their stake alive a bit longer.

Early in the Great Depression, Young had formed what may have been the first distressed investing firm: Young, Kolbe and Company, which sorted among the countless bankrupt corporations of the day.[205] In 1935, J. P. Morgan had foreclosed on a large block of Alleghany shares that the Van Sweringens had posted as collateral for a loan that they could not pay. Ball was the successful bidder at the sale, for $3.1 million—recall that Alleghany had spent more than $100 million on MoPac, and the company owned controlling stakes in the C&O, the Erie, and the Pere Marquette as well, along with other investments—and when Ball looked to sell a few years later, Young, Kolbe teamed up with Allan Kirby, heir to the Woolworth fortune, to buy him out at $6.4 million (see figure 5.6).[206] Their primary target was the durable C&O, but they also looked to salvage whatever value they could from Alleghany's MoPac stake.

By 1953, Alleghany held 396,000, or about 48 percent, of the MoPac common shares, a reduction from the 499,200 (60 percent) that the Van Sweringens had originally bought back in 1929.[207] In 1948, Alleghany sold all its MoPac bonds, and previously it had sold its preferred shares.[208] This left it as a pure common shareholder, which allowed it to advocate the shareholder position

5.6 Left to right: Senator Burton Wheeler, Allen P. Kirby, and Robert R. Young, May 1937.

more plainly. In many respects, there was more than a bit of the Scott-Gould antimonopolist getup here, as Alleghany, the speculative vehicle owned by a parade of speculators, took up the cause of the retail stock investor.[209]

Nevertheless, Young was quite adept at public relations and government lobbying: "Flush with millions, he began the bitter attacks on the railroad industry that marked his stormy career . . . [he] launched a publicity campaign whose high point was the famous newspaper ad that said: 'A hog can cross the country without changing trains—but you can't.' He lashed out fiercely at 'goddam bankers' (his favorite phrase) for their control of the railroads, set himself up as the champion of the people in a crusade to revitalize U.S. railroads. And all the while, he strengthened and expanded Alleghany's holdings."[210] Soon he had many in Congress fighting for shareholders "trapped" in section 77 proceedings.[211]

In 1948, responding to this public lobbying, Congress enacted a new, streamlined reorganization procedure that allowed modifications to one or more classes of securities if approved by 75 percent of that class.[212] A similar reorganization process was first proposed a few years earlier by Senator Wheeler, but that version was pocket-vetoed by President Truman.[213]

Reorganization under section 20b—also known as the Mahaffie Act, after the ICC commissioner who first suggested it—did not have to comply with the *Boyd* rule of liquidation or "absolute" priority, opening the possibility of revamping bond debt while leaving shareholders in place.[214] The act simply required that the ICC make findings that a plan was just and reasonable, in the best interest of the railroad and of each effected class, as well as in the public interest.[215] In many respects, the Mahaffie Act, albeit limited to railroads, was much like the still-existing English scheme of arrangement process where a class of securities can be restructured upon a 75 percent vote, without putting the entire company and its capital structure into a reorganization proceeding.[216]

Congress was motivated by what it perceived as the ICC's stinginess in section 77 plans. In particular, the commission was so conservative in its valuations that the junior creditors and shareholders were routinely zeroed out. That had the effect of leaving the senior creditors, where the large insurance companies dominated, holding the new equity, which in many cases quickly traded at premium prices given the booming Cold War economy.[217] One railroad successfully moved to dismiss its case with its shares trading at around $300 while the ICC was proposing to eliminate them in its pending plan. A Senate committee bemoaned the ICC's efforts, which it asserted had resulted in "the forfeiture of over $500,000,000 of railroad bonds and creditors' claims and $2,000,000,000 of railroad preferred and common stock."[218]

. . .

Congress promoted the Mahaffie Act as a tool for protecting small shareholders, the "widows and orphans" of legal folklore, from unwarranted investment losses. But "it turned out that one of the largest widows and orphans was Wall Street financier Robert R. Young."[219] With the failure of the 1949 plan, MoPac's board quickly set about using section 20b to save Alleghany's stake in MoPac.[220]

Under the proposed section 20b plan, Missouri Pacific would be organized on a stand-alone basis, with a Gulf Coast Lines plan to follow, after completion of the parent company's plan. Bondholders would get new bonds with lower coupons and extended maturities, and in some cases, Texas and Pacific preferred shares were given in exchange for overdue coupon payments. MoPac preferred shareholders would get two new preferred shares for each old one—to account for accumulated and unpaid dividends—but the new shares would be noncumulative and pay at a lower rate. Common shareholders would ride through untouched, save for a reduction in par value.[221] The allure to Alleghany (and Young) was obvious.

Moody's noted that market prices for MoPac securities declined after the section 20b plan was made public, and stated that the rating agency had five core objections to the plan:

- The large proposed cash payments would apparently drain the company of its liquid resources, raising the question as to whether it would meet the test of "being in the best public interest."
- The plan increases debt, fails to provide for capital and sinking funds, and possibly does not fully safeguard the company against further financial difficulties under adverse operating conditions.
- The plan provides little incentive for holders of first and refunding bonds to accept a lower coupon rate. Ultimately, 75 percent of each class of security holder must assent to make the plan effective.
- Bondholders and preferred stockholders are requested to make sacrifices, whereas the common is left practically unscathed. This raises the question as to whether the plan is fair and equitable.
- The proposal does not provide for a subsidiary, International Great Northern Railroad.

Because of the foregoing we [Moody's] believe that investors should regard this new proposal with considerable caution.[222]

T. C. Davis petitioned the district court for permission to file the proposed plan with the ICC.[223] The board's counsel was no other than former Montana senator Wheeler, now a practicing attorney in Washington after losing his reelection bid.[224] The Protective Committee for Secured Serial 5-1/4% Bonds of Missouri Pacific Railroad and others objected that the 20b plan was impractical and would result in the potential breakup of the MoPac system since the debtors would be reorganized separately or distributed (in the case of the Texas and Pacific) as part of the plan.[225] The court denied the petition, writing that "the Debtor's plan would, in my opinion, require drastic revision in order to prevent the company from becoming an immediate candidate for a new Section 77 proceeding. In view of its violation of the principle of a system reorganization, found by the Commission and the Courts to be in the public interest, I believe that the submission of this plan to the Commission could do nothing more than delay the final confirmation of a plan in the Section 77 proceedings."[226]

Davis was probably not helped by having signed some of Young's more bellicose advertisements and public letters, including ads that suggested that the judge was in cahoots with trustee Thompson, a topic that the judge asked about when Davis was on the stand in support of his 20b petition.[227] The ad in question, entitled "Congress be Damned!" appeared in several papers nationwide, including the *St. Louis Post Dispatch*, where the judge was bound to see it.[228]

. . .

The Missouri Pacific section 77 case was one of the first large corporate reorganizations to feature attorneys of both genders—for example, the common shareholder's committee was for a time represented by Helen Walter Munsert, who was admitted to the Illinois bar in 1935.[229] The numbers remained small, however.

After the war, the railroad was also compelled to address the question of equal service to its customers. The railroad was under increasing public pressure to follow its Midwest competitors in fully desegregating its operations, and it received a round of bad press in the early 1950s when a group of women traveling south for a conference had to change their seats when the MoPac train crossed into Texas.[230]

In 1954, shortly after the *Brown v. Board of Education* ruling, the president of Southeast Missouri State College asked Dearmont for his opinion on "whether or not we should proceed to admit colored applicants this fall, if there are any." Dearmont was an alumnus of the college and sat on its board. At the same time, he was a director of the Fund for the Republic, an institution funded by the Ford Foundation that promoted free speech and civil liberties in the face of McCarthyism.[231]

He responded to the college president with full-throated support for equality in admissions, arguing that "negroes are citizens and entitled to equal treatment under the law and . . . they have just as much right to freely use the facilities of the State institution as any other citizens."[232] That said, the railroad was hardly racing to embrace integration in its own operations. And in a 1961 speech at Lindenwood College, where he was a member of the board, Dearmont would argue that to support democracy, Americans must be "more diligent than ever in our efforts to preserve the good influence of the home because of the growing trend among women to enter the work-a-day world."[233]

In short, the railroad and its senior leadership were struggling to address a changing world at the same time that they were trying to get out of bankruptcy.

. . .

The 1949 plan was being contemplated by the appellate courts so slowly that in July 1951, the group of institutional investors asked the ICC to withdraw it because of changed circumstances. These creditors did not actually want to have the plan withdrawn, but rather wanted to get the issue on the table and resolved while everyone was waiting for the Supreme Court to consider the appeal.[234] That is, the request was made with the hope that the ICC would not withdraw the plan, but it would not turn out that way.

The request suspended confirmation of the plan, hearings on which had been held in June. The voting period ended February 15, 1951, and resulted in its approval by fourteen classes and disapproval by three classes, all representing junior securities slated for little or no recoveries. Hearings before the ICC on the potential withdrawal were held late in the year, with some three hundred pages of additional briefing in February 1952. The core issue was whether there had been new developments "which were not provided for in the plan, and which in the opinion of the Commission make it necessary or expedient for the Commission to reexamine or reconsider and, if necessary, to revise such plan."

Anticipating Justice Frankfurter, one group of bondholders argued:

> Time destroys the relevance of even uncontroverted evidence developed in the past and the conclusions drawn therefrom. Time even more ruthlessly destroys conclusions based upon predictions as to what the future will reveal. Time has again emphatically refuted the conclusions of the Commission and added another demonstration of the fallacy of the conceptions upon which the Commission has predicated its several Plans of Reorganization. Obsolete conceptions, evidence and predictions can only lead to wrong conclusions. The latest available evidence must be considered and weighed to test the validity of prior conceptions, predictions and conclusions, and to provide the basis for the employment of different procedures when old procedures are no longer adequate.[235]

MoPac's board similarly filed a brief arguing that "failure to recall the plan would cast the full responsibility for its resulting unfairness and inequity squarely upon the Commission and upon the Commission alone."[236]

With the process dragging toward 1953, the district court eventually ordered the case back to the ICC.[237] The always comprehensive commission held hearings on June 3, 4, 5, 8, 9, 10, 11, 12, 15, 16, 17, 18 and 19, 1953, and in early 1954, a proposed report finally was issued recommending extensive changes in the 1949 plan.

Shortly before the ICC's report came out, the trustee, now well into his seventies, undoubtedly realized that he could not go down this road again if he wanted to complete the case in his lifetime. Thus, Thompson asked the court for permission to abandon his disinterest and inject himself into the plan process, "and generally to take such further or other action which in his judgment may expedite the reorganization of Debtor Companies."[238]

When the court approved his request, the trustee sent a letter to the key participants in the case, inviting their input on moving the case forward.[239] He called a series of meetings in St. Louis with the major stakeholders on the key question of whether the case should stay in section 77 or proceed via a revised section 20b plan.[240] And he sent Dearmont, along with other MoPac executives, to New York to canvass investors.[241] Thompson and Dearmont also negotiated with specific groups: for example, Dearmont was in frequent contact with Eli Black, a former rabbi turned investor, who headed a group of preferred shareholders.[242] Black came to St. Louis and eventually agreed to support the trustee's proposals.

Thompson then sought to get the parties to sign a stipulation that would amend the ICC's latest plan to create an "Agreed System Plan." This name reflected the groupwide nature of the reorganization, in contrast to company-by-company reorganization under section 20b, which MoPac's board continued to encourage.[243] All the various MoPac subsidiaries in bankruptcy would be combined into a single corporate entity, the Missouri Pacific Railroad.

The key change under the trustee's plan was the preferred shares that the ICC was going to give to certain bondholders were replaced with income bonds. The old preferred shareholders were then to receive class A shares, which had full voting rights and noncumulative dividend rights up to $5 per year. New class B shares, which also had voting rights and rights to dividends after the class A ones were paid, would be given for every twenty shares of old common stock turned in. In short, common shareholders were reduced to a small fraction of the voting power of the reorganized company and were given potential, if remote, divided rights.[244] But from the shareholders' (and Alleghany's) perspectives, this was a better outcome than elimination since it retained the potential for upside indefinitely.[245]

The major players all signed up. But Alleghany, which was originally supportive, almost tanked the entire effort when Young proposed changes to the stipulation at the last minute.[246] Among other things, he wanted to change the class B structure so the old common shares would be exchanged on a one-for-one basis and the new B shares would be given the right to elect one director to the new board. Dearmont fired back a lengthy letter to John L. J. Hart,

Allegany's Colorado-based counsel: "The changes in the instrument which you propose are so substantial and constitute such a departure from the basic principles which Mr. Neff [MoPac's current CEO; Baldwin had passed away in 1946] and I discussed with Mr. Young . . . March 19th, and which Mr. Young accepted at that time, and they differ so much from the terms that have been under discussion with you since that date that they necessarily raise the question in our minds as to whether you really are interested in a settlement of the Missouri Pacific case."[247]

Dearmont wrote that unless Young rescinded his requested changes, "we will advise the parties that Mr. Thompson's efforts to negotiate a settlement have failed so that they may proceed to file such Exceptions [to the ICC revised plan] as they may care to file without further delay." Hart largely withdrew Young's requested changes on April 23, following a telephone conversation with Dearmont that same day.[248]

Hart did push for an agreement—ultimately memorialized in a side letter between the key parties—that the new MoPac charter would not allow changes to the rights of class A or B without a separate vote by each class.[249] The letter agreement, and more specifically the resulting changes to the corporate documents, would prove quite significant after the bankruptcy.

In May, Thompson filed a new petition with the ICC, presenting the stipulation and the Agreed System Plan.[250] The insurance companies—the remnants of the Stedman committee—refused to sign, but they did not actively object to the plan before either the ICC or the court. The signing parties had hoped to avoid another hearing before the commission, but some holdouts insisted, so "all the experts were once again brought forward and the familiar arguments heard . . . There came a representative from the rail management with a tale of possible future woes and a plea for a relatively low capitalization, followed on the stand by the cheery economists drawing their fees from Alleghany."[251]

The ICC adopted Thompson's plan and sent it to the district court.[252] Commissioner Mahaffie concurred in the result but noted some concerns. The railroad was still heavily indebted.[253] He further argued that the class B stock was a mistake since the old common stock "has, at most, only a nuisance value," and thus "the 'B' stock is . . . principally valuable as a token for speculation. Consequently, its relation to the 'A' stock and to the debentures and income bonds which precede it is reasonably sure to cause trouble."[254] He would prove quite correct.

The court held three days of hearings in December 1954, all stage-managed by Dearmont.[255] It approved the plan and sent it out for voting in February 1955.[256] The inevitable appeal to the Eighth Circuit was rejected in September, and an appeal to the Supreme Court was likewise turned away in early 1956.[257]

The docket records that the ballots were sent to the court in wooden crates. Sadly, the crates are no more, but the ballots still exist in the National Archives in Kansas City: great big bundles of black, photostatic copies bound together by cloth straps.[258]

"In all but two of the classes more than two-thirds of those voting accepted the plan. In Class 3 (capital stock of [Gulf Coast] both that publicly held and that pledged under Missouri Pacific 5 1/4 percent secured serial bonds) only 59.17 percent of those voting voted to accept the plan; in Class 19 (the Missouri Pacific 5 1/4 percent secured serial bonds) only 63.94 percent of those voting voted to accept the plan."[259] The two objecting classes were not as close to real approval as they appeared since MoPac owned a sizable share of the Gulf Coast's stock—for example, only about 35 percent of class 3 supported the plan if MoPac was excluded.[260]

The court nonetheless confirmed the plan, and then another round of appeals inexorably commenced.[261] Reorganization managers were appointed to implement the plan, although the court grumbled about Alleghany's decision to name T. C. Davis to the group.[262] The managers retained Cravath, Swaine & Moore, historically MoPac and Kuhn Loeb's attorneys, as their counsel. De Forest Billyou, a senior associate at the firm and future professor at New York University, managed the extensive paperwork needed to fold the Missouri Pacific System into the single corporate entity of the Missouri Pacific Railroad, while getting everyone the new securities they were entitled to.[263]

Finally in March 1956, *The New York Times* would write, "The Missouri Pacific Railroad Company, first major railroad to go into reorganization under Section 77 of the Bankruptcy Act after it was passed in 1933, yesterday was the last one out."[264] A new board was named by the parties—Dearmont was named by Thompson and Black by the preferred shareholders.[265] Both would serve until the early 1960s.[266] The presidents of Chase and Chemical Bank were also named to the fifteen-member board. Dearmont was vice president and general counsel.

• • •

Dearmont was elevated to president in 1957.[267] In the early 1960s, he served as chairman of the board while Downing Jenks, formerly of the Rock Island Railroad, was appointed president.[268] "Relying on shipping chemicals from the Gulf to northern cities, with 16 percent of its traffic coming from grain, MoPac . . . developed into a well-run and well-managed railroad."[269]

MoPac would resume buying Texas and Pacific shares, including a large block from the estate of Frank Gould (George's younger brother).[270] But when it hoped to use a merger with the Texas and Pacific to eliminate its own dual-class share structure, the Supreme Court said the class B shareholders must be given a separate vote.[271] Hart's handiwork bound Alleghany to MoPac into the 1970s, when Alleghany ultimately extracted the value that Mahaffie had foreseen from the class B shares.[272]

Under the settlement that the parties negotiated, the old class A became voting convertible preferred shares, while each share of class B was exchanged for
16 shares of new common stock and $850 in cash, and the majority preferred
shareholder immediately announced a tender offer for 400,000 shares of the
new common shares at $100 per share, in which Alleghany agreed to sell all its
new common shares.[273] In short, Alleghany sold out for $2,450 per old class B
share, or about $52 million in total.[274]

The Van Sweringens had paid a bit over $40 million for their original com-
mon stock position back in 1929, which had ebbed and flowed in size through
the decades of Alleghany's ownership.[275] Obviously, it took quite a while to
realize the return, but that is still not bad for something that was essentially an
afterthought to Young and Kirby's original investment.[276] On the other hand,
some class B speculators clearly lost out under the deal—at the end of 1972, the
B shares had been trading as high as $8,926 per share.

The Texas and Pacific's federal charter disappeared in 1976 as it became one
with MoPac.[277] MoPac then briefly considered a merger with the Southern Railway before being instead taken over by the Union Pacific, which took over the
Western Pacific at the same time.[278] A decade later, Union Pacific also absorbed
the Southern Pacific.[279] Ironically, once the Union Pacific owned both the Texas
and Pacific (MoPac) and then the Southern Pacific, the old Texas and Pacific
line became much more active, being a faster way across the Lone Star State
than Southern Pacific's winding southern route.

• • •

Section 77 had taken control away from the Goulds, Morgans, and Kuhn
Loebs of the world and given it to the ICC. But the ICC did not really want
to exercise that control, and thus it left it up to other parties, like Alleghany,
to exercise whatever control they could in the new corporate reorganization
universe.[280] Alleghany's power in section 77 was largely negative—it could prevent a plan but could not impose a plan itself. And in future cases, without the
roller-coaster extremes of economic depression and world war, investors might
not even have that level of interest in the section 77 process.

For example, "unlike previous railroad bankruptcies where the roads had
positive [operating returns] and their failures stemmed from their inability to
pay interest on amortized debt, the bankruptcies of the 1970s were operating
failures as well as financial ones."[281] The debtors were so deeply distressed that
shareholders were unlikely to recover anything no matter what happened.

A common theme of the New Deal corporate bankruptcy reforms, which we
see again in chapter 6, is that the reformers identified real problems with the
old system but did not provide real solutions. The old edifice was destroyed,
but the new system did not provide a workable replacement.

CHAPTER 6

THE END OF AN ERA

Whether Chapter XI is used for large corporations or small ones, the system of reorganization it offers is unsatisfactory to creditors, except on grounds of economy and speed. Insofar as it is or can be used for large corporations, or corporations with publicly held securities, it has all the procedural weaknesses of the equity receivership and the 77B proceeding, and some new ones peculiarly its own.

—Eugene Rostow and Lloyd Cutler (1939)

On the Harvard Business School's "Great American Business Leaders of the 20th Century" webpage, the entry for William T. Grant reads as follows:

Grant opened his department store operation in 1906 with a 25 cent-limit on all merchandise. Grant created this 25 cent niche market at a time when department store prices began at 50 cents and Kresge and Woolworth sold their merchandise at 5 cents and 10 cents. At the end of World War I, when Grant had established a chain of 30 stores, the 25 cent-limit on merchandise was raised to one dollar. W. T. Grant Company evolved into one of the largest retailing companies in the nation. By the time of Grant's death in 1972, the company had nearly 1,200 [stores], sales of $1.2 billion, and 60,000 employees.[1]

Less than five years later, all the Grants stores were gone. All 60,000 employees lost their jobs.

. . .

Corporate restructuring began with railroads because those were the first giant corporations, but after World War II, railroads no longer held the central place in American economic life. Big corporations of all types grew and collapsed, and they were increasingly more significant than railroads. Corporate bankruptcy expanded to meet this broader need.[2]

At first, these corporations were addressed by receiverships, but during the Great Depression, Congress recognized the trend and began enacting statutes that covered nonrail corporate debtors.[3] The year after enacting section 77 for railroads, Congress enacted section 77B for other corporations.[4] That statute allowed the debtor to remain in possession of its estate and consummate a plan upon the vote of two-thirds of the creditors in a class. The provision expressly allowed for creditor voting before a case was filed—the predecessor to today's prepackaged chapter 11 cases.[5]

Section 77B "eliminated the hocus-pocus of the friendly creditor's bill, the ancillary receiverships and the necessity for sale, as the majority or two-thirds could bind non-depositors. However, it introduced a new concept, the debtor in possession, and the debtor and underwriter were still influential and consents to plans were often obtained before court approval. These features gave the advocates of more government control ground for continued criticism, although most criticisms were carried over from the old equity receivership."[6] The same year that section 77B was enacted, the Securities Exchange Act of 1934 instructed the newly formed Securities and Exchange Commission (SEC) to conduct a study of corporate reorganization.

The commission, largely under the direction of the head of the reorganization section and later commissioner (and then Supreme Court justice) William O. Douglas, produced an eight-volume, four-thousand-page report.[7] Central to the report's finding was that self-appointed protective committees lead to great abuses of power and conflicts of interest, and through these committees, large institutional investors could control the outcome of reorganizations.[8] The SEC's proposed solution was more government oversight to protect small investors.

This was a major switch for Douglas, who had bluntly rejected governmental oversight of committees when suggested by Max Lowenthal in the pages of the *Harvard Law Review*.[9] In contrast to Lowenthal, Douglas was not worried that bankers dominated the committees initially formed in section 77 cases, writing that "from the point of view of those interested in effectuating a sensible, workable plan of reorganization, their presence is highly desirable in order that their technical skill and knowledge may be fully utilized."[10] Douglas pointed to the Stedman Committee (discussed in chapter 5) as an example of a well-constituted, independent committee, ignoring the actual independent bond-holder committee that was also formed in the MoPac case. But Douglas was ambitious if he was anything, and he quickly reformed his thinking to bring it in line with the broader New Deal consensus, which Lowenthal clearly reflected.[11]

The SEC also noted that prearranged reorganizations put tremendous pressure on courts to approve them and avoid the costs of sending the parties back to "square one."[12] The commission argued that section 77B had only increased the use of such quick reorganizations, but such high-speed reorganizations "should not be permitted to have the imprimatur of federal courts placed on their plans so easily and so expeditiously."[13] That is, bankruptcy discharges should be granted only to reorganizations that had been properly scrutinized by the courts.

Thus, while section 77B was only four years old, Douglas proclaimed that "the necessary reforms call for fundamental revisions in, and a rather complete overhauling of, the statute. Only by such methods can real protection be provided those investors whose interests are involved in these proceedings."[14]

. . .

The Chandler Act of 1938 replaced section 77B with two new business reorganization provisions: chapters X and XI.[15] The provisions of chapter X represented the joint work of the National Bankruptcy Conference (which had originally proposed basic edits of section 77B) and the SEC.[16] It required that trustees be appointed in every case involving a large corporate debtor and prohibited any Wall Street bankers and lawyers who had engaged with a debtor before bankruptcy from reorganizing the company in bankruptcy.[17]

The SEC was given a large role in proceedings, somewhat akin to that of the ICC in section 77 proceedings, albeit with more judicial ability to move on without the agency if necessary.[18] All plans had to comply with the "absolute priority rule"; that is, the liquidation order of payment, such that shareholders would often be eliminated in chapter X plans. Chapter X then was more often about protecting public bondholders and the general public interest in the conduct of corporate reorganizations.

On the other hand, under chapter XI, which represented the direct successor of the old composition under section 12 of the 1898 Bankruptcy Act, the debtor remained in possession of its estate.[19] "Its philosophy is that of composition, not equity reorganization, and, as applied to corporations, these are historically distinct points of view about insolvency administration."[20]

The SEC had no formal role, and there was no absolute priority rule.[21] The plan could only adjust secured claims consensually, shareholders could be diluted but not eliminated, and only a debtor could propose a plan. Unlike chapter X, there was no cramdown provision that allowed for confirmation of a plan over the vote of a dissenting (unsecured) class.[22] And while under chapter X, plans were approved by two-thirds in dollar amount of a class, under chapter XI, the approval vote was half in both number and amount. Committees could be formed under procedures fairly similar to the old receivership days— that is, they were formed by the creditors themselves, with limited input from the court.

In hearings on the Chandler bill, one key witness argued that chapter XI would "relieve the courts of the burden of the great multitude of little cases that have come in under section 77B and do not belong there." He went on to explain that chapter X addressed "corporate reorganizations," while chapter XI "opens the relief to individuals and small corporations."[23]

Likewise, Representative Walter Chandler, writing in the *American Bar Association Journal*, explained that under his new bankruptcy law, "section 12 of the Act of 1898 has been removed, and its general purposes have been incorporated into four separate chapters, Nos. X, XI, XII, and XIII," and he described chapter X as applicable to "corporations" and chapter XI as applicable to "small businesses." He further observed that "most of the large American corporations being publicly owned, the protection of the investors therein, and the preservation of useful enterprises giving large employment involve the public welfare and justify the special treatment accorded in Chapter X."[24]

Indeed, it seems clear that "Congress intended Chapter X for the reorganization of big corporations, and Chapter XI for the relief of small debtors, incorporated and unincorporated. But the forty-odd experts who worked eight years revising the Act omitted from it any formula for determining which corporate debtors should be rehabilitated under Chapter X and which under Chapter XI."[25] In short, "although it was the purpose of Chapter X to give reorganization procedures a good scrubbing," from 1938 until the Chandler Act's repeal in 1978, corporate debtors often attempted to reorganize under chapter XI.[26] The problem was recognized almost from the act's inception, but Congress never did fix it.[27]

That said, as shown in figure 6.1, it would be an overstatement to say that chapter X was dying or its use was in substantial decline. There was an average of just over 105 (median, 101) cases a year between 1950 and 1975, and 127 (median, 115) for 1965 through 1975.

And contrary to the received wisdom, there were examples of successful chapter X cases.[28] One of the first big chapter X cases involved McKesson & Robbins, which filed for bankruptcy following a multimillion-dollar accounting scandal and the suicide of its president, F. Donald Coster (aka Philip Musica).[29] Trustee William Jed Wardall oversaw a successful reorganization plan that righted the company, which exists to this day.[30]

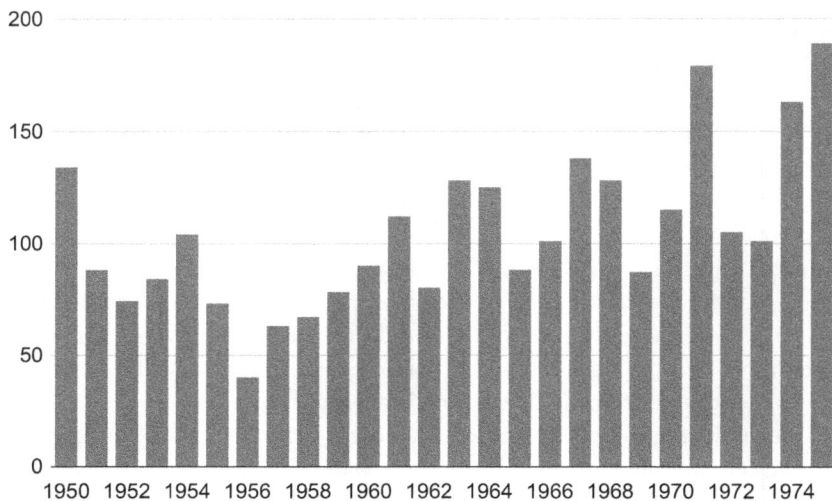

6.1 Number of chapter X cases by year, 1950–1975.

Source: Securities and Exchange Commission (SEC).

In 1977, the SEC told Congress that "this Commission has been intimately involved in every major reorganization case since Chapter X was enacted in 1938, and we have found no lack of vitality in this superb statute. In the last 15 months we filed reports in no less than 11 cases, with an aggregate valuation of $500 million, each providing substantial participation for public investors. The largest of these, Interstate Stores, Inc., which is solvent and valued at over $200 million, began in Chapter XI but was transferred to Chapter X, and its reorganization will soon be completed."[31]

Interstate emerged as Toys "R" Us in 1978—with the judge calling it one of the most successful chapter X cases—and operated effectively until its (ironic) recent death under modern chapter 11.[32] And likewise there were many unsuccessful chapter XI cases—Grants being prime among them.[33]

• • •

Grants stores (in modern times, they dropped the apostrophe, but many older locations were still marked as "W. T. Grant"; see figure 6.2) began life as a kind of dime-store competitor before moving slightly more upscale over time.[34] In the 1920s, it benefited from the phenomenon of people taking advantage of improved transportation—reliable trains, buses, and private cars—to shop in city centers. The company particularly opened stores in second- and third-tier

6.2 W. T. Grant Co. in downtown Tampa in the 1920s.

Robertson and Fresh (firm), "W. T. Grant Co. in Downtown Tampa" (1900). Robertson and Fresh Collection of Tampa Photographs. Image 2112. https://digitalcommons.usf.edu/robertson_and_fresh/2112. The photograph's date is given as January 1900, but the automobiles and clothing appear to this author as being more consistent with the 1920s.

cities across the country, despite having their headquarters in Manhattan. And like many chain stores of that age, Grants focused mostly on white, middle-class women, who were thought to represent the bulk of shoppers.[35]

A Grants chief executive officer (CEO) said that the entire goal of any retail business was "finding out who your customer is, and then giving her the merchandise at the price she wants it."[36] Of course, he then went on to say that "a retail business is four things: merchandise, money, method, and men."[37] Indeed, despite aiming to sell predominantly to women, it seems that Grants never had a woman among its senior executives, and only a small handful of the store managers were women. The list of officers in their 1974 annual report (the last one that the company would put out) has a glut of "Johns," but no obvious women. Prior years appear similar.

After the war, Grants stores, which often featured lunch counters or restaurants, were the subject of increasing protests across the South, where the company followed local Jim Crow laws.[38] Grants also began to face complaints from its investors and customers in the North about its discriminatory policies.[39] And once the issue of discrimination against customers was resolved, the question of discrimination against employees remained.[40]

Grants did appoint Asa T. Spaulding, the head of North Carolina Mutual Life Insurance—reportedly the largest African American–owned business in the United States at the time—to its board in 1964.[41] The company still had eight segregated lunch counters at this point, and his appointment could be dismissed as tokenism, inasmuch as Spaulding would remain the only African American executive at Grants, and upon his retirement in early 1975, there were once again none.[42]

At the same time, middle-class women were reducing their trips to urban centers. Grants responded as other chain stores did, by building larger stores outside of cities, with parking lots (see figure 6.3).[43] The largest of these stores were called "Grant City," the "s" having vanished in the enlargement. As of 1970, the company had opened 195 new stores in the past five years, mostly in "new shopping center and free-standing stores so as to take advantage of the growth of the suburban market."[44] By 1974, the company reported that "during the five years ended January 31, 1974, the Company opened 369 new and larger stores, while 272 smaller stores were closed. The average size of the new stores opened during this five-year period was approximately 70,000 square feet. The Company is currently opening new stores in three basic standard sizes—56,000, 94,000 and 163,000 square feet."[45] More and bigger stores, in short. From

6.3 A suburban Grants store, c.1972.

W. T. Grant Company 1972 Annual Report.

1963 to 1973, Grants opened 612 new stores—more than 430 after 1969—and expanded the size of 91 others.[46]

In these bigger stores, they began selling larger, more expensive goods, like furniture and appliances.[47] Grants only offered store-branded electronics and large appliances, labeled "Bradford" after Bradford County, Pennsylvania, where W. T. Grant was born. Grants began to offer customer financing for these larger purchases.

The company was the darling of the financial press in the mid- to late-1960s.[48] In a 1965 article, *Barron's* waxed enthusiastic about Grants' record profits and general success.[49] A similar *Barron's* article in 1969 gushed that,

> spurred by an aggressive store expansion program and a growing stress on big-ticket merchandise, W. T. Grant is expected to ring up its eighth straight year of higher sales and profits. In the fiscal year ended January 31, 1969, the nation's second-largest variety store chain registered net of $37.90 million, or $2.83 per share, up 14.9 percent from $32.56 million, or $2.50 per share, a year earlier. Sales reached the billion-dollar mark for the first time, totaling $1.09 billion vs. $979.5 million last year. Aided by an increasing number of new store openings, Grant may gross $1.24 billion this fiscal year. . . .
>
> With the expansion into higher-ticket items, credit sales also have grown. Last year, credit sales rose 12 percent over 1967 to $262.82 million, accounting for 24 percent of total sales. This percentage is expected to mount.[50]

In less than five years, nearly every one of these points would be seen as a blunder.[51]

In figure 6.4, we can see that the problems really took off around 1968. The size of the company's receivables, which were mostly customer charge accounts, showed a massive increase that would continue into the 1970s. Grants was increasingly financing these customer balances with short-term borrowing, which spiked at the same time.

Grants' 1971 Annual Report told shareholders that "by wisely putting our dollars to work, by prudently borrowing, and by carefully supervising all resources we are able to open more stores, maintain adequate inventories, and carefully administer the growing accounts receivable brought about by increased credit sales." But it turned out that credit sales were not actually managed by the corporation, but instead by the hundreds of individual store managers at Grants locations across the country.

These managers decided whether a customer received a line of credit, at the very same time that they were required to meet certain sales targets. Obvious conflicts of interest abounded. Moreover, customers could obtain lines of credit at several different stores and Grants would likely never know about it, since records were not centralized. When Grants mostly sold basic clothing

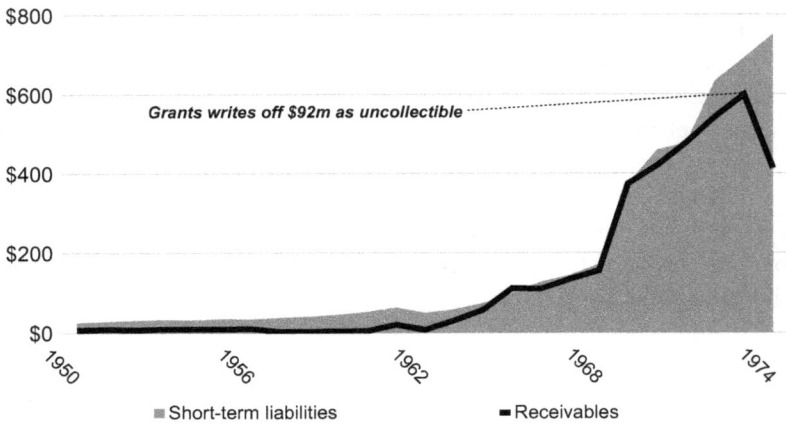

Grants writes off $92m as uncollectible

6.4 Receivables and short-term liabilities for Grants (millions)

Figures taken from annual reports and Form 10-Ks.

and other low-priced goods, this was less of a problem than when it began to sell major appliances. Some customers in New England, where Grants stores were often located close together, reportedly would buy a washing machine at one store, a refrigerator at another, a television at another, and a couch at yet another, all on credit. Some customers in Texas and California had home addresses in Mexico.[52]

At the same time, Grants was confusing customers; in 1970, *Forbes* called the company "The Great What-Is-It."[53] Some of its stores looked like the old Grants stores—essentially five-and-dimes—while others, especially the Grant City stores, were almost more like a Sears or JCPenney store, with large furniture, auto repair, and appliance departments.[54] A later Grants' CEO would observe that the company really had at least three kinds of stores: variety, urban, and suburban.[55] Even Grants' board members expressed bewilderment regarding whom the company was targeting as its customers.[56]

Grants was initially dismissive of the concern:

To convert a chain of approximately 1,000 successful limited variety stores to a Company with approximately half of its units composed of Grant City or "full line" stores, while at the same time adding all of the necessary back up services, merchandise distribution centers, data processing, and major appliance warehousing, home delivery and service in a relatively short span of time was not easily accomplished. Our image may have become blurred. We do have both small and large stores. This has to be. Ten years ago, from Maine to California,

Grants operated small stores with limited merchandise assortments. Today in hundreds of communities the Grant City store is recognized as a store with complete assortments of merchandise for the home and family.[57]

As the quote indicates, not only was Grants' image with consumers becoming confused, but its costs were rising as it added infrastructure to support sales of products that required much more support than the merchandise that Grant had previously carried. For example, it had never previously delivered merchandise to customers' homes. Now it had a fleet of trucks to deliver large furniture and appliances.

Originally, Grants financed customer charge account balances by borrowing in money markets—selling very short-term notes to securities investors. But in 1970, Penn Central—the ungainly 1968 amalgamation of the New York Central

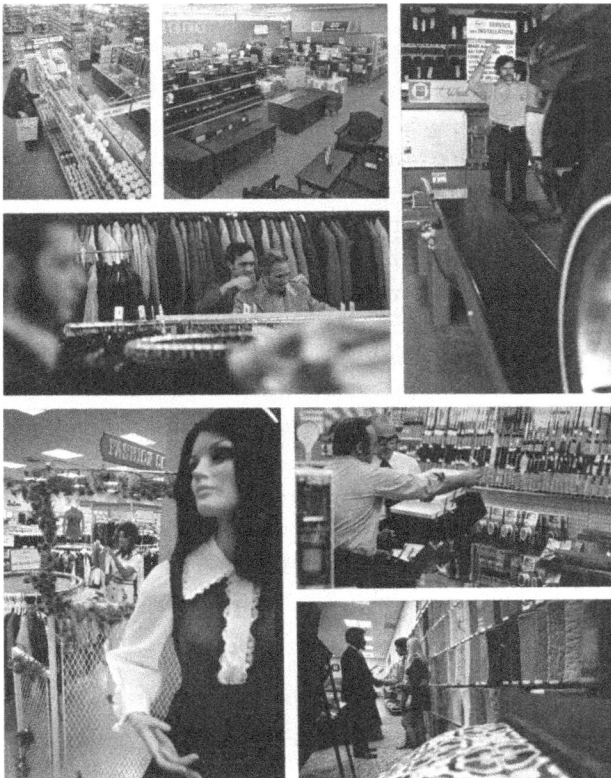

6.5 From auto repair to appliances to suits to hairspray: the offerings of a Grants store.

W. T. Grant Company 1972 Annual Report

and Pennsylvania railroads—had filed the largest American bankruptcy (section 77) case to date.[58] That filing dislocated the money markets and alerted investors to the risk of loss in previously risk-free commercial paper.[59]

Grants, with ballooning short-term debt levels, was downgraded shortly thereafter, which forced it to switch to borrowing from its banks. In June 1973, it borrowed $100 million under a five-year unsecured term loan from a group of eight large banks headed by Morgan Guaranty Trust Company (the postwar merger of J. P. Morgan's banking arm with the previously affiliated Guaranty Trust).[60] This loan carried interest rates of between 8 to 10 percent, whereas the company's long-term bonds had previously been issued at 4.75 percent. The effective interest rate on the term loan was even higher than the stated rate because the loan required the company to keep a 15 percent "compensating balance" on deposit with the banks. That is, Grants was borrowing $100 million, and paying interest on that amount, but got to use only $85 million.

In part, all of this reflected rising market interest rates, but it also reflected Grants' declining creditworthiness. And it quickly became clear that $100 million was nowhere near enough.

In 1973, customers had more than $600 million outstanding in more than 2.9 million accounts.[61] Robert Anderson, a future Grants CEO, would observe that Grants had more customer accounts than Sears, a much larger retailer.[62] Moreover, Grants was increasingly paying more for its own financing, thus earning less on the spread between what it paid and what its customers paid. For example, while in 1967 it reported paying $3.7 million in interest to finance customer accounts, by 1971 it was paying more than $17 million.[63] And as the American economy slowed, Grants continued to incur costs of new stores and new infrastructure as all the while its customers were financing more of their purchases and repaying less of them.

By 1974, the country was in a recession, and Grants' board expressly discussed the need to "not go after delinquencies so hard as they might have otherwise in the hopes that economic conditions were going to improve and these customers were going to be able to get back on a current basis."[64] At about the same time, the company extended the time that an account could be delinquent before it was written off, and the company had long had a policy of treating an account as current if *any* payment had been made on it, no matter how small.[65] Customers could make a token payment to get current on their accounts and then walk out of the store with a new appliance.[66]

At that same time, the company "felt it prudent to reduce its borrowing in the commercial paper field and place a greater reliance on its banks for short-term loans."[67] That quote, from the 1973 annual report issued in early 1974, suggests that the financing adjustment was far more voluntary than it was. Grants maintained relationships with more than a thousand banks—every store had an account with a local bank. Most of those banks offered Grants a line of credit, apparently because they wanted to be able to say that they were lenders on a loan to Grants with Morgan Guaranty, but they never really expected that it would be used. But, cut off from the money markets, Grant was starting to do just that.[68]

As the money market commercial paper ran off, it was refinanced with bank debt.[69] By January 1974, the company had more than $493 million in short-term bank loans outstanding.[70] By the fall, the number would grow to more than $553 million.[71] In the first quarter, Grants applied to Morgan for an increase in the company's credit line.[72]

Nevertheless, it was only by August of that year that Grants stopped paying dividends on its common shares—and throughout the early 1970s, it had been paying more than $20 per share per year, or more than $20 million per year in total.[73] In June 1974, the company lured John Sundman from the Singer Company to become vice president of finance and bring Grants' accounting and credit practices up to date. Among his first moves was to change the company over to bank-issued credit cards, like Master Charge and BankAmericard, deemphasizing the in-house credit program, which was in worse shape than anyone realized at this point.[74]

• • •

In early July, Grants' chairman and CEO resigned at the request of the board. The company had reported a $6.9 million loss in the first quarter and followed it with a $3.9 million loss in the second.[75] This followed a 78 percent drop in profits in 1973.[76]

Throughout 1974, the company was constantly swatting at rumors that it would soon file for bankruptcy.[77] An April "Heard on the Street" column in the *Wall Street Journal* opened bluntly: "Mention W. T. Grant Co. on Wall Street and chances are you'll get a snide remark about the retail chain's alleged failure to pay its bills on time or the conjecture that it won't be around in a couple of years."[78] In December, a *Barron's* column was entitled "Grant's Tomb?"—the reference here being to the company's new corporate headquarters, a fifty-four-story tower in Times Square that was just completed in 1972—quite a change for a publication that in the 1960s was Grants' biggest cheerleader.[79]

The column expressed opposition to rumors that the Federal Reserve was pressuring banks to "go easy" on Grants and thus avoid the broader economic effects of Grants' failure on suppliers and employees.[80] A few days before the *Barron's* column, *Women's Wear Daily* had reported that Grants' lead banks were worried that its collapse "could have a devastating impact on the economy as well as themselves."[81]

The banks indeed approached the Federal Reserve about possible support for a lending program, with one banker noting that it had recently helped to prop up real estate investment trusts (REITs).[82] And the Federal Reserve apparently did contact at least one small bank in the lending group, when that bank refused to go along with the New York banks' plans.[83] But no lending plan was forthcoming.

About the same time that Grant was asking Morgan for an expanded credit line, Morgan put the company on its internal "special review list," which indicated that Morgan viewed Grants as a "problem" credit risk.[84] In March, before Sundman was hired, the company had given Morgan a set of handwritten projections for the coming year in connection with its new loan application, which probably did not inspire great confidence.[85]

In September, Grants signed a $600 million loan deal with more than 140 banks.[86] This lending facility would refinance the existing short-term loans and give Grants about $50 million in new funding. Morgan was the lead bank, as it had been on the prior term loan, acting as a point of contact for the other banks; one of its senior partners had long sat on Grants' board.[87] And it was a trustee for the company's senior bonds as well.[88]

Some skeptics suggested that the bank loan was odd, and they wondered again if the Federal Reserve was not ultimately behind it.[89] *The Economist* quoted one banker who stated that "the Federal Reserve pushed for the loan because it didn't want a company its size to go out of business."[90]

Grants actually looked a lot like the aforementioned REITs, who were also squeezed out of the commercial paper market after Penn Central's collapse and found themselves increasingly reliant on commercial bank lending. As Professor Minsky observed regarding the REITs, "Banks were accepting paper from institutions that could no longer sell their paper on the open market. Obviously, at some stage in this process, even the bankers must have known that they were making loans to organizations whose creditworthiness was suspect. Making loans because of other than profit-making considerations is characteristic of lender-of-last-resort operations. When the commercial banks refinanced the REITs as the open market closed, they were acting as surrogate lenders of last resort."[91] The banks played the same role with Grants until they decided that they had gone far enough. That is, by switching to secured bank financing, Grants had given the banks control of its fate.[92] While in earlier reorganizations bankers had seized control, here the bankers were handed control by management on a platter.

The banks made the loan despite knowing that Grants had a serious problem with its customer credit operations. The later testimony of Morgan's representative was quite direct:

Q: Prior to the closing of the loan agreement, were you aware that Grant's credit organization and its credit reporting organization could be improved?
A: Yes.

Q: Were you of the opinion that it was lousy?

A: Yes.

Q: Prior to the closing of the loan agreement, were you aware that the Grant credit operation was in trouble?

A: You mean that Grant was in trouble because of the credit operation?

Q: Well—

A: Yes.

Q: Were you aware of the extent of delinquencies prior to the closing of the loan agreement?

A: We were given certain figures, and we were, therefore, aware of what people thought the delinquencies were.

Q: Were they extraordinarily high?

A: They were large.[93]

For the first time, Grants was required to borrow on a secured basis: The banks received a lien on the company's receivables and its 51 percent stake in Zeller's, a Canadian retailer based in Montreal, operating more than 150 stores.[94] At the same time, the $24 million in outstanding senior bonds got an equivalent lien, under an indenture provision called a "negative pledge clause" that entitled the bondholders to a lien equal to any other lien that Grants might hand out.[95] Half of these bonds were registered in the name of 185 holders; and the other half held in "bearer" form, with one insurance company holding $2.9 million of the latter.[96]

In one fell swoop, Grants had obtained $625 million in secured debt— actually $725 million, because the term lenders became secured too, as they also had a negative pledge clause in their agreements.[97] There is a real question as to whether the company would not have been better off filing for bankruptcy before this point, while all its debt remained unsecured.[98]

But regardless of the many rumors of a pending bankruptcy, apparently no such filing was ever considered by the board or senior management, despite the presence of bankers, law firm partners, and CEOs on the company's board. While the management of Grants, going back at least a decade before 1974, bears responsibility for the state of the company, the outcome of the eventual bankruptcy case can be largely pinned on the lack of leadership from the board in the early- to mid-1970s, once the problems became palpable.

In August, the company had appointed James Kendrick as CEO and president.[99] Kendrick had held similar positions at Zeller's. But the board was still scouting for a "superstar" executive who could turn Grants around, apparently at the urging of the banks.[100]

In 1975, Grants announced that Robert Anderson, a senior vice president at Sears, had agreed to a lucrative five-year deal.[101] Anderson became president, and Kendrick remained as CEO.[102] Notably, Anderson's compensation was guaranteed by the lead banks, likely making him somewhat hesitant to confront the banks going forward. To show his faith in the company, Anderson agreed to buy 100,000 shares of Grants common stock at a bit over $4 per share—and he took out a loan from a Chicago bank to do so.

In early 1975, before Anderson started, the company announced that it faced a staggering $175 million loss for the prior year, and it would close 126 stores and lay off more than 12,600 people.[103] Kendrick attributed most of the loss to the credit program, which he was trying to get a handle on.[104] To a large degree, he was now paying the price for his predecessors' lack of transparency.[105]

Business Week quoted one unnamed Grants banker, mixing his transportation metaphors, saying that while he had "a sinking feeling that Grant is going to go down the Penn Central tracks, the banks have so many millions involved that we have little choice but to go along and hope that it flies."[106] *The Economist* responded to the announced loss with an article sassily entitled "$67.50 off!"—a reference to the share price, which had been at $70 in 1971—that once again suggested that the banks were keeping the company alive only because of pressure from the Federal Reserve "to prevent a rash of bankruptcies among the department chain's 8,000 suppliers."[107] A shareholder resolution at that year's annual meeting asked the company to retain business consultants to evaluate "the mental, emotional and psychological fitness of all members of present management."[108]

Suppliers started to get nervous about shipping to a company that had "lien-ed up" most of its assets, so in May, the company granted trade creditors a lien on inventory.[109] Under the terms of the senior bonds, the bondholders got a $24 million lien on inventory as well.[110] At about the same time, the banks agreed to consolidate the loan among the 27 largest lenders and extend the maturity date to the end of March 1976. Grants used income from sales to pay off the debt owed to 116 of the smaller banks.[111]

• • •

Anderson then decided to visit some Grants stores, in anticipation of his taking the new job. One wonders why he did not do this before signing his contract and deciding to buy all those Grants shares, and certainly the results also call into question whether the banks were doing any diligence at all before lending millions of dollars. It does seem that Grants' blue-chip reputation might have been taken as given by many who interacted with the company.[112]

Anderson started his tour in Connecticut. When he bought a cup of coffee from the lunch counter, he noticed that most of the seat cushions were split. During the tour, he asked why the store was so dark: "I asked them to turn the lights on, and they said the lights were on, but maybe 40 percent of the light bulbs were operative."[113] The manager said that he had no money left in the repair budget for new bulbs. The store in Springfield, Massachusetts, had tarps hanging from the ceiling to catch water leaking in, even though the building was new, and in Pontiac, Michigan, the store had rows of empty shelves from lack of inventory.[114]

At the May annual meeting, the company announced a first-quarter loss of just under $54 million. But Kendrick received warm applause from shareholders when he announced that Grants was "off the critical list." Nevertheless, the empty shelves remained, as the offer of a lien to vendors was dismissed as confusing.[115] The trade creditors found it easier to just ship to other retailers.[116]

In August, the banks agreed to subordinate their lien in favor of up to $300 million of new inventory delivered after August 6.[117] An open letter from Anderson to vendors was published in *Women's Wear Daily*, trumpeting the "vote of confidence from the banks."[118] And indeed both the prior lien agreement and the subordination agreement show the banks making some real effort to save the company, which is easy to overlook given subsequent events.[119]

At the same time, Anderson announced that Grants was getting out of the business of selling appliances, electronics, and furniture.[120] This was consistent with his vision of transforming it into a clothing retailer that focused on what he repeatedly termed "young marrieds."[121]

The attempts to appease vendors and buy time from the banks left Grants' capital structure tied in knots. Table 6.1 attempts to make some sense of it.

The subordination agreement did not directly change these priorities, but trade creditors that delivered after August 6 would be entitled to grab up to $300 million of the banks' recovery on inventory under their second lien, to the extent that the post–August 6 trade was still unpaid. There presumably was some degree of overlap between those trade creditors that were secured and those that were entitled to benefit from the subordination agreement.[122]

And the landlords were a significant group of Grants' creditors as well; the company did not own any of its own stores (or the new corporate headquarters, for that matter) and paid about $115 million a year in rent.[123] Then there were

TABLE 6.1 Grants' capital structure

Asset	Creditors	Claims
Customer receivables and Zeller's	→ Senior bonds	→ $24 million
	→ Banks	→ $641 million
Inventory	First claim	
	→ Senior bonds	→ $24 million
	→ Trade creditors	→ $70 million
	Second claim	
	→ Banks	→ $641 million

subordinated bondholders (just under $94 million) and the shareholders, of which there were more than 18,700 in the early 1970s.[124]

· · ·

"1975 was marked by New York City's financial crisis, the failure of W. T. Grant and Company, the need for Consolidated Edison to sell assets to New York state in order to meet payment commitments, and the walking bankruptcy of Pan Am."[125] In March 1975, the Rock Island Railroad, a major Midwestern railroad that stretched from Chicago to New Mexico, filed its third and final bankruptcy case—it would be liquidated, but not before trying to barge its way into the MoPac–Texas and Pacific merger.[126]

For Grants, the end came suddenly, evidently triggered by Anderson's concern that he might face personal liability for securities law violations. It all began in the summer of 1975, when Anderson demanded that the company start to prepare its budget on a bottom-up basis—starting with the individual stores—rather than the top down, or corporate headquarters–initiated budgets that Grants had typically done. This was no easy task for Sundman to achieve: The computers of the era were not flexible, and Grants was barely computerized anyway. Indeed, its cash registers were so antiquated that it could not tell if a $200 purchase related to a washing machine or a lifetime supply of thumbtacks.[127]

Finally, on the morning of Monday, September 22, Sundman was able to present a draft budget to Anderson and Kendrick. The "loss was far, far greater than the previous projection."[128] In particular, while the July budget had projected a loss of $70 million for the year, the new bottom-up projections showed a loss of $299 million.[129] On Tuesday, the new projections were presented to the board: "After extensive discussion, the board requested management to reexamine those projections in every respect, and report back to the board."[130]

Despite the preliminary nature of the projections, Anderson was clearly becoming a bit unnerved about the securities law implications, and he arranged a meeting with Martin Lipton, a partner of Wachtell, Lipton, Rosen & Katz, for Wednesday evening at Lipton's home. Lipton asked to see documents and suggested that Anderson ask Joseph Hinsey—a partner at White & Case and member of the Grants board—about the disclosure issues arising from the new draft budget.

Anderson later testified:

> Joe Hinsey—this was still Wednesday night—responded to my question by saying that he had been looking at this for quite some time in terms of the disclosure question, that he really wasn't prepared to respond immediately that evening.
>
>   I said, "Well, I'm asking it as an officer of the Grant Company." I said, "I am concerned. We are at the position of negative net worth."[131]

Anderson would continue to be troubled that the company had "negative net worth"—that is, it was insolvent—although the significance of that fact standing alone is unclear.

On Thursday, at a previously scheduled meeting, the projections were presented to the banks, "but on a preliminary basis and with the clear indication that they were subject to revision in their entirety."[132] Anderson then announced that he had retained separate counsel. Lipton told Anderson that evening that he agreed that the new projections should be disclosed in an SEC filing; and they arranged to meet Friday afternoon with representatives of Morgan Stanley, Grants' investment bankers.

Anderson was meeting with the company's bankers, with his own counsel, without notifying either the board, the CEO, the chief financial officer (CFO), company counsel, or anyone else at Grants. At some point late in the day, those at the Friday meeting decided that they should ask Kendrick to come over and join them. Before his arrival, the parties had decided that Grants' financial situation needed to be disclosed, trading would be halted on Monday, and the company should prepare to file a chapter XI petition. Again, these would seem to be decisions for the board, not the company president and his personal attorney.

Kendrick was told all this when he arrived at Morgan Stanley, and he later reported that he was "flabbergasted."[133] At some point during the day, Lipton and a representative from Morgan Stanley reached out to an SEC commissioner.[134] Joe Hinsey, of White and Case, who actually was company counsel at this point (in addition to being a board member), was told all about it by Anderson in a phone call Friday night, in which he was asked to come to an officers' meeting on Saturday and a board meeting on Sunday.[135]

Later, Kendrick, Sundman, and Hinsey would maintain that Anderson's unilateral actions had at least forced the bankruptcy filing to happen sooner than it might have.[136] They also expressed anger and frustration that he did not involve them or the board generally at an earlier stage. Sundman also expressed frustration that the subordination agreement was not given adequate time to work.

At some point on the weekend, Wachtell was finally retained as company bankruptcy counsel, and on the following Thursday, October 2, the company filed its bankruptcy petition under chapter XI in New York.[137] The petition estimated the company's assets at $1,016,776,000, and liabilities were $1,030,556,000. The petition was signed not only by Leonard Rosen, of Wachtell, but also by Professor Lawrence King of New York University, who was "of counsel" to the firm. King's inclusion on the early pleadings was a recognition of the importance of the case, and its mammoth size relative to the typical chapter XI.

As New York University law school dean Troy McKenzie has observed: "The W. T. Grant case demonstrated how adept counsel had become at pushing the boundary between Chapter X and Chapter XI. The company was listed on the New York Stock Exchange and had more than $1 billion in debt. If any firm fell within the contemplation of Chapter X, it was W. T. Grant. Yet counsel were able to persuade the court that the case should remain in Chapter XI."[138] It was the second-largest bankruptcy filing ever in the United States, exceeded only by Penn Central's 1970 section 77 case, and far larger than any other chapter XI case. In its petition, it reported more than 35,500 shareholders.[139]

But it is unclear if the case would have remained in chapter XI: Grants was liquidated before the expiration of the time under Bankruptcy Rule 11–15 for the SEC to seek to transfer the case to chapter X.[140] And the New York District Court's ruling just a year before that Arlan's Department Stores—a retailer about a tenth of the size of Grants—must be reorganized under chapter X would seem to have been quite applicable to the Grants case if the SEC had made such a move.[141]

The Creditors Committee that was formed in the Grants case recognized the real possibility of conversion to chapter X, and "to increase the possibility that Grant will stay in Chapter XI, it was suggested that some of the safeguards present in Chapter X be incorporated into the Chapter XI case. It was suggested, for example, that the committee retain independent auditors; that there be recommendation to the SEC that it actively participate in the case; and that debenture holders organize themselves into unofficial committees."[142] This discussion plainly conceded that chapter X offered protections that chapter XI did not.

· · ·

Women's Wear Daily broke the news under the headline "A $1 Billion Bust."[143] The *Atlanta Constitution* published a picture of an empty Grants store under the headline "Why W. T. Grant Filed Bankruptcy."

Morgan wrote off $35 million of its stake in the Grants loan—with one Morgan executive stating that "we don't make many mistakes, but when we do make one, it's a beaut."[144] Morgan would ultimately write off more than half of its $97 million exposure to Grants.[145] The *Wall Street Journal* reported that "the Federal Reserve System aggressively supplied reserves to the banking network Friday, apparently in response to the collapse of W. T. Grant Co."[146]

In his affidavit supporting the petition, Anderson attributed the collapse to "a variety of factors, including, over-expansion involving the opening or enlargement of approximately 439 stores between the fiscal years ended 1969 and 1974, the entry into leases upon terms and at locations which have proven to be unfavorable, over-expansion of merchandise lines, especially major appliances and furniture, inadequate inventory control and an over-liberal credit policy which resulted in excessive chargeoffs and bad debts."[147] He also estimated that the debtor would lose $10.7 million during the thirty days following petition.[148]

On October 15, a meeting of the general creditors was convened in the Grand Ballroom of the Americana Hotel in New York City.[149] Crowds of creditors mobbed the sign-in tables outside, and John Ingraham of Citibank and Harvey Miller of Weil, Gotshal & Manges were inside on the stage. Ingraham had been appointed bank representative, and the banks had retained Weil Gotshal to represent them at the meeting and on a committee.[150]

The banks had previously decided it would be an eleven-member committee, and the banks would take six of the seats, with Ingraham as chair.[151] The purpose of the meeting was to hear from Leonard Rosen, of Wachtell, about the debtor's plan for its chapter XI case, as well as Anderson's vision for the "New Grants."[152] The meeting also elected five trade creditors to fill out the remaining slots on the committee. The entire slate would then be presented to Judge John J. Galgay, the bankruptcy judge presiding over the case. A separate committee of secured trade creditors formed in Newark in late October.[153]

Miller, Rosen, and Lipton, the attorney Anderson first consulted, had all previously worked together at Seligson & Morris, a firm headed by New York University bankruptcy professor Charles Seligson.[154] In 1965, Miller and Seligson went to Weil, while the others formed Wachtell.

The company quickly announced two rounds of store closings. In the first, 301 stores were to be closed, and then it asked the judge for permission to close 277 more. The first closures were west of the Mississippi, but the closure wave soon moved east, and more than two-thirds of the company's stores were closed.[155] Anderson's "New Grants" would be focused on about 300 to 400 stores in the northeast.

Initially, Grants attempted to liquidate the closing stores itself, as debtor in possession. It yielded something like 18 percent of the retail value of the inventory, which was very disappointing.[156] Companies existed that would buy inventory in bulk, but Grants' complicated three-way inventory lien situation dissuaded most of them from offering anything that Grants thought that the secured trade creditors committee and the banks might accept.

The Sam Nassi Company offered a solution. The company's founder—whose anti-tie wearing, California ways were unlike anything the New York based Grants and its bankers had ever seen—proposed to sell Grants inventory with Grants staff, overseen by Nassi's people.[157] They would use a combination of bombastic advertising and time pressure to generate much higher returns than Grants had achieved to date.

For example, in California, Nassi proposed to consolidate all Grants' inventory into ten metropolitan areas. Of the 114 stores in those areas, he would immediately close 34 and conduct the sales in the remaining 80. During the second week, the sales would be consolidated into 50 stores, and during the third and final week, only 10 stores would be selling. After three weeks, he would sell any residual inventory to traditional liquidators.[158] Merchandise would be subjected to increasing discounts as the sale progressed.

Nassi offered that approximately the first third of the inventory's retail value, net of his costs, would go to Grants. After that, Grants and Nassi would share the proceeds. Grants' consultants noted that in theory, Nassi could make millions on this deal, but since Grants had never been able to liquidate inventory for anything near one-third of its list price, this seemed like a great deal for Grants. The bankruptcy court approved Nassi's retention on October 29.[159]

The standard form of his advertisements used in connection with Grants is shown in figure 6.4, although this version relates to Grants' subsequent attempts to use Nassi's techniques without paying Nassi. Anyone who has experienced an American going-out-of-business sale in the last few decades—for

6.6 Grants' going-out-of-business advertisement: specific store locations would be listed at the bottom.

W. T. Grant Company, 1976.

Blockbuster Video, Borders, Caldor, or Bed Bath and Beyond, for example—has seen this basic Nassi-inspired form in use.[160]

At the first official meeting of creditors held on November 19, Rosen provided an update on the debtor's case. He announced that Kendrick and Sundman were no longer with the company—and Anderson had become the CEO. Anderson would disparage both in his later depositions in the case. Anderson felt that Sundman, the CFO, did not understand the retail business, but their inability to work together certainly did not help matters as the company struggled.

Harvey Miller, on behalf of the creditors' committee, voted the claim of Genesco, Inc. in the sum of $559,611.96 in favor of appointment of the committee as constituted at the Americana Hotel. O. D. Glaus, Jr., of Genesco, was one of the trade members of that committee; in the absence of any objection, the committee was appointed.[161] The court also named Charles Rodman—a former attorney with Wall Street firm Sullivan and Cromwell, who was then serving as chair of the Grand Union Company—as standby trustee, after Miller once again voted the Genesco claim.[162] He was to be on call to become a trustee if the case converted to a liquidation.

The committee had been holding meetings long before it was officially appointed. Its first meeting commenced on October 17, at 7:30 A.M. in the Grants boardroom in Times Square.[163] The meetings would typically last all day.[164] A young associate—Richard Krasnow of Weil Gotshal—was tasked with taking the minutes.

Martin Lipton led the presentation of the company's cash flow situation at the first meeting and updated the committee on the status of market trading of the company's securities. Consultants reported on the store closing plans, as well as plans to reduce the staff at the corporate headquarters. Anderson reported that he had sent teams to the mid-Atlantic and Northeastern stores to evaluate those stores that would make up his "New Grants."

The committee met again on October 21, at 8 A.M., and October 23, again at 8, and again on October 30, although this time they did not gather until 2:30 P.M. At least five meetings were held in November. By this point, Lipton had stepped back and the meetings were being run by Rosen, the company's lead bankruptcy attorney, and Anderson. One wonders if this was the most productive use of Anderson's (or Rosen's) time during these days.

At the December 2 meeting, again at 8 A.M., the company's consultants reported on the projected results for some 490 "keeper" stores that would comprise the New Grants.[165] The consultants estimated that for fiscal year 1976 (January 31, 1976, to January 31, 1977), the reorganized company would lose about $31 million. Rosen then noted that the company was already considering closing about fifty additional stores, which would shrink operations even further. Rosen also advised he was in constant communication with the SEC, in large part to forestall any move by them to convert the case to chapter X. Nassi reported that he was achieving recoveries of more than 60 percent of retail prices on the inventory at the closed stores—it appears he ultimately received about $5 million from the Grants engagement.[166]

In early January 1976, the banks told the bankruptcy court that "time and again the Banks have cooperated with Grant, and we expect that they will continue to do so unless it appears that rehabilitation is not feasible."[167] But in mid-December, the banks had pushed the committee to retain several consultants, including the investment bank Donaldson, Lufkin & Jenrette (DLJ), to advise on the feasibility of any plan that Grants might present.[168] In fact, these consultants were also going to be offered as expert witnesses in case the banks decided to force Grants into a liquidation.[169] The question of whether rehabilitation was feasible was one that the banks expected to have a large say in.

• • •

At the January 20, 1976, creditors' committee meeting, Grants presented a proposed business plan for "New Grants," based around 359 stores and about 35,000 employees. About half of the stores would be in strip malls, and Grants would sell 266 product lines "with emphasis on casual wear and leisure oriented products."[170] Shortly thereafter, Anderson outlined his vision for Grants in an interview with *The New York Times*, where he stated that "we are aiming at the young marrieds, the ages 21 to 30, with incomes from $12,000 to $17,000 [about $68,000 to $98,000 today], the budget-minded shopper who wants casual and leisure apparel with good values."[171]

On the morning of February 3, the committee convened at DLJ's offices.[172] Two teams of consultants presented reports: one headed by Robert E. Brooker and another from DLJ. DLJ had visited thirty stores in the New Grants area as part of its analysis. The consultants generally concluded that Grants would probably break even by 1978, but it would take six to eight years to really know if Anderson's plan was working.

In the executive session that followed, the committee held an extensive discussion about Grants' viability and whether it should be placed in liquidation. The members also discussed the possibility that the SEC might move to put the company into chapter X, which would likely result in no recovery for the subordinated bondholders or equity, given the application of the absolute priority rule. It is doubtful that the last were real concerns, given that no shareholders or subordinated bondholders were on the committee. More plausibly, the committee was also concerned that Grants had plans to buy large amounts of merchandise in the coming months. They ultimately agreed to meet again three days hence.

The next day, Leonard Rosen presented the outline of a reorganization plan to representatives of the largest bank creditors.[173] It is unclear if he knew about

TABLE 6.2 Reorganization plan for grants

	Proposed distributions				
Class	Estimated claims	Cash	Subordinated notes	Preferred stock (%)	Common stock (%)
Banks	340	60	55	100	10
Secured trade	110	70	40		8
Senior bondholders	24	20	4		2
General unsecured creditors	500				70
Old shareholders					10

the consultants' presentation at the committee meeting the day before. The plan provided for payments in cash, subordinated bonds, preferred stock, and new common stock to creditors. The proposed distributions are shown in table 6.2, in millions of dollars, but the result would be that the general unsecured creditors— which included the $90 million of subordinated bondholders and the $300 million subordinated bank claim—would end up controlling the company.

The cash payments would come from the proceeds of the store liquidations and leave Grants with about $127 million in cash for operations. One Wachtell attorney involved in preparing the plan said that he felt they had offered a path to reorganization.[174]

• • •

But the banks were not inclined to take it. The committee met again on February 6 as planned, and the banks were unified in their belief that Grants should be liquidated.[175] Clearly, they had discussed their position in advance, as each bank speaker built on the prior speakers to make the case that the committee owed a fiduciary duty to all creditors not to dissipate the bankruptcy estate. Behind the banks' comments was the reality that they had little faith in Grants' management, even Anderson, and worried that Anderson's plans would result in the alienation of traditional Grants customers in search of new customers that might never materialize.[176] After hearing this onslaught from the banks, the trade creditors asked for a recess so they could caucus.

The committee resumed the discussion, and in the afternoon they decided to invite Rosen to join them. He discussed the advantages of his reorganization plan for the remaining Grants employees and suggested that the company could position itself as an acquisition target for a chain looking to expand into the northeast. He noted that the proposed capital structure set Grants up to obtain outside financing in future years, since the only debt would be already subordinated.

The committee then phoned Anderson and others to ask them to join the meeting. Anderson may have oversold the case for reorganizing Grants, while at the same time pointing some fingers. The committee minutes report: "Mr. Anderson said that he felt that the Company can and should be saved. He mentioned that he took the job because he thought he had the support of the financial community. However, he said that he had not received adequate financing to allow for a free flow of merchandise. Nevertheless, the stores are 'pretty well stocked' at the present time. For Mr. Anderson, the question was how much the Committee wanted to save a 'great American enterprise.'"[177] The committee adjourned for three days, with the caution that their discussion must remain confidential.

The meeting resumed at noon on February 9 at Weil Gotshal's offices in the General Motors Building near Central Park. The chair announced that the committee would hear from Grants accountants, consultants, and then DLJ. At the start of the meeting, Phillip Potter from Davis Polk, counsel to the banks, circulated an opinion letter from Brooker, and a partner from DLJ circulated a similar letter. The Brooker letter argued that it would take at least three years to implement Anderson's plan, and the DLJ letter stated that "seven to eight years would probably transpire before management would conclude that the transformation was completed."[178] In the early years, both experts predicted greater losses than Grants' management was currently forecasting.

Grants' accountant from Coopers and Lybrand then acknowledged that it would take at least two years for the company to show a profit, and he could not really tell if Grants was presently viable. He further noted that Grants needed to develop a proper system of inventory management, which would allow it to understand which departments were selling and what they were selling, and implementing such a system would take time and money.

The DLJ partner noted that Anderson's plan involved a high degree of risk, and Sears was having trouble convincing customers that it was a real source of fashion apparel. He did note that Kmart—itself a derivative of Grants' old variety competitor, S. S. Kresge—was just beginning to move into the northeast, so Grants had a window to develop its position in the market.

The committee then went into executive session. The representative from Morgan stated that his bank believed that continued investment in Grants was high risk, and "if a speedy liquidation was possible, the size of the estate could exceed $400,000,000 which, if invested in appropriate bonds, could result in a return higher than the company [Grants] would earn operating through 1980."[179] That, of course, would do little for Grants' employees, but a former Davis Polk attorney conceded that the employees did not loom large in this discussion.[180]

The Morgan representative then moved that the committee seek to convert the Grants case to a liquidation—then called "adjudication," the equivalent of today's chapter 7. The Chase representative quickly seconded the resolution. After extensive discussion, the committee voted: All the banks voted in favor of the resolution, and most of the trade creditors were against it, except for Genessco, which voted with the banks for liquidation.[181] One committee attorney told me that he sensed that Glaus, the Genesco representative, took his fiduciary duties to the estate quite seriously.[182] And while the banks did not absolutely need Genesco's vote, it certainly helped the banks to sidestep the unmistakable "banks versus trade creditors" narrative."[183] The final vote was thus 7 to 4, and the committee adjourned late Monday evening.

The New York Times and *Women's Wear Daily* had the story by Wednesday morning, with the latter's front page proclaiming "End of Line for Grant's."[184] On Thursday, the news spread nationwide, along with the further news that Grants would not attempt to fight the banks' move.[185] On Friday, Judge Galgay signed an order allowing Grants to conduct going-out-of-business sales at its remaining stores, although the company would not formally convert to liquidation until April.[186]

The SEC fumed. The agency later testified in front of the Senate that Grants was "a concrete illustration of what may and does occur without the safeguards for public investors which chapter X provides."[187] It further noted that under the Bankruptcy Rules, the SEC had until March to move to convert the case to chapter X, but the banks decided to liquidate the company in February.[188] Anderson testified in the bankruptcy court that the banks' move to convert to liquidation essentially killed the company with trade creditors, foreclosing any possibility of successfully converting to chapter X thereafter. The SEC argued that "the banks, after the filing for chapter XI, had given us to understand that the first step would be to liquidate the unprofitable stores and hold for reorganization the remaining stores."[189] In short, the SEC felt that it had been misled.

Marvin Jacobs, the SEC associate regional director, argued that the company should have been in chapter X from inception. He complained:

> We will never know if Grant could have been saved because of the lack of disinterested trustees and a thorough investigation of the company. Anderson is crying all the way to the bank. If he had resisted the banks, he would have had a conflict. All the banks saw was this pool of cash, and they figured, "Why spin our wheels—let's liquidate."
>
> The whole thing has been a horrible situation; haste had been the watchword here. They took a big public company which should have been a Chapter X proceeding and ran it into the ground.[190]

On the other hand, many of the other participants suggested that "nobody" wanted to be in chapter X.[191]

"Nobody" in this instance means company management and their professionals, who would have been supplanted in chapter X by a trustee and the trustee's professionals. As one contemporary commentator observed, "The format for whacking up the fees provides an overpowering stimulus toward Chapter XI. Any attorney with so much as a passing interest in making money will opt for XI, and at the outset the choice is up to debtor's attorney."[192] One of the obvious flaws with the Chandler Act, and chapter X, was that there was no one major stakeholder motivated to insist on a chapter X filing. Once Congress left the door open to chapter XI, which the Supreme Court refused to close, it was never likely that chapter X would see extensive use, especially since most corporate advisors were never going to steer their clients in that direction when it could be avoided

That is not to say that chapter X was otherwise perfect. The quality of the trustee appointed by the district court allegedly could vary widely, and there were complaints of raw patronage rivaling the receivership days.[193] Like the ICC, the SEC was often the perceived source of slowdowns in reorganizations— but it is notable that while after the war, section 77 cases still took an average of seven years, chapter X cases took only a little over two years, a figure that compares favorably with "free fall" cases under present-day chapter 11.[194] To be sure, the SEC was reluctant to devote staff resources to a department whose work would ebb and flow with the health of the broader economy, and once the old New Dealers left the agency, the interest in restructuring declined tremendously.[195]

All were important issues that Congress should have addressed long before 1975, along with the fundamental issue of what cases belonged in chapter X in the first place.

• • •

The committee continued to meet throughout the remainder of the chapter XI case. At their first meeting after the court's liquidation order, Anderson advised them that all remaining Grants stores had closed "as of the evening of February 12, 1976, and that only one or two employees will remain at the stores to receive merchandise." Anderson noted that he would continue to work for about six more weeks, and Grants would be terminating about $23 million in open purchase orders.[196] Rodman began attending the meetings in March, and on April 8, the committee met for the last time.[197]

The "Grants" sign came down from the corporate headquarters in Times Square in March.[198] Rodman stepped in as a trustee in April and retained Weil Gotshal as his counsel. When the banks filed an action demanding the store sale proceeds, Rodman responded with a counterclaim that the banks should be subordinated because of their domination of Grants' management.[199]

For Morgan, having a senior executive on the board and indeed chairing the audit committee and spearheading Anderson's hiring, while also leading the bank group, holding more than $64 million of the $562 million of bank debt, and acting as indenture trustee for the senior bonds, was not a good look. During the chapter XI case, it resigned from the board and as a trustee, but that was late in the game.[200] Unhelpfully, two of the other banks with the biggest stakes in the loans, Chase ($89.4 million) and Citibank ($90.9 million), had acted as indenture trustees for the subordinated bonds.[201] Recall that the Citibank representative was the chair of the committee during the chapter XI case.

More than a year of litigation and depositions followed, until in 1978, the trustee entered into a settlement with the banks.[202] At that point, the trustee had already reached settlements with the secured trade creditors, which were given the option of taking 90 percent payment immediately or waiting for more, and the senior bondholders, which received payment of the full face amount of their bonds (without interest).[203]

The banks agreed to set aside $35 million to pay unsecured creditors other than the subordinated bondholders, a pro rata distribution. They also agreed to set aside about $95 million, pending a settlement with the subordinated bondholders. In the meantime, the banks would get an allowed claim of $650 million and an initial distribution of $161 million.[204] Trade creditors whose claims were related to orders from August through October 1975 also had the benefit of the subordination agreement with the banks. As part of the compromise, the trustee agreed not to sue the 116 small banks whose loans were paid by Grants just before the bankruptcy.

The $35 million for unsecured creditors was spread across about $85 million in claims asserted by some 32,000 creditors. The creditors received interim distributions of 20 percent and 10 percent in 1978 and 1981.[205] Those trade creditors that were protected by the subordination agreement then received their remaining 70 percent payment from the banks, who then took over their claims. The final payment of 9.5 percent of unsecured claims did not occur until 1985, when Judge Tina Brozman, who was by then presiding over the case, approved the distribution despite a single creditor's pending appeal.[206]

After the trustee's settlement with the banks was approved, the subordinated bondholders took over the trustee's arguments and then some. There was about $92 million of the 4-3/4 percent subordinated convertible debentures outstanding, held by just over 2,400 investors. The largest single holder held $11 million.[207] There was apparently enough there to warrant a payoff of more than 20 percent to the bondholders when all was said and done.[208]

The estate also distributed $4.1 million to 17,378 former employees in vacation pay benefits and $9.72 million to 25,866 employees in severance pay, based on rulings from Judge Galgay.[209] This represented full payment of the severance claims and more than 77 percent of the vacation claims.

Landlord claims—for early termination of leases—were paid about 40 percent. Several store leases were sold to Caldor, Bradlees, and Ames, among others, setting up the landlords for another round of bankruptcies in the 1990s. The luckier landlords were transferred to two newer chains that were just expanding: Target and Wal-Mart.[210] The Grants location in Pittsburgh became a Saks Fifth Avenue that operated until 2012.[211]

In total, the Grants estate distributed more than $780 million before the case was closed in 1993 by Judge Cornelius Blackshear, one of the earliest African American bankruptcy judges in the country.[212] Richard Krasnow, who had been there from the early days and was now a partner, appeared for the successor trustee—Rodman had passed away, as had Judge Galgay.[213] And while female attorneys had been a rarity in the Missouri Pacific case, and unheard of in both of our receivership cases, several appeared in Grants, most visibly Jacqueline Taubes and Marsha Goldstein of Weil Gotshal.[214] Slow change, sometimes glacially slow, was happening in the corporate bankruptcy system.

Grants ultimately paid about $10 million to the various professionals who worked on the case.[215] The banks recovered about 84 percent of their claims. That they did not receive full payment, despite their seniority and the ample size of the trustee's recoveries, reflects the chapter XI penchant for widespread distributions, unhindered by the so-called absolute priority rule, as well as the nontrivial nature of the claims against the banks, as difficult as it may have been to actually "win" those claims.

Indeed, Morgan paid $2.8 million in 1981 to settle a securities lawsuit by Grants' shareholders.[216] Former directors paid the trustee about $2 million (about $7.7 million in 2023), and Ernst and Ernst, Grants' former auditors, agreed to pay a similar amount.[217] Again, none of the settlements were huge, but they were not peanuts either.

Into the 1990s, Grants would still rank among the biggest corporate bankruptcy cases ever.[218] But it was the last big case under the first generation of corporate reorganization statutes, enacted in response to the Great Depression.

Like section 77, chapter X gave the power formerly exercised by banks and insiders to an agency that was somewhat reluctant to exercise it. The banks stepped into the void, but only because Grants' board gave them that opening back in 1974. More effective managers might have considered chapter X, but doing so would have required them to go against the advice that they were undoubtedly receiving from their professionals.

Often, it was thought that the debtor had all the control in chapter XI because it was the only party who could propose a plan, but in a situation like Grants', where the debtor had put liens on all of its assets and thus became dependent on its lenders for liquidity, the power shifted. Indeed, once in bankruptcy,

Grants' court-approved agreement with the banks stipulated that the banks would immediately cease granting the company credit (and all loans would be called) if a motion to transfer the case to chapter X were filed.[219] The agreement made the SEC uneasy that any move to transfer the case would kill it and leave the agency with the blame—further power to the banks.[220]

Grants, then, is ultimately a story of corporate governance failure in the context of a poorly designed (and maintained) corporate bankruptcy system. The bankruptcy system would be different going forward, but it is doubtful whether the governance of companies in Grants' position has improved. And a changed corporate bankruptcy system does not necessarily mean a better corporate bankruptcy system.

PART III

MODERNIZATION?

CHAPTER 7

THE DEREGULATION OF CORPORATE BANKRUPTCY

Throughout the late 1960s and early 1970s, Congress discussed a comprehensive revision of American bankruptcy law—both personal and corporate—that finally came to a resolution in 1978. The first serious effort at changing corporate reorganization came in 1973 from the Commission on the Bankruptcy Laws of the United States, appointed in 1970 to "study, analyze, evaluate and recommend changes" in the existing Bankruptcy Act. The commission proposed a single reorganization chapter to avoid the chapter X versus chapter XI conundrum. The proposal to consolidate the chapters was spearheaded by Professor Lawrence King, who was an adviser to the commission and, as noted in chapter 6, one of Grants' early bankruptcy attorneys.[1]

A bankruptcy-focused administrative agency would take over for the SEC, and there would have been a presumption that a trustee would be appointed in larger cases.[2] Fights over that presumption might have looked a lot like the fights regarding chapter choice, although at least the other issues behind the choice—like the absolute priority rule and the dual process of court and SEC—would have been decided.[3]

The commission's proposal was introduced in Congress, but there was a competing bill proposed by the National Conference of Bankruptcy Judges. This "Judges Bill," as it was called, started with the commission's bill but then stripped out the proposed bankruptcy agency in favor of a much weaker "director," who would handle some basic administrative tasks in bankruptcy cases, leaving more work for judges.[4] Indeed, it was estimated that under the commission's bill, there would be less need for bankruptcy judges, and thus we see at least some of what was motivating the Judges Bill.

Neither bill was enacted as drafted, in part because the Watergate hearings consumed the attention of the relevant congressional committees. Once Richard Nixon had flown off to California after his resignation as president, and a new vice president was approved, the commission's bill and the Judges Bill were again introduced as H.R. 31 and H.R. 32, respectively, in 1975. Both houses held extensive hearings on the bills—the House committee held thirty-five separate hearings on topics ranging from the bankruptcy court system to international aspects of bankruptcy.[5]

Harvey Miller, testifying for the National Bankruptcy Conference, told the House committee that "in the Grant case, involving some 40,000 public investors, the threat of a potential chapter X conversion had in my view a very prejudicial effect on the ability of that corporation to reorganize . . . We submit if there was a consolidated chapter, we wouldn't have these problems; we wouldn't have the enormous amount of time that is devoted to battling as to whether you should be in chapter X, or chapter XI."[6] Of course, the very fact that Grants had so many public investors supported the SEC's argument that the chain should have been in chapter X in the first place—the uncertainty was created by the decision to try to force the massive case into chapter XI, like an elephant into a shoebox.

Miller repeatedly argued that the threat of conversion to chapter X was a "sword of Damocles" hanging over corporate bankruptcy cases, but we should recall that Miller represented the creditor perspective in the Grants case—first banks, then committee, then trustee—and not the debtor (as he would do so often after 1978). While the banks had obtained a court order allowing them to terminate financing upon conversion to chapter X, they would have faced the stay against collecting on their liens, while chapter XI had no effect on secured creditors, leaving them in the driver's seat.

Eventually, a synthesis bill was drafted and introduced in the House on January 4, 1977, as H.R.6.[7] The bill was marked up in committee and ultimately reintroduced as H.R.8200 in July 1977.[8] The Senate responded with S.2266, which approached business reorganization from a completely different direction than the House bill.[9]

In particular, while both bills consolidated corporate bankruptcy into a single "chapter 11," the Senate bill had an overlay of special rules for publicly traded debtors. The Senate defined such public companies as "a debtor who, within 12 months prior to the filing of a petition for relief under this chapter, had outstanding liabilities of $5 million or more, exclusive of liabilities for goods, services, or taxes and not less than 1,000 security holders."[10]

Public status triggered the mandatory appointment of a trustee and an advisory role for the SEC. Section 1130(a)(7) of S.2266 mandated the application of the "absolute priority rule" in public cases, even where all classes of creditors and equity interests consented to the plan.

And section 1125(f) of the Senate bill prohibited solicitation of acceptances from investors before court approval of the plan, even when all applicable securities laws were complied with. In short, for companies that qualified as "public," the Senate bill would have kept much of chapter X in place, in a somewhat updated form, while all other companies would have reorganized under what we know today as chapter 11, which was (and is) essentially a supercharged version of old chapter XI.

The Senate Bill reflected the influence of Aaron Levy, head of the SEC's reorganization section.[11] Levy was "steeped in the New Deal tradition," and believed in chapter X's approach to public-company corporate bankruptcy.[12] But why did the Senate embrace the New Deal approach to public companies? That is harder to answer.

Senator Dennis DeConcini, who headed the Senate effort, seemed quite supportive of the idea that public investors—both bondholders and shareholders—needed protection from institutional players in bankruptcy. But the Senate's ultimate willingness to concede to the House's approach on business bankruptcy has led some to suggest that the embrace of the SEC vision was mostly about creating a bargaining chip for later negotiations about the final form of the broader bankruptcy law.[13]

The SEC did receive some support, although notably, almost none of it came from bankruptcy practitioners. For example, Harold Tyler, former district court judge and a named partner of New York's Patterson, Belknap, Webb & Tyler, testified that H.R.8200 was a step backward regarding protection of public investors, whereas the Senate bill "eschews this backward approach and allows us to retain the essence of Chapter X by permitting in appropriate cases a public trustee to protect debt and equity holders in reorganizing a public company."[14]

But in the end, the only reflection of the Senate's approach that survived was one that provided for automatic appointment of an examiner (i.e., investigator) in cases with more than $5 million of debt.[15] This echoed the Senate's old trigger for a trustee, although it omitted the requirement of one thousand or more security holders, which might have made the provision more targeted, especially since the dollar figure was not among those Bankruptcy Code provisions indexed for inflation.

The examiner would simply investigate the debtor rather than run it. Indeed, the 1978 Code would expressly prohibit the examiner from ever becoming the trustee.[16] And ultimately both the bankruptcy courts and the parties would become adept at evading even this small concession in favor of the Senate's New Deal–inspired approach.[17] Those who push the issue—that is, rely on what the statute actually says—risk facing the wrath of an angry bankruptcy judge.[18]

Neither bill revived the idea of the Bankruptcy Administration. While such an agency made lots of policy sense, particularly concerning personal bankruptcy, it was opposed by every lawyer in the United States who had ever filed a bankruptcy case. Lost business trumped good policy: Many of those small-town lawyers were quite influential with their representatives in Congress, and a bankruptcy attorney in Minnesota, Raeder Larson, was instrumental in getting the American Bar Association to come out against the commission's bill. As a result, the idea was quietly dropped.[19]

While the SEC and Chief Justice Warren Burger (who opposed the creation of dozens of new bankruptcy judges) fought the new Bankruptcy Code to the bitter end, President Jimmy Carter ultimately did sign the bill, on the last day he could.[20] And thus chapter 11, the corporate bankruptcy law that the United States still uses to this day, was enacted. It was based on the idea that "the parties involved should be able to negotiate a plan even to the point that those holding senior interests allow junior interests to realize some distribution and, if such a plan is acceptable based on informed consent, the court should not be hamstrung by an inflexible standard in determining whether the plan should be confirmed."[21] As a result, there is no absolute priority rule unless a class votes against a plan—under a two-part standard that blends old chapters X and XI and requires more than half the creditors in number, and two-thirds in amount, to approve.[22] The SEC has largely vanished in corporate bankruptcy over time, despite chapter 11's provision that they "may raise and may appear and be heard on any issue in a case under this chapter."[23]

Some of the SEC's role was assumed by the Office of the United States Trustee, an agency within the US Department of Justice. Congress charged the US Trustee with "watchdog" responsibilities in chapter 11 cases and gave it standing to be heard on any issue in any case or proceeding.[24] Nevertheless, as the bankruptcy courts have developed more of a "deal" mentality in chapter 11 throughout the years, they have become increasingly resistant to the notion that a party with no economic interest in the case could upend the process.[25]

. . .

Sections 1102(b)(1), 1121(a), and 1126(b) of the 1978 Bankruptcy Code permit what is termed "prepackaged" plans by allowing plans to be simultaneously filed with petitions, authorize the conversion of prepetition committees into official committees, and allow votes solicited prepetition to be counted and considered for plan confirmation. This represents a return to section 77B's approach to prebankruptcy solicitation of plans, which was expressly prohibited under chapter X but allowed under chapter XI.

Upon passage of the Code, and enactment of chapter 11, the SEC expressed concern that junior creditors and stockholders would lack bargaining power without a trustee to represent them.[26] They were not wrong to worry.

Trustees could be appointed, but there was no presumption of a trustee. Indeed, just the opposite: The presumption was that the debtor would remain in possession of its own estate, keeping the business operating.[27] And the Code expressly prohibited appointment of a trustee based solely on "the number of holders of securities of the debtor or the amount of assets or liabilities of the debtor."[28] In short, courts were prohibited from embracing the SEC and Senate approach through the back door of the discretionary powers granted by the Code.

After the Enron and WorldCom scandals in the early 2000s, Congress amended the trustee provision to require that the US Trustee ask for appointment of a trustee if "there are reasonable grounds to suspect" that the debtor's current managers or directors "participated in actual fraud, dishonesty, or criminal conduct."[29] But in cases where a trustee might be called for, like Enron or more recently the cryptocurrency broker FTX, parties have learned to replace senior management just before the bankruptcy commences.

Often a new senior executive, sometimes called a "chief restructuring officer (CRO)" and hired from a financial consulting firm, takes the helm.[30] But this move (at least standing alone) neglects state corporate law, which actually identifies the board as the source of control of a corporation. In part to address this, more recent cases have also seen the appointment of a number of "independent" directors to the board, who often are charged with investigating past acts, in an effort to head off the appointment of an examiner (despite the Code's unqualified requirement of such in larger cases).

Of course, neither a CRO nor independent board members are truly independent in the same way that a trustee under old chapter X or modern chapter 11 would be, since they were chosen by prior management. Moreover, it has been observed that many "independent" directors are repeat players who often are associated with large investors (like private equity firms) or their law firms.[31]

. . .

Given the frequency that the business press reports on chapter 11 cases—think of FTX, WeWork, Johnson & Johnson's baby powder subsidiary (three attempts as of now), Rite Aid, Vice Media, American Airlines (or most any other big airline), General Motors, J. Crew, Enron, Circuit City, Bed Bath & Beyond, or Revlon, for example—figure 7.1 might come as a bit of a surprise, especially when compared with its counterpart, figure 6.1. This graph shows all the large chapter 11 cases in the LoPucki database—which includes all publicly traded debtors that had assets of more than $100 million in 1980 dollars (about $355 million in 2022). 1,190 cases in total, as of the end of 2022.

The graph shows there are (on average) fewer large chapter 11 cases per year than there were chapter X cases. While figure 6.1 showed an average of 105 chapter X cases per year between 1950 and 1975, figure 7.1 shows an average of

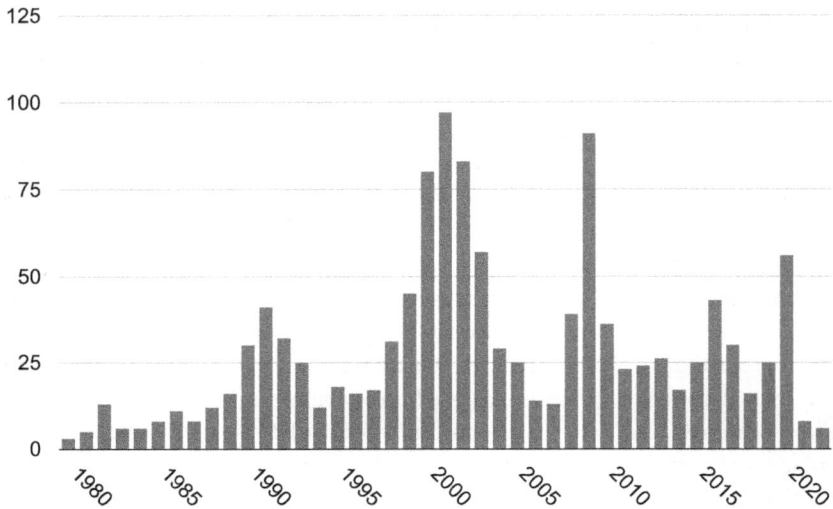

7.1 Large chapter 11 cases by year, from 1980 to 2022.

Source: Florida-UCLA-LoPucki Bankruptcy Research Database.

about 28 (median 24) large chapter 11 cases per year between 1980 and 2022. Now the two graphs here measure slightly different things—figure 7.1 covers *large* public chapter 11 cases, while figure 6.1 has *all* chapter X cases, so in theory the difference might be made up of a plethora of small, publicly traded bankrupt companies under chapter X. Why those companies would have ended up in chapter X, and not chapter XI, should make us question this hypothesis.

So if the number of big corporate bankruptcy cases has not changed in any meaningful way—indeed, figure 7.1 suggests that perhaps the numbers have declined—why do chapter 11 and corporate bankruptcy seem much more common these days? One obvious answer is greater press coverage, facilitated by a growing mainstream business press, and the use of chapter 11 by more companies that are in the public eye. While Grants was an obvious exception, along with Penn Central and the other railroads, many companies that failed in the pre-1978 days were comparatively obscure. Modern chapter 11, on the other hand, has been embraced as a necessary tool by several well-known companies—key early examples include Texaco in 1987, Federated Department Stores in 1990, and R. H. Macy & Co. (Macy's) in 1992.

• • •

The Texaco case is an example of the use of chapter 11 in ways that the 1978 Congress could never have imagined.[32] At the time, the company was the third-largest oil producer in the world, and quite solvent, but then a Houston jury awarded Pennzoil damages of $10.5 *billion* plus interest after a busted transaction where Texaco allegedly "stole" a target away from Pennzoil. The number was eventually reduced, but with interest, it still totaled about $11 billion. And under Texas law, to appeal that verdict, Texaco would have had to post a bond at least equal to that amount. Instead, Texaco filed chapter 11. It could have negotiated a deal with Pennzoil outside of bankruptcy, but filing for bankruptcy flipped the bargaining power—instead of Pennzoil threatening to send the sheriff to grab Texaco's assets, Texaco now had the benefit of an automatic stay and the first crack at proposing a plan that could settle the matter.[33]

An even earlier, novel use of chapter 11 came in the 1982 Johns Manville case. Denver-based building and forest products concern Johns Manville was the one of the largest corporations in the United States, with over $2 billion in sales—in addition to being the world's single biggest asbestos producer.[34] In the forty years preceding Manville's bankruptcy, it was estimated that some 18 million people had been exposed to the substance, with 250,000 likely to die early because of it.[35]

John A. McKinney, Johns Manville's chairman and CEO, lambasted the tort system as a nightmare and unworkable, arguing that some victims who were deserving of compensation had received nothing from the courts, while others who were only slightly injured had won extremely large judgments.[36] Thus, despite being apparently solvent according to its SEC reports, on August 26, 1982, Manville filed a chapter 11 petition.

McKinney's goal was to have the bankruptcy court address all present and future asbestos claims, determine how much the company would need to pay, and then clear the company of all its asbestos liability in perpetuity.[37] Critics of this approach argued that it was an attempt by Manville to escape responsibility for paying its debts, and they were especially skeptical of any exculpation of liability that might arise in the future because of the delayed nature of asbestos-related diseases.[38]

In an early win for Manville in late August 1982, Judge Burton R. Lifland (who would preside over several of the key early chapter 11 cases) refused to lift the stay on all pending lawsuits that automatically arose upon the chapter 11 filing.[39] Judge Lifland gave Manville until early 1983 to present a formal reorganization plan.[40] That deadline would be extended many times, in what would ultimately be a six-year reorganization process that would culminate, in the words of one commentator, in "legal history."[41]

Proposed plans bounced back and forth, and there was much tension among the various creditor groups throughout the early years of the case. Judge Lifland himself expressed disappointment that Manville and the creditors had not been able to work out a consensual reorganization plan because the bankruptcy would now likely be "mired in years of litigation."[42] Despite this, he would refuse a motion to dismiss the proceedings in January 1984.[43]

Then on March 15, 1985, the *Wall Street Journal* reported that Leon Silverman, a New York lawyer appointed by the bankruptcy court to represent people with *future* asbestos claims against Manville, was drafting a new proposal for a restructuring plan.[44] A little over a month later, it was announced that the plan included a trust fund capable of paying $2 billion to $4 billion to asbestos victims over two decades, funded by a $1.6 billion bond issued by Manville, $600 million in insurance funds, and 90 percent of the company's common and preferred stock.[45]

Reaction to the plan was mixed, with Manville officials expressing concern that the plan was too costly, while George Hahn, counsel for the shareholders' committee, criticized the stock dilution as "far too excessive." However, committees for both asbestos claimants and commercial creditors appeared to like many of the plan's provisions, with one attorney representing asbestos claimants stating that "we really couldn't have gotten more than what's in this." The parties would negotiate the terms of the Silverman plan over the next several months.[46]

In August 1985, Manville and Silverman tentatively arrived at what *The New York Times* described as a "breakthrough" plan.[47] In addition to the bond issuance, $600 million in insurance funds, and the contribution of 90 percent of the company's common and preferred stock toward the funding of the trust, the new plan included a court order making Manville immune from further asbestos-related lawsuits and set aside $50 million to pay property damage claims, which would later be increased to $125 million.[48]

However, the plan still required the approval of its commercial creditors, who wanted Manville to pay interest that could exceed $100 million on money that the company owed when it filed, and stockholders, who opposed the proposed issuance of Manville stock to fund the trust. On the other hand, Manville secured the approval of a group representing 19 percent of the 4.6 million preferred shares outstanding in July 1986, whose votes (unlike the common shareholders) were required for the plan to be confirmed under the Bankruptcy Code.

Removing the final impediment to court approval, Manville's commercial creditors accepted a proposal in December 1986 to receive 100 percent of their principal in the form of $247.5 million in cash and a $225 million bond payable over four-and-a-half years, with a portion of the interest that they were owed funded by common stock, warrants, and a separate bond. In addition, holders of common stock would receive 6 percent of the 48 million shares outstanding upon Manville's reemergence, with potential further dilution to a 2 percent stake in the company, while for holders of preferred stock, each $5.40 preferred share would be swapped for 2.16 new common shares—a total of 10 million shares—plus one share of new series B preferred stock, paying a $2.70 annual dividend starting seven years after Manville's emergence from bankruptcy.[49]

After more than four years of negotiations among various interest groups, Judge Lifland issued a forty-eight-page ruling and opinion on December 18, 1986, finding that the plan met the statutory requirements for confirmation. The plan was approved by all creditors, but not the common stock, which, as the lowest rung on the liquidation payment ladder, were easily "crammed down" in conformance with chapter 11's absolute priority rule for nonconsensual plans.[50]

Nearly two years later, after myriad appeals, the trust was fully established and Manville finally emerged from bankruptcy, ending a six-year saga that created a $2.5 billion trust and illustrated how to utilize the new Bankruptcy Code to address mass tort litigation.[51]

But the story was not over.

In February 1989, Manville trustees filed a report in Bankruptcy Court in Manhattan indicating that the trust would run out of money by the end of the year if settlements continued at their current rate.[52] Then, on June 1, 1990, judges in New York reopened Manville's bankruptcy proceeding by ordering Judge Lifland to drastically overhaul the procedures for compensating the victims.[53] Manville was finally authorized on July 23, 1993, to make its first disbursement—$154 million—to asbestos disease claimants.[54]

In addition to creating a mechanism for dealing with aggregate litigation in bankruptcy, Manville pioneered the concept of a "third-party release." That is, a release of a nondebtor's potential joint liability with the debtor. In Manville, the insurance companies that contributed to funding the trust wanted to make sure that their payments were the end of the matter. In future cases, such releases would be far more controversial.

• • •

Manville is the best known of the novel uses of chapter 11—spawning waves of other asbestos companies and other corporate tortfeasors like A. H. Robbins. That company failed to warn women about defective and dangerous intrauterine devices for years, but it followed the Manville model (claims trust, future claims representative, third-party releases) and discharged its liability.[55]

Another unanticipated use of chapter 11 in these early years was to break collective bargaining agreements—a century after Jay Gould used the Texas and Pacific's receivership to break the Knights of Labor. In 1983, Continental Airlines filed a chapter 11 petition claiming that deregulation of the airline industry and competition from new, low-fare, nonunion airlines had resulted in massive losses.[56] It shut down for a couple of days, laid off all its 12,000 employees, and then agreed to hire back about 25 percent of them at half wages and benefits. The airline's CEO, Frank Lorenzo—who also controlled its parent holding company, Texas Air—announced that the airline would seek to reject the existing collective bargaining agreements under section 365 of the Bankruptcy Code, and the employees went on strike.[57]

In the end, Lorenzo's tactics largely worked: "Within months, Continental experienced a pronounced turnaround. It quickly dropped 25 of its money-losing routes and added highly traveled, profitable routes as a discount airline. Its labor costs have dipped to just 22 percent of operating costs, down from 36 percent before the filing. Other cost cutting saved $200 million a year."[58]

Since then, nearly every major American airline has filed chapter 11 at least once—and some have filed several times.[59] Continental itself was back in 1990. TWA used its third case to sell itself to American Airlines. In 2013, American used its own chapter 11 to facilitate a merger with US Airways, which itself had twice reorganized.[60] While an operating airline would have avoided chapter X like the plague, chapter 11 has become quite routine for airlines foreign and domestic, contributing to the belief that corporate bankruptcy has become more common.[61]

· · ·

While the frequent use of new chapter 11 by consumer-facing companies, like airlines and retailers, certainly fueled the perception that corporate bankruptcy was on the rise, it was also true that mainstream companies were far more indebted than they had been in the past. As a result, they were far more likely to experience bankruptcy, which had previously been reserved for companies in disrupted industries—like railroads, northeastern manufacturing concerns, and poorly managed retailers.

In previous years, it was hard for distressed companies to get into too much debt so long as their business continued to operate as designed: "Historically, low-rated companies had borrowed money short term on a senior, secured basis from banks, and longer term from insurance companies in private placements (although some companies were too low-rated to qualify for the private placements). But those loans had been laden with restrictive covenants. The other source of capital, of course, was equity offerings—but those diluted the value of the stock already outstanding. Furthermore, the equity markets had been so depressed through the seventies that for many companies . . . an equity offering was not even an option."[62]

Grants could be seen as an example of this model—albeit swollen to a tremendous size. Many companies that needed funding and could not get money from banks or insurance companies could try to reorganize under either chapter X or chapter XI, but imposing large losses on trade creditors was not a recipe for future success, and chapter XI was useless against secured creditors or shareholders.

But then came Drexel Burnham Lambert and Michael Milken. High-yield debt has existed for a long time. Recall that the Texas and Pacific's Rio Grande division bonds were trading between 70 and 75 in 1883, after trading at par during the Thomas Scott years.[63] Somebody who bought these at 70 got the 6 percent coupon but also were entitled to repayment at 100 in 1930, meaning that their actual yield was *potentially* much higher than the coupon. Of course, there is a lot of strain placed on the word "potentially"—that extra yield reflected the risk of nonpayment, which in the case of the Texas and Pacific became quite real in 1885.

High-yield bonds issued by former investment grade companies that have fallen on hard times are called "fallen angels."[64] Beginning in the late 1970s, just as Congress was enacting the Bankruptcy Code, Milken launched the modern high-yield market by selling new bonds from companies with below-investment grade ratings. These bonds were high yield—or, more casually, *junk*—from inception.[65]

At first, they were used to finance shaky companies. Junk bonds offered these companies access to the bond market, which meant fewer covenants and more funding than banks and insurance companies had previously provided.[66] Then Drexel Burnham Lambert also began underwriting high-yield bonds to finance mergers and acquisitions, or leveraged buyouts (LBOs). These LBOs involved buying out the old shareholders with lots of borrowed money, in the form of junk bonds.

As Professor Bratton has explained:

LBOs involve leverage so high that restructured companies sometimes start life at or near insolvency. As is usual with restructuring transactions, acquirers "take out" stockholders with the proceeds of new borrowing. The target does not receive proceeds of this borrowing, even though its assets are pledged to secure the debt . . .

An LBO does not occur because promoters, managers, and financiers decide to improve a corporation for the good of preexisting investors; it occurs because it offers sure profits for the equity taken out and a chance for extravagant, but high-risk, profits for the promoters and managers who take control and for the financiers who help them. Preexisting creditors share this risk, but get no compensation in the form of a higher interest rate or an option to exit at face value. These creditors' "upside," if the corporation recovers, is to return to their original position—holding a fixed coupon that bars them from further "upside" possibilities.[67]

In its heyday, Drexel had half the market for new junk debt.

• • •

A classic example of the 1980s LBO was Safeway Stores, Inc.[68] Susan Faludi won a Pulitzer Prize for her account of the deal, in which Drexel obtained more than $42 million worth of fees from the both the winning and losing bidders.[69] The winning bidder, KKR, bought the company for $2 billion in junk bonds and about $130 million of its own money. Safeway quickly sold bits of itself, which allowed it to pay off its junk bonds and avoid bankruptcy, unlike many other LBO targets. It was a great success for KKR, eventually netting the firm $7.2 billion on its comparatively small investment.

But as part of the LBO process, Safeway fired over 54,000 employees, or almost one-third of its workforce; Faludi noted the number of suicides and sudden deaths among the laid-off employees. Academics had trumpeted what she called "the putative benefits" of LBOs, but few before had focused on the enormous human costs—especially for workers who had devoted a lifetime to a single employer. Faludi sardonically noted that after the LBO, Safeway changed its longtime corporate slogan from "Safeway Offers Security" to "Targeted Returns on Current Investment."

In 2014, Safeway was the subject of yet another LBO—this time, it was taken over by Cerberus Capital Management, which already had the Albertson's chain under its control.[70] Safeway's price was $9 billion, of which almost $8 billion was debt. Within a few years, the unions were complaining that Cerberus was looting the company.[71] In particular, the unions noted that Cerberus had collected hundreds of millions of dollars in fees and dividends, while employee pensions remained underfunded. Somewhat surprisingly, it eventually agreed to contribute more to the pension fund.

. . .

Shortly after the first Safeway LBO, Milken pled guilty to six counts of securities and tax violations. He paid $600 million in fines, agreed to a lifetime ban from the finance industry, and served twenty-two months in jail. Drexel collapsed into its own chapter 11 case soon afterward. Executive Life Insurance, one of Drexel's in-house buyers of its junk bonds, also went down, destroying many investors' retirement savings. In 2020, President Donald Trump pardoned Milken.[72]

By "the fall of 1991, there were over 150 pending federal civil lawsuits against Drexel, its managers, and Milken, plus the claims of more than nine thousand creditors in the bankruptcy proceeding."[73] Chapter 11 was the obvious solution.[74] Drexel's ultimate chapter 11 plan included Milken making a contribution toward payment of creditors in exchange for a release from any personal liability.[75] The "third-party release" had moved away from insurance companies to relieving individual bad actors of the need to file their own bankruptcy cases for their own misdeeds.[76]

And the junk bond market remained in place, along with LBOs—these days promoted by private equity firms.[77] Indeed, one of the biggest private equity firms, Apollo Global Management, was founded by three former Drexel Burnham Lambert bankers, Marc Rowan, Josh Harris, and Leon Black, the son of Eli Black from MoPac.[78] Another large private equity firm established around the same time was called the Texas Pacific Group. After spending its early years explaining that it was *not* the railroad, it is today called TPG Inc.[79]

As a result of these developments, beginning in the 1980s lots of companies had capital structures that looked like Grants' or worse, without necessarily having the extreme management problems that company did. And it was all quite intentional, unlike with Grants.

In the struggle to make their bond payments, many companies would inflict self-harm with extreme cost cutting or new financing or corporate engineering that would make future corporate reorganizations far more complicated than anything that the drafters of the 1978 Code might have envisioned.[80] For example, a common move in private equity deals is to split the debtor from its real estate—making two companies where there once was one. The real estate company then leases the stores, hotels, or even hospitals back to the operating company that runs the debtor's business. Both companies are overloaded with debt. The challenge is that the operating company no longer has control over its key assets, while the real estate company is frequently left entirely dependent on the operating company making rent payments for its own survival—each has its own set of creditors, with their own incentives, while neither company is complete standing alone.

A recent example resulting in chapter 11, as is so often the case, is Steward Health Care, operator of more than thirty hospitals nationwide. Its former owners, Cerberus Capital, split off its ownership of the hospitals in a transaction that allowed Cerberus to extract millions of dollars from the company.[81] A hospital operator without hospitals makes little sense, while a real estate company is not likely to start providing medical care. Finance for finance's sake, in short.

When it filed for chapter 11 in May 2024, Steward said that it had over $9 billion in total liabilities, including $1.2 billion in loans, $6.6 billion in long-term rent obligations (to the aforementioned real estate company), nearly $1 billion in unpaid bills from medical vendors and suppliers, and $290 million in unpaid employee wages and benefits.[82] Yet the company blamed insufficient government reimbursement rates, along with an increase in labor costs, as the causes of its chapter 11 filing. Indeed.

Moreover, it is often difficult to tell which kind of debtor a company is— management always has an incentive to say that the problem is solely "too much debt" because the alternative has big implications for their continued role in the company. The advent of private equity targets, loaded with debt, might also suggest that the LoPucki database, the source of figure 7.1, undercounts the number of big chapter 11 cases. Namely, because most companies that undergo an LBO do so to pay off (get rid of) the public shareholders, they will not be eligible for inclusion in the LoPucki database when they later file for bankruptcy. At the very least, these companies might help explain the apparent reduction in the number of large chapter 11 cases compared with chapter X cases.

These private equity debtors are right at home in the broader story of corporate reorganization that began back in 1885. Sophisticated players run a company until it falls down and then use the reorganization system to impose most of the costs of failure on smaller parties, be they tort claimants or employees. It worked for Jay Gould, and as we will see in the final chapters, it continues to work for private equity sponsors and distressed debt investors.

. . .

Before taking on the complex restructuring maneuvers of more recent vintage in chapter 8, we might conclude the 1980s with the archetypal chapter 11 case of that decade, at least for many students of chapter 11: Eastern Airlines (figure 7.2). Under one reading, Eastern demonstrated that chapter 11 had not gone far enough in slaying the specter of the New Deal. For many of these

7.2 An Eastern Airlines plane at JFK airport in the 1980s.

Tony Henshaw / Alamy Stock Photo.

critics, corporate bankruptcy should be more about selling companies and less about restructuring them. Restructuring was seen as an offense to the pure market approach of sales or liquidations. That is, the market and businesspeople would take care of any needed rejiggering of the debtor's operations.

Eastern Airlines was founded by World War I ace Eddie Rickenbacker in 1928 and was the first large airline to ply the north-south routes along the eastern seaboard. Eastern was already on the ropes back in 1975, when it hired former astronaut Frank Borman to take charge. In the early years, Borman had some degree of success, obtaining worker agreements to reduce the company's labor costs in the interest of saving the larger enterprise.

But when those cuts failed to stop Eastern's annual losses—indeed, the losses grew even bigger when the industry was deregulated in the late 1970s—the relationship between Borman and the employees soured. The employees resisted further cuts, Borman began imposing them unilaterally, and he threatened to either shut down the company or sell it if the unions did not come to terms.

He eventually took the latter course, selling out to Frank Lorenzo's Texas Air. Eastern was the second major airline that Lorenzo had attempted to add to his stable. He first bid on TWA, with financial backing from Drexel Burnham (represented in the deal by Leon Black). But the TWA unions so loathed Lorenzo after the Continental bankruptcy that they ran to embrace Carl Icahn, another corporate raider, in his place.[83] So Lorenzo bought Eastern instead.

He began a program of driving out mechanics, whom he thought were overpaid, for small rule infractions. More than 840 were fired by 1989. Video cameras were installed in 1986 to help with this process. One union representative said, "This is not union busting 101 . . . this is advanced union busting."[84]

After a few years of tension, everything came to a head. On March 4, 1989, the International Association of Machinists struck Eastern Air Lines (figure 7.3). Pilots and flight attendants walked out in support. The job actions trapped thousands of passengers at Miami International Airport—as one paper reported: "About 2,200 cruise passengers are booked on Eastern, and reticketing becomes a nightmare."[85]

Five days later, Eastern filed for chapter 11 in New York, despite being based in Miami.[86] An affiliate incorporated in New York filed first, and then the main company filed as a related case. This basic move has allowed many debtors to file in New York over the years—most notably, General Motors in 2009. Judge Lifland took charge of the Eastern case.

Over the course of the next year, Lorenzo and Eastern's creditors would negotiate back and forth over the terms and vision of Eastern's reemergence. This process began in earnest in September 1989, when Eastern made a variety of proposals to its creditors to revitalize the operation: (1) raising $100 million in financial markets, (2) dropping plans to prepay a total of approximately $200 million in debt, and (3) finding a way for Eastern's parent, Texas Air, to

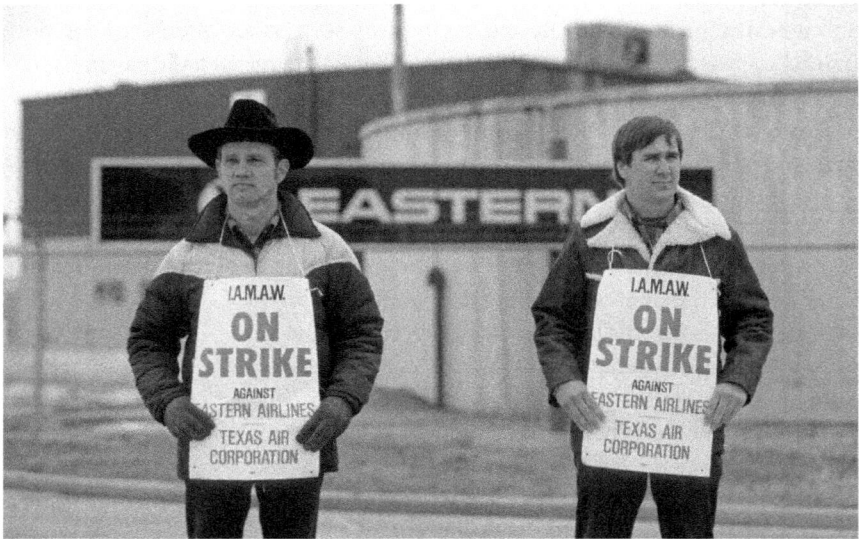

7.3 Eastern Airlines employees on strike in Atlanta, 1989.

ZUMA Press, Inc. / Alamy Stock Photo.

provide all or part of a $99 million payment due Eastern's pension plan on September 15.[87]

This ultimately culminated in a deal struck between Eastern and its creditors a month later, whereby Eastern would sell $1.8 billion in assets and would emerge from bankruptcy law protection at two-thirds of its former size.[88] The plan also would have given creditors a 40 percent equity stake in lieu of some cash payments.[89] This plan was announced in February 1990, almost a year after the strike began.[90]

However, the solace that this new agreement brought would be short lived, as less than a week later, the examiner whom Judge Lifland had previously appointed issued a report indicating that Texas Air had been "cherry picking" Eastern's assets for the benefit of Continental.[91] In response, Eastern's creditors began to threaten to call for the bankruptcy court to liquidate Eastern, especially if Texas Air did not shoulder a larger role in the effort to reorganize it.[92]

Adding to their concerns, Eastern's president announced two days later that the airline expected to lose $330 million that year, which was $185 million more than it had predicted in January—just a few months earlier. Less than a week later, in early April, Eastern's creditors voted against any further withdrawals from Eastern's escrow accounts (which had been funded with proceeds from asset sales) and took the extraordinary step of requesting that Judge Lifland appoint a trustee.[93] In mid-April, the judge appointed Martin Shugrue, a former Continental executive, as Eastern's trustee, wresting control from Lorenzo.[94] Lorenzo would ultimately resign from Eastern later that August.[95]

In some respects, it was Grants all over again, but slower. Eastern's business struggles would continue; even though Eastern had restored two-thirds of its flights and introduced lower fares, the aftermath of the thirteen-month strike had left many travelers reluctant to book with the airline. Eastern would continue to drain its escrow funds until it ultimately ceased operations in late January 1991.[96] Eastern was then able to raise $250 million by selling its airport gates and its fleet of airplanes.[97]

Many subsequent critics would charge that Judge Lifland had been too concerned about the employees and kept Eastern sheltered in chapter 11 too long. A more "efficient" result would have been to lift the debtor's exclusive right to propose a plan earlier (it was automatically lifted once the trustee was appointed) and let the creditors quickly decide the airline's fate.

The *Economist* charged that Eastern was just one example of the reality that "America's bankruptcy laws are too kind to managers."[98] On the other hand, the *Financial Times* argued that "from the beginning, the public's fascination with the strike and bankruptcy at Eastern Airlines has been far greater than the business significance of America's seventh largest air carrier would have appeared to justify."[99] The same might hold for bankruptcy academics as well.

* * *

As my bankruptcy professor noted many years ago (long before I entered law school or gave a care about corporate bankruptcy):

> The issue in the W. T. Grant proceeding was control. There was no trustee because there was, in theory, neither a liquidation nor a reorganization, just a simple debtor-controlled arrangement affecting unsecured creditors . . . The debtor, influenced by creditors, petitioned for the sale of certain assets; once these were sold, the creditors pulled the rug and took the proceeds.
>
> Under the Bankruptcy Code there is no SEC. Nor is there any troublesome question about whether a public company is involved or a trustee should be appointed. The whole move may be swift and sure, and not only perfectly legal but, to all appearances, ethically correct as well.[100]

In short, it is not clear that the enactment of chapter 11 changed all that much, but it did effectively bless the approach that the insiders used in Grants. They no longer had to worry about the SEC, a trustee, or often even the court. They were free to structure the case as they pleased. The New Deal style chapter X was gone, but was the replacement an improvement, or simply a return to the pre–New Deal past?

Chapter 11, as a congressionally enacted statute, obviously was more stable than the old, rickety receivership system. But the two are similar in the sense that they are both extremely flexible and subject to repurposing by any nearby controlling party—Gould and Morgan before, and, as we will see in the coming chapters, private equity firms and distressed debt funds today. The new controllers are perhaps less widely known, but they bend the corporate bankruptcy system just as skillfully as their predecessors.

And nothing in chapter 11 really addresses the basic problem in the Grants case: Debtors still file too late.[101] Modern management does not face being displaced by a trustee, as in chapter X, but they still tend to take on more and more debt in the hope of avoiding bankruptcy. The gamble for revival is always the first move. And management faces little penalty for doing so.

CHAPTER 8

THE ALWAYS EVOLVING CHAPTER 11

The fact that a little western company incorporated in an eastern State can come down to this little eastern State, far removed from any investor interest, and far removed from any local interest, and reorganize, has put the security holders and the investors to a great disadvantage. Furthermore, it has meant that with that choice your reorganizers have been able occasionally to get into courts where the atmosphere is a little more friendly, and where they will not be very closely scrutinized or examined.

—William O. Douglas, 1937

The 1980s ended (and the 1990s commenced) with a slew of academic commentary on chapter 11 and whether it should be replaced by something else. For those steeped in then ascendant law and economics movement, "something else" normally involved some sort of automated bankruptcy process that would bypass the future Judge Liflands. None of the proposals were particularly likely to work in the real world—they all seemed to hinge on improbably simple capital structures, wonderfully rational investors, and frictionless markets.

But chapter 11 itself was already changing by the 1990s. Indeed, given the flexibility of the 1978 statute, even as adulterated by subsequent amendments, it is hardly surprising that it has gone through several waves of change in the nearly fifty years since enactment. Ultimately, the willingness of the bankruptcy judges to accept such adaptations is key to the continued viability of the chapter. But much as with receiverships, which eventually faced a "crackdown" from the US Supreme Court, it is also possible that bankruptcy courts will at some point tolerate too much and awaken the slumbering and distracted legislature or the bankruptcy-shy appellate courts.[1]

Since 1990, about two-thirds of the big cases have filed their chapter 11 petitions in one of three jurisdictions: New York City (including White Plains), Wilmington, or Houston.[2] The last is a new entrant in this market in the last decade; previously, it received only a handful of energy cases.

But as I write this book, Houston's new status is under threat because of a conflict-of-interest scandal that has resulted in the sudden resignation of one of its leading jurists, while New Jersey is making a run to take its place as a favored jurisdiction. The latter is primarily being employed by debtors represented by law firm Kirkland & Ellis; that firm was highly influential in developing Houston as a favored jurisdiction.

Other law firms have since also filed cases in New Jersey, despite their debtors' limited (or recent) connections with the Garden State. A notable example was the Washington State–based fitness company BowFlex (also known as Nautilus), represented by Sidley Austin, which in March 2024 filed for bankruptcy in New Jersey—some 3,000 miles from its headquarters.[3] The filing seemed to be based on the prior filing of a subsidiary—BowFlex New Jersey LLC—which, according to the New Jersey Department of Revenue and Enterprise Services webpage, was formed in February 2024.[4] If that works, American corporate debtors can file pretty much wherever they want.

Even more recently, Intrum AB, a Swedish debt collection company, filed a chapter 11 petition in Houston (more than 5,200 miles from Stockholm), despite having no connections to the United States whatsoever.[5] How? Basically, it embraced the BowFlex model: "Intrum AB of Texas LLC" was formed a few weeks before the bankruptcy petition was filed, and it gratuitously signed on to all its parent company's debts.

The Houston court decided that this was all perfectly fine. So apparently any company, anywhere in the world, can reorganize in Houston, so long as they pay to form a Texas limited liability company (LLC). In short, in modern chapter 11, blatant forum shopping is largely tolerated, at least by the courts that are eager to see the big cases.

Within these favored jurisdictions, the central parties to the reorganizations—namely, the handful of large law firms, financial advisers, and lenders that make frequent appearances—develop techniques that can be exported to the minority of cases that file elsewhere.[6]

Delaware became extremely popular in the 1990s, when it had only one or two bankruptcy judges.[7] These judges would permit attorneys to submit their "first day" motions—in the days of paper filings, these typically filled a thick, black, three-ring binder, with requests ranging from paying employees and customers, to retaining professionals, to entering into bankruptcy financing agreements—in draft form, for the judge's staff to review.[8] The attorneys could then revise them before filing based on the comments received.

Debtor's counsel would then fax notice of a planned filing the next morning to the largest creditors—which, especially if not on the East Coast, faced a scramble to get to the courthouse in time for the subsequent first-day hearing. Some then discovered that Wilmington does not have a public airport—in the dial-up internet era, it sometimes took a while to figure out that Philadelphia International Airport was the nearest. Experienced counsel, especially from New York, would already know the drill—and head to the Metroliner early the next morning.

The Delaware bankruptcy court eventually faced a backlash against many of these tendencies in the early part of this century, and thereafter it adopted more traditional practices, but the jurisdiction has remained popular, in large part because the judges see so many large corporate reorganization cases, as state of incorporation is always a potential place to file. As such, the judges are steeped in the procedures developed by the larger law firms that handle such cases.

The four leading jurisdictions—Delaware, New Jersey, New York, and Houston—received about three-quarters of all large chapter 11 cases in 2024. And the broader reason why all the noted jurisdictions are favored is because the judges therein are seen as more likely to accept a novel use of chapter 11, particularly if they believe that the reorganization in question has widespread support. The difficulties with that widely adopted approach to the judicial role are developed further in subsequent chapters of this book, but for now, we need to understand the story of chapter 11's evolution between 1990 and 2024.

• • •

By the 1990s, creditors had enough experience with chapter 11 in operation that they began to understand how to exercise control of cases. That is, while many commentators continued to complain that chapter 11 was too "debtor friendly," creditors had already taken over. Particularly by the middle of the decade, senior creditors would demand debtors short-circuit their case by selling their assets under section 363 of the Code. Often this demand was made by the prepetition lenders, who became the postpetition lenders by extending new senior money to the company.

The "DIP lenders," as lenders to the debtor in possession are called, would demand that the new (postbankruptcy) loan be used to pay off the old (prebankruptcy) loan to the same lenders. A recent example involved retailer Big Lots, which filed a chapter 11 petition in September 2024. The company obtained a $708 million DIP loan, consisting of a $550 million secured loan that paid off prebankruptcy secured debt and a $157.5 million superpriority credit facility that paid off $122.5 million of preexisting term loans. Overall, the $700 million DIP loan provided just $35 million of new cash to the company. Big Lots expected to close a 363 sale and emerge from bankruptcy by the end of 2024, although its original sale plans fell through, delaying its exit and ultimately leading to its liquidation.[9]

This sort of a roll-up slightly improves the priority of the loans, which go from being not only a secured debt, but also an administrative expense of the bankruptcy. But the real motivation is that administrative expenses must be paid in full under chapter 11 and are not susceptible to being "crammed down."[10] In short, the senior lenders regain the same powerful stature that they had in the Grants case by acting as DIP lenders under a roll-up.

And if the lender put a short timeline on the postpetition lending, it can force a quick sale of the debtor's assets because nothing else is possible in the time allotted or the limited funding provided.[11] On the other hand, if the debtor cannot find a willing buyer, liquidation sometimes became inevitable, again not unlike what happened decades before with Grants. The liquidation of electronics retailer Circuit City in 2009 and the resulting loss of more than 34,000 jobs provide a key example.[12] That Circuit City offered an employee stock purchase plan, while engaging for years in buying back its own stock, made the collapse sting a bit more.

The company listed assets of $3.4 billion and debts of $2.3 billion when it filed its petition. Its DIP loan provided it with just $50 million in new money, and the remainder of the loan rolled up $898 million in prebankruptcy loans in exchange for $30 million in fees.[13] The DIP loans were paid in full as part of the store liquidation process; it was estimated that general unsecured creditors would receive at most 13.5 cents on the dollar.[14] Notably, the liquidation occurred by way of a chapter 11 plan; traditional chapter 7 was never invoked.

More typical is a quick, lender-mandated 363 sale process that turns the bankruptcy estate into a pool of cash.[15] The senior lenders take their cut and exit stage right. Everyone else remains to fight over what's left. During the 2008 financial crisis, 363 sales reached the mainstream of American consciousness when they were used in the Lehman Brothers, General Motors, and Chrysler chapter 11 cases.[16] But, as shown in figure 8.1, these sorts of cases became common in the mid-1990s and have remained common long after the financial crisis.

For example, in 2001, TWA was sold in a 363 sale to American Airlines during the former's third and final bankruptcy case.[17] In the late 1990s, lots of failed roll-ups of various industries were unwound through 363 sales, when the attempt to consolidate a particular industry proved misguided or at least poorly executed. Once the debtor was disaggregated, there was not much left

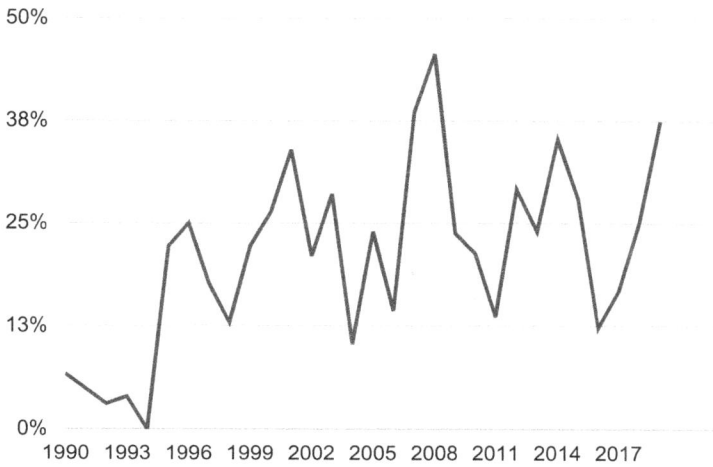

8.1 Section 363 sales as percent of total cases (1990–2020).

Source: Florida-UCLA-LoPucki Bankruptcy Research Database.

to reorganize—just a holding company with lots of debt and few assets beyond some office supplies.

In Lehman, the brokerage business was sold to Barclays during the first week of the case, while the residue of the business was liquidated.[18] In the automotive cases, the "good" assets were sold to buyers that were newly created, which then took over running the business, somewhat like the process used in the railroad receiverships. The DIP lenders in both auto cases were the US and Canadian governments, but they were just as eager as other senior lenders to get their money out of the bankruptcy process, and thus they pushed a speedy timeline.[19]

Chrysler's plans to close 789 dealerships, plus General Motors' plan to likewise prune its dealership network in bankruptcy, meant that while the automakers themselves survived the financial crisis, many small businesses did not. Corporate bankruptcy under chapter 11 continued to favor large players.

• • •

While 363 sales were becoming more common (i.e., after about 1995), cases were also increasingly becoming prenegotiated. These seem to be distinct trends, at least among the public companies in the LoPucki dataset: prenegotiated cases rarely feature 363 sales and vice versa. In part, this may reflect the frequency with which 363 sales are driven by senior lenders, who may be less inclined to worry about lining up a deal with junior creditors. And conversely, many prenegotiated transactions treat senior lenders pretty well, which likely reduces the temptation to seek a 363 sale.

In the early days, many of these deals were memorialized in documents called "lockup agreements." Consider, for example, the following:

> During the first quarter of 2001, a group of holders of Prandium 9-3/4 percent Senior Notes formed an Informal Committee of noteholders and engaged Klee, Tuchin, Bogdanoff & Stern LLP, as counsel. After lengthy negotiations, the Company and the Informal Committee reached an agreement in principle on the terms of a restructuring of Prandium's long term debt. . . .Thereafter, Prandium and the members of the Informal Committee negotiated and entered into a lock-up agreement dated April 1, 2002 (the "Prandium Lockup Agreement"), outlining the terms and provisions of a chapter 11 reorganization plan that the Informal Committee would support.[20]

In this arrangement, the agreement was simply to support a plan, but the plan itself was largely traditional and followed the normal pathways. The large bondholders formed a committee, negotiated a deal with the debtor, which then filed for bankruptcy, and asked the other bondholders if they would like to join the deal.[21] They likely had little practical choice in the matter.

More recently, the same basic concept has been rebranded a "restructuring support agreement (RSA)." Although the new term has been most widely used in the past decade, its first use actually seems to date to a 2004 chapter 11 case involving one of Donald Trump's numerous casino bankruptcies.[22] While both lockups and RSAs bind creditors to support a reorganization, modern RSAs are typically more elaborate and aggressive than the old lockup agreements.

For example, by the 1990s, Guitar Center was the largest seller of musical instruments in the United States (see figure 8.2). In 2007, it was purchased by private equity firm Bain Capital, which naturally borrowed enthusiastically to fund the deal, and Guitar Center was responsible for paying all that debt back. In 2014, the company entered into a debt-to-equity exchange with Ares Management, a private equity investor that specializes in financial distress, who swapped $500 million in debt for preferred stock that gave it a controlling interest in Guitar Center. Bain retained partial ownership of the company, as well as representation on the board. At the same time, Guitar Center refinanced its remaining debt through issuing new senior secured notes and senior unsecured notes, and obtained a new revolving credit facility. In short, it made its capital structure more convoluted in an effort to avoid bankruptcy.

In 2020, the pandemic prompted the company to close its five-hundred-odd locations and furlough about 9,000 of its 13,000 employees, which greatly impaired its ability to service its immense debt load. We will come back to Guitar Center in chapter 9, but for now, the important point is that before it

8.2 A Guitar Center store in Manhattan on October 27, 2020, the day of the company's chapter 11 filing.

NurPhoto SRL / Alamy Stock Photo.

filed for bankruptcy, it had entered into an RSA with key stakeholders, including Ares, new equity investors Brigade Capital Management and the Carlyle Group, and "supermajorities of its noteholder groups." Brigade, Ares, and Carlyle would each own a third of the postreorganization equity.

The RSA set forth specific details of a plan that would be supported by all who signed the agreement. It also provided for the sale of certain securities in the reorganized debtor to specific parties, and for specific parties to provide DIP financing to Guitar Center while it was in bankruptcy. The RSA also included very specific deadlines—or milestones—for when the court would enter specific orders or when the debtor would seek specific relief. Very little was left to chance, and the bankruptcy court was presented with a deal to be approved on a take-it-or-leave-it basis. Somewhere Jay Gould and Isaac Wistar were jealous.

• • •

Further contributing to the changing face of chapter 11, in 2005 the Bankruptcy Code's personal bankruptcy provisions were extensively amended, and various creditor groups used the opportunity to promote their particular interests with regard to the Code's business provisions. Commercial landlords got time limits on the debtor's ability to reject store leases—making it harder for the modern-day Grants to sort through their many leases in a sensible fashion.[23] Either the debtor must conduct substantial prebankruptcy planning, assuming that it has the time to do so, or risk foregoing significant value from beneficial leases.

In a world of precarious brick-and-mortar retail, these issues become even more salient. Aware of these issues, DIP lenders often will structure loans on the supposition that the debtor's inventory will be sold in a going-out-of-business sale, since there is a real risk that the leases will have to be rejected before any sort of reorganization is possible. That in turn means that DIP lenders provide less lending because there is less value to backstopping such lending. While the landlords clearly thought that the new time limit was a good idea back in the 1990s, when they first started lobbying for the provision, it is not clear that is still true today.

And those who still thought of chapter 11 in terms of Eastern Airlines used the 2005 amendments to obtain limits on the bankruptcy court's ability to extend the debtor's exclusive right to propose a plan. As amended, the Code provides that the 120-day period during which the debtor has the exclusive right to file a chapter 11 plan "may not be extended beyond a date that is 18 months" after the petition date. In addition, the 180-day period during which only the debtor may solicit votes for a plan may not be extended beyond twenty months after the filing date—a strange jumble of days and months there. Notably, competing plans are still quite rare, although in part, that is no doubt because so many big cases are prenegotiated.

The biggest change was the vast expansion of the "safe harbors" that apply to derivatives and other financial instruments. A routine supply contract can now be recast as a forward or a swap, and thus immune from the automatic stay and the debtor's power to assume or reject.

This expansion of the safe harbors had big implications in particular for the many LBO-rooted chapter 11 cases. Typically, if the debtor failed soon after the LBO, the payments to the old shareholders might be clawed back as a voidable transfer based on the argument that the debtor company did not receive fair value in the deal. Indeed, it is not clear that a target company gets *any* value for paying off its old shareholders in new debt.[24] What does a corporation care who its shareholders are? But since the advent of the safe harbors, payments to old shareholders are increasingly immune from attack.

The biggest example of this involved the busted LBO of the Tribune Company. A year after its 2007 LBO, in which public shareholders received over $8 billion in payments funded with new debt, Tribune—the owner of the *Chicago Tribune* and the *Los Angeles Times* (figure 8.3), among other key newspapers—filed for bankruptcy.

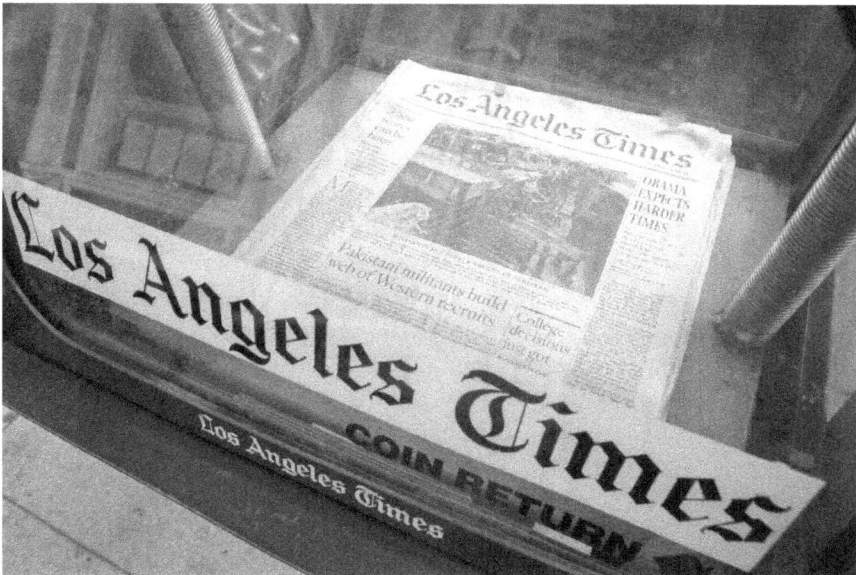

8.3 *Los Angeles Times* offices on the day that its parent company filed its chapter 11 petition.

ZUMA Press, Inc./Alamy Stock Photo.

Section 546(e) of the Bankruptcy Code bars the avoidance of transfers that are made "in connection with a securities contract" and "by or to (or for the benefit of)" a "financial institution." The Second Circuit held that section 546(e)'s requirement that the transfer be "by or to" a financial institution was satisfied because Tribune, as the transferor, itself qualified as a "financial institution" under the statutory definition. This was because the Bankruptcy Code defines a "financial institution" to include not only banks and other entities commonly known as "financial institutions," but also "customers" of such financial institutions when the financial institution is acting as their "agent" in connection with a securities contract.[25]

The Second Circuit held that Tribune qualified as a statutory "financial institution" because Tribune was a "customer" of Computershare Trust Company (the depositary for the LBO), and Computershare acted as Tribune's "agent" in the transaction. None of this analysis was particularly deep—the court, for example, seems to have assumed an agency relationship without much actual evidence that such was the case—but the result was that LBOs may not be challenged as voidable transfers, absent unusual facts where a financial institution is not involved in the closing.

A more recent decision comes to a similar result in a case involving more than $1 billion doled out to shareholders in Sycamore Partners' 2014 buyout of shoe retailer Nine West.[26] So long as the private equity funds do not start paying in cryptocurrency or sacks of gold, almost every LBO will be immune because payments are typically made through a financial institution to and for customers of a financial institution, which seems to be sufficient in the Second Circuit (which importantly includes New York).

Other safe harbors protect derivative transactions. Harvey Miller, representing Lehman in its mammoth bankruptcy case in 2008, felt that the safe harbors had allowed millions of dollars in value to leak out of the estate.[27] And as noted, there are nonderivative supply contracts—especially those that involve commodities—that can easily fall within the safe harbors and thus are immune from assumption, rejection, or the automatic stay.

Every creditor and stakeholder would like to be excused from the effects of a large company's bankruptcy. But only the big players have the ability to achieve such blessings from Congress.

· · ·

As discussed in chapter 7, asbestos maker Johns Manville pioneered the use of "third-party releases" in chapter 11. In that case, the releases mostly went to insurance companies, which wanted to be sure that if they paid the policy limit, or something close to it, into the trust fund, they would not have to pay yet again in parallel litigation. Cases like Drexel Burnham expanded the concept to protect other parties—such as Michael Milken—from their own potential liability in exchange for a contribution to funding the debtor's plan. By doing so, the Drexel Burnham bankruptcy case helped those nondebtor parties get something like a bankruptcy discharge without having to file bankruptcy themselves.

In short, two strands of third-party release cases exist. One is centered around mass torts, the other around releases for related parties within the corporate group for fiduciary duty claims and the like. The mass tort strand obviously has its roots in Manville—and Congress ultimately blessed the Manville approach, albeit in provisions that are expressly limited to asbestos—but other tortfeasors, including Dow Corning (breast implants), several Catholic archdioceses (sexual assault), and the Boy Scouts (sexual assault), have used the same model. Professors Foohey and Odinet argue that the goal of such cases is twofold: "to bypass procedural justice and to shut down discussion of their purported wrongdoings."[28] The Drexel Burnham, or corporate affiliates, line of cases are arguably more prevalent but also more likely to fly under the radar, as the press is likely to examine a case that does not involve large numbers of individual tort victims.[29]

The two strands came together in Purdue Pharma. "Purdue's bankruptcy was occasioned by a health crisis that was, in significant part, of its own making: an explosion of opioid addiction in the United States over the past two decades, which can be traced largely to the over-prescription of highly addictive medications, including, specifically and principally, Purdue's proprietary, OxyContin."[30] Purdue was (and still is for now) owned and controlled by members of the Sackler family. The Sackler family chose White Plains as the venue to file Purdue's chapter 11 case—with nothing more than recently leased office space as a real connection, along with an silly argument that White Plains was actually "kind of" close to its Connecticut headquarters—because it was thought to be a court that would allow them to bind dissenting tort claimants to releases of nondebtor members of the Sackler family, based on prior decisions like *Drexel*.[31]

The US solicitor general, who sought Supreme Court review of the Second Circuit's decision upholding the chapter 11 plan, argued in her brief to the Supreme Court that between 2008 and 2016, Purdue recognized that its insolvency was looming and paid out approximately $11 billion "to the Sackler family member trusts and holding companies" and thus "drained Purdue's total assets by 75 percent." Under the chapter 11 plan, which was approved by Judge Robert D. Drain, whose visage is shown on the banner in figure 8.4, the Sacklers

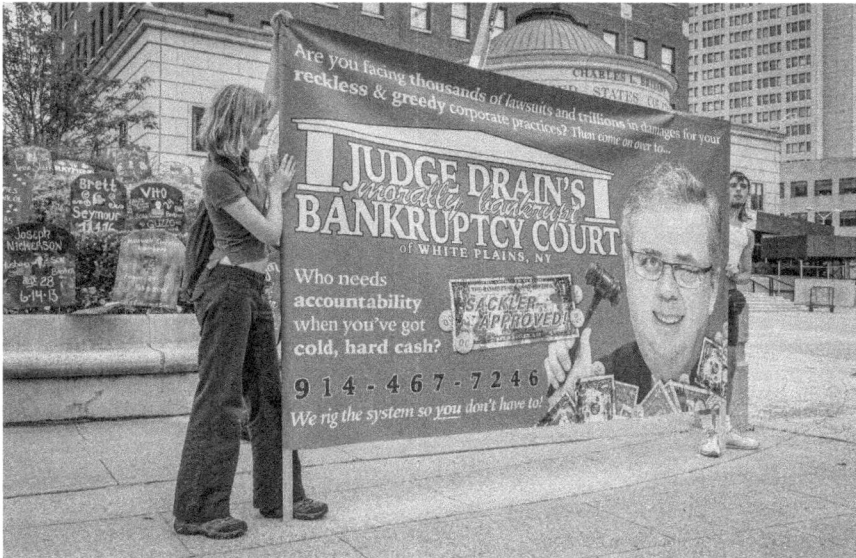

8.4 Protesters outside the White Plains bankruptcy court where the Purdue Pharma case was pending, 2021.

Sipa USA / Alamy Stock Photo.

received a release from all liability in exchange for an (eventual) contribution to the plan of $6 billion.[32] By most estimates, they would still have at least $5 billion after bankruptcy; in short, like Milken before them, they aimed to use the chapter 11 process get a bankruptcy discharge while remaining quite wealthy.

New York District Judge Colleen McMahon reversed the bankruptcy court, and the Second Circuit reversed her. The Second Circuit held that bankruptcy courts have the authority to impose nonconsensual releases of third-party claims in limited circumstances.

The Second Circuit articulated seven factors that courts should consider before imposing such releases: (1) whether there is an identity of interests between the debtors and related third parties; (2) whether claims against the debtor and the third party are intertwined; (3) the scope of the releases; (4) whether the releases are essential to the reorganization's success; (5) the third party's contribution of "substantial assets" to the reorganization; (6) whether the affected claimholder classes "overwhelmingly" support the releases; and (7) whether the plan provides fair payment of the enjoined claims.

Many of the factors are highly subjective—for example, what makes an asset "substantial?"—and the notion of widespread support ignores votes that come in because of a lack of perceived other options, just as the myriad bondholders jumped to "support" plans in receiverships, lest they get left behind in empty corporate shells. Really, the key question is whether third parties can buy a discharge in somebody else's bankruptcy case.

The Supreme Court agreed to consider the case.[33] In late June 2024, the case was finally decided, with the majority stating that "the question we face . . . boils down to whether a court in bankruptcy may effectively extend to *nondebtors* the benefits of a Chapter 11 discharge usually reserved for *debtors*." By a vote of 5–4, the Court answered that question "no."[34]

The majority made clear that their concern was not with claims that belonged in any sense to the company or its bankruptcy estate. Instead, the claims being released belonged to the tort victims, and as such the Bankruptcy Code, including chapter 11, did not and could not address them without express statutory authority. And the majority more generally rejected the notion that chapter 11 existed to solve all problems of failed negotiations among corporate claimants: "Bankruptcy law may serve to address some collective-action problems, but no one (save perhaps the dissent) thinks it provides a bankruptcy court with a roving commission to resolve all such problems that happen its way, blind to the role other mechanisms (legislation, class actions, multi-district litigation, consensual settlements, among others) play in addressing them."

The Court looked back through history and noted that every bankruptcy statute that Congress has ever enacted "from 1800 until 1978, generally reserved the benefits of discharge to the debtor who offered a 'fair and full surrender of [its] property.' Sturges v. Crowninshield, 4 Wheat. 122, 176 (1819)." Conversely, the Supreme Court majority observed that under the plan approved by the bankruptcy court, the owners of the debtor (Purdue) would have received the equivalent of a discharge "without securing the consent of those affected or placing anything approaching their total assets on the table for their creditors."

Consensual third-party releases remain a possibility—and as this book was going to print, the Sacklers upped their offer by over a billion dollars to achieve successful confirmation of a new plan; although about half of that would be held back to pay for the Sacklers' own legal bills, if too many creditors sued outside the plan—but short of that (or congressional action), corporate bankruptcy will no longer provide an out for companies and individuals that happen to be associated with corporate debtors.[35] The Court has shifted the bargaining power, ever so slightly, in favor of the outsiders. And at the same time, the Court also cast some doubt on the common assumption that anything approved by most creditors is always permissible in corporate bankruptcy.

. . .

Of course, these various aspects of change did not instantaneously transform chapter 11. Instead, there was a period from the mid-1990s through at least the 2008 financial crisis where there were a mix of cases. Some followed the new models, while others looked more like those from the 1980s.

Take the 1997 chapter 11 case of Levitz Furniture, which I worked on as a junior attorney representing the debtor.[36] The company had about $1.7 billion in assets and more than 5,000 employees who sold furniture in stores across the country. It also had more than $1 billion in debt and big losses the year before the filing. The company filed a traditional chapter 11 case, with no prepackaged plan or 363 sales. It closed several stores, laid off lots of employees, negotiated a plan, confirmed it, and emerged from bankruptcy about three years later.[37] There was nothing particularly novel about the case.

Or, more recently, Delphi Corporation, an auto parts manufacturer, filed for chapter 11 in New York in 2005.[38] It too filed and negotiated a traditional plan, which was confirmed in 2008.

These sorts of cases underline the gradual nature of chapter 11's evolution. While there was certainly an academic tendency in the early twenty-first century to suggest that "all" chapter 11 cases featured controlling lenders and quick 363 sales, the reality was otherwise.[39] If we refer back to figure 8.1, we see that both Levitz and Delphi happened at a time when 363 sales were frequently in use. But these cases also remind us that 363 sales never represented even most large corporate bankruptcy cases.

That said, it is true that leading up to the 2008 financial crisis, many debtors followed the basic path laid out by Grants: As distress approached, their debt became increasingly secured. Changes in the nonbankruptcy law of security interests at the start of the century allowed lenders to sweep up collateral in a comprehensive fashion that Grants' lenders could have only dreamed of. These changes in turn facilitated the rise of the 363 sale, with lenders using their controlling position to avoid the two or three years that a traditional chapter 11 case might take in that era.

But after Lehman's collapse, interest rates were low and lending was free and easy, and senior lenders no longer had obvious ways to exercise power over distressed companies. At the same time, the free flow of credit meant that private equity firms were snatching up companies like never before, since funding for LBOs was widely available. That in turn leads to current-day chapter 11, with all its problems and complications.

PART IV

REFORM?

CHAPTER 9

MODERN CHAPTER 11 AND THE GHOSTS OF THE PAST

The personal objectives of reorganizers are significant chiefly in terms of control of the reorganization. The emoluments of control are the stakes of reorganization. Control means profits and protection. Managements and bankers seek perpetuation of that control for the business patronage it commands, which they may take for themselves or allot to others, as they will. They seek, also, to perpetuate that control in order to stifle careful scrutiny of the past history of the corporation.

—Securities and Exchange Commission, 1937

resent-day chapter 11 is a strange place, where it seems that most anything goes, so long as it is packaged in an RSA outwardly supported by most creditors. Further confounding the situation is the reality that the more often courts accept the deal placed before them, the less likely creditors are to object, since doing so will be seen as throwing good money after bad. What is the point of funding an objection if the court is going to approve the plan anyway? That in turn shrinks the size of the objector pool and pumps up the numbers who "consent," all the while telling us very little about what is actually going on in the case.

In 2023, something like 27 percent of large chapter 11 cases featured RSAs that stage-managed the case before the process was begun.[1] And even those without an RSA featured more than their fair share of shenanigans, largely because of their heavy debt loads and sophisticated creditors, particularly private funds, holding key parts of that debt. Smaller investors—even smaller institutional investors—are increasingly left on the sidelines. As one debt investor recently observed, "If you don't own hundreds of millions of bonds, you're going to be left outside the big boy table in terms of negotiations."[2]

And courts play the role of the ineffectual parent—threatening consequences that never (or at least rarely) seem to occur.[3]

• • •

Yellow Corp., which since the dawn of the twenty-first century was attempting to roll up the legacy (i.e., prederegulation) less-than-truckload (LTL) shipping market, provides a recent exemplar of modern chapter 11 dynamics, even without an RSA. In August 2023, it shut down and filed for chapter 11 to liquidate (figure 9.1), despite evidently being solvent and thus quite able to pay its creditors.[4] Its problem: It could not get along with the Teamsters, which represented Yellow's 22,000 unionized workers (out of 30,000 total).[5]

The chapter 11 filing came just three years after Yellow received $700 million in pandemic-era loans from the federal government under the CARES

9.1 Yellow Corp. trucks parked at a terminal in Orlando, August 2023, after the chapter 11 filing.

Sipa USA / Alamy Stock Photo.

Act. Echoes of MoPac and the Van Sweringens surrounded the transaction, as the company owed large amounts of debt to a lender group led by Apollo, and the CARES Act loans were supposed to go only to companies that needed to be supported during the pandemic because of their importance to national security. Apollo had strong ties to President Donald Trump's administration, including loans to the Kushner Companies, while Yellow's chief executive served on the administration's coronavirus economic task force. US Defense Department staff recommended that the loan be denied, but a June 2020 call between Treasury Secretary Steve Mnuchin and Defense Secretary Mark Esper led to the loan being approved nonetheless.[6]

Yellow had about $1.5 billion of outstanding debt when it filed for bankruptcy. While immediately after deregulation the new nonunion LTL carriers started with an obvious cost advantage, repeated concessions by the union helped close much of the gap between Yellow and those firms. More recently, a shortage of drivers nationally, which helped lift wages at the nonunion carriers, also improved Yellow's situation.

Yellow operated for years with each of its many acquisitions remaining a separate brand under the parent company. Indeed, as of late 2023, its webpage still trumpeted its many brands: "As the holding company for a portfolio of proven trucking brands that include Holland, New Penn, Reddaway and YRC Freight, Yellow operates one of the largest, most comprehensive logistics and less-than-truckload (LTL) networks in North America, with local, regional, national and international capabilities."[7] That some of these companies were in competition with each other might resurface memories of the Richmond Terminal.

Nevertheless, Yellow continued to limp along with a massive debt load, borrowing more and more rather than taking the obvious step of entering chapter 11. Just as companies filed too late under chapter X, they continue to file too late under chapter 11.

In the summer of 2023, Yellow missed payments to union pension and health insurance funds, bringing on a threat from the Teamsters that they would go on strike on July 24. At the eleventh hour, the union agreed to keep working and to give Yellow another month to make the payments.

When it filed for chapter 11 and decided to liquidate, Yellow blamed it all on the union, which Yellow had sued in federal court—that $1.5 billion of debt apparently was *not* an issue.[8] Undoubtedly, the donnybrook with the union did little to inspire customer confidence, but Yellow somehow found a way to pay bonuses totaling about $4.6 million to executives in the weeks before the bankruptcy filing.[9]

Meanwhile, Apollo was adapting the J. P. Morgan "community of interest" playbook for the new century. It offered a $643 million DIP loan—quite something for a liquidation. But only $142.5 million of that was new money; the rest was a payoff of Apollo's entire prepetition loan, which would have given it an effective veto over any plan that did not pay it in full. Arguably, a roll-up should be rejected out of hand in a liquidation case.

The proposed loan came with a healthy 17 percent interest rate, a $7.125 million closing fee, and another variable fee that could reach as high as $25 million, for total fees of as much as $32 million. The DIP loan also provided that Yellow would get the court to approve rules for its auction within ten days of filing for bankruptcy, with Apollo given the right to vet those rules, and the DIP loan would last only ninety days, or just long enough to sell and not think about any real sort of reorganization (or investigation of Apollo).

This loan highlights the reality that Apollo, although largely known as a private equity house, is much more of a lender these days—with nearly $500 billion of loans outstanding.[10] But it continues to sponsor private equity funds as well. In short, it wears just as many hats as J. P. Morgan did a century before.

The proposed loan was so clearly rewarding that several other would-be lenders jumped in to offer better terms. Apollo, seeing its opportunity slipping away, sold out (reportedly at par) to Citadel Credit Master Fund LLC, which teamed up with a Boston-based hedge fund that owned about 40 percent of Yellow's common shares, to provide a $212 million DIP loan. The shareholders' role as DIP lender will provide strong power in the ongoing liquidation sales.

But in no case will those 30,000 workers be getting their jobs back—reportedly many of the drivers have found new, nonunion employment, which is certainly better than nothing but obviously not quite the same. The real estate has already sold for about $1.9 billion, and in early 2024, the bankruptcy judge approved a $82.9 million sale of twenty-three shipping centers to six other trucking companies. The company has already managed to pay off several of its senior creditors, including the US government.

There is an unsecured creditors' committee made up of nine creditors, including the Teamsters and the Central States Pension Fund. The ultimate size of the union claims is key to the whole case, given the backstory here.[11]

Having laid off most of their employees, save for a few well-bonused executives, Yellow then decided that it was unable to maintain and eventually sell its large fleet of trucks—about 12,000 cabs and more than twice as many trailers. So the debtor has hired professional liquidators to take over the task.[12] The liquidators agreed to take a sliding percentage, which ramped up with the size of the sale proceeds. Somewhere Sam Nassi is smiling.

Yellow is being run in bankruptcy by the inevitable "chief restructuring officer," lest anyone get the idea that a trustee might be appropriate for a company that has plainly stated that it will not reorganize.[13] In this context, the "chief restructuring officer" title is a bit odd—"I'm the chief restructuring officer in charge of liquidation. Please don't call me a trustee."

Of course, the whole case is odd since in a world of rational actors—that is, the world that most corporate reorganization theory resides in—an apparently solvent company would not file for bankruptcy simply because management and union representatives are unable to speak civilly to one another. In March 2024, the company's share price was about $5.35—in a liquidation case.

As one commentator observed: "The stock of a small-cap trucking company is just a boring stock, but the stock of a bankrupt company is an absurd lottery ticket, and that is just more fun. Yellow went from being a boring stock that had lost value to being a silly stock that has gone up, and that's how modern finance works, I guess."[14] The attraction of the stock noticeably faded in September 2024, when the bankruptcy court refused to knock out a pension claim that may ultimately exceed $6.5 billion.[15] Then, in November, the judge agreed to reconsider his ruling, leaving the entire issue in flux.[16]

. . .

As discussed in earlier chapters, an increasing number of the modern chapter 11 debtors are wholly owned by private equity firms—or more precisely, funds managed by private equity firms. Companies owned by private equity firms are different creatures, inasmuch as they have a single shareholder rather than the vague mass of shareholders that own most public companies. As *the* shareholder, a private equity fund also has strong incentives to stay as far from the absolute priority rule as possible. Not only does liquidation cut off the equity interest itself, but it also cuts off the management fees that portfolio companies pay to their private equity owners. Section 363 sales are particularly unattractive since the postsale process looks a lot like a standard liquidation.

As such, private equity–owned debtors—I will call them PODs for short—typically take one of two approaches to financial distress. First, whenever possible, they attempt to reorganize outside of chapter 11, where the absolute priority rule can be held safely at bay.[17] Second, when chapter 11 becomes inevitable, PODs have strong incentives to ensure a highly structured process that reduces the risk of loss of control by making the plan "consensual," and thus not subject to the absolute priority rule under modern chapter 11. In many respects, PODs, and their private equity "sponsors," will act much as Jay Gould or J. P Morgan did a century ago, deferring to those with power and ignoring those without.

In October 2006, Harrah's Entertainment Inc. (later renamed Caesars Entertainment Corporation) was the subject of a takeover offer from the previously noted private equity firms Apollo and TPG. These sponsors contributed $6 billion of their own capital—of which the two lead investors actually put in only $1.325 billion each, the remainder came from outside coinvestors—and then added $19.5 billion of debt to Caesars' existing $4.5 billion of debt.[18] All of this happened just in time for the 2008 financial crisis.

Frumes and Indap's *The Caesars Palace Coup*—in many ways the twenty-first-century counterpart to Max Lowenthal's *The Investor Pays*—recounts

Apollo and TPG's machinations in the months leading up to the very contin-uous bankruptcy, as well as the story of the case itself. In short, the sponsors shifted assets to other entities, paid certain large creditors who could thwart their plans, and promoted an RSA to confirm a chapter 11 plan that would have allowed them to retain ownership and obtain releases for their prior behavior. It is likely only because they pushed matters so far, and the case somehow ended up in Chicago rather than one of the favored jurisdictions that might have rushed it through, that Apollo and TPG were ultimately called to account.[19] An examiner found "assets were removed from [Caesars] to the detriment of [Cae-sars] and its creditors," and suggested billions of dollars of potential liability.[20] Junior creditors were ultimately paid about two-thirds of their claims, while everyone above them was paid in full.

In many respects, Caesars was a crude predecessor to the POD cases of today, which feature a simple two-step process: liability management exer-cise (LME) followed by RSA. An RSA, as we have already noted, is a deal between a group of creditors and a debtor (or, more realistically, the debtor's owners). LMEs are also sometimes called "liability management transac-tions (LMTs)."

Such a transaction is a prebankruptcy maneuver allegedly designed to gain "runway," or time to consider the debtor's options, but most often it is just used to set up a subsequent chapter 11 case in a way that benefits the debtor's private equity owner and some select group of creditors working with the sponsors. In 2023, one bond rating agency counted more than forty-five LME transactions, with more than twenty in the first half of 2024.[21]

These LMEs can take a variety of forms. The two most common are the following:

- Debt exchanges where the borrower issues additional debt to an existing lender that is senior to existing debt of the same class (up-tiering)
- Transfers key assets to a new subsidiary, which can take on additional debt (drop-down financing)

What an LME is really about is pitting one group of creditors against another and then favoring the winner that provides new, low-risk financing to the debtor in exchange for favorable treatment of all their claims (pre- and post-LME/LMT).

The same rating agency wrote that "LMTs generally constitute or delay issuer defaults rather than prevent them and can materially lower first-lien recoveries . . . issuers undertaking LMTs before bankruptcy showed lower par-weighted recoveries for first-lien debt than those who did not. The weighted average recovery for issuers that either emerged or were expected to emerge in 2024 after conducting an LMT is 23 percent, compared to 53 percent for those who had not conducted an LMT."[22]

For example, in the much-debated Serta Simmons Bedding LME, Serta and some of its lenders entered into an up-tier transaction, with those lenders providing new first-tier superpriority debt and exchanging their existing first- and second-lien debt for second-tier superpriority debt. The $814 million of old first-lien lenders who did not participate in the LME went from being at the top of the capital structure to somewhere near the bottom, despite still holding first-lien debt, because both tiers of superpriority debt was now ahead of them. The transaction provided Serta with an additional $200 million in liquidity, but Serta ultimately filed for bankruptcy nonetheless.

Even more recently, movie theater chain AMC announced plans to seek a new loan by moving collateral, including 175 theaters and intellectual property including its brand name, out of the reach of existing creditors. It stated that this "drop-down" deal will help it avoid bankruptcy, but the ultimate aims may be simply to protect favored creditors in a future chapter 11 case.[23] When some creditors sued, the movie theater chain ultimately reached a deal to dismiss the litigation in exchange for new money from the settling creditors.[24]

In 2024, there were at least fifty LMEs among major companies.[25]

• • •

A POD can bake the terms of the LME transaction into an RSA, often with a supportive DIP loan agreement, which gives the participating creditors control over the subsequent chapter 11 case. The bankruptcy court is left with the unpalatable choice of either upending this deal—and unleashing a maelstrom of litigation—or swallowing hard and accepting it. In most recent cases, the latter course has been preferred.

Of course, rejiggering the capital structure to either avoid chapter 11 or preordain a particular result tends to lead to extreme capital structure complexity on top of the already extreme complexity that exists in most PODs because of their LBO. From the PODs' perspective, that might not be a bad thing, in that it will make it harder for outsiders, like the financial press, noisy bankruptcy professors, or even bankruptcy courts, to follow what is ultimately happening in a reorganization; and the big players can then do what they want, without any pesky "law" getting in their way.

Consider, for example, Neiman Marcus (figure 9.2). In 2013, Ares and the Canada Pension Plan Investment Board acquired Neiman's in a $6 billion LBO that replaced debt from an earlier LBO in 2005. The two investors put in about $1 billion and borrowed the rest. The retailer struggled for the next several years under its massive debt load. And then came the pandemic.[26]

By the time Neiman's filed its chapter 11 petition in May 2020—in Houston, despite its historic association with Dallas—it had a $900 million senior secured revolving credit facility, a $100 million last-out term loan facility, a $2.3 *billion*

9.2 Shoppers line up outside the closing Neiman Marcus store in Hudson Yards in New York on Saturday, August 29, 2020.

Richard Levine / Alamy Stock Photo.

senior secured term loan facility, $561.7 million in second-lien notes, $730.5 million in senior secured 8 percent third-lien notes, $497.8 million 8.75 percent third-lien notes, $80.7 million 8 percent senior cash pay notes, $56.6 million unsecured pay-in-kind (PIK) toggle notes, and $125 million senior debentures.[27] The PIK toggle feature means that the debtor gets to choose whether to pay coupons in cash or further debt—"toggling" between the options until maturity of the debt. In many ways, this is the modern version of the income bonds that were common in railroad receiverships.

The company ultimately signed an RSA with 78 percent of their first-lien lenders, 99 percent of second-lien lenders, 70 percent of third-lien lenders, 78 percent of debentures, and 100 percent of the equity ownership (both shareholders).[28] The RSA featured a DIP loan provided by select term loan lenders, which then were able to obtain:

- A DIP backstop fee equal to about 1.5 percent of the new equity
- A DIP exit fee equal to about 3.3 percent of the new equity
- A backstop fee that totaled $11.3 million in cash
- An exit term loan participation fee equal to 30 percent of Neiman Marcus postreorganization equity, "payable ratably to each 2019 Term Loan Lender,

2013 Term Loan Lender, 2028 Debenture Holder, Second Lien Noteholder, and/or Third Lien Noteholder who participates in the Exit Facility, based on such party's commitment percentage to fund the Exit Facility."

This was in addition to what these creditor-lenders would get on their claims—the term loan holders were already getting more than 87 percent of the equity of the reorganized company under the plan before dilution by the items listed here.

For the two largest term loan holders—Pacific Investment Management Co. (PIMCO) and Davidson Kempner Capital Management—the various DIP fees were substantial additional recoveries on their claims, given in exchange for providing a DIP loan that already featured a floating interest rate equal to an index *plus* 11–12 percent and very strong protections under the Bankruptcy Code. In short, a low-risk, high-return loan even before considering all of the equity handed out to the lenders.

The plan essentially gave the company to two senior creditors—PIMCO and Davidson Kempner—in a very convoluted way, gave its former owners a pass on anything that they had done wrong in the past, and left everyone else with little or no recovery. The plan was on track for a swift confirmation until the creditors' committee alleged that Ares had previously looted Neiman of key assets.

· · ·

The Neiman Marcus case is but one illustration of how the growth of PODs in recent years has encouraged the use of highly complex RSAs that structure a case in a way that is agreeable to the private equity fund owners and their more sophisticated creditors. A case that is controlled by the terms of an RSA is a case where the powerful creditors, who get a say in the drafting of the RSA, and the large equity holders run the show. This is part of a larger trend that Melissa Jacoby has termed "bankruptcy à la carte," which "extracts the tools of Chapter 11 meant to be available only as part of a package deal and redistributes the benefits."[29] In short, 1885 all over again.[30]

The new reality allows large creditors to obtain a greater recovery than those in their own class. For example, in Nieman Marcus, those creditors who backstopped the DIP Loan got a backstop fee that other senior lenders did not. In theory, this fee was to compensate those lenders that promise to take up parts of the DIP loan that other senior creditors refuse to fund. But given the economics of the loan and its attractiveness even without the fee, the backstop fee could and should be considered additional return to a subset of the senior lenders. What institutional creditor in 2020 (when base interest rates fell to zero during the pandemic) was going to turn down a hefty, double-digit yield on an almost risk-free loan?

Other RSAs provide even more flagrant examples.[31] Bankruptcy Code section 1123(a)(4) provides that "a plan shall . . . provide the same treatment for each claim or interest of a particular class."[32] Nevertheless, modern chapter 11 cases routinely involve plans in which certain bondholders (those that sign the RSA) get a better recovery than those that do not.

Peabody Energy Corporation is the most notorious example of the end run around 1124(a)(4), although the role of the backstop fees is often missed by commentators, who focus on other outrages. In 2016, Peabody was the world's largest private-sector coal company, but it was weighed down by debt from its poorly timed $5.2 billion acquisition of Macarthur Coal of Australia in 2011.[33] After filing for chapter 11, the company commenced an adversarial proceeding to resolve a prepetition dispute between the secured and senior-unsecured creditors over the scope of the secured creditors' liens. The court sent the parties to mediation—how one "mediates" the interpretation of a contract is a head-scratcher—and the mediation produced an RSA.

As of the petition date, Peabody had approximately $4.3 billion of secured obligations and $4.5 billion in unsecured indebtedness. The plan agreed to as part of the RSA included, among other things, a $1.5 billion equity sale through a $750 million rights offering of common stock and $750 million private placement that involved an exclusive sale of discounted preferred stock to "qualifying" creditors, initially defined to mean those creditors that signed the RSA.

The private placement of the preferred stock was contentious, especially given that the first version of this offering represented little more than a flagrant attempt by the plan proponents to grab most of the debtor's preferred equity (and the benefits that went with it) despite holding only 40 percent of the debt in the relevant class. Eventually, the plan was revised such that these holders were given the right to purchase the first 22.5 percent of preferred shares, other creditors that signed on shortly thereafter would share the next 5 percent of the preferred shares with the original creditors, and those creditors that signed on still later in the process were permitted to join the other participating noteholders to purchase their pro rata share of the remaining 72.5 percent of preferred equity. Note that the original creditors were still given quite favorable treatment, getting the exclusive right to 22.5 percent of the preferred shares and then participating pro rata in the next two rounds of shares as well.

The preferred shares were offered at a 35 percent discount to the reorganized debtor's value as stated in the plan, and shares purchased through this mechanism were in addition to the recoveries that creditors would receive under the plan.[34] The discriminatory nature of the offer has been the subject of much comment.

But of equal import and interest is that the creditors that bought the preferred shares also agreed to backstop the common stock offering. That is, if any of the common shares went unsold, the creditors that signed on to the preferred share offer would have to buy the common shares as well. The creditors received a fee for providing this backstop, equal to about 8 percent of the reorganized Peabody's equity.

Because securities in these chapter 11 rights offerings are typically presented at a substantial discount of the value attributed to the reorganized debtor in the plan, there would seem to be minimal risk that the backstop will ever be used in most cases. And logically, the greater the discount to plan value being offered to rights offering investors, the lower the backstop fee should be. Said another way, the backstop fee is to pay for the degree of risk that a "backstopper" is taking, and a backstop fee makes no sense unlinked from the degree of risk (i.e., the magnitude of the plan value discount).

The Peabody plan provided for exit financing commitments of $1.5 billion in new money: $750 million to be raised through the private placement of preferred equity, as noted, sold at a 35 percent discount to the agreed-upon debtor value in the plan, and $750 million to be raised through the offering of common stock sold at a 45 percent discount to the agreed-upon value in the plan. Nevertheless, Peabody paid a standard backstop fee despite the apparent low risk that a backstop would come into play in its case.

Then consider that the Peabody plan proponents received an outsized portion of the backstop fee because they ensured that they would receive more of the preferred shares than anyone else. Indeed, one law firm has estimated that the proponents ended up with about two-thirds of the preferred shares—and thus two-thirds of the backstop fee—when all was said and done. And we might also note that a 40 percent stake in a single class of debt is just about the right amount to give creditors a veto over confirmation of a chapter 11 plan—which requires approval of two-thirds of creditors (by number).

Overpaying for a backstop that will never likely be used is one obvious way of bypassing the intraclass equity requirement of section 1124(a)(4). But as the Eighth Circuit observed, the caselaw is well developed that unequal payments, based on factors outside of membership in the class, are no problem at all.[35] The court was unwilling to consider whether this caselaw made any sense.

Shortly after the Peabody plan was confirmed, Reuters wrote that Elliot Associates, a well-known hedge fund, "gained roughly 25 percent of Peabody—the world's largest private sector coal producer—through stock offerings at discounts between 35 percent and 45 percent. The stock is trading more than double the offering price."[36]

Return as well to the case of Guitar Center, noted in chapter 8. In a pre-bankruptcy maneuver, it had one class of noteholders make an interest payment in exchange for a new class of "superpriority secured notes," which got a lien that surpassed the old secured notes' liens while also carrying a hefty 10 percent coupon and very nice treatment under the company's subsequent bankruptcy plan.

Moreover, the lenders under the "superpriority secured notes" were given the exclusive rights to provide a term DIP loan to Guitar Center. Under the RSA, that DIP loan was also to be paid in full upon plan confirmation. The opportunity to provide new money is itself a valuable right, which in this case was conferred on a subset of the broader noteholder class with no market test. In short, by the time the debtor made it to bankruptcy, the Code's equal treatment norm was already violated. The inevitable reply, that the extra return to favored creditors comes not from their existing claim but from the provision of new money, rings hollow when the chance to provide that new money was limited to the select class in the first instance.

Indeed, recall that Jay Gould's Missouri Pacific got the upper hand in the Texas and Pacific reorganization by paying bond coupons as they came due, and then also that the superpriority secured notes were created to reflect the privileged bondholders' payment of Guitar Center's bond coupons on the eve of its chapter 11. Some things never change.

• • •

The growth of PODs also suggests that debtors will increasingly file too late, which as noted is a problem with chapter 11 generally, but this is apt to be pushed to an extreme in the private equity case. Namely, because PODs shun bankruptcy, there will be a tendency to try to avoid filing, even if doing so inflicts real damage on the operating business. In this respect, we see a return to Grants (discussed in chapter 6), where maintenance of the business is deferred to facilitate debt payments. By the time the company actually enters bankruptcy, it may have alienated customers or otherwise harmed the business beyond repair. For example, Caesars customers complained about slow check-ins, long lines, and bad service after the LBO, when hundreds of supposedly "redundant" positions were eliminated.[37] Prioritization of debt payments over customer service is but one obvious drawback of the private equity model.

In an even more keen example, on September 18, 2017, Toys "R" Us, Inc. and twenty-four affiliated debtors each filed a voluntary petition for relief under chapter 11 in the United States Bankruptcy Court for the Eastern District of Virginia (Richmond Division).[38] At the same time, the Canadian subsidiary commenced parallel proceedings under the Companies' Creditors Arrangement Act in the Ontario Superior Court of Justice. Toys "R" Us was based in New Jersey—indeed, according to Moody's, the taxes that it paid represented about 2.5 percent of the budget of Wayne, New Jersey—but this was during a period when Richmond was making an attempt to challenge the other leading chapter 11 jurisdictions of choice, so it became especially popular for retail debtors.

Toys "R" Us had been making more than $450 million in interest payments on its debt every year, the result of its $6.6 billion LBO in 2005.[39] Its operating income in 2017 just about equaled its debt payments—leaving no margin to actually run the business.[40] These interest payments were in addition to the millions in dividends and management fees that the company paid to its new owners: Bain Capital, KKR & Co., and Vornado Realty—the latter is a REIT, the other two private equity firms. One estimate put payments to the three owners at more than $450 million during the thirteen years that they controlled Toys "R" Us.[41]

When it filed for bankruptcy, Toys "R" Us pointed to the usual suspects in any modern retail case: Amazon, Walmart, and Target.[42] But the *Financial Times* argued that "the blame is perhaps to be placed most squarely on its private equity ownership."[43] As one retail industry publication noted:

> The retailer, especially after its 2005 leveraged buyout, continually under-invested in its business and employees, according to current and former employees.
>
> Stores went without maintenance. Dust collected on the floors and rafters as cleaning services were cut back. Employees grappled with expanding work loads. Knowledgeable staff were let go in cost-cutting campaigns. Key customer satisfaction metrics were fudged. Shrink increased. Key IT systems failed at the worst times.[44]

Its own CEO admitted in SEC reports that Toys "R" Us had fallen behind "on various fronts, including with regard to general upkeep and the condition of our stores," language that he would repeat verbatim in the bankruptcy filing.[45]

"The company eliminated positions, loading responsibilities onto other workers. Schedules became unpredictable. Employees had to pay more for fewer benefits."[46] The heavy debt load also left the company unable to develop its online presence.

Toys "R" Us had 866 stores in the United States and more than 750 international stores. Upon filing, the company immediately announced a round of store closings, and more rounds of closings followed.[47]

The CEO announced his plan for a "new" Toys "R" Us, which included investing $65 million in its stores. Among other things, the company hoped to add playrooms where kids could try out toys and spaces for birthday parties. The company also said that it would spend $72 million from 2018 to 2021 to raise wages and to reward and keep its best employees. Somewhat unusually, these initiatives were to be funded with a DIP loan.[48]

As with most PODs, the corporate and capital structure of Toys "R" Us was a mess: The stores had been split into separate real estate finance arms, and the company's more than $5 billion debt was made of fifteen different credit instruments, many with liens on various bits of the company's assets.[49] In many respects, the PODs are like the old railroads, with the corporate structure sliced and diced to support the claims of myriad creditors.

At the first day hearing in the chapter 11 case, the debtors announced that they had secured over $3.1 billion in three separate debtor-in-possession financing facilities. The most senior piece of the DIP loan was nominally $2.3 billion, but it provided only $170 million of new money, the remainder being a rollover of the prebankruptcy senior loan. The middle layer was a $450 million DIP loan funded by an ad hoc group holding about half of the prepetition Term Loan B-4, who were willing to consensually prime their prepetition liens. This group was ultimately made up of funds managed by Oaktree Capital Management, L.P.; Angelo, Gordon & Co., L.P.; Franklin Mutual Advisers, LLC; Highland Capital Management, LP; and Solus Alternative Asset Management LP.[50]

Solus, a distressed debt investor, would be the public face of this group that would play a key role in the case. Franklin had the biggest stake in the DIP loan ($99.7 million) of the group, but Solus had the biggest stake in the underlying B-4 loan ($221 million), apparently as the result of postbankruptcy purchases.[51] The B-4 lenders had a lien on the Toys "R" Us intellectual property: the logo with the vaguely Cyrillic spelling, the giraffe, the earworm of a theme song, and whatnot.

The 2017 holiday sales came in well below even the worst estimates, producing earnings approximately $250 million below the DIP budget.[52] A retail trade publication reported that "Toys R Us consistently priced higher than key competitors, according to data shared with *Retail Dive* at the time, and its price matching strategy was out of step with modern practices. Meanwhile, many customers avoided purchasing the retailer's giftcards following its Chapter 11 filing, lawyers said in court later. Making matters even worse, years of underinvestment in IT systems led to numerous operational flubs, leaving many customers furious after orders they purchased online shipped late or not at all."[53] More store closings were quickly announced.

Toys 'R' Us reached a deal with another private equity firm, Sycamore Partners, to reorganize around 400 US stores.[54] But the B-4 lenders determined that the best way to maximize their recoveries was to liquidate all the debtors' remaining US stores and begin a wind-down of the operations.

Forty-two years after the banks made a similar decision in the Grants case, the B-4 lenders decided to stop funding Toys "R" Us. They held a critical piece of secured debt with a face value of $668 million—a small chunk of the more than $5 billion outstanding—and consistently stated that they "were exercising their rights as creditors and their duties to generate returns to their investors."[55]

Some 33,000 workers lost their jobs. And suppliers felt that they had been used to build up the recoveries of senior creditors. For example, Toys "R" Us owed Crayola nearly $2 million for goods shipped since the start of 2018, and those goods would be sold off in the liquidation as "inventory," to the benefit of senior creditors. Basic Fun Inc., maker of Lincoln Logs and other classic toys, would file its own chapter 11 case in 2024, noting $6 million in unpaid Toys "R"

9.3 A Toys "R" Us store in Dublin, California, during a going-out-of-business sale, April 21, 2018.

Sheila Fitzgerald / Shutterstock.

Us invoices. The trade creditors would ultimately receive about $180 million, with a chance for more depending on senior creditor recoveries, on $800 million in unpaid invoices.

As with Grants, Toys "R" Us is on some level the story of too much debt, addressed too late. But unlike Grants, once it went through its LBO, Toys "R" Us was always meant to have its heavy-duty debt load, and it seems unlikely that its owners, which ultimately controlled its governance, would have ever decided to reorganize earlier. After all, reorganization meant likely loss of investment unless the creditors could be corralled into an extremely favorable RSA. Perhaps that might have happened earlier, especially if the owners had been willing to put in new money, but it seems that there was little drive to revamp the company before it failed. Perhaps the flow of dividends and fees from Toys "R" Us was "good enough."

Faced with a tremendous public backlash generated by the failure of employees to receive promised severance benefits, KKR and Bain ultimately made a small token payment of $2 million (out of total claims of $75 million) to the employees. The funds also set up a $20 million hardship fund for former employees. "Solus and Angelo, Gordon & Co. . . . have said they recognize the hardship on the laid-off workers, but they don't believe they are responsible for the retailer's liquidation or for helping to fund workers' severance benefits."[56]

The settlement came as Kirkland and Ellis, which represented Toys "R" Us in the chapter 11 case, was awarded $56 million in legal fees. Kirkland had represented Bain in the initial acquisition of the company. As with J. P. Morgan and Kuhn, Loeb & Co., reorganization remains highly lucrative for those that control the process.

• • •

The outer extremes to which the modern chapter 11 process can be stretched is well illustrated by Belk, Inc.'s bankruptcy, which Professor LoPucki has termed "lawless."[57] The clothing retail company filed chapter 11 on February 23, 2021 with fourteen affiliated debtors in the Southern District of Texas (Houston). Twenty hours later, it was out of bankruptcy.

The company's CFO stressed the urgency of the situation, saying that "absent confirmation today, the entire enterprise will be at risk, threatening severe damage to the business, the loss of approximately 17,000 jobs, the closing of 291 stores, and the disappearance of a value maximizing—and fully consensual—restructuring."[58] But to paraphrase Dylan Thomas, the bankruptcy papers address every issue about the case, except "why?" Why did so much turn on the case getting out of bankruptcy on the very day that it started? The RSA required confirmation in a single day, but nowhere do the court papers indicate who or what had demanded this, or why it was so important.

The CFO's declaration in support of the bankruptcy filing contains perhaps two arguments in favor of a speedy chapter 11 case: First, the company had arranged no DIP financing; and second, nearly everybody affected by the plan supported it. The first point was entirely self-created, and the second was entirely vacuous. If everyone supported the plan, then why would the case need to go so fast? There is still no answer there. And in a move reminiscent of the receivership days, when the plaintiff's name would be filled in later, the CFO's declaration contains all the support for the standard chapter 11 "first day" motions in an appendix, which presumably could be attached to anyone's declaration as needed.

The CFO's declaration also devotes but one sentence to the 2015 LBO.[59] In December of that year, Sycamore Partners bought the company for about $3 billion. The debt included about $1.8 billion in the form of a first-lien loan, a $800 million revolving credit facility, and $600 million as a second-lien term loan. The senior debt was largely funded by traditional financial institutions—Credit Suisse, Deutsche Bank, Jefferies, Nomura, Royal Bank of Canada, Wells

Fargo, and Morgan Stanley—while the second-lien debt was taken by GSO Capital, an affiliate of the Blackstone Group. Just nine months after the LBO, Belk paid Sycamore a $135 million dividend.[60]

But no—the bankruptcy was entirely the fault of COVID-19 and the resulting shutdowns. And perhaps it was, in the very loose sense that the company had no margin for error in its operations after the LBO saddled it with so much debt.

The CFO also submitted a separate declaration in support of confirming the plan.[61] Paragraph 9 of that declaration is entitled "The Plan Enjoys Unanimous Voting Support," but a close reading of that text suggests that it is just as slippery as anything put forth by Jay Gould. "Voting support" is not quite the same thing as "support," it turns out.

The paragraph itself states that the plan is support by "approximately 99 percent in principal amount of First Lien Term Loan Claims (Class 4)." And the chart thereafter actually shows that 96.9 percent (by number) and 99 percent (by dollar amount) of the claims in that class voted. The result was unanimous of those who voted, but that is not actually the standard under the Bankruptcy Code, which looks to *all* creditors in a class.[62] Beyond that, this latter declaration is mostly devoted to justifying the releases granted under the plan to the sponsors and others. The confirmation brief likewise points to the mostly self-imposed deadlines as a reason for quickly confirming the plan.[63]

It appears that nobody got "hurt" in the Belk case, but this case raises several important issues. Perhaps most fundamentally, are there any rules left in chapter 11? That is, is there nothing left to the chapter 11 that may not be modified by the apparent consent of the parties?

In invoking a government-sanctioned process like chapter 11, the debtor-firm is agreeing to abide by a structure adopted by policymakers. Indeed, the move from receivership to statute was in part about providing a more potent reorganization system, while at the same time addressing the perceived unfairness of aspects of receiverships. But if today a debtor can get in and out of chapter 11 without really engaging in any of the process, is the governmental system now not totally under the control of the large players?

In short, have we not gone back to the days of Jay Gould, but with a more powerful, statutory reorganization system? In some sense, it might be the worst combination of all the historical eras—a statute that all the key players assume exists solely to facilitate deals among the key players. All other policy considerations are ignored.

The problem with Belk is not the outcome of the case as much as the easy assumption that it could be done. For no explained reason, the company was run through chapter 11 in less than a day, and the clear expectation was that the court would not say "no." That provides a pretty clear indication of where the law of corporate restructuring is at this moment—namely, a world where almost anything goes, so long as it gets sufficient creditor support. And courts will not consider the argument that such support comes, at least in part, from creditors that perceive a lack of other viable options.

Prebankruptcy transactions create more complex ultimate restructuring, but they have value to shareholders who maintain control for a bit longer and select groups of creditors who get a higher priority or better treatment in the subsequent chapter 11 case. Courts accept practically any terms in an RSA, so long as they have broad support. But the support issue is entirely circular, in that creditors that expect courts to approve the RSA will accept their fate and sign on rather than incur the expenses of a pointless fight.

Courts are unwilling to "look behind the curtain" regarding these transactions or the RSAs that dictate the outcome of a chapter 11 case, and there is an incremental ratchet effect, wherein each new "outrage" becomes accepted and the next case works off that new, more aggressive base. Eventually a court might finally stop the ratchet—and perhaps the recent decision in *Serta*, where an appellate court for the first time found an LME to violate the terms of a loan agreement, will turn out to be such a case—but that will simply mean that the status quo at that point will be frozen.[64] We are so far beyond what was originally intended when corporate reorganization was first codified that only new legislative action will rectify things, as I discuss further in the next and final chapter.

· · ·

Ironically, Belk, despite its speedy reorganization, was still in trouble in late 2023, expecting lower revenues for the year. While that is itself problematic, the bigger issue appears to be the company's still heavy capital structure. In announcing a ratings downgrade in early 2023, S&P observed that "we believe the company's capital structure is unsustainable and will likely be addressed through some type of restructuring. Belk's turn-around efforts have not succeeded in a sustained improvement in EBITDA and cash flow since the 2021 bankruptcy emergence. The capital structure put in place at that time required significant improvement in profitability to become sustainable and this looks increasingly unlikely . . . We also view liquidity as constrained by Belk's very large debt burden totaling $1.9 billion as of the third quarter." In July 2024, Sycamore's ride finally came to an end; it turned over control of the company to the creditors.[65] Whether another chapter 11 is in its future remains to be seen.

CHAPTER 10

CHAPTER 11 GOING FORWARD

We often go on discussing problems in terms of old ideas when the solution of the problem depends upon getting rid of the old ideas, and putting in their place concepts more in accord with the present state of ideas and knowledge.

—John Dewey 1926

By early 2024, Robertshaw, a manufacturer of controls for home appliances and industrial pumps, had an array of debt that would have been right at home in a nineteenth-century railroad, as shown in table 10.1.

The company was taken over by private equity firm One Rock Capital Partners in 2018—the seller was the prior private equity owner, Sun Capital Partners, so Robertshaw had been living with debt for a good while.

The very modern part of the Robertshaw story is that until 2023, the sixth and seventh layers of debt (indicated in italics in the table) were the first-lien ($510 million) and second-lien ($110 million) loans resulting from the most recent LBO. At the time, the company also had about $50 million in senior bank debt, originally owed to Deutsche Bank and PNC Bank but since taken over by Invesco, which hoped to control the restructuring.

TABLE 10.1 Robertshaw debts

First-out superpriority term loan	$218 million
Second-out superpriority term loan	$381 million
Third-out superpriority term loan	$72.8 million
Fourth-out superpriority term loan	$22.8 million
Fifth-out superpriority term loan	$29.2 million
Sixth-out term loan	*$78.9 million*
Seventh-out term loan	*$16.3 million*

But when Robertshaw began to experience financial troubles—the company, of course, points to the pandemic, not its debt as the cause—a group of debt investors set up an ad hoc committee. Rumors abounded that the company (or its sponsor) helped set up the committee; again, all very reminiscent of the good old days of Jay Gould, Isaac Wistar, and every other railroad receivership that followed. These lenders arranged to repay Invesco, keeping the restructuring for themselves.[1]

The result was several lawsuits filed in New York State court, and the five "superpriority" layers of debt shown in the table. The first tier represented the new money that creditors provided to Robertshaw. Much of the remainder refinanced old LBO debt, including the old bank debt, leaving behind the $95 million that belonged to creditors that did not get their own invitations to the party.

Those creditors, who previously thought they were at the top of the heap, now found themselves sitting behind $700 million of new senior debt.[2] They would ultimately receive no recovery whatsoever in the bankruptcy that followed.

Even those that got an invitation to the party were refinanced into the second through fifth tiers, while the truly select (namely, the three large creditors that would join with the sponsor to buy the company in the subsequent bankruptcy) had their old debt refinanced into only the second or third tier. These special creditors slinked up the priority structure relative to their previously equal-ranked fellow lenders.

And then the company, based in Illinois, incorporated in Delaware, and being sued in New York naturally decided to file its chapter 11 case in Houston.[3] No doubt the court was chosen because it had previously shrugged at similar creditor abuse of fellow lenders in the Serta Simmons Bedding chapter 11 case, which we discussed in chapter 9.[4]

In *Serta*, existing lenders Apollo and Angelo Gordon were pushed to the back of the line by fellow lenders Eaton Vance and Invesco. And while the appeals court eventually reversed the bankruptcy court's decision in *Serta*, that ruling came too late for the creditors in the Robertshaw situation, and one wonders if the Houston bankruptcy court would have distinguished it anyway.[5] Indeed, the *Serta* opinion is already seen as something to be avoided rather than a real obstacle to aggressive LMEs.

In Robertshaw, Invesco, the ostensible winner in *Serta*, was left out in the cold—what goes around comes around. The bankruptcy judge observed that "Invesco engaged in acts it now calls bad faith, including using its status as the top lender to amend the company's credit agreement several times without informing other lenders and planning an Invesco-controlled bankruptcy filing."[6]

Three of the Robertshaw creditors, including Eaton Vance, large owners of the first and second superpriority loans shown in table 10.1, along with the sponsor, ended up owning the company when all was said and done.[7] Such is the way of modern chapter 11: Create a new senior class and give them special

10.1 A Robertshaw device installed in Indonesia, October 2021.

Kalken/Shutterstock.

treatment in the subsequent bankruptcy. The sponsor is happy to do that if they get to salvage some of their investment.[8]

• • •

At the very end of 2024, Party City and The Container Store filed for chapter 11, while SWF Holdings I Corp., a window-dressing company, iHeart Communications, Inc., and Veritas all executed multibillion-dollar LMEs.

Party City's filing was its second, coming fourteen months after its first. The company commenced going-out-of-business sales at over seven hundred locations. Fabric and crafts retailer JOANN Inc. likewise filed a second chapter 11 eight months after its first, on January 15. The Container Store's plan, which converted debt to equity and gave the DIP lenders 64 percent of the equity, was confirmed on January 24, just over a month after filing.

Ligado Networks, a satellite communications company, filed for chapter 11 on January 7, with $8.6 billion of debt. The RSA in its case provided for a DIP facility loan of up to $442 million of new money and a roll-up of prepetition debt of up to $497 million. The RSA had 88 percent creditor support.

With more than a hundred billion dollars of debt maturing in the coming years, much of it issued by private equity–owned companies, we can expect chapter 11 mischief to continue for the foreseeable future.[9] The need for reform seems patent.

At the same time, the widely acknowledged dysfunction of our national legislature makes it easy to dismiss any effort to change corporate bankruptcy as futile. Nevertheless, assuming (hoping) that the dysfunction is not permanent, this chapter briefly considers how a revised corporate bankruptcy system might take shape, in light of the historical lessons of the prior chapters.

There is a tendency, especially in academia, to assume that corporate bankruptcy developed to maximize returns to creditors and support a super-efficient American corporate capital market. Instead, as this book has shown, corporate bankruptcy settled in its modern form because Jay Gould wanted to keep control of his railroad, and to achieve that, he had to work out a compromise with a few other wealthy investors. Nobody else was invited to the table; at heart, that is the foundation of modern corporate bankruptcy.

Understanding that corporate restructuring was initially created largely to serve the interests of powerful players and to suppress the interests of the less powerful who might get in the way has important implications for chapter 11, as well as how we might approach a reconsidered version of our corporate bankruptcy system. Moreover, the current state of chapter 11—nasty and brutish, in short—makes a lot more sense if we push back the start of modern restructuring to the Jay Gould days and reconsider the sainting of J. P. Morgan.

Chapter 11 itself is the direct product of the extreme push to deregulation that swelled in the late 1970s.[10] While deregulation often worked well, sometimes it did not—the revived freight railroad industry on the one hand, compared with domestic air travel and the lack thereof in many US locations that previously had functioning airports on the other.[11] With regard to statutory corporate reorganization, chapter X, with the prominent role given to the SEC, stands at one extreme, but chapter 11 stands at the other. As with air travel, it seems like an opportune time to reconsider the arrangement.

Deregulation probably made corporate bankruptcy a better system for the big players, but at what cost? Has the exclusion of smaller players left the system open to charges of injustice? It is likely that in any corporate bankruptcy system, there will always be winners and losers—inherent in bankruptcy is the idea that there is not enough to go around—but if the winners are *always* the sophisticated players, we might ask why they need backing from a government-funded bankruptcy system.

• • •

In the last two chapters, I have sketched the rough-and-tumble turn that chapter 11 has taken in the twenty-first century. Modern corporate bankruptcy is noted for the extent to which "dominant interests strategically use Chapter 11 to overturn the customary commercial expectations of less powerful parties."[12]

As we have seen, this basic problem is not new. One constant theme throughout the history of American corporate reorganization is insider control. From Gould's and Wistar's machinations, to Charles Coster and Morgan's takeover of the Richmond Terminal, to the Van Swerigans' early unsuccessful attempts to control MoPac's reorganization and Robert Young's more successful efforts to stop the process until he got paid, to the banks' control of Grants' fate, to the present day, with its PODs, controllers have sought power in restructurings with the minimum possible actual investment.

Professor Brudney observed years ago that "bankruptcy reorganization is a substitute for the equity receivership as a procedure for readjusting participations in an enterprise that has failed but is economically worth continuing."[13] But if statutory reorganization is supposed to offer something more than receivership, it must certainly start with fair treatment of all participants in the debtor company, inasmuch as ultimately "the shape of bankruptcy law is an expression of distributional norms . . . and interest group politics, rather than an exercise in economic efficiency."[14] A statutory structure and judicial power are harnessed in support of economic goals, but policy choice spreads well beyond simple maximization of creditor returns.

So to consider reform of chapter 11, or corporate reorganization more generally, we must first consider the policy goals that are to underly the system. Once we identify those goals, we can better see the needed reforms.

• • •

In 1978, the drafters of the Bankruptcy Code and chapter 11 highlighted key goals like saving jobs, businesses relationships, and communities.[15] Somehow along the way, the aim of chapter 11 became maximizing the size of the bankruptcy estate.[16] That in turn has facilitated extensive deference to deals that purport to have the support of most creditors—in large part because it is assumed that quick, consensual chapter 11 cases achieve the goal of maximizing the size of the pie. This goes hand in hand with a vacuous concept of "maximization" that essentially means nothing more than a deal that is profitable to the most vocal or powerful creditors.[17]

Another strand of corporate bankruptcy thinking views chapter 11 as primarily targeted to the problem of the holdup creditor, which demands better treatment in exchange for consent.[18] Robert Young fits the mold nicely, even if he was a MoPac shareholder. But an excessive focus on holdouts not only tends to support excessive deference to deals, but it also acknowledges only a single strand of the arguments in favor of codifying corporate bankruptcy in the first instance.

Certainly, the insiders that advocated for section 77 and its successors, such as section 77B, wanted greater power against holdouts. But equally important as a matter of policy, and motivation for congressional action, was the argument that insiders overly dominated the existing receivership process to their advantage. Max Lowenthal's contributions loom large here.[19]

Moreover, not all corporate reorganization systems have had strong powers to deal with holdouts: Chapter XI notably lacked a cramdown power, and section 77's was of limited utility, as MoPac showed all too well. Canada's Companies' Creditors Arrangement Act, which is widely used and seen as the equivalent of modern chapter 11, also lacks a cramdown power.[20] As such, focus on holdouts can hardly be the primary point of a good reorganization statute.

• • •

To facilitate chapter 11 reform, we need to first shake off both the narrow conception of the chapter's goals that we have accepted in the past decades and the myth that reorganization in its present form is preordained and clearly desirable.

To begin, one obvious and fundamental reform is enforcement of the already existing "rules" of the game. For example, as noted, the Code already states that plans must "provide the same treatment for each claim or interest of a particular class," but the courts have adopted a crabbed reading of this provision, holding that it does not sweep up treatment of a creditor on account of separate legal rights.[21] Thus, if the company borrows even a token amount of money from one bondholder prebankruptcy, this might provide the basis for different treatment of that bondholder compared to other bondholders.

Part of the difficulty of enforcing the existing terms of chapter 11 is that in a debtor-in-possession system, there is no neutral party that can tell the bankruptcy court the story of the case.[22] Everyone who appears before the court is by definition pursuing some goal—leaving the judge overseeing a chapter 11 as isolated from the reality of the process as Judge Don Pardee, who oversaw the Texas and Pacific receivership. The only information that comes to the judge is what the parties want the court to know. Large players dictate the terms of a deal that is then presented to everyone else on a "take it or leave it" basis, and then to the bankruptcy court as something that "everyone" is supporting. In this respect, nothing much has changed from the receivership days, when "the plan drafted in the largest railroad reorganization in the country's history (the reorganization of a middle western and western railroad) was prepared by a New York banker and his lawyer behind locked doors in a hotel at White Sulphur Springs . . . Security holders were then required to accept the plan in toto, without opportunity before taking action to suggest changes."[23]

The New Dealers saw this problem, but their solution (chapter X) never worked as designed, in large part because insiders were able to use chapter XI in its place. But even today, insider control remains. And to the extent that the enactment of chapter 11 in 1978 was designed to take us back to the "golden age" of receiverships, and the "deal culture" that such a return entailed, we should worry that chapter 11 is rooted in a problematic history.

In the modern world of chapter 11, like the world of receiverships more than a century ago, it is very difficult for courts to figure out what is actually going on. Thus, while I have noted my basic concern that bankruptcy judges have become too willing to accept "deals" and too reluctant to look behind those deals, it is also true that they are not apt to do so without better sources of information. Returning to something like a chapter X trustee—or perhaps the Canadian monitor, who advises the court without running the business—might provide courts with a trusted source of information.[24]

One of the chief purported drawbacks of chapter X, which led insiders to shun it, was the belief that trustees could not operate large businesses—they could only liquidate them. One obvious fix would be to refine the role of the trustee and move away from the all-powerful, chapter 7 or liquidation-style trustee. For example, the trustee might take over the power of the board, without necessarily displacing operational management. Indeed, this is reportedly what frequently happened in chapter X—the trustee would retain senior operational management to help run the business.

At the very least, some sort of neutral party in the case, which is not a stakeholder in any sense, can provide the court with vision in the reorganization. That, combined with a clarified version of what it means to provide equal treatment to all creditors within a class, would go a long way toward addressing the present chapter 11 free-for-all.

On the other hand, if we decide that it makes good policy to have a restructuring mechanism that allows quick approval of deals among sophisticated parties, it makes sense to separate that from the general corporate bankruptcy provisions. A separate provision could offer assurances that smaller parties are first cleared from the field. Not only trade creditors and employees but also retail investors should be paid in full, or otherwise be left untouched by the process, so they do not become squashed by the giants. A stand-alone chapter of the Code, perhaps modeled on the old section 20b of the Interstate Commerce Act (discussed in chapter 5, in connection with MoPac), which applies only to qualified institutional buyers (QIBs), might make some sense.[25]

In all cases, there remains the question of what to do about forum shopping in corporate chapter 11 cases. On the one hand, it is understandable that debtor-companies would seek out experienced jurists, who would appreciate the distinct challenges that a large corporate debtor faces. On the other hand, too often those understandable sentiments are mere cover for a more dubious reality—for example, the desire to have a judge who defers to sophisticated parties. Implementing reform becomes nearly impossible if the parties can always seek out the weakest version of those reforms.

And the image of the corporate bankruptcy system is tarnished by the defaulting company picking its own judge—just as Lowenthal noted the distastefulness of the Milwaukee Road (or more frankly, Kuhn, Loeb) picking the judge to oversee its own receivership. The recent disclosures about the conflicts of interest that a Houston bankruptcy judge operated under also revealed the clubby nature of modern large company chapter 11, including a report that when the judge in question conducted an arbitration for a case pending before the other Houston chapter 11 judge, he met with several of the participating attorneys for dinner that evening.[26] Obviously, most participants in a corporate bankruptcy do not get such access to the judge, but when those insiders also decide where a chapter 11 case files, the results are insidious.

A circuit-level group of judges certified to work on complex cases within the circuit might address the core concerns here. Each large case would be randomly assigned to a sophisticated, experienced judge from the regional complex case panel, leading to the desired judicial competencies, without allegations of judge-shopping.

A hard-and-fast rule for what constitutes a complex case—perhaps more than $100 million in liabilities and more than one hundred likely claimants, for example—would be needed to avoid the chapter X versus chapter XI mess that we saw with Grants. Debtors would be required to file in the district of their corporate headquarters—the long-term headquarters itself, not where some officers might happen to be at the moment of filing or where some newly minted subsidiary is purportedly located.

Debtors that require deep operational restructurings could file under the chapter X–style provision, essentially chapter 11 but with a trustee, but those that were content with a straightforward balance sheet revamp could use the section 20b–style provision. The latter would also incentivize early restructurings and plans that leave smaller players untouched, in that they would not feature a trustee.

There remains the broader policy question of whether the Code should facilitate these creditor fights or shut them down. The creditors involved are hardly sympathetic—nobody sheds any tears over Apollo's ill treatment in the Serta bankruptcy, to take but one example, because we all know that Apollo has done the same or worse in other cases. As the bankruptcy court noted, "The Objecting Lenders acquired the majority of their loan holdings long after the original issuance and in anticipation of negotiating and executing a [transaction] to the exclusion of the PTL Lenders—exactly what they complain was done to them using the same provisions of the 2016 Credit Agreement."[27] But regardless of the nature of the creditors, the initial question lingers.

The fights themselves are inefficient, in that they utilize judicial resources and invite legal and other professional expenses in efforts to head off future opportunism. In a recent opinion, a English High Court judge wrote that

> I was horrified to discover that the Plan Company has spent around US$150 million on professional fees in negotiating with its secured creditors from December 2022 and then putting forward the Plan and taking it to this hearing. That is an enormous sum of money, even taking account of the fact that it includes the costs of the supporting creditors as well. The Group actually raised US$250 million of new money while the Plan was being negotiated, but that was principally to fund the professional fees for getting the Plan through. The witness . . . said that he was deeply uncomfortable with this and I agree with his comment that there seems to be something wrong with the restructuring industry, particularly in the US, where the costs appear to be out of control.[28]

He attributed a large amount of the cost in that case to the debtor's extremely aggressive posture toward the dissenting creditor, a criticism that probably runs ultimately to the debtor's counsel, Kirkland and Ellis, which dominates the representation of large corporate debtors these days, just as Cravath (Kuhn, Loeb's favorite firm) dominated in an earlier era. In 1917, it was observed that a small number of law firms dominated "the task of supervising the legal phases of the work of reorganizing and refinancing great corporate enterprises."[29] Again, very little has changed.

And of course, there also remains the real chance that others will get caught in the crossfire—the employees of Toys "R" Us, for example, had no say in the battle that led to that company's demise. Neither did Grants' employees. In the extreme, the debtor and a select group of creditors can even utilize modern chapter 11 to keep alive a firm that would be better off liquidated.[30]

Conversely, if certain creditors will benefit most from liquidation even if the firm is otherwise viable, they might be able to pay the debtor's controllers enough to make liquidation happen, despite what would be best for the debtor's stakeholders generally. That is, they might undermine the very purpose of corporate reorganization.

More broadly, the ability of creditors to steal value from each other has obvious (if hard-to-quantify) effects on the wider economy. If lenders are unable to rely on enforcement of their lending agreements, that will decrease the availability (and increase the cost) of credit for all firms in the economy. Because these costs chiefly are felt outside the corporate bankruptcy system, they are easy for participants within the system to ignore, but that does not decrease the significance of the costs. The latter should be of concern to policymakers, particularly in Congress, even if bankruptcy courts view it as beyond their remit.

Perhaps the easiest solution would simply be to require disaggregation of the deals that are presented to bankruptcy courts. Long ago, reorganization expert Walter Blum suggested that there should be "a restriction on trimming new securities with rococo qualities which tend to be misleading and make intelligent judgment by investors more difficult."[31] The basic point seems equally valid today.

At present, large corporate debtors often arrive at bankruptcy court with an RSA, which in turn references a DIP loan agreement, a postbankruptcy financing agreement, and various other contracts. The RSA promises consensus among its signatories, and the debtor will sell it to the court as providing a clear path out of chapter 11. But what creditors are getting from these various agreements is very hard to evaluate when the provisions are interlinked and each agreement supports the other, without any indication of the total value of the provisions.

If, for example, the Bankruptcy Code required that DIP loans stand alone as loan agreements that had to be repaid in cash—with no rights to receive special treatment under the debtor's plan or rights to participate in the loan contingent on voting for the plan—the ability to police compliance with the basic rules of chapter 11 would be greatly enhanced. To similar effect might be a rule that required sale of the reorganized debtor's shares for cash, with no special allocations to best-loved bondholders or the sponsors. Not only would this improve the apparent legitimacy of chapter 11, but it would provide better insights into what is going on in corporate bankruptcy cases. The latter would facilitate court—and trustee, if the "chapter X" model was adopted—oversight of the process.

Courts might also contemplate the ratio of new money provided under DIP loans to the fees that the debtor incurs thereunder. For example, in Circuit City, the debtor paid $30 million in fees to get $50 million in new money, netting only $20 million in a case that seems to have been run for the benefit of the senior lenders in all respects. The lenders got the benefit of selling the company in a way that maximized their return, while also charging the company a handsome price for its own funeral.

We might also consider the relationship of old debt rolled over to new money. For example, in Yellow Corp.'s proposed DIP loan, nearly $650 million of old loans were being repaid, for new money of just over $142 million of new money. The rolled-over debt was about six times the new money, without even considering the $32 million in proposed fees. Toys "R" Us's most senior DIP loan rolled over billions of old debt and provided but $170 million of new money.

It is hard to set a precise rule, but it seems that senior lenders already benefit from having the case in chapter 11 (compared with chapter 7), so why should they reap even more bounty through a DIP loan? At the very least, courts might raise these issues and ask additional questions when the loans are obviously rewarding to the lenders as senior creditors.

Finally, we might also consider tightening up the safe harbors for securities and derivatives trades. The safe harbors themselves were designed to protect trading markets. As such, there is no obvious reason why they should apply to a debtor-issuer's repurchase of its own securities—such as in an LBO. Likewise, why should the debtor's procurement of commodities for use in its operations be subject to safe harbors? Again, this seems like a loophole opened for sophisticated parties to exploit, while other vendors have to play by the rules.

Ultimately, true reform will need to involve a clean break from the legacy that Jay Gould left us. No easy task.

And, unlike in 1978, modern chapter 11 now competes in a global market for corporate reorganization.[32] Large corporate debtors have their choice of reorganizing in the United States—or London, Amsterdam, or Singapore. The Jay Goulds of the new century can consider which place best serves their interests and which one will best maintain their control.

ACKNOWLEDGMENTS

J ennifer R. Hoyden provided key advice and assistance from the very start of this project, and without her, this book would never have happened.

The book was supported by the amazing staff at Seton Hall's Peter W. Rodino, Jr. Law Library—particularly Sara Gras, Sara Klein, and Christy Smith. Their hard work and diligence tracking down and getting access to sources was indispensable.

Thank you to Louise Harrison of the London Metropolitan Archives; Lindsay Closterman, Jessica Hopkins, and Stephen Spence of the National Archives at Kansas City; Sophia Southard of the State Historical Society of Missouri; Joanna Bouldin of the East Tennessee History Center; and Jenny Sweeney and Barbara Rust of the National Archives at Fort Worth, Texas, for facilitating my visits to review the many archival documents that support this book. Similar thanks as well to David Huelsing of the Missouri Pacific Historical Society Archives, who provided vital material regarding the Texas and Pacific.

And thank you as well to the London office of Deutsche Bank for granting me access to the Morgan, Grenfell & Co. (J. S. Morgan & Co.) papers.

Thanks to Professor Lynn LoPucki for putting together his database of publicly traded chapter 11 cases, which helps to illustrate the later chapters of this book. I truly understand how much work collecting a database of that size by hand entails, and value that he spent a sizable part of his career doing so.

I am also grateful to one of my former bosses at Skadden, Arps, Michael L. Cook, who put me in touch with several leading attorneys who had worked on the W. T. Grant case. Thanks as well to Harold S. Novikoff, Richard P. Krasnow, and Stephen H. Case, who allowed me to record our conversations. My thanks as well to Al Togut and Bill Rochelle for their thoughts on W. T. Grant. I also greatly appreciate that another of my former bosses at Skadden, Arps, Richard Levin, agreed to discuss the enactment of the 1978 Bankruptcy Code on video.

Special thanks to the two anonymous reviewers of the manuscript, as well as the anonymous reviewers of the initial proposal, who helped improve this book at each step.

My Seton Hall colleague Illya Beylin provided helpful comments on early drafts of the chapters.

The project was supported by sabbatical leave from Seton Hall University during the 2023–2024 academic year, and I appreciate the university's continued commitment to scholarship in an age where the finances of higher education can be challenging.

I am also grateful for the research assistance provided by Samuel J. Brownsword, Seton Hall Law Class of 2025, and for the support and advice provided by Christian P. Winting, my former editor at Columbia University Press, and Brian Smith, also of Columbia University Press, the editor who saw me through to the end.

NOTES

Introduction

1. Bruce H. Mann, *Republic of Debtors: Bankruptcy in the Age of American Independence* (Harvard University Press, 2002), 207–8.
2. Louise Story and Peter Lattman, "Short on Time and Options, Lawyers Remade Chrysler," *The New York Times*, June 14, 2009.
3. Elizabeth Warren, "Bankruptcy Policy," *University of Chicago Law Review* 54, no. 3 (1987): 767. Accord Riz Mokal, "What Is an Insolvency Proceeding? Gategroup Lands in a Gated Community," *International Insolvency Review*, 31, no. 3 (2022): 423.
4. The 1978 Bankruptcy Code was a major revision of the prior 1898 Bankruptcy Act, and it provides for reorganization and liquidation for individuals, businesses, and municipalities. Pub. L. No. 95–598, 92 Stat. 2549 (1978). The Bankruptcy Code itself has been amended from time to time since its enactment, including significant amendments in 1984, 2005, and 2019. Although bankruptcy is governed by federal law, state law plays an important role in bankruptcy. The property interests owned by the debtor and the rights of creditors in such property are determined under state law (or other applicable nonbankruptcy law, like federal intellectual property law).
5. Sarah Pei Woo, "Regulatory Bankruptcy: How Bank Regulation Causes Fire Sales," *Georgetown Law Journal* 99, no. 6 (August 2011): 1620–22; William W. Bratton, "Corporate Debt Relationships: Legal Theory in a Time of Restructuring," *Duke Law Journal* 1989, no. 1 (February 1989): 114. See also Ferdinand Fairfax Stone, "The Case of the Ladies' Handbags: A Study in Receivership Procedure," *Virginia Law Review* 24 (June 1938): 851–52.
6. Sarah Paterson, "Rethinking Corporate Bankruptcy Theory in the Twenty-First Century," *Oxford Journal of Legal Studies* 36, no. 4 (2016): 710.
7. Janis Sarra, *Creditor Rights and the Public Interest: Restructuring Insolvent Corporations* (University of Toronto Press, 2003), 66.

8. Philip J. Stern, *Empire, Incorporated: The Corporations That Built British Colonialism* (Harvard University Press, 2023), 44.

9. See generally John Dewey, "The Historic Background of Corporate Legal Personality," *Yale Law Journal* 35, no. 6 (April 1926): 655–73. See also Monell v. Dep't of Soc. Servs. of City of New York, 436 U.S. 658, 687–88, 98 S. Ct. 2018, 2034, 56 L. Ed. 2d 611 (1978); Morton J. Horwitz, *The Transformation of American Law, 1870–1960: The Crisis of Legal Orthodoxy* (Oxford University Press, 1992), chap. 3; Herbert Hovenkamp, *Enterprise and American Law, 1836–1937* (Harvard University Press, 1991), 14–16.

10. The stock or shares did not obtain all these features overnight; rather, I describe the ultimate result.

11. This was a long-standing problem. The Virginia Company requested an amendment to its charter in 1612 to allow it to expel investors who refused to pay what they had promised. Stern, *Empire, Incorporated*, 55.

12. In the very early days, before the colonization of the New World, many English corporate charters and corporate shares had expiration dates.

13. The price of British government bonds is quoted in terms of price per £100 face value, which may be the source of this pricing convention.

14. "The mortgagee acquires a sort of contingent interest in the property, redeemable in the event the owner-mortgagor defaults on her loan." James Y. Stern, "The Essential Structure of Property Law," *Michigan Law Review* 115 (May 2017): 1184.

15. Stephen J. Lubben, "A New Understanding of the Bankruptcy Clause," *Case Western Reserve Law Review* 64, no. 2 (Winter 2013): 319–412.

16. 11 U.S.C. section 362(a).

17. Recent versions of this story can be found in Sarah Paterson, *Corporate Reorganization Law and Forces of Change* (Oxford University Press, 2020), and Douglas G. Baird, *The Unwritten Law of Corporate Reorganizations* (Cambridge University Press, 2022). Probably the most widely read version can be found in Ron Chernow, *The House of Morgan* (Atlantic Monthly Press, 1990), 67–70.

18. As University of Pennsylvania professor David Skeel noted in a recent Brookings Institute report: "Complaints about insider control of Chapter 11 were rising even before the recent pandemic. The pressure has steadily increased during the pandemic, due both to the pandemic and to the confluence of highly controversial bankruptcy filings by Purdue Pharma, USA Gymnastics, the Boy Scouts, and others." https://www.brookings.edu/research/the-populist-backlash-in-chapter-11/.

19. Lynn M. LoPucki, "Chapter 11's Descent into Lawlessness," *American Bankruptcy Law Journal* 96, no. 2 (Spring 2022).

1. The Early Days of Corporate Reorganization and Texas Railroads

1. See generally Albert Fishlow, "Internal Transportation in the Nineteenth and Early Twentieth Centuries," in *The Cambridge Economic History of the United States*, ed. Stanley L. Engerman and Robert E. Gallman, 543–642; Frank Walker Stevens, *The Beginnings of the New York Central Railroad; A History* (G. P. Putnam, 1926).

2. Maury Klein, *Unfinished Business: The Railroad in American Life* (University of Rhode Island, 1994), 8–12. Many of the Southeastern railroads obviously needed to be rebuilt after the war, but rebuilding was still distinct from new construction, as was common in the West.

3. Richard White, *Railroaded: The Transcontinentals and the Making of Modern America* (W. W. Norton, 2011), 20–25.
4. White, *Railroaded*.
5. David Cannadine, *Victorious Century: The United Kingdom, 1800–1906* (Allen Lane, 2017), 371. For information on the early Canadian Pacific, see Pierre Berton, *The National Dream: The Great Railway, 1871–1881* (McClelland and Stewart, 1970).
6. Jere W. Roberson, "The South and the Pacific Railroad, 1845–1855," *Western Historical Quarterly* 5, no. 2 (April 1974): 163.
7. Kevin Waite, *West of Slavery: The Southern Dream of a Transcontinental Empire* (University of North Carolina Press, 2021), chap. 6.
8. Kevin Starr, *Inventing the Dream: California Through the Progressive Era* (Oxford University Press, 1986), 53; Kevin Starr, *Americans and the California Dream, 1850–1915* (Oxford University Press, 1973), 108, 135–36, 416. See also Patt Morrison, "Confederate Sentiment in Southern California Ran Deeper Than You Might Know," *Los Angeles Times*, April 12, 2024; Albert Lucian Lewis, "Los Angeles in the Civil War Decades," PhD diss., University of Southern California, 1970.
9. Waite, *West of Slavery*, chap. 3.
10. See generally Emmie Giddings W. Mahon and Chester V. Kielman, "George H. Giddings and the San Antonio-San Diego Mail Line," *Southwestern Historical Quarterly* 61, no. 2 (1957): 220–39.
11. Jere W. Roberson, "To Build a Pacific Railroad: Congress, Texas, and the Charleston Convention of 1854," *Southwestern Historical Quarterly*, 78, no. 2 (October 1974): 134.
12. Santa Clara County v. Southern Pacific Railway Co., 118 U.S. 394, 397 (1886). Act of Texas Legislature, February 16, 1852, Incorporating Texas Western Railroad Company. This early railroad also went by other names, but the name was changed to the Southern Pacific Railroad Company by the Act of Texas Legislature, August 16, 1856.
13. Act of Texas Legislature, February 16, 1852, section 2.
14. Act of Texas Legislature, February 16, 1852, sections 7, 8, 15.
15. Act of Texas Legislature, January 30, 1854.
16. Act of Texas Legislature, August 3, 1856. See also the Act of August 26, 1856 (amending the Act of August 3). Note that these two acts bookend the change in name of the Southern Pacific; there was a lot of railroad activity that month in the state legislature.
17. S. S. McKay, "Texas and the Southern Pacific Railroad, 1848–1860," *Southwestern Historical Quarterly* 35, no. 1 (July 1931): 2. McKay was a longtime professor of history at Texas Technological College (now Texas Tech University), https://www.tshaonline.org/handbook/entries/mckay-seth-shepard.
18. Randolph Campbell, "Slaveholding in Harrison County, 1850–1860, a Statistical Profile," *East Texas Historical Journal* 11, no. 1 (1973): 21.
19. Randolph Campbell, "Human Property: The Negro Slave in Harrison County, 1850–1860," *Southwestern Historical Quarterly* 76, no. 4 (April 1973): 384. Campbell notes that "Negro slaves made up 52 percent of the county's total population of 11,822 in 1850 and 58 percent of the 15,001 people living there in 1860." A. B. Armstrong, "Origins of the Texas and Pacific Railway," *Southwestern Historical Quarterly*, 56, no. 4 (April 1953): 495. See also Theodore Kornweibel, "Railroads and Slavery," *Railroad History* no. 189 (Fall-Winter 2003): 34–59.
20. Aaron W. Marrs, "The Iron Horse Turns South: A History of Antebellum Southern Railroads," *Enterprise & Society* 8, no. 4 (2007): 789.
21. S. G. Reed, *A History of the Texas Railroads* (St. Clair, 1941), 102.

22. Reed, *A History of the Texas Railroads*, 103. Andrew Forest Muir, "The Thirty-Second Parallel Pacific Railroad in Texas to 1872" (PhD diss., University of Texas, 1949), 164.
23. John Bakeless credits them with five miles of track, but this seems doubtful and certainly must be considered the upper limit of what they actually built. John Edwin Bakeless, "History of the Missouri Pacific Railroad" (unpublished manuscript, 1957), 150. The manuscript is available through the Missouri Pacific Historical Society.
24. Texas and Pacific 1875 Annual Report, p. 7.
25. *Davis v. Gray*, 83 U.S. 203, 224, 21 L. Ed. 447 (1872).
26. Mark W. Summers, *Railroad, Reconstruction, and the Gospel of Prosperity* (Princeton University Press, 1984), 151–52.
27. Lewis H. Haney, *Congressional History of Railways in the United States* (Augustus M. Kelley, 1968), 114.
28. Haney, *Congressional History*, 152.
29. Will Guzmán, *Civil Rights in the Texas Borderlands: Dr. Lawrence A. Nixon and Black Activism* (University of Illinois Press, 2015), 17–18.
30. Christopher Bean, "'A Most Singular and Interesting Attempt': The Freedmen's Bureau at Marshall, Texas," *Southwestern Historical Quarterly* 110, no. 4 (April 2007): 468.
31. "From Louisville," *The Philadelphia Inquirer*, March 27, 1886.
32. *The Texas Almanac for 1869 and Emigrant's Guide to Texas* (Unknown, 1869), 78.
33. C. Vann Woodward, *Reunion and Reaction: The Compromise of 1877 and the End of Reconstruction* (Little, Brown & Co., 1951), 70–71. For more background on the general, see Michael Burlingame, *Abraham Lincoln: A Life* (Johns Hopkins University Press, 2013), 200–12.
34. R. W. Kostal, *Law and English Railway Capitalism, 1825–1875* (Oxford University Press, 1994, 2004 reprint), chaps. 1 and 2.
35. Cardinal Goodwin, *John Charles Frémont: An Explanation of His Career* (Stanford University Press, 1930), 246–47.
36. Forbes v. Memphis, E P & P R Co, 9 F. Cas. 408, 410 (C.C.W.D. Tex. 1872).
37. Lawrence M. Friedman, *A History of American Law*, 3rd ed. (Touchstone, 2005), 390.
38. Hyman P. Minsky, "The Evolution of Financial Institutions and the Performance of the Economy," *Journal of Economic Issues* 20, no. 2 (1986): 347.
39. Naomi R. Lamoreaux, "Entrepreneurship, Business Organization, and Economic Concentration," in *The Cambridge Economic History of the United States*, vol. 2, ed. Stanley L. Engerman and Robert E. Gallman (Cambridge University Press. 2000), 418–21.
40. See V. Markham Lester, *Victorian Insolvency: Bankruptcy, Imprisonment for Debt, and Company Winding-up in Nineteenth-Century England* (Clarendon Press and Oxford University Press, 1995), chap. 6.
41. Barton v. Barbour, 104 U.S. 126, 135 (1851).
42. For example, see N.Y. Laws of 1850, chap. 140. In Texas, see the Act of December 19, 1857, section 5.
43. Morgan County v. Thomas, 76 Ill. 120, 147 (1875); Commonwealth v. Cent. Pass. Ry. Co., 52 Pa. 506, 512 (1866); Vilas v. Milwaukee & P. du C. Ry. Co., 17 Wis. 497, 502 (1863). See also Houston & Texas Central Ry. Co. v. Shirley, 54 Tex. 125, 137–38 (1880) ("But clearly the purchaser of property at a sale under an execution or deed of trust assumes no personal liability for the debts of the former owner; and if by such a purchase the chartered rights and corporate existence and privileges of a corporation pass under the control of the purchaser, it still does not follow that its liabilities also attach to him").
44. Witherspoon & Lane v. Texas Pac. R. Co., 48 Tex. 309, 319 (1877).
45. Adrian H. Joline, "Railway Reorganizations," *American Lawyer* 8 (1900): 508.

46. Philip J. Stern, *Empire, Incorporated: The Corporations That Built British Colonialism* (Harvard University Press, 2023), 165–66.
47. Stern, *Empire, Incorporated*, 5–7. See also Herbert Hovenkamp, *Enterprise and American Law, 1836–1937* (Harvard University Press, 1991), 12–13.
48. William W. Bratton, "The New Economic Theory of the Firm: Critical Perspectives from History," *Stanford Law Review* 41, no. 6 (1989): 1484–86; Naomi R. Lamoreaux, "Partnerships, Corporations, and the Theory of the Firm," *American Economic Review* 88, no. 2 (1998): 66. "Yet there was still a long ideological distance to travel between the first general incorporation laws, which continued to impose many restrictions on corporate financing and structure, and the New Jersey incorporation law, first enacted in 1889, whose major premise was that a corporation could do virtually anything it wanted." Morton J. Horwitz, "Santa Clara Revisited: The Development of Corporate Theory," *West Virginia Law Review* 88, no. 2 (Fall 1985): 187.
49. J. S. Morgan & Co. papers, London Metropolitan Archives, HC3.1.2.1 (Alexander Trotter to the First Mortgage Bondholders of the Ohio and Mississippi Railroad Company, dated December 22, 1858).
50. I discuss the 1868 sale in the chapter itself. The earlier sales are recounted in Stevenson v. Texas Ry. Co., 105 U.S. 703, 706, 26 L. Ed. 1215 (1881). One sale happened in 1861, which raises interesting questions of the legality of a sale conducted while Texas was in rebellion. An opinion letter found in Missouri Pacific Historical Society, MF4 (1122–1947) suggests that there were actually four judicial sales: 1858, 1859, 1861, and 1868. Some of these were foreclosures and others followed sheriff's levies.
51. Missouri Pacific Historical Society, MF6 (0654–0707) (various levies, verdicts, and foreclosures related to the 1868 sale). It appears that the Hall group utilized a mix of sheriff's sales and foreclosures to obtain the railroad's assets. See also Missouri Pacific Historical Society, MF4 (1122–1947). The documents relevant to this point are scattered throughout the latter file, often in duplicate copies, much to the joy of researchers past, present, and future. A handwritten copy of the document creating the "new" Southern Pacific, dated May 5, 1868, with handwritten edits and insertions, can be found in that file as well.
52. Missouri Pacific Historical Society, MF6 (0849–0859) (presale stockholder list). The 1872 stock list, by comparison and showing fewer than thirty holders, can be found at Missouri Pacific Historical Society, MF6 (0708–0730).
53. Missouri Pacific Historical Society, MF4 (2245–2490) (handwritten letter from the widow of Oliver P. Garr, dated June 26, 1890). Garr appears on the 1868 shareholder list. A letter dated March 1890 from the Southern Pacific in San Francisco, noting the confusion of the names, also appears in the same file with a handwritten note from the widow on the back.
54. "Texas and Pacific," *The Economist*, January 27, 1883.
55. N.Y. Laws of 1874, chap. 430.
56. "Trust Sale of the Southern Pacific Rail Road," *The Texas Republican*, May 15, 1868. The sale notice itself is dated May 6.
57. Even within a state, the results might be problematic:

> What disastrous consequences would have resulted, if each judgment creditor had been allowed to seize and sell separate portions of the road, at different sales, in the six different Counties through which it passed, and to different purchasers! Would not this valuable property have been utterly sacrificed—the rights and interests of the creditors, as well as the objects and intentions of the Legislature in granting this charter, entirely defeated?
>
> Macon & W.R. Co. v. Parker, 9 Ga. 377, 394 (1851).

58. J. H. Baker, *An Introduction to English Legal History*, 4th ed. (Oxford University Press, 2007), chap. 6, and lectures I and II of Frederic William Maitland, A. H. Chaytor, W. J. Whittaker, and John Brunyate, *Equity: A Course of Lectures* (Cambridge University Press, 1936), where Professor Maitland (at page 18) explains that "we ought to think of equity as supplementary law." See also Stephen N. Subrin, "How Equity Conquered Common Law: The Federal Rules of Civil Procedure in Historical Perspective," *University of Pennsylvania Law Review* 135 (April 1987): 914–21.

59. Baker, *English Legal History*, 111–13.

60. Bennet William Heath, *Practical Treatise on the Appointment, Office, and Duties of a Receiver, Under the High Court of Chancery* (A. Maxwell & Son, 1849), 2. For more on the development of receivership law in the United States, see Ralph Ewing Clark, *A Treatise on the Law and Practice of Receivers*, 3rd ed., vol. 2 (W. H. Anderson Co., 1959), sections 3–10.

61. J. S. Morgan & Co. papers, London Metropolitan Archives, HC3.1.2.1. ("Alexander Trotter to the First Mortgage Bondholders Of The Ohio And Mississippi Railroad Company," dated Dec. 22, 1858). See also Morgan v. New York & Albany Railroad Co., 1843 WL 5303 (N.Y. May 2, 1843).

62. Pittsburgh, Fort Wayne and Chicago Railway, *Statement of the Trustees Relative to the Reorganization* (Baker & Godwin, 1862), 4.

63. *Statement of the Trustees*, 5.

64. Among the receivers were Samuel Tilden, future governor of New York and Democratic candidate in the disputed 1876 US presidential election, and John Edgar Thomson of the Pennsylvania Railroad, who had arranged the 1856 merger that formed the debtor-railroad. "Pittsburgh, Fort Wayne and Chicago Railway," *Railway Times*, May 31, 1862.

65. In a later case, the US Supreme Court acknowledged the different types of receiverships. Duparquet Huot & Moneuse Co. v. Evans, 297 U.S. 216, 220, 56 S. Ct. 412, 414, 80 L. Ed. 591 (1936).

66. For instance, see Louisville Trust Co. v. Louisville & C. Ry. Co., 174 U.S. 674, 676–77, 687–88 (1899); Brassey v. N.Y. & N.E.R. Co., 19 F. 663, 669 (C.C.D. Conn. 1884).

67. Edward H. Levi and James Wm. Moore, "Bankruptcy and Reorganization: A Survey of Changes," *University of Chicago Law Review* 5, no. 1 (1937): 4.

68. Edward H. Levi and James Wm. Moore, "Bankruptcy and Reorganization: A Survey of Changes. II," *University of Chicago Law Review* 5, no. 2 (1938): 225–26.

69. James Byrne, "The Foreclosure of Railroad Mortgages in the United States Courts," in *Some Legal Phases of Corporate Financing, Reorganization and Regulation* (McMillan, 1917), 79–81.

70. Harold G. Wren, "American Law of Railroad Reorganization," (JSD diss., Yale Law School, 1957), 22–23.

71. Taylor v. the Philadelphia & Reading R Co., 7 F. 381, 384 (C.C.E.D. Pa. 1881) ("The custody of the property of this railroad devolves upon the receivers appointed by the court. They are custodians of it for the benefit of the creditors. As the object of the whole proceeding is the preservation of the property for the benefit of the creditors").

72. Sage v. Central Railroad Co., 99 U.S. 334, 339 (1878) ("The amount required is so large usually, that it is beyond the reach of ordinary purchasers . . . the first-mortgage bondholders are the only party that can become the purchasers, and they only, because they need not pay their bid in cash").

73. Max Lowenthal, *The Investor Pays* (A. A. Knopf, 1936), 219, 245.

74. Dewing Stone Arthur, *Financial Policy of Corporations* (Ronald Press, 1920), vol. 5, 122.

75. William Z. Ripley, *Railroads: Finance & Organization* (Longmans, Green, and Co., 1920), 398–99. The author explains that "considerable transfer of securities may occur during the progress of events. Quite commonly the small shareholders sell out, usually at bottom prices. And speculative manipulation in the interest of insiders, as in the Chicago Great Western reorganization of 1909, may sometimes take place."

76. Joseph C. Simpson, "Comments on the Railroad Reorganization Provisions of the Bankruptcy Act of 1973," *The Business Lawyer* 30, no. 4 (1975): 1209.

77. John D. Ayer, "Rethinking Absolute Priority After *Ahlers*," *Michigan Law Review* 87, no. 5 (1989): 971.

78. Sidney Post Simpson, "Fifty Years of American Equity," *Harvard Law Review* 50, no. 2 (1936): 191.

79. Henry V. Poor, *Manual of the Railroads of the United States: 1870–71* (H. V. & H. W. Poor, 1871), 394.

80. "The Late Col. R. B. Hall: Funeral Services at the Christian Church To-Day," *Courier-Journal*, June 2, 1869.

81. "Marshall O. Roberts Dead," *The New York Times*, September 12, 1880.

82. "W. C. Hall Sued for a Settlement of His Accounts as Executor," *Courier-Journal*, April 6, 1889. In 1867, Hall was listed as a director of a newly formed Louisville bank. "Kentucky." *Bankers' Magazine and Statistical Register* 1 (3rd Series), no. 10 (1867): 786. Missouri Pacific Historical Society, MF4 (1122–1947) (charter of the new Southern Pacific, dated May 5, 1868). Missouri Pacific Historical Society, MF16 (1517–1566). Under the agreement, Roberts purchased 5,500 shares. The *1870 Annual Report*, for the fiscal year ending in April, indicates 6,861 shares outstanding. *Annual Report to the Stockholders of the Southern Pacific Railroad Company of Texas, for the year ending April 30, 1870*, 6.

83. Act of Texas Legislature, July 27, 1870, section 3.

84. Missouri Pacific Historical Society, MF16 (1581–1640).

85. "Local Miscellany: Southern Trans-Continental Railway Meeting of the Corporators," *New York Tribune*, November 1, 1870.

86. "Southern Pacific Road: Shall Freemont [*sic*] Have a Hand in the Pie?" *Republican Banner*, June 22, 1870.

87. "Forty-First Congress: Senate. Cables. Certification of Bank Checks. Railroad Bill. Tax Bill. Steamships. Texas Pacific Railroad Bill. House. Bridges. Minnesota State U. Department of Internal Revenue. Money Due Maine. Railroad. Correspondent of New York Post. Currency Bill. An Exciting Scene. National Junction Railroad. Miscellaneous Bills," *The Cincinnati Daily Enquirer*, June 23, 1870.

88. "Fremont's Fraud: The Memphis and El Paso Railroad–Four Millions and a Half Picked Up in Paris," *The Cincinnati Daily Enquirer*, June 3, 1870.

89. "To the Pacific: Memphis, El Paso Railroad. A Card from Gen. Fremont," *New York Tribune*, January 10, 1870.

90. "Railway on the Thirty-Second Parallel," *New York Tribune*, May 4, 1870.

91. Albert J. Churella, "The Pennsylvania Railroad in the Trans-Mississippi West," *Railroad History*, 208 (Spring-Summer 2013): 64–82.

92. James A. Ward, "J. Edgar Thomson and Thomas A. Scott: A Symbiotic Partnership?" *Pennsylvania Magazine of History and Biography*, 100, no. 1 (January 1976): 37–65.

93. Eric Foner, *Reconstruction: America's Unfinished Revolution, 1863–1877*, updated ed. (HarperPerennial, 2014), 462.

94. William G. Thomas, *The Iron Way: Railroads, the Civil War, and the Making of Modern America* (Yale University Press, 2011), 201.

95. Woodward, *Reunion and Reaction*, 68–70. C. K. Brown, "The Southern Railway Security Company: An Early Instance of the Holding Company," *North Carolina Historical Review*, 6, no. 2 (April 1929): 158–70.

96. Quoted in Julius Grodinsky, *Transcontinental Railway Strategy, 1869–1893: A Study of Businessmen* (University of Pennsylvania Press, 1962), 18.

97. J. S. Morgan & Co. papers, London Metropolitan Archives, HC3.1.23 (1871).

98. Albert J. Churella, *The Pennsylvania Railroad*, vol. 1 (University of Pennsylvania Press, 2012), 413.

99. Churella, *The Pennsylvania Railroad*, 409.

100. In his recent book, Professor Langlois glosses over the question of divided loyalties by simply observing that "Carnegie and Scott used their insider connections to set up corporations that were essentially part of the Pennsylvania Railroad group." Richard N. Langlois, *The Corporation and the Twentieth Century* (Princeton University Press, 2023), 63. The word "essentially" is doing a lot more work here than the casual reader might surmise.

101. H. W. Brands, *American Colossus* (Doubleday: 2010), 78–79.

102. Maury Klein, *Union Pacific: The Birth of a Railroad, 1862–1893* (Doubleday, 1987), 303.

103. Susie J. Pak, *Gentlemen Bankers: The World of J. P. Morgan* (Harvard University Press, 2013), 221.

104. Virginia H. Taylor, *The Franco-Texan Land Company* (University of Texas Press, 1969), 63–66.

105. "Chapter of History: General Fremont's Southern Pacific Railroad–How a Railroad Three Miles Long Earned Half a Million," *Courier-Journal*, August 21, 1870.

106. Albert V. House Jr., "Post-Civil War Precedents for Recent Railroad Reorganization," *Mississippi Valley Historical Review* 25, no. 4 (March 1939): 514.

107. Douglas Campbell, *Opening Argument Before the Judiciary Committee of the House of Representatives* (Washington, DC, 1878), 22–26.

108. Forbes v. Memphis, E P & P R Co, 9 F. Cas. 408, 410 (C.C.W.D. Tex. 1872).

109. Taylor, *The Franco-Texan Land Company*, 71–72.

110. 16 Stat. 573. In this act, the railroad was called the "Texas Pacific Railroad Company"; in 1872, the name was changed to the Texas *and* Pacific *Railway* Company, which I use throughout.

111. 16 Stat. 573, section 9.

112. 16 Stat. 573, section 1.

113. 16 Stat. 573, section 23. A handwritten version of the rider adding section 23 to the bill is in the Texas and Pacific Corporate files, which might suggest that the railroad's promoters were responsible for opening the door to the Southern Pacific. Missouri Pacific Historical Society, MF4 (1122–1947). Whoever wrote the rider also corrected the spelling of "Marshall O. Roberts" in the bill.

114. 16 Stat. 573, section 1.

115. Rebecca Edwards, *New Spirits: Americans in the "Gilded Age,"* 3rd ed. (Oxford University Press, 2015), 16.

116. Summers, *Railroad, Reconstruction, and the Gospel of Prosperity*, 289.

117. Foner, *Reconstruction*, 467.

118. Act of May 24, 1871; Act of November 21, 1871.

119. Act of May 2, 1873.

120. Missouri Pacific Historical Society, MF15 (0775–0878) (Affidavit of Charles E. Satterlee, June 1892, both quotes).

121. Summers, *Railroad, Reconstruction, and the Gospel of Prosperity*, 166.

122. Dolores Greenberg, *Financiers and Railroads, 1869–1889: A Study of Morton, Bliss & Company* (University of Delaware Press, 1980), 43.

123. "Texas Pacific Railroad," *Cincinnati Daily Enquirer*, April 17, 1871. The press reports seem to come from Roberts's speech, in which he urged the incorporators to allow Roberts *and his associates* to buy 11,000 of the projected 20,000 shares to be sold, "being a controlling interest in the company."

124. *New York Tribune*, March 28, 1871 (notice of the April 15 meeting). The notice appeared again in the same paper on April 10.

125. "The Texas Pacific Railroad," *New York Tribune*, April 17, 1871. "The Texas Pacific Railroad: Meeting of the Incorporation," *Republican Banner*, April 19, 1871.

126. "The Texas Pacific Railroad—Election of Directors Deferred," *New York Tribune*, April 18, 1871.

127. "The Texas Pacific Railroad: Meeting of the Incorporation—the Preliminary Issue of Stock All Subscribed For," *Republican Banner*, April 19, 1871.

128. *New York Tribune*, May 19, 1871.

129. Missouri Pacific Historical Society, MF6 (1893–1899).

130. U.S. Congress, Senate, Letter from the Secretary of the Interior, 48th Cong., 1st sess., December 20, 1883, Ex. Doc. No. 27, 11.

131. Ralph N. Traxler, "Collis P. Huntington and the Texas and Pacific Railroad Land Grant," *New Mexico Historical Review* 34, no. 2 (April 1959): 121.

132. "Washington: Railroad Legislation in 1871," *New York Tribune*, February 24, 1876.

133. Churella, *The Pennsylvania Railroad*, 420.

134. Missouri Pacific Historical Society, MF16 (1581–1640).

135. Missouri Pacific Historical Society, MF16 (1517–1566).

136. Missouri Pacific Historical Society, MF16 (1581–1640).

137. *Report Made to the President and Executive Board of the Texas Pacific Railroad by General G. P. Buell, Chief Engineer*, New York, dated July 1871.

138. "Affairs in New York," *The Baltimore Sun*, July 31, 1871.

139. Taylor, *The Franco-Texan Land Company*, 85.

140. "Tom Scott and His Railroads," *Cincinnati Daily Enquirer*, January 31, 1872.

141. Printed record in Stevenson v. Texas Ry. Co., 105 U.S. 703, 26 L. Ed. 1215 (1881), at 592 (Deposition of Marshall O. Roberts, September 4, 1875).

142. "The Texas Pacific Railroad Company," *The Commercial and Financial Chronicle*, March 2, 1872 (dating the resignation to February 16).

143. "Look to Congress!" *The Road*, February 1, 1879.

144. Missouri Pacific Historical Society, MF6 (1900–1938). The March 21, 1872, vote in favor of the deal can be found in Missouri Pacific Historical Society, MF6 (0708–0730). In the tally, 11,864 of the 12,500 outstanding shares voted in favor, which was unanimous among the shares that voted—Scott controlled 6,256 shares at this point, so the outcome was never really in doubt.

145. Printed record in Stevenson v. Texas Ry. Co., 105 U.S. 703, 26 L. Ed. 1215 (1881), at 804 (Thomas A. Scott, Answer to Interrogatories, undated). Among the debts paid in the acquisition was about $200,000 owed to Marshall Roberts. Details of the debts paid to Marshall and the "Louisville Association" can be found in Missouri Pacific Historical Society, MF4 (1122–1947) (letter from W. C. Hall to Scott, dated November 2, 1872, and letter from Smith to Hart, dated November 9, 1872). The Louisville group accepted Texas and Pacific notes as payment of their debt.

146. Indenture dated March 30, 1872: Southern Transcontinental Railway Company to Texas Pacific Railroad Company. See also Missouri Pacific Historical Society, MF16 (1517–1566).

147. Indenture dated March 21, 1872: Southern Pacific Railroad Company to Texas Pacific Railroad Company. Copies of both indentures can be found in various places, including the Texas and Pacific 1872 Annual Report. Copies of the minutes of the March shareholders meeting, also dated March 21, can be found in Missouri Pacific Historical Society, MF4 (1122–1947). Several shareholder proxies regarding the meeting also appear near the minutes in the file.

148. Davis v. Gray. Articles of agreement between Enoch L. Fancher, of the city, county and state of New York, as trustee, party of the first part; John A. C. Gray, of the same place, as receiver of the Memphis, El Paso & Pacific Railroad Company, and as trustee, party of the second part, and the Texas & Pacific Railway Company, a corporation created by and existing under the laws of the United States, party of the third part, dated June 12, 1873.

149. Texas and Pacific 1875 Annual Report, 8–9.

150. The Texas and Pacific Railway Company, 29 ICC Val. Rep. 525, 582 (1929).

151. Printed record in Stevenson v. Texas Ry. Co., 105 U.S. 703, 26 L. Ed. 1215 (1881), at 809 (Thomas A. Scott, Answer to Interrogatories, undated). The Texas and Pacific 1875 annual report (7) states that before the 1868 sale, the Southern Pacific built between the state border westward, while the twenty miles in Louisiana was actually owned by the Vicksburg, Shreveport and Texas Railroad Company and operated under a lease by the Southern Pacific. The sale united the parts under a single corporation called the Southern Pacific Railroad Company, which was then purchased by the Texas and Pacific. As of late 1885, it appeared that the Texas and Pacific still leased this small bit of its line. Missouri Pacific Railway Company v. the Texas and Pacific Railway Company, box 683 (petition for appointment of receivers, dated December 15, 1885, para. 4).

152. See Texas & Pacific Railway Co. v. City of Marshall, 136 U.S. 393, 396, 10 S. Ct. 846, 847, 34 L. Ed. 385 (1890).

153. Missouri Pacific Historical Society, MF4 (2028–2035).

154. 29 ICC Val. Rep., at 547. The 1875 Annual Report states that it was $40,000 per mile of the first type of bond.

155. Missouri Pacific Historical Society, MF4 (1122–1947) (transcript of testimony of Frank S. Bond, from pleadings in Commonwealth v. Texas and Pacific).

156. Missouri Pacific Historical Society, MF4 (1122–1947) (receipt dated November 22, 1872). Interesting, as noted earlier, Roberts bought 5,500 shares from the Southern Pacific under the deal with Hall, so Scott (or Roberts before him) had acquired additional shares along the way.

157. Annual Report of the California & Texas Railway Construction Co., dated June 4, 1874, at 7.

158. "Financial and Commercial," The Philadelphia Inquirer, September 2, 1872.

159. Missouri Pacific Historical Society, MF6 (0730–0735) (memorandum of agreement between the Texas and Pacific—signed by Scott—and John Harold of Liverpool and Robert E. Randall of Philadelphia).

160. Missouri Pacific Historical Society, MF4 (0941–0953) (prospectus for 1873 construction bonds).

161. Greenberg, Financiers and Railroads, 55.

162. "Col. Tom Scott: Arrival of the Great American Railway Monarch," San Francisco Chronicle, August 21, 1872.

163. "Tom Scott's New Road," San Francisco Chronicle, August 23, 1872.

164. That distance was about what the San Antonio to San Diego stagecoach managed to cover in about two months before the Civil War, but that required nonstop travel, with relay teams of mules.

165. "Col. Scott's Reception: His Triumphal Journey to San Diego," *San Francisco Chronicle*, August 28, 1872.

166. An ad for real estate sales in San Diego, using similar phrasing as the pamphlet, appears in *Harper's Weekly*, July 27, 1872 (90), which suggests that real estate interests were behind the publication.

167. J. R. Perkins, *Trails, Rails and War: The Life of General G. M. Dodge* (Bobbs-Merrill, 1929), 251. Perkins's biography has to be handled with care; it reads as propaganda.

168. *Annual Report of the California & Texas Railway Construction Co.*, dated June 4, 1874, 7.

169. Wallace D. Farnham, "Grenville Dodge and the Union Pacific: A Study of Historical Legends," *Journal of American History* 51, no. 4 (March 1965): 632–50.

170. Klein, *Union Pacific*, 19.

171. Farnham, "Grenville Dodge."

172. Tempel v. Dodge, 89 Tex. 69, 69, 32 S.W. 514, 514 (1895).

173. Richard C. Overton, *Gulf to Rockies* (University of Texas Press, 1953), 93–94. See also *Dodge Book X*, part 1, 657 (Dodge to Washburn, October 8, 1881).

174. "Grenville M. Dodge," *Railway Age Gazette*, January 7, 1916.

175. Missouri Pacific Historical Society, MF6 (1165–1216) (California & Texas letter dated May 14, 1873).

176. W. J. Burton, "History of the Missouri Pacific" (unpublished manuscript, July 1, 1956), 643.

177. Missouri Pacific Historical Society, MF9 (1759–1769).

178. "Worse Than Modocs: An Unoffending Negro Tortured and Murdered by 'Respectable' White Citizens of Texas," *The New York Times*, June 12, 1873.

179. Missouri Pacific Historical Society, MF9 (1770–1780).

180. Missouri Pacific Historical Society, MF9 (1781–1785).

181. Burton, "History of the Missouri Pacific," at 643.

182. Edwards, *New Spirits*, 41.

183. Cannadine, *Victorious Century*, 371.

184. On Cooke's role during the war, see Bray Hammond, *Sovereignty and an Empty Purse; Banks and Politics in the Civil War* (Princeton University Press, 1970), 289, 335–36.

185. Charles P. Kindleberger and Robert Z. Aliber, *Manias, Panics, and Crashes: A History of Financial Crises*, 5th ed. (John Wiley & Sons, 2005), 137.

186. An involuntary bankruptcy petition was later filed against the firm, and some blamed the ensuing depression on the bankruptcy case and presented it as grounds for repeal of the existing bankruptcy statute, even though the case was filed almost two weeks after the firm collapsed. Charles Warren, *Bankruptcy in United States History* (Harvard University Press), 114–15. The bankruptcy case was still pending as late as 1884. "Preemptory Sale," *The Philadelphia Inquirer*, May 8, 1884 (notice of sale of various parcels of real estate by the trustee). It may have been wound down in 1885. "Estate of Jay Cooke & Co," *The Philadelphia Inquirer*, March 19, 1885 (small classified notice requesting that creditors claim the remaining dividends).

187. Jay Sexton, *Debtor Diplomacy* (Oxford University Press, 2005), 236–39.

188. Christoph Nitschke, "Theory and History of Financial Crises: Explaining the Panic of 1873," *Journal of the Gilded Age and Progressive Era* 17, no. 2 (2018): 229. "Crash Reverberations," *The Atlanta Constitution*, October 2, 1873.

189. "The Money Market and Financial Situation," *The Commercial and Financial Chronicle*, November 8, 1873. George Heckman Burgess and Miles C. Kennedy, *Centennial History of the Pennsylvania Railroad Company, 1846–1946* (Pennsylvania Railroad Co., 1949), 349.

190. Grodinsky, *Transcontinental Railway Strategy*, 46; Summers, *Railroad, Reconstruction, and the Gospel of Prosperity*, 277. See also J. S. Morgan & Co. papers, London

Metropolitan Archives, HC3.1.23 (1876) (documents related to the winding-up of the company).

191. Nicolas Barreyre, "The Politics of Economic Crises: The Panic of 1873, the End of Reconstruction, and the Realignment of American Politics," *Journal of the Gilded Age and Progressive Era* 10, no. 4 (2011): 408.

192. "Railroad Interests," *New York Tribune*, October 29, 1873.

193. Union Pacific R. Co. v. United States, 99 U.S. 700, 723, 25 L. Ed. 496 (1878).

194. Thomas, *The Iron Way: Railroads, the Civil War, and the Making of Modern America*, 199.

195. John F. Stover, *American Railroads*, 2nd ed. (University of Chicago Press, 1997), 70–71.

196. "The Scott Railroad Interests," *New York Tribune*, November 6, 1873.

197. White, *Railroaded*, 94.

198. Annual Report of the California & Texas Railway Construction Co., dated June 4, 1874, 5–6.

199. J. S. Morgan & Co. papers, London Metropolitan Archives, HC3.1.1(25) (copy of telegram sent to Drexel Morgan New York, dated September 22, 1873). Formally, the loan was made by the London & San Francisco Bank (an institution located in the same building as J. S. Morgan & Co.), which itself borrowed from the London Joint Stock Bank, and the loan was guaranteed by J. S. Morgan. The latter ultimately paid off on the guaranty and negotiated repayment directly with the borrowers. This may be the loan that Andrew Carnegie discusses in his autobiography, although his account of it is unclear, at times suggesting that it was a loan to the Construction Company. *The Autobiography of Andrew Carnegie* (Constable & Co. Ltd. 1920), 173. Carnegie writes that his refusal to guaranty the loan "marked another step in the total business separation which had to come between Mr. Scott and myself. It gave more pain than all the financial trials to which I had been subjected up to that time."

200. The fourth piece of the Drexel-Morgan operation was Drexel, Harjes and Company in Paris. Dan Rottenberg, *The Man Who Made Wall Street* (University of Pennsylvania Press, 2001), 101–2. See also Kathleen Burk, *Morgan Grenfell, 1838–1988: The Biography of a Merchant Bank* (Oxford University Press, 1989), 36–37.

201. J. S. Morgan & Co. papers, London Metropolitan Archives, HC3.1.1(25) (telegram, Scott to J. S. Morgan, October 5, 1873).

202. See the papers in J. S. Morgan & Co. papers, London Metropolitan Archives, HC3.1.1(25) generally. There are indications that the borrowers were already in distress when the loan was made, with a note in the file stating that the transaction was "altogether done from notions of aiding an escape from difficulties by the parties in Philadelphia." Nonetheless, the Texas and Pacific collateral was accepted.

203. Annual Report of the California & Texas Railway Construction Co., 9.

204. "California & Texas Construction Company," *The Commercial and Financial Chronicle*, December 13, 1873.

205. *Dodge Book IX*, part 1, 5 (Dodge to Scott, January 2, 1874).

206. J. S. Morgan & Co. papers, London Metropolitan Archives, HC3.15.8 (letter from George Cabot Ward, dated October 26, 1874).

207. 29 ICC Val. Rep. at 546. Texas and Pacific 1875 Annual Report; see also Supplement Report to the Texas and Pacific 1874 Annual Report.

208. Missouri Pacific Historical Society, MF4 (1122–1947) (transcript of testimony of Frank S. Bond, from pleadings in Commonwealth v. Texas and Pacific).

209. The Construction Company continued to exist, however, until at least 1890. Missouri Pacific Historical Society, MF4 (2245–2490) (letter from Wistar dated January 1890, regarding scheduling the annual meeting).

210. J. S. Morgan & Co. papers, London Metropolitan Archives, HC3.15 (Scott to J. S. Morgan, May 18, 1875).

211. Thus, in 1882, the railroad paid off 314 of the first-lien bonds (worth $3,140) and immediately issued new consolidated bonds in the same amount. "Texas Pacific," *The Commercial and Financial Chronicle*, November 4, 1882. Of course, once the first-lien bonds were entirely paid off, the consolidated bonds, with a second lien, would effectively become first-lien bonds with regard to the wonky rectangle.

212. For example, see the 1885 edition of Poor, *Manual of the Railroads of the United States*, 834, which reports, "Land securities received, $731,278.32; land notes received, $943,297.67; cash, $1,608.18—total, $1,676,184.17."

213. Texas and Pacific 1878 Annual Report, 6–7.

214. Sexton, *Debtor Diplomacy*, 246. See also Hammond, *Sovereignty and an Empty Purse*, 357.

215. Joshua D. Wolff, *Western Union and the Creation of the American Corporate Order, 1845–1893* (Cambridge University Press, 2013), 16.

216. "The Week," *The Nation*, January 18, 1877. See also "The South and the Texas-And-Pacific Job," *The Nation*, February 8, 1877. The Half Breeds were led by James G. Blaine, who was probably just as corrupt as Roscoe Conkling, the leader of the "Stalwart" or traditional Republicans; thus the term "reform" is used loosely. Lewis L. Gould, *The Republicans: A History of the Grand Old Party* (Oxford University Press, 2014), 74–76.

217. "The Week," *The Nation*, May 3, 1887.

218. White, *Railroaded*, 95.

219. Colton Letters, as reproduced in Salvador A. Ramirez, *The Octopus Speaks: The Colton Letters, Edited, with Notes and Introduction* (Carlsbad, CA: Tentacled Press, 1982), December 8, 1874 (Huntington to Scott).

220. Colton Letters, December 9, 1874 (Scott to Huntington).

221. See the letter reprinted in Texas and Pacific Railroad, Speech of Hon. Henry W. Blair, of New Hampshire in the House of Representatives—Monday, January 20, 1879—Against the Bill Providing for a Subsidy to the Texas and Pacific Railroad (Washington, DC: 1879), 13–14.

222. *Dodge Book IX*, part 1, 127 (Dodge to Scott, December 19, 1874); at 215 (same, January 12, 1875); and at 225 (same, January 26, 1875). All three were written from Washington, D.C.

223. "Personal," *Post* (Pittsburgh), December 20, 1875. The appointment was officially announced in late December, but in October, Brown sat for an interview with the *Atlanta Constitution*, where he sure sounded like a Texas and Pacific employee. "The Pacific Road," *The Atlanta Constitution*, October 10, 1875.

224. "Brown, John Calvin," in *New American Supplement to Encyclopedia Britannica*, vol. 1 (Werner Co., 1899).

225. Helen Hershkoff and Fred Smith Jr., "Reconstructing Klein," *University of Chicago Law Review* 90, no. 8 (December 2023): 2107–108, 2136–140.

226. Mark Wahlgren Summers, *The Ordeal of the Reunion: A New History of Reconstruction* (University of North Carolina Press, 2014), 147–48. Sam Davis Elliot, *John C. Brown of Tennessee: Rebel, Redeemer, and Railroader* (University of Tennessee Press, 2017), 153–59, 280–81.

227. Woodward, *Reunion and Reaction*, 38.

228. Joshua W. Caldwell, *Sketches of the Bench and Bar of Tennessee* (Ogden Bros. & Co., 1898), 294.

229. "Alexander H. Stephens," *Boston Globe*, September 27, 1877. In the interview, Stephens notes that at that point, he had supported the Texas and Pacific for at least five years.

230. Scott Reynolds Nelson, *Iron Confederacies: Southern Railways, Klan Violence, and Reconstruction* (University of North Carolina Press, 1999), 182.
231. "Themes in Money Centers," *New York Tribune*, January 27, 1875 (letter from Scott to the paper).
232. "The Texas Pacific Railroad," *St. Louis Dispatch*, January 24, 1876. See also Starr, *Inventing the Dream*, 199–203, 236.
233. Brook Thomas, "Ruiz de Burton, Railroads, Reconstruction," 80, no. 3 *ELH* (Fall 2013): 871–95.
234. Lloyd J. Mercer, *Railroads and Land Grant Policy: A Study in Government Intervention* (Academic Press, 1982), 45–46.
235. Summers, *Railroad, Reconstruction, and the Gospel of Prosperity*, 172–74.
236. Colton Letters, March 22, 1876; August 7, 1876 (all, Huntington to Colton).
237. Colton Letters, February 26, 1876 (Huntington to Colton).
238. Colton Letters, February 2, 1878 (Huntington to Colton).
239. Cerinda W. Evans, *Collis Porter Huntington*, vol. 1 (Mariners' Museum, 1954), 252.
240. Grodinsky, *Transcontinental Railway Strategy*, 67.
241. Colton Letters, September 11, 1878 (Huntington to Colton).
242. Colton Letters, October 4, 1878 (Huntington to Colton). "Gen. Sherman's Trip," *The Washington Post*, October 9, 1879.
243. Samuel DeCanio, *Democracy and the Origins of the American Regulatory State* (Yale University Press, 2015), 160. The most famous of the several efforts that Scott made was during the controversy surrounding the 1876 presidential election, but this too failed. Michael Les Benedict, *Preserving the Constitution: Essays on Politics and the Constitution in the Era of Reconstruction* (Fordham University Press, 2006), 198–99.
244. Grodinsky, *Transcontinental Railway Strategy*, 60.
245. C. Loyal (María Amparo Ruiz de Burton), *The Squatter and the Don* (S. Carson & Co., 1885), 320–21.

2. Jay Gould and the Texas and Pacific

1. Vincent P. Carosso, *Investment Banking in America: A History* (Harvard University Press, 1970), 29.
2. Elroy Dimson, Paul Marsh, and Mike Staunton, *Global Investment Returns Yearbook* (UBS, 2024).
3. See Milton Friedman and Anna Jacobson Schwartz, *A Monetary History of the United States, 1867–1960* (Princeton University Press, 1963), 42–44, 77–78.
4. Oscar Osburn Winther, "The Rise of Metropolitan Los Angeles, 1870–1900," *Huntington Library Quarterly* 10, no. 4 (1947): 391–93.
5. Kevin Starr, *Inventing the Dream: California Through the Progressive Era* (Oxford University Press, 1986), 36.
6. Starr, *Inventing the Dream*, 40–41, 132–33, 140–46. See generally Glenn Dumke, "The Boom of the 1880s in Southern California," *Southern California Quarterly* 76, no. 1 (1994): 99–114.
7. Stuart Daggett, *Chapters on the History of the Southern Pacific* (Ronald Press Co., 1922), 127.
8. Franklin Hoyt, "Railroad Development in Southern California: 1868 to 1900" (PhD diss., University of Southern California, 1951), 339.

9. Colton Letters, as reproduced in Salvador A. Ramirez, *The Octopus Speaks: The Colton Letters, Edited, with Notes and Introduction* (Tentacled Press, 1982), January 31, 1878 (Colton to Huntington).

10. "Railways in Japan," *Daily American*, March 31, 1881. Correspondence from the engineer to Philadelphia, dated as late as 1877, can be found in Missouri Pacific Historical Society, MF4 (1122–1947).

11. "The Texas Pacific and the South," *The New York Times*, October 2, 1878.

12. "A Very Bad Cause," *Courier-Journal*, October 12, 1878. See also "The War on the Texas Pacific," *Courier-Journal*, October 5, 1878.

13. "Necessity of Competition," *San Francisco Chronicle*, September 5, 1878.

14. Richard White, "Information, Markets, and Corruption: Transcontinental Railroads in the Gilded Age," *Journal of American History* 90, no. 1 (2003): 43.

15. On October 16, Scott met with the visiting mayor of Baltimore, which puts the stroke in the second half of the month. "Visitors from Baltimore," *The Philadelphia Inquirer*, October 17, 1878.

16. "Urged to Take a Respite," *The Philadelphia Inquirer*, October 31, 1878. "President Scott Sails for Europe," *The Philadelphia Inquirer*, November 4, 1878. See also "Local Summary," *The Philadelphia Inquirer*, November 5, 1878, which states, "The Switzerland, of the Red Star line, sailed yesterday, taking out a cargo valued at $128,453. Among the cabin passengers are Colonel Scott and family," and "Colonel Scott Sails for Europe," *North American*, November 5, 1878; "The Last Two Years . . .", *North American*, November 4, 1878.

17. "Personal," *New York Tribune*, November 6, 1878. "Colonel Thomas A. Scott's Illness," *The New York Times*, November 10, 1878.

18. "Colonel Tom Scott: Authoritative Contradiction of the Story of His Paralysis," *The Cincinnati Daily Enquirer*, November 14, 1878.

19. "Return of President Scott," *The Philadelphia Inquirer*, September 11, 1879.

20. "A Wooden Horse," *Courier-Journal*, January 7, 1879.

21. "Why This Opposition?" *San Francisco Chronicle*, January 22, 1879.

22. Texas and Pacific Railroad, "Speech of Hon. Henry W. Blair, of New Hampshire in the House of Representatives,—Monday, January 20, 1879—Against the Bill Providing for a Subsidy to the Texas and Pacific Railroad" (Washington, DC: 1879), 7. This printed version of the speech is more than twenty pages, in small, single-spaced type, although about four pages represents Blair's dissent from the House committee's prior approval of a subsidy bill (reprinted in even smaller type).

23. Richard White, *Railroaded: The Transcontinentals and the Making of Modern America* (W. W. Norton, 2011), 129.

24. Henry V. Poor, *Manual of the Railroads of the United States: 1879* (H. V. & H. W. Poor, 1879), 877.

25. "The Texas and Pacific Railway," *The New York Times*, August 13, 1879.

26. "The Texas Pacific," *The Baltimore Sun*, August 16, 1879.

27. "Trustee's Notice" (classified ad), *The New York Times*, August 4, 1879.

28. "Their Big Chief," *Courier-Journal*, November 9, 1879.

29. "Track Talk," *Daily Inter Ocean*, November 11, 1879.

30. "Financial Condition of the Texas and Pacific," *The Cincinnati Daily Enquirer*, November 24, 1879.

31. "Col. Thomas Scott, President of the Pennsylvania Railroad, Denies the Rumor That Gen. Grant Is to Become President of the Pennsylvania Railroad, Also One That Col. Scott Intends Giving up the Texas Pacific." *Lowell Daily Citizen*, November 17, 1879.

32. "Southern Pacific Railways," *The Philadelphia Inquirer*, December 9, 1879.
33. The Southern Pacific arrived in Tucson in March 1880. "The First Locomotive," *The Atlanta Constitution*, March 19, 1880. See also "Southern Pacific Railway," *New York Tribune*, April 25, 1880.
34. "The Texas Pacific Contract," *Courier-Journal*, January 7, 1880.
35. Hoyt, "Railroad Development in Southern California," 259–60.
36. Reproduced in Hoyt, "Railroad Development in Southern California," 340.
37. Missouri Pacific Historical Society, MF6 (0554–0560).
38. "South Pacific Railways," *The Philadelphia Inquirer*, December 9, 1879. The San Francisco papers reported similar news in late November. "The Southern Pacific," *San Francisco Chronicle*, November 28, 1879.
39. "The Texas Pacific: Jay Gould Reaching out for Its Control," *The Cincinnati Daily Enquirer*, December 10, 1879. The *New York Tribune* had the story a few days later with a bit more detail. "The Texas Route to the Pacific," *New York Tribune*, December 16, 1879.
40. Maury Klein, *The Life and Legend of Jay Gould* (John Hopkins University Press, 1986), 258.
41. Klein, *The Life and Legend of Jay Gould*, is the key biography of Gould, although I am somewhat less forgiving of Gould's insider dealing than Professor Klein. However, Professor Klein is surely right that much of what Gould has been criticized for was also done by Huntington, Scott, and even the near-sainted (at least in recent years) J. P. Morgan.
42. John Steele Gordon, *The Scarlet Woman of Wall Street* (Weidenfeld & Nicolson, 1988), chap. 13.
43. "Men of Many Millions," *The Washington Post*, April 25, 1885. On both events, see generally Charles Francis Adams, Jr., and Henry Adams, *Chapters of Erie* (Waveland Press, 2002; orig. 1871).
44. Maury Klein, *Union Pacific: The Birth of a Railroad, 1862–1893* (Doubleday, 1987), 309.
45. Eugene V. Debs, "Jay Gould," *Locomotive Fireman's Magazine* 13, no. 5 (May 1889): 390–91.
46. Julius Grodinsky, *Jay Gould: His Business Career* (University of Pennsylvania Press, 1957), 269–314.
47. Joshua D. Wolff, *Western Union and the Creation of the American Corporate Order, 1845–1893* (Cambridge University Press, 2013), 208–31, 257–59.
48. Robert E. Pattison et al., *Report of the United States Pacific Railway Commission [and Testimony Taken by the Commission]* (US Government Publishing Office, 1887), 477, 505–6 (testimony of Jay Gould).
49. *St. Louis Dispatch*, December 14, 1880.
50. Dolores Greenberg, *Financiers and Railroads, 1869–1889: A Study of Morton, Bliss & Company* (University of Delaware Press, 1980), 69.
51. "On to Mexico," *St. Louis Dispatch*, December 25, 1880.
52. Pattison et al., *Report of the United States Pacific Railway Commission*, 506. See also Klein, *The Life and Legend of Jay Gould*, 251, 260.
53. J. S. Morgan & Co. papers, London Metropolitan Archives HC3.1.1.(13) (letter from DM New York to JSM London, dated April 28, 1880).
54. Philip H. Burch, Jr., *Elites in American History* (Holmes & Meier, 1981), 71.
55. Klein, *The Life and Legend of Jay Gould*, 225.
56. Pacific Railway Improvement Company, at 107–8. Pacific Railway Improvement Company, at 110.

57. "Jay Gould's Credit Mobilier," *The New York Times*, January 6, 1880.
58. *The Philadelphia Inquirer*, March 25, 1880. "Finance and Commerce," *The Washington Post*, January 28, 1880. See also Julius Grodinsky, *Transcontinental Railway Strategy, 1869–1893: A Study of Businessmen* (University of Pennsylvania Press, 1962), 189–90.
59. Klein, *The Life and Legend of Jay Gould*, 266.
60. "Ex-Judge Dillon, Noted Lawyer, Dies," *The New York Times*, May 6, 1914.
61. Charles R. Geisst, *Wall Street: A History*, updated ed. (Oxford University Press, 2012), 70.
62. "Missouri, Kansas, and Texas," *Railway World*, January 31, 1880.
63. Grodinsky, *Jay Gould: His Business Career*, 255. See also Klein, *The Life and Legend of Jay Gould*, 320–21.
64. Henry Clews, *Fifty Years in Wall Street* (John Wiley & Sons, 2006; orig. 1906), 349. George Wheeler, *Pierpont Morgan & Friends: The Anatomy of a Myth* (Prentice-Hall, 1973), 162–63.
65. Pacific Railway Improvement Company, at 107, 111. Pullman signed in Chicago, in front of another commissioner.
66. Pacific Railway Improvement Company, at 110.
67. *The New York Times*, January 6, 1880; *The Philadelphia Inquirer*, January 2, 1880. *Fidelity Insurance, Trust, and Safe Deposit Co. v. Texas and Pacific Railway Co.*, No. 93, C.C.N.D. Texas, Bill of Complaint, dated June 16, 1886, at paragraph "twelfth."
68. *The Philadelphia Inquirer*, January 3, 1880.
69. *The New York Times*, January 6, 1880 (story dated January 2, "from the Cincinnati Commercial").
70. "Finance and Trade," *Chicago Tribune*, January 25, 1880. See also Missouri Pacific Historical Society, MF9 (1814–1821), annual report, dated June 30, 1880.
71. "Financial Affairs," *The New York Times*, September 14, 1881, which reports that: "The Pacific Railway Improvement Company gives notice that the tenth installment of 10 per cent. upon subscriptions for the extensions of the Texas and Pacific Railway will be due Sept. 22 at the office of Messrs. Woerishoffer & Co., No. 54 Exchange-place. The balance of stock due upon subscriptions and bonds appertaining to the seventh installment of 10 per cent. will be ready for delivery on that date."
72. *Courier-Journal*, March 26, 1881 (classified ad). "The Backbone Railroad," *The New York Times*, January 10, 1885. "The Money Market," *New York Tribune*, September 10, 1881. See also Grodinsky, *Jay Gould: His Business Career*, 255–56.
73. *New York Tribune*, May 13, 1882 (classified ad).
74. *Montreal Herald and Daily Commercial Gazette*, May 15, 1882.
75. Missouri Pacific Railroad Co. et al., 40 ICC Valuation Rep. 249, 489 (1933).
76. *The New York Times*, November 29, 1882.
77. *Railway Age*, February 1880.
78. "Port of Galveston," *Galveston Daily News*, March 6, 1881.
79. "The Yearly Consumption of Rails," *Railway Gazette*, September 2, 1881.
80. W. J. Burton, "History of the Missouri Pacific" (unpublished manuscript, July 1, 1956), 667–68.
81. Edward J. M. Rhoads, "The Chinese in Texas," *Southwestern Historical Quarterly* 81, no. 1 (1977): 8. The author also notes (in a footnote on the same page) that while it is frequently said that Chinese workers built the Texas and Pacific, there is little actual evidence of this. As I note in chapter 3, many Chinese immigrants were employed to maintain the Rio Grande Division during the mid- to late-1880s. It is entirely possible that some authors confused maintenance and construction. "Miriam and Ira D.

Wallach Division of Art, Prints, and Photographs: Photography Collection," New York Public Library. "Indians Laborers, Employed by the Southern Pacific Railway, near El Paso," New York Public Library Digital Collections, https://digitalcollections.nypl.org /items/510d47e1-b1e2-a3d9-e040-e00a18064a99.

82. George W. Rafter, "Railroad-Building on the Texas Frontier," *Engineering Magazine*, vol. II (1891–1892): 36–38.

83. "Texas Topics," *Courier-Journal*, July 5, 1881.

84. Will Guzmán, *Civil Rights in the Texas Borderlands: Dr. Lawrence A. Nixon and Black Activism* (University of Illinois Press, 2015), 14.

85. "The Texas and Pacific," *Courier-Journal*, July 27, 1881.

86. Rafter, "Railroad-Building on the Texas Frontier": 35, 41.

87. "A New Pacific Railway in Sight," *New York Tribune*, August 12, 1880.

88. James E. Vance, *The North American Railroad: Its Origin, Evolution, and Geography* (Johns Hopkins University Press, 1995), 206.

89. Rafter, "Railroad-Building on the Texas Frontier": 32.

90. *The Philadelphia Inquirer*, January 2, 1882.

91. Grodinsky, *Transcontinental Railway Strategy*, 426.

92. American Railway Improvement Company, documents filed with the Colorado Secretary of State's Office, Incorporation Book 4 (12), Book 10 (444 and 594), and Book 15 (159); obtained from the Colorado State Archives, at 12–15.

93. American Railway Improvement Company, at 12.

94. American Railway Improvement Company, at 12, articles III and IV.

95. *Dodge Book X*, part 1, at 103 (Dodge to Baldwin, June 24, 1880).

96. American Railway Improvement Company, at 13–14, article VIII; *Railway World*, August 28, 1880.

97. 16 Stat. 573, section 22. That section provides, in full:

> That the New Orleans, Baton Rouge, and Vicksburg Railroad Company, chartered by the State of Louisiana, shall have right to connect, by the most eligible route to be selected by said company, with the said Texas Pacific Railroad at its eastern terminus, and shall have the right of way through the public land to the same extent granted hereby to the said Texas Pacific Railroad Company; and in aid of its construction from New Orleans to Baton Rouge, thence by the way of Alexandria, in said State, to connect with the said Texas Pacific Railroad Company at its eastern terminus, there is hereby granted to said company, its successors and assigns, the same number of alternate sections of public lands per mile, in the State of Louisiana, as are by this act granted in the State of California to said Texas Pacific Railroad Company; and said lands shall be withdrawn from market, selected, and patents issued therefor, and opened for settlement and pre-emption, upon the same terms and in the same manner and time as is provided for and required from said Texas Pacific Railroad Company, within said State of California: Provided, that said company shall complete the whole of said road within five years from the passage of this act.

> That is, "ten alternate sections of land per mile on each side of said railroad" (see section 9). Those connected to the construction company relied on an opinion from Judge Dillon, which argued that the last passage of section 22 only gave Congress an option to cancel the grant. Materials regarding the New Orleans Pacific Railway Company, Opinion of John F. Dillon and Wager Swayne, dated December 20, 1883; *Schulenberg v.*

Harriman, 88 U.S. 44, 55, 22 L. Ed. 551 (1874) ("The words are merely definitive of the condition, for the non-performance of which the legislature may thereafter declare a forfeiture, and are to be construed in connection with the whole act, and in the light of the objects to be accomplished thereby").

As with the section of the original Texas and Pacific bill that allowed the Southern Pacific to connect to the road, discussed in chapter 1, the section regarding the New Orleans, Baton Rouge was added to the bill by a handwritten rider that can be found in the Texas and Pacific corporate records. Missouri Pacific Historical Society, MF4 (1122–1947).

98. Nathaniel Means, "Sugarcane, Cotton Fields, and High Water: Building the Louisiana Branch of the Texas and Pacific Railroad," *Louisiana History: The Journal of the Louisiana Historical Association* 45, no. 4 (2004): 448.

99. Act of General Assembly of Louisiana, April 30, 1877, repealing an act incorporating the New Orleans, Baton Rouge and Vicksburg Railroad Company. Hayes withdrew the troops in April.

100. Act of the General Assembly of the State of Louisiana, no. 14 of 1876.

101. *Dodge Book X*, part 1, at 77 (Scott and Gould to Wheelock, April 3, 1880).

102. *Dodge Book X*, part 1, at 99 (Bond to Scott and Gould, June 23, 1880). "Managing the Railroads," *The New York Times*, April 17, 1880.

103. *Dodge Book X*, part 1, at 113.

104. *Dodge Book X*, part 1, at 105 (Dodge to Tichenor, July 2, 1880).

105. New Orleans Pacific Railway Company (Dodge affidavit dated October 17, 1882).

106. J. S. Morgan & Co. papers, London Metropolitan Archives, HC3.15 (Scott to J. S. Morgan, August 23, 1880). The letter shows that the Pacific Railway Improvement Company was not simply a Gould operation. Indeed, the letter opens by stating, "I am about taking charge of the New Orleans Pacific Road," and makes no mention of Gould at all.

107. 16 Stat. 573, section 16.

108. New Orleans Pacific Railway Company (board resolution, dated December 29, 1880).

109. New Orleans Pacific Railway Company (deed, dated January 5, 1880—this is undoubtedly an error, though, because the commissioner certificates put the date as 1881).

110. The firm is known today as Simpson Thacher & Bartlett. New Orleans Pacific Railway Company (board resolution, dated December 29, 1880).

111. New Orleans Pacific Railway Company (stockholders list, dated November 28, 1881).

112. New Orleans Pacific Railway Company (various proxies and adopted resolution, dated December 9, 1881).

113. Klein, *The Life and Legend of Jay Gould*, 258–59. See also "The Backbone Railroad," *The New York Times*, January 10, 1885.

114. *Dodge Book X*, part 1, at 193. The memorandum appears between two letters dated November 17, 1880, both to Gould.

115. New Orleans Pacific Railway Company (indenture dated June 20, 1881). Board resolutions and minutes regarding the transaction, along with a copy of the aforementioned indenture, can be found in Missouri Pacific Railway Company v. the Texas and Pacific Railway Company, no. 11,181, case files, National Archives at Fort Worth, box 676.

116. "Construction Companies," *Railway Gazette*, January 6, 1882.

117. Meyers v. Scott, 2 N.Y.S. 753, 754 (Gen. Term 1888).

118. American Railway Improvement Company, at 595, 159–163.

119. "President Scott's Resignation," *New York Tribune*, May 3, 1880; "Colonel T. A. Scott Resigns," *New York Tribune*, May 2, 1880.

120. "The Texas and Pacific Railroad," *The New York Times*, August 11, 1880; "The Texas and Pacific," *Daily American*, August 12, 1880.

121. *Dodge Book X*, part 1, at 117 (Bond to Dodge, August 5, 1880).

122. "Overland Railroads," *San Francisco Chronicle*, March 6, 1881.

123. "Railroad Matters," *Daily American*, November 11, 1880.

124. "The Texas and Pacific Road," *Courier-Journal*, November 15, 1880.

125. "Col. Scott on the South," *Courier-Journal*, November 27, 1880.

126. "Death of a Coast Merchant Abroad," *San Francisco Chronicle*, February 19, 1898. See also Franklin Hoyt, "Railroad Development in Southern California: 1868 to 1900" (PhD diss., University of Southern California, 1951), 340.

127. "Overland Railroads."

128. "The Railroads," *Courier-Journal*, March 25, 1881.

129. "Personal," *New York Tribune*, April 1, 1881; "The Texas and Pacific and Col. Scott," *The Baltimore Sun*, April 15, 1881.

130. "Rail and Tie," *The Philadelphia Inquirer*, April 13, 1881.

131. Grodinsky, *Jay Gould: His Business Career*, 263.

132. *The New York Times*, May 12, 1881 (classified ad). The office address was 195 Broadway; the present Western Union building (at the same address) was built during the World War I era.

133. "At Rest," *The Philadelphia Inquirer*, May 23, 1881. The paper attributed Scott's strokes to a head injury that he had sustained years earlier in a train wreck.

134. Richard J. Orsi, *Sunset Limited: The Southern Pacific Railroad and the Development of the American West, 1850–1930* (University of California Press, 2005), 22.

135. The board resolutions can be found in Missouri Pacific Railway Company v. the Texas and Pacific Railway Company, no. 11,181, case files, National Archives at Fort Worth, box 671, among other places.

136. Missouri Pacific Railway Company v. the Texas and Pacific Railway Company, no. 11,181, case files, National Archives at Fort Worth, box 668 (documentary evidence submitted in New Mexico litigation, which includes several letters between the parties).

137. Exhibit D of complaint in Texas Pacific Railway Co. v. Southern Pacific Railroad Co. of New Mexico, dated May 11, 1881.

138. "Notes of Points for the Complainant," Texas Pacific Railway Co. v. Southern Pacific Railroad Co. of New Mexico.

139. Complaint, dated May 11, 1881, and amendments thereto, in Texas Pacific Railway Co. v. Southern Pacific Railroad Co. of New Mexico.

140. Missouri Pacific Railway Company v. the Texas and Pacific Railway Company, no. 11,181, case files, National Archives at Fort Worth, box 676 (complaint dated July 23, 1881).

141. Missouri Pacific Railway Company v. the Texas and Pacific Railway Company, no. 11,181, case files, National Archives at Fort Worth, box 673 (letter from Huntington to Satterlee, June 21, 1881).

142. John F. Dillon, *The Law and Jurisprudence of England and America* (Little Brown & Co., 1894), 222–23. He tells the story somewhat differently in his deposition of 1893, giving more credit to Gould for coming up with the legal arguments. Missouri Pacific Railway Company v. the Texas and Pacific Railway Company, no. 11,181, case files, National Archives at Fort Worth, box 671 (deposition of John F. Dillon, November 18, 1893).

143. Affidavit of Charles Crocker, dated June 11, 1881, in Texas Pacific Railway Co. v. Southern Pacific Railroad Co. of New Mexico.

144. Missouri Pacific Railway Company v. the Texas and Pacific Railway Company, no. 11,181, case files, National Archives at Fort Worth, box 671 (deposition of Grenville Dodge, July 3, 1893); Charles S. Potts, *Railroad Transportation in Texas* (University of Texas, 1909), 54.

145. Missouri Pacific Railway Company v. the Texas and Pacific Railway Company, no. 11,181, case files, National Archives at Fort Worth, box 668 (deposition of Collis P. Huntington, September 19, 1893).

146. Missouri Pacific Railway Company v. the Texas and Pacific Railway Company, no. 11,181, case files, National Archives at Fort Worth, box 668 (deposition of Collis P. Huntington, September 19, 1893). See also Missouri Pacific Railway Company v. the Texas and Pacific Railway Company, no. 11,181, case files, National Archives at Fort Worth, box 671 (deposition of Amos Lawrence Hopkins, November 18, 1893); Missouri Pacific Railway Company v. the Texas and Pacific Railway Company, no. 11,181, case files, National Archives at Fort Worth, box 671 (deposition of John F. Dillon, November 18, 1893).

147. Agreement between Collis P. Huntington and Jay Gould, November 20, 1881.

148. Lloyd J. Mercer, *Railroads and Land Grant Policy: A Study in Government Intervention* (Academic Press, 1982), 46. See also Agreement between Collis P. Huntington and Jay Gould, November 20, 1881, Articles I, X.

149. 23 Stat. 337. Southern Pacific R. Co. v. United States, 189 U.S. 447, 452, 23 S. Ct. 567, 569, 47 L. Ed. 896 (1903). See also "Stopping a Great Railroad Swindle," *The New York Times*, January 23, 1884; "The Texas Pacific Grant: The Central Pacific Still Trying to Secure the Lands," *The New York Times*, July 17, 1883.

150. Klein, *The Life and Legend of Jay Gould*, 271, 305. Professor Klein seems to accept the Texas and Pacific position, while I am more skeptical.

151. "Financial," *Bradstreet's*, August 11, 1883.

152. Grodinsky, *Transcontinental Railway Strategy*, 172.

153. Missouri Pacific R. Co. v. U.S., 1934 WL 31814, at *3. See also Missouri Pacific R. Co. v. U.S., 4 F. Supp. 449, 450 (E.D. Ky. 1933), *aff'd*, 293 U.S. 524, 55 S. Ct. 121, 79 L. Ed. 636 (1934).

154. Affidavit of Charles Crocker, dated June 11, 1881, in Texas Pacific Railway Co. v. Southern Pacific Railroad Co. of New Mexico. See also Missouri Pacific Railway Company v. the Texas and Pacific Railway Company, no. 11,181, case files, National Archives at Fort Worth, box 668 (deposition of Collis P. Huntington, September 19, 1893). There were also press reports from early 1880 that the Southern Pacific was grading a route from El Paso to San Antonio. "The Southern Pacific Nearing Completion," *St. Louis Dispatch*, April 24, 1880.

155. "Wanted an Outlet to Gulf," *The Philadelphia Inquirer*, October 27, 1880.

156. Missouri Pacific Railway Company v. the Texas and Pacific Railway Company, no. 11,181, case files, National Archives at Fort Worth, box 668 (deposition of Collis P. Huntington, September 19, 1893).

157. "The Jay Gould Railroads," *Los Angeles Times*, November 9, 1882. The line from New Orleans to El Paso was about 1,200 miles long, with the wonky rectangle adding the remaining miles to the system.

158. "Texas Consolidations," *Daily Inter Ocean*, July 8, 1882.

159. *Dodge Book X*, part 2, at 779 (Dodge to Montgomery, April 15, 1882); at 1027–28 (Eddy to Dodge, May 16, 1883, reporting comments of others on "Dodge style of construction"); at 1049 (Hayes to Dodge, June 27, 1883, "The Eastern Division has always been doing very well and about earning its fixed charges, but the Rio Grande Div. has been falling behind and the New Orleans Div. also"). See also "The Financial World," *The New York Times*, November 4, 1883.

160. Klein, *The Life and Legend of Jay Gould*, 305.
161. Testimony of John C. Brown, in US Congress, House, *Investigation of Labor Troubles Part 2*, 49th Cong., 2nd sess., 1887, Report No. 4174.
162. "Railroad Earnings in June," *The Commercial and Financial Chronicle*, July 12, 1884.
163. *Dodge Book X*, part 2, at 1011 (Hayes to Dodge, March 11, 1883).
164. "From Wall Street," *The Baltimore Sun*, October 13, 1883.
165. Klein, *The Life and Legend of Jay Gould*, 317.
166. J. S. Morgan & Co. papers, London Metropolitan Archives, HC3.1.1(40) (promissory notes, various dates in 1882, Gould to Drexel, Morgan & Co., New York).
167. Edwin G. Burrows and Mike Wallace, *Gotham* (Oxford University Press, 1999), 1042–43; Klein, *The Life and Legend of Jay Gould*, 326. See also Jean Edward Smith, *Grant* (Simon & Schuster, 2001), 618–22.
168. "Wall Street Greatly Excited," *New York Tribune*, May 14, 1884.
169. Texas & Pacific Ry. Co. v. Marlor, 123 U.S. 687 (1887).
170. "Texas and Pacific Bondholders," *The New York Times*, November 2, 1883.
171. Burrows and Wallace, *Gotham*, 1010–11. The renamed hotel would collapse in 1973, killing several. "Broadway Central Hotel Collapses," *The New York Times*, August 4, 1973.
172. Townsend Ludington, "The Portuguese Heritage—First and Second Generation American Born: The Example of the Two Dos Passoses," *Govea-Brown* 1, no. 2 (1980): 7–8. See also Melvin Landsberg, "John R. Dos Passos: His Influence on the Novelist's Early Political Development," *American Quarterly* 16, no. 3 (1964): 474.
173. Adrian H. Joline, *Method and Conduct of the Reorganization of Corporations* (Self-published, 1910), 8.
174. Marlor v. Texas & P.R. Co., 21 F. 383, 384–85 (C.C.S.D.N.Y. 1884) ("It is elementary that when a promise is in the alternative, to pay in money or in some other medium of payment, the promisor has an election either to pay in money or in the equivalent, and after the day of payment has elapsed without payment the right of election on the part of the promisor is gone, and the promisee is entitled to payment in money"), *aff'd* Texas & P. Ry. Co. v. Marlor, 123 U.S. 687, 8 S. Ct. 311, 31 L. Ed. 303 (1887). See also "Suing Texas and Pacific," *The New York Times*, August 28, 1884.
175. Statement of Agreed Facts, in Texas & P. Ry. Co. v. Marlor. In his correspondence with Gould and Dillon, Dos Passos reported that he represented about $2 million in bondholders, but only $150,000 of that was the subject of the lawsuit. Later, he brought suits on behalf of more bondholders.
176. Bond for Damages and Costs, in Texas & P. Ry. Co. v. Marlor, at 125.
177. Missouri Pacific Historical Society, MF4 (1122–1947) (Satterlee statement of "Securities of the Company Deposited as Collateral").
178. Missouri Pacific Historical Society, MF6 (0860–0915) (Jeffery to Satterlee, January 10, 1902). "Affairs of the Railways: Texas and Pacific Coupons," *The New York Times*, June 4, 1884; "The Financial World," *The New York Times*, July 6, 1884. Notices that a bank would "pay" the coupons appeared in newspapers, without making it clear that the coupons were actually being bought rather than paid. *New York Tribune*, June 4, 1884 (classified ad), 7.
179. "The Texas and Pacific," *St. Louis Dispatch*, June 4, 1884. See also "Railway Notes," *Montreal Daily Witness*, June 10, 1884; "Application Made for Receivership," *Detroit Free Press*, June 5, 1884.
180. "Texas and Pacific: The Sensation in Wall Street Yesterday," *The Philadelphia Inquirer*, June 4, 1884.
181. Grodinsky, *Jay Gould: His Business Career*, 403.

182. The shareholder lists that do exist simply provide the names of the shareholders, not the size of their stakes. For example, see the list attached to the 1883 annual report in Missouri Pacific Historical Society, MF9 (1833–1854).

183. Grodinsky, *Jay Gould: His Business Career*, 351. His account is supported by the anonymous writer in "The Texas and Pacific Road," *The New York Times*, December 25, 1885 (letter to the editor, signed "X"), who also writes that Gould sold the securities from the construction company as soon as he got them, if not earlier.

184. Klein, *The Life and Legend of Jay Gould*, 330. Professor Klein argues that Gould controlled the Texas and Pacific "not through stock ownership but through an operating contract with the Missouri Pacific."

185. The circular is reprinted in "Texas and Pacific," *The Commercial and Financial Chronicle*, July 26, 1884.

186. Missouri Pacific Historical Society, MF5 (0007–1265) (report dated July 18, 1884).

187. "Relief of the Texas and Pacific," *New York Tribune*, July 22, 1884. The indenture for the new "Terminal Division" bonds can be found in Missouri Pacific Historical Society, MF6 (0775–0848).

188. "The Financial World," *The New York Times*, July 27, 1884.

189. "Still Waiting," *The Philadelphia Inquirer*, June 6, 1884; "Notes about Railroads," *The New York Times*, October 30, 1884.

190. "Texas and Pacific Negotiations," *New York Tribune*, November 19, 1884; "Meeting of the Texas and Pacific Bondholders," *The Philadelphia Inquirer*, November 25, 1884.

191. One example of another such interest was the Philadelphia Mortgage and Trust Co. *The Philadelphia Inquirer*, September 27, 1886.

192. "Texas and Pacific," *The Economist*, December 13, 1884.

193. The new circulars to bondholders are reproduced in *The Philadelphia Inquirer*, December 11, 1884.

194. "Railroad Notes," *The New York Times*, November 16, 1884. See also "Texas and Pacific Finances," *The New York Times*, March 4, 1885; "The Texas and Pacific," *Daily American*, February 7, 1885.

195. The report is in Missouri Pacific Historical Society, MF12 (0001–0043) (report dated February 5, 1885).

196. "Many Suits Against a Road," October 16, 1884; "Attaching a Railroad's Property," *The New York Times*, October 15, 1884.

197. Grodinsky, *Jay Gould: His Business Career*, 409.

198. "Left for the Southwest," *The Philadelphia Inquirer*, November 21, 1885.

3. The Start of Corporate Bankruptcy

1. Julius Grodinsky, *Jay Gould: His Business Career* (University of Pennsylvania Press, 1957), 440.

2. Bradley Hansen, "The People's Welfare and the Origins of Corporate Reorganization: The Wabash Receivership Reconsidered," *Business History Review* 74, no. 3 (2000): 379–80.

3. Charles Francis Adams, Jr., and Henry Adams, *Chapters of Erie* (Waveland, 2002; orig. 1871), 72, 81. He was appointed receiver by a New York state court in the first instance, and by the federal district court in the second.

4. The most famous example, which predates modern chapter 11, is Albro Martin, "Railroads and the Equity Receivership: An Essay on Institutional Change," *Journal*

of Economic History 34, no. 3 (1974): 685–709. See also James W. Ely, *Railroads and American Law* (University Press of Kansas, 2001), 177–78. More recent examples in the legal literature are Troy A. McKenzie, "Bankruptcy and the Future of Aggregate Litigation: The Past as Prologue?" *Washington University Law Review* 90, no. 3 (2013): 855, and Gerald Berk, "Corporate Power and Its Discontents," *Buffalo Law Review* 53, no. 5 (2006): 1421. One the earliest examples is Thomas L. Greene, "Commercial Basis for Railway Receiverships," *American Law Register and Review* 42, no. 6 (1894): 419–20.

5. Dewing calls Wabash "the first of our American railway systems of any considerable size to throw itself into the hands of receivers," and I agree, but I argue that the second such case was more consequential. Arthur S. Dewing, *The Financial Policy of Corporations*, vol. II, 5th ed. (Ronald, 1953), 1243.

6. Robert T. Swaine, *The Cravath Firm and Its Predecessors*, vol. I (Privately printed by Ad, 1948), 378 (emphasis mine). Some time earlier, James Byrne wondered why counsel had adopted such a strange approach. James Byrne, "The Foreclosure of Railroad Mortgages in the United States Courts," in *Some Legal Phases of Corporate Financing, Reorganization and Regulation* (McMillan, 1917), 85–86. He goes on to make clear that the "friendly creditor" approach, which would result in diversity jurisdiction, was the preferred method. See also McIlhenny v. Binz, 80 Tex. 1, 7, 13 S.W. 655, 657 (1890), writ dismissed sub nom. Houston, East & West Texas Railway Co. v. Binz, 145 U.S. 641, 12 S. Ct. 982, 36 L. Ed. 854 (1892).

7. Securities and Exchange Commission, *Report on the Study and Investigation of the Work, Activities, Personnel and Functions of Protective and Reorganization Committees*, Part 8 (1940), 24.

8. Stephen J. Lubben, "Railroad Receiverships and Modern Bankruptcy Theory," *Cornell Law Review* 89 (September 2004): 1442. See also Stephen J. Lubben, "Fairness and Flexibility: Understanding Corporate Bankruptcy's Arc," *University of Pennsylvania Journal of Business Law* 23 (Fall 2020): 147, n66.

9. Key examples of this confusion can be seen in D. H. Chamberlain, "New-Fashioned Receiverships," *Harvard Law Review* 10, no. 3 (1896): 142, and Arthur S. Dewing, "The Procedure of Contemporary Railroad Reorganization," *American Economic Review* 9, no. 1 (1919): 12–13; and they likely influenced later authors regarding the importance of the Wabash case. Garrard Glenn noted that years earlier, Chief Justice Salmon P. Chase had outlined the perils of the debtor seeking equitable relief on its own petition: Namely, "the debtor can file a bill; but it may get nowhere, because the court will not act upon it if a creditor seasonably protests," Garrard Glenn, "Basis of the Federal Receivership," *Columbia Law Review* 25, no. 4 (1925): 442–44. He goes on to explain that "it is more logical for a creditor to file the bill than for the debtor to file it, for then the court can treat the plaintiff as representative of his class; and, in so doing, it can temporarily remove the assets from the reach of all creditors in order to effectuate a distribution on the basis of equality."

10. The story here is drawn from "A Chapter of Wabash," *North American Review*, 146, no. 375 (February 1888): 178–93.

11. "Russell Sage: The Father of the Put and Call System Getting Poor," *St. Louis Dispatch*, February 27, 1885; Maury Klein, *The Life and Legend of Jay Gould* (John Hopkins University Press, 1986), 329–30.

12. Klein, *The Life and Legend of Jay Gould*, 330.

13. Grodinsky, *Jay Gould: His Business Career*, 417. A good discussion of receivers' certificates can be found in Union Trust Co. of New York, v. Illinois Midland Ry. Co., 117 U.S. 434, 451, 6 S. Ct. 809, 818, 29 L. Ed. 963 (1886).

14. There is an interesting comparison here with the "up-tier" transactions of recent years. See chapter 9.
15. H. Roger Grant, *Follow the Flag: A History of the Wabash Railroad Company* (Cornell University Press, 2004), 65.
16. "Men of Many Millions," *The Washington Post*, April 25, 1885.
17. Atkins v. Wabash Ry., 29 F. 161 (C. C. N. D. Ill. 1886).
18. Grodinsky, *Jay Gould: His Business Career*, 439.
19. Grant, *Follow the Flag*, 68.
20. "Upon the Staked Plains," *The Sun*, January 4, 1885.
21. Missouri Pacific Historical Society, MF5 (0007–1265) (undated report to the board). The report was likely prepared for the March 1885 annual meeting.
22. "Wall Street Worry," *Courier-Journal*, March 9, 1885.
23. "The Texas and Pacific Road," *The New York Times*, December 25, 1885 (letter to the editor, signed "X").
24. "The Texas Pacific Strike," *Boston Globe*, March 9, 1885. See also "The Railroad Strikers," *The Evening Star*, March 9, 1885; "Texas and Pacific Shopmen to Strike," *The Sun*, March 1, 1885; Klein, *Life and Legend of Jay Gould*, 357.
25. "Railway Collision," *The Philadelphia Inquirer*, April 28, 1885.
26. "The St. Louis Collision," *Daily American*, April 30, 1885.
27. Missouri Pacific Historical Society, MF5 (0007–1265) (typed report dated December 8, 1885, with physical signatures).
28. All three are directly quoted from Missouri Pacific Historical Society, MF5 (0007–1265).
29. "Texas and Pacific," *The Philadelphia Inquirer*, December 12, 1885. See also "Financial and Commercial," *The Sun*, December 11, 1885.
30. *Report of the Committee Appointed to Examine the Physical and Financial Condition of the Property*, dated December 8, 1885 (with board resolutions dated December 16).
31. "Texas and Pacific," *Railway News*, January 2, 1886. The company apparently attempted to obscure the fact that the petition was filed before the board met. "Money Market," *Brooklyn Daily Eagle*, December 16, 1885.
32. Missouri Pacific Railway Company v. the Texas and Pacific Railway Company, no. 11,181, case files, National Archives at Fort Worth, box 683 (petition dated December 15, 1885). "Railroad Interests," *New York Tribune*, December 17, 1885; "Financial and Commercial," *The Sun*, December 17, 1885. The news reached London quickly, reflecting the stable cable connections that had developed by this time. "The United States," *The Times*, December 18, 1885.
33. Missouri Pacific Railway Company v. the Texas and Pacific Railway Company, box 671 (answer dated December 15, 1885; docket no. 2).
34. Recall that the Texas and Pacific operated under a federal corporate charter. Allen v. Texas & Pacific Ry. Co., 25 F. 513, 513 (C.C.E.D. La. 1885). Unlike modern bankruptcy petitions (which are signed by a representative of the debtor), the petition and the answer were only signed by counsel for the respective railroads.
35. "Railway Affairs in America," *Railway News*, January 16, 1886; "Texas and Pacific," *The Commercial and Financial Chronicle*, January 9, 1886.
36. "Mr. Jay Gould's Conjuring," *The Statist*, January 30, 1886.
37. "Morning Dispatches," *Daily Evening Bulletin* (San Francisco), December 17, 1885 (reprinting a story from the *New York Herald*).
38. "Financial," *Christian Union*, January 14, 1886.
39. Missouri Pacific Railway Company v. the Texas and Pacific Railway Company, box 683 (order dated December 16, 1885, docket no. 8). The original order signed by Judge

Pardee is a strange patchwork of handwritten and typed text; in one case, a typed paragraph appears to be glued onto a page that is otherwise handwritten. Somebody (presumably the judge) also edited the typed text substantially, suggesting that receivership practices had not yet developed to the point where the court would accept the order as presented by counsel.

40. In re Higgins, 27 F. 443, 444 (C.C.N.D. Tex. 1886). The filing of such ancillary cases was expressly authorized by the original order. In subsequent litigation after the reorganization had concluded, the Texas Supreme Court tended to ignore the ancillary receivership. Texas & P. Ry. Co. v. Gay, 86 Tex. 571, 596, 26 S.W. 599, 608 (1894), aff'd, 167 U.S. 745, 17 S. Ct. 1000, 42 L. Ed. 1209 (1897).

41. "Railroad Interests," *New York Tribune*, December 17. 1885. The article includes Sage discussing both the plans for the receivership and the recent board meeting.

42. Missouri Pacific Historical Society, MF5 (0007–1265). Although date-stamped on the same day as the order physically signed by the judge, which as noted previously had significant handwritten additions and deletions, this version is cleanly typed throughout.

43. "Pulaski," *Daily American*, January 13, 1886; "The Railroads," *St. Louis Globe-Democrat*, December 27, 1885.

44. Missouri Pacific Historical Society, MF5 (0007–1265) (Dillon and Swayne to Farrar and Kruttschnitt, November 3, 1887).

45. See, for example, Missouri Pacific Railway Company v. the Texas and Pacific Railway Company, box 681 (letter from Dickson to Howe, February 4, 1887). Both receiverships were still pending during the Texas and Pacific case. *New York Tribune*, November 20, 1887, 2, features articles about all three cases.

46. Thus, in 1938, when receiverships were coming to an end, one commentator explained in connection with contemporary receivership:

> Valeria Coriell, claiming that she had no adequate recovery at law, then sued on this note for the appointment of a receiver with the usual allegation of multiplicity of suits and dissipation of assets. It is not pretended that she was more than a convenient non-resident "dummy," who lent name and diverse citizenship to a suit planned and negotiated by the bank creditors and the debtor himself. As was the accepted tradition in these suits, the debtor filed an answer admitting all the complaints of the bill and joined in the prayer for the appointment of a receiver.

Ferdinand Fairfax Stone, "The Case of the Ladies' Handbags: A Study in Receivership Procedure," *Virginia Law Review* 24 (June 1938): 835. The author goes on to note that "in many cases the same counsel drew both the answer and the bill," which we also see in the Texas and Pacific case.

47. Missouri Pacific Railway Company v. the Texas and Pacific Railway Company, box 683 (Brown's oath of office, dated December 16, 1885, docket no. 9). "Railway Affairs in America." Sheldon would not take his oath until January 8, 1886. Missouri Pacific Railway Company v. the Texas and Pacific Railway Company, box 683 (docket no. 29).

48. "The East Bound Pool," *St. Louis Dispatch*, February 22, 1886.

49. Missouri Pacific Historical Society, MF16 (1644–1692) (Brown and Abrams to Satterlee and George Gould, as trustees, August 16, 1886).

50. *Investigation of Labor Troubles in Missouri, Arkansas, Kansas, Texas, and Illinois*, 49th Congress, 2d sess., House Report 4174, 68.

51. "The Texas and Pacific Railroad," *Republican Banner*, April 19, 1871.

52. Allan Peskin, *Garfield* (Kent State University Press, 1999), 93, 96, 408.

53. Lionel A. Sheldon biographical material and essay (1888), BANC MSS C-D 801; Lionel A. Sheldon to H. H. Bancroft (1886), BANC MSS P-O 70; the Bancroft Library, University of California, Berkeley.

54. Lionel A. Sheldon biographical material and essay (1888).

55. Peskin, *Garfield*, 551.

56. Lionel A. Sheldon biographical material and essay (1888).

57. "Railroad Personals," *Los Angeles Times*, January 26, 1887.

58. Missouri Pacific Railway Company v. the Texas and Pacific Railway Company, box 667 (various statements regarding compensation of receivers).

59. Missouri Pacific Railway Company v. the Texas and Pacific Railway Company, box 665 (testimony of Julius Kruttschnitt, April 1, 1893, 5). See also Missouri Pacific Railway Company v. the Texas and Pacific Railway Company, box 667 (Sheldon statement dated March 4, 1886); Missouri Pacific Railway Company v. the Texas and Pacific Railway Company, box 675 (motion, docket no. 48, requesting approval to lease offices in New Orleans and Dallas—and order authorizing same, docket no. 49).

60. "El Paso to Be a Second Denver," *New York Tribune*, January 25, 1886.

61. Missouri Pacific Historical Society, MF5 (0007–1265) (Wistar to Satterlee, January 4, 1886, referencing earlier telegram from Gould to Wistar).

62. Missouri Pacific Historical Society, MF5 (0007–1265). Wistar's annotated draft is dated January 3, and the original that he marked up is undated, as is the retyped version incorporating Wistar's changes.

63. This scaling-down of existing shareholders seems to be Wistar's idea, in place of Gould's original plan to charge each shareholder a $8 assessment—one might suspect that this early version was designed to force Wistar to make all the hard choices since it offered little to appeal to the consolidated bondholders. In short, Gould's first plan may not have been a real plan, but rather a bargaining technique. Missouri Pacific Historical Society, MF5 (0007–1265) (undated "term sheets" with Wistar's changes to shareholder treatment at the bottom of the second copy).

64. *Dodge Book XI*, part 1, at 371 (Dodge to Tyler, April 24, 1886); at 371 (Dodge to Walters, April 13, 1886); at 329 (Dodge to Brown, March 8, 1886); and at 327 (Dodge to Tyler, March 6, 1886).

65. Here too, Dodge seems to have been taken in by Gould, writing to one congressman in 1884 that Gould had recently "bought 10,000 shares of it and laid it away for keeps." *Dodge Book XI*, part 1, at 27 (Dodge to Kellogg, January 25, 1884).

66. Grodinsky, *Jay Gould: His Business Career*, 443.

67. Missouri Pacific Railway Company v. the Texas and Pacific Railway Company, box 683 (petition for appointment of receivers, dated December 15, 1885, para. 15). By the end of the case, MoPac was only claiming $1.3 million. Missouri Pacific Historical Society, MF5 (0007–1265) (Final Report of Committee on Reorganization, December 5, 1888, at 5).

68. Missouri Pacific Railway Company v. the Texas and Pacific Railway Company, box 667 (inventory of New York Office, dated February 10, 1886). Among the contents of the New York Office, beyond two safes, three desks, and twelve volumes of Texas statutes, was more than $4.2 million in Memphis, El Paso bonds. A receipt for $500,000 of these bonds—given as "additional collateral" for more than $1 million loaned in December 1884—is dated October 22, 1885. Missouri Pacific Historical Society, MF5 (0007–1265).

69. Missouri Pacific Historical Society, MF5 (0007–1265) (receipt from MoPac, dated October 15, 1884).

70. "Charles E. Satterlee Dead," *The New York Times*, June 18, 1912. Missouri Pacific Historical Society, MF5 (0007–1265) (telegram, Wistar to Satterlee, January 7, 1886). See

also "Texas and Pacific," *The Commercial and Financial Chronicle*, January 9, 1886, and "Texas and Pacific," *The Philadelphia Inquirer*, January 8, 1886, which discuss the rumors on Wall Street regarding the plan.

71. Missouri Pacific Historical Society, MF5 (0007–1265) (letter, Wistar to Satterlee, dated January 4, 1886).

72. "Fighting for a Railroad," *The New York Times*, January 11, 1886. The *New York Tribune* said that it was William Bond, rather than Frank Bond, who was suggested. "Texas and Pacific Case," *New York Tribune*, January 10, 1886.

73. All of the Dos Passos pleadings can be found in Missouri Pacific Railway Company v. the Texas and Pacific Railway Company, box 682.

74. He chaired a shareholder committee as that company was winding down. J. S. Morgan & Co. papers, London Metropolitan Archives, HC3.1.23 (To the Stockholders of the Southern Railway Securities Company, October 16, 1876). C. K. Brown, "The Southern Railway Security Company: An Early Instance of the Holding Company," *North Carolina Historical Review*, 6, no. 2 (April 1929): 161.

75. Missouri Pacific Railway Company v. the Texas and Pacific Railway Company, box 682 (order dated January 9, 1886).

76. Sheldon's bond can be found in Missouri Pacific Railway Company v. the Texas and Pacific Railway Company, box 683 (with notation from court approving same, dated January 11, 1886).

77. Missouri Pacific Historical Society, MF5 (0007–1265) (telegram, Gould to Satterlee, January 10, 1886).

78. "General Railroad News," *The Philadelphia Inquirer*, January 15, 1886.

79. "Texas and Pacific," *Rhodes' Journal of Banking*, XIII, February 1886; "Texas Pacific Reorganization Plan," *Bradstreet's*, January 9, 1886.

80. "Texas and Pacific," *The Commercial and Financial Chronicle*, January 9, 1886.

81. Missouri Pacific Historical Society, MF5 (0007–1265) (resolution dated March 5, 1886). See also Henry V. Poor, *Manual of the Railroads of the United States 1885* (H. V. & H. W. Poor, 1885), 834, which shows that the board, as elected under the bondholder deal in early 1885, included Wistar, Markoe, Winsor, and Hutchinson, all of Philadelphia.

82. "Texas and Pacific," *Railway Gazette*, April 16, 1886; "New York Stocks," *Pittsburgh Commercial Gazette*, April 8, 1886.

83. "Texas and Pacific," *The New York Times*," March 6, 1886.

84. "They Cannot Agree," *The Philadelphia Inquirer*, April 22, 1886.

85. "The Texas and Pacific," *New York Tribune*, April 22, 1886; "Notes of Various Interest," *The New York Times*, April 23, 1886.

86. "The Gossip of New York," *The Washington Post*, May 2, 1886.

87. Plan dated April 27, 1886. Hereinafter, this is referred to as the "original Wistar plan." A copy from the Princeton University Library is readily available online in Google Books and is sometimes mistaken for the final plan. See also "Texas and Pacific," *Railway Gazette*, April 30, 1886.

88. Drexel, Morgan & Co., syndicate records, Morgan Library and Museum (ARC 105, vol. 1, 127).

89. Klein, *The Life and Legend of Jay Gould*, 351.

90. Missouri Pacific Railway Company v. the Texas and Pacific Railway Company, box 683 (docket no. 28). The report is undated, but docket number 29 is dated January 8, 1886. The entire paragraph is based on this report.

91. Missouri Pacific Railway Company v. the Texas and Pacific Railway Company, box 667 (Sheldon statement dated March 4, 1886).

92. Robert Worth Miller, "The Lost World of Gilded Age Politics," *Journal of the Gilded Age and Progressive Era* 1, no. 1 (2002): 59.

93. "Back to Work," *Courier-Journal*, March 17, 1885. The agreement, which is just two pages long, can be found in "The Official History of the Great Strike of 1886," which is appended to the back of the Eighth Annual Report of the Bureau of Labor Statistics of the State of Missouri for the year ending December 31, 1886. The "Official History" purports to be purely factual, but it is heavily tilted against the Knights of Labor.

94. Arnold M. Paul, *Conservative Crisis and the Rule of Law: Attitudes of Bar and Bench, 1887–1895* (Cornell University Press, 1960), 19.

95. The agreement was set forth on the letterhead of the "Missouri Pacific Company . . . and Texas and Pacific Railway Company" and signed by two officers who held the same positions in both railroads. Poor, *Manual of the Railroads of the United States 1885*. The agreement was also introduced into the record by several witnesses at the congressional hearings, discussed later in this chapter. In his testimony before Congress, Gould argued that the agreement applied only in Missouri and Kansas because the governors of those states had encouraged and signed it, and indeed the terms of the contract are focused on those two states. On the other hand, it seems that until 1886, everyone had assumed that the agreement applied to the entire MoPac system, which included the Texas and Pacific at the point when the deal was struck.

96. "Receiver Brown," *Atlanta Constitution*, March 10, 1886.

97. *Investigation of Labor Troubles in Missouri, Arkansas, Kansas, Texas, and Illinois*, 49th Congress, 2d sess., House Report 4174, part 2. Hall's testimony, which this paragraph is based on, begins on page 353.

98. Ruth A. Allen, *The Great Southwest Strike* (University of Texas Press, 1942), 50.

99. Sheldon (letter).

100. This is as reprinted in "Strike Moves," *Fort Worth Gazette*, March 15, 1886, at 1.

101. "Ordered out by Knights," *The Sun*, March 7, 1886.

102. "Striking," *Los Angeles Times*, March 10, 1886.

103. Gerald N. Grob, *Workers and Utopia: A Study of Ideological Conflict in the American Labor Movement, 1865–1900* (Northwestern University Press, 1961), 60–61.

104. See generally Theresa A. Case, "Blaming Martin Irons: Leadership and Popular Protest in the 1886 Southwest Strike," *Journal of the Gilded Age and Progressive Era* 8, no. 1 (2009), 51–81.

105. Allen, *Great Southwestern Strike*, 52.

106. Sheldon (letter).

107. Theresa A. Case, *The Great Southwest Railroad Strike and Free Labor* (Texas A&M University Press, 2010), 163.

108. *Investigation of Labor Troubles in Missouri, Arkansas, Kansas, Texas, and Illinois*, 49th Congress, 2d sess., House Report 4174, part 2, 211.

109. *Investigation of Labor Troubles in Missouri, Arkansas, Kansas, Texas, and Illinois*, part 2, 204.

110. Hoxie was a longtime railroad manager, who, among other things, was involved in the formation of Union Pacific's notorious construction company.

111. Grob, *Workers and Utopia*, 68.

112. "The Great Strike Ended," *The New York Times*, March 29, 1886.

113. Klein, *The Life and Legend of Jay Gould*, 361.

114. Klein, *The Life and Legend of Jay Gould*, 361–62.

115. Nell Irvin Painter, *Standing at Armageddon: The United States, 1877–1919* (W. W. Norton, 1989), 42–43.

116. Grob, *Workers and Utopia*, 65. See also Case, *The Great Southwest Railroad Strike*, 146–47.

117. Missouri Pacific Railway Company v. the Texas and Pacific Railway Company, boxes 673 and 675, contain the petitions.

118. An example can be found in Missouri Pacific Railway Company v. the Texas and Pacific Railway Company, box 670 (order dated March 11, 1886).

119. Missouri Pacific Railway Company v. the Texas and Pacific Railway Company, box 683 (report of special master, dated March 24, 1886, docket no. 108).

120. Missouri Pacific Railway Company v. the Texas and Pacific Railway Company, box 682 (Protective Intelligence Co. invoice dated March 31, 1886).

121. "A Crisis Approaching," *The Washington Post*, March 15, 1886.

122. Missouri Pacific Railway Company v. the Texas and Pacific Railway Company, box 682 (L. Graham & Son, Book and Job Printers, invoice dated March 24, 1886); Missouri Pacific Railway Company v. the Texas and Pacific Railway Company, box 682 (statement of R. B. Pleasants, dated April 3, 1886; docket no. 112).

123. Missouri Pacific Railway Company v. the Texas and Pacific Railway Company, box 670 (affidavit of W. L. Cabell, dated May 3, 1886).

124. "The Railway Strike," *Frank Leslie's Illustrated Newspaper*, April 17, 1886; "Almost a Riot at Fort Worth," *The New York Times*, April 3, 1886.

125. In re Higgins, 27 F. 443, 445–46 (C.C.N.D. Tex. 1886).

126. *New York Tribune*, April 19, 1886 (editorial; no title) and "In Contempt Of Court: Judge Pardee's Decision At Dallas The Texas Pacific Strikers Subjecting Themselves To An Unlimited Penalty," in the same issue. The same paper editorialized the next day that "[t]he interests of labor are in danger when the reckless hierarchy brings them in conflict with the law." April 20, 1886 (editorial; no title). See also "Strikes In The Law's Eye: Judge Pardee Defines The Legal Status Of The Knights Of Labor," *New York Times*, April 19, 1886; "What Judge Pardee Says," *Hartford Daily Current*, April 19, 1886.

127. Matthew Hild, *Greenbackers, Knights of Labor, and Populists: Farmer-Labor Insurgency in the Late-Nineteenth-Century South* (University of Georgia Press, 2007), 74.

128. Alan M. Kraut, *The Huddled Masses: The Immigrant in American Society, 1880–1921* (Harlan Davidson, 1982), 100–1. See generally Yucheng Qin, "A Century-Old 'Puzzle': The Six Companies' Role in Chinese Labor Importation in the Nineteenth Century," *Journal of American-East Asian Relations* 12, no. 3/4 (2003): 225–54.

129. Case, *The Great Southwest Railroad Strike*, 180.

130. "Chinamen Tortured and Robbed," *The New York Times*, December 1, 1886.

131. "Greek Meets Greek," *The New York Times*, August 2, 1888. See also "Chinese Labor," *Daily Picayune*, August 1, 1888.

132. "A Shrewd Chinaman," *St. Louis Globe-Democrat*, November 26, 1886.

133. 47 Cong. Ch. 126, May 6, 1882, 22 Stat. 58.

134. "Sherman," *Galveston Daily News*, July 20, 1884.

135. Mark T. Banker, *Appalachians All: East Tennesseans and the Elusive History of an American Region* (University of Tennessee Press, 2010), 91.

136. William Joseph MacArthur, Jr., "Charles McClung McGhee, Southern Financier," PhD diss., University of Tennessee, 1975, 12.

137. Charles McClung McGhee papers, East Tennessee History Center, Calvin M. McClung Historical Collection of the Knox County Public Library, box 1 (autobiography of McGhee, no date); Benjamin Franklin Cooling III and Benjamin Franklin Cooling, *To the Battles of Franklin and Nashville and Beyond: Stabilization and Reconstruction in Tennessee and Kentucky, 1864–1866* (University of Tennessee Press, 2011), 38; Maury Klein, *The Great Richmond Terminal: A Study in Businessmen and Business*

Strategy (University of Virginia Press, 1970), 44. See also MacArthur, "Charles McClung McGhee, Southern Financier," 14. The *National Cyclopedia of American Biography*, cited in note 139, states that he was "commissioned in the staff department army owing to his ill-health."

138. "Col. C. M. McGhee Has Passed Away," *Nashville American*, May 6, 1907.

139. "McGhee, Charles McClung," in *The National Cyclopedia of American Biography*, vol. 12 (James T. White and Co., 1904), 198. The board minutes for the consolidation are reprinted in Fairfax Harrison, *History of the Legal Development of the Railroad System of the Southern Railway Company* (Washington, DC, 1901), 666–70.

140. Charles McClung McGhee papers, box 2 (notice of meeting of purchase and reorganization committee, July 2, 1886, signed by Olcott).

141. "Sale of the East Tennessee Virginia & Georgia for $10,850,000," *Daily American*, May 26, 1886.

142. His investment could have started from the inception of the Texas and Pacific, as that would have coincided with McGhee's connection with Scott, but unfortunately, McGhee's surviving records do not go back to the 1870s.

143. McGhee Letterbook (February 1888 to February 1889) (Amount of Securities and Where Placed, February 25, 1888). A note at the bottom of the list suggests that $5,000 of the New Orleans bonds were being held for "Mrs. Tyson."

144. Missouri Pacific Historical Society, MF5 (0007–1265) (McGhee, Hill, and Rice to Satterlee, April 20, 1886); "Notes of Various Interests," *The New York Times*, April 20, 1886; *The Commercial and Financial Chronicle*, April 24, 1886. Confusingly, the *Chronicle* had two stories about the formation of the committee: the second makes no mention of the first story. *The Commercial and Financial Chronicle*, May 22, 1886.

145. Grodinsky, *Jay Gould: His Business Career*, 443. Unfortunately, from this point onward in his book, Professor Grodinsky seems to lose the plot of the receivership, crediting Fry, and then J. P. Morgan, with roles far beyond what the evidence supports.

146. The circular, dated June 5, 1886, went to the bondholders of the Rio Grande Division, Texas and Pacific Railway Company.

147. Securities and Exchange Commission, *Report on the Study and Investigation of the Work, Activities, Personnel and Functions of Protective and Reorganization Committees* (1937–1940), part I, ed. Adelaide R. Hasse, 888.

148. A description of the process in its fully formed state can be found in Indus. & Gen. Trust v. Tod, 180 N.Y. 215, 220–23, 73 N.E. 7, 7–9 (1905).

149. Adrian H. Joline, *Method and Conduct of the Reorganization of Corporations* (Self-published, 1910), 12–13.

150. Habirshaw Electric Cable Co. v. Habirshaw Electric Cable Co., 296 F. 875, 881 (2d Cir. 1924). Also see generally Max Lowenthal, *The Investor Pays* (A. A. Knopf, 1936), chap. 16.

151. Missouri Pacific Railway Company v. the Texas and Pacific Railway Company, box 674 (motion dated May 19, 1886).

152. Missouri Pacific Railway Company v. the Texas and Pacific Railway Company, box 675 (letter dated May 20, 1886, White & Saunders to Denegre).

153. "Texas and Pacific Reorganization," *Courier-Journal*, April 27, 1886. Missouri Pacific Railway Company v. the Texas and Pacific Railway Company, box 667 (telegram from Satterlee, as trustee, to counsel for receivers).

154. "Texas and Pacific Reorganization," *New York Tribune*, May 19, 1886. "Texas and Pacific Reorganization," *The Philadelphia Inquirer*, June 17, 1886.

155. "Texas and Pacific Reorganization Plans," *St. Louis Globe-Democrat*, July 10, 1886; "Texas and Pacific Reorganization," *The Philadelphia Inquirer*, July 2, 1886.

156. Missouri Pacific Historical Society, MF5 (0007–1265) (Gould to Dos Passos, May 4, 1886).
157. Missouri Pacific Historical Society, MF5 (0007–1265) (Dos Passos to Burr, Clews, Bloodgood, September 14, 1886).
158. "Texas and Pacific Railway," *The Railway Times* June 12, 1886.
159. "Money Market," *The Times*, June 9, 1886.
160. Dorothy R. Adler, *British Investment in American Railways, 1834–1898* (University Press of Virginia, 1970), 147–48.
161. Bill Smith, *Robert Fleming: 1845–1933* (Whittingehame House, 2000), 26–28. Robert Fleming & Co., originally based in Dundee, remained a notable City of London bank and manager of investment trusts until it was taken over by JPMorgan Chase in 2000.
162. Smith, *Robert Fleming: 1845–1933*, 53–54, 87–88. Mira Wilkins, *The History of Foreign Investment in the United States to 1914* (Harvard University Press, 1989), 209, 223.
163. McGhee papers, Transatlantic Cablegram, dated June 24, 1886, from Fleming in London to McGhee in NY.
164. One of the Philadelphia members of Wistar's committee (Newcomer) also had ties to Baltimore and Walters; they were both large investors in Scott's southern railroad venture.
165. For instance, see Charles McClung McGhee papers, box 2 (Tyler to McGhee, June 19, 1886).
166. Smith, *Robert Fleming: 1845–1933*, 91.
167. Dolores Greenberg, *Financiers and Railroads, 1869–1889: A Study of Morton, Bliss & Company* (University of Delaware Press, 1980), 167. Charles McClung McGhee papers, box 2 (investment banks to Olcott, August 2, 1886, referring to prior oral agreement with Fleming).
168. Drexel, Morgan & Co., syndicate records, 166; J. S. Morgan & Co. papers, HC3.1.1.(101) (J. S. Morgan received a $500,000 stake in the syndicate).
169. Fleming had long been a client of J. S. Morgan in London. J. S. Morgan & Co. papers, HC2.18 (various loan agreements from the 1870s, typically collateralized with Erie or Union Pacific securities).
170. Charles McClung McGhee papers, box 2 (Kuhn, Loeb to McGhee, August 17, 1886—acknowledging the assignment).
171. "Gould's Hand Exposed," *The New York Times*, July 24, 1886.
172. Klein, *The Life and Legend of Jay Gould*, 352.
173. "Miscellaneous Railroad Intelligence," *New York Tribune*, July 15, 1886.
174. Charles McClung McGhee papers, box 2 (Fleming to McGhee, July 26, 1886). The letterhead suggests that this letter was written from London, but given Fleming's presence shortly before and after in the United States (in an era when it often took ten days to cross), that seems unlikely. Perhaps Fleming brought the stationery (or even the letter itself) with him.
175. Cyrus Adler, *Jacob H. Schiff: His Life and Letters.* vol. 1 (Doubleday, 1928), 124.
176. Vincent P. Carosso, *Investment Banking in America: A History* (Harvard University Press, 1970), 19.
177. Carosso, *Investment Banking*, 33. Naomi W. Cohen, *Jacob H. Schiff: A Study in American Jewish Leadership* (Brandeis University Press, 1999), 6.
178. Ron Chernow, *The Warburgs* (Random House, 1993), 46–48.
179. Charles McClung McGhee papers, box 2 (Beard to McGhee, July 24, 1886).
180. "The New Texas and Pacific Committee," *New York Tribune*, July 28, 1886.

181. Copies of the memo with the plan outline can be found in Drexel, Morgan & Co., syndicate records, 165.2; and J. S. Morgan & Co. papers, HC3.1.1 (101). Notices regarding the proposed plan can be found in *New York Tribune*, August 5, 1886; *The New York Times*, August 8, 1886.

182. "Money-Market and City Intelligence," *The Times*, July 31, 1886.

183. "Trade and Commerce," *Montreal Herald*, August 2, 1886; "The Financial World," *The New York Times*, August 8, 1886; "Commerce and Finance," *Galveston Daily News*, August 10, 1886; "Texas and Pacific," *The Baltimore Sun*, August 10, 1886.

184. "Railroad Interests," *The Baltimore Sun*, August 9, 1886. Newcomber and Winters had invested together starting with Scott's Southern Railway Security Company.

185. Drexel, Morgan & Co., syndicate records, 165.2.

186. A total of $167,000 was still outstanding at the time.

187. J. S. Morgan & Co. papers, HC3.1.1 (101).

188. J. S. Morgan & Co. papers, HC3.1.1 (101) (telegram dated August 6, 1886, from Drexel Morgan NY to J. S. Morgan).

189. The numbers given here and in this paragraph come from a chart in J. S. Morgan & Co. papers, HC3.1.1 (101).

190. "Financial Affairs," *The New York Times*, December 30, 1888.

191. "Financial Affairs," *The New York Times*, December 31, 1890.

192. Drexel, Morgan & Co., syndicate records, 165. See also Charles McClung McGhee papers, box 2.

193. "Texas and Pacific," *The Philadelphia Inquirer*, August 5, 1886.

194. J. S. Morgan & Co. papers, HC3.1.1 (101). The trading price is noted in handwriting next to a copy of the notice of the offer.

195. "Railroad Interests," *New York Tribune*, August 4, 1886.

196. Wistar's account is hard to square with the available evidence regarding the receivership and almost seems to be another case altogether. Among other things, Fleming goes unmentioned. Isaac J. Wistar, *Autobiography of Isaac Jones Wistar, 1827–1905* (Wistar Institute of Anatomy and Biology, 1914), 492–93.

197. Charles McClung McGhee papers, box 2 (Brown to McGhee, August 3, 1886).

198. The *New York Tribune* had the basic terms the following morning, which provides further evidence that the deal was being driven by New York. "Uniting Texas and Pacific Interests," *New York Tribune*, August 11, 1886.

199. Missouri Pacific Historical Society, MF5 (0007–1265) (telegram, Gould to Wistar, August 10, 1886).

200. "Under a Modified Plan," *The New York Times*, August 12, 1886.

201. McGhee papers, letter dated August 11, 1886 from KL and Drexel Morgan to syndicate members, addressed to McGhee at bottom.

202. "Who Is Issac L. Rice?" *Wall Street Journal*, September 8, 1893.

203. Dos Passos received the $50,000 that Gould had previously promised him, which was $10,000 more than Bullitt received for his work on the case. Rice received $10,000. Missouri Pacific Historical Society, MF5 (0007–1265) (Final Report of Committee on Reorganization, December 5, 1888, at 13).

204. Shortly afterward, Gould would assign $330,000 of his interest in the syndicate to Sage and $100,000 to two other investors (split evenly between them). J. P. Morgan & Co. syndicate records (vol 1, 166).

205. Adler, *British Investment in American Railways*, 176.

206. Klein, *The Life and Legend of Jay Gould*, 352.

207. Missouri Pacific Railway Company v. the Texas and Pacific Railway Company, box 672 (affidavit of Charles J. Canda, dated June 11, 1887). The affidavit details the committee's holding in connection with the eventual settlement.

208. Missouri Pacific Railway Company v. the Texas and Pacific Railway Company, box 683 (motion regarding settlement, dated June 11, 1887). Copies of the agreement and other materials regarding the settlement can also be found in box 675.

209. Missouri Pacific Historical Society, MF5 (0007–1265) (Wistar to Satterlee, December 9, 1887).

210. The trust recently converted to a Delaware corporation. A list of the lands in question, along with a resolution of the Texas and Pacific executive committee, dated August 2, 1887, approving the same, can be found in Missouri Pacific Historical Society, MF4 (1122–1947).

211. See Texas Pacific Land Corporation, https://www.texaspacific.com. These statistics are valid as of August 2023.

212. Kevin Crowley, "AI Boom Propels a Wild-West-Era Texas Landowner to 230% Stock Rally," *Bloomberg*, November 25, 2024.

213. The signed settlement memorandum is in Missouri Pacific Historical Society, MF5 (0007–1265).

214. McGhee Letterbook (McGhee to G. Gould, August 31, 1888). See also McGhee Letterbook (McGhee to Brown, July 26, 1888).

215. See, for example, Missouri Pacific Historical Society, MF5 (0007–1265) (Brown to Wistar, December 31, 1887, and Brown to Wistar, December 26, 1887).

216. McGhee Letterbook (McGhee to Schiff, February 17, 1888).

217. McGhee Letterbook (McGhee to Wistar, April 16, 1888).

218. Adrian Joline discussed the Texas and Pacific and the desire to retain the federal charter in his 1910 lectures at Harvard Business School, which provides some indication of the case's lasting importance to the reorganization bar. Adrian H. Joline, *Method and Conduct of the Reorganization of Corporations* (Self-published, 1910), 99–100.

219. "Texas and Pacific," *El Paso Times*, November 10, 1887; "Financial and Commercial," *The Sun*, November 10, 1887; "Sale of a Railway," *The Times*, November 10, 1887; "American Financial Markets," *The Guardian*, October 6, 1887. The Texas sales foreclosed the Rio Grande Division and the wonky rectangle. The sales in Louisiana foreclosed the Terminal and New Orleans Pacific bonds.

220. The receivers' receipts dated November 8 and 10, 1887, can be found in Missouri Pacific Historical Society, MF5 (0007–1265).

221. "Commercial and Financial Notes," *The Guardian*, February 3, 1888.

222. Missouri Pacific Railway Company v. the Texas and Pacific Railway Company, box 676 (motion dated November 30, 1887, order date same day, docket nos. 910 and 911). As noted, Mrs. Sheldon had visited Pasadena in 1887, and Sheldon himself visited in 1886. "Personal News," *Los Angeles Times*, October 3, 1886. They would live there for the remainder of their lives.

223. The railroad had lobbied, without success, for such a federal law. A legal bill for this effort can be found in Missouri Pacific Historical Society, MF5 (0007–1265). Interestingly, it appears that MoPac initially hired the law firm in question.

224. "Texas and Pacific Reorganization," *The Philadelphia Inquirer*, February 3, 1888.

225. Charles McClung McGhee papers, box 5 (Schiff to Wistar, March 12, 1888).

226. Missouri Pacific Railway Company v. the Texas and Pacific Railway Company, box 671 (petition and answers, filed and dated by court January 23, 1888). George Gould signed the petition on behalf of the railroad.

227. "Texas and Pacific," *The Commercial and Financial Chronicle*, March 10, 1888; "Railroad Notes," *The Philadelphia Inquirer*, January 21, 1887. The applications to the court to permit the new mortgages can be found in Missouri Pacific Railway Company v. the Texas and Pacific Railway Company, box 678; and the court's order on the mortgages, dated January 23, 1888, in Missouri Pacific Railway Company v. the Texas and Pacific Railway Company, box 680.

228. Missouri Pacific Historical Society, MF5 (0007–1265) (committee minutes dated April 20, 1888, referencing agreement among the parties of April 10).

229. In re Scott's Trust, 322 Pa. 1, 7 (1936).

230. Missouri Pacific Historical Society, MF5 (0007–1265) (Final Report of Committee on Reorganization, December 5, 1888, at 8).

231. "End of Receivership," *Austin Daily Statesman*, October 16, 1888. "Texas and Pacific," *The Commercial and Financial Chronicle*, May 12, 1888.

232. Missouri Pacific Railway Company v. the Texas and Pacific Railway Company, box 672 (order dated October 26, 1888, docket no. 1253). See also Missouri Pacific Railway Company v. the Texas and Pacific Railway Company, box 676 (order dated October 24, 1888, docket no. 1251).

233. Missouri Pacific Historical Society, MF6 (0457–0552) (annual report for year ending December 31, 1888). The report also notes that most of the bridges built on the Rio Grande Division "during the years 1880, 1881, 1882, had to be renovated during the year 1888."

234. Missouri Pacific Historical Society, MF5 (0007–1265) (balance sheet as of November 30, 1887, showing receivers' certificates sold). The receivers also realized over $1 million from selling the old iron rails for scrap. Missouri Pacific Historical Society, MF5 (0007–1265) (Final Report of Committee on Reorganization, December 5, 1888, at 9).

235. Missouri Pacific Historical Society, MF6 (0457–0552) (salaries as of January 1889).

236. In 1899, or more than a decade later, the president was making $7,200 per year and the general manager, who actually supervised the operations in Texas, $10,000. In 1908, those same positions received $15,000 and $16,000, respectively. Missouri Pacific Historical Society, MF6 (0457–0552).

237. Missouri Pacific Historical Society, MF5 (0007–1265; Final Report of Committee on Reorganization, December 5, 1888, at 7–8).

238. The Drake Committee agreed to take care of untendered Land Grant bonds.

239. "Suing the Texas and Pacific Road," *New York Tribune*, December 1, 1888.

240. Missouri Pacific Historical Society, MF5 (0007–1265; Dale to Satterlee, August 15, 1889).

241. The 1900 annual report shows both McGhee and Wistar still serving. By 1903, they both had stepped down. Wistar passed away in 1905, McGhee in 1907.

242. "Texas & Pacific Plan," *The New York Times*, May 7, 1924. See also Texas & Pacific Readjustment, 86 I.C.C. 808 (1924).

243. The other transcontinentals lost their federal charters as the result of foreclosure sales during receiverships.

244. Julius Grodinsky, *Transcontinental Railway Strategy, 1869–1893: A Study of Businessmen* (University of Pennsylvania Press, 1962), 167, 173.

245. Missouri Pacific Historical Society, MF5 (0007–1265; Choate to G. Gould, July 28, 1899). The letter concludes with the argument that "once the western terminus [is] secured for handling the great oriental trade—now in its infancy, you could construct the Yuma-Sierra Blanca gap at your pleasure." A 1957 interview with Choate can be found in the June 1965 issue of the *Journal of San Diego History*, but it does not touch on the letter to Gould.

4. The Bankers Take Charge

1. Maury Klein, *The Great Richmond Terminal: A Study in Businessmen and Business Strategy* (University of Virginia Press, 1970), chap. 2 (biographies of Brice and Thomas).
2. Joseph T. Lambie, *From Mine to Market: The History of Coal Transportation on the Norfolk and Western Railway* (New York University Press, 1954), 115–20. See also Mira Wilkins, *The History of Foreign Investment in the United States to 1914* (Harvard University Press, 1989), 223.
3. The Richmond and Danville was first formed under Acts of Assembly of Virginia 1846–47, chap. 117. John F. Stover, "The Pennsylvania Railroad's Southern Rail Empire," *Pennsylvania Magazine of History and Biography* 81, no. 1 (1957): 31–34.
4. E. G. Campbell, *The Reorganization of the American Railroad System, 1893–1900* (Columbia University Press, 1938), 15.
5. "Jay Gould in the South," *The Financial Times t*, February 4, 1891.
6. "New Railroad Syndicate," *The New York Times*, June 16, 1880. Klein, *The Great Richmond Terminal*, 174. See also Karin A. Shapiro, *New South Rebellion: The Battle Against Convict Labor in the Tennessee Coalfields, 1871–1896* (University of North Carolina Press, 1998), 25. See also McGhee Letterbook (August 1886 to February 1888; McGhee to Inman, June 30, 1887).
7. "The Wall Street Deal," *Atlanta Constitution*, January 21, 1887.
8. McGhee Letterbook (February 1888 to February 1889; Amount of Securities and Where Placed, February 25, 1888).
9. McGhee box 6 (Kimball to McGhee, August 4, 1888).
10. McGhee Letterbook (February 1888 to February 1889; McGhee to Fleming, September 22, 1888).
11. Lease of the East Tennessee, Virginia and Georgia Railway Company to the Richmond and Danville Railroad Company, October 17, 1888.
12. McGhee Letterbook (February 1888 to February 1889; McGhee to Inman, October 22, 1888).
13. *East Tennessee Annual Report* 1889, at 9; Thouron v. East Tennessee V. & G. Ry. Co., 38 F. 673, 674 (C.C.E.D. Tenn. 1889). See also "Injunction Against a Deal," *The New York Times*, November 25, 1888.
14. As indicated in the 1892 edition of Henry V. Poor, *Manual of the Railroads of the United States* (H. V. & H. W. Poor, 1892). Richmond Terminal also owned $6.5 million worth of the East Tennessee's second preferred shares (which were junior to the shares issued in the 1886 reorganization, but senior to the common shares). Swaine, perhaps breaching client confidence, states that the Norfolk and Western "assisted" the plaintiffs in the lease litigation. Robert T. Swaine, *The Cravath Firm and Its Predecessors*, vol. I (Privately printed at Ad, 1948), 387.
15. "A Huge Railroad Deal," *The New York Times*, October 23, 1888. Confusingly, there was another railroad in the area called the Georgia Railroad and Banking Company, so I call the *Central* Railroad and Banking Company of Georgia the "Georgia Central" throughout.
16. Clarke v. Central Railroad & Banking Co of Georgia, 50 F. 338, 340 (C.C.S.D. Ga. 1892).
17. Klein, *The Great Richmond Terminal*, 232. See also "Railway Combination in the United States," *The Economist*, November 8, 1890. Klein has them at the second largest, after the Santa Fe, while *The Economist* has them fourth, after the Santa Fe, the Missouri Pacific (Gould) system, and the Pennsylvania.
18. "Financial Review," *Banking Law Journal* 6, no. 5 (1892), 234–36.

19. McGhee Letterbook (February 1888 to February 1889; Amount of Securities and Where Placed, February 25, 1888).

20. "Jay Gould and the Richmond Terminal," *Financial Times*, January 24, 1891.

21. Klein, *The Great Richmond Terminal*, 234.

22. "News About Railroads," *The New York Times*, July 30, 1891.

23. "The Southern Railroads of America," *The Economist*, October 31, 1891.

24. Poor's 1892 has Gould, Sage, and Dillion reelected in March 1892, but the 1893 edition (showing a new board elected in September 1892) no longer includes any of the three men, but it does include George Gould. Poor, *Manual of the Railroads of the United States*. Reliability is an issue with Poor's, which shows McGhee as being from Atlanta in the Richmond Terminal listings.

25. McGhee box 12 (Satterlee to McGhee, December 3, 1892, noting Gould's death the prior day).

26. Julius Grodinsky, *Jay Gould: His Business Career* (University of Pennsylvania Press, 1957), 593.

27. All figures are taken from *The Commercial and Financial Chronicle*, Investor Supplement, March 1892.

28. Richmond and West Point Terminal Railway and Warehouse Company and Frederic P. Olcott, Alfred Sully, and James B. Pace, preferred stock, trust agreement dated December 6, 1886.

29. The indentures and mortgages associated with these bonds are noted in the bibliography under "Corporate Documents." I have indicated the respective issue in parentheses, as the names of the documents do not always clearly indicate which bond they relate to.

30. In the nineteenth century, long-term leases were often used when mergers were not possible, such as when the railroad in question had a charter granted by the state legislature that prohibited mergers without legislative consent.

31. Poor, *Manual of the Railroads of the United States*, 1891.

32. "Stocks Dormant," *The Philadelphia Inquirer*, July 16, 1891.

33. "A Big Deficit, But Dividends All the Same," *New York Herald*, August 8, 1891, 4.

34. Fairfax Harrison, *History of the Legal Development of the Railroad System of the Southern Railway Company* (Washington: 1901), 691.

35. McGhee Letterbook (February 1889 to February 1892; McGhee to Walters, September 16, 1891).

36. *Fifth Annual Report of East Tennessee, Virginia & Georgia Railway Company*, for the fiscal year ending June 30, 1891.

37. J. F. Stover, *The Railroads of the South, 1865–1900* (University of North Carolina Press 1955), 250–51.

38. J. S. Morgan & Co. papers, London Metropolitan Archives, HC3.1.1 (40).

39. "President Inman's Statement," *Wall Street Journal*, August 10, 1891.

40. The letter is reproduced in *To the Shareholders of the Richmond and West Point Terminal Railway and Warehouse Company*, dated December 16, 1891.

41. Klein, *The Great Richmond Terminal*, 238–39.

42. He was also one of the original investors in Gould and Scott's Pacific Railway Improvement Company. See chapter 2 of this book for more information.

43. "Richmond Terminal Stockholders," *New York Tribune*, December 9, 1891.

44. *To the Shareholders of the Richmond and West Point Terminal Railway and Warehouse Company.*

45. "The American Cotton Market," *The Guardian*, December 16, 1891.

46. "Railroad Interests," *New York Tribune*, December 19, 1891.
47. Clarence W. Barron, Arthur Pound, and Samuel Taylor Moore, *More They Told Barron: Conversations and Revelations of an American Pepys in Wall Street* (Harper, 1931), 181.
48. "Richmond Terminal Affairs," *The New York Times*, December 29, 1891.
49. "A New Scheme," *Atlanta Constitution*, January 13, 1892.
50. *To the Holders of Securities of the Richmond and West Point Terminal Railway and Warehouse Company and of Its Auxiliary Corporations*, New York, March 1, 1892 (hereinafter "Olcott Plan").
51. Olcott Plan, 3.
52. Stover, *The Railroads of the South*, 251. See also C. R.R. & Banking Co. of Ga. v. Farmers' Loan & Tr. Co., 79 F. 158, 159 (C.C.S.D. Ga. 1897) (Pardee, J.).
53. A notice to securityholders regarding this plan appeared in the *Boston Daily Advertiser*, March 24, 1892, at 2. A half-page notice for the same plan appears in *The Nation: A Weekly Journal Devoted to Politics, Literature, Science, and Art*, March 24, 1892, iii.
54. Stuart Daggett, *Railroad Reorganization* (Houghton Mifflin, 1908), 172.
55. "The Plan Abandoned," *New York Tribune*, May 17, 1892.
56. Klein, *The Great Richmond Terminal*, 254.
57. "Olcott Plan a Failure," *The New York Times*, May 17, 1892; "Richmond Terminal," *The Philadelphia Inquirer*, May 17, 1892. See also 35th Annual Report of the Richmond and Danville Railroad Co., dated September 30, 1882, which mentions Clyde's involvement with the annual meeting; the 36th Annual Report, dated September 30, 1883, which lists him as a board member; the 37th Annual Report Annual Report, dated September 30, 1884, where Clyde is again listed as a board member; and the 38th Annual Report, dated September 30, 1995, where he nominated the board members (including himself). But the 43rd Annual Report, dated June 30, 1890, shows him off the board.
58. Daggett, *Railroad Reorganization*, 174.
59. This was reprinted in "Richmond Terminal," *The New York Times*, May 27, 1892.
60. Harold van B. Cleveland and Thomas F. Huertas, *Citibank, 1812–1970* (Harvard University Press, 1985), 33.
61. "Business: All Paths Unite!" *Time*, March 26, 1934.
62. "Anthony J. Drexel Is Dead," *The New York Times*, July 1, 1893.
63. Kathleen Burk, *Morgan Grenfell, 1838–1988: The Biography of a Merchant Bank* (Oxford University Press 1989), 48–51.
64. Vincent P. Carosso, *The Morgans: Private International Bankers, 1854–1913* (Harvard University Press, 1987), 260–61.
65. Carosso, *The Morgans*, 266.
66. Susie J. Pak, *Gentlemen Bankers: The World of J. P. Morgan* (Harvard University Press, 2013), 49.
67. "The Business Career of Charles H. Coster," *The New York Times*, March 18, 1900. See also Carosso, *The Morgans*, 168.
68. John Moody and George Kibbe Turner, "The Masters of Capital in America: Morgan: The Great Trustee," *McClure's Magazine* (November 1910): 24.
69. Jean Strouse, *Morgan: American Financier* (Random House, 1999), 320.
70. Campbell, *The Reorganization of the American Railroad System*, 148.
71. Douglas G. Baird, *Elements of Bankruptcy*, 7th ed. (Foundation Press, 2022), 61. Moody and Turner (in 1910) are an early example of the tendency to credit Morgan with the invention of corporate reorganization, with the aim of protecting mistreated bondholders. Moody and Turner, *The Masters of Capital in America*, 22–24.

72. David A. Skeel, *Debt's Dominion: A History of Bankruptcy Law in America* (Princeton University Press, 2001), 66.

73. Pak, *Gentlemen Bankers*, 217.

74. Securities and Exchange Commission, *Report on the Study and Investigation of the Work, Activities, Personnel and Functions of Protective and Reorganization Committees* (1937–1940), part II, ed. Adelaide R. Hasse (hereinafter "SEC Report"), 171.

75. Lance E. Davis and Robert J. Cull, "International Capital Movements, Domestic Capital Markets, and American Economic Growth, 1820–1914," in *The Cambridge Economic History of the United States*, ed. Stanley L. Engerman and Robert E. Gallman, 740 (Cambridge University Press).

76. "Foreign Capital in American Railways," *Railway Age*, November 3, 1911.

77. Davis and Cull, "International Capital Movements," 744.

78. Moody and Turner, *The Masters of Capital in America*, 17.

79. Klein, *The Great Richmond Terminal*, 249.

80. Albro Martin, *Railroads Triumphant: The Growth, Rejection, and Rebirth of a Vital American Force* (Oxford University Press, 1992), 334. See generally Klein, *The Great Richmond Terminal*.

81. Louis D. Brandeis, *Other People's Money: and How the Bankers Use It* (F. A. Stokes, 1914; Harper Torchbook ed., 1967), 7.

82. Max Lowenthal, *The Investor Pays* (A. A. Knopf, 1936), 163–65.

83. SEC Report, part I, at 874.

84. Drexel, Morgan & Co., syndicate records, Morgan Library & Museum, ARC 107, vol. 3, 137.1.

85. Drexel, Morgan & Co., syndicate records, ARC 107; vol. 3, 137.2.

86. "Railroads of the South," *Atlanta Constitution*, June 11, 1892; "Railroad News," *Atlanta Constitution*, June 7, 1892.

87. Drexel, Morgan & Co., syndicate records, ARC 107; vol. 3, 137.10.

88. A copy of the petition is in Southern Railway Co v. Carnegie Steel Co., 176 U.S. 257 (1900), case record, 1–19.

89. Southern Railway Co v. Carnegie Steel Co., 19–22 (order dated June 15, 1892).

90. Southern Railway. Co. v. Carnegie Steel Co., 267 (1900).

91. Harrison, *History of the Legal Development of the Railroad System*, 37.

92. Harrison, *History of the Legal Development of the Railroad System*, 692–93; McGhee box 11 (Fink to McGhee, June 26, 1892). See also Cent. Tr. Co. v. Ingersoll, 87 F. 427, 427-28 (6th Cir. 1898).

93. Drexel, Morgan & Co., syndicate records, ARC 107; vol. 3, 137.5. All the Clyde-Morgan correspondence that follows can be found in vol. 3, section 137.

94. "Railway Traffic," *Atlanta Constitution*, July 26, 1892.

95. "Financial World," *The New York Times*, July 3, 1892.

96. McGhee Letterbook (ETV&G, June 1892 to November 1894; McGhee to Fink, August 19, 1892).

97. For example, see the agreement dated June 27, 1892, by and between the undersigned holders of the Extension and General Mortgage Bonds of the East Tennessee, Virginia and Georgia Railroad and Georgia Railway Company.

98. "To the Stockholders of the Richmond and West Point Terminal Railway and Warehouse Company," *The New York Times*, September 11, 1892.

99. "It Looks Like Harmony," *New York Tribune*, February 3, 1893; "Assistance Asked," *Atlanta Constitution*, February 3, 1893.

100. "This Is Business," *Atlanta Constitution*, April 14, 1893. See also the notice published on page 18 of *The New York Times*, May 28, 1893.

101. J. S. Morgan & Co. papers, HC3.1.1 (115). The syndicate agreement is dated April 18.

102. J. S. Morgan & Co. papers, HC3.1.1 (115) (N. M. Rothchild & Son to J. S. Morgan, February 9, 1894); J. S. Morgan & Co. papers, HC3.1.1 (115) (syndicate agreement dated April 18, 1893, signed by N. M. Rothchild & Son). The latter committed Rothchild to take $500,000 of the $3.25 million that J. S. Morgan had agreed to give toward funding the syndicate. Similar documents from other investors are in the same file—J. S. Morgan kept about $ 1.75 million for itself and subsyndicated the remainder to seven investors, of which Rothchild had one of the biggest pieces. J. S. Morgan & Co. papers, HC3.1.1 (115) (three undated foolscap sheets, with calculations).

103. "Here Is the Plan," *Atlanta Constitution*, May 24, 1893.

104. J. S. Morgan & Co. papers, HC3.1.1 (115). An interesting development, given the rumors that Olcott was angry with Morgan for muscling in on the Richmond Terminal Reorganization. Barron, *More They Told Barron*, 145 (Barron's story is that Olcott felt that Morgan had "knifed him"). And indeed, Morgan had stepped down from the board of the Central Trust reportedly because of the tension. "Richmond Terminal Affairs," *The New York Times*, July 2, 1892.

105. Lowenthal, *The Investor Pays*, 180–183.

106. J. S. Morgan & Co. papers, HC3.1.1 (115) (circular dated May 22, 1893).

107. By 1914, about one-third of the railroad was subject to a first lien resulting from these bonds. Letter to Holders of Richmond & Danville Consolidated Mortgage Six Percent bonds, from J. P. Morgan & Co., dated December 7, 1914, with attachment.

108. Plan and Agreement for the Reorganization of Richmond and West Point Terminal Railway and Warehouse Company et al., dated May 1, 1893, at 11–12. Copies of the May 1893 version of the plan can be found in various places, including J. S. Morgan & Co. papers, HC3.1.1 (115).

109. Plan and Agreement for the Reorganization of Richmond and West Point Terminal Railway and Warehouse Company et al., dated May 1, 1893, at 10.

110. Plan and Agreement for the Reorganization of Richmond and West Point Terminal Railway and Warehouse Company et al., dated May 1, 1893, at 15.

111. Plan and Agreement for the Reorganization of Richmond and West Point Terminal Railway and Warehouse Company et al., dated May 1, 1893, at 19, 22.

112. Daggett, *Railroad Reorganization*, 184.

113. For example, a notice for payment of assessments on the common stock appears on page 14 of the *New York Tribune*, June 24, 1893.

114. David W. Blight, *Frederick Douglass: Prophet of Freedom* (Simon & Schuster, 2018), 732.

115. Charles Hoffmann, "The Depression of the Nineties," *Journal of Economic History* 16, no. 2 (1956), 138.

116. "Railroad Reorganization," *The New York Times*, November 6, 1893.

117. Daniel Schulman, *The Money Kings: The Epic Story of the Jewish Immigrants Who Transformed Wall Street and Shaped Modern America* (Alfred A. Knopf, 2023), 199–209, and Maury Klein, *The Life & Legend of E. H. Harriman* (University of North Carolina Press, 2000), 106–15, 166–67. See also Cleveland and Huertas, *Citibank*, 37–40; "The Baltimore and Ohio," *The New York Times*, July 1, 1899. Like the Texas and Pacific before it, the Baltimore and Ohio reorganized without a foreclosure to save its original charter.

118. Albert C. Stevens, "Analysis of the Phenomena of the Panic in the United States in 1893," *Quarterly Journal of Economics* 8, no. 2 (1894), 128.

119. J. S. Morgan & Co. papers, HC3.1.1 (115) (New York to London, August 29, 1893).

120. "Richmond Terminal Affairs Unpromising," *Wall Street Journal*, November 4, 1893.

121. "Southern Railroad Business," *Wall Street Journal*, December 28, 1893.

122. J. S. Morgan & Co. papers, HC3.1.1 (115) (Modified Plan of Reorganization, revision of January 22, 1894).

123. J. S. Morgan & Co. papers, HC3.1.1 (115) (Modified Plan of Reorganization, revision of February 1, 1894).

124. Plan and Agreement for the Reorganization of Richmond and West Point Terminal Railway and Warehouse Company et al., dated May 1, 1893, at 22.

125. East Tennessee Reorganization Mortgage, Southern Railway to Central Trust Company of New York, Trustee, October 2, 1894, and the Modified Plan of Reorganization, at 10.

126. J. S. Morgan & Co. papers, HC3.1.1 (115) (telegram dated February 9, 1894).

127. J. S. Morgan & Co. papers, HC3.1.1 (115) (Heseltine, Powell & Co. to J. S. Morgan & Co., February 15, 1894).

128. Augustus J. Veenendaal, Jr., *Slow Train to Paradise: How Dutch Investment Helped Build American Railroads* (Stanford University Press, 1996), 92.

129. Klein, *The Great Richmond Terminal*, 281.

130. Klein, *The Great Richmond Terminal*, 265, 277–79.

131. McGhee box 14 (Coster to McGhee, February 28, 1894).

132. "New Plan for Terminal," *New York Tribune*, March 2, 1894; "Richmond Terminal," *Atlanta Constitution*, March 4, 1894.

133. Drexel, Morgan & Co., syndicate records, ARC 107; vol. 3, 229.6.

134. J. S. Morgan & Co. papers, HC3.1.1 (115) (undated memorandum with totals); Drexel, Morgan & Co., syndicate records, ARC 107; vol. 3, 229.8.

135. "Under a New Name," *Atlanta Constitution*, June 19, 1894.

136. Central Trust Co. of New York v. East Tennessee, V & G R Co., 73 F. 661, 661 (C.C.N.D. Ga. 1895); Clyde v. Richmond & D.R. Co., 65 F. 336, 337 (C.C.N.D. Ga. 1894); Clyde v. Richmond & D.R. Co., 63 F. 21, 23 (C.C.D.S.C. 1894). See also "Richmond Terminal," *Wall Street Journal*, April 15, 1893.

137. R. Scott Huffard, Jr., *Engines of Redemption: Railroads and the Reconstruction of Capitalism in the New South* (University of North Carolina Press, 2019), 202. See also "An Important Tour of Inspection," *Atlanta Constitution*, June 12, 1892; "What It Means to Atlanta," *Atlanta Constitution*, May 28, 1892.

138. Campbell, *The Reorganization of the American Railroad System*, 157. See also "Mr. Spencer's Career," *New York Tribune*, November 30, 1906; "Samuel Spencer," *Railway Age*, December 7, 1906.

139. See "By-the-Bye in Wall Street," *Wall Street Journal*, July 24, 1935, which writes wistfully of Spencer "quitting college preliminaries to rush into the volunteer ranks of soldier." To similar effect is "Builders of Georgia," *Atlanta Constitution*, November 5, 1942, which mentions the monument to Spencer in Atlanta, then at the train station.

140. Burke Davis, *The Southern Railway: Road of the Innovators* (University of North Carolina Press, 1985), 19.

141. Steven G. Collins, "Progress and Slavery on the South's Railroads," *Railroad History*, no. 181 (1999), 17. Most prewar Southern railroads were built with the labor of enslaved people, although some in Tennessee also used Irish immigrants. R. S. Cotterill, "Southern Railroads, 1850–1860," *Mississippi Valley Historical Review* 10, no. 4 (1924), 404.

142. Theodore Kornweibel, "'Not at All Proper for Women': Black Female Railroaders," *Railroad History*, no. 201 (2009), 9.

143. Huffard, *Engines of Redemption*, 200.

144. Douglas A. Blackmon, *Slavery by Another Name: The Re-enslavement of Black Americans from the Civil War to World War II* (Doubleday, 2008), 343.

145. Scott Reynolds Nelson, *Iron Confederacies: Southern Railways, Klan Violence, and Reconstruction* (University of North Carolina Press, 1999), 173.

146. 163 U.S. 537 (1896).

147. Barbara Young Welke, *Recasting American Liberty: Gender, Race, Law, and the Railroad Revolution, 1865–1920* (Cambridge University Press, 2001), 348.

148. Moody was the founder of Moody's Investor Services, which is still a major bond-rating agency today.

149. John Moody, *The Railroad Builders: A Chronicle of the Welding of the States* (Yale University Press, 1919), 188–89.

150. To the best of my knowledge, none of the leading Morgan biographies, nor Professor Klein's important Richmond Terminal volume, engages with Moody's text on this issue.

151. Blight, *Frederick Douglass*, 741–44.

152. Pak, *Gentlemen Bankers*, 47.

153. "The Southern Railway Plans," *New York Tribune*, July 6, 1894; "The New Southern Railway," *The New York Times*, July 1, 1894.

154. Southern Railway First Annual Report, dated August 22, 1895.

155. Floyd W. Mundy, *Earning Power of Railroads* (Oliphant & Co., 1935), 656. See also "The Common Stockholder," *Railway Age*, March 29, 1924 (discussing the first dividend on common stock).

156. Floyd W. Mundy, *Earning Power of Railroads* (Oliphant & Co., 1947), 506.

157. The connection that Chernow draws between assessments and voting trusts is plainly erroneous. Ron Chernow, *The House of Morgan* (Atlantic Monthly Press, 1990), 68.

158. J. P. Morgan & Co. syndicate records, Morgan Library & Museum, ARC 110; vol. 3, 101.

159. *Report of the Money Trust Investigation: Investigation of Financial and Monetary Conditions in the United States Under House Resolutions Nos. 429 and 504: Before a Subcommittee of the Committee on Banking and Currency* (hereinafter "Money Trust Investigation Report"), 40.

160. The preferred shares were active in the market, but press reports about the common were few and far between until early 1914 (when the railroad first broached the idea of terminating the trust).

161. "Answers to Inquirers," *Wall Street Journal*, July 14, 1913.

162. Hearing Before a Subcommittee of the Committee on Naval Affairs, United States Senate, Under Senate Resolution 291. Statement of Fairfax Harrison on Behalf of Southern Railway Company, 33.

163. Money Trust Investigation: Investigation of Financial and Monetary Conditions in the United States Under House Resolutions Nos. 429 and 504: Before a Subcommittee of the Committee on Banking and Currency, part 15, 1046–47.

164. "Stock Exchange Notice," *Wall Street Journal*, January 16, 1915.

165. Campbell, *The Reorganization of the American Railroad System*, 160.

166. Mundy, *Earning Power of Railroads* (1902), 110. See also Mundy, *Earning Power of Railroads* (1936), 173.

167. Letter to Holders of Richmond & Danville Consolidated Mortgage Six Percent Bonds, from J. P. Morgan & Co., dated December 7, 1914, with attachment.

168. Daggett, *Railroad Reorganization*, 191.

169. *In Memoriam, Samuel Spencer* (Atlanta, 1910). See also "Spencer Killed in Wreck," *The New York Times*, November 30, 1906. Also killed in Spencer's car was Philip George Schuyler, a former Union army general from New York and member of the prominent Hamilton and Schuyler families. The *New York Times* reported that he was "associated" with the J. P. Morgan–affiliated New York Life Insurance Company. "Gen. Schuyler, Veteran, Sporting and Clubman," *The New York Times*, November 30, 1906.

170. "Atlanta City Council OKs Removal of Railroad Statue with Confederacy Ties," *Atlanta Constitution*, April 20, 2021. According to the article, the city owns the statue.

171. Atlanta History Center, https://www.atlantahistorycenter.com/blog/samuel-spencer -memorial/.

172. Joline, whom I quoted in chapter 1, had represented the Central Trust Company (and perhaps also the railroads) in the receiverships. Clyde v. Richmond & D.R. Co., 55 F. 445 (C.C.E.D. Va. 1893). See also "Keeping Hands Off," *Atlanta Constitution*, December 30, 1893.

173. "Changes of Railroad Ownership or Control in 1907," *Railway Gazette*, January 3, 1908.

174. Except for this matter, the committee had given its final accounting to the Southern in September 1896.

175. Klein, *The Great Richmond Terminal*, 283.

176. Norfolk Southern Corp.–Control–Norfolk & W.R. Co. and Southern R. Co., 366 I.C.C. 173 (1982). Both railroads were acquired by a holding company—Norfolk Southern *Corporation*—and later the Southern's name was changed to Norfolk Southern *Railway*. On September 1, 1998, Norfolk and Western merged into Norfolk Southern Railway (the old Southern). In short, the Southern still exists as a renamed subsidiary of the holding company. Form 10-K: Norfolk Southern Railway Co., for the year ended December 31, 2004, at 2. See also Form 10-K: Norfolk Southern Corporation, for the year ended December 31, 2010, at K3. Confusingly, Norfolk Southern Railway is also the name of a railroad that the Southern acquired in the early 1970s.

177. Form 10-K: Norfolk Southern Railway Co., for the year ending December 31, 1993. The "Southern Railway Company First Consolidated Mortgage 5 Percent Gold Bonds, due July 1, 1994" document heads the list of outstanding securities on the cover. Note that this 10-K is for the operating subsidiary (namely, the former Southern Railway).

178. Klein, *The Great Richmond Terminal*, 284.

179. Money Trust Investigation Report, 148.

180. Vincent P. Carosso, *Investment Banking in America: A History* (Harvard University Press, 1970), 40–41.

181. Southern Railway Co. et al., 37 ICC Val. Rep. 1, 230 (1931).

182. Chernow, *The House of Morgan*, 69.

183. Carosso, *The Morgans*, 500.

184. Carosso, *The Morgans*, 372.

185. Moody and Turner, *The Masters of Capital in America*, 24.

186. J. P. Morgan & Co. syndicate records, ARC 110; vol. 3, 100.

187. Martin Horn, *J. P. Morgan & Co. and the Crisis of Capitalism* (Cambridge University Press, 2022), 18.

188. "Frederick Lisman, Rail Bond Expert," *The New York Times*, February 15, 1940. F. J. Lisman, "Protective Committees for Security Holders," *Harvard Business Review*, XIII, no. 1 (October 1934): 20.

5. The Statutes Arrive

1. Ron Chernow, *The House of Morgan* (Atlantic Monthly Press, 1990), 68.

2. 208 U.S. 90 (1908).

3. De Forest Billyou, "Corporate Reorganization Under State and Federal Statutes," *University of Illinois Law Forum* 1958, no. 4 (Winter 1958): 557.

4. For a discussion of both the MoPac and Texas and Pacific receiverships, see Stuart Daggett, "Recent Railroad Failures and Reorganizations," *Quarterly Journal of Economics*,

32, no. 3 (1918): 459–60, 470–1, 480, 483, 485. Professor Daggett aptly noted that MoPac's reorganization was not "radical," and he doubted whether it would be sufficient to allow the railroad to weather another economic downturn. The Texas and Pacific's reorganization was not completed as of the time of his article—eventually, the railroad would be greatly buoyed by the discovery of oil in western Texas in the 1920s, and as a result, it avoided the fate of its parent company during the Great Depression.

5. Max Lowenthal, "The Case of The Missouri Pacific," *Harper's Monthly Magazine* (December 1, 1934): 89, 92.

6. Investigation of Railroads, Holding Companies and Affiliated Companies: Hearings Before a Subcommittee of the Committee on Interstate Commerce, United States Senate (hereinafter, "Investigation of Railroads"), Additional Report of July 29, 1944, 5. The other two members of the trust were identified in later hearings: "Mr. James N. Wallace, as I recall, was the then president or chairman of the Central Trust Co., the present Central Hanover Bank & Trust Co. Mr. Robert Winsor was a partner of Kidder, Peabody & Co. Mr. Wallace was chairman of the stockholders' protective committee, and Mr. Winsor was a member of that committee," Investigation of Railroads, part 13, 5594.

7. Investigation of Railroads, part 13, 5606.

8. Floyd W. Mundy, *Earning Power of Railroads* (Oliphant & Co., 1925), 467. The Missouri Pacific's receivership also provided an opportunity to merge the old Iron Mountain into MoPac, formalizing a relationship that had existed since Jay Gould's time.

9. Just over $24 million of the income bonds were issued in the first Texas and Pacific receivership (the subject of chapter 3), and more than $23.7 million were ultimately held by the Iron Mountain, and thus MoPac.

10. Lowenthal, "The Case of the Missouri Pacific," 92.

11. Investigation of Railroads, part 13, 5655.

12. Dan N. Baycot, "A Discussion of All Phases of Missouri Pacific's Operations during the 10-Year Period Ending with 1929," *An Analysis of Missouri Pacific RR* (Railroad Analyses Inc., 1934), 1.

13. W. J. Burton, "History of the Missouri Pacific" (unpublished manuscript, July 1, 1956), 769–70.

14. Baycot, "A Discussion of All Phases of Missouri Pacific's Operations," 18.

15. Investigation of Railroads, Additional Report of July 29, 1944, 2, 19–20. The tendency of receiverships to leave railroads with heavy fixed costs was common. Stephen J. Lubben, "Railroad Receiverships and Modern Bankruptcy Theory," *Cornell Law Review* 89, no. 6 (September 2004): 1462–63.

16. Melville J. Ulmer, *Capital in Transportation, Communications, and Public Utilities: Its Formation and Financing* (Princeton University Press, 1960), 169.

17. James Stuart Olson, *Saving Capitalism: The Reconstruction Finance Corporation and the New Deal, 1933–1940* (Princeton University Press, 1988), 99; F. J. Lisman, "Railroad Bonds," *Annals of the American Academy of Political and Social Science*, 88, no. 1 (1920): 59.

18. 228 U.S. 482, 33 S. Ct. 554, 57 L. Ed. 931 (1913). See also Samuel Spring, "Upset Prices in Corporate Reorganization," *Harvard Law Review* 32, no. 5 (1919): 508–13.

19. Jerome Frank, "Some Realistic Reflections on Some Aspects of Corporate Reorganization," *Virginia Law Review* 19, no. 6 (1932–1933): 552.

20. Robert T. Swaine, "Reorganization of Corporations: Certain Developments of the Last Decade," *Columbia Law Review* 27, no. 8 (1927): 902.

21. Kansas City Southern Ry. Co. v. Guardian Trust Co., 240 U.S. 166, 172, 36 S. Ct. 334, 335, 60 L. Ed. 579 (1916).

22. Douglas G. Baird, *The Unwritten Law of Corporate Reorganizations* (Cambridge University Press, 2022), 42. See also Guar. Tr. Co. of New York v. Missouri Pac. Ry. Co., 238 F. 812, 818 (E.D. Mo. 1916), which involved MoPac's receivership.

23. Case v. Los Angeles Lumber Products Co., 308 U.S. 106, 116, 60 S. Ct. 1, 8, 84 L. Ed. 110 (1939).

24. Harkin v. Brundage, 276 U.S. 36, 52, 48 S. Ct. 268, 274, 72 L. Ed. 457 (1928); Shapiro v. Wilgus, 287 U.S. 348, 355, 53 S. Ct. 142, 145, 77 L. Ed. 355 (1932); Nat'l Sur. Co. v. Coriell, 289 U.S. 426, 435 (1933); First Nat. Bank v. Flershem, 290 U.S. 504, 515 (1934).

25. Harkin v. Brundage, 276 U.S. 36, 52 (1928).

26. Henry J. Friendly, "Some Comments on the Corporate Reorganizations Act," *Harvard Law Review* 48, no. 1 (1934): 43.

27. Shapiro v. Wilgus, 287 U.S. 348, 356 (1932).

28. People of State of Michigan, by Haggerty, v. Michigan Trust Co., 286 U.S. 334, 345, 52 S. Ct. 512, 515, 76 L. Ed. 1136 (1932).

29. First Nat. Bank of Cincinnati v. Flershem, 290 U.S. 504, 517, 54 S. Ct. 298, 303, 78 L. Ed. 465 (1934).

30. May Hosiery Mills v. F. & W. Grand 5-10-25 Cent Stores, 59 F.2d 218, 221 (D. Mont. 1932), rev'd, 64 F.2d 450 (9th Cir. 1933).

31. Lowenthal, "The Case of the Missouri Pacific," 92–93.

32. See William W. Bratton, "Corporate Debt Relationships: Legal Theory in a Time of Restructuring," *Duke Law Journal* 1989, no. 1 (February 1989): 165–67.

33. Investigation of Railroads, part 11, 4666.

34. Herbert H. Harwood, *Invisible Giants: The Empires of Cleveland's Van Sweringen Brothers* (Indiana University Press, 2003), 89–90.

35. Kevin Starr, *Inventing the Dream: California Through the Progressive Era* (Oxford University Press, 1986), 105–6.

36. Harwood, *Invisible Giants*, 91.

37. John F. Stover, *American Railroads*, 2nd ed. (University of Chicago Press, 1997), 202.

38. Investigation of Railroads, part 11, 4668–69.

39. Investigation of Railroads, part 6, 1991–92. With regard to Guaranty Trust, in particular, see also Investigation of Railroads, part 1, 111. See also Harold van B. Cleveland and Thomas F. Huertas, *Citibank, 1812–1970* (Harvard University Press, 1985), 56.

40. For instance, see Investigation of Railroads, part 4, 1245–47.

41. Investigation of Railroads, part 1, Exhibit 83.

42. Edward M. Lamont, *The Ambassador from Wall Street: The Story of Thomas W. Lamont, J. P. Morgan's Chief Executive* (Lyons, 2023), 253.

43. Investigation of Railroads, part 1, 191–195.

44. Martin Horn, *J. P. Morgan & Co. and the Crisis of Capitalism* (Cambridge University Press, 2022), 1225–26. See also Arthur E. Wilmarth, *Taming the Megabanks: Why We Need a New Glass-Steagall Act* (Oxford University Press, 2020), 131–32.

45. Vincent P. Carosso, *Investment Banking in America: A History* (Harvard University Press, 1970), 341.

46. Investigation of Railroads, part 25, exhibit A-84.

47. Investigation of Railroads, part 2, 448; Investigation of Railroads, part 11, 4655–56. According to calculations by the Guaranty Company of New York, "The original investment by Alleghany Corporation in the securities of the Missouri Pacific amounted to $76,101,506 in the Preferred and Common Stock and $23,409,061 in the Convertible 5½s, a total of $99,510,567," Investigation of Railroads, part 11, Exhibit 1434.

48. Investigation of Railroads, part 1, 141. The other was Douglas & Co., and it may have had a similar origin story. Investigation of Railroads, part 11, Exhibits 1364–1365.
49. Baldwin had moved to MoPac in 1923 from another Kuhn, Loeb railroad, the Illinois Central. Investigation of Railroads, part 13, 5595–96.
50. Investigation of Railroads, part 11, Ex. 1436.
51. Chernow, *The House of Morgan*, 414–15.
52. Investigation of Railroads, part 1, 173–5, Exs. 70, 71.
53. Investigation of Railroads, part 2, Exs. 99a, b, c, d.
54. Investigation of Railroads, part 13, 5697–707.
55. Investigation of Railroads, part 12, 5035. See also "Missouri Pacific Had Wyer on Pan Before Early Truman Probe," *Newsday*, October 6, 1952; Missouri Pacific Reorganization Proceedings, William A. Wise Law Library, University of Colorado Law School, motion no. 892.
56. Elroy Dimson, Paul Marsh, and Mike Staunton, *Global Investment Returns Yearbook* (UBS, 2024).
57. Harold Palmer, *Investment Salvage in Railroad Reorganizations* (Harper & Brothers, 1938), 91.
58. Philipp Blom, *Fracture: Life and Culture in the West, 1918–1938* (Atlantic Books, 2015), 333–40. See also Lamont, *The Ambassador from Wall Street*, 380.
59. Horn, *J. P. Morgan & Co. and the Crisis of Capitalism*, 171.
60. Investigation of Railroads, part 3, 1163. Most of the proceeds went to pay off $43 million of bonds that were maturing in April 1931. See also J. P. Morgan & Co. syndicate records, Morgan Library & Museum, ARC 119; vol. 12, 97.
61. Dearmont Folder 2928 (agreement dated October 1, 1932, between J. P. Morgan and MoPac).
62. Investigation of Railroads, part 12, Exhibit 1565.
63. Daniel A. Schiffman, "Shattered Rails, Ruined Credit: Financial Fragility and Railroad Operations in the Great Depression," *Journal of Economic History* 63, no. 3 (2003), 806. See also Milton Friedman and Anna Jacobson Schwartz, *A Monetary History of the United States, 1867–1960* (Princeton University Press, 1963), 319–20, 379–80.
64. Lowenthal, "The Case of the Missouri Pacific," 96.
65. Wilmarth, *Taming the Megabanks*, 110.
66. Stock Exchange Practices: Hearings Before the Committee on Banking and Currency, United States Senate, Seventy-third Congress, part 1, 766.
67. "Bailing out the Van Sweringens," *New Republic*, April 19, 1933.
68. "Missouri Pacific Allowed to Borrow $2,234,800 More," *Boston Globe*, March 1, 1933; "Morgans Got RFC Money," *Boston Globe*, December 19, 1936; Horn, *J. P. Morgan & Co.*, 174. See also Investigation of Railroads, part 3, 1174; Investigation of Railroads, part 6, 2050; Wilmarth, *Taming the Megabanks*, 116.
69. "It's Fun to Be Fooled," *New Republic*, May 3, 1933.
70. Harwood, *Invisible Giants*, 254.
71. Olson, *Saving Capitalism*, 119.
72. Olson, *Saving Capitalism*, 100.
73. Jesse H. Jones, *Fifty Billion Dollars: My Thirteen Years with the RFC, 1932–1945* (Macmillan, 1951), 121–26.
74. Morgan's testimony regarding the voting trust in the Richmond Terminal reorganization was quoted in chapter 4. Wilmarth, *Taming the Megabanks*, 124.
75. Investigation of Railroads, part 1, 11, 49, 75.

76. Katie Louchheim, *The Making of the New Deal: The Insiders Speak* (Harvard University Press, 1983), 242–43. See also Lamont, *The Ambassador from Wall Street*, 405–6.

77. Oral interview with Max Lowenthal by Jerry N. Hess, September 20, 1967, at 3–9.

78. Michael J. Cohen, *Truman and Israel* (University of California Press, 1990), 78–80.

79. Max Lowenthal, *The Investor Pays* (A. A. Knopf, 1936).

80. William Polatsek, "Wreck of the Old 77," *Cornell Law Quarterly* 34, no. 4 (1948–1949), 544 n68.

81. This is a common practice in receiverships. Securities and Exchange Commission, *Report on the Study and Investigation of the Work, Activities, Personnel and Functions of Protective and Reorganization Committees (1937–1940)*, vol. I, ed. Adelaide R. Hasse (hereinafter "SEC Report"), 258. Lowenthal, *The Investor Pays*, 113–7, 131–42.

82. Joseph L. Weiner, "Book Review," *Harvard Law Review* 47, no. 4 (1934): 721.

83. "Other People's Money," *New Republic*, August 21, 1935.

84. David G. McCullough, *Truman* (Simon & Schuster, 1992), 231–34.

85. Chernow, *The House of Morgan*, 414; "Truman Statement Called Libel," *The New York Times*, October 29, 1937. See also Horn, *J. P. Morgan & Co. and the Crisis of Capitalism*, 311.

86. 2 Stat. 19 (1800). Bruce Mann provides the definitive account of the 1800 Bankruptcy Act in *Republic of Debtors: Bankruptcy in the Age of American Independence* (Harvard University Press, 2002).

87. 5 Stat. 440 (1841). See generally Rafael I. Pardo, "Rethinking Antebellum Bankruptcy," *University of Colorado Law Review* 95, no. 4 (2024): 995–1087; Edward J. Balleisen, "Vulture Capitalism in Antebellum America: The 1841 Federal Bankruptcy Act and the Exploitation of Financial Distress," *Business History Review* 70, no. 4 (1996): 473–516.

88. *Congressional Globe*, vol. 12, 27th Cong., 3d sess., 69.

89. 14 Stat. 517 (1867).

90. Section 37, 14 Stat. at 535.

91. 18 Stat. 178 (1874).

92. 20 Stat. 99 (1878).

93. Stephen J. Lubben, "A New Understanding of the Bankruptcy Clause," *Case Western Reserve Law Review* 64, no. 2 (Winter 2013): 385–90.

94. Corporations could not file voluntary bankruptcy petitions until 1910.

95. In The Matter of an Inquiry into the Administration of Bankrupts' Estates Conducted Before Hon. Thomas D. Thacher, Judge of the United States District Court for the Southern District of New York, Pursuant to the Petition of the Association of the Bar of the City of New York, the New York County Lawyers' Association, and the Bronx County Bar Association, and the Orders of Said Court Made Thereon, commonly referred to as the "Donovan Report," dated March 22, 1930.

96. *Report to the President on the Bankruptcy Act and Its Administration in the Courts of the United States, Dated December 5, 1931* (hereinafter "Thacher Report").

97. Thacher Report, at 7.

98. Texas and Pacific Railway Co. Annual Report for the year ending December 31, 1888.

99. The proposed reorganization section is printed starting on page 91 of the Thacher Report.

100. S. 3866, 72d Cong., 1st Sess. (1932). Garrard Glenn, *The Law Governing Liquidation* (Baker, Voorhis & Co., 1935), 572.

101. Justice Harlan Fiske Stone, dissenting in United States v. Chicago, M., St. P. & P.R. Co., involving the much-discussed Milwaukee Road receivership, provides a nice example of somebody who might fit within this frame: "No one familiar with the financial and

corporate history of this country could say, I think, that railroad credit and the marketability of railroad securities have not been profoundly affected, for long periods of time, if not continuously, by the numerous railroad reorganizations, in the course of which junior security holders have found it impossible to save more than a remnant of their investment, and that only by the assumption of a heavy burden of expense, too often the result of wasteful and extravagant methods of reorganization," 282 U.S. 311, 337, 51 S. Ct. 159, 167, 75 L. Ed. 359 (1931).

102. Earl Latham, *The Politics of Railroad Coordination 1933–1936* (Harvard University Press, 1959), 26–33. Eastman sets forth the reform position in a January 31, 1933, letter to Senator Hastings, introduced into the record at a later congressional hearing by Lowenthal. Railroad Reorganization: Hearings Before the United States House Committee on the Judiciary, Special Subcommittee on Bankruptcy and Reorganization, Seventy-Eighth Congress, 1st sess., 144.

103. "Would Press Mergers," *The New York Times*, September 18, 1932.

104. Lowenthal, *The Investor Pays*, 156.

105. Lowenthal, *The Investor Pays*, 256.

106. Lowenthal, *The Investor Pays*, 260.

107. Lowenthal, *The Investor Pays*, 169–10.

108. Lowenthal, *The Investor Pays*, 268.

109. Robert T. Swaine, "A Decade of Railroad Reorganization Under Section 77 of the Federal Bankruptcy Act," *Harvard Law Review* 56, no. 7 (1943): 1038; E. Merrick Dodd Jr., "Reorganization Through Bankruptcy: A Remedy for What?" *Harvard Law Review* 48, no. 7 (May 1935): 1103–10. See also Joseph C. Simpson, "Comments on the Railroad Reorganization Provisions of the Bankruptcy Act of 1973," *The Business Lawyer* 30, no. 4 (1975): 1209–10.

110. "Bill Would Facilitate Railway Reorganizations," *Railway Age*, December 17, 1932.

111. Dearmont Folder 2934 (Cravath etc. proof of claim, dated August 29, 1933).

112. Robert T. Swaine, "Corporate Reorganization Under the Federal Bankruptcy Power," *Virginia Law Review* 19, no. 4 (1933): 327–28.

113. "Bankruptcy Bill Aids Rails' Plans," *Wall Street Journal*, March 2, 1933. See also 47 Stat. 1474 (1933).

114. Glenn, *The Law Governing Liquidation*, 598.

115. "Text of Amendment to Bankruptcy Act," *The New York Times*, March 2, 1933. The law also added a new section 74, which provided an additional composition provision for individual debtors, partnerships and decedents' estates; section 75, which applied to farmers; and sections 78 to 80, which related to distressed municipalities.

116. "New Law Eases Bankrupts' Cares," *Newsweek*, March 11, 1933.

117. A good overview of the statute as enacted in 1933 can be found in Lloyd K. Garrison, "Reorganization of Railroads Under the Bankruptcy Act," *University of Chicago Law Review* 1, no. 1 (May 1933): 71–80.

118. Ecker v. Western Pacific R. Corp., 318 U.S. 448, 468, 63 S. Ct. 692, 705, 87 L. Ed. 892 (1943).

119. Churchill Rodgers and Littleton Groom, "Reorganization of Railroad Corporations Under Section 77 of the Bankruptcy Act," *Columbia Law Review* 33, no. 4 (1933): 584.

120. For example, in Delaware, appraisal rights (or dissenters' rights) grant a stockholder the right to an appraisal by the Delaware Court of Chancery of the fair value of the stockholder's shares that are being "cashed out" in a merger. See Delaware General Corporation Law, section 262.

121. Section 77(e), 49 Stat. 911 (1935).

122. Leslie Craven and Warner Fuller, "The 1935 Amendments of the Railroad Bankruptcy Law," *Harvard Law Review* 49, no. 8 (1936): 1278.

123. Missouri Pacific Reorganization Proceedings, petition no. 1, order no. 1, petition no. 2, order no. 2, petition no. 3, and order no. 3. The original MoPac petition can be found in In re Missouri Pacific Railroad Company, case files, National Archives at Kansas City, box 1. The court's order directing the printing of the record—which resulted in the documents that I cite as "Missouri Pacific Reorganization Proceedings"—can be found in the same box.

124. Dearmont Folder 3126 (Excerpt from Minutes of Meeting of Missouri Pacific Railroad Company Held at Cleveland, Ohio, on March 31, 1933).

125. "Missouri Pacific Goes into Bankruptcy," *St. Louis Dispatch*, March 31, 1933.

126. "MOP's Future," *Time*, December 3, 1934.

127. Keith L. Bryant, Jr., "Southern Railway," in Keith L. Bryant, *Encyclopedia of American Business History and Biography: Vol. 1, Railroads in the Age of Regulation, 1900–1980* (Bruccoli Clark Layman, 1988), 411. A full list of the major section 77 cases in the 1930s can be found in Joseph C. Simpson, "Comments on the Railroad Reorganization Provisions of the Bankruptcy Act of 1973," *The Business Lawyer* 30, no. 4 (1975): 111. Among the larger railroads to quickly take advantage of the new statute were the following: as noted, the Missouri Pacific Railway Company, filed on March 31, 1933 (in St. Louis); Chicago and Eastern Illinois, April 18, 1933 (in Chicago); St. Louis & San Francisco Railway Company (the Frisco), May 16, 1933 (in St. Louis); Chicago, Rock Island and Pacific Railway Company (the Rock Island), June 7, 1933 (in Chicago); and Chicago, Indianapolis & Louisville (the Monon), December 30, 1933 (in Chicago). Two brothers held key positions in the reorganizations pending in St. Louis: Guy Thompson, trustee of MoPac, and Frank A. Thompson, counsel to the trustee in the Frisco case. These family relations would lead to Robert Young's claims that the judge and the Thompsons were somehow in cahoots.

128. Olson, *Saving Capitalism*, 100, 120–23.

129. "Business & Finance: Receiverships," *Time*, April 10, 1933. See also De Forest Billyou, "Railroad Reorganization Since Enactment of Section 77," *University of Pennsylvania Law Review* 96, no. 6 (1948): 795.

130. In re Missouri Pacific Railroad Company, case files, box 77 (Transcript of hearing, Wednesday, December 15, 1954), at 43.

131. Missouri Pacific Reorganization Proceedings, motion no. 40. See also Max Lowenthal, "The Railroad Reorganization Act," *Harvard Law Review* 47, no. 1 (1933): 28–29. Early in the case, a group of creditors asked either that the case be dismissed or that a trustee be appointed, but the court denied both motions. A transcript of the hearing on these early motions can be found in In re Missouri Pacific Railroad Company, case files, box 1 (Transcript of hearing, May 6, 1933), which reveals that the court initially had serious constitutional concerns about section 77.

132. Missouri Pacific Reorganization Proceedings, answer no. 40.

133. Missouri Pacific Reorganization Proceedings, order no. 40; In re Missouri Pacific Railroad Company, case files, box 1 (bankruptcy petition of Missouri Pacific Railroad Company, dated March 31, 1933—petitions for the other two main debtors are also in this box). See also Missouri Pacific Reorganization Proceedings, order no. 45; "Mrs. Shields Is Wed to Guy A. Thompson," *The New York Times*, October 13, 1933. Also consistent with past practices, the court appointed special masters. Missouri Pacific Reorganization Proceedings, order no. 42.

134. Missouri Pacific Reorganization Proceedings, order no. 43.

135. Missouri Pacific Reorganization Proceedings, order no. 71.
136. Investigation of Railroads, part 14, 6432. Such unequal salaries had been common in receiverships. Lowenthal, *The Investor Pays*, 127.
137. Missouri Pacific Reorganization Proceedings, order no. 416; "Baldwin Out as Trustee," *The New York Times*, December 27, 1935. Thompson's compensation went up to $30,000 thereafter. Missouri Pacific Reorganization Proceedings, order no. 71-A. See also Missouri Pacific Reorganization Proceedings, motion no. 892 (reporting on Baldwin's role with regard to the share repurchases); Dearmont Folder 3126 (extracts from board minutes).
138. William Miller Collier, *Collier on Bankruptcy*, 14th ed. (M. Bender, 1940), para. 77.07.
139. Missouri Pacific Reorganization Proceedings, petition no. 8, order no. 8. In re Missouri Pacific Railroad Company, case files, In re Missouri Pacific Railroad Company, case files, box 1 (orders dated April 27, April 14). See also Missouri Pacific Reorganization Proceedings, motion 207, order no. 10a. After he ceased serving as trustee, Baldwin was paid $53,000 per year, which might suggest that his trustee salary was in addition to his regular salary. Missouri Pacific Reorganization Proceedings, order no. 871.
140. Missouri Pacific Reorganization Proceedings, motion no. 5, order no. 5.
141. Missouri Pacific Reorganization Proceedings, petition no. 41, file no. 287, petition no. 314, master's report no. 41, motion no. 41-D, exceptions no. 41a. See also Missouri Pacific Reorganization Proceedings, motion no. 234-A- (3).
142. In re Missouri Pacific Railroad Company, case files, box 1 (MoPac Binder, vol. 1, 14). In re Missouri Pacific Railroad Company, case files, In re Missouri Pacific Railroad Company, case files, box 1 (MoPac Binder, vol. 1, 128—Mantis and Oris are each listed).
143. In re Missouri Pacific Railroad Company, case files, box 1 (MoPac Binder, vol. 1, 385).
144. In re Missouri Pacific Railroad Company, case files, box 1 (MoPac Binder, vol. 1, 346).
145. This was presumably either the heir (or a descendant) of the founder of the champagne company since the namesake had died in 1899. In re Missouri Pacific Railroad Company, case files, box 1 (MoPac Binder, vol. 1, 311).
146. In re Missouri Pacific Railroad Company, case files, box 1 (MoPac Binder, vol. 2).
147. In re Missouri Pacific Railroad Company, case files, box 1 (MoPac Binder, vol. 2, 915).
148. The bond data comes from *An Analysis of Missouri Pacific RR* by Railroad Analyses, Inc., February 10, 1934.
149. On the origins of the crisis, see Peter Conti-Brown and Sean H. Vanatta, "The Logic and Legitimacy of Bank Supervision: The Case of the Bank Holiday of 1933," *Business History Review* 95, no. 1 (2021): 102–3.
150. Dearmont Folder 3126 (extract from board minutes of March 31, 1933, meeting).
151. Floyd W. Mundy, *Earning Power of Railroads* (Oliphant & Co., 1935).
152. Martin Daunton, *The Economic Government of the World: 1933–2023* (Farr, Straus and Giroux, 2023), 50–54.
153. In re Missouri Pac. R. Co., 7 F. Supp. 1, 3 (E.D. Mo. 1934).
154. Norman v. Baltimore & Ohio Railroad Co., 294 U.S. 240, 294, 55 S. Ct. 407, 410, 79 L. Ed. 885 (1935). The court took the MoPac case while the Eighth Circuit was still considering the appeal from the district court. United States v. Bankers Trust Co, 293 U.S. 548, 55 S. Ct. 145, 79 L. Ed. 652 (1934).
155. "Justices Split on Gold Case," *Washington Post*, January 10, 1935.
156. SEC Report, part II, at 67. The Frisco receivership became the Frisco section 77 case in May 1933.
157. Investigation of Railroads, part 13; Exhibit 1755.
158. Missouri Pacific Reorganization Proceedings, petition no. 174.

159. This deposit agreement is among those discussed in Max Lowenthal, "The Stock Exchange and Protective Committee Securities," *Columbia Law Review* 33, no. 8 (1933): 1293–328. See also Lowenthal, "The Railroad Reorganization Act," 38–39, 44, 54–55.

160. Investigation of Railroads, part 14, Ex. 1745.

161. "Truman Boosts Proposed Rail Reorganization," *Washington Post*, November 11, 1937.

162. "'Old Bird' Pecks at Missouri Pacific's Operators," *Newsweek*, August 10, 1935.

163. Lowenthal, "The Case of the Missouri Pacific," 97.

164. Form D-1 (Registration Statement on File with Federal Trade Commission), Protective Committee for St. Louis, Iron Mountain and Southern Railway Company Rive and Gulf Divisions First Mortgage 4 Percent Bonds Due May 1, 1933. The Securities Division of the Federal Trade Commission enforced the provisions of the 1933 act only between May 27, 1933, and September 4, 1934.

165. Trust Indenture Act of 1939, Pub. L. No. 253; 53 Stat. 1149, codified at 15 U.S.C. sections 77aaa–77bbbb. 90 Stat. 56 (1976). See Friedman v. Chesapeake & Ohio Railway Co., 261 F. Supp. 728, 731 (S.D.N.Y. 1966), aff'd, 395 F.2d 663 (2d Cir. 1968); see also Dabney v. Alleghany Corp., 164 F. Supp. 28, 30 (S.D.N.Y. 1958). The exemption would be repealed after the 1970 Penn Central section 77 case, discussed in chapter 6.

166. Dearmont Folder 2932 (ICC brief dated February 1, 1938, at 3); Missouri Pacific Reorganization Proceedings, order nos. 394, 394-A. See also "MOP's No. 23," *Time*, August 12, 1935.

167. Missouri Pacific Reorganization Proceedings, at 12006 (ICC report), at 12275 (supplemental order), and at 12245 (supplemental report). A helpful three-page summary can be found at 12003.

168. Missouri Pacific Reorganization Proceedings, Objections to Plan No. 1523; Objections to Plan No. 1526.

169. In re Missouri Pac. R. Co., 39 F. Supp. 436, 450 (E.D. Mo. 1941).

170. Dearmont Folder 3126 (extract of board meeting minutes of November 18, 1941, authorizing executive committee to take all steps that counsel recommends to oppose the plan—includes letter from Alleghany offering to lend $25,000 to support these efforts).

171. Missouri Pacific Reorganization Proceedings, motion no. 1935. Missouri Pacific Reorganization Proceedings, order no. 1953.

172. Missouri Pacific Reorganization Proceedings, Vote on Plan No. 2038.

173. 318 U.S. 523, 63 S. Ct. 727, 87 L. Ed. 959 (1943).

174. In re Missouri Pac. R. Co., 50 F. Supp. 936 (E.D. Mo. 1943).

175. H. Craig Miner, *The Rebirth of the Missouri Pacific, 1956–1983* (Texas A&M University Press, 1983), 9–10.

176. Joseph C. Simpson, "Comments on the Railroad Reorganization Provisions of the Bankruptcy Act of 1973," *The Business Lawyer* 30, no. 4 (1975): 1216.

177. Missouri Pacific Reorganization Proceedings, motion no. 944, petition no. 958, petition no. 1122, answer no. 958. The board ultimately retained the Cleveland organization as consultants and had some success seeking reimbursement from the bankruptcy estate for these expenses. Missouri Pacific Reorganization Proceedings, order nos. 1122 and 1123.

178. Missouri Pacific Reorganization Proceedings, petition no. 474, petition no. 515, supp. order 515. See also Dearmont Folder 2923 (various letters, dated April 1936, congratulating Dearmont on his appointment).

179. "Russell L. Dearmont Is Dead; Headed MoPac Many Years," *St. Louis Globe-Democrat*, January 12, 1967, 1. Dearmont also served as chair of the board of directors of the St. Louis Federal Reserve Bank from 1946 to 1953, key years of the MoPac reorganization.

180. "'2-Year Job' Brings Missouri Lawyer Railroad Presidency," *St. Louis Globe-Democrat*, May 17, 1957.

181. In re Missouri Pacific Railroad Company, case files, box 77 (Transcript of hearing, Wednesday, December 15, 1954), at 50. The case was originally in front of District Judge Charles Breckenridge Faris. When he was appointed to the US Court of Appeals for the Eighth Circuit in 1935, the case was briefly reassigned to Judge Charles B. Davis before going to Judge George Moore, who was the primary judge on the case until its conclusion in the 1950s. See also In re Missouri Pacific Railroad Company, case files, box 77 (Transcript of hearing, Wednesday, December 17, 1954), at 429–30.

182. See Adrian H. Joline, *Method and Conduct of the Reorganization of Corporations* (Self-published, 1910), 11, where he writes: "I think that it is most improper for the receivers to have anything to do with reorganizations. They are officers of court and represent all the interests; hence they should be unbiased and impartial. In New York the Federal court has expressly disapproved of their identifying themselves with any plan. It is a good rule."

183. Wright v. Group of Institutional Invs., 163 F.2d 1022 (8th Cir. 1947). See also Missouri Pacific Reorganization Proceedings, at page 25317 (mandate of 8th Circuit).

184. Missouri Pacific Reorganization Proceedings, petition no. 2963; In re Missouri Pacific Railroad Company, case files, box 77 (petition of the Group of Institutional Investors Holding First and Refunding Mortgage 5 Percent Bonds of Missouri Pacific Railroad Company for Allowance for and Reimbursement of Expenses, dated May 17, 1956). The Institutional Investors retained Cadwalader, Wickersham & Taft, Lowenstein's old firm.

185. "I.C.C. Modifies M. P. Reorganization Plan," *Railway Age*, August 20, 1949.

186. State of Texas v. Group of Institutional Invs., 191 F.2d 265, 277 (8th Cir. 1951).

187. Chemical Bank & Trust Co. v. Group of Institutional Investors, 343 U.S. 982, 987, 72 S. Ct. 1018, 1020, 96 L. Ed. 1372 (1952) (Frankfurter, J. concurring).

188. OF 22, "Missouri Pacific Railroad Company," in box 156 of official file (letter dated June 10, 1952).

189. Frederick M. Myers, Jr., and Lucien Hilmer v. Missouri Pacific Railroad Company, 248 F.2d 177 (8th Cir. 1957). See also Missouri Pacific Reorganization Proceedings, motion no. 3297.

190. The reference here was likely to Charles D. Mahaffie, who was prominent in railroad reorganizations and up for reappointment in 1952. During the Senate hearings on his reappointment, several senators asked him about his support for the 1949 "forfeiture plan." On the other hand, Mahaffie was the namesake of the Mahaffie Act, which he supported based on his own frustrations with section 77. Hearings Before the Committee on Interstate and Foreign Commerce, United States Senate, Eighty-second Congress, Second Session, on the Nomination of Charles D. Mahaffie, of the District of Columbia, to be an Interstate Commerce Commissioner for the Term Expiring December 31, 1958, Reappointment.

191. Missouri Pacific Reorganization Proceedings, file nos. 1904, 2154.

192. The estate had nearly $100 million in cash by 1953, about equal to the amount of the still-outstanding bonds, although there were decades of missed coupons and unpaid preferred dividends to deal with as well. Hearing Before the Committee on Interstate & Foreign Commerce, United States Senate, Eighty-third Congress, First Session, on S. 978, U.S. Senate, March 23, 1953 (see Dearmont's testimony in particular).

193. Missouri Pacific Reorganization Proceedings, petition no. 6935; Missouri Pacific Reorganization Proceedings, motion no. 4562; Missouri Pacific Reorganization Proceedings, motion no. 4335; Missouri Pacific Reorganization Proceedings, motion no. 3278;

Missouri Pacific Reorganization Proceedings, motion no. 3279; Missouri Pacific Reorganization Proceedings, motion no. 3297; Missouri Pacific Reorganization Proceedings, petition no. 2538; Missouri Pacific Reorganization Proceedings, petition no. 2509; Missouri Pacific Reorganization Proceedings, motion no. 2166; Missouri Pacific Reorganization Proceedings, motion no. 2093; Dearmont Folder 2950 (Dearmont to Alsop, May 28, 1948).

194. Dearmont Folder 2953 (statements of Thompson and Dearmont).

195. Dearmont Folder 2940 (Terminal Shares settlement papers); Folder 2939 (same); Missouri Pacific Reorganization Proceedings, petition no. 2946; Missouri Pacific Reorganization Proceedings, petition no. 2928; Missouri Pacific Reorganization Proceedings, petition no. 2202; " 'Mop' Will Buy Alleghany Firm Unit Holdings," *New York Tribune*, March 15, 1940. See also Missouri Pacific Reorganization Proceedings, motion no. 2594 (settlement of litigation against Estate of O. P. Van Sweringen and others).

196. Hearing Before the Committee on Interstate & Foreign Commerce, United States Senate, Eighth Congress, First Session, on S. 249, U.S. Senate, 1947, at 579–81. See also Missouri Pacific Reorganization Proceedings, petition no. 3023.

197. Miner, *The Rebirth of the Missouri Pacific*, 10. See also Missouri Pacific Reorganization Proceedings, motion no. 3862 ("Motion of Trustee for Authority to Purchase 126 Diesel Locomotive Units for Debtor Lines"). The Southern was the first railway to make this switch, in 1953.

198. Dearmont Folder 2944; Folder 2950 (Dearmont to Alleghany, April 24, 1948); see also Missouri Pacific Reorganization Proceedings, motion no. 4615.

199. The cars were still in use in 1963, when MoPac renumbered its passenger cars—even though the ICC outlawed segregation in interstate travel in 1955. Robert J. Wayner, *Car Names, Numbers and Consists* (Wayner Publications, 1972), 178–80.

200. Miner, *The Rebirth of the Missouri Pacific*, 12; Thomas G. Paterson, *On Every Front: The Making of the Cold War* (Norton, 1979), chap. 1.

201. Ex parte Baldwin, 291 U.S. 610, 612, 54 S. Ct. 551, 552, 78 L. Ed. 1020 (1934).

202. Alleghany Corp. v. Comm'r of Internal Revenue, 28 T.C. 298, 301–2 (1957).

203. Investigation of Railroads: Role of Life Insurance Companies.

204. "Alleghany Corp. Accused of Moves to Delay Mo. Pac. Reorganization," *St. Louis Dispatch*, April 21, 1953; "Young Opposes Plan for MOP in Plea to Holders: Bays Present Program Is as Unfair as Older One Contested by Alleghany," *New York Tribune*, August 7, 1947; "Young Answers Attack on Alleghany MOP Plan: Chairman Says More Bondholders Recognize That Stedman Proposal 'Is Insupportable on Merits,'" *Wall Street Journal*, February 2, 1942.

205. Charles V. Bias, "Robert B. Young," in Keith L. Bryant, *Encyclopedia of American Business History and Biography: V. 1, Railroads in the Age of Regulation, 1900–1980* (Bruccoli Clark Layman, 1988), 495–96.

206. Harwood, *Invisible Giants*, 278–80; "Age of Innocence," *Time*, May 17, 1937; "Ball Sells Van Sweringen Properties," *Railway Age*, May 1, 1937. The sale did not go entirely smoothly and was followed by years of disputes. "Chesapeake & Ohio Control Regained by Alleghany Corp.," *Wall Street Journal*, April 22, 1942; "$8,000,000 Suits Settled out of Court," *Railway Age*, March 7, 1942; "Alleghany Stock Reverts to Ball," *The New York Times*, May 7, 1939. See also Young v. Bradley, 142 F.2d 658 (6th Cir. 1944); Robert E. Bedingfield, "Allan Kirby, Head of Alleghany, Dies," *The New York Times*, May 3, 1973; and Investigation of Railroads, vol. 1. The exhibits in the last include many relevant corporate documents regarding the various sales. The main volume includes Ball's testimony before the committee.

207. The common stock sales took place between 1948 and 1953. Shortly after the reorganization, Alleghany brought its stake back above 50 percent. Beth Kracklauer, "The Alleghany Record," *Wall Street Journal*, April 25, 1961 (advertisement, 21).

208. "Alleghany Sells Entire Holding of Bonds of Missouri Pacific," *New York Tribune*, February 3, 1948.

209. Robert R. Young, "A Strange Alliance for Monopoly, *Atlantic Monthly Magazine* (December 1946): 47.

210. "End of the Line," *Time*, February 3, 1958.

211. See, for example, the letter from the Chair of the Senate Interstate and Foreign Commerce Committee to the ICC, dated October 1951, regarding the MoPac plan. Dearmont Folder 2953. See also Miner, *The Rebirth of the Missouri Pacific*, 7.

212. April 9, 1948, chap. 180, 62 Stat. 162. It was enacted as section 20b of the Interstate Commerce Act.

213. Memorandum of Disapproval, dated August 13, 1946; Gregory L. Schneider, *Rock Island Requiem: The Collapse of a Mighty Fine Line* (University Press of Kansas, 2013), 19–20. The provision had its roots in a series of temporary Depression-era statutes, mostly appearing as chapter XV of the Bankruptcy Act, that had allowed similar reorganizations.

214. "Dream World for Busted Rail Stockholders," *Barron's National Business and Financial Weekly*, August 16, 1948.

215. De Forest Billyou, "Corporate Reorganization Under State and Federal Statutes," *University of Illinois Law Forum* 1958 (Winter 1958): 581.

216. John A. E. Pottow, "Modular Bankruptcy: Toward a Consumer Scheme of Arrangement," *Cardozo Law Review* 45, no. 3 (February 2024): 739–44; Sarah Paterson, "Debt Restructuring and Notions of Fairness," *Modern Law Review* 80, no. 4 (2017): 612. See also Alan W. Kornberg and Sarah Paterson, "Out-of-Court vs Court-Supervised Restructurings," in Rodrigo Olivares-Caminal, Randall Guynn, Alan Kornberg, Sarah Paterson, Eric McLaughlin, and Daivinder Singh, *Debt Restructuring*, 3rd ed. (Oxford, 2022), 224–47.

217. Joseph C. Simpson, "Comments on the Railroad Reorganization Provisions of the Bankruptcy Act of 1973," *The Business Lawyer* 30, no. 4 (1975): 1221–23.

218. Quoted in Simpson, "Comments on the Railroad Reorganization Provisions," 1222.

219. Schneider, *Rock Island Requiem*, 20.

220. Dearmont Folder 2958 (Resolution adopted at meeting of the Board of Directors of the Missouri Pacific Railroad Company held January 26, 1953); "MoPac Reorganization Under Mahaffie Act Sought by Directors," *Wall Street Journal*, January 27, 1953. See also Dearmont Folder 3126 (extracts of board meeting minutes, January 26, 1953).

221. Debtor's proposed plan for the reorganization of the Missouri Pacific Railroad Company under section 20b (the Mahaffie Act).

222. Dearmont Folder 2959 (Moody's Bond Survey, February 9, 1953).

223. Missouri Pacific Reorganization Proceedings, petition no. 4150. A copy of Wheeler's draft ICC application can be found in Dearmont Folder 2961, as well as a typewritten copy of the Davis petition. See also Dearmont Folder 2962. The railroad had attempted to get the statute amended so it could bypass the court, but the legislation did not pass. Hearing Before the Committee on Interstate & Foreign Commerce, United States Senate, Eighty-third Congress, First Session, on S. 978, U.S. Senate, March 23, 1953.

224. Dearmont Folder 2967 (brief in support of 20b petition). Wheeler and his son received about 15,000 MoPac common shares from Alleghany in March 1952. Dearmont Folder 2956.

225. Missouri Pacific Reorganization Proceedings, answer nos. 4150-A, 4150.

226. Missouri Pacific Reorganization Proceedings, opinion no. 4150. See also Dearmont Folder 2970 (telegrams to key parties in the case re the judge's decision, all dated May 25, 1953).

227. Dearmont Folder 2965 (transcript of hearing, April 10, 1953).

228. It appeared in the St. Louis paper on November 21, 1951.

229. In re Missouri Pacific Railroad Company, case files, box 77 (Transcript of hearing, Wednesday, December 15, 1954), at 40.

230. "Missouri-Pacific Asked to End JC," *Afro-American*, November 10, 1951; "Attacks Crowding of Negroes on Jim Crow Cars," *Atlanta Daily World*, November 4, 1951; "Beauticians Forced into Segregation," *New Journal and Guide*, September 1, 1951.

231. Dearmont Folder 2965 (expense report related to fund activities); Folder 2972 (letter dated July 2, 1953). See also Andrea Walton, "Ford's Fund for the Republic: A 1950s-Era Foundation As Educator," *American Educational History Journal* 42, no. 1 (2015): 111–26.

232. Dearmont Folder 906 (Letter dated August 9, 1954).

233. "Dearmont Speaks at Lindenwood," *St. Louis Globe-Democrat*, September 25, 1961.

234. Robert Crown Law Library, Stanford Law School, vol. IX, no. 4, at 2 ("The purpose of the petition was to bring the issue on for hearing by the Commission at as early a date as possible so that the already protracted reorganization not be further delayed").

235. Robert Crown Law Library, vol. IX, no. 5, at 1–2.

236. Robert Crown Law Library, vol. IX, no. 6, at 5.

237. Missouri Pacific Reorganization Proceedings, petition no. 3850, order nos. 3850, 3850-A.

238. Missouri Pacific Reorganization Proceedings, motion no. 4272. The section 77 trustee would later be given the responsibility of preparing a plan in the first instance. Collier, *Collier on Bankruptcy*, para. 77.13.

239. Dearmont Folder 3128 (letter dated January 11, 1954).

240. Dearmont Folder 2070 (notes of conference, January 21, 1954); Folder 2984 (notes of conference, March 9, 1954).

241. In re Missouri Pacific Railroad Company, case files, box 77 (Transcript of hearing, Wednesday, December 15, 1954), at 59–70 (testimony of Guy Thompson).

242. Dearmont Folder 3048 (letter to E. M. Black, October 17, 1955); Folder 3046 (letter to E. M. Black, December 19, 1955). Black would later launch one of the first leveraged buyouts in the United States, that of the once-mighty United Brands (or United Fruit), which sold Chiquita bananas. Matt Garcia, *Eli and the Octopus: The CEO Who Tried to Reform One of the World's Most Notorious Corporations* (Harvard University Press, 2023); Thomas P. McCann and Henry Scammell, *An American Company: The Tragedy of United Fruit* (Crown Publishers, 1976). Garcia massively overstates Black's role in the MoPac reorganization.

243. Dearmont Folder 2993 (transcript of telephone call with T. C. Davis, May 26, 1954); see also Dearmont Folder 2985 (undated memo, with a cover letter dated April 1954, stating, "It will be helpful if creditors call or wire Col. T. C. Davis and tell him they will not support his proposed 20b effort").

244. Dearmont Folder 2956 (stipulation and agreement, dated May 11, 1954); folder 2965 (further signature pages for stipulation); folder 2980 (markup of stipulation).

245. Dearmont Folder 3096 (letter from T. C. Davis to shareholders, dated February 28, 1956). Alleghany spent more than $540,000 to achieve this end, including more than $180,000 to White & Case (its New York counsel) and more than $80,000 to Holland & Hart in Colorado. Alleghany Corp. v. Comm'r, 28 T.C. 298, 301 (1957). White & Case was also paid about $70,000 from the bankruptcy estate.

246. Dearmont Folder 2986 (letter dated April 21, 1954, Hart to Dearmont. "Mr. Young has instructed me . . .").
247. "L. W. Baldwin Died on May 14," *Railway Age*, May 25, 1946. See also Missouri Pacific Reorganization Proceedings, motion no. 2967. Baldwin was receiving $60,000 per year at the time of his death. Dearmont Folder 2987 (Dearmont to Hart, undated copy).
248. Dearmont Folder 2987 (Hart to Dearmont, April 23, 1954).
249. Dearmont Folder 2990 (letter dated May 6, 1954, from Dearmont to Thompson; letter dated May 4, 1954, from Hart to Dearmont; letter dated May 3, 1954, from Hart to Dearmont). See also Dearmont Folder 2987 (copy of letter dated April 29, 1954, from Hart to Dearmont).
250. Dearmont Folder 2988 (Petition of Guy A. Thompson, Trustee, Presenting a Proposed Agreed System Plan for Debtor Companies, dated May 10, 1954).
251. Miner, *The Rebirth of the Missouri Pacific*, 13.
252. Missouri Pacific Railroad Co. Reorganization, 290 I.C.C., 477, 588 (1954).
253. See also "Missouri Pacific: The Reorganized Road Carries a Heavy Load of Debt," *Barron's*, December 24, 1956.
254. 290 I.C.C., at 625.
255. Transcripts for all three days can be found in In re Missouri Pacific Railroad Company, case files, box 77.
256. In re Missouri Pac. R. Co., 129 F. Supp. 392 (1955).
257. Missouri Pac. R. Co. 5 1/4 Secured Serial Bondholders' Comm. v. Thompson, 225 F.2d 761 (8th Cir. 1955).
258. For example, see In re Missouri Pacific Railroad Company, case files, box 90. See also Missouri Pacific Reorganization Proceedings, motion no. 4560 (Motion of Trustee with Respect to Employment of J. P. Morgan & Co. Incorporated to Assist the Interstate Commerce Commission in Processing and Counting Ballots on Plan of Reorganization Received from Creditors and Stockholders.).
259. In re Missouri Pac. R. Co., 135 F. Supp. 102, 104 (E.D. Mo. 1955), *aff'd sub nom.* Missouri Pac. R. Co. 5 1/4 Secured Serial Bondholders' Comm. v. Thompson, 229 F.2d 898 (8th Cir. 1956). See also Missouri Pacific Reorganization Proceedings, order no. 4590.
260. Missouri Pacific Reorganization Proceedings, objection no. 4590-A.
261. Missouri Pacific Reorganization Proceedings, opinion no. 4590; Dearmont Folder 3124 (memorandum of confirmation proceedings, with appearances, July 21, 1955); "U.S. Supreme Court Won't Block MP Reorganization," *Railway Age*, February 6, 1956.
262. In re Missouri Pacific Railroad Company, case files, box 77 (Proposed Designation of a Reorganization Manager, dated March 23, 1955).
263. Missouri Pacific Reorganization Proceedings, report no. 4726, at 37772–73. See also Dearmont Folders 3022, 3134, 3202 (various notes and letters from and to Billyou, some with attachments or enclosures). Minutes from one of the reorganization manger meetings can be found in Dearmont Folder 3099.
264. "Railroad Empire Rolls out of a Generation of Trusteeship," *The New York Times*, March 2, 1956; "MoPac Wins Its Freedom," *Time*, March 12, 1956. See also Missouri Pacific Reorganization Proceedings, petition no. 4715.
265. 1955 Annual Report; Missouri Pacific Reorganization Proceedings, motion no. 4702.
266. 1961 Annual Report. Black left the board after the 1962 election. "Local Business Notes," *St. Louis Dispatch*, April 11, 1962. The 1962 Annual Report shows Dearmont as a general board member (no longer chair). See also Dearmont Folder 981 (Dearmont to Neff,

August 10, 1956), which indicates some suspicions that Black was leaking MoPac information to Wall Street.

267. "Dearmont Gets Top MoPac Post," *Railway Age*, May 27, 1957; "Dearmont Heads Mop; Fight Ends," *New York Tribune*, May 17, 1957.

268. Miner, *The Rebirth of the Missouri Pacific*, 50.

269. Schneider, *Rock Island Requiem*, 212.

270. Miner, *The Rebirth of the Missouri Pacific*, 28; "MoPac Now Has 80 Percent of T. & P. Voting Stock, Plans Joint Tax Return," *Wall Street Journal*, December 12, 1958. See also Dearmont Folder 3191, containing the minutes of a board meeting on September 17, 1956: "The President then stated that he would like to recommend that $1,000,000 of the proposed purchase fund be applied to the purchase of Common Stock of The Texas and Pacific Railway Company, from time to time, in small lots so that the purchases would not effect the market prices. He pointed out that the proposed purchase of this stock would be a step toward our acquiring an 80 percent ownership in the Company which would permit us to include it in our consolidated income tax returns."

271. Levin v. Mississippi River Fuel Corp., 386 U.S. 162, 170, 87 S. Ct. 927, 932, 17 L. Ed. 2d 834 (1967).

272. The story behind the failed merger attempt is recounted in Miner, *The Rebirth of the Missouri Pacific*, 86–111.

273. "Missouri Pacific Recapitalization Is Agreed Upon," *Wall Street Journal*, October 16, 1972; "Alleghany Plans to Settle Case," *The New York Times*, October 16, 1972. See also Missouri Pacific Railroad Company Securities, 347 ICC 377 (1973). There were about 635,000 new common shares outstanding after the transaction and before the tender offer.

274. The return figure is based on the following calculation: 39,731 (total class B outstanding in 1973, which was the amount issued under the plan) times .535 (the percentage Alleghany owned) times $2,450. Even as late as 1973, there were 922 distinct class B shareholders, of which Alleghany was only one.

275. The Van Sweringens had also purchased MoPac convertible bonds and preferred shares around the same time to make up their total MoPac investment of almost $100 million. See *supra*.

276. The day after he acquired Alleghany, Young reportedly asked Thompson, "Did I get the Missouri Pacific?" Dearmont Folder 2956 (draft case history as of early 1952, at 19). Beginning in 1964, the class B shares had paid some dividends, totaling just under $2 million by the time of the settlement.

277. "Merger of 2 Railroads Is Completed by MoPac," *Wall Street Journal*, October 18, 1976; see also Missouri Pac. R. Co.-Merger-T&P and C&EI, 348 I.C.C. 414 (1976).

278. S. Pac. Transp. Co. v. I.C.C., 736 F.2d 708, 711 (D.C. Cir. 1984); "Road to Success: Missouri Pacific Is Highballing down It," *Barron's*, January 31, 1977. In 1982, the three-way Union Pacific–Missouri Pacific–Western Pacific merger was approved by the ICC. MoPac became a Union Pacific subsidiary thereafter. On January 1, 1997, Missouri Pacific actually merged with Union Pacific Railroad, with Union Pacific Railroad remaining as the surviving corporation.

279. "U.S. Approves $5.4-Billion Rail Merger," *Los Angeles Times*, July 4, 1996.

280. Joseph C. Simpson, "Comments on the Railroad Reorganization Provisions of the Bankruptcy Act of 1973," *The Business Lawyer* 30, no. 4 (1975): 1210.

281. Howard H. Lewis, *Derailed by Bankruptcy: Life After the Reading Railroad* (Indiana University Press, 2015), 22.

6. The End of an Era

1. Harvard Business School, "William T. Grant," Great American Business Leaders of the 20th Century, https://www.hbs.edu/leadership/20th-century-leaders/details?profile=william _t_grant.

2. In re Philadelphia Rapid Transit Co., 8 F. Supp. 51, 53 (E.D. Pa.), *aff'd sub nom.* Wilson v. Philadelphia Rapid Transit Co., 73 F.2d 1022 (3d Cir. 1934).

3. See generally P. *Jackson Report, Receivership and Bankruptcy Proceedings in United States Courts,* S. Doc. No. 268, 74th Cong., 2d sess., 4–6 (1936).

4. 48 Stat. 912. Garrard Glenn, *The Law Governing Liquidation* (Baker, Voorhis & Co., 1935), 569, 597.

5. See generally Joseph L. Weiner, "Corporate Reorganization: Section 77B of the Bankruptcy Act," *Columbia Law Review* 34, no. 7 (1934): 1173–97.

6. Benjamin Wham, "Chapter X of the Chandler Act: A Study in Reconciliation of Conflicting Views," *Virginia Law Review* 25, no. 4 (1939): 390.

7. Securities and Exchange Commission (SEC), *Report on the Study and Investigation of the Work, Activities, Personnel and Functions of Protective and Reorganization Committees (1937–1940),* ed. Adelaide R. Hasse (hereinafter "SEC Report").

8. SEC Report, part VIII.

9. David A. Skeel, *Debt's Dominion: A History of Bankruptcy Law in America* (Princeton University Press, 2001), 122. See also Dalia T. Mitchell, "From Vulnerable to Sophisticated: The Changing Representation of Creditors in Business Reorganizations," *New York University Journal of Law and Business* 16, no. 1 (Fall 2019): 147–52.

10. William O. Douglas, "Protective Committees in Railroad Reorganizations," *Harvard Law Review* 47, no. 4 (1934): 573.

11. Max Lowenthal, "The Railroad Reorganization Act," *Harvard Law Review* 47, no. 1 (1933): 18–58.

12. SEC Report, part I, 871.

13. SEC Report, part I, 872.

14. Revision of the Bankruptcy Act: Hearing Before the Committee on the Judiciary, House of Representatives, Seventy-fifth Congress, First Session on H.R. 6439 and H.R. 8046 (hereinafter "House Hearings"), 163.

15. Pub. L. No. 75–696, 52 Stat. 840 (1938). See also 11 U.S.C. sections 501–676 (chapter X), 701–99 (chapter XI) (repealed 1978). There was also a special chapter for real estate–related reorganizations, which I omit from this discussion. The original Chandler Bill introduced in the House in the 75th Congress was H.R. 6439. Hearings were held on the bill before the Committee on the Judiciary of the House in June 1937, and it was amended and reintroduced as H.R. 8046. John Gerdes, a professor at New York University, redrafted the reorganization provisions included in H.R. 6439, section 12, II into short sections, each dealing with a single subject, which then became chapter X. Hearings were held before a subcommittee of the Committee on the Judiciary of the Senate in November 1937 and January and February 1938.

16. House Hearings, 163. See generally John Gerdes, "Corporate Reorganizations: Changes Effected by Chapter X of the Bankruptcy Act," *Harvard Law Review* 52, no. 1 (1938): 1–39.

17. Jonathan C. Lipson, "Understanding Failure: Examiners and the Bankruptcy Reorganization of Large Public Companies," *American Bankruptcy Law Journal* 84, no. 1 (Winter 2010): 10; Vincent Carosso, "Washington and Wall Street: The New Deal and Investment Bankers, 1933–1940," *Business History Review* 44, no. 4 (Winter 1970): 438. Section

156 of chapter X required the appointment of a disinterested trustee if the debtor's liabilities were $250,000 or more.

18. Gerard McCormack, "Control and Corporate Rescue: An Anglo-American Evaluation," *International and Comparative Law Quarterly* 56, no. 3 (2007): 538–39.

19. SEC v. American Trailer Rentals Co., 379 U.S. 594, 604 (1965). See also Vern Countryman, "A History of American Bankruptcy Law," *Commercial Law Journal* 81, no. 6 (June/July 1976): 231.

20. Eugene V. Rostow and Lloyd N. Cutler, "Competing Systems of Corporate Reorganization: Chapters X and XI of the Bankruptcy Act," *Yale Law Journal* 48, no. 8 (1939), 1353.

21. The rule briefly appeared in the statute but was quickly eliminated by Congress.

22. Alfred N. Heuston, "Corporate Reorganizations Under the Chandler Act," *Columbia Law Review* 38, no. 7 (1938): 1236–38.

23. House Hearings, 39.

24. Walter Chandler, "The Revised Bankruptcy Act of 1938," *American Bar Association Journal* 24, no. 11 (1938): 883.

25. Rostow and Cutler, *Competing Systems of Corporate Reorganization*, 1334. See generally H.R. Rep. No. 1409 on H.R. 8046 (the Chandler Act), 75th Cong., 1st sess., 48 (1937), where, for example, the report assumes that the new law would put an end to the debtor-in-possession concept in large cases, something that would be true only if chapter X were the sole forum for such cases (42).

26. Richard W. Jennings, "Mr. Justice Douglas: His Influence on Corporate and Securities Regulation," *Yale Law Journal* 73, no. 6 (1964): 939–41.

27. Rostow and Cutler, "Competing Systems of Corporate Reorganization," 1337–38.

28. Jacob J. Kaplan, Daniel J. Lyne, and C. Keefe Hurley, "The Reorganization of the Waltham Watch Company: A Clinical Study," *Harvard Law Review* 64, no. 8 (1951): 1262–86. https://doi.org/10.2307/1337081.

29. "Coster's Dual Existence Unique in the Criminal History of City," *The New York Times*, December 16, 1938. See also In the Matter of McKesson & Robbins, Inc., 1940 SEC LEXIS 1528; "Drug Mystery," *Time*, December 19, 1938.

30. "McKesson Leaves the Court," *Time*, April 7, 1941.

31. Bankruptcy Reform Act of 1978: Hearings on S. 2266 and H.R. 8200 Before the Subcommittee on Improvements in Judicial Machinery of the Senate Committee on the Judiciary, 95th Cong., (1977), at 623 (hereinafter "Senate Bankruptcy Hearings").

32. "Judge Approves Substantial Part of Plan for Reorganization of Interstate Stores," *Wall Street Journal*, January 30, 1978.

33. A prior case from the early 1960s stayed in chapter XI despite the SEC's appeals all the way to the Supreme Court, only to see the company liquidate shortly after the plan was approved. Sidney Rutberg, *Ten Cents on the Dollar: The Bankruptcy Game* (Simon and Schuster, 1973), 132–33.

34. Peter Scott and James T. Walker, "'The Only Way Is Up': Overoptimism and the Demise of the American Five-and-Dime Store, 1914-1941," *Business History Review* 91, no. 1 (2017): 100. See also "The W. T. Grant Story–It Rose from Failure," *Women's Wear Daily*, October 3, 1975.

35. Alison Isenberg, *Downtown America: A History of the Place and the People Who Made It* (University of Chicago Press, 2004), 83–100.

36. In re W. T. Grant, case files, National Archives at Kansas City, box 1 (Deposition of Robert H. Anderson, May 18, 1976, at 38).

37. In re W. T. Grant, case files, box 1 (Deposition of Robert H. Anderson, May 18, 1976, at 22–23).

38. "4 Chains List 112 Cities Where Segregation Ends," *Women's Wear Daily*, October 19, 1960.

39. "W. T. Grant Counter Policy Unchanged," *Los Angeles Sentinel*, May 5, 1960; "W. T. Grant Defends Lunch Counter Racial Bar," *The New York Times*, April 27, 1960.

40. Traci Parker, *Department Stores and the Black Freedom Movement: Workers, Consumers, and Civil Rights from the 1930s to the 1980s* (University of North Carolina Press, 2019), 165–73.

41. "Negroes Named to Board of 2 Giant Firms," *New Amsterdam News*, June 27, 1964.

42. "W. T. Grant Co. Honors Spaulding," *New Journal and Guide*, June 7, 1975; "Negroes in Business," *The New York Times*, June 26, 1964.

43. "W. T. Grant Confirms 1-Stop Unit," *Women's Wear Daily*, October 17, 1962.

44. Grants prospectus dated April 28, 1970, at 8.

45. Grants prospectus dated May 30, 1974, at 11.

46. In re W. T. Grant, case files, box 48 (Affidavit Under Local Bankruptcy Rule XI-2, at para. 13). "Investigating the Collapse of W. T. Grant," *Business Week*, July 19, 1976; "How W. T. Grant Lost $175 Million Last Year," *Business Week*, February 24, 1975. See also "Five W. T. Grant Stores Open Today," *Women's Wear Daily*, July 24, 1969.

47. "New W. T. Grant Unit to Open Monday," *Hartford Courant*, March 21, 1971.

48. "Upgrading at Grant's," *Financial World*, April 2, 1969.

49. "W. T. Grant to Ring up Best Profits Year Ever," *Barron's National Business and Financial Weekly*, February 22, 1965.

50. "Variety Adds Fresh Spice to Growth of W. T. Grant," *Barron's National Business and Financial Weekly*, April 21, 1969.

51. "Trouble at W. T. Grant's," *The New York Times*, December 15, 1974.

52. "Probe of Grants' Bears Millions Lost in Big Credit Push," *Women's Wear Daily*, February 4, 1977; "Grant Testimony Shows It Lacked Curbs on Budget, Credit and Had Internal Woes," *Wall Street Journal*, February 4, 1977. See also National Bankruptcy Archives, Biddle Law Library, University of Pennsylvania Carey Law School (interview of Harvey Miller, October 30, 2013, at 33).

53. "The Great What-Is-It," *Forbes*, January 15, 1970.

54. In re W. T. Grant, case files, box 1 (Deposition of Robert H. Anderson, May 18, 1976, at 140, 191).

55. In re W. T. Grant, case files, box 1 (Deposition of Robert H. Anderson, May 18, 1976, at 191).

56. In re W. T. Grant, case files, box 5 (Deposition of DeWitt Peterkin, Jr., August 10, 1976, at 10–11, 21–22).

57. 1973 Annual Report, 2.

58. 327 I.C.C. 475 (1966). Edward I. Altman, "Predicting Railroad Bankruptcies in America," *Bell Journal of Economics and Management Science* 4, no. 1 (1973): 184.

59. Allan H. Meltzer, *A History of the Federal Reserve*, vol. 2, book 1 (University of Chicago Press, 2009), 605–8. See also Hyman P. Minsky, *Stabilizing an Unstable Economy* (McGraw Hill, 2008), 73; Kenneth V. Handal, "The Commercial Paper Market and the Securities Acts," *University of Chicago Law Review* 39, no. 2 (Winter 1972): 376–78. The SEC entered into a settlement with Goldman Sachs in 1974 regarding its commercial paper sales after the agency argued that that Goldman had failed to conduct a reasonable investigation of Penn Central and had implicitly represented to its customers that Penn Central was creditworthy.

60. In re W. T. Grant, case files, box 11 (Memorandum of Morgan Guaranty Trust Company, dated January 9, 1976, at 5). See also Harold van B. Cleveland and Thomas F. Huertas, *Citibank, 1812–1970* (Harvard University Press, 1985), 242, 269.

61. 1973 Annual Report, 3.
62. Oral interview of Harold S. Novikoff, retired partner in the law firm of Wachtell, Lipton, Rosen & Katz, March 31, 2023.
63. Form 10-K, for year ending January 31, 1971, at 3.
64. In re W. T. Grant, case files, box 6 (Deposition of DeWitt Peterkin, Jr., September 8, 1976, at 188).
65. In re W. T. Grant, case files, box 6 (Deposition of DeWitt Peterkin, Jr., September 8, 1976, at 191–94).
66. In re W. T. Grant, case files, box 77 (minutes of committee meeting, October 17, 1975).
67. 1973 Annual Report, 26.
68. Oral interview of Richard P. Krasnow, retired partner in the law firm of Weil, Gotshal & Manges, February 24, 2023. In re W. T. Grant, case files, box 77 (minutes of committee meeting, October 17, 1975). See also "A Tardy Aid Package That Couldn't Work," *Washington Post*, May 2, 1976.
69. Oral interview of Stephen H. Case, retired partner in the law firm of Davis Polk & Wardwell, February 10, 2023. See also In re W. T. Grant, case files, box 2 (hearing transcript, May 11, 1978, at 126–32) (hereinafter "Settlement Transcript (May 11)").
70. "W. T. Grant Is Seeking $600 Million Credit from 200-Bank Group," *Wall Street Journal*, August 27, 1974. See also In re W. T. Grant, case files, box 11 (Memorandum of Morgan Guaranty Trust Company, dated January 9, 1976, at 6).
71. "Grant Signs on the Dotted Line," *Women's Wear Daily*, October 7, 1974.
72. In re W. T. Grant, case files, box 2 (Deposition of John P. Schroeder, January 17, 1978, at 15).
73. "W. T. Grant Loss Widened in Half: Payout Omitted," *Wall Street Journal*, August 28, 1974.
74. Those cards are today's Mastercard and Visa, respectively.
75. "Grant's Second Period Loss Was $3,893,253," *Women's Wear Daily*, August 28, 1974; "3 Chains up in April Despite Retail Static," *Women's Wear Daily*, May 24, 1974.
76. "Profit Drop Led to Grant Chief's Quitting," *The New York Times*, July 6, 1974.
77. "Problems Over, Grant's Chairman Tells Complaining Stockholders," *The New York Times*, May 1, 1974.
78. "Heard on the Street," *Wall Street Journal*, April 24, 1974.
79. "Grant's Tomb?" *Barron's National Business and Financial Weekly*, December 9, 1974.
80. "Fed Reaffirms Encouragement of Bank Credit for Big Firms in Liquidity Squeeze," *American Banker*, August 30, 1974. See also "A Tardy Aid Package That Couldn't Work"; "Fed Watching Some 'Vulnerable' Firms," *St. Louis Dispatch*, March 5, 1975; Congressional Record, March 14, 1975, at 6728.
81. "Banks Fear Rip in Economy If Grant's Fails," *Women's Wear Daily*, December 4, 1974.
82. In re W. T. Grant, case files, box 2 (Deposition of John P. Schroeder, January 17, 1978, at 53–57). For a good discussion of the REIT crisis of the early 1970s, see Minsky, *Stabilizing an Unstable Economy*, 68–71.
83. Davita Silfen Glasberg, *The Power of Collective Purse Strings: The Effects of Bank Hegemony on Corporations and the State* (University of California Press, 1989), 41. See also In re W. T. Grant, case files, box 2 (Deposition of John P. Schroeder, January 17, 1978, at 148–49).
84. In re W. T. Grant, case files, box 2 (Deposition of John P. Schroeder, January 17, 1978, at 47–48).
85. In re W. T. Grant, case files, box 2 (Deposition of John P. Schroeder, January 17, 1978, at 27, 32).

86. In re W. T. Grant, case files, box 11 (Memorandum of Morgan Guaranty Trust Company, dated January 9, 1976, at 7).

87. Glasberg, *The Power of Collective Purse Strings*, 35.

88. Indenture, dated January 1, 1962, 4¾ Percent Sinking Fund Debentures Due January 1987.

89. "The Federal Reserve: Doctor to Sick Companies?" *Forbes*, February 1, 1975.

90. "It's Get-Tough Time at W. T. Grant," *The Economist*, October 19, 1974.

91. Minsky, *Stabilizing an Unstable Economy*, 71.

92. Glasberg, *The Power of Collective Purse Strings*, 49–53.

93. In re W. T. Grant, case files, box 2 (Deposition of John P. Schroeder, January 17, 1978, at 143).

94. In re W. T. Grant, case files, box 1 (transcript of hearing, June 18, 1976, at 6–10).

95. Indenture, section 4.03.

96. In re W. T. Grant, case files, box 77 (minutes of committee meeting, November 12, 1975, at 5).

97. Oral interview of Harold S. Novikoff. In re W. T. Grant, case files, box 11 (Memorandum of Morgan Guaranty Trust Company, dated January 9, 1976, at 8).

98. Oral interview of Harold S. Novikoff.

99. "W. T. Grant Names Kendrick Chairman President and Chief," *The New York Times*, August 15, 1974.

100. Oral interview of Richard P. Krasnow, retired partner in the law firm of Weil, Gotshal & Manges, October 26, 2023; oral interview of Harold S. Novikoff.

101. The terms of his employment are set forth in the Proxy Statement, dated April 28, 1975. See also "Anderson Inked 5-Year Pact with Grant's for $1,250,000," *Women's Wear Daily*, May 5, 1975.

102. "Grant Picks Anderson, Sears Aide, as President and Operating Chief," *Wall Street Journal*, April 23, 1975.

103. "W. T. Grant, Facing $175-Million Loss to Close 126 Stores and Lay off 12,600," *The New York Times*, January 17, 1975.

104. "Grant Expects Loss for This Year Will Total $175 Million," *Women's Wear Daily*, January 17, 1975.

105. "How the Boom Went Bust," *Washington Post*, May 3, 1976.

106. "How W. T. Grant Lost $175 Million Last Year."

107. *The Economist*, January 25, 1975.

108. Proxy Statement, dated April 28, 1975, at 12.

109. "W. T. Grant Offers Liens on Inventory," *The New York Times*, May 24, 1975. See also Inventory Security Agreement, dated May 15, 1975, in In re W. T. Grant, case files, box 49.

110. In re W. T. Grant, case files, box 76 (hearing transcript, November 19, 1975, at 20–21). See also "Notice of Second Supplemental Indenture," *Wall Street Journal*, May 22, 1975.

111. Isadore Barmash, "Grant Will Meet Debt Obligations," *The New York Times*, May 29, 1975. See also In re W. T. Grant, case files, box 11 (Memorandum of Morgan Guaranty Trust Company, dated January 9, 1976, at 12).

112. Oral interview of Richard P. Krasnow, October 26, 2023; oral interview of Stephen H. Case.

113. In re W. T. Grant, case files, box 1 (Deposition of Robert H. Anderson, May 18, 1976, at 135).

114. In re W. T. Grant, case files, box 1 (Deposition of Robert H. Anderson, May 18, 1976, at 141, 149).

115. In re W. T. Grant, case files, box 1 (Deposition of Robert H. Anderson, May 19, 1976, at 220–1).

116. Oral interview of Stephen H. Case.

117. In re W. T. Grant, case files, box 2 (hearing transcript, May 15, 1978, at 27–35) (hereinafter "Settlement Transcript (May 15)").
118. "An Open Letter to W. T. Grant Vendors," *Women's Wear Daily*, August 13, 1975.
119. Oral interview of Stephen H. Case.
120. "W. T. Grant Co. Says Major Appliance Line Will Be Phased Out," *Wall Street Journal*, August 27, 1975.
121. In re W. T. Grant, case files, box 1 (Deposition of Robert H. Anderson, May 18, 1976, at 191).
122. The figures in this paragraph are taken from In re W. T. Grant, case files, box 11 (Memorandum of Morgan Guaranty Trust Company, dated January 9, 1976, at 9–11, 14–5).
123. In re W. T. Grant, case files, box 48 (Affidavit Under Local Bankruptcy Rule XI-2, at para. 15).
124. Form 10-K, for year ending January 31, 1971, at 7.
125. Minsky, *Stabilizing an Unstable Economy*, 15–16.
126. Gregory L. Schneider, *Rock Island Requiem: The Collapse of a Mighty Fine Line* (University Press of Kansas, 2013), 6–7, 165–66.
127. Oral interview of Stephen H. Case.
128. In re W. T. Grant, case files, box 1 (Deposition of Robert H. Anderson, May 19, 1976, at 272).
129. In re W. T. Grant, case files, box 1 (Deposition of Robert H. Anderson, May 19, 1976, at 282–85).
130. In re W. T. Grant, case files, box 2 (Deposition of Joseph Hinsey, May 23, 1977, at 12).
131. In re W. T. Grant, case files, box 1 (Deposition of Robert H. Anderson, May 19, 1976, at 274–75).
132. In re W. T. Grant, case files, box 2 (Deposition of Joseph Hinsey, May 23, 1977, at 12, 15).
133. In re W. T. Grant, case files, box 7 (Deposition of James G. Kendrick, October 19, 1976, at 768–69).
134. In re W. T. Grant, case files, box 1 (Deposition of Robert H. Anderson, May 19, 1976, at 279).
135. In re W. T. Grant, case files, box 2 (Deposition of Joseph Hinsey, May 23, 1977, at 12).
136. In re W. T. Grant, case files, box 7 (Deposition of James G. Kendrick, October 19, 1976, at 770–77); In re W. T. Grant, case files, box 2 (Deposition of Joseph Hinsey, May 23, 1977, at 17–19).
137. The petition can be found in In re W. T. Grant, case files, box 48. Wachtell's retention application states that they switched to representing the company on September 27, but the board met on September 28. In re W. T. Grant, case files, box 48 (Affidavit of Proposed Attorney, dated October 2, 1975). See also In re W. T. Grant, case files, box 1 (Deposition of Robert H. Anderson, May 19, 1976, at 280), where Anderson indicated that Wachtell became counsel on Sunday.
138. Troy A. McKenzie, "Bankruptcy and the Future of Aggregate Litigation: The Past as Prologue," *Washington University Law Review* 90, no. 3 (2013): 880–81.
139. In re W. T. Grant, case files, box 48 (exhibit A to the petition).
140. National Bankruptcy Archives (2004 interview of Leonard Rosen by Randall J. Newsome, at 28).
141. In re Arlan's Dep't Stores, Inc., 373 F. Supp. 520, 525 (S.D.N.Y. 1974). See also In re Arlan's Dep't Stores, Inc., 615 F.2d 925 (2d Cir. 1979).
142. In re W. T. Grant, case files, box 77 (minutes of committee meeting, October 30, 1975, at 9).
143. *Women's Wear Daily*, October 3, 1975.
144. Ron Chernow, *The House of Morgan* (Atlantic Monthly Press, 1990), 618.
145. "Turning the Corner," *Barron's National Business and Financial Weekly*, May 24, 1976.
146. *Wall Street Journal*, October 6, 1975.

147. In re W. T. Grant, case files, box 48 (Affidavit Under Local Bankruptcy Rule XI-2, at para. 13).
148. In re W. T. Grant, case files, box 48 (Affidavit Under Local Bankruptcy Rule XI-2, at para. 12).
149. In re W. T. Grant, case files, box 49 (Application for Order Authorizing Retention of Attorneys by Creditors' Committee, at para. 2).
150. Oral interview of Richard P. Krasnow, February 24, 2023. See also National Bankruptcy Archives (interview of Harvey Miller, October 30, 2013, at 37). Miller reports that Chase contacted the firm.
151. In re W. T. Grant, case files, box 10 (Application of Ballon, Stoll & Itzler for Allowance as Co-Counsel to Creditors' Commtttee, at 9–10).
152. Isadore Barmash, "Grant Urges First Creditors' Meeting Not to Force It to Court Trusteeship," *The New York Times*, October 16, 1975.
153. In re W. T. Grant, case files, box 77 (minutes of committee meeting, October 21, 1975).
154. Rutberg, *Ten Cents on the Dollar*, 166–67.
155. In re W. T. Grant, case files, box 11 (Memorandum of Morgan Guaranty Trust Company, dated January 9, 1976, at 21); In re W. T. Grant, case files, box 49 (Application for Order Authorizing Debtor-in-Possession to Close Additional Stores and Transfer and Consolidate Merchandise Inventories, dated December 1975, with the day left blank). The order on the foregoing, dated December 19, is in the same box.
156. "Nassi: The Liquidator and the Giants," *Women's Wear Daily*, November 13, 1975.
157. Oral interview of Richard P. Krasnow, February 24, 2023.
158. Oral interview of Richard P. Krasnow, February 24, 2023. In re W. T. Grant, case files, box 77 (minutes of committee meeting, October 23, 1975).
159. In re W. T. Grant, case files, box 48 (Order Authorizing Debtor-in-Possession to Retain Sam Nassi Company, Inc. to Supervise the Conduct of Store Liquidation Sales).
160. James F. Peltz, "Liquidators of Failed Retailers Fast Becoming a New Growth Industry," *Los Angeles Times*, December 11, 1990.
161. In re W. T. Grant, case files, box 49 (order designating official creditors' committee, dated November 19, 1975). See also In re W. T. Grant, case files, box 49 (order authorizing retention of attorneys by creditors' committee, dated November 26, 1975).
162. In re W. T. Grant, case files, box 76 (transcript of creditors' meeting). See also National Bankruptcy Archives (interview of Harvey Miller, October 30, 2013, at 41–42).
163. In re W. T. Grant, case files, box 77 (minutes of committee meeting, October 17, 1975).
164. Oral interview of Richard P. Krasnow, February 24, 2023.
165. In re W. T. Grant, case files, box 77 (minutes of committee meeting, December 2, 1975).
166. In re W. T. Grant, case files, box 77 (minutes of committee meeting, January 8, 1976).
167. In re W. T. Grant, case files, box 11 (Memorandum of Morgan Guaranty Trust Company, dated January 9, 1976, at 22).
168. In re W. T. Grant, case files, box 77 (minutes of committee meeting, December 16, 1975). The minutes vaguely report that "after lengthy discussion, with two abstentions, a majority of the Committee voted to retain the consultants on the foregoing basis."
169. Oral interview of Stephen H. Case.
170. In re W. T. Grant, case files, box 77 (minutes of committee meeting, January 20, 1976).
171. Isadore Barmash, "W. T. Grant Is Planning New Outlook for Stores," *The New York Times*, January 22, 1976.
172. In re W. T. Grant, case files, box 77 (minutes of committee meeting, February 3, 1976).
173. In re W. T. Grant, case files, box 77 (minutes of committee meeting, February 6, 1976). The plan is outlined in the minutes and in an exhibit to the minutes, which provides the basis of table 6.2.

174. Oral interview of Harold S. Novikoff.
175. In re W. T. Grant, case files, box 77 (minutes of committee meeting, February 6, 1976).
176. Oral interview of Stephen H. Case; oral interview of Richard P. Krasnow, October 26, 2023.
177. In re W. T. Grant, case files, box 77 (minutes of committee meeting, February 6, 1976, at 6).
178. In re W. T. Grant, case files, box 77 (minutes of committee meeting, February 9, 1976). The letters are appended to the minutes.
179. In re W. T. Grant, case files, box 77 (minutes of committee meeting, February 9, 1976, at 10).
180. Oral interview of Stephen H. Case. Interestingly, at the end of 1975, the committee chair, John Ingraham of Citibank, had said that "the banks were highly sensitive to the issue of the number of jobs hanging in the balance, the interest of landlords and the public interests involved," In re W. T. Grant, case files, box 77 (minutes of committee meeting, November 24, 1975, at 13–14).
181. Voting for liquidation: Continental Illinois, Chase Manhattan Bank, Manufacturers Hanover Trust Company, Bank of America, Morgan Guaranty Trust Company of New York, Genesco, Inc., and First National City Bank.
182. See also Jack Egan, "'The Risk Was Too Great,'" *Washington Post*, May 5, 1976.
183. Oral interview of Richard P. Krasnow, October 26, 2023.
184. *Women's Wear Daily*, February 11, 1976; Isadore Barmash, "Grant Adjudication as Bankrupt Urged," *The New York Times*, February 11, 1976.
185. "W. T. Grant Agrees to Liquidate," *Washington Post*, February 12, 1976.
186. "Grant's Officially Bankrupt," *Women's Wear Daily*, April 14, 1976; Isadore Barmash, "Judge Signs Order to Liquidate Grant Company Within 60 Days," *The New York Times*, February. 13, 1976.
187. Senate Bankruptcy Hearings, at 634.
188. *42nd Annual Report of the SEC*, for the year ended June 30, 1976, at 160.
189. Senate Bankruptcy Hearings, at 638.
190. "Investigating the Collapse of W. T. Grant," *Business Week*, July 19, 1976.
191. National Bankruptcy Archives (interview of Leonard Rosen, April 25, 2007, at 7).
192. Rutberg, *Ten Cents on the Dollar*, 140.
193. Martin I. Klein, "Chapter XI of the Bankruptcy Act: A Retailer's Biggest Markdown," *Commercial Law Journal* 82, no. 5 (May 1977): 160; Henry S. Blum, "The Chandler Act and the Courts," *American Bar Association Journal* 27, no. 4 (1941): 234.
194. Altman, *Predicting Railroad Bankruptcies*, 189. In the context of chapter 11, "free fall" refers to a case filed without any agreed-upon course of action with creditors, such as a restructuring support agreement (RSA). See chapter 8 of this book for more information.
195. Oral interview of Richard Levin, partner in the law firm of Jenner & Block, November 15, 2023. See also Senate Bankruptcy Hearings, at 587, where one witness (John J. Jerome, partner at Milbank, Tweed, Hadley & McCloy) stated: "There is no way in the world, in my judgment, that the SEC staff could have dealt with W. T. Grant."
196. In re W. T. Grant, case files, box 1 (minutes of committee meeting, February 19, 1976).
197. In re W. T. Grant, case files, box 1 (minutes of committee meeting, February 24, 1976). All the minutes for the meetings after the decision to liquidate can be found in In re W. T. Grant, case files, box 1.
198. "W. T. Grant's Signs Coming Down," *The New York Times*, March 13, 1976. The building, still sometimes called the "W. T. Grant Building," remains in Times Square and is now called One Astor Plaza.
199. Settlement Transcript (May 11), at 13–17.
200. In re W. T. Grant, case files, box 49 (Application of Morgan Guaranty Trust Company of New York, as Trustee Under an Indenture, for an Order Authorizing It to Resign as

Trustee and Directing the Debtor to Appoint a Successor Trustee, dated December 2, 1975); In re W. T. Grant, case files, box 46 (Agreement of Compromise and Settlement, dated as of February 24, 1978).

201. The 4 Percent Convertible Subordinated Debentures, due 1990, and the 4.75 Percent Convertible Subordinated Debentures, due 1996. See also In re W. T. Grant, case files, box 46 (Agreement of Compromise and Settlement, dated as of February 24, 1978). Morgan, Citibank, and Chase were the only banks with stakes of more than $50 million. Bank of America, Continental Illinois, and Manufacturers Hanover were all in the next tier, holding about $45 million each, with Bankers Trust and Chemical Bank holding slightly smaller stakes.

202. In re W. T. Grant, case files, box 46 (Agreement of Compromise and Settlement, dated as of February 24, 1978). See also In re W.T. Grant Company, 4 Bankr. Ct. December 597 (Bankr. S.D.N.Y. 1978).

203. 578 F.2d 1372 (2d Cir. 1978). See also In re W. T. Grant, case files, box 46 (Lubeskie to Secured Suppliers Committee, August 8, 1977).

204. In re W. T. Grant, case files, box 46 (Pardo to Galgay, July 31, 1981).

205. In re W. T. Grant, case files, box 46 (Krasnow to Galgay, July 16, 1981).

206. In re W. T. Grant, case files, box 46 (order dated November 15, 1985).

207. In re W. T. Grant, case files, box 77 (minutes of committee meeting, November 12, 1975).

208. 20 B.R. 186 (S.D.N.Y. 1982), aff'd, 699 F.2d 599 (2d Cir. 1983), cert denied, Cosoff v. Rodman, 464 U.S. 822, 104 S. Ct. 89, 78 L.Ed.2d 97 (1983). See also In re W.T. Grant Co., 6 B.R. 762 (Bankr. S.D.N.Y. 1980).

209. "More Grant Severance Pay Upheld," Women's Wear Daily, January 10, 1980. The banks appealed the issue all the way to the Supreme Court. "Grant's Creditor Loses Bid on Severance Pay," Women's Wear Daily, January 16, 1980.

210. "Target Stores Opening Houston, Omaha Units," Women's Wear Daily, November 3, 1976.

211. "New, Larger Saks Planned in Pittsburgh," Women's Wear Daily, June 21, 1976.

212. "Notice of Final Meeting of Creditors and of Filing of Trustee's Final Report and Account," The New York Times, March 1, 1993.

213. "John J. Galgay, 66; A Bankruptcy Judge in U.S. District Court," The New York Times, May 31, 1984.

214. In re W. T. Grant Co., 119 B.R. 898 (S.D.N.Y. 1990), aff'd, 935 F.2d 1277 (2d Cir. 1991). See also Settlement Transcript (May 11), at 2; In re W. T. Grant, case files, (case docket, first page); oral interview of Richard P. Krasnow, February 24, 2023.

215. "It's Expensive to Go Broke," Forbes, February 1, 1977.

216. "Morgan Guaranty Will Pay $2.8 Million to Settle Class Suit," Wall Street Journal, August 18, 1981.

217. "Settlement Proposed in Grant's Suit," Women's Wear Daily, March 5, 1981.

218. "The Price of Distress," The Economist, April 27, 1991.

219. In re W. T. Grant, case files, box 48 (certificate of indebtedness of debtor in possession).

220. Senate Bankruptcy Hearings, at 639–40.

7. The Deregulation of Corporate Bankruptcy

1. Report of the Commission on the Bankruptcy Laws of the United States, part 1, at xv–xvi.

2. David A. Skeel, Debt's Dominion: A History of Bankruptcy Law in America (Princeton University Press, 2001), 143, 176.

3. Robert J. Rosenberg, "Corporate Rehabilitation Under the Bankruptcy Act of 1973: Are Reports of the Demise of Chapter XI Greatly Exaggerated?" *North Carolina Law Review* 53 (6) (1975): 1154–55. Oral interview of Richard Levin, partner in the law firm of Jenner & Block, November 15, 2023.

4. Oral interview of Richard Levin.

5. Oral interview of Richard Levin.

6. Bankruptcy Act Revision: Hearings Before the House of Representatives, Subcommittee on Civil and Constitutional Rights of the Committee on the Judiciary on H.R.31 and H.R.32, 94th Congress (1976), at 1901–2.

7. Bruce G. Carruthers and Terence C. Halliday, *Rescuing Business: The Making of Corporate Bankruptcy Law in England and the United States* (Oxford University Press, 1998), 83–84.

8. Nancy L. Ross, "Smoothing the Road from Insolvency," *Washington Post*, August 16, 1977.

9. Report to Accompany S.2266; Senate Report No. 95–989.

10. The definition was in section 1101(3) of the Senate bill.

11. Skeel, *Debt's Dominion*, 180.

12. Oral interview of Richard Levin.

13. Oral interview of Richard Levin.

14. Senate Bankruptcy Hearings, at 898–99.

15. 11 U.S.C. section 1004(c)(2).

16. 11 U.S.C. section 321(b).

17. A recent appellate court decision ordering the appointment of an examiner suggests that, at least in some circuits, the trend has gone too far. In re FTX Trading Ltd., No. 23–2297, 2024 WL 204456 (3d Cir. January 19, 2024).

18. Jonathan C. Lipson, "'Special': Remedial Schemes in Mass Tort Bankruptcies," *Texas Law Review* 1773 101, no. 7 (2023): 1794.

19. Oral interview of Richard Levin.

20. "Carter Expected to Sign Revised Bankruptcy Bill," *Washington Post*, October 10, 1978. See also "Chief Justice Hit Ceiling, Sen. DeConcini Charges," *Washington Post*, October 7, 1978; Kenneth N. Klee, "Legislative History of the New Bankruptcy Law," *DePaul Law Review* 28, no. 4 (1979): 956–57.

21. Lawrence P. King, "Chapter 11 of the 1978 Bankruptcy Code," *American Bankruptcy Law Journal* 53, no. 2 (Spring 1979): 108.

22. Sally McDonald Henry, "Chapter 11 Zombies," *Indiana Law Review* 50, no. 2 (2017): 587–88.

23. 11 U.S.C. section 1109(a).

24. 28 U.S.C. section 586; 11 U.S.C. section 307.

25. For example, see In re Houghton Mifflin Harcourt Publ'g Co., 474 B.R. 122 (Bankr. S.D.N.Y. 2012).

26. "Going for Broke: New Bankruptcy Law Called Quicker, Faster, But It Disturbs Critics," *Wall Street Journal*, November 15, 1978.

27. 11 U.S.C. sections 1101(1); 1107; 1108.

28. 11 U.S.C. section 1104(a)(1).

29. 11 U.S.C. § 1104.

30. Douglas G. Baird, *Elements of Bankruptcy*, 7th ed. (Foundation, 2022), 229.

31. See generally Jared A. Ellias, Ehud Kamar, and Kobi Kastiel, "The Rise of Bankruptcy Directors," *Southern California Law Review* 95, no. 5 (2022). In the abstract, the authors summarize their conclusion thusly: "While these directors claim to be neutral experts

that act to maximize value for the benefit of creditors, we argue that they suffer from a structural bias because they often receive their appointment from a small community of repeat private equity sponsors and law firms."

32. Michael A. Hiltzik, "Texaco Files for Bankruptcy Relief: Seeks Legal Protection to Fend off Asset Seizure in Pennzoil Dispute," *Los Angeles Times*, April 13, 1987.

33. Stephen Labaton, "Texaco Files to End Bankruptcy," *The New York Times*, December 22, 1987.

34. Thomas J. Lueck, "Manville Submits Bankruptcy Filing to Halt Lawsuits," *The New York Times*, August 27, 1982.

35. "A Glimmer in the Asbestos Gloom," *The New York Times*, February 6, 1984.

36. "Manville Asserts U.S. Must Share Costs of Asbestos Damage Claims," *The New York Times*, August 28, 1982.

37. Tamar Lewin, "Business and the Law; Manville Case: Game Strategy," *The New York Times*, March 22, 1983.

38. Barnaby J. Feder, "Manville Outlines a Plan on Claims," *The New York Times*, January 28, 1983. "Business and the Law; Manville Case: Game Strategy."

39. Tamar Lewin, "Manville's Plaintiffs Set Back by Bankruptcy Court Ruling," *The New York Times*, August 31, 1982.

40. "Manville Outlines a Plan on Claims."

41. "Manville Ready to Emerge from Bankruptcy," *Los Angeles Times*, November 26, 1988.

42. "Manville Plan Sets Claim Guidelines," *The New York Times*, November 22, 1983.

43. Tamar Lewin, "Manville's Chapter 11 Bid Upheld," *The New York Times*, January 24, 1984.

44. In re Johns-Manville Corp., 45 B.R. 833, 835 (S.D.N.Y. 1984). See also "Leon Silverman, 93, Dies; Lawyer Led Inquiry of Labor Secretary," *The New York Times*, February 3, 2015. Jonathan Dahl, "Manville Claimants Draft Plan to Settle Asbestos Lawsuits," *Wall Street Journal*, March 15, 1985.

45. Jonathan Dahl, "Plan for Manville to Pay Claimants Stirs Controversy," *Wall Street Journal*, April 25, 1985.

46. Cynthia F. Mitchell, "Manville Plan Effectively Is Cleared by Judge," *Wall Street Journal*, December 17, 1986.

47. Richard W. Stevenson, "'Breakthrough' Plan Advances at Manville," *The New York Times*, August 2, 1985. See also Kenneth N. Gilpin and Todd S. Purdum, "New York Lawyer Aims to End Manville Fight," *The New York Times*, August 6, 1985.

48. Cynthia F. Mitchell, "Manville Concludes Plan to Settle Claims of Property Damage Linked to Asbestos," *Wall Street Journal*, August 25, 1986.

49. Cynthia F. Mitchell, "Manville, Its Bankruptcy Plan in Hand, Girds for the Long Haul to Pay Its Debts," *Wall Street Journal*, December 18, 1986.

50. "Manville Revamping Confirmed by Judge as 'Fair, Equitable,'" *Wall Street Journal*, December 19, 1986.

51. "After 6 Years, Manville Is out of Bankruptcy," *The New York Times*, November 29, 1988.

52. Stephen Labaton, "Manville Trust Fund in Trouble," *The New York Times*, February 7, 1989.

53. Stephen Labaton, "Revamping Ordered for Manville's Fund on Asbestos Claims," *The New York Times*, June 2, 1990. See also Scot J. Paltrow, "Manville Told to Boost Asbestos Trust Quickly," *Los Angeles Times*, August 7, 1990.

54. Barnaby J. Feder, "Court Frees Manville Funds," *The New York Times*, July 24, 1993.

55. Melissa B. Jacoby, "Fake and Real People in Bankruptcy," *Emory Bankruptcy Developments Journal* 39, no. 3 (2023): 504–5. See also In re A. H. Robins Co., Inc., 880 F.2d 694 (4th Cir. 1989).

56. "Continental Airlines Files for Bankruptcy," *Los Angeles Times*, September 25, 1983.
57. In re Continental Airlines Corp., 901 F.2d 1259, 1261 (5th Cir. 1990).
58. Robert E. Dallos, "Continental to File Plan to End Its Bankruptcy," *Los Angeles Times*, September 5, 1985.
59. Doug Cameron and Michael Peel, "Carriers Rely on Chapter 11," *Financial Times*, September 18, 2001.
60. Jad Mouawad, "Merger of American and US Airways Is Waved Ahead," *The New York Times*, November 27, 2013. See also Chico Harlan, "Landing a Mega-merger: The Last Days of US Airways," *Washington Post*, September 25, 2015.
61. Dominic Chopping, "Scandinavian Airline SAS Wipes out Shareholders as Part of Rescue Deal," *Financial Times*, October 3, 2023.
62. Connie Bruck, *The Predators' Ball: The Junk-Bond Raiders and the Man Who Staked Them* (Simon and Schuster, 1988), 45.
63. See chapter 2.
64. To be sure, it is not clear that the Texas and Pacific ever was "investment grade."
65. "Stars of the Junkyard: Drexel Burnham Lambert's Legacy," *The Economist*, October 21, 2010.
66. Ira M. Millstein, *The Activist Director: Lessons from the Boardroom and the Future of the Corporation* (Columbia University Press, 2017). 119.
67. William W. Bratton, "Corporate Debt Relationships: Legal Theory in a Time of Restructuring," *Duke Law Journal* 1989, no. 1 (February 1989): 152–53.
68. Jane Seaberry, "Safeway Agrees to Buyout," *Washington Post*, July 28, 1986.
69. "The Reckoning: Safeway LBO Yields Vast Profits But Exacts a Heavy Human Toll," *Wall Street Journal*, May 16, 1990. See also *Leveraged Buyouts: Case Studies of Selected Leveraged Buyouts*, GAO Report, dated September 1991.
70. Anjli Raval and Ed Hammond, "Cerberus Leads $9bn Bid to Merge Safeway and Albertsons," *Financial Times*, March 6, 2014.
71. Chris Cumming, "Cerberus in Union's Crosshairs as Firm Prepares Albertsons IPO," *Wall Street Journal*, January 31, 2020.
72. "Executive Grant of Clemency, Michael Robert Milken," https://www.justice.gov/pardon/page/file/1250056/dl.
73. Millstein, *The Activist Director*, 128.
74. Brett Duval Fromson, "The Last Days of Drexel Burnham," *Fortune*, May 21, 1990.
75. In re Drexel Burnham Lambert Group, Inc., 960 F.2d 285 (2d Cir. 1992).
76. Melissa B. Jacoby, *Unjust Debts: How Our Bankruptcy System Makes America More Unequal* (New Press, 2024), 175.
77. William J. Magnuson, *For Profit: A History of Corporations* (Basic Books, 2022), 247–48.
78. Max Frumes and Sujeet Indap, *The Caesars Palace Coup: How a Billionaire Brawl over the Famous Casino Exposed the Power and Greed of Wall Street* (Diversion Books, 2021), 19.
79. Frumes and Indap, *The Caesars Palace Coup*, 22.
80. Brendan Ballou, *Plunder: Private Equity's Plan to Pillage America* (PublicAffairs, 2023), 4–6; Jeffrey C. Hooke, *The Myth of Private Equity: An Inside Look at Wall Street's Transformative Investments* (Columbia University Press, 2021), 143–44.
81. Mark Arsenault, Liz Kowalczyk, Robert Weisman, and Adam Piore, "Inside the Rise and Fall of Steward Health Care's Ralph de la Torre," *Boston Globe*, March 29, 2024. See also Sabrina Willmer, "Cerberus Quadruples Money After Unusual Exit from Hospital Giant," *Bloomberg*, May 27, 2021.
82. Case No. 24-90213. See in particular docket no. 38 (declaration of CRO).
83. Bruck, *The Predators' Ball*, 173–78.

84. Kenneth M. Jennings, "Union-Management Tumult at Eastern Airlines: From Borman to Lorenzo," *Transportation Journal* 28, no. 4 (1989): 16.

85. Tom Stieghorst, "The Strike at Eastern Wild Week Emotions Run High as Eastern Strike Yields Triumph and Despair," *Sun Sentinel*, March 12, 1989.

86. "Eastern Airlines in Bankruptcy File," *The Times*, March 10, 1989; "Eastern Airlines' Flight Path to Bankruptcy," *The Telegraph*, March 10, 1989.

87. Caleb Solomon, "Eastern Air Seeks to Alter Revamp Plan to Compensate for Projected Cash Gap," *Wall Street Journal*, September 1, 1989.

88. Bridget O'Brian, "Eastern Air's Creditors Ask Experts to Present Options for Reorganization," *Wall Street Journal*, October 18, 1989.

89. Roger Lowenstein, "Eastern Air Business Proposal Retreats from Pledges to Pay Debts in Full, Cash," *Wall Street Journal*, January 26, 1990.

90. Bridget O'Brian, "Eastern Airlines and Unsecured Creditors Settle: Repayment Plan Is Key Step Toward the Resolution of Chapter 11 Process," *Wall Street Journal*, February 23, 1990.

91. Keith Bradsher, "Texas Air Accused on Eastern Deals: Broad Shortchanging Seen—$280 Million Will Be Paid Eastern Tie to Parent Criticized," *The New York Times*, March 2, 1990.

92. Bridget O'Brian, "Eastern's Creditors Threaten to Move for Liquidation," *Wall Street Journal*, March 30, 1990.

93. Agis Salpukas, "Eastern's Fate Clouded by Creditors' Move," *The New York Times*, April 5, 1990.

94. Wade Lambert and Bridget O'Brian, "Trustee Named to Take Helm of Eastern Air: Judge Appoints Shugrue, Wrests Control of Carrier from Texas Air, Lorenzo," *Wall Street Journal*, April 19, 1990.

95. Eric Weiner, "Lorenzo, Head of Continental Air, Quits Industry in $30 Million Deal," *The New York Times*, August 10, 1990.

96. Agis Salpukas, "Eastern Airlines Is Shutting Down and Plans to Liquidate Its Assets: Eastern Airlines Decides It Will Shut Down," *The New York Times*, January 19, 1991.

97. Peter Pae and Bridget O'Brian, "Eastern Slots, Gates Are Purchased by Two Carriers," *Wall Street Journal*, February 19, 1991.

98. "A New Ending for Chapter 11," *The Economist*, February 24, 1990.

99. Anatole Kaletsky, "The Hawk of Texas Gets His Wings Clipped," *Financial Times*, April 10, 1989.

100. Walter W. Miller, Jr., "Bankruptcy Code Cramdown Under Chapter 11: New Threat to Shareholder Interests," *Boston University Law Review* 62, no. 5 (November 1982): 1107.

101. Carruthers and Halliday, *Rescuing Business*, 266.

8. The Always Evolving Chapter 11

1. See generally Stephen J. Lubben, "Fairness and Flexibility: Understanding Corporate Bankruptcy's Arc," *University of Pennsylvania Journal of Business Law* 23, no. 1 (Fall 2020): 132–78.

2. Florida-UCLA-LoPucki Bankruptcy Research Database. Data is through the end of 2022.

3. Case No. 24–12364.

4. NJ Department of the Treasury, Division of Revenue & Enterprise Services, "Business Name Search," https://www.njportal.com/DOR/BusinessNameSearch/Search/BusinessName.

5. "Companies from Afar Tap Houston Bankruptcy Court Despite Minimal Local Ties," *Wall Street Journal*, January 16, 2025.

6. George W. Kuney, "Hijacking Chapter 11," *Emory Bankruptcy Developments Journal* 21 (2004): 26.

7. See generally Lynn M. LoPucki, *Courting Failure: How Competition for Big Cases Is Corrupting the Bankruptcy Courts* (University of Michigan Press, 2005), which details the rise of the Southern District of New York and the District of Delaware as the two leading corporate bankruptcy venues.

8. There is some similarity here to the prefiling meetings with the judge that happened in receiverships.

9. "Big Lots Approved for Last-Minute Sale of 200 to 400 Stores," *Reuters*, December 31, 2024.

10. 11 U.S.C. section 1129(a)(9).

11. Harvey R. Miller, "Chapter 11 in Transition—From Boom to Bust and into the Future," *American Bankruptcy Law Journal* 81, no. 4 (Fall 2007): 390.

12. "Circuit City to Shut Down," *The New York Times*, January 16, 2009.

13. In re Circuit City Stores, Inc., 441 B.R. 496 (Bankr. E.D. Va. 2010).

14. Disclosure Statement with Respect to Joint Plan of Liquidation of Circuit City Stores, Inc. and Its Affiliated Debtors and Debtors in Possession and Its Official Committee of Creditors Holding General Unsecured Claims, Case No. 08-35653 (KRH).

15. In re Chrysler LLC, 576 F.3d 108, 113 (2d Cir. 2009). The Second Circuit's decision was vacated on the ground that the case became moot before the Supreme Court could hear an appeal.

16. Stephanie Ben-Ishai and Stephen J. Lubben, "Involuntary Creditors and Corporate Bankruptcy," *UBC Law Review* 45, no. 2 (June 2012): 264–66; Stephanie Ben-Ishai and Stephen J. Lubben, "Sales or Plans: A Comparative Account of the 'New' Corporate Reorganization," *McGill Law Journal/Revue de Droit de McGill* 56, no. 3 (2010): 596–98.

17. "American Unveils Deal to Buy TWA," *Washington Post*, January 11, 2001.

18. In re Lehman Bros. Holding Inc., 492 B.R. 191, 196 (Bankr. S.D.N.Y. 2013), *aff'd* 526 B.R. 481 (S.D.N.Y. 2014), *aff'd* 645 F. App'x 6 (2d Cir. 2016).

19. In re General Motors Corp., 407 B.R. 463, 491–92 (Bankr. S.D.N.Y. 2009).

20. Exhibit 99.2 (Prandium, Inc. and FRI-MRD Corporation Offering Memorandum and Disclosure Statement) to Prandium, Inc. Form 8-K, dated April 1, 2002. I represented the debtor in this case.

21. "Decora Industries Inc.: Chapter 11 Bankruptcy Filed with Noteholders' Pact Set," *Wall Street Journal*, December 6, 2000.

22. "Trump Hotels & Casino Resorts Announces Banking Relationship with Morgan Stanley; Investment Bank Selected to Joint Lead Company's $500 Million Financing," Trump Entertainment Resorts press release, dated October 26, 2004. https://www.hospitalitynet.org/news/4021046.html.

23. 11 U.S.C. section 365(d)(4).

24. Mellon Bank, N.A. v. Metro Communications, Inc., 945 F2d 635, 645–46 (3d Cir. 1991).

25. Section 101(22)(A) of the Bankruptcy Code defines a qualifying "financial institution" not only to include traditional banks, trust companies, and the like, but also a customer of such a financial institution when the financial institution "is acting as agent or custodian for [the] customer . . . in connection with a securities contract."

26. In re Nine West LBO Securities Litigation, 87 F. 4th 130 (2d Cir. 2023). See also In re Boston Generating, LLC, 2024 WL 4234886 (2nd Cir. September 19, 2024); Petr v. BMO Harris Bank N.A., 95 F.4th 1090 (7th Cir. 2024).

27. "A Legal Lion Dismantles Lehman Brothers," *International Herald Tribune*, December 15, 2008. See also Stephen J. Lubben, "Lehman's Derivative Portfolio: A Chapter 11 Perspective," in Denis Faber and Niels Vermunt, *Bank Failure: Lessons from Lehman Brothers* (Oxford University Press, 2017), 59–74.

28. Pub. L. No. 103–394, 108 Stat. 4106 (1994). Pamela Foohey and Christopher K. Odinet, "Silencing Litigation Through Bankruptcy," *Virginia Law Review* 109, no. 6 (October 2023): 1266.

29. See, for example, In re Home Holdings, Inc., No. 98 CIV. 5690 (DAB), 2001 WL 262750, at *2 (S.D.N.Y., March 16, 2001), which I should note that I worked on as a junior attorney.

30. In re Purdue Pharma, L.P., 635 B.R. 26, 34 (S.D.N.Y. 2021), rev'd and remanded, 69 F.4th 45 (2d Cir. 2023), cert. granted sub nom. Harrington v. Purdue Pharma L.P., No. (23A87), 2023 WL 5116031 (U.S. August 10, 2023).

31. Melissa B. Jacoby, *Unjust Debts: How Our Bankruptcy System Makes America More Unequal* (New Press, 2024), 182–83.

32. Laura N. Coordes, "Bankruptcy Overload," *Georgia Law Review* 57 (2023): 1161–62.

33. "What the Supreme Court's Decision to Hear the Purdue Pharma Case Means," *The New York Times*, August 11, 2023.

34. Harrington v. Purdue Pharma L. P., No. 23–124, 2024 WL 3187799 (U.S. June 27, 2024).

35. "Purdue and Sackler Family Agree to $7.4bn Opioid Settlement with US States," *Financial Times*, January 23, 2025. As the Court explained, "We hold only that the bankruptcy code does not authorize a release and injunction that, as part of a plan of reorganization under Chapter 11, effectively seeks to discharge claims against a nondebtor without the consent of affected claimants."

36. Case No. 97–01842, D. Del.

37. "Levitz, Seaman to Combine Some Operations," *Los Angeles Times*, April 8, 2000; "Levitz Furniture to Close 27 Stores and Cut 1,000 Jobs," *The New York Times*, December 22, 1998.

38. Case No. 05–44481, S.D.N.Y.

39. Douglas G. Baird and Robert K. Rasmussen, "The End of Bankruptcy," *Stanford Law Review* 55, no. 3 (2002): 751–89; David A. Skeel, "Creditors' Ball: The 'New' New Corporate Governance in Chapter 11," *University of Pennsylvania Law Review* 152, no. 2 (2003): 917–51.

9. Modern Chapter 11 and the Ghosts of the Past

1. Based on my hand count of the RSAs in the 166 large (over $100 million in debt, for profit) chapter 11 cases filed by December 19, 2024.

2. "How Distressed Debt Brought a Billionaire's Satellite Empire Crashing to Earth," *Financial Times*, February 16, 2024.

3. A notable but rare recent exception is the appeals court's recent reversal of the bankruptcy court in *Serta*, which is discussed later in this chapter. In re Serta Simmons Bedding, L.L.C., No. 23–20181, 2024 WL 5250365 (5th Cir., December 31, 2024).

4. The case is Yellow Corp. 23–11069, US Bankruptcy Court District of Delaware.

5. In re Yellow Corporation, et al., Debtors., No. 23–11069 (CTG), 2024 WL 1313308, at *1 (Bankr. D. Del. March 27, 2024).

6. Yeganeh Torbati and Jeff Stein, "Trump Officials Overruled Pentagon to Approve Pandemic Loan, Emails Show," *Washington Post*, April 27, 2022.

7. Yellow, "Corporate Profile," https://investors.myyellow.com/corporate-profile (as of December 12, 2023).

8. The case against the union was Yellow Corp. et al. v. International Brotherhood of Teamsters et al., 6:23-cv-01131 (D. Kan. 2023), in the District of Kansas. The court has since dismissed the matter.

9. Jonathan Randles and Amelia Pollard, "Trucker Yellow Paid Managers Millions Just Before Bankruptcy," *Bloomberg*, September 14, 2023.

10. Ebrahim Poonawala, "Citigroup, Apollo Join Forces in $25 Billion Private Credit Push," *Bloomberg*, September 26, 2024.

11. In re Yellow Corporation, et al., Debtors., No. 23–11069 (CTG), 2024 WL 1313308, at *4 (Bankr. D. Del. March 27, 2024).

12. Yellow Corporation, Form 8-K, dated October 23, 2023.

13. The chief restructuring officer's declaration in support of the chapter 11 filing appears as docket no. 14 in the case.

14. Matt Levine, "IRL's Users Were Not IRL," *Bloomberg*, August 7, 2023.

15. Steven Church, "Bankrupt Trucker Yellow Loses Ruling over $6.5 Billion in Pension Debts," *Bloomberg*, September 17, 2024.

16. Evan Ochsner, "Yellow Bankruptcy Judge to Reconsider Pension Debt Ruling," *Bloomberg*, November 5, 2024.

17. See generally Stephen J. Lubben, "Protecting Ma and Pa: Bond Workouts and the Trust Indenture Act in the 21st Century," *Cardozo Law Review* 44, no. 1 (October 2022): 81–144.

18. Max Frumes and Sujeet Indap, *The Caesars Palace Coup: How a Billionaire Brawl over the Famous Casino Exposed the Power and Greed of Wall Street* (Diversion Books, 2021), 31, 35.

19. Frumes and Indap, *The Caesars Palace Coup*, 295.

20. In re Caesars Entertainment Operating Co., Inc., No. 15 B 1145 (Bankr. N.D. Ill.), docket no. 3401.

21. Fitch Ratings, "Liability Management Transactions as DDEs" (June 14, 2024). https://www.fitchratings.com/research/corporate-finance/terms-conditions-series-liability-management-transactions-as-ddes-14-06-2024.

22. Fitch Ratings, "Serta Ruling Will Not Slow Pace of Liability Management Transactions" (January 29, 2025). https://www.fitchratings.com/research/corporate-finance/serta-ruling-will-not-slow-pace-of-liability-management-transactions-29-01-2025.

23. Max Frumes and Kartikeya Dar, "AMC Launches LME Struck with 1L, 2L Groups—Aims to Loop in Remaining 1Ls with Fee Incentives" (July 22,2024). https://9fin.com/insights/amc-launches-lme-struck-with-1l-2l-groups-aims-fee-incentives.

24. Luca Casa, "AMC Entertainment Rallied After Settlement Deal," *Bloomberg* (July 8, 2025).

25. Fitch Ratings, "Serta Ruling Will Not Slow."

26. James Fontanella-Khan and Sujeet Indap, "Neiman Marcus: How a Creditor's Crusade Against Private Equity Power Went Wrong," *Financial Times*, October 4, 2020.

27. Layla Ilchi, "What to Know About Neiman Marcus' Bankruptcy," *Women's Wear Daily*, July 24, 2020.

28. Neiman Marcus Grp. Ltd. LLC, Bankr. S.D. Tex., No. 20–32519. The Disclosure Statement, which is the source of much of the following discussion, can be found at docket number 772. The DIP Financing motion is docket number 104, and the First Day Declaration is docket number 86.

29. Melissa B. Jacoby, "Shocking Business Bankruptcy Law," *Yale Law Journal Forum* 131 (2021–2022): 411.

30. Vincent S. J. Buccola, "Sponsor Control: A New Paradigm for Corporate Reorganization," *University of Chicago Law Review* 90, no. 1 (2023): 41–42.

31. The discussion of Peabody that follows is based on that in Stephen J. Lubben, "Holdout Panic," *American Bankruptcy Law Journal* 96, no. 1 (Winter 2022): 22–25.

32. 11 U.S.C. section 1123(a)(4), in full provides:

    (a) Notwithstanding any otherwise applicable nonbankruptcy law, a plan shall—

    (4) provide the same treatment for each claim or interest of a particular class, unless the holder of a particular claim or interest agrees to a less favorable treatment of such particular claim or interest.

33. John W. Miller and Matt Jarzemsky, "Peabody Energy Files for Chapter 11 Bankruptcy Protection," *Wall Street Journal*, April 14, 2016.

34. Two classes were eligible to buy the preferred shares: Projected recoveries under the plan were 52.4 percent on second-lien note claims and 22.1 percent on unsecured notes.

35. In re Peabody Energy Corp., 933 F.3d 918, 925 (8th Cir. 2019) ("Here, the opportunity to participate in the Private Placement was not 'treatment for' the participating creditors' claims. It was consideration for valuable new commitments made by the participating creditors."). As I suggest in the text, it is unclear that the commitment was all that valuable.

36. "The Energy Patch: Where Rights Offerings Are "Sexy" Again," *Reuters*, August 1, 2017.

37. Frumes and Indap, *The Caesars Palace Coup*, 50–51.

38. The case is In re Toys "R" Us Inc., 17–34665. The CEO First Day Declaration, cited in this discussion, is docket number 20. The CFO First Day Declaration is docket number 30.

39. CEO First Day Declaration, para. 19.

40. Amy Merrick, "How Toys 'R' Us Succumbed to Its Nasty Debt Problem," *The New Yorker*, September 21, 2017.

41. Brendan Ballou, *Plunder: Private Equity's Plan to Pillage America* (PublicAffairs, 2023), 62.

42. CEO First Day Declaration, paras. 54, 86.

43. Sujeet Indap, James Fontanella-Khan, Kara Scannell, and Joe Rennison, "Toys 'R' Us Buckles Under Private Equity Ownership," *Financial Times*, September 21, 2017.

44. Ben Unglesbee, "Inside the 20-Year Decline of Toys 'R' Us," *RetailDive*, June 26, 2018.

45. That is probably because the junior attorney who drafted the CEO's declaration lifted it from the SEC reports.

46. Bryce Covert, "The Demise of Toys 'R' Us Is a Warning," *The Atlantic*, June 13, 2018.

47. Paul Ziobro and Lillian Rizzo, "Toys 'R' Us Plans to Close Another 200 Stores; Retailer's Corporate Staff Would Also Suffer Layoffs Following a Disappointing Holiday Season," *Wall Street Journal*, February 22, 2018; "Toys 'R' Us to Shut About 180 Stores in Bid to Exit Bankruptcy," *Bloomberg*, January 24, 2018.

48. CEO First Day Declaration, para. 13.

49. CEO First Day Declaration, para. 13.

50. Third Amended Statement of Ad Hoc Group of B-4 Lenders Pursuant to Bankruptcy Rule 2019, dated June 29, 2018 (docket no. 3637).

51. In the first 2019 statement, dated October 18, 2017, Solus was listed as having $31.4 million of the DIP loan and $40.6 million of the B-4 loan, and there were additional members of the ad hoc group. Docket no. 609. Notably, Angelo, Gordon's stake shrank as the case progressed.

52. "Toys 'R' Us Is in Danger of Breaching a Covenant with Its Lenders," Canadian National Broadcasting Corp., February 22, 2018.

53. Ben Unglesbee, "Toys 'R' Us' Fatal Journey Through Chapter 11," *RetailDive*, September 18, 2018.

54. Matthew Townsend, Lauren Coleman-Lochner, and Eliza Ronalds-Hannon, "Toys 'R' Us Nearly Had a Deal to Save Itself," *Bloomberg*, June 5, 2018.

55. Suzanne Kapner and Michael Outou, "Five Investors Sealed Fate of Toys 'R' Us," *Wall Street Journal*, August 24, 2018.

56. Lillian Rizzo, "Toys 'R' Us Owners to Create Severance Fund for Former Employees," *Wall Street Journal*, September 28, 2018.

57. See generally Lynn M. LoPucki, "Chapter 11's Descent into Lawlessness," *American Bankruptcy Law Journal* 96, no. 2 (Spring 2022): 247–310.

58. In re Belk, Inc., Case No. 21–30630 (Bankr. S.D. Texas) (Houston). Docket No. 8 is the CFO Declaration, which is the source of this quote.

59. CFO Declaration, para. 15.

60. CFO Declaration, para. 36.

61. Docket no. 25.

62. 11 U.S.C. section 1126(c) provides for counting votes based on the "allowed claims of such class held by creditors."

63. Docket no. 16. In particular, see paragraph 3, which provides: "As of the Petition Date, the Debtors have limited to no cash reserves on hand and no committed debtor-in-possession financing. Additionally, the milestones under the RSA require that the Debtors obtain confirmation of the Plan by February 24, 2021. Accordingly, it is imperative that the Debtors obtain confirmation of the Plan at the first-day hearing and that Restructuring Transactions be implemented promptly thereafter."

64. In re Serta Simmons Bedding, L.L.C., 125 F.4th 555 (5th Cir. 2024).

65. Evan Clark, "The Retail Debt Cycle: When Lenders Become Owners," *Women's Wear Daily*, August 22, 2024.

10. Chapter 11 Going Forward

1. Jonathan Randles, "Invesco-Bain Debt Brawl Spills out into Open After Shock Payment," *Bloomberg*, April 18, 2024. See also In re Robertshaw US Holding Corp., 662 B.R. 146, 156 (Bankr. S.D. Tex. 2024).

2. Becky Yerak, "Top-Ranking Lenders See Diminishing Recoveries in Bankruptcy," *Wall Street Journal*, May 14, 2024.

3. In re Robertshaw US Holding Corp., Docket No. 4:24-bk-90052 (Bankr. S.D. Tex. February 15, 2024). The first-day declaration, which tells much of the story, is docket no. 19.

4. In re Serta Simmons Bedding, LLC, No. 23–90020, 2023 WL 3855820, at *13 (Bankr. S.D. Tex. June 6, 2023). See also "Big Debt Investors Dealt Blow in Mattress Maker Bankruptcy Ruling," *Financial Times*, March 28, 2023.

5. In re Serta Simmons Bedding, L.L.C., No. 23–20181, 2024 WL 5250365 (5th Cir. December 31, 2024).

6. Akiko Matsuda, "Judge Denies Invesco Bid to Retake Control of Robertshaw Restructuring," *Wall Street Journal*, June 20, 2024.

7. Akiko Matsuda, "Robertshaw Beats Appeals Court Stay by an Hour to Seal Bankruptcy Sale," *Wall Street Journal*, October 3, 2024.

8. Jonathan Randles, "Bain Director Said Debt Deal Took Invesco 'Behind the Woodshed,'" *Bloomberg*, May 23, 2024.

9. Antoine Gara and Amelia Pollard, "Private Equity Groups' Assets Struggling Under Hefty Debt Loads, Moody's Says," *Financial Times*, October 10, 2024.
10. Dalia T. Mitchell, "From Vulnerable to Sophisticated: The Changing Representation of Creditors in Business Reorganizations," *New York University Journal of Law and Business* 16, no. 1 (Fall 2019): 166.
11. Ganeshi Sitaraman, "Why Airlines Don't Fly to Your City and Other Problems Washington Caused," *Politico*, November 14, 2023.
12. Diane Lourdes Dick, "The Chapter 11 Efficiency Fallacy," *Brigham Young University Law Review* 2013, no. 4 (2013): 814.
13. Victor Brudney, "The Investment-Value Doctrine and Corporate Readjustments," *Harvard Law Review* 72, no. 4 (1959): 676.
14. Adam J. Levitin, "Bankrupt Politics and the Politics of Bankruptcy," *Cornell Law Review* 97, no. 6 (September 2012): 1405.
15. For example, see 124 Cong. Rec. 32,392 (1978).
16. Toibb v. Radloff, 501 U.S. 157, 163, 111 S. Ct. 2197, 2201, 115 L. Ed. 2d 145 (1991).
17. Melissa B. Jacoby, "Unbuilding Business Bankruptcy Law," *North Carolina Law Review* 101, no. 6 (September 2023): 1711.
18. Compare Anthony J. Casey, "Chapter 11's Renegotiation Framework and the Purpose of Corporate Bankruptcy," *Columbia Law Review* 120, no. 7 (2020): 1709–70, and Stephen J. Lubben, "Holdout Panic," *American Bankruptcy Law Journal* 96, no. 1 (Winter 2022): 1–28. See also Sarah Paterson, "Rethinking Corporate Bankruptcy Theory in the Twenty-First Century," *Oxford Journal of Legal Studies* 36, no. 4 (2016): 717–18.
19. See Max Lowenthal, *The Investor Pays* (A. A. Knopf, 1936), and chapter 5 of this book.
20. See generally Virginia Torrie, *Reinventing Bankruptcy Law: A History of the Companies' Creditors Arrangement Act* (University of Toronto Press, 2020).
21. 11 U.S.C. section 1123(a)(4).
22. See Michelle M. Harner and Jamie Marincic, "Committee Capture—An Empirical Analysis of the Role of Creditors' Committees in Business Reorganizations," *Vanderbilt Law Review* 64, no. 3 (April 2011): 789–90.
23. Max Lowenthal, "The Railroad Reorganization Act," *Harvard Law Review* 47, no. 1 (1933): 42. This is the receivership of the Milwaukee Road, which Lowenthal covered in his book *The Investor Pays*. The New York banker was Jerome J. Hanauer, of Kuhn Loeb & Co., and the attorney was Robert Swaine, of Cravath, Swaine and Moore, which was the bank's longtime counsel. They were undoubtedly at The Greenbrier, a very large hotel built by the Chesapeake & Ohio Railway, at the time (1925) owned by the Van Sweringen brothers.
24. See generally Oscar Couwenberg and Stephen J. Lubben, "Mitigating by Monitoring: Saving Corporate Restructuring from Controllers' Opportunism," *Chicago-Kent Law Review* 98, no. 2 (2023): 361–90.
25. A QIB is an institution included within one of the categories of institutional "accredited investors" as defined in SEC rule 501 of regulation D, acting on its own account or the accounts of other QIBs.
26. Sujeet Indap, "The Downfall of the Judge Who Dominated Bankruptcy in America," *Financial Times*, November 21, 2023. See also Ramon Antonio Vargas, "New Orleans Archdiocese Bankruptcy Parties Wary of Turnaround Expert After WSJ Investigation," *The Guardian*, October 6, 2024; Alexander Gladstone, Andrew Scurria, and Akiko Matsuda, "This Judge Made Houston the Top Bankruptcy Court. Then He Helped His Girlfriend Cash In," *Wall Street Journal*, June 19, 2024.

27. In re Serta Simmons Bedding, LLC, No. 23–90020, 2023 WL 3855820, at *13 (Bankr. S.D. Tex. June 6, 2023).
28. In re CB&I UK Ltd. [2024] EWHC 398 (Ch), at para. 19.
29. "Introductory Note," in Francis Lynde Stetson, James Byrne, and Paul D. Cravath, *Some Legal Phases of Corporate Financing, Reorganization and Regulation* (McMillan, 1917), viii.
30. Diane Lourdes Dick, "Alliance Politics in Corporate Debt Restructurings," *Emory Bankruptcy Developments Journal* 39, no. 2 (2023): 322.
31. Walter J. Blum, "The Law and Language of Corporate Reorganization," *University of Chicago Law Review* 17, no. 4 (1950): 584.
32. See generally Oscar Couwenberg and Stephen J. Lubben, "Good Old Chapter 11 in a Pre-insolvency World: The Growth of Global Reorganization Options," *North Carolina Journal of International Law* 46, no. 2 (2021): 353–88.

BIBLIOGRAPHY

Archival Materials

American Railway Improvement Company. Document filed with the Colorado Secretary of State's Office. Incorporation Book 4, 12. Colorado State Archives.

American Railway Improvement Company. Document filed with the Colorado Secretary of State's Office. Book 10, 444 and 594. Colorado State Archives.

American Railway Improvement Company. Document filed with the Colorado Secretary of State's Office. Book 15, 159. Colorado State Archives.

Dearmont, Russel L. Papers, 1929–1965. State Historical Society of Missouri. C2665.

Drexel, Morgan & Co. Syndicate records. ARC 105 and 107. Morgan Library and Museum, New York.

General Grenville Dodge Collection, Council Bluffs Public Library, Iowa.

In re Missouri Pacific Railroad Company, case files, National Archives at Kansas City.

    Record Group: 21

    Creator: U.S. District Court for the Eastern (St. Louis) Division of the Eastern District of Missouri.

    Series: Bankruptcy Act of 1898 Dockets, 1898 to 1978

    National Archives Identifier: 6002241. https://catalog.archives.gov/id/6002241

    Case 6935, In re Missouri Pacific Railroad Company

In re W.T. Grant, case files, National Archives at Kansas City

    Record Group: 578

    Creator: U.S. Bankruptcy Court for the New York Division of the Southern District of New York.

    Series: Bankruptcy Dockets, 1971 to 1993

    National Archives Identifier: 140093965. https://catalog.archives.gov/id/140093965

    75-B-1735, W.T. Grant Company

J. P. Morgan & Co. Syndicate records. ARC 108, 110, and 119. Morgan Library and Museum, New York.

J. S. Morgan & Co. Papers. London Metropolitan Archives.

McClung, Calvin M. Historical Collection of the Knox County Public Library, Knoxville, Tennessee.

McClung McGhee, Charles. Papers. East Tennessee History Center, Knoxville, Tennessee.

Missouri Pacific Historical Society, St. Louis. Files are named based on microfilm reels and image numbers, even though they are now in pdf form.

Missouri Pacific Railway Company v. The Texas and Pacific Railway Company. No. 11,181, case files, National Archives at Fort Worth.
Record Group: 21
Creator: U.S. Circuit Court of the New Orleans Division of the Eastern District of Louisiana.
Series: Circuit General Case Files, 1837–1911
National Archives Identifier: 251421
https://catalog.archives.gov/id/251421
Record Group: 21
Creator: U.S. Circuit Court of the New Orleans Division of the Eastern District of Louisiana.
Series: Dockets, 1837–1911
National Archives Identifier: 4597303. https://catalog.archives.gov/id/4597303

Missouri Pacific Reorganization Proceedings. Call number KF 1546.R2 M53. William A. Wise Law Library, University of Colorado Law School, Boulder.

National Bankruptcy Archives. Biddle Law Library, University of Pennsylvania Carey Law School, Philadelphia.

Pacific Railway Improvement Company. Certificate of Organization for the Pacific Railway Improvement Company in the Secretary of the State's Records, Articles of Incorporation–Joint Stock Companies, RG 006:32, v.13 (Box 5). Connecticut State Library, Hartford.

Robert Crown Law Library. Call number KF2379.M5 M57. Stanford Law School, Stanford, CA.

S. New York C. C. U.S. No.97. The Texas and Pacific Railway Company, plaintiff in error, vs. Henry S. Marlor, filed October 13, 1884.

Southern R. Co v. Carnegie Steel Co., 176 U.S. 257 (1900), case record.

Stevenson v. Texas Ry. Co., 105 U.S. 703, 26 L. Ed. 1215 (1881).

Texas & P R Co v. Gay, 167 U.S. 745 (1897), case record.

Texas & Pacific Ry. Co. v. Marlor, 123 U.S. 687 (1887), case record.

Harry S. Truman Library and Museum. OF 22, "Missouri Pacific Railroad Company" in Box 156 of Official File. Independence, Missouri.

U.S. Congress, Senate. Letter from the Secretary of the Interior, 48th Cong., 1st sess., December 20, 1883. Ex. Doc. No. 31. Materials regarding the New Orleans Pacific Railway Company.

Lionel A. Sheldon biographical material and essay, [1888], BANC MSS C-D 801; Lionel A. Sheldon to H. H. Bancroft, [1886], BANC MSS P-O 70
The Bancroft Library, University of California, Berkeley

Interviews

Stephen H. Case (retired partner in the law firm of Davis Polk & Wardwell), with author, February 10, 2023. Recorded Zoom call.

Richard P. Krasnow (retired partner in the law firm of Weil, Gotshal & Manges), with author, February 24, 2023 (part 1) and October 26, 2023 (part 2). Recorded Zoom calls.

Richard Levin (partner in the law firm of Jenner & Block), with author, upstate New York, Nov. 15, 2023. Video recording.

Max Lowenthal (former aid to Senator Truman) by Jerry N. Hess, September 20, 1967. Transcript, Harry S. Truman Library & Museum.

Harold S. Novikoff (retired partner in the law firm of Wachtell, Lipton, Rosen & Katz), with author, March 31, 2023. Recorded Zoom call.

Corporate Documents

Missouri Pacific (and affiliates)

Annual Reports, various years.

Debtor's proposed plan for the reorganization of the Missouri Pacific Railroad Company under section 20b (Mahaffie Act).

Form D-1 (Registration Statement with Federal Trade Commission), Protective Committee for St. Louis, Iron Mountain and Southern Railway Company Rive and Gulf Divisions First Mortgage 4 Percent Bonds due May 1, 1933, with ancillary documents. Reprinted in Philip M. Payne, *Plans of Corporate Reorganization* (Foundation, 1934).

Trustee Annual Reports, various years.

An Analysis of Missouri Pacific RR by Railroad Analyses, Inc., February 10, 1934.

Richmond Terminal (and affiliates)

Agreement dated June 27, 1892, by and between the undersigned holders of the Extension and General Mortgage Bonds of the East Tennessee, Virginia and Georgia Railway Company.

Annual Reports, various years, various railroads.

Deed, Richmond and Danville Railroad Company to Isaac Davenport, Jr., and George B. Roberts, dated October 5, 1874 (6 percent consolidated mortgage bonds, due 1915).

Deed, Richmond and Danville Railroad Company to Central Trust Co. of New York, dated February 1, 1882 (6 percent debenture bonds, due 1927).

East Tennessee Reorganization Mortgage, Southern Railway to Central Trust Company of New York, Trustee, October 2, 1894.

Equipment and Sinking Fund Five Percent Mortgage, Richmond and Danville Railroad Company to Central Trust Co. of New York, dated September 3, 1889 (5 percent equipment mortgage bonds, due 1909).

Form 10-K: Norfolk Southern Railway, for the year ended December 31, 1993.

Form 10-K: Norfolk Southern Railway, for the year ended December 31, 2004.

Form 10-K: Norfolk Southern Corporation, for the year ended December 31, 2010.

Lease of the East Tennessee, Virginia and Georgia Railway Company to the Richmond and Danville Railroad Company, October 17, 1888.

Letter to holders of Richmond & Danville Consolidated Mortgage Six Percent bonds, from J. P. Morgan & Co., dated December 7, 1914, with attachment.

Plan and agreement for the reorganization of Richmond and West Point Terminal Railway and Warehouse Company et al., dated May 1, 1893.

Plan and agreement for the reorganization of Richmond and West Point Terminal Railway and Warehouse Company et al., dated May 1, 1893.

Plan of reorganization, as modified, dated February 20, 1894.

Reorganization agreement of East Tennessee, Virginia and Georgia Railway Company's FIVE Per Cent, Cincinnati Extension Mortgage Gold Bonds, dated April 7, 1894.

Richmond and West Point Terminal Railway and Warehouse Company and Frederic P. Olcott, Alfred Sully and James B. Pace, preferred stock, trust agreement, dated December 6, 1886.

Richmond and Danville Railroad Company to Central Trust Co. of New York, Consolidated Mortgage, dated October 22, 1886 (5 percent consolidated mortgage bonds, due 1936), with supplemental agreement, same date.

Southern Railway Company, Plan of Organization, dated December 4, 1894, with bylaws of same date.

To the holders of securities of the Richmond and West Point Terminal Railway and Warehouse Company and of its auxiliary corporations, New York, March 1, 1892.

To the shareholders of the Richmond and West Point Terminal Railway and Warehouse Company, dated December 16, 1891.

Texas & Pacific (and affiliates)

Agreement between Collis P. Huntington and Jay Gould, November 20, 1881, and amendments.

Annual Reports, various years.

Annual Report of the California & Texas Railway Construction Co., dated June 4, 1874.

Indenture dated March 21, 1872—Southern Pacific Railroad Company to Texas Pacific Railroad Company.

Indenture dated March 30, 1872—Southern Transcontinental Railway Company to Texas Pacific Railroad Company.

Pleadings from Texas and Pacific Railway Co. v. Southern Pacific Railroad Co. of New Mexico, District Court of the Third Judicial District, Territory of New Mexico.

Report of the committee appointed to examine the physical and financial condition of the property, dated December 8, 1885 (with board resolutions dated December 16).

Report made to the president and executive board of the Texas Pacific Railroad by General G. P. Buell, chief engineer, dated New York, July 1871.

Southern Pacific Railroad Company (Texas) Annual Reports, various years.

To the bondholders of the Rio Grande Division, Texas and Pacific Railway Company, dated June 5, 1886.

Traffic agreement (and joint track contract), dated September 1, 1886.

W. T. Grant

Annual Reports, various years.

SEC Forms 10-K, registration statements, and proxy statements, various years.

Indenture, dated January 1, 1962, 4¾ percent sinking fund debentures due January 1987.

Other Companies

Pittsburgh, Fort Wayne and Chicago Railway, *Statement of the Trustees Relative to the Reorganization*. New York: Baker & Godwin, 1862.

Prandium, Inc. Form 8-K, dated April 1, 2002, with exhibits.

Yellow Corporation, Form 8-K, dated October 23, 2023.

Articles

"Affairs in New York." *The Baltimore Sun*, July 31, 1871.

"After 6 Years, Manville Is out of Bankruptcy." *The New York Times*, November 29, 1988.

"Age of Innocence." *Time*, May 17, 1937.

"AI Boom Propels a Wild-West-Era Texas Landowner to 230 Percent Stock Rally." *Bloomberg*, November 25, 2024.

"Alexander H. Stephens." *Boston Globe*, September 27, 1877. "Allan Kirby, Head of Alleghany, Dies." *The New York Times*, May 3, 1973.

"Alleghany Corp. Accused of Moves to Delay Mo. Pac. Reorganization." *St. Louis Dispatch*, April 21, 1953.

"Alleghany Plans to Settle Case." *The New York Times*, October 16, 1972.

"Alleghany Sells Entire Holding of Bonds of Missouri Pacific." *New York Tribune*, February 3, 1948.

"Alleghany Stock Reverts to Ball." *The New York Times*, May 7, 1939.

Altman, Edward I. "Predicting Railroad Bankruptcies in America." *Bell Journal of Economics and Management Science* 4, no. 1 (1973): 184–211. https://doi.org/10.2307/3003144.

"Almost a Riot at Fort Worth." *The New York Times*, April 3, 1886.

"The American Cotton Market." *The Guardian*, December 16, 1891.

"American Financial Markets." *The Guardian*, October 6, 1887.

"American Unveils Deal to Buy TWA." *Washington Post*, January 11, 2001.

"Anderson Inked 5-Year Pact with Grant's for $1,250,000." *Women's Wear Daily*, May 5, 1975.

"Answers to Inquirers." *Wall Street Journal*, July 14, 1913.

"Anthony J. Drexel Is Dead." *The New York Times*, July 1, 1893.

"Application Made for Receivership." *Detroit Free Press*, June 5, 1884.

Armstrong, A. B. "Origins of the Texas and Pacific Railway." *Southwestern Historical Quarterly* 56, no. 4 (1953): 489–97. http://www.jstor.org/stable/30240722.

Arsenault, Mark, Liz Kowalczyk, Robert Weisman, and Adam Piore. "Inside the Rise and Fall of Steward Health Care's Ralph de la Torre." *Boston Globe*, March 29, 2024.

"Assistance Asked." *Atlanta Constitution*, February 3, 1893.

"Atlanta City Council OKs Removal of Railroad Statue with Confederacy Ties." *Atlanta Constitution*, April 20, 2021.

"At Rest." *The Philadelphia Inquirer*, May 23, 1881.

"Attaching a Railroad's Property." *The New York Times*, October 15, 1884.

"Attacks Crowding of Negroes on Jim Crow Cars." *Atlanta Daily World*, November 4, 1951.

Ayer, John D. "Rethinking Absolute Priority after *Ahlers*." *Michigan Law Review* 87, no. 5 (1989): 963–1025. https://doi.org/10.2307/1289227.

"The Backbone Railroad." *The New York Times*, January 10, 1885.

"Back to Work." *Courier-Journal*, March 17, 1885.

"Bailing out the Van Sweringens." *New Republic*, April 19, 1933.

Baird, Douglas G., and Robert K. Rasmussen. "The End of Bankruptcy." *Stanford Law Review* 55, no. 3 (2002): 751–89. https://doi.org/10.2307/1229669.

"Baldwin Out as Trustee." *The New York Times*, December 27, 1935.

Balleisen, Edward J. "Vulture Capitalism in Antebellum America: The 1841 Federal Bankruptcy Act and the Exploitation of Financial Distress." *Business History Review* 70, no. 4 (1996): 473–516. https://doi.org/10.2307/3117313.

"Ball Sells Van Sweringen Properties." *Railway Age*, May 1, 1937.

"The Baltimore and Ohio." *The New York Times*, July 1, 1899.

"Bankruptcy Bill Aids Rails' Plans." *Wall Street Journal*, March 2, 1933.

"Bankrupt Trucker Yellow Loses Ruling over $6.5 Billion in Pension Debts." *Bloomberg*, September 17, 2024.

"Banks Fear Rip in Economy If Grant's Fails." *Women's Wear Daily*, December 4, 1974.

Barmash, Isadore. "Grant Adjudication as Bankrupt Urged." *The New York Times*, February 11, 1976.

Barmash, Isadore. "Grant Urges First Creditors' Meeting Not to Force It to Court Trusteeship." *The New York Times*, October 16, 1975.

Barmash, Isadore. "Grant Will Meet Debt Obligations." *The New York Times*, May 29, 1975.

Barmash, Isadore. "Judge Signs Order to Liquidate Grant Company Within 60 Days." *The New York Times*, February. 13, 1976.

Barmash, Isadore. "W. T. Grant Is Planning New Outlook for Stores." *The New York Times*, January 22, 1976.

Barreyre, Nicolas. "The Politics of Economic Crises: The Panic of 1873, the End of Reconstruction, and the Realignment of American Politics." *Journal of the Gilded Age and Progressive Era* 10, no. 4 (2011): 403–23. http://www.jstor.org/stable/23045120.

Bean, Christopher. "'A Most Singular and Interesting Attempt': The Freedmen's Bureau at Marshall, Texas." *Southwestern Historical Quarterly* 110, no. 4 (2007): 464–85. http://www.jstor.org/stable/30239530.

"Beauticians Forced into Segregation." *New Journal and Guide*, September 1, 1951.

Berk, Gerald. "Corporate Power and Its Discontents." *Buffalo Law Review* 53, no. 5 (2006): 1419–26.

Ben-Ishai, Stephanie, and Stephen J. Lubben. "Involuntary Creditors and Corporate Bankruptcy." *U.B.C. Law Review* 45, no. 2 (June 2012): 253–82.

Ben-Ishai, Stephanie, and Stephen J. Lubben. "Sales or Plans: A Comparative Account of the 'New' Corporate Reorganization." *McGill Law Journal/Revue de Droit de McGill* 56, No. 3 (2010): 591–627.

"Big Debt Investors Dealt Blow in Mattress Maker Bankruptcy Ruling." *Financial Times*, March 28, 2023.

"A Big Deficit, But Dividends All the Same." *New York Herald*, August 8, 1891.

"Big Lots Approved for Last-Minute Sale of 200 to 400 Stores." *Reuters*, December 31, 2024.

"Bill Would Facilitate Railway Reorganizations." *Railway Age*, December 17, 1932.

Billyou, De Forest. "Railroad Reorganization Since Enactment of Section 77." *University of Pennsylvania Law Review* 96, no. 6 (1948): 793–821. https://doi.org/10.2307/3309494.

Billyou, De Forest. "Railroad Reorganization Under Section 20b of the Interstate Commerce Act." *Virginia Law Review* 39, no. 4 (1953): 459–98.

Billyou, De Forest. "Corporate Reorganization Under State and Federal Statutes." *University of Illinois Law Forum* 1958, no. 4 (Winter 1958): 556–84.

Blum, Henry S. "The Chandler Act and the Courts." *American Bar Association Journal* 27, no. 4 (1941): 232–36. http://www.jstor.org/stable/25713102.

Blum, Walter J. "The Law and Language of Corporate Reorganization." *University of Chicago Law Review* 17, no. 4 (1950): 565–603. https://doi.org/10.2307/1597862.

Bratton, William W. "Corporate Debt Relationships: Legal Theory in a Time of Restructuring." *Duke Law Journal* 1989, no. 1 (February 1989): 92–172.

Bratton, William W. "The New Economic Theory of the Firm: Critical Perspectives from History." *Stanford Law Review* 41, no. 6 (1989): 1471–527. https://doi.org/10.2307/1228806.

"'Breakthrough' Plan Advances at Manville." *The New York Times*, August 2, 1985.

"Broadway Central Hotel Collapses." *The New York Times*, August 4, 1973.

Brown, C. K. "The Southern Railway Security Company: An Early Instance of the Holding Company." *North Carolina Historical Review* 6, no. 2 (1929): 158–70. http://www.jstor.org/stable/23515196.

Brudney, Victor. "The Investment-Value Doctrine and Corporate Readjustments." *Harvard Law Review* 72, no. 4 (1959): 645–94. https://doi.org/10.2307/1338297.

Buccola, Vincent S. J. "Sponsor Control: A New Paradigm for Corporate Reorganization." *University of Chicago Law Review* 90, no. 1 (2023): 1–48. https://www.jstor.org/stable /27222236.

"Builders of Georgia." *Atlanta Constitution*, November 5, 1942.

"Business: All Paths Unite!" *Time*, March 26, 1934.

"The Business Career of Charles H. Coster." *The New York Times*, March 18, 1900.

"Business & Finance: Receiverships." *Time*, April 10, 1933.

"Business and the Law; Manville Case: Game Strategy." *The New York Times*, March 22, 1983.

"By-the-Bye in Wall Street." *Wall Street Journal*, July 24, 1935.

Campbell, Randolph. "Human Property: The Negro Slave in Harrison County, 1850–1860." *Southwestern Historical Quarterly* 76, no. 4 (1973): 384–96. http://www.jstor.org/stable /30238206.

Campbell, Randolph. "Slaveholding in Harrison County, 1850–1860, A Statistical Profile." *East Texas Historical Journal* 11, no. 1 (1973): 18–27.

Carosso, Vincent. "Washington And Wall Street: The New Deal And Investment Bankers, 1933–1940." *Business History Review* 44, no. 4 (Winter, 1970): 425–45.

"Carriers Rely on Chapter 11." *Financial Times*, September 18, 2001.

"Carter Expected to Sign Revised Bankruptcy Bill." *Washington Post*, October 10, 1978.

Case, Theresa A. "Blaming Martin Irons: Leadership and Popular Protest in the 1886 Southwest Strike." *Journal of the Gilded Age and Progressive Era* 8, no. 1 (2009): 51–81. http:// www.jstor.org/stable/40542736.

Casey, Anthony J. "Chapter 11's Renegotiation Framework and The Purpose Of Corporate Bankruptcy." *Columbia Law Review* 120, no. 7 (2020): 1709–70. https://www.jstor.org/stable /26958731.

"Cerberus Leads $9bn Bid to Merge Safeway and Albertsons." *Financial Times*, March 6, 2014.

Chamberlain, D. H. "New-Fashioned Receiverships." *Harvard Law Review* 10, no. 3 (1896): 139–49. https://doi.org/10.2307/1321754.

Chandler, Walter. "The Revised Bankruptcy Act Of 1938." *American Bar Association Journal* 24, no. 11 (1938): 880–931. http://www.jstor.org/stable/25713821.

"Changes of Railroad Ownership or Control in 1907." *Railway Gazette*, January 3, 1908.

"Chapter of History: General Fremont's Southern Pacific Railroad–How a Railroad Three Miles Long Earned Half a Million." *Courier-Journal*, August 21, 1870.

"A Chapter of Wabash." *North American Review* 146, no. 375 (February 1888): 178–93. http:// www.jstor.org/stable/25101422.

"Charles E. Satterlee Dead." *The New York Times*, June 18, 1912.

"Chief Justice Hit Ceiling, Sen. DeConcini Charges." *Washington Post*, October 7, 1978.

"Chesapeake & Ohio Control Regained by Alleghany Corp." *Wall Street Journal*, April 22, 1942.

"Chinamen Tortured and Robbed." *The New York Times*, December 1, 1886.

"Chinese Labor." *Daily Picayune*, August 1, 1888.

Chopping, Dominic. "Scandinavian Airline SAS Wipes out Shareholders as Part of Rescue Deal." *Financial Times*, October 3, 2023.

Churella, Albert J. "The Pennsylvania Railroad in the Trans-Mississippi West." *Railroad History*, no. 208 (2013): 64–82. http://www.jstor.org/stable/43524688.

"Circuit City to Shut Down." *The New York Times*, January 16, 2009.

Clark, Evan. "The Retail Debt Cycle: When Lenders Become Owners." *Women's Wear Daily*, August 22, 2024.

Collins, Steven G. "Progress and Slavery on the South's Railroads." *Railroad History*, no. 181 (1999): 6–25. http://www.jstor.org/stable/43524014.

"Col. C. M. McGhee Has Passed Away." *Nashville American*, May 6, 1907.

"Colonel Scott Sails for Europe." *North American*, November 5, 1878

"Colonel T. A. Scott Resigns." *New York Tribune*, May 2, 1880.

"Colonel Thomas A. Scott's Illness." *The New York Times*, November 10, 1878.

"Colonel Tom Scott: Authoritative Contradiction of the Story of His Paralysis." *The Cincinnati Daily Enquirer*, November 14, 1878.

"Col. Scott's Reception: His Triumphal Journey to San Diego." *San Francisco Chronicle*, August 28, 1872.

"Col. Scott on the South." *Courier-Journal*, November 27, 1880.

"Col. Thomas Scott, President of the Pennsylvania Railroad, Denies the Rumor That Gen. Grant Is to Become President of the Pennsylvania Railroad, Also One That Col. Scott Intends Giving up the Texas Pacific." *Lowell Daily Citizen*, November 17, 1879.

"Col. Tom Scott: Arrival of the Great American Railway Monarch." *San Francisco Chronicle*, August 21, 1872.

"Commerce and Finance." *Galveston Daily News*, August 10, 1886.

"Commercial and Financial Notes." *The Guardian*, February 3, 1888.

"Companies from Afar Tap Houston Bankruptcy Court Despite Minimal Local Ties." *Wall Street Journal*, January 16, 2025.

"Construction Companies." *Railway Gazette*, January 6, 1882.

Conti-Brown, Peter, and Sean H. Vanatta. "The Logic and Legitimacy of Bank Supervision: The Case of the Bank Holiday of 1933." *Business History Review* 95, no. 1 (2021): 87–120. https://doi.org/10.1017/S0007680520000896.

"Continental Airlines Files for Bankruptcy." *Los Angeles Times*, September 25, 1983.

Coordes, Laura N. "Bankruptcy Overload." *Georgia Law Review* 57, no. 3 (2023): 1133–206.

"Coster's Dual Existence Unique in the Criminal History of City." *The New York Times*, December 16, 1938.

Cotterill, R. S. "Southern Railroads, 1850–1860." *Mississippi Valley Historical Review* 10, no. 4 (1924): 396–405. https://doi.org/10.2307/1892932.

Countryman, Vern. "A History of American Bankruptcy Law." *Commercial Law Journal* 81, no. 6 (June/July 1976): 226–33.

Countryman, Vern. "Scrambling to Define Bankruptcy Jurisdiction: The Chief Justice, the Judicial Conference, and the Legislative Process." *Harvard Journal on Legislation* 22, no. 1 (Winter 1985): 1–46.

Couwenberg, Oscar, and Stephen J. Lubben. "Good Old Chapter 11 in a Pre-insolvency World: The Growth of Global Reorganization Options." *North Carolina Journal of International Law* 46, no. 2 (2021): 353–88.

Couwenberg, Oscar, and Stephen J. Lubben. "Mitigating by Monitoring: Saving Corporate Restructuring from Controllers' Opportunism." *Chicago-Kent Law Review* 98, no. 2 (2023): 361–90.

"Crash Reverberations." *The Atlanta Constitution*, October 2, 1873.

Craven, Leslie, and Warner Fuller. "The 1935 Amendments of the Railroad Bankruptcy Law." *Harvard Law Review* 49, no. 8 (1936): 1254–85. https://doi.org/10.2307/1333023.

"A Crisis Approaching." *The Washington Post*, March 15, 1886.

Cumming, Chris. "Cerberus in Union's Crosshairs as Firm Prepares Albertsons IPO." *Wall Street Journal*, January 31, 2020.

Daggett, Stuart. "Recent Railroad Failures and Reorganizations." *Quarterly Journal of Economics* 32, no. 3 (1918): 446–86.

Dallos, Robert E. "Continental to File Plan to End Its Bankruptcy." *Los Angeles Times*, September 5, 1985.

"Dearmont Gets Top MoPac Post." *Railway Age*, May 27, 1957.

"Dearmont Heads Mop; Fight Ends." *New York Tribune*, May 17, 1957.

"Dearmont Speaks at Lindenwood." *St. Louis Globe-Democrat*, September 25, 1961.

"Death of a Coast Merchant Abroad." *San Francisco Chronicle*, February 19, 1898.

Debs, Eugene V. "Jay Gould." *Locomotive Fireman's Magazine* 13, no. 5 (May 1889): 390–1.

"Decora Industries Inc.: Chapter 11 Bankruptcy Filed with Noteholders' Pact Set." *Wall Street Journal*, December 6, 2000.

Dewing, Arthur S. "The Procedure of Contemporary Railroad Reorganization." *American Economic Review* 9, no. 1 (1919): 1–33. http://www.jstor.org/stable/1803592.

Dewey, John. "The Historic Background of Corporate Legal Personality." *Yale Law Journal* 35, no. 6 (April 1926): 655–73.

Dick, Diane Lourdes. "The Chapter 11 Efficiency Fallacy." *Brigham Young University Law Review* 2013, no. 4 (2013): 759–824. https://www.proquest.com/scholarly-journals/chapter-11 -efficiency-fallacy/docview/1506884643/se-2.

Dick, Diane Lourdes. "Alliance Politics in Corporate Debt Restructurings." *Emory Bankruptcy Developments Journal* 39, no. 2 (2023): 285–328.

Dodd, E. Merrick, Jr. "Reorganization Through Bankruptcy: A Remedy for What." *Harvard Law Review* 48, no. 7 (May 1935): 1100–37.

Douglas, William O. "Protective Committees in Railroad Reorganizations." *Harvard Law Review* 47, no. 4 (February 1934): 565–89.

"Dream World for Busted Rail Stockholders." *Barron's National Business and Financial Weekly*, August 16, 1948.

"Drug Mystery." *Time*, December 19, 1938.

Dumke, Glenn. "The Boom of the 1880s In Southern California." *Southern California Quarterly* 76, no. 1 (1994): 99–114. https://doi.org/10.2307/41171704.

"The East Bound Pool." *St. Louis Dispatch*, February 22, 1886.

"Eastern Airlines in Bankruptcy File." *The Times*, March 10, 1989.

"Eastern Airlines' Flight Path to Bankruptcy." *The Telegraph*, March 10, 1989.

"Eastern Airlines and Unsecured Creditors Settle: Repayment Plan Is Key Step Toward the Resolution of Chapter 11 Process." *Wall Street Journal*, February 23, 1990.

"Eastern Air's Creditors Ask Experts to Present Options for Reorganization." *Wall Street Journal*, October 18, 1989.

"Eastern Air Seeks to Alter Revamp Plan to Compensate for Projected Cash Gap." *Wall Street Journal*, September 1, 1989.

"Eastern's Creditors Threaten to Move for Liquidation." *Wall Street Journal*, March 30, 1990.

"Eastern Slots, Gates Are Purchased by Two Carriers." *Wall Street Journal*, February 19, 1991.

"$8,000,000 Suits Settled out of Court." *Railway Age*, March 7, 1942.

Ellias, Jared A., Ehud Kamar, and Kobi Kastiel. "The Rise of Bankruptcy Directors." *Southern California Law Review* 95, no. 5 (2022): 1083–136.

"El Paso to Be a Second Denver." *New York Tribune*, January 25, 1886.

"End of the Line." *Time*, February 3, 1958.

"End of Receivership." *Austin Daily Statesman*, October 16, 1888.

"The Energy Patch: Where Rights Offerings Are "Sexy" Again." *Reuters*, August 1, 2017.

"Estate of Jay Cooke & Co." *The Philadelphia Inquirer*, March 19, 1885.

"Ex-Judge Dillon, Noted Lawyer, Dies." *The New York Times*, May 6, 1914.

Farnham, Wallace D. "Grenville Dodge and the Union Pacific: A Study of Historical Legends." *Journal of American History* 51, no. 4 (1965): 632–50. https://doi.org/10.2307/1889805.

Feder, Barnaby J. "Court Frees Manville Funds." *The New York Times*, July 24, 1993.

Feder, Barnaby J. "Manville Outlines a Plan on Claims." *The New York Times*, January 28, 1983.

"The Federal Reserve: Doctor to Sick Companies?" *Forbes*, February 1, 1975.

"Fed Reaffirms Encouragement of Bank Credit for Big Firms in Liquidity Squeeze." *American Banker*, August 30, 1974.

"Fed Watching Some 'Vulnerable' Firms." *St. Louis Dispatch*, March 5, 1975.

"Fighting for a Railroad." *The New York Times*, January 11, 1886.

"Finance and Commerce." *The Washington Post*, January 28, 1880.

"Finance and Trade." *Chicago Tribune*, January 25, 1880.

"Financial." *Bradstreet's*, August 11, 1883.

"Financial." *Christian Union*, January 14, 1886.

"Financial Affairs." *The New York Times*, December 30, 1888.

"Financial Affairs." *The New York Times*, December 31, 1890.

"Financial and Commercial." *The Philadelphia Inquirer*, September 2, 1872.

"Financial and Commercial." *The Sun*, December 11, 1885.

"Financial and Commercial." *The Sun*, December 17, 1885.

"Texas and Pacific." *El Paso Times*, November 10, 1887.

"Financial and Commercial." *The Sun*, November 10, 1887.

"Financial Condition of the Texas and Pacific." *The Cincinnati Daily Enquirer*, November 24, 1879.

"Financial Review." *Banking Law Journal* 6, no. 5 (1892), 234–36.

"The Financial World." *The New York Times*, November 4, 1883.

"The Financial World." *The New York Times*, July 6, 1884.

"The Financial World." *The New York Times*, July 27, 1884.

"The Financial World." *The New York Times*, August 8, 1886.

"Financial World." *The New York Times*, July 3, 1892.

"The First Locomotive." *The Atlanta Constitution*, March 19, 1880.

Fitch Ratings, "Liability Management Transactions as DDEs" (June 14, 2024). https://www.fitchratings.com/research/corporate-finance/terms-conditions-series-liability-management-transactions-as-ddes-14-06-2024.

Fitch Ratings, "Serta Ruling Will Not Slow Pace of Liability Management Transactions" (January 29, 2025). https://www.fitchratings.com/research/corporate-finance/serta-ruling-will-not-slow-pace-of-liability-management-transactions-29-01-2025.

"Five W. T. Grant Stores Open Today." *Women's Wear Daily*, July 24, 1969.

Fontanella-Khan, James, and Sujeet Indap. "Neiman Marcus: How a Creditor's Crusade Against Private Equity Power Went Wrong." *Financial Times*, October 4, 2020.

Foohey, Pamela, and Christopher K. Odinet. "Silencing Litigation through Bankruptcy." *Virginia Law Review* 109, no. 6 (October 2023): 1261–330.

"Foreign Capital in American Railways." *Railway Age*, November 3, 1911.

"Forty-First Congress: Senate. Cables. Certification of Bank Checks. Railroad Bill. Tax Bill. Steamships. Texas Pacific Railroad Bill. House. Bridges. Minnesota State U. Department of Internal Revenue. Money Due Maine. Railroad. Correspondent of New York Post. Currency Bill. An Exciting Scene. National Junction Railroad. Miscellaneous Bills." *The Cincinnati Daily Enquirer*, June 23, 1870.

"4 Chains List 112 Cities Where Segregation Ends." *Women's Wear Daily*, October 19, 1960.

Frank, Jerome. "Some Realistic Reflections on Some Aspects of Corporate Reorganization." *Virginia Law Review* 19, no. 6 (1932–1933): 541–70.

"Frederick Lisman, Rail Bond Expert." *The New York Times*, February 15, 1940.

"Fremont's Fraud: The Memphis and El Paso Railroad–Four Millions and a Half Picked Up in Paris." *The Cincinnati Daily Enquirer*, June 3, 1870.

"From Louisville." *The Philadelphia Inquirer*, March 27, 1886.

"From Wall Street." *The Baltimore Sun*, October 13, 1883.

Fromson, Brett Duval. "The Last Days of Drexel Burnham." *Fortune*, May 21, 1990.

Gara, Antoine, and Amelia Pollard. "Private Equity Groups' Assets Struggling Under Hefty Debt Loads, Moody's Says." *Financial Times*, October 10, 2024.

Garrison, Lloyd K. "Reorganization of Railroads Under the Bankruptcy Act." *University of Chicago Law Review* 1, no. 1 (May 1933): 71–80.

"General Railroad News." *The Philadelphia Inquirer*, January 15, 1886.

"Gen. Schuyler, Veteran, Sporting and Clubman." *The New York Times*, November 30, 1906.

Gerdes, John. "Corporate Reorganizations: Changes Effected by Chapter X of the Bankruptcy Act." *Harvard Law Review* 52, no. 1 (1938): 1–39. https://doi.org/10.2307/1333622.

Gilpin, Kenneth N., and Todd S. Purdum. "New York Lawyer Aims to End Manville Fight." *The New York Times*, August 6, 1985.Glenn, Garrard. "Basis of the Federal Receivership." *Columbia Law* Review 25, no. 4 (1925): 434–46.

Gladstone, Alexander, Andrew Scurria, and Akiko Matsuda. "This Judge Made Houston the Top Bankruptcy Court. Then He Helped His Girlfriend Cash In." *Wall Street Journal*, June 19, 2024.

"A Glimmer in the Asbestos Gloom." *The New York Times*, February 6, 1984.

"Going for Broke: New Bankruptcy Law Called Quicker, Faster, but It Disturbs Critics." *Wall Street Journal*, November 15, 1978.

"The Gossip of New York." *The Washington Post*, May 2, 1886.

"Gould's Hand Exposed." *The New York Times*, July 24, 1886.

"Grant Expects Loss for This Year Will Total $175 Million." *Women's Wear Daily*, January 17, 1975.

"Grant Picks Anderson, Sears Aide, as President and Operating Chief." *Wall Street Journal*, April 23, 1975.

"Grant's Creditor Loses Bid on Severance Pay." *Women's Wear Daily*, January 16, 1980.

"Grant's Officially Bankrupt." *Women's Wear Daily*, April 14, 1976.

"Grant's Second Period Loss Was $3,893,253." *Women's Wear Daily*, August 28, 1974.

"Grant Signs on the Dotted Line." *Women's Wear Daily*, October 7, 1974.

"Grant's Tomb?" *Barron's National Business and Financial Weekly*, December 9, 1974.

"Grant Testimony Shows It Lacked Curbs on Budget, Credit and Had Internal Woes." *Wall Street Journal*, February 4, 1977.

"The Great Strike Ended." *The New York Times*, March 29, 1886.

"The Great What-Is-It." *Forbes*, January 15, 1970.

"Greek Meets Greek." *The New York Times*, August 2, 1888.

Greene, Thomas L. "Commercial Basis for Railway Receiverships." *American Law Register and Review* 42, no. 6 (1894): 417–25.

"Grenville M. Dodge." *Railway Age Gazette*, January 7, 1916.

Handal, Kenneth V. "The Commercial Paper Market and the Securities Acts." *University of Chicago Law Review* 39, no. 2 (Winter 1972): 362–402.

Hansen, Bradley. "The People's Welfare and the Origins of Corporate Reorganization: The Wabash Receivership Reconsidered." *Business History Review* 74, no. 3 (2000): 377–405. doi:10.2307/3116432.

Harlan, Chico. "Landing a Mega-merger: The Last Days of US Airways." *Washington Post*, September 25, 2015.

Harner, Michelle M., and Jamie Marincic. "Committee Capture—An Empirical Analysis of the Role of Creditors' Committees in Business Reorganizations." *Vanderbilt Law Review* 64, no. 3 (April 2011): 747–810.

"Heard on the Street." *Wall Street Journal*, April 24, 1974.

Henry, Sally McDonald. "Chapter 11 Zombies." *Indiana Law Review* 50, no. 2 (2017): 579–618.

"Here Is the Plan." *Atlanta Constitution*, May 24, 1893.

Hershkoff, Helen, and Fred Smith Jr. "Reconstructing Klein." *University of Chicago Law Review* 90, no. 8 (December 2023): 2101–72.

Heuston, Alfred N. "Corporate Reorganizations Under the Chandler Act." *Columbia Law Review* 38, no. 7 (1938): 1199–241. https://doi.org/10.2307/1116829.

Hiltzik, Michael A. "Texaco Files for Bankruptcy Relief: Seeks Legal Protection to Fend off Asset Seizure in Pennzoil Dispute." *Los Angeles Times*, April 13, 1987.

Hoffmann, Charles. "The Depression of the Nineties." *Journal of Economic History* 16, no. 2 (1956): 137–64. http://www.jstor.org/stable/2114113.

Horwitz, Morton J. "Santa Clara Revisited: The Development of Corporate Theory." *West Virginia Law Review* 88, no. 2 (Fall 1985): 173–224.

House, Albert V., Jr. "Post-Civil War Precedents for Recent Railroad Reorganization." *Mississippi Valley Historical Review* 25, no. 4 (Mar. 1939): 505–22.

"How the Boom Went Bust." *Washington Post*, May 3, 1976.

"How Distressed Debt Brought a Billionaire's Satellite Empire Crashing to Earth." *Financial Times*, February 16, 2024.

"How W. T. Grant Lost $175 Million Last Year." *Business Week*, February 24, 1975.

"A Huge Railroad Deal." *The New York Times*, October 23, 1888.

"I.C.C. Modifies M. P. Reorganization Plan." *Railway Age*, August 20, 1949.

Ilchi, Layla. "What to Know About Neiman Marcus' Bankruptcy." *Women's Wear Daily*, July 24, 2020.

"An Important Tour of Inspection." *Atlanta Constitution*, June 12, 1892.

Indap, Sujeet, James Fontanella-Khan, Kara Scannell, and Joe Rennison. "Toys 'R' Us Buckles Under Private Equity Ownership." *Financial Times*, September 21, 2017.

Indap, Sujeet. "The Downfall of the Judge Who Dominated Bankruptcy in America." *Financial Times*, November 21, 2023.

"Injunction Against a Deal." *The New York Times*, November 25, 1888.

"Investigating the Collapse of W. T. Grant." *Business Week*, July 19, 1976.

"Invesco-Bain Debt Brawl Spills out into Open After Shock Payment." *Bloomberg*, April 18, 2024.

"It Looks Like Harmony." *New York Tribune*, February 3, 1893.

"It's Expensive to Go Broke." *Forbes*, February 1, 1977.

"It's Fun to Be Fooled." *New Republic*, May 3, 1933.

"It's Get-Tough Time at W. T. Grant." *The Economist*, October 19, 1974.

Jacoby, Melissa B. "Fake and Real People in Bankruptcy." *Emory Bankruptcy Developments Journal* 39, no. 3 (2023): 497–522.

Jacoby, Melissa B. "Shocking Business Bankruptcy Law." *Yale Law Journal Forum* 131 (2021–2022): 409–27.

Jacoby, Melissa B. "Unbuilding Business Bankruptcy Law." *North Carolina Law Review* 101, no. 6 (September 2023): 1703–62.

"The Jay Gould Railroads." *Los Angeles Times*, November 9, 1882.

"Jay Gould and the Richmond Terminal." *Financial Times*, January 24, 1891.

"Jay Gould's Credit Mobilier." *The New York Times*, January 6, 1880.

Jennings, Kenneth M. "Union-Management Tumult at Eastern Airlines: From Borman to Lorenzo." *Transportation Journal* 28, no. 4 (1989): 13–27. http://www.jstor.org/stable/20713006.

Jennings, Richard W. "Mr. Justice Douglas: His Influence on Corporate and Securities Regulation." *Yale Law Journal* 73, no. 6 (1964): 920–74. https://doi.org/10.2307/794628.

"John J. Galgay, 66; A Bankruptcy Judge in U.S. District Court." *The New York Times*, May 31, 1984.

Joline, Adrian H. "Railway Reorganizations." *American Lawyer* 8, no. 11 (November 1900): 507–14

"Judge Approves Substantial Part of Plan for Reorganization of Interstate Stores." *Wall Street Journal*, January 30, 1978.

"Justices Split on Gold Case." *Washington Post*, January 10, 1935.

Kaletsky, Anatole. "The Hawk of Texas Gets His Wings Clipped." *Financial Times*, April 10, 1989.

Kaplan, Jacob J., Daniel J. Lyne, and C. Keefe Hurley. "The Reorganization of the Waltham Watch Company: A Clinical Study." *Harvard Law Review* 64, no. 8 (1951): 1262–86. https://doi.org/10.2307/1337081.

Kapner, Suzanne, and Michael Outou. "Five Investors Sealed Fate of Toys 'R' Us." *Wall Street Journal*, August 24, 2018.

"Keeping Hands Off." *Atlanta Constitution*, December 30, 1893.

King, Lawrence P. "Chapter 11 of the 1978 Bankruptcy Code." *American Bankruptcy Law Journal* 53, no. 2 (Spring 1979): 107–32.

Klee, Kenneth N. "Legislative History of the New Bankruptcy Law." *DePaul Law Review* 28, no. 4 (1979): 941–60.

Klein, Martin I. "Chapter XI of the Bankruptcy Act: A Retailer's Biggest Markdown." *Commercial Law Journal* 82, no. 5 (May 1977): 159–69.

Kornweibel, Theodore. "'Not at All Proper for Women': Black Female Railroaders." *Railroad History*, no. 201 (2009): 6–29. http://www.jstor.org/stable/43525226.

Kornweibel, Theodore. "Railroads and Slavery." *Railroad History*, no. 189 (2003): 34–59. http://www.jstor.org/stable/43504849.

Kuney, George W. "Hijacking Chapter 11." *Emory Bankruptcy Developments Journal* 21, no. 1 (2004): 19–112.

Labaton, Stephen. "Manville Trust Fund in Trouble." *The New York Times*, February 7, 1989.

Labaton, Stephen. "Revamping Ordered for Manville's Fund on Asbestos Claims." *The New York Times*, June 2, 1990.

Labaton, Stephen. "Texaco Files to End Bankruptcy." *The New York Times*, December 22, 1987.

Lamoreaux, Naomi R. "Partnerships, Corporations, and the Theory of the Firm." *American Economic Review* 88, no. 2 (1998): 66–71. http://www.jstor.org/stable/116894.

Landsberg, Melvin. "John R. Dos Passos: His Influence on the Novelist's Early Political Development." *American Quarterly* 16, no. 3 (1964): 473–85. https://doi.org/10.2307/2710937.

"The Last Two Years . . .", *North American*, November 4, 1878.

"The Late Col. R. B. Hall: Funeral Services at the Christian Church To-Day." *Courier-Journal*, June 2, 1869.

"Left for the Southwest." *The Philadelphia Inquirer*, November 21, 1885.

"A Legal Lion Dismantles Lehman Brothers." *International Herald Tribune*, December 15, 2008.

"Leon Silverman, 93, Dies; Lawyer Led Inquiry of Labor Secretary." *The New York Times*, February 3, 2015.

Levi, Edward H., and James Wm. Moore. "Bankruptcy and Reorganization: A Survey of Changes." *University of Chicago Law Review* 5, no. 1 (1937): 1–40. https://doi.org/10.2307/1596866.

Levi, Edward H., and James Wm. Moore. "Bankruptcy and Reorganization: A Survey of Changes. II." *University of Chicago Law Review* 5, no. 2 (1938): 219–59. https://doi.org/10.2307/1596975.

Levine, Matt. "IRL's Users Were Not IRL." *Bloomberg*, August 7, 2023.

Levitin, Adam J. "Bankrupt Politics and the Politics of Bankruptcy." *Cornell Law Review* 97, no. 6 (September 2012): 1399–460.

"Levitz Furniture to Close 27 Stores and Cut 1,000 Jobs." *The New York Times*, December 22, 1998.

"Levitz, Seaman to Combine Some Operations." *Los Angeles Times*, April 8, 2000.

Lewin, Tamar. "Manville's Chapter 11 Bid Upheld." *The New York Times*, January 24, 1984.

Lipson, Jonathan C. "'Special': Remedial Schemes in Mass Tort Bankruptcies." *Texas Law Review* 101, no. 7 (2023): 1773–802.

Lipson, Jonathan C. "Understanding Failure: Examiners and the Bankruptcy Reorganization of Large Public Companies." *American Bankruptcy Law Journal* 84, no. 1 (Winter, 2010): 1–77.

Lisman, F. J. "Protective Committees for Security Holders." *Harvard Business Review* XIII, no. 1 (October 1934): 19–32.

Lisman, F. J. "Railroad Bonds." *Annals of the American Academy of Political and Social Science* 88, no. 1 (1920): 57–62. https://doi.org/10.1177/000271622008800108.

"Local Miscellany: Southern Trans-Continental Railway Meeting of the Corporators." *New York Tribune*, November 1, 1870.

"Local Summary." *The Philadelphia Inquirer*, November 5, 1878."

"Look to Congress!" *The Road*, February 1, 1879.

LoPucki, Lynn M. "Chapter 11's Descent into Lawlessness." *American Bankruptcy Law Journal* 96, no. 2 (Spring 2022): 247–310.

Lowenstein, Roger. "Eastern Air Business Proposal Retreats from Pledges to Pay Debts in Full, Cash." *Wall Street Journal*, January 26, 1990.

Lowenthal, Max. "The Case of The Missouri Pacific." *Harper's Monthly Magazine* (December 1, 1934): 87–98.

Lowenthal, Max. "The Railroad Reorganization Act." *Harvard Law Review* 47, no. 1 (1933): 18–58. https://doi.org/10.2307/1332105.

Lowenthal, Max. "The Stock Exchange and Protective Committee Securities." *Columbia Law Review* 33, no. 8 (1933): 1293–328. https://doi.org/10.2307/1115561.

Lubben, Stephen J. "Fairness and Flexibility: Understanding Corporate Bankruptcy's Arc." *University of Pennsylvania Journal of Business* Law 23, no. 1 (Fall 2020): 132–78.

Lubben, Stephen J. "Holdout Panic." *American Bankruptcy Law Journal* 96, no. 1 (Winter 2022): 1–28.

Lubben, Stephen J. "A New Understanding of the Bankruptcy Clause." *Case Western Reserve Law Review* 64, no. 2 (Winter 2013): 319–412.

Lubben, Stephen J. "The Overstated Absolute Priority Rule." *Fordham Journal of Corporate & Financial Law* 21, no. 4 (2016): 581–606.

Lubben, Stephen J. "Protecting Ma and Pa: Bond Workouts and the Trust Indenture Act in the 21st Century." *Cardozo Law Review* 44, no. 1 (October 2022): 81–144.

Lubben, Stephen J. "Railroad Receiverships and Modern Bankruptcy Theory." *Cornell Law Review* 89, no. 6 (September 2004): 1420–75.

Ludington, Townsend. "The Portuguese Heritage—First and Second Generation American Born: The Example of the Two Dos Passoses." *Govea-Brown* 1, no. 2 (1980): 5–14.

Lueck, Thomas J. "Manville Submits Bankruptcy Filing to Halt Lawsuits." *The New York Times*, August 27, 1982.

"L. W. Baldwin Died on May 14." *Railway Age*, May 25, 1946.

Mahon, Emmie Giddings W., and Chester V. Kielman. "George H. Giddings and the San Antonio-San Diego Mail Line." *Southwestern Historical Quarterly* 61, no. 2 (1957): 220–39. http://www.jstor.org/stable/30241927.

"Managing the Railroads." *The New York Times*, April 17, 1880.

Mann, Ronald J. "Bankruptcy and the Entitlements of the Government: Whose Money Is It Anyway." *New York University Law Review* 70, no. 5 (November 1995): 993–1058

"Manville Asserts U.S. Must Share Costs of Asbestos Damage Claims." *The New York Times*, August 28, 1982.

"Manville Claimants Draft Plan to Settle Asbestos Lawsuits." *Wall Street Journal*, March 15, 1985.

"Manville Plan Effectively Is Cleared by Judge." *Wall Street Journal*, December 17, 1986.

"Manville Plan Sets Claim Guidelines." *The New York Times*, November 22, 1983.

"Manville Ready to Emerge from Bankruptcy." *Los Angeles Times*, November 26, 1988.

"Manville Revamping Confirmed by Judge as 'Fair, Equitable." *Wall Street Journal*, December 19, 1986.

"Manville's Plaintiffs Set Back by Bankruptcy Court Ruling." *The New York Times*, August 31, 1982.

"Many Suits Against a Road." October 16, 1884.

Marrs, Aaron W. "The Iron Horse Turns South: A History of Antebellum Southern Railroads." *Enterprise & Society* 8, no. 4 (2007): 784–9. http://www.jstor.org/stable/23700764.

"Marshall O. Roberts Dead." *The New York Times*, September 12, 1880.

Martin, Albro. "Railroads and the Equity Receivership: An Essay on Institutional Change." *Journal of Economic History* 34, no. 3 (1974): 685–709. http://www.jstor.org/stable/2116758.

Matsuda, Akiko. "Judge Denies Invesco Bid to Retake Control of Robertshaw Restructuring." *Wall Street Journal*, June 20, 2024.

Matsuda, Akiko. "Robertshaw Beats Appeals Court Stay by an Hour to Seal Bankruptcy Sale." *Wall Street Journal*, October 3, 2024.

McCormack, Gerard. "Control and Corporate Rescue: An Anglo-American Evaluation." *International and Comparative Law Quarterly* 56, no. 3 (2007): 515–51. http://www.jstor.org/stable/4498088.

McKay, S. S. "Texas and the Southern Pacific Railroad, 1848–1860." *Southwestern Historical Quarterly* 35, no. 1 (1931): 1–27. http://www.jstor.org/stable/30235386.

McKenzie, Troy A. "Bankruptcy and the Future of Aggregate Litigation: The Past as Prologue?" *Washington University Law Review* 90, no. 3 (2013): 839–94.

"McKesson Leaves the Court." *Time*, April 7, 1941.

Means, Nathaniel. "Sugarcane, Cotton Fields, and High Water: Building the Louisiana Branch of the Texas and Pacific Railroad." *Louisiana History: The Journal of the Louisiana Historical Association* 45, no. 4 (2004): 445–61. http://www.jstor.org/stable/4234060.

"Meeting of the Texas and Pacific Bondholders." *The Philadelphia Inquirer*, November 25, 1884.

"Men of Many Millions." *The Washington Post*, April 25, 1885.

"Merger of 2 Railroads Is Completed by MoPac." *Wall Street Journal*, October 18, 1976.

Merrick, Amy. "How Toys 'R' Us Succumbed to Its Nasty Debt Problem." *The New Yorker*, September 21, 2017.

Miller, Harvey R. "Chapter 11 in Transition—From Boom to Bust and into the Future." *American Bankruptcy Law Journal* 81, no. 4 (Fall 2007): 375–404.

Miller, John W., and Matt Jarzemsky. "Peabody Energy Files for Chapter 11 Bankruptcy Protection." *Wall Street Journal*, April 14, 2016.

Miller, Walter W., Jr. "Bankruptcy Code Cramdown Under Chapter 11: New Threat to Shareholder Interests." *Boston University Law Review* 62, no. 5 (November 1982): 1059–114.

Miller, Worth Robert. "The Lost World of Gilded Age Politics." *Journal of the Gilded Age and Progressive Era* 1, no. 1 (2002): 49–67. http://www.jstor.org/stable/25144285.

Minsky, Hyman P. "The Evolution of Financial Institutions and the Performance of the Economy." *Journal of Economic Issues* 20, no. 2 (1986): 345–53. http://www.jstor.org/stable/4225715.

"Missouri Pacific Allowed to Borrow $2,234,800 More." *Boston Globe*, March 1, 1933.

"Missouri Pacific Had Wyer on Pan Before Early Truman Probe." *Newsday*, October 6, 1952.

"Missouri Pacific: The Reorganized Road Carries a Heavy Load of Debt." *Barron's*, December 24, 1956.

"Mrs. Shields Is Wed to Guy A. Thompson." *The New York Times*, October 13, 1933.

"Mr. Jay Gould's Conjuring." *The Statist*, January 30, 1886.

"Mr. Spencer's Career." *New York Tribune*, November 30, 1906.

"Miscellaneous Railroad Intelligence." *New York Tribune*, July 15, 1886.

"Missouri-Pacific Asked to End JC." *Afro-American*, November 10, 1951.

"Missouri Pacific Goes into Bankruptcy." *St. Louis Dispatch*, March 31, 1933.

"Missouri Pacific Recapitalization Is Agreed Upon." *Wall Street Journal*, October 16, 1972.

Mitchell, Cynthia F. "Manville Concludes Plan to Settle Claims of Property Damage Linked to Asbestos." *Wall Street Journal*, August 25, 1986.

Mitchell, Dalia T. "From Vulnerable to Sophisticated: The Changing Representation of Creditors in Business Reorganizations." *New York University Journal of Law and Business* 16, no. 1 (Fall 2019): 123–84.

Mokal, Riz. "What Is an Insolvency Proceeding? Gategroup Lands in a Gated Community." *International Insolvency Review* 31, no. 3 (2022): 418–73. https://doi.org/10.1002/iir.1470

"Money Market." *Brooklyn Daily Eagle*, December 16, 1885.

"Money Market." *The Times*, June 9, 1886.

"Money-Market and City Intelligence." *The Times*, July 31, 1886.

Moody, John, and George Kibbe Turner. "The Masters of Capital in America: Morgan: The Great Trustee." *McClure's Magazine* (November 1910): 3–24.

"MoPac Now Has 80 Percent of T. & P. Voting Stock, Plans Joint Tax Return." *Wall Street Journal*, December 12, 1958.

"MoPac Reorganization Under Mahaffie Act Sought by Directors." *Wall Street Journal*, January 27, 1953.

"MoPac Wins Its Freedom." *Time*, March 12, 1956.

"MOP's Future." *Time*, December 3, 1934.

"MOP's No. 23." *Time*, August 12, 1935.

"'Mop' Will Buy Alleghany Firm Unit Holdings." *New York Tribune*, March 15, 1940.

"More Grant Severance Pay Upheld." *Women's Wear Daily*, January 10, 1980.

"Morgan Guaranty Will Pay $2.8 Million to Settle Class Suit." *Wall Street Journal*, August 18, 1981.

"Morgans Got RFC Money." *Boston Globe*, December 19, 1936.

Morrison, Patt. "Confederate Sentiment in Southern California Ran Deeper Than You Might Know." *Los Angeles Times*, April 12, 2024

Mouawad, Jad. "Merger of American and US Airways Is Waved Ahead." *The New York Times*, November 27, 2013.

"Nassi: The Liquidator and the Giants." *Women's Wear Daily*, November 13, 1975.

"Necessity of Competition." *San Francisco Chronicle*, September 5, 1878.

"Negroes in Business." *The New York Times*, June 26, 1964.

"Negroes Named to Board of 2 Giant Firms." *New Amsterdam News*, June 27, 1964.

"A New Ending for Chapter 11." *The Economist*, February 24, 1990.

"New, Larger Saks Planned in Pittsburgh." *Women's Wear Daily*, June 21, 1976.

"New Law Eases Bankrupts' Cares." *Newsweek*, March 11, 1933.

"A New Pacific Railway in Sight." *New York Tribune*, August 12, 1880.

"New Plan for Terminal." *New York Tribune*, March 2, 1894.

"New Railroad Syndicate." *The New York Times*, June 16, 1880.

"News About Railroads." *The New York Times*, July 30, 1891.

"The New Southern Railway." *The New York Times*, July 1, 1894.

"A New Scheme." *Atlanta Constitution*, January 13, 1892.

"The New Texas and Pacific Committee." *New York Tribune*, July 28, 1886.

"New W. T. Grant Unit to Open Monday." *Hartford Courant*, March 21, 1971.

"New York Stocks." *Pittsburgh Commercial Gazette*, April 8, 1886.

Nitschke, Christoph. "Theory and History of Financial Crises: Explaining the Panic of 1873." *Journal of the Gilded Age and Progressive Era* 17, no. 2 (2018): 221–40. doi:10.1017/S1537781417000810.

"Notes About Railroads." *The New York Times*, October 30, 1884.

"Notes of Various Interests." *The New York Times*, April 20, 1886.

"Notice of Final Meeting of Creditors and of Filing of Trustee's Final Report and Account." *The New York Times*, March 1, 1993.

"Notice of Second Supplemental Indenture." *Wall Street Journal*, May 22, 1975.

"Notes of Various Interest." *The New York Times*, April 23, 1886.

"The Plan Abandoned." *New York Tribune*, May 17, 1892.

"Olcott Plan a Failure." *The New York Times*, May 17, 1892.

"'Old Bird' Pecks at Missouri Pacific's Operators." *Newsweek*, August 10, 1935.

"On to Mexico." *St. Louis Dispatch*, December 25, 1880.

"An Open Letter to W. T. Grant Vendors." *Women's Wear Daily*, August 13, 1975.

"Ordered out by Knights." *The Sun*, March 7, 1886.

"Other People's Money." *New Republic*, August 21, 1935.

"Overland Railroads." *San Francisco Chronicle*, March 6, 1881.

"The Pacific Road." *The Atlanta Constitution*, October 10, 1875.

Paltrow, Scot J. "Manville Told to Boost Asbestos Trust Quickly." *Los Angeles Times*, August 7, 1990.

Pardo, Rafael I. "Rethinking Antebellum Bankruptcy." *University of Colorado Law Review* 95, no. 4 (2024): 995–1087.

Paterson, Sarah. "Debt Restructuring and Notions of Fairness." *Modern Law Review* 80, no. 4 (2017): 600–23. http://www.jstor.org/stable/26647063.

Paterson, Sarah. "Rethinking Corporate Bankruptcy Theory in the Twenty-First Century." *Oxford Journal of Legal Studies* 36, no. 4 (2016): 697–723. http://www.jstor.org/stable/26363440.

Peltz, James F. "Liquidators of Failed Retailers Fast Becoming a New Growth Industry." *Los Angeles Times*, December 11, 1990.

"Personal." *New York Tribune*, April 1, 1881.

"Personal." *New York Tribune*, November 6, 1878.

"Personal." *Post* or *Daily Morning Post*, December 20, 1875.

"Pittsburgh, Fort Wayne and Chicago Railway." *Railway Times*, May 31, 1862.

"Plan for Manville to Pay Claimants Stirs Controversy." *Wall Street Journal*, April 25, 1985.

Polatsek, William. "Wreck of the Old 77." *Cornell Law Quarterly* 34, no. 4 (1948–1949): 532–69.

Poonawala, Ebrahim. "Citigroup, Apollo Join Forces in $25 Billion Private Credit Push." *Bloomberg*, September 26, 2024.

"Port of Galveston." *Galveston Daily News*, March 6, 1881.

Pottow, John A. E. "Modular Bankruptcy: Toward a Consumer Scheme of Arrangement." *Cardozo Law Review* 45, no. 3 (February 2024): 721–88.

"Preemptory Sale." *The Philadelphia Inquirer*, May 8, 1884.

"President Inman's Statement." *Wall Street Journal*, August 10, 1891.

"President Scott Sails for Europe." *The Philadelphia Inquirer*, November 4, 1878.

"President Scott's Resignation." *New York Tribune*, May 3, 1880

"The Price of Distress." *The Economist*, April 27, 1991.

"Probe of Grants' Bears Millions Lost in Big Credit Push." *Women's Wear Daily*, February 4, 1977.

"Problems over, Grant's Chairman Tells Complaining Stockholders." *The New York Times*, May 1, 1974.

"Profit Drop Led to Grant Chief's Quitting." *The New York Times*, July 6, 1974.

"Pulaski." *Daily American*, January 13, 1886.

"Purdue and Sackler Family Agree to $7.4bn Opioid Settlement with US States." *Financial Times*, January 23, 2025.

Qin, Yucheng. "A Century-Old 'Puzzle': The Six Companies' Role in Chinese Labor Importation in the Nineteenth Century." *Journal of American-East Asian Relations* 12, no. 3/4 (2003): 225–54. http://www.jstor.org/stable/23613231.

Rafter, George W. "Railroad-Building on the Texas Frontier." *Engineering Magazine* vol. II (1891–92): 29–41.

"Railroad Earnings in June." *The Commercial and Financial Chronicle*, July 12, 1884.

"Railroad Empire Rolls out of a Generation of Trusteeship." *The New York Times*, March 2, 1956.

"Railroad Interests." *The Baltimore Sun*, August 9, 1886.

"Railroad Interests." *New York Tribune*, October 29, 1873.

"Railroad Interests." *New York Tribune*, December 17, 1885.

"Railroad Interests." *New York Tribune*, August 4, 1886.

"Railroad Interests." *New York Tribune*, December 19, 1891.

"Railroad Matters." *Daily American*, November 11, 1880.

"Railroad News." *Atlanta Constitution*, June 7, 1892.

"Railroad Notes." *The New York Times*, November 16, 1884.

"Railroad Notes." *The Philadelphia Inquirer*, January 21, 1887.

"Railroad Personals." *Los Angeles Times*, January 26, 1887.

"Railroad Reorganization." *The New York Times*, November 6, 1893.

"The Railroads." *Courier-Journal*, March 25, 1881.

"The Railroads." *St. Louis Globe-Democrat*, December 27, 1885.

"Railroads of the South." *Atlanta Constitution*, June 11, 1892.

"The Railroad Strikers." *The Evening Star*, March 9, 1885.

"Rail and Tie." *The Philadelphia Inquirer*, April 13, 1881.

"Railway Affairs in America." *Railway News*, January 16, 1886.

"Railway Collision." *The Philadelphia Inquirer*, April 28, 1885.

"Railway Combination in the United States." *The Economist*, November 8, 1890.

"Railways in Japan." *Daily American*, March 31, 1881.

"Railway Notes." *Montreal Daily Witness*, June 10, 1884.

"Railway on the Thirty-Second Parallel." *New York Tribune*, May 4, 1870.

"The Railway Strike." *Frank Leslie's Illustrated Newspaper*, April 17, 1886.

"Railway Traffic." *Atlanta Constitution*, July 26, 1892.

Randles, Jonathan. "Bain Director Said Debt Deal Took Invesco 'Behind the Woodshed,'" *Bloomberg*, May 23, 2024.

Randles, Jonathan, and Amelia Pollard. "Trucker Yellow Paid Managers Millions Just Before Bankruptcy." *Bloomberg*, September 14, 2023.

"Receiver Brown." *Atlanta Constitution*, March 10, 1886.

"The Reckoning: Safeway LBO Yields Vast Profits but Exacts a Heavy Human Toll." *Wall Street Journal*, May 16, 1990.

"Relief of the Texas and Pacific." *New York Tribune*, July 22, 1884.

"Return of President Scott." *The Philadelphia Inquirer*, September 11, 1879.

Rhoads, Edward J. M. "The Chinese in Texas." *Southwestern Historical Quarterly* 81, no. 1 (1977): 1–36. http://www.jstor.org/stable/30238491.

"Richmond Terminal." *Atlanta Constitution*, March 4, 1894.

"Richmond Terminal." *The New York Times*, May 27, 1892.

"Richmond Terminal." *The Philadelphia Inquirer*, May 17, 1892.

"Richmond Terminal." *Wall Street Journal*, April 15, 1893.

"Richmond Terminal Affairs." *The New York Times*, December 29, 1891.

"Richmond Terminal Affairs." *The New York Times*, July 2, 1892.

"Richmond Terminal Affairs Unpromising." *Wall Street Journal*, November 4, 1893.

"Richmond Terminal Stockholders." *New York Tribune*, December 9, 1891.

"'The Risk Was Too Great,'" *Washington Post*, May 5, 1976.

Rizzo, Lillian. "Toys 'R' Us Owners to Create Severance Fund for Former Employees." *Wall Street Journal*, September 28, 2018.

"Road to Success: Missouri Pacific Is Highballing down It." *Barron's*, January 31, 1977.

Roberson, Jere W. "To Build a Pacific Railroad: Congress, Texas, and the Charleston Convention of 1854." *Southwestern Historical Quarterly* 78, no. 2 (1974): 117–39. http://www.jstor.org/stable/30240992.

Roberson, Jere W. "The South and the Pacific Railroad, 1845–1855." *Western Historical Quarterly* 5, no. 2 (1974): 163–86. https://doi.org/10.2307/967035.

Rodgers, Churchill, and Littleton Groom. "Reorganization of Railroad Corporations Under Section 77 of the Bankruptcy Act." *Columbia Law Review* 33, no. 4 (1933): 571–616. https://doi.org/10.2307/1115487.

Rosenberg, Robert J. "Corporate Rehabilitation Under the Bankruptcy Act of 1973: Are Reports of the Demise of Chapter XI Greatly Exaggerated?" *North Carolina Law Review* 53, no. 6 (1975): 1149–96.

Ross, Nancy L. "Smoothing the Road from Insolvency." *Washington Post*, August 16, 1977.

Rostow, Eugene V., and Lloyd N. Cutler. "Competing Systems of Corporate Reorganization: Chapters X and XI of the Bankruptcy Act." *Yale Law Journal* 48, no. 8 (1939): 1334–76. https://doi.org/10.2307/792526.

"Russell L. Dearmont Is Dead; Headed MoPac Many Years." *St. Louis Globe-Democrat*, January 12, 1967.

"Russell Sage: The Father of the Put and Call System Getting Poor." *St. Louis Dispatch*, February 27, 1885.

"Sale of the East Tennessee Virginia & Georgia for $10,850,000." *Daily American*, May 26, 1886.

"Sale of a Railway." *The Times*, November 10, 1887.

Salpukas, Agis. "Eastern Airlines Is Shutting Down and Plans to Liquidate Its Assets: Eastern Airlines Decides It Will Shut Down." *The New York Times*, January 19, 1991.

Salpukas, Agis. "Eastern's Fate Clouded by Creditors' Move." *The New York Times*, April 5, 1990.

"The St. Louis Collision." *Daily American*, April 30, 1885.

"Samuel Spencer." *Railway Age*, December 7, 1906.

Schiffman, Daniel A. "Shattered Rails, Ruined Credit: Financial Fragility and Railroad Operations in the Great Depression." *Journal of Economic History* 63, no. 3 (2003): 802–25. http://www.jstor.org/stable/3132308.

Scott, Peter, and James T. Walker. "'The Only Way Is Up': Overoptimism and the Demise of the American Five-and-Dime Store, 1914–1941." *Business History Review* 91, no. 1 (2017): 71–103. http://www.jstor.org/stable/26291050.

"The Scott Railroad Interests." *New York Tribune*, November 6, 1873.

Seaberry, Jane. "Safeway Agrees to Buyout." *Washington Post*, July 28, 1986.

"Settlement Proposed in Grant's Suit." *Women's Wear Daily*, March 5, 1981.

"Sherman." *Galveston Daily News*, July 20, 1884.

"A Shrewd Chinaman." *St. Louis Globe-Democrat*, November 26, 1886.

Simpson, Joseph C. "Comments on the Railroad Reorganization Provisions of the Bankruptcy Act of 1973." *Business Lawyer* 30, no. 4 (1975): 1207–49. http://www.jstor.org/stable/40685444.

Simpson, Sidney Post. "Fifty Years of American Equity." *Harvard Law Review* 50, no. 2 (1936): 171–251.

Sitaraman, Ganeshi. "Why Airlines Don't Fly to Your City and Other Problems Washington Caused." *Politico*, November 14, 2023.

Skeel, David A. "Creditors' Ball: The 'New' New Corporate Governance in Chapter 11." *University of Pennsylvania Law Review* 152, no. 2 (2003): 917–51. https://doi.org/10.2307/3313038.

"The Southern Pacific." *San Francisco Chronicle*, November 28, 1879.

"The Southern Pacific Nearing Completion." *St. Louis Dispatch*, April 24, 1880.

"Southern Pacific Railway." *New York Tribune*, April 25, 1880.

"Southern Pacific Railways." *The Philadelphia Inquirer*, December 9, 1879.

"Southern Pacific Road: Shall Freemont Have a Hand in the Pie?" *Republican Banner*, June 22, 1870.

"Southern Railroad Business." *Wall Street Journal*, December 28, 1893.

"The Southern Railroads of America." *The Economist*, October 31, 1891.

"The Southern Railway Plans." *New York Tribune*, July 6, 1894.

"South Pacific Railways." *The Philadelphia Inquirer*, December 9, 1879.

"Spencer Killed in Wreck." *The New York Times*, November 30, 1906.

Spring, Samuel. "Upset Prices in Corporate Reorganization." *Harvard Law Review* 32, no. 5 (1919): 489–515. https://doi.org/10.2307/1327925.

"Stars of the Junkyard: Drexel Burnham Lambert's Legacy." *The Economist*, October 21, 2010.

Stern, James Y. "The Essential Structure of Property Law." *Michigan Law Review* 115, no. 7 (May 2017): 1167–212.

Stevens, Albert C. "Analysis of the Phenomena of the Panic in the United States in 1893." *Quarterly Journal of Economics* 8, no. 2 (1894): 117–48. https://doi.org/10.2307/1883708.

"Still Waiting." *The Philadelphia Inquirer*, June 6, 1884.

"Stock Exchange Notice." *Wall Street Journal*, January 16, 1915.

"Stocks Dormant." *The Philadelphia Inquirer*, July 16, 1891.

Stone, Ferdinand Fairfax. "The Case of the Ladies' Handbags: A Study in Receivership Procedure." *Virginia Law Review* 24, no. 8 (June 1938): 831–62

"Stopping a Great Railroad Swindle." *The New York Times*, January 23, 1884.

Story, Louise. and Peter Lattman. "Short on Time and Options, Lawyers Remade Chrysler." *The New York Times*, June 14, 2009.

Stover, John F. "The Pennsylvania Railroad's Southern Rail Empire." *Pennsylvania Magazine of History and Biography* 81, no. 1 (1957): 28–38. http://www.jstor.org/stable/20088936.

"The Strike at Eastern Wild Week Emotions Run High as Eastern Strike Yields Triumph and Despair." *Sun Sentinel*, March 12, 1989.

"Strike Moves." *Fort Worth Gazette*, March 15, 1886.

"Striking." *Los Angeles Times*, March 10, 1886.

Subrin, Stephen N. "How Equity Conquered Common Law: The Federal Rules of Civil Procedure in Historical Perspective." *University of Pennsylvania Law Review* 135, no. 4 (April 1987): 909–1002.

"Suing Texas and Pacific." *The New York Times*, August 28, 1884.

"Suing the Texas and Pacific Road." *New York Tribune*, December 1, 1888.

Swaine, Robert T. "Corporate Reorganization Under the Federal Bankruptcy Power." *Virginia Law Review* 19, no. 4 (1933): 317–33. https://doi.org/10.2307/1066680.

Swaine, Robert T. "A Decade of Railroad Reorganization Under Section 77 of the Federal Bankruptcy Act." *Harvard Law Review* 56, no. 7 (1943): 1037–58. https://doi.org/10.2307/1334988.

Swaine, Robert T. "Reorganization of Corporations: Certain Developments of the Last Decade." *Columbia Law Review* 27, no. 8 (1927): 901–31. https://doi.org/10.2307/1113840.

"A Tardy Aid Package That Couldn't Work." *Washington Post*, May 2, 1976.

"Target Stores Opening Houston, Omaha Units." *Women's Wear Daily*, November 3, 1976.

"Texas Air Accused on Eastern Deals: Broad Shortchanging Seen—$280 Million Will Be Paid." *The New York Times*, March 2, 1990.

"Texas Consolidations." *Daily Inter Ocean*, July 8, 1882.

"The Texas Pacific." *The Baltimore Sun*, August 16, 1879.

"Texas and Pacific." *The Baltimore Sun*, August 10, 1886.

"Texas and Pacific." *The Commercial and Financial Chronicle*, July 26, 1884.

"Texas and Pacific." *The Commercial and Financial Chronicle*, January 9, 1886.

"Texas and Pacific." *The Commercial and Financial Chronicle*, January 9, 1886.

"Texas and Pacific." *The Commercial and Financial Chronicle*, March 10, 1888.

"Texas and Pacific." *The Commercial and Financial Chronicle*, May 12, 1888.

"The Texas and Pacific." *Courier-Journal*, July 27, 1881.

"The Texas and Pacific." *Daily American*, August 12, 1880.

"The Texas and Pacific." *Daily American*, February 7, 1885.

"Texas and Pacific." *The Economist*, January 27, 1883.

"The Texas and Pacific." *The Economist*, December 13, 1884.

"The Texas and Pacific." *New York Tribune*, April 22, 1886.

"Texas and Pacific." *The Philadelphia Inquirer*, December 12, 1885.

"Texas and Pacific." *The Philadelphia Inquirer*, January 8, 1886.

"Texas and Pacific." *The Philadelphia Inquirer*, August 5, 1886.

"Texas and Pacific." *Railway Gazette*, April 16, 1886.

"Texas and Pacific." *Railway Gazette*, April 30, 1886.

"Texas and Pacific." *Railway News*, January 2, 1886.

"Texas and Pacific." *Rhodes' Journal of Banking*, XIII, February 1886.

"The Texas and Pacific." *St. Louis Dispatch*, June 4, 1884.

"Texas and Pacific Bondholders." *The New York Times*, November 2, 1883.

"Texas and Pacific Case." *New York Tribune*, January 10, 1886.

"The Texas and Pacific and Col. Scott." *The Baltimore Sun*, April 15, 1881.

"Texas and Pacific Finances." *The New York Times*, March 4, 1885.

"The Texas Pacific Grant: The Central Pacific Still Trying to Secure the Lands." *The New York Times*, July 17, 1883.

"The Texas Pacific: Jay Gould Reaching out for Its Control." *The Cincinnati Daily Enquirer*, December 10, 1879.

"Texas and Pacific Negotiations." *New York Tribune*, November 19, 1884.

"Texas & Pacific Plan." *The New York Times*, May 7, 1924.

"Texas Pacific Railroad," *Cincinnati Daily Enquirer*, April 17, 1871."The Texas and Pacific Railroad." *The New York Times*, August 11, 1880.

"The Texas Pacific Railroad." *New York Tribune*, April 17, 1871.

"The Texas and Pacific Railroad." *Republican Banner*, April 19, 1871.

"The Texas Pacific Railroad." *St. Louis Dispatch*, January 24, 1876.

"The Texas Pacific Railroad Company." *The Commercial and Financial Chronicle*, March 2, 1872.

"The Texas Pacific Railroad—Election of Directors Deferred." *New York Tribune*, April 18, 1871.

"The Texas Pacific Railroad: Meeting of the Incorporation." *Republican Banner*, April 19, 1871.

"The Texas Pacific Railroad: Meeting of the Incorporation—the Preliminary Issue of Stock All Subscribed For." *Republican Banner*, April 19, 1871.

"The Texas and Pacific Railway." *The New York Times*, August 13, 1879.

"Texas and Pacific Reorganization." *Courier-Journal*, April 27, 1886.

"Texas and Pacific Reorganization." *New York Tribune*, May 19, 1886.

"Texas and Pacific Reorganization." *The Philadelphia Inquirer*, June 17, 1886.

"Texas and Pacific Reorganization." *The Philadelphia Inquirer*, July 2, 1886.

"Texas and Pacific Reorganization." *The Philadelphia Inquirer*, February 3, 1888.

"Texas Pacific Reorganization Plan." *Bradstreet's*, January 9, 1886.

"Texas and Pacific Reorganization Plans." *St. Louis Globe-Democrat*, July 10, 1886.

"The Texas and Pacific Road." *Courier-Journal*, November 15, 1880.

"The Texas and Pacific Road." *The New York Times*, December 25, 1885

"Texas and Pacific: The Sensation in Wall Street Yesterday." *The Philadelphia Inquirer*, June 4, 1884.

"Texas and Pacific Shopmen to Strike." *The Sun*, March 1, 1885.

"The Texas Pacific and the South." *The New York Times*, October 2, 1878.

"The Texas Pacific Strike." *Boston Globe*, March 9, 1885.

"The Texas Route to the Pacific." *New York Tribune*, December 16, 1879.

"Texas Topics." *Courier-Journal*, July 5, 1881.

"Their Big Chief." *Courier-Journal*, November 9, 1879.

"Themes in Money Centers." *New York Tribune*, January 27, 1875.

"They Cannot Agree." *The Philadelphia Inquirer*, April 22, 1886.

"This Is Business." *Atlanta Constitution*, April 14, 1893.

Thomas, Brook. "Ruiz De Burton, Railroads, Reconstruction." *ELH* 80, no. 3 (2013): 871–95. http://www.jstor.org/stable/24475545.

"3 Chains up in April Despite Retail Static." *Women's Wear Daily*, May 24, 1974.

"Tom Scott and His Railroads," *Cincinnati Daily Enquirer*, January 31, 1872.

"Tom Scott's New Road." *San Francisco Chronicle*, August 23, 1872.

"To the Pacific: Memphis, El Paso Railroad. A Card from Gen. Fremont." *New York Tribune*, January 10, 1870.

"Top-Ranking Lenders See Diminishing Recoveries in Bankruptcy." *Wall Street Journal*, May 14, 2024.

Torbati, Yeganeh, and Jeff Stein. "Trump Officials Overruled Pentagon to Approve Pandemic Loan, Emails Show." *Washington Post*, April 27, 2022.

"To the Stockholders of the Richmond and West Point Terminal Railway and Warehouse Company." *The New York Times*, September 11, 1892.

Townsend, Matthew, Lauren Coleman-Lochner, and Eliza Ronalds-Hannon. "Toys 'R' Us Nearly Had a Deal to Save Itself." *Bloomberg*, June 5, 2018.

"Toys 'R' Us Is in Danger of Breaching a Covenant with Its Lenders." Canadian National Broadcasting Corp., February 22, 2018.

"Toys 'R' Us to Shut About 180 Stores in Bid to Exit Bankruptcy." *Bloomberg*, January 24, 2018.

"Track Talk." *Daily Inter Ocean*, November 11, 1879.

"Trade and Commerce." *Montreal Herald*, August 2, 1886.

"Trustee's Notice" (classified ad), *The New York Times*, August 4, 1879.

"Turning the Corner." *Barron's National Business and Financial Weekly*, May 24, 1976.

Traxler, Ralph N. "Collis P. Huntington and the Texas and Pacific Railroad Land Grant." *New Mexico Historical Review* 34, no. 2 (April 1959): 117–33.

"Truman Boosts Proposed Rail Reorganization." *Washington Post*, November 11, 1937.

"Trustee Named to Take Helm of Eastern Air: Judge Appoints Shugrue, Wrests Control of Carrier from Texas Air, Lorenzo." *Wall Street Journal*, April 19, 1990.

Turner, Charles W. "The Virginia Southwestern Railroad System at War 1861—1865." *Railway and Locomotive Historical Society Bulletin*, no. 71 (1947): 71–84. http://www.jstor.org/stable/43520013.

"'2-Year Job' Brings Missouri Lawyer Railroad Presidency." *St. Louis Globe-Democrat*, May 17, 1957.

"Under a Modified Plan." *The New York Times*, August 12, 1886.

"Under a New Name." *Atlanta Constitution*, June 19, 1894.

Unglesbee, Ben. "Inside the 20-Year Decline of Toys 'R' Us." *RetailDive*, June 26, 2018.

Unglesbee, Ben. "Toys 'R' Us' Fatal Journey Through Chapter 11." *RetailDive*, September 18, 2018.

"The United States." *The Times*, December 18, 1885.

"Uniting Texas and Pacific Interests." *New York Tribune*, August 11, 1886.

"Upgrading at Grant's." *Financial World*, April 2, 1969.

"Upon the Staked Plains." *The Sun*, January 4, 1885.

"Urged to Take a Respite." *The Philadelphia Inquirer*, October 31, 1878.

"U.S. Approves $5.4-Billion Rail Merger." *Los Angeles Times*, July 4, 1996.

"U.S. Supreme Court Won't Block MP Reorganization." *Railway Age*, February 6, 1956.

Vargas, Ramon Antonio. "New Orleans Archdiocese Bankruptcy Parties Wary of Turnaround Expert After WSJ Investigation." *The Guardian*, October 6, 2024.

"Variety Adds Fresh Spice to Growth of W. T. Grant." *Barron's National Business and Financial Weekly*, April 21, 1969.

"A Very Bad Cause." *Courier-Journal*, October 12, 1878.

"Visitors from Baltimore." *The Philadelphia Inquirer*, October 17, 1878.

"The Wall Street Deal." *Atlanta Constitution*, January 21, 1887.

"Wall Street Greatly Excited." *New York Tribune*, May 14, 1884.

"Wall Street Worry." *Courier-Journal*, March 9, 1885.

Walton, Andrea. "Ford's Fund for the Republic: A 1950s-Era Foundation as Educator." *American Educational History Journal* 42, no. 1 (2015): 111–26.

"Wanted an Outlet to Gulf." *The Philadelphia Inquirer*, October 27, 1880.

"The War on the Texas Pacific." *Courier-Journal*, October 5, 1878.

Ward, James A. "J. Edgar Thomson and Thomas A. Scott: A Symbiotic Partnership?" *Pennsylvania Magazine of History and Biography* 100, no. 1 (1976): 37–65. http://www.jstor.org/stable/20091028.

Warren, Elizabeth. "Bankruptcy Policy." *University of Chicago Law Review* 54, no. 3 (1987): 775–814. https://doi.org/10.2307/1599826.

Warren, Elizabeth, and Jay Lawrence Westbrook. "Contracting out of Bankruptcy: An Empirical Intervention." *Harvard Law Review* 118, no. 4 (2005): 1197–254. http://www.jstor.org/stable/4093379.

"Washington: Railroad Legislation in 1871." *New York Tribune*, February 24, 1876.

"W. C. Hall Sued for a Settlement of His Accounts as Executor." *Courier-Journal*, April 6, 1889.

Weiner, Eric. "Lorenzo, Head of Continental Air, Quits Industry in $30 Million Deal." *The New York Times*, August 10, 1990.

Weiner, Joseph L. "Book Review." *Harvard Law Review* 47, no. 4 (1934): 719–21. https://doi.org/10.2307/1332010.

Weiner, Joseph L. "Corporate Reorganization: Section 77B of the Bankruptcy Act." *Columbia Law Review* 34, no. 7 (1934): 1173–97. https://doi.org/10.2307/1116101.

Wham, Benjamin. "Chapter X of the Chandler Act: A Study in Reconciliation of Conflicting Views." *Virginia Law Review* 25, no. 4 (1939): 389–97. https://doi.org/10.2307/1068272.

"What It Means to Atlanta." *Atlanta Constitution*, May 28, 1892.

"What the Supreme Court's Decision to Hear the Purdue Pharma Case Means." *The New York Times*, August 11, 2023.

White, Richard. "Information, Markets, and Corruption: Transcontinental Railroads in the Gilded Age." *Journal of American History* 90, no. 1 (2003): 19–43. https://doi.org/10.2307/3659790.

"Who Is Issac L. Rice?" *Wall Street Journal*, September 8, 1893.

"Why This Opposition?" *San Francisco Chronicle*, January 22, 1879.

Willmer, Sabrina. "Cerberus Quadruples Money After Unusual Exit from Hospital Giant." *Bloomberg*, May 27, 2021.

Winther, Oscar Osburn. "The Rise of Metropolitan Los Angeles, 1870–1900." *Huntington Library Quarterly* 10, no. 4 (1947): 391–405. https://doi.org/10.2307/3815801.

Woo, Sarah Pei. "Regulatory Bankruptcy: How Bank Regulation Causes Fire Sales." *Georgetown Law Journal* 99, no. 6 (August 2011): 1615–70.

"A Wooden Horse." *Courier-Journal*, January 7, 1879.

"Worse Than Modocs: An Unoffending Negro Tortured and Murdered by 'Respectable' White Citizens of Texas." *The New York Times*, June 12, 1873.

"Would Press Mergers." *The New York Times*, September 18, 1932.

"W. T. Grant Agrees to Liquidate." *Washington Post*, February 12, 1976.

"W. T. Grant Co. Honors Spaulding." *New Journal and Guide*, June 7, 1975

"W. T. Grant Confirms 1-Stop Unit." *Women's Wear Daily*, October 17, 1962.

"W. T. Grant Co. Says Major Appliance Line Will Be Phased Out." *Wall Street Journal*, August 27, 1975.

"W. T. Grant Counter Policy Unchanged." *Los Angeles Sentinel*, May 5, 1960.

"W. T. Grant Defends Lunch Counter Racial Bar." *The New York Times*, April 27, 1960.

"W. T. Grant, Facing $175-Million Loss to Close 126 Stores and Lay off 12,600." *The New York Times*, January 17, 1975.

"W. T. Grant Is Seeking $600 Million Credit from 200-Bank Group." *Wall Street Journal*, August 27, 1974.

"W. T. Grant Loss Widened in Half: Payout Omitted." *Wall Street Journal*, August 28, 1974.

"W. T. Grant Names Kendrick Chairman President and Chief." *The New York Times*, August 15, 1974.

"W. T. Grant Offers Liens on Inventory." *The New York Times*, May 24, 1975.

"W. T. Grant to Ring up Best Profits Year Ever." *Barron's National Business and Financial Weekly*, February 22, 1965.

"W. T. Grant's Signs Coming Down." *The New York Times*, March 13, 1976.

"The Yearly Consumption of Rails." *Railway Gazette*, September 2, 1881.

"Yellow Bankruptcy Judge to Reconsider Pension Debt Ruling." *Bloomberg*, November 5, 2024.

"Young Answers Attack on Alleghany MOP Plan: Chairman Says More Bondholders Recognize That Stedman Proposal 'Is Insupportable on Merits." *Wall Street Journal*, February 2, 1942.

"Young Opposes Plan for MOP in Plea to Holders: Bays Present Program Is as Unfair as Older One Contested by Alleghany." *New York Tribune*, August 7, 1947.

Young, Robert R. "A Strange Alliance for Monopoly." *Atlantic Monthly Magazine* (December 1946): 43–50.

Ziobro, Paul, and Lillian Rizzo, "Toys 'R' Us Plans to Close Another 200 Stores; Retailer's Corporate Staff Would Also Suffer Layoffs Following a Disappointing Holiday Season." *Wall Street Journal*, February 22, 2018.

Books and Manuscripts

Adams, Charles Francis, Jr., and Henry Adams. *Chapters of Erie*. Waveland, 2002 (1871).

Adler, Cyrus. *Jacob H. Schiff: His Life and Letters*. vol. 1. Doubleday, 1928.

Adler, Dorothy R. *British Investment in American Railways, 1834–1898*. University Press of Virginia, 1970.

Allen, Ruth A. *The Great Southwest Strike*. University of Texas Press, 1942.

Baird, Douglas G. *Elements of Bankruptcy*. 7th ed. Foundation, 2022.

Baird, Douglas G. *The Unwritten Law of Corporate Reorganizations*. Cambridge University Press, 2022.

Baker, J. H. *An Introduction to English Legal History*. 4th ed. Oxford University Press, 2007.

Bakeless, John Edwin. "History of the Missouri Pacific Railroad." Unpublished manuscript, 1957. https://archives.nypl.org/mss/182

Ballou, Brendan. *Plunder: Private Equity's Plan to Pillage America*. PublicAffairs, 2023.

Banker, Mark T. *Appalachians All: East Tennesseans and the Elusive History of an American Region*. University of Tennessee Press, 2010.

Barron, Clarence W., Arthur Pound, and Samuel Taylor Moore. *More They Told Barron: Conversations and Revelations of an American Pepys in Wall Street*. Harper, 1931.

Benedict, Michael Les. *Preserving the Constitution: Essays on Politics and the Constitution in the Era of Reconstruction*. Fordham University Press, 2006.

Berton, Pierre. *The National Dream: The Great Railway, 1871–1881*. McClelland and Stewart, 1970.

Blackmon, Douglas A, *Slavery by Another Name: The Re-enslavement of Black Americans From the Civil War to World War II*. Doubleday, 2008.

Blight, David W. *Frederick Douglass: Prophet of Freedom*. Simon & Schuster, 2018.

Blom, Philipp. *Fracture: Life and Culture in the West, 1918–1938*. Atlantic Books, 2015.

Brandeis, Louis D. *Other People's Money: and How the Bankers Use It*. F. A. Stokes, 1914 (Harper Torchbook edition, 1967).

Brands, H. W. *American Colossus*. Doubleday, 2010.

"Brown, John Calvin." In *New American Supplement to Encyclopedia Britannica*, vol. 1 Werner Co., 1899.

Bruck, Connie. *The Predators' Ball: The Junk-Bond Raiders and the Man Who Staked Them*. Simon & Schuster, 1988.

Bryant, Keith L., *Encyclopedia of American Business History and Biography: V. 1, Railroads in the Age of Regulation, 1900–1980*. Bruccoli Clark Layman, 1988.

Burch, Philip H., Jr. *Elites in American History*. Holmes & Meier, 1981.

Burgess, George Heckman, and Miles C. Kennedy. *Centennial History of the Pennsylvania Railroad Company, 1846–1946*. Penn. R.R. Co., 1949.

Burk, Kathleen. *Morgan Grenfell, 1838–1988: The Biography of a Merchant Bank*. Oxford University Press, 1989.

Burlingame, Michael. *Abraham Lincoln: A Life*, vol. 2. Reprint ed. Johns Hopkins University Press, 2013.

Burns, James MacGregor. *Roosevelt: The Soldier of Freedom*. Harcourt Brace Jovanovich, 1970.

Burrows, Edwin G., and Mike Wallace. *Gotham*. Oxford University Press, 1999.

Burton, W. J. "History of the Missouri Pacific." Unpublished manuscript, July 1, 1956. Corporate files of the Missouri Pacific Railroad, St. Louis, Missouri.

Caldwell, Joshua W. *Sketches of the Bench and Bar of Tennessee*. Ogden Bros., 1898.

Campbell, E. G. *The Reorganization of the American Railroad System, 1893–1900*. Columbia University Press, 1938.

Cannadine, David. *Victorious Century: The United Kingdom, 1800–1906*. Allen Lane, 2017.

Carnegie, Andrew. *The Autobiography of Andrew Carnegie*. Constable & Co., 1920.

Carosso, Vincent P. *Investment Banking in America, a History*. Harvard University Press, 1970.

Carosso, Vincent P. *The Morgans: Private International Bankers, 1854–1913*. Harvard University Press, 1987.

Carruthers, Bruce G., and Terence C. Halliday. *Rescuing Business: The Making of Corporate Bankruptcy Law in England and the United States*. Oxford University Press, 1998.

Case, Theresa A. *The Great Southwest Railroad Strike and Free Labor*. Texas A&M University Press, 2010.

Chernow, Ron. *The House of Morgan*. Atlantic Monthly Press, 1990.

Chernow, Ron. *The Warburgs*. Random House, 1993.

Churella, Albert J. *The Pennsylvania Railroad*, vol. 1. University of Pennsylvania Press, 2012.

Clark, Ralph Ewing. *A Treatise on the Law and Practice of Receivers*, vol. 2. 3rd ed. W. H. Anderson, 1959.

Cleveland, Harold van B., and Thomas F. Huertas. *Citibank, 1812–1970*. Harvard University Press, 1985.

Cohen, Michael J. *Truman and Israel*. University of California Press, 1990.

Cohen, Naomi Wiener. *Jacob H. Schiff: A Study in American Jewish Leadership*. Brandeis University Press, 1999.

Collier, William Miller. *Collier on Bankruptcy*, 14th ed. M. Bender, 1940 (loose-leaf, updated to 1978).

Cooling, Benjamin Franklin, III, and Cooling, Benjamin Franklin. *To the Battles of Franklin and Nashville and Beyond: Stabilization and Reconstruction in Tennessee and Kentucky, 1864–1866*. University of Tennessee Press, 2011.

Daggett, Stuart. *Chapters on the History of the Southern Pacific*. Ronald, 1922.

Daggett, Stuart. *Railroad Reorganization*. Houghton Mifflin, 1908.

Daunton, Martin. *The Economic Government of the World: 1933–2023*. Farr, Straus and Giroux, 2023.

Davis, Burke. *The Southern Railway: Road of the Innovators*. University of North Carolina Press, 1985.

DeCanio, Samuel. *Democracy and the Origins of the American Regulatory State*. Yale University Press, 2015.

Dewing, Arthur S. *The Financial Policy of Corporations*, 4th ed. Ronald, 1920.

Dewing, Arthur S. *The Financial Policy of Corporations*, 5th ed. Ronald, 1953.

Dillon, John F. *The Law and Jurisprudence of England and America*. Little Brown & Co., 1894.

Dimson, Elroy, Paul Marsh, and Mike Staunton. *Global Investment Returns Yearbook*. UBS, 2024.

Edwards, Rebecca. *New Spirits: Americans in the "Gilded Age."* 3rd ed. Oxford University Press, 2015.

Elliot, Sam Davis. *John C. Brown of Tennessee: Rebel, Redeemer, and Railroader*. University of Tennessee Press, 2017.

Ely, James W. *Railroads and American Law*. University Press of Kansas, 2001.

Engerman, Stanley L., and Robert E. Gallman, eds. *The Cambridge Economic History of the United States*. Vol 2. Cambridge University Press, 2000.

Evans, Cerinda W. *Collis Porter Huntington*, vol. 1. Mariners' Museum, 1954.

Faber, Denis, and Niels Vermunt. *Bank Failure: Lessons from Lehman Brothers*. Oxford University Press, 2017.

Foner, Eric. *Reconstruction: America's Unfinished Revolution, 1863–1877*. Updated ed. HarperPerennial, 2014.

Friedman, Lawrence M. *A History of American Law*, 3rd ed. Touchstone, 2005.

Friedman, Milton, and Anna Jacobson Schwartz. *A Monetary History of the United States, 1867–1960*. Princeton University Press, 1963.

Frumes, Max, and Sujeet Indap. *The Caesars Palace Coup: How a Billionaire Brawl Over the Famous Casino Exposed the Power and Greed of Wall Street*. Diversion Books, 2021.

García, Matt. *Eli and the Octopus: The CEO Who Tried to Reform One of the World's Most Notorious Corporations*. Harvard University Press, 2023.

Geisst, Charles R. *Wall Street: A History*. Updated ed. Oxford University Press, 2012.

Glasberg, Davita Silfen. *The Power of Collective Purse Strings: The Effects of Bank Hegemony on Corporations and the State*. University of California Press, 1989.

Glenn, Garrard. *The Law Governing Liquidation*. Baker, Voorhis & Co., 1935.

Goodwin, Cardinal. *John Charles Frémont: An Explanation of His Career*. Stanford University Press, 1930.

Gordon, John Steele. *The Scarlet Woman of Wall Street*. Weidenfeld & Nicolson, 1988.

Gould, Lewis L. *The Republicans: A History of the Grand Old Party*. Oxford University Press, 2014.

Grafton, Anthony. *The Footnote: A Curious History*. Harvard University Press, 1997 (rev. ed. 1999).

Grant, H. Roger. *Follow the Flag: A History of the Wabash Railroad Company*. Cornell University Press, 2004.

Greenberg, Dolores. *Financiers and Railroads, 1869–1889: A Study of Morton, Bliss & Company*. University of Delaware Press, 1980.

Grob, Gerald N. *Workers and Utopia: A Study of Ideological Conflict in the American Labor Movement, 1865–1900*. Northwestern University Press, 1961.

Grodinsky, Julius. *Jay Gould: His Business Career, 1867–1892*. University of Pennsylvania Press, 1957.

Grodinsky, Julius. *Transcontinental Railway Strategy, 1869–1893: A Study of Businessmen*. University of Pennsylvania Press, 1962.

Guzmán, Will. *Civil Rights in the Texas Borderlands: Dr. Lawrence A. Nixon and Black Activism*. University of Illinois Press, 2015.

Hammond, Bray. *Sovereignty and an Empty Purse; Banks and Politics in the Civil War*. Princeton University Press, 1970.

Haney, Lewis H. *Congressional History of Railways in the United States*. Augustus M. Kelley, 1968.

Harrison, Fairfax. *A History of the Legal Development of the Railroad System of Southern Railway Company*. Southern Railway Company, 1901.

Harwood, Herbert H. *Invisible Giants: The Empires of Cleveland's Van Sweringen Brothers*. Indiana University Press, 2003.

Heath, Bennet William. *Practical Treatise on the Appointment, Office, and Duties of a Receiver, Under the High Court of Chancery*. A. Maxwell & Son, 1849.

Hild, Matthew. *Greenbackers, Knights of Labor, and Populists: Farmer-Labor Insurgency in the Late-Nineteenth-Century South*. University of Georgia Press, 2007.

Horwitz, Morton J. *The Transformation of American Law, 1870–1960: The Crisis of Legal Orthodoxy*. Oxford University Press, 1992.

Hooke, Jeffrey C. *The Myth of Private Equity: An Inside Look at Wall Street's Transformative Investments*. Columbia University Press, 2021.

Horn, Martin. *J. P. Morgan & Co. and the Crisis of Capitalism*. Cambridge University Press, 2022.

Hovenkamp, Herbert. *Enterprise and American Law, 1836–1937*. Harvard University Press, 1991.

Hoyt, Franklin "Railroad Development in Southern California: 1868 to 1900." PhD diss., University of Southern California, 1951.

Huffard, R. Scott. *Engines of Redemption: Railroads and the Reconstruction of Capitalism in the New South*. University of North Carolina Press, 2019.

Isenberg, Alison. *Downtown America: A History of the Place and the People Who Made It*. University of Chicago Press, 2004.

Jacoby, Melissa B. *Unjust Debts: How Our Bankruptcy System Makes America More Unequal*. New Press, 2024.

Joline, Adrian H. *Method and Conduct of the Reorganization of Corporations*. Self-published, 1910.

Jones, Jesse H. *Fifty Billion Dollars; My Thirteen Years with the RFC, 1932–1945*. Macmillan, 1951.

Kindleberger, Charles P., and Robert Z. Aliber. *Manias, Panics, and Crashes: A History of Financial Crises*. 5th ed. John Wiley & Sons, 2005.

Klein, Maury. *The Great Richmond Terminal: A Study in Businessmen and Business Strategy*. University of Virginia Press, 1970.

Klein, Maury. *The Life & Legend of E. H. Harriman*. University of North Carolina Press, 2000.

Klein, Maury. *The Life and Legend of Jay Gould*. John Hopkins University Press, 1986.

Klein, Maury. *Unfinished Business: The Railroad in American Life*. University of Rhode Island, 1994.

Klein, Maury. *Union Pacific: The Birth of a Railroad, 1862–1893*. Doubleday, 1987.

Klein, Maury. *Union Pacific: Volume II, 1894–1969*. New ed. University of Minnesota Press, 1989.

Kostal, R. W. *Law and English Railway Capitalism, 1825–1875*. Clarendon Press, 1994 (2004 reprint).

Kraut, Alan M. *The Huddled Masses: The Immigrant in American Society, 1880–1921*. Harlan Davidson, 1982.

Lambie, Joseph T. *From Mine to Market. The History of Coal Transportation on the Norfolk and Western Railway*. New York University Press, 1954.

Lamont, Edward M. *The Ambassador from Wall Street: The Story of Thomas W. Lamont, J. P. Morgan's Chief Executive*. Lyons, 2023.

Langlois, Richard N. *The Corporation and the Twentieth Century*. Princeton University Press, 2023.

Latham, Earl. *The Politics of Railroad Coordination 1933–1936*. Harvard University Press, 1959.

Lester, V. Markham. *Victorian Insolvency: Bankruptcy, Imprisonment for Debt, and Company Winding-up in Nineteenth-Century England*. Clarendon and Oxford University Press, 1995.

Lewis, Albert Lucian. "Los Angeles in the Civil War Decades." PhD diss., University of Southern California, 1970.

Lewis, Howard H. *Derailed by Bankruptcy: Life After the Reading Railroad*. Indiana University Press, 2015.

LoPucki, Lynn M. *Courting Failure: How Competition for Big Cases Is Corrupting the Bankruptcy Courts*. University of Michigan Press, 2005.

Louchheim, Katie. *The Making of the New Deal: The Insiders Speak*. Harvard University Press, 1983.

Lowenthal, Max. *The Investor Pays*. A. A. Knopf, 1936.

Loyal, C [María Amparo Ruiz de Burton]. *The Squatter and the Don*. S. Carson & Co., 1885.

Lubben, Stephen J. *The Law of Failure: A Tour Through the Wilds of American Business Insolvency Law*. Cambridge University Press, 2018.

MacArthur, William Joseph, Jr. "Charles McClung McGhee, Southern Financier." PhD diss., University of Tennessee, 1975. https://trace.tennessee.edu/utk_graddiss/2652.

Magnuson, William J. *For Profit: A History of Corporations*. Basic Books, 2022.

Maitland, Frederic William, A. H. Chaytor, W. J. Whittaker, and John Brunyate. *Equity: A Course of Lectures*. Cambridge University Press, 1936.

Mann, Bruce H. *Republic of Debtors: Bankruptcy in the Age of American Independence*. Harvard University Press, 2002.

Martin, Albro. *Railroads Triumphant: The Growth, Rejection, and Rebirth of a Vital American Force*. Oxford University Press, 1992.

McCann, Thomas P., and Henry Scammell. *An American Company: The Tragedy of United Fruit*. Crown Publishers, 1976.

McCullough, David G. *Truman*. Simon & Schuster, 1992.

Meltzer, Allan H. *A History of the Federal Reserve*. Vol. 2., book 1. University of Chicago Press, 2009.

Mercer, Lloyd J. *Railroads and Land Grant Policy: A Study in Government Intervention*. Academic, 1982.

Millstein, Ira M. *The Activist Director: Lessons from the Boardroom and the Future of the Corporation*. Columbia University Press, 2017.

Miner, H. Craig. *The Rebirth of the Missouri Pacific, 1956–1983*. Texas A&M University Press, 1983.

Minsky, Hyman P. *Stabilizing an Unstable Economy*. McGraw Hall, 2008.

Moody, John. *The Railroad Builders: A Chronicle of the Welding of the States*. Yale University Press, 1919.

Mundy, Floyd W. *Earning Power of Railroads*. Oliphant & Co, various years.

Nelson, Scott Reynolds. *Iron Confederacies: Southern Railways, Klan Violence, and Reconstruction*. University of North Carolina Press, 1999.

Olivares-Caminal, Rodrigo, Randall Guynn, Alan Kornberg, Sarah Paterson, Eric McLaughlin, and Dalvinder Singh. *Debt Restructuring*. 3rd ed. Oxford University Press, 2022.

Olson, James Stuart. *Saving Capitalism: The Reconstruction Finance Corporation and the New Deal, 1933–1940*. Princeton University Press, 1988.

Orsi, Richard J. *Sunset Limited: The Southern Pacific Railroad and the Development of the American West, 1850–1930*. University of California Press, 2005.

Overton, Richard C. *Gulf to Rockies*. University of Texas Press, 1953.

Painter, Nell Irvin. *Standing at Armageddon: The United States, 1877–1919*. W.W. Norton, 1989.

Pak, Susie J. *Gentlemen Bankers*. Harvard University Press, 2013.

Palmer, Harold. *Investment Salvage in Railroad Reorganizations*. Harper & Brothers, 1938.

Parker, Traci. *Department Stores and the Black Freedom Movement : Workers, Consumers, and Civil Rights from the 1930s to the 1980s*. University of North Carolina Press, 2019.

Paterson, Sarah. *Corporate Reorganization Law and Forces of Change*. Oxford University Press, 2020.

Paterson, Thomas G. *On Every Front: The Making of the Cold War*. Norton, 1979.

Pattison, Robert E. et al. *Report of the United States Pacific Railway Commission [and Testimony Taken by the Commission]*. US Government Publishing Office, 1887.

Paul, Arnold M. *Conservative Crisis and the Rule of Law: Attitudes of Bar and Bench, 1887–1895*. Cornell University Press, 1960.

Perkins, J. R. *Trails, Rails and War: The Life of General G. M. Dodge*. Bobbs-Merrill, 1929.

Peskin, Allan. *Garfield*. Kent State University Press, 1999.

Poor, Henry V. *Manual of the Railroads of the United States*. H.V. & H.W. Poor, various years.

Potts, Charles S. *Railroad Transportation in Texas*. University of Texas, 1909.

Ramirez, Salvador A. *The Octopus Speaks: The Colton Letters, Edited, with Notes and Introduction*. Tentacled, 1982.

Reed, S. G. *A History of the Texas Railroads*. St. Clair, 1941.

Resnick, Alan N., and Eugene M. Wypyski. *Bankruptcy Reform Act of 1978: A Legislative History*. William S. Hein & Co., 1979.

Ripley, William Z. *Railroads: Finance & Organization*. Longmans, Green, and Co., 1920.

Rottenberg, Dan. *The Man Who Made Wall Street*. University of Pennsylvania Press, 2001.

Rutberg, Sidney. *Ten Cents on the Dollar; the Bankruptcy Game*. Simon & Schuster, 1973 (BeardBooks edition, 1999).

Sarra, Janis. *Creditor Rights and the Public Interest: Restructuring Insolvent Corporations*. University of Toronto Press, 2003.

Schneider, Gregory L. *Rock Island Requiem: The Collapse of a Mighty Fine Line*. University Press of Kansas, 2013.

Schulman, Daniel. *The Money Kings: The Epic Story of the Jewish Immigrants Who Transformed Wall Street and Shaped Modern America*. Alfred A. Knopf, 2023.

Sexton, Jay. *Debtor Diplomacy*. Oxford University Press, 2005.

Shapiro, Karin A. *New South Rebellion: The Battle Against Convict Labor in the Tennessee Coalfields, 1871–1896*. University of North Carolina Press, 1998.

Skeel, David A. *Debt's Dominion: A History of Bankruptcy Law in America*. Princeton University Press, 2001.

Smith, Bill. *Robert Fleming: 1845–1933*. Whittingehame House, 2000.

Smith, Jean Edward. *Grant*. Simon & Schuster, 2001.

Starr, Kevin. *Americans and the California Dream, 1850–1915*. Oxford University Press, 1973.

Starr, Kevin. *Inventing the Dream: California Through the Progressive Era*. Oxford University Press 1986.

Stern, Philip J. *Empire, Incorporated: The Corporations That Built British Colonialism*. Harvard University Press, 2023.

Stetson, Francis Lynde, James Byrne, and Paul D. Cravath. *Some Legal Phases of Corporate Financing, Reorganization and Regulation*. MacMillan, 1917.

Stevens, Frank Walker. *The Beginnings of the New York Central Railroad; A History*. G. P. Putnam, 1926.

Stover, John F. *American Railroads* 2nd ed. University of Chicago Press, 1997.

Stover, J. F. *The Railroads of the South, 1865–1900*. University of North Carolina Press, 1955.

Strouse, Jean. *Morgan: American Financier*. Random House, 1999.

Summers, Mark Wahlgren. *The Ordeal of the Reunion: A New History of Reconstruction*. University of North Carolina Press, 2014.

Summers, Mark W. *Railroad, Reconstruction, and the Gospel of Prosperity*. Princeton University Press, 1984.

Swain, Henry H. *Economic Aspects of Railroad Receiverships*. Macmillan Company, 1898.

Swaine, Robert T. *Cravath Firm and Its Predecessors*. priv. print by Ad, 1948. Multiple volumes.

Taylor, Virginia H. *The Franco-Texan Land Company*. University of Texas Press, 1969.

Texas Almanac for 1869 and Emigrant's Guide to Texas. Unknown, 1869.

Thomas, William G. *The Iron Way: Railroads, the Civil War, and the Making of Modern America*. Yale University Press, 2011.

Torrie, Virginia. *Reinventing Bankruptcy Law: A History of the Companies' Creditors Arrangement Act*. University of Toronto Press, 2020.

Ulmer, Melville J. *Capital in Transportation, Communications, and Public Utilities: Its Formation and Financing*. Princeton University Press, 1960.

Vance, James E. *The North American Railroad: Its Origin, Evolution, and Geography*. Johns Hopkins University Press, 1995.

Veenendaal, Augustus J., Jr. *Slow Train to Paradise: How Dutch Investment Helped Build American Railroads*. Stanford University Press, 1996.

Waite, Kevin. *West of Slavery: The Southern Dream of a Transcontinental Empire*. University of North Carolina Press, 2021.

Warren, Charles. *Bankruptcy in United States History*. Harvard University Press, 1935.

Wayner, Robert J. *Car Names, Numbers and Consists*. Wayner Publications, 1972.

Welke, Barbara Young. *Recasting American Liberty: Gender, Race, Law, and the Railroad Revolution, 1865–1920*. Cambridge University Press, 2001.

Wheeler, George. *Pierpont Morgan & Friends: The Anatomy of a Myth*. Prentice-Hall, Inc., 1973.

White, Richard. *Railroaded: The Transcontinentals and the Making of Modern America*. W.W. Norton, 2011.

Wilkins, Mira. *The History of Foreign Investment in the United States to 1914*. Harvard University Press, 1989.

Wilmarth, Arthur E., *Taming the Megabanks: Why We Need a New Glass-Steagall Act*. Oxford University Press, 2020.

Wistar, Isaac J. *Autobiography of Isaac Jones Wistar, 1827–1905*. Wistar Institute of Anatomy and Biology, 1914.

Wolff, Joashua D. *Western Union and the Creation of the American Corporate Order, 1845–1893*. Cambridge University Press, 2013.

Woodward, C. Vann. *Reunion and Reaction: The Compromise of 1877 and the End of Reconstruction*. Little, Brown & Co., 1951.

Wren, Harold G. "American Law of Railroad Reorganization." JSD diss., Yale Law School, 1957.

INDEX

absolute priority rule, 217, 247
Acela train, 20
Act of March 3, 1871, 28
African Americans, 28, 37, 93
Agreed System Plan (MoPac), 172, 173
A. H. Robbins, 217
Albertson's, 220
Alleghany Corporation, 147, 158, 166, 169;
    common shares sold by, 175; Great
    Depression and, 148; J. P. Morgan and
    Company and, 167; MoPac and, 174;
    Young and, 172
Allen, Ruth, 88
AMC theaters, 249
American Airlines, 230
American Bar Association Journal, 179
American Railway Improvement Company,
    58, 59, 60, 62, 85
American South, 14, 15
Ames, Frederick L., 55
A. M. Kidder Co., 95
Anderson, Eliza, 158
Anderson, Ernest, 158
Anderson, Robert, 186, 189–193
Anderson, Virginia, 158
Angelo, Gordon & Co., L.P., 256, 263

Apollo Global Management, 221, 245–246,
    263, 269
Apple, 6
Ares Management, 232, 233, 249, 251
Arizona, 63
Articles of Confederation, 114
asbestos, 215, 216, 217, 236
assessments, 22
asset sale, 34
Astor, John Jacob, 25
Atchison, Topeka and Santa Fe Railway, 108
Atlanta Constitution, 194
Austin, Texas, 52

backstop fees, 250, 251, 252, 253
Bain Capital, 232, 255, 257
Baker, George F., 120, 133
Baldwin, Lewis W., 147, 156
Ball, Corinne, 2
Baltimore and Ohio (B&O), 156
BankAmericard, 187
Bankers Trust, 147, 161, 162
Bank of New York, 95, 160
Bankruptcy Act of 1800, 152
Bankruptcy Act of 1898, 153, 155, 178, 275n4
Bankruptcy Administration, 212

Bankruptcy Code, 1, 4, 211; Burger and, 212; personal bankruptcy provisions of, 233; section 365 of, 217; section 546(e) of, 235; section 1123(a)(4) of, 252; section 1124(a)(4) of Bankruptcy Code, 253; tort victims and, 238. *See also specific chapters*
Bankruptcy Code, 1978, 212, 266, 275n4
Bankruptcy Court, 217
bankruptcy courts, 228; in Delaware, 229; Supreme Court and, 239
bankruptcy judges, 228, 267
Barclays, 231
Barnum, William Milo, 60, 61
Barron's, 183
Basic Fun Inc., 256
Baton Rouge, Louisiana, 59
Beard, Charles, 161
Bear Flag Revolt (California), 17
Bed Bath and Beyond, 197
Belk, Inc., 258, 259, 260
Big Lots, 229–230
Big Spring, Texas, 58
Billyou, De Forest, 174
Black, Eli, 172, 221
Black, Leon, 221
"Black Friday" panic, 50
Blackshear, Cornelius, 204
Blackstone Group, 259
Blair, Henry W., 49
Blockbuster Video, 197
Blum, Walter, 270
B&O. *See* Baltimore and Ohio
Bond, Frank, 50, 54, 62, 85
bondholders, 7, 85, 102, 108; Consol, 71; Eastern Division, 86; of East Tennessee, Virginia and Georgia Railroad, 131; foreign, 123, 138; Gulf Coast, 161; Iron Mountain committee of, 161; Land Grant, 104; New Orleans Pacific Railway Company, 86; noninsider, 23
bond market, 7
Borders, 197
Borman, Frank, 223
BowFlex New Jersey LLC, 228
Boy Scouts, 236
Bradley, Joseph P., 27
Brandeis, Louis, 124, 144, 150
Bratton, William W., 219
Brice, Calvin S., 111, 112, 113, 114, 145

Brigade Capital Management, 233
British Empire, 19
Brown, John Calvin, 42, *43*, 62, 78, 81; Congress and, 93; McGhee and, 103; repairs to Rio Grande Division, 97; report on condition of Texas and Pacific Railway Company, 87–88; role in receivership, 89; salary of, 107
Brown v. Board of Education, 170
Brozman, Tina, 203
Brudney, Victor, 265
Budge, Henry, 119
Buffalo Soldiers, 57
Bullitt, John C., 71, 80, 108
Burger, Warren, 212
business bankruptcy, 1, 4, 153
Business Week, 190
Byrne, James, 298n6

Caesars Entertainment Corporation, 247
Caesars Palace Coup, The (Frumes and Indap), 247
Caldor, 197
California, 14, 17; Northern, 140; Southern, 106. *See also specific cities*
California & Texas Railway Construction Company, 34, 36, 39; Dodge and, 56; T. Scott and, 35; Texas and Pacific Railway Company and, 40
Calker, Fritz van, 158
Canada Pension Plan Investment Board, 249
capital structure, 8; of Belk, Inc., 260; of Grants stores, *191*, 200, 221; of MoPac, 142, 158, *159*, 166; of Texas and Pacific Railway Company, 79; of Toys "R" Us, 255
Cardozo, Benjamin, 143
CARES Act, 244, 245
Carlyle Group, 233
Carnegie, Andrew, 26, 286n199
Carter, Jimmy, 212
Catholic archdioceses, 236
Central Pacific, 42, 48, 63
Central Railroad and Banking Company of Georgia, 114
Central Trust Company, 95, 100, 128
Cerberus Capital Management, 220, 221
Chandler, Walter, 179, 332n15

Chandler Act of 1938, 2, 178, 179
chapter 7, 4
chapter 11, 2, 81, 210, 264; absolute priority rule, 217; airlines use of, 218; bankruptcy à la carte and, 251; of Belk, Inc., 258–259; Big Lots and, 229–230; changes to, 227–228, 233; companies filing too late, 245; company management under, 8; difficulty of enforcing, 267; drafters of, 266; Drexel Burnham Lambert case, 220; Eastern Airlines and, 234; enactment of, 212; favoring large players, 231; forum shopping and, 228; free-for-all nature of, 268; Guitar Center and, *233*; impact of, 225; important cases in, 9; J. P. Morgan and, 2; jurisdictions for, 229; large cases by year, *214*; Levitz Furniture and, 239; Macarthur Coal and, 252; modern, *214*, 247, 271; Neiman Marcus and, 249; New Deal and, 222; novel use of, 215; path out of, 270; present-day, 243; Purdue Pharma and, 237; reform of, 266; Robertshaw and, 262; RSA and, 243–244; securities in rights offerings of, 253; stability of, 226; Steward Health Care filing, 221; third-party releases in, 217, 236; tort victims and, 238; Toys "R" Us and, 258; unanticipated use of, 217; voting and, 96
chapter X, 178, 179, 180, *180*, 201–202, 265; airlines and, 218; chapter XI and, 269; companies filing too late, 245; Miller on, 210; New Deal and, 225–226, 267; s.2266 and, 211; section 77 of Bankruptcy Act and, 204
chapter XI, 178, 179, 180, 193, 201–202; chapter X and, 269; debtors and, 204; Grants stores case, 203; largest case of, 194; s.2266 and, 211; secured creditors and, 218
Chase Bank, 147, 174, 203
Chemical Bank, 174
Chesapeake and Ohio (C&O), 106, 145, 146
Chicago Tribune, 234
child labor, 87
Chinese workers, 57, 92, 93, 291n81
Christian Union, 80
Chrysler, 230, 231
Circuit City, 230
Citadel Credit Master Fund LLC, 246

Citibank, 195, 203
Civil War (U.S.), 13, 15, 85, 94, 132; corporations and, 19; PRR and, 26
Clayton Antitrust Act, 145
Clyde, William, 120, 125, 126, 127
C&O. *See* Chesapeake and Ohio
Cold War, 165, 168
collective bargaining, 218
Colorado, 58
Colorado Eagle (train), 140
Colton, David, 44
Commercial and Financial Chronicle, 86
commercial landlords, 234
common law, 20
common shares, 102, 175, 252–253
common stock, 103, 115, 149, 252
community of interests, 137, 245
Companies' Creditors Arrangement Act, 254, 266
Confederacy, 15, 42, 85, 94
Confederate army, 16
Confederate sympathizers, 14
Congress, US, 38, 332n15; Brown and, 93; Chapter XI and, 202; gold clauses and, 158, 160; J. Gould and, 81; Great Depression and, 177; J. Pierpont Morgan and, 134; T. Scott and, 41, 48; SEC and, 180
Congressional Money Trust committee, 136
congressional subsidies, 41
consensual third-party releases, 239
Constitution, US, 8
consumer-facing companies, 218
Container Store, 264
Continental Airlines, 217
convict labor, 87, 92, 93
Cooke, Jay, 38
Cooke and Company, 38
Coolidge, Calvin, 150
"Cornerstone Speech" (Stephens), 43
corporate bankruptcy reforms, New Deal, 175
corporate bonds, 7
corporate law, 26
corporate reorganization, 1, 26, 108, 122, 137, 312n71; business bankruptcy and, 153; codification of, 152; global market for, 271; private equity debtors and, 222; reform of, 266; statutes, 204; system, 74

corporate restructuring, 264
corporate structures, 8
corporations: borrowing money, 7; Civil
    War and, 19; early, 18; form of, 6
Coster, Charles, 120, 121, *121*, 128, 131, 135, 142
Coster, F. Donald, 179
COVID-19, 259
Cravath, Swaine & Moore, 154, 174, 269
Crayola, 256
Crédit Mobilier of America, 35, 38
Credit Suisse, 258
Crocker, Charles, 42, 63, 65, 67

Daggett, Stuart, 119, 135
Dallas, Texas, 37, 38
Davidson Kempner Capital Management,
    251
Davis, T. C., 166, 169, 174
Davis Polk, 200–201
Dearmont, Russell L., 164, *164*, 170, 172,
    173, 174
Debs, Eugene, 51
debtor-corporations, 2, 5, 22
debtor-in-possession, 8, 267
debtors, 204, 259
debtor's counsel, 229
DeConcini, Dennis, 211
Delaware, 228, 229, 322n120
Delphi Corporation, 239
Democratic Party, 41, 59
Department of Justice, US, 212
Department of the Interior, US, 37
deposit agreements, 96
deposited securities, 96
deregulation, 265
derivatives, 234, 236
Deutsche Bank, 258, 261
Dickens, Charles, 20
Dickson, Samuel, 71
Dillon, John F., 54, 63, 64, *64*, 70, 75
Dillon, Sidney, 54, 114
Dime Savings Bank, 160
DIP loans, 229–230, 231, 233, 348n51;
    Guitar Center and, 254; for liquidation,
    245; Nieman Marcus and, 251;
    predecessor to, 128; RSA featuring, 250,
    264, 270; structure of, 234; supportive,
    249; Toys "R" Us and, 255, 256; for Yellow
    Corp., 246

dividends, 6
DLJ. *See* Donaldson, Lufkin & Jenrette
Dodge, Grenville, 36, 37, 42, 54, 58,
    84; California & Texas Railway
    Construction Company and, 56;
    sued by shareholders, 61; Wheelock
    and, 60
Domain Land Company, 34
Donaldson, Lufkin & Jenrette (DLJ), 198,
    200
Donovan, William J., 153
Dos Passos, John R., 68, *68*, 69, 70, 72, 81,
    85, 97
Douglas, William O., 177–178, 227
Dow Corning, 236
Drain, Robert D., 237
Drake Committee (Texas and Pacific),
    104–105
Drew, Daniel, 50
Drexel, Anthony, 71, 120
Drexel Burnham Lambert, 219, 220, 236
Drexel & Co., 39, 86
Drexel Morgan, 39, 98, 120, 129; Clyde
    and, 126, 127; First National Bank, 128;
    in-house railroad operations expert, 124;
    Kuhn, Loeb & Co. and, 107; Richmond
    Terminal and, 123; unpaid assessments
    and, 130
dust bowl, 148

early corporations, 18
Eastern Airlines, 222, *222*; annual losses of,
    223; chapter 11 and, 234; labor strikes
    by employees of, 224, *224*; Lorenzo
    resignation from, 225
Eastman, Joseph, 154
East Tennessee, Virginia, and Georgia
    Railroad and Railway, 94, 95, 98, 111,
    112, *112*, 114; bonds of, 115; Cincinnati
    extension of, 130; Dutch bondholders of,
    131; leases held by, 116; preferred shares
    of, 113; Richmond Terminal and, 119
East Tennessee "Improvement and
    Equipment 5s" (bonds), 133
East Tennessee Reorganization Mortgage
    Bonds, 130, 133
Eaton Vance, 263
Economist, The, 115, 188, 190, 225
Elliot Associates, 253

El Paso, Texas, 15, 45, 49, 50, 52, 54, 65
English Bankruptcy Act of 1869, 152
English law, 20
Enron scandal, 213
equity, 20, 23; interest, 247
Erie Railroad, 50, 98, 147
Esper, Mark, 245
Europe, 48
Executive Life Insurance, 220

face value, 6
Faludi, Susan, 220
Faris, Charles Breckenridge, 326n181
favored jurisdictions, 228
federal circuit judges, 21, 22
Federal Reserve, 188
Federal Trade Commission, 162
Felsenheld, David, 62
female attorneys, 204
Fidelity Trust and Safe Deposit Company, 98
Fifth (Southern) Circuit, 27
Financial Chronicle, 97
financial crisis, 2008, 239
financial instruments, 234
Financial Times, 113, 225, 255
Fink, Henry, 126
first day motions, 229
First Nat. Bank v. Flershem, 144
First National Bank, 120, 125, 128, 133, 147
Fisk, James, 50, 69
Fleming, Robert, 95, 98, 100, 103, 104, 112
Foohey, Pamela, 236
Forbes, 184
Ford Foundation, 170
foreclosure, 19, 279n51; receivers and, 20; reorganization plans and, 20; traditional process of, 21
foreclosure sales, 105, 133; limitations of, 20; Pardee confirmation of, 106
foreign bondholders, 123, 138
foreign railroad investment, 123
Forrest, Nathan Bedford, 132, 135
Fort Worth, Texas, 29, 38, 40, 54, 65
Fort Worth Belt Railway, 148
42nd Ohio Volunteer Infantry, 81
forum shopping, 228, 268
Frankfurter, Felix, 150, 154, 165, 171
Franklin Mutual Advisers, LLC, 256

Frémont, John C., 17, 18, 25, 28, 30, 31
Friendly, Henry, 143
friendly creditor approach, 298n6
Frumes, Max, 247
Fry, Charles M., 95, 100
FTX, 213
Fund for the Republic, 170

Galgay, John J., 195, 204
Galveston, Texas, 52, 67, 140
Garfield, James A., 81, 82
general bankruptcy law, 152
General Motors, 223, 230, 231
Genesco, Inc., 197, 201
Georgia, 48
Georgia Central, 115, 117, 124, 135
Gilded Age, 17
gold clauses, 158, 160
Goldstein, Marsha, 204
Gould, Frank, 174
Gould, George, 104, 108, 114, 119, 140
Gould, Jay, 2, 7, 9, 50, *51*, 62; American Railway Improvement Company and, 58; assets of, 53; Congress and, 81; corporate reorganization system and, 74; Crocker and, 63; Debs on, 51; declining health of, 115; Dos Passos and, 97; Knights of Labor and, 87; litigation by, 65; losses faced by, 73; McGhee and, 99; Missouri Pacific and, 55, 70; Missouri Pacific bonds and, 68; *New York Times* on, 71; Powderly and, 90; power as controlling shareholder, 108; Pullman and, 54; reorganization and, 122; reorganization plan negotiated by, 83, 85; short-term notes signed by, 75; Supreme Court and, 70; Texas and Pacific Railway Company and, 55; Western Union and, 52; Wistar and, 103, 104; workers' pay cut by, 77
Gould-Huntington agreement, 66, 67
Gould-Southwestern system, 140
governmental participation, 5
Grand Union Company, 197
Grant, Ulysses S., 27, 41, 49
Grant, William T., 2, 176, 183
Grant and Ward panic of 1884, 95
Grant City stores, 184

Grants stores, 180–182, *181*, *182*, 205, 218;
    Annual Report, 1971, 183; ballooning
    short-term debt levels, 186; *Business
    Week* and, 190; capital structure of, *191*,
    200, 221; Chapter XI case, 203; Creditors
    Committee for, 194; customer base
    of, 184–185, 199; employees of, 270;
    going-out-of-business advertisement,
    196; in-house credit program of, 187;
    J. P. Morgan and Company and, 204;
    landlord claims and, 204; liquidation
    of, 195–196, 201; loan deal signed by,
    188; losses projected by, 192; negative
    net worth of, 193; *New York Times* and,
    198, 201; products at, *185*; receivables
    and short-term liabilities for, *184*;
    reorganization plan for, 198, 199, *199*;
    SEC and, 194, 201; secured debt obtained
    by, 189; *Women's Wear Daily* and, 187, 191
Gray, John A. C., 27, 28, 32, 34
Great Depression, 5, 26, 100, 145; Alleghany
    Corporation and, 148; Congress and, 177;
    Young and, 167
Green, John P., 54
Greenberg, Dolores, 35
Grodinsky, Julius, 54, 70
*Group of Institutional Investors v. Chicago,
    Milwaukee, St. Paul & Pacific Railroad
    Company*, 163
GSO Capital, 259
Guaranty Trust Company, 147
Guitar Center, 232, 233, *233*, 253, 254
Gulf Coast Lines, 140, 169; bondholders, 161;
    sold to MoPac, 162

Hall, Charles, 88, 89, 90, 93
Hall, R. B., 17, 19, 20, 24
Hall, W. C., 24, 97
Hamilton-Jefferson conflicts, 41
Harkin v. Brundage, 143
Harrah's Entertainment Inc., 247
Harriman, Edward Henry, 115, 129, 135
Harris, Josh, 221
Hart, E. B., 54
Hart, John L. J., 172, 173
Harvard Law Review, 177
Harvard Law School, 150
Hastings-Michener Bill, 153
Hayes, Rutherford B., 59

health insurance funds, 245
Henry Clews & Co, 38
Highland Capital Management, LP, 256
high-yield bonds, 219
Hilmer, Lucian, 165
Hing, Sam, 93
Hinsey, Joseph, 192, 193
Hoover, Herbert, 149, 153, 155
Hopkins, Mark, 42
House of Representatives, 48
Houston, Texas, 52, 228, 262
Howard County, Texas, 81
Hoxie, H. M., 90, 303n110
H.R.6, 210
H.R. 6439, 332n15
H.R.8200, 210, 211
Huidekoper, Frederic W., 125
Humphreys, Solon, 54, 75
Huntington, Arabella, 145
Huntington, Collis Potter, 42, 44–45, 48, 63,
    66, 145
Huntington, Henry E., 145
Hutchinson, John N., 86

Icahn, Carl, 223
ICC. *See* Interstate Commerce Commission
iHeart Communications, Inc., 264
income bonds, 69, 83
Indap, Sujeet, 247
Ingraham, John, 195
Inman, John H., 117
In re Metropolitan Railway Receivership
    (Supreme Court, US), 139
insider-shareholders, 38
institutional investors, 171, 177, 244
International Association of Machinists, 223
International & Great Northern Railroad,
    52, 140
Interstate Commerce Act, 268
Interstate Commerce Commission (ICC),
    55, 150, 155, 162–163; Agreed System
    Plan, 172, 173; hearings held by, 172;
    institutional investors and, 171; valuation
    errors by, 165
Interstate Stores, Inc., 180
Intrum AB, 228
Invesco, 261, 262, 263
Investor Pays, The (Lowenthal), 150, 163, 247
Iowa, 36

Irish workers, 57, 93
Iron Mountain, 62, 75, 158, 166; bondholders committee, 161; Eastern Division bondholders and, 86; MoPac and, 63, 218n8; T. Scott and, 52
Irons, Martin, 89, 90, 93

Jacobs, Marvin, 201
Jacoby, Melissa, 251
JCPenney, 184
Jefferies, 258
Jefferson, Texas, 25
Jenks, Downing, 174
Jim Crow laws, 166, 182
JOANN Inc., 264
Jobs, Steve, 6
Johns Manville, 215, 216, 236
Johnson, Andrew, 42
Joline, Adrian H., 18, 69, 135, *136*, 308n218
Jonesville, Texas, 15
J. P. Morgan and Company, 1, 98, 100, 135, 136, 138, 147; Alleghany Corporation and, 167; chapter 11 and, 2; Grants stores and, 204; Southern Railway Company and, 137
J. S. Morgan & Co., 39, 40
Judges Bill, 209–210
judge-shopping, 268
judicial sale, 19

Kendrick, James, 189, 191, 193
Kentucky, 17
Kimball, Frederick J., 113
King, Lawrence, 209
Kirby, Allen P., *167*
Kirkland and Ellis, 228, 258, 269
KKK. *See* Ku Klux Klan
KKR & Co., 220, 255, 257
Klein, Maury, 27, 90, 118, 123, 135, 290n41
Knights of Labor, 77, 87–89, 90, 92
Korean War, 165
Krasnow, Richard, 197, 204
Kugler & Co., 147
Kuhn, Loeb & Co., 98, 100, 124, 139; Drexel Morgan syndicate and, 107; Milwaukee Road receivership and, 154; MoPac and, 139, 140, 145; Stedman and, 160
Ku Klux Klan (KKK), 28, 42, 132
Kushner Companies, 245

labor strikes, 77, 87, 88, 91–93; by Eastern Airlines employees, 224, *224*; by International Association of Machinists, 223; Teamsters and, 245
La Guardia, Fiorello, 154, 155
land grant bonds, 35, 36, 40, 41, 61, 77, 97, 104
Land Grant committee (Texas and Pacific), 105
land grants, 49, 59, 66, 69; New Orleans Pacific Railway Company and, 61; purchase of, 36; from Texas, 16, 27, 29, 30, 41; for Texas and Pacific Railway Company, 28
land reform, 87
Lanier, Charles, 133
Larson, Raeder, 212
LBOs. *See* leveraged buyouts
Lehman, Mayer, 95, 100
Lehman Brothers, 230, 231, 236, 240
lender-of-last-resort operations, 188
less-than-truckload (LTL), 244, 245
leveraged buyouts (LBOs), 219, 220, 221, 222, 261; of Belk, Inc., 258–259; funding for, 240; immunity of, 236; Neiman Marcus and, 249; of Toys "R" Us, 254–255, 257; of Tribune Company, 234, 235
Levitz Furniture, 239
Levy, Aaron, 211
liability management exercise (LME), 248–249, 263, 264
liability management transactions (LMTs), 248
Life and Legend of Jay Gould, The (Klein), 290n41
life insurance companies, 149
Lifland, Burton R., 215, 217, 223; Shugrue and, 225; Texas Air and, 224
Ligado Networks, 264
Lincoln Logs, 256
Lipton, Martin, 192
liquidation, 8, 18, 247, 270; of Circuit City, 230; DIP loans for, 245; of Grants stores, 195–196, 201; rules of, 4–5
liquidation priority rule, 143. *See also* absolute priority rule
Lisman, Frederick, 137
LME. *See* liability management exercise
LMTs. *See* liability management transactions

lockup agreements, 232
London Joint Stock Bank, 286n199
London & San Francisco Bank, 286n199
long-term financing, 142
Longview, Texas, 34, 37
LoPucki, Lynn M., 213, 222, 231, 258
Lorenzo, Frank, 217–218, 223, 225
Los Angeles, California, 47
Los Angeles Times, 234, 235
Louisiana, 15, 16, 17, 20, 24, 30, 58, 91. *See
    also specific cities*
Louisville Courier-Journal, 48, 50
Louisville Southern, 116
Lowenthal, Max, 150, 151, 152, 161, 163,
    177–178, 247
LTL. *See* less-than-truckload

Macarthur Coal, 252
Mahaffie, Charles D., 173, 326n190
Mahaffie Act, 168, 169
Manhattan Elevated Railroad, 52
Manual of the Railroads of the United States
    (Poor), 24, 49
Markoe, John, 86
Marshall, Texas, 15, 16, 24, 28, 29
marshals, U.S., 91, 92
Master Charge, 187
McCarthyism, 170
McGhee, Charles McClung, 94, 94–95,
    98; Brown and, 103; J. Gould and, 99;
    Norfolk and Western Railway and, 112;
    Richmond Terminal and, 113, 114; Texas
    and Pacific Railway Company and, 111;
    Walters and, 117; Wistar and, 105
McKay, Seth Shepard, 15
McKenzie, Troy, 193
McKinney, John A., 215
McMahon, Colleen, 238
Memphis, El Paso and Pacific Railroad
    Company, 16–17, 18, 34; Gray and, 28;
    land grants for, 27; Texas state legislature
    purchase of, 25
Mexican workers, 57, 93
Miami International Airport, 223
Midland, Texas, 75, 76
Milken, Michael, 219, 220
Miller, Harvey, 2, 195, 197, 210, 236
Milwaukee Road receivership, 154
Minsky, Hyman, 18, 188

Mississippi River, 74
Missouri, Kansas & Texas Railway (MKT),
    52, 54
Missouri Pacific (MoPac), 52, 55, 56, 73,
    83, 84, 156, 172, 221, 254; Alleghany
    Corporation and, 174; American Railway
    Improvement Company and, 60; in
    bankruptcy for twenty-three years,
    164; capital structure of, 142, 158, 159,
    166; claim of, 102; common stock, 103,
    149; counsel for, 81; Cravath, Swaine &
    Moore, 154; earnings of, 163; J. Gould
    and, 70; Gulf Coast Lines sold to, 162;
    Iron Mountain and, 63, 218n8; Kuhn,
    Loeb & Co. and, 139, 140, 145; map of,
    141, 141; receiver appointment to, 79;
    scandal around, 148; second-lien bonds
    bought by, 108; section 20b plan and,
    169; section 77 case of, 170; Southern
    Railway and, 175; Stedman committee of,
    160, 161, 165; subsidiaries combined into
    Missouri Pacific Railroad, 172; Terminal
    bonds and, 100; Texas and Pacific
    Railway Company and, 140, 174; Truman
    and, 152; voting control of, 147; workers
    on strike at, 77
MKT. *See* Missouri, Kansas & Texas
    Railway
Mnuchin, Steve, 245
monetary reform, 87
money markets, 185, 187
Money Trust, 134, 150
Moody, John, 121, 132
Moody's, 169, 254
MoPac. *See* Missouri Pacific
Morgan, J. Pierpont, 9, 101, 104, 115, 135,
    146; Clyde and, 126; Congress and,
    134; Drexel Morgan and, 120; foreign
    bondholders and, 123; Money Trust
    hearings and, 150; Northern Pacific
    Railroad and, 142; reorganization and,
    122; Richmond Terminal and, 133
Morgan, J. S., 101, 120, 131
Morgan Guaranty Trust Company, 186
Morganization plans, 122
Morgan Stanley, 259
Morosini, G. P., 58
Morse, Samuel F. B., 41
mortgage bonds, 102

Munsert, Helen Walter, 170
Musk, Elon, 7

Nation, The, 41
National Bankruptcy Conference, 210
National City Bank, 147
National Conference of Bankruptcy Judges, 209
Native Americans, 36, 57, 58
Nazi Party, 158
Neiman Marcus, 249, 250, *250*, 251
Nelson, Scott Reynolds, 43
Newark, New Jersey, 27
Newcomer, Benjamin F., 86
New Deal, 1, 4, 137, 150, 154, 158; approach to public companies, 211; chapter 11 and, 222; chapter X and, 225–226, 267; consensus, 178; corporate bankruptcy reforms, 175; reform efforts of, 9
New Hampshire, 49
New Jersey, 27, 228
New Mexico, 16, 63, 65
New Orleans, Louisiana, 15, 65, 66, 67
New Orleans, Texas and Mexico Railway, 140
New Orleans Division (Texas and Pacific), 76, 84
New Orleans Pacific Railway Company, 59, 98; bondholders, 86; construction bonds, 60; land grants and, 61
New York Central, 145, 156, 185
New York City, 17, 53
New York Herald, 117
New York Life Insurance Co., 137
New York Stock Exchange, 147
New York Times, 48, 59, 86, 102, 127, 174; on J. Gould, 71; Grants stores and, 198, 201; on Johns Manville, 216
New York Tribune, 39
Nickel Plate, 145
Nine West, 236
Nomura, 258
nonemployee tort claimants, 2
noninsider bondholders, 23
nonpaying shareholders, 131
Norfolk and Western Railway, 112, 113, 118
North Carolina Mutual Life Insurance, 182
Northeastern Texas, 25
Northern California, 140

Northern Pacific Railway Company, 38, 142
Northern Pacific Railway Co. v. Boyd, 142, 168
Northern railroads, 16
Northwestern Mutual, 158

Oakland, California, 140
Oakman, Walter, 119, 124, 126
Oaktree Capital Management, L.P., 256
Odinet, Christopher K., 236
Office of the United States Trustee, 212, 213
Olcott, Frederick, 95, 100, 102, 118
Olcott-Fleming committee, 100, 103, 104
One Rock Capital Partners, 261

Pacific Electric Railway, 145
Pacific Investment Management Co. (PIMCO), 250
Pacific Railway Improvement Company, 53, *53*, 54, 56, 58, 291n71; building west, 57; shareholders of, 55
Palestine, Texas, 52
Panic of 1873, 38, 47, 95
Panic of 1893, 153
Pardee, Don, 80, 81, 82, 85, 91, 267; foreclosure sales confirmed by, 106; Knights of Labor and, 92
Paris, Texas, 29
Parsons, Richard C., 31
Party City, 264
par value, 6
Patterson, Belknap, Webb & Tyler, 211
pay-in-kind (PIK) toggle notes, 250
Payne, Oliver H., 119
Peabody Energy Corporation, 252, 253
Pecora, Ferdinand, *146*
Pendergast machine, 164–165
Penn Central, 188, 194
Pennsylvania Company, 26
Pennsylvania Railroad (PRR), 25, 33, 38, 52, 100; Civil War and, 26; T. Scott and, 48, 49, 61; Texas and Pacific Railway Company and, 39
Pennzoil, 215
Pere Marquette Railway, 147
Perkins, William H., 119
personal bankruptcy provisions, 233
Philadelphia and Reading Railroad Company, 22

Philadelphia Inquirer, 48, 67, 105, 117
Pierrepont, Edwards, 25, 32
PIK. *See* pay-in-kind
PIMCO. *See* Pacific Investment
    Management Co.
Pittsburgh, Fort Wayne and Chicago
    Railway, 20, 26
Plessy v. Ferguson, 132
PNC Bank, 261
PODs. *See* private equity–owned debtors
Poor, Henry, 24, 49
Potter, Phillip, 200
Powderly, Terrance, 89, 90
Powers, Richard C., 30
prebankruptcy solicitation of plans, 212

preferred shares and stock, 130, 252
private equity firms, 221, 247, 256
private equity funds, 236
private equity–owned debtors (PODs), 222,
    247, 249, 251, 254
Progressive Era, 150
PRR. *See* Pennsylvania Railroad
Prudential Insurance, 160
public-company corporate bankruptcy, 211
Pueblo, Colorado, 140
Pullman, Geo. M., 54
Purdue Pharma, 237, *237*

qualified institutional buyers (QIBs), 268,
    350n25

race, 132–133, 182
Railroad Builders, The (Moody), 132
railroads: crossing state lines, 20;
    English developers of, 17; failed, 129;
    infrastructure related to, 18; insolvencies
    of, 20; quasi-public nature of, 18; as
    single-state operations, 21; Southeastern,
    276n2; type of, 13; after World War
    II, 177. *See also specific lines; specific
    railroads*
Reading *Railroad*, 22
Reagan, Ronald, 113
real estate investment trusts (REITs), 188,
    255
receivers, 20; appointment of, 22;
    appointment to Missouri Pacific, 79;
    traditional function of, 21

receiverships, 20, 34, 78, 142, 153; bad
    reputation of, 23, *24*; Brown role in, 89;
    form of, 80; institution of, 22; judicial
    pushback against, 144–145; Milwaukee
    Road, 154; of Texas and Pacific Railway
    Company, 122; viability of, 143
Reconstruction, 28, 81
Reconstruction Finance Corporation
    (RFC), 149, 156, 166
REITs. *See* real estate investment trusts
reorganization committee, 86
reorganization plans, 179; foreclosure and,
    20; J. Gould negotiation of, 83, 85; for
    Grants stores, 198, 199, *199*; intermediate
    creditors, 143; Johns Manville, 215;
    receivership and, 20
Republican Party, 28, 45
restructuring support agreement (RSA),
    232, 233, 243–244, 248–249; DIP loans
    and, 254, 264, 270; Neiman Marcus and,
    250; Peabody Energy Corporation and,
    252; terms in, 260; of Toys "R" Us, 257
Retail Dive, 256
RFC. *See* Reconstruction Finance
    Corporation
R. H. Macy & Co., 214
Rice, Isaac G., 104
Richmond and Danville Railroad, 112, *112*,
    119, 120; assets of, 133; common stock of,
    115; receivership petition against, 124;
    slavery and, 132
Richmond Terminal, 112, *112*, 113, 124, 132,
    310n14; bonds of, *116*; common shares
    of, 115; cuts at, 128; Drexel Morgan
    and, 123; East Tennessee, Virginia and
    Georgia Railroad and, 119; exposé
    on, 137; Inman and, 117; McGhee and
    shares of, 114; J. Pierpont Morgan and,
    133; Morganization plans and, 122;
    Oakman and, 126; Olcott and, 118;
    railroads ostensibly controlled by, 115;
    reorganization of, 129, 135, 136, 138;
    shareholders of, 127; Standard Oil and,
    119
Rickenbacker, Eddie, 223
Rio Grande Division, 54, 56, 60, 67–68, 76,
    84; Chinese workers and, 93; in disrepair,
    96; quality of work of, 58; repairs to, 97
Ripley, William Z., 123

Roberts, Marshall Owen, 24, 25, 30, 31, 85, 283n145; on board of Texas and Pacific Railway Company, 33; named president of Texas and Pacific Railway Company, 32

Robertshaw, 261, *262*, *263*; financial troubles of, 262; Invesco and, 263

Rock Island Railroad, 174, 192

Rodman, Charles, 197, 202

Roosevelt, Franklin D., 154, 155

Rosen, Leonard, 195, 198

Roster, Reuben, 125

Rowan, Marc, 221

Royal Bank of Canada, 258

RSA. *See* restructuring support agreement

Ruiz de Burton, María Amparo, 44, 45

S.2266, 210–211

Sackler family, 237, 239

safe harbors (in Bankruptcy Code), 234, 236

Safeway Stores, Inc., 220

Sage, Russell, 54, 55, 70, 75, 114

St. Louis Post Dispatch, 170

Salomon, William, 118

Sam Nassi Company, 195–196, 197, 198, 246

San Antonio, Texas, 52, 66

San Antonio & San Diego Mail (SA&SD), 14

San Diego, California, *37*, 47, 50, 62, 108

San Francisco Chronicle, 48

SA&SD. *See* San Antonio & San Diego Mail

Satterlee, C. E., 85, 86, 95, 108

Schiff, Jacob, *99*, 115, 118, 129; McGhee and, 95, 100, 112; Money Trust hearings and, 150; Olcott-Fleming committee and, 103; reorganization and, 122; Texas and Pacific Railway Company and, 120; Wistar and, 106

Scott, Thomas A., 25, 26, 27, 31, *33*; American Railway Improvement Company and, 58; California & Texas Railway Construction Company and, 35; Congress and, 41, 48; death of, 62; Dodge and, 36; health of, 62; Huntington and, 42; Iron Mountain and, 52; J. S. Morgan & Co. and, 39; PRR and, 48, 49; Ruiz de Burton and, 44; Southern Trans-Continental Railway Company and, 34; stepping down from PRR, 61; Texas and Pacific Railway Company and, 33, 40, 47

Scott, William T., 15

Scottsville, Texas, 15

Sears, 184

SEC. *See* Securities and Exchange Commission

Second Circuit, 235, 236, 238

section 12 of 1898 Bankruptcy Act, 178

section 20b plan, 169. *See also* Mahaffie Act

section 77B of Bankruptcy Act, 177–178, 179, 212, 277

section 77 of Bankruptcy Act, 155, 156, 157, 163, 164, 168, 170, 175, 194, 204, 277

section 546(e) of Bankruptcy Code, 235

section 1123(a)(4) of Bankruptcy Code, 252

section 1124(a)(4) of Bankruptcy Code, 253

secured bonds, 17

secured creditors, 218

Securities and Exchange Commission (SEC), 74, 122, 124, 162; as bankruptcy-focused administrative agency, 209; chapter X and, 265; Congress and, 180; Grants stores and, 194, 201; Levy and, 211; Office of the United States Trustee and, 212; as perceived source of slowdowns, 202; on prearranged reorganizations, 178; protecting small investors, 177

Seligson, Charles, 195

Serta Simmons Bedding, 249, 262–263, 269

Shapiro v. Wilgus, 143

shareholders, 7, 23, 84; common, 169; Dodge sued by, 61; insider, 38; insider-shareholders, 38; nonpaying, 131; of Pacific Railway Improvement Company, 55; preferred, 169; private equity firms and, 247; of Southern Pacific Railroad Company, 35; of Southern Trans-Continental Railway Company, 31, *31*

Sheldon, Lionel A., 30, 81, *82*; Knights of Labor and, 90; repairs to Rio Grande Division, 97; report on condition of Texas and Pacific Railway Company, 87–88; resignation of, 106

Sherman, George, 128

Sherman, Texas, 29, 37

Sherman and Sterling, 154

short-term notes, 75

Shreveport, Louisiana, 16, 17, 24, 34, 40

Shugrue, Martin, 225

Sierra Blanca, Texas, 66, 108
Silverman, Leon, 216
Simpson, John Woodruff, 60
Singer Company, 187
Six Companies, 92
Skeel, David, 122
slavery, 14, 15, 132
Slocum, Joseph J., 54
Socorro, New Mexico, 82
Solus Alternative Asset Management LP, 256, 348n51
Southeastern railroads, 276n2
Southern California, 47, 106
Southern District of Texas (Houston), 258
Southern Pacific Railroad Company, 14, 15, 16–17, 24, 32, 42; building east, 57; foreclosure sales and, 19; Gould-Huntington agreement and, 66, 67; Huntington and, 44; New Mexico and, 63; New Orleans and, 65; as "The Octopus," 43; San Diego and, 50; shareholders of, 35; special board meeting of, 34
Southern Railway Company, 128, 130, 132, 138; C. Coster and, 135; J. P. Morgan and Company and, 137; MoPac and, 175
Southern Railway Security Company, 26, 38, 42, 85, 95, 112
Southern Trans-Continental Railway Company, 25, 28, 30; bond donations to, 32; T. Scott and, 34; shareholders of, 31, 31
S&P 500, 105
Spaulding, Asa T., 182
special masters, 21
Spencer, Samuel, 124, 125, 126, 128, 132, 135
Speyer & Co., 118
Squatter and the Don, The (Ruiz de Burton), 44, 45
S. S. Kresge, 200
Standard Oil, 119
Stanford, Leland, 42, 45
State of Michigan v. Michigan Trust Co., 144
statutory law, 5
Stedman, John, 160, 161, 165, 178
Stephens, Alexander H., 43, 48
Steward Health Care, 221
Stewart, W. R., 25
stockholders, 23

Stokes, Edward Stiles, 69
Stone, Harlan Fiske, 321n101
Sugar Trust, 69
Sullivan and Cromwell, 197
Sun, The, 75
Sun Capital Partners, 261
Sundman, John, 187, 188, 192, 193, 197
Supreme Court, US, 21, 28, 38, 69, 124, 132, 142–143, 165; bankruptcy courts and, 239; Chapter XI and, 202; crackdown from, 228; J. Gould and, 70; In re Metropolitan Railway Receivership, 139
Swaine, Robert, 154
SWF Holdings I Corp., 264
Sycamore Partners, 236, 256, 258–259

Taft, William Howard, 143
Tappen, Frederick D., 119
Taubes, Jacqueline, 204
Teamsters, 244, 245
Tehachapi Pass, 65
10th Cavalry, 57
Texaco, 214–215
Texarkana, Texas, 29, 37, 52
Texas, 14, 20; land grants from, 16, 27, 29, 30, 41; Northeastern, 25, 67; slave economy within, 15; Southern District of Texas (Houston), 258; state legislature of, 25. See also specific cities
Texas Air, 217, 223, 224
Texas and Pacific Railway Company, 7, 28, 29, 30, 37, 56, 57, 169, 254; Bond and, 54; bonds from, 34, 39; charter of, 58; Chinese workers and, 93; complex capital structure of, 79; Confederacy and, 42; congressional subsidies for, 41; counsel for, 81; debt of, 77; Dodge and, 36, 37; Eastern Division, 67, 70, 71, 84, 86; 1875 annual report, 284n151; Fourth Annual Report, 40; J. Gould and, 52, 55; Gould-Huntington agreement and, 66, 67; Iron Mountain and, 62; Joline and, 308n218; Kuhn, Loeb & Co. and, 139; land grants for, 49; litigation and, 70; map of, 141, 141; McGhee and, 111; MoPac and, 140, 174; MoPac claims against, 84; never under bondholder control, 108; New Mexico, 65; Olcott-Fleming committee and, 100; Parsons

and, 31; PRR and, 39; quality of work
of, 58; receivership of, 122; receivership
petition, 3; reorganization of, 74, 136;
repairs to, 102; report on condition of,
87–88; rights in Arizona, 63; Roberts
named president of, 32; Roberts on
board of, 33; sale of, 32; San Diego
lawsuit against, 50; Schiff and, 120;
T. Scott and, 33, 40, 47; strikers
and, 91; *Third Annual Report*, 40,
41; underperforming, 68; wings of,
84; Wistar and, 86; workers on strike
at, 77
Texas Pacific Group, 221
Texas Pacific Land Trust, 105
Thacher, Thomas, 60, 153
Third Annual Report (Texas and Pacific
Railway Company), 40, 41
third-party releases, 217, 236
Thomas, Anthony J., 128
Thomas, Dylan, 258
Thomas, Samuel, 111, 112, 113, 114, 128,
138, 145
Thompson, Guy A., 156–157, *157*, 165, 172
Thomson, J. Edgar, 25, 26, 27, 280n64
363 sales, 230, *231*, 240, 247
TIA. *See* Trust Indenture Act
Tilden, Samuel, 280n64
Todd, J. Kennedy, 100
tort claimants, 8
tort litigation, 217
tort victims, 215, 217, 236, 238
Toyah, Texas, 58
Toys "R" Us, 180, 254–258, *257*, 270
TPG Inc., 221, 248
transcontinental railroads, 13–14
Tribune Company, 234, 235
Truman, Harry S., 150, *151*, 152, 161,
165, 168
Trump, Donald, 220, 232, 245
Trust Indenture Act (TIA), 162
Turner, George Kibbe, 121
TWA, 218, 223, 230

Union Pacific, 25, 35, 129; chartered by
Congress, 38; Dodge and, 36; J. Gould
and, 53; J. Gould buying shares in, 50
Union Pacific–Central Pacific line, 38
union pension funds, 245

United States Bankruptcy Court for the
Eastern District of Virginia (Richmond
Division), 254
unpaid assessments, 130
unsecured trade creditors, 23
unskilled workers, 92, 93
Untermyer, Samuel, 150
Utah, 36

Vanderbilt, Cornelius, 50
Van Sweringen, Mantis James, 145, *146*, 147,
148, 161, 165
Van Sweringen, Oris Paxton, 145, *146*, 147,
148, 161, 165
Veritas, 264
Vicksburg Railroad Company, 59, 60, 61
Vornado Realty, 255

Wabash, St. Louis, & Pacific Railroad Co.,
54, 73–74, 90–91
Wachtell, Lipton, Rosen & Katz, 192,
193, 199
wage system, 87
Wall Street Journal, 130, 134, 194, 216
Walters, William T., 85, 98, 100, 117
Wardall, William Jed, 179
Warren, Elizabeth, 4
Washington, D.C., 27
Washington Post, 75
Waskom, Texas, 15
watered stock, 6
Webber, Paine, 147
Weil, Gotshal & Manges, 195, 197, 200, 202
Wells Fargo, 258–259
Western Union, 52, 53
WeWork, 213
Wheeler, Burton K., 150, *167*, 168
Wheelock, Edward B., 60, 61
White, Richard, 14, 39
White & Case, 192
Wilmington, Delaware, 229
Winsor, Robert, 86
Wistar, Isaac, 71, 72, 77–78, 80, 83–85,
301n63; J. Gould and, 103, 104; McGhee
and, 105; proposed plan of, 97, 99, 103;
Schiff and, 106; securities deposited
with, 98; Texas and Pacific Railway
Company and, 86
Wistar-Fleming committee, 104

Wistar-Fleming plan, 106
Woerishoffer, C. F., 54, 58
Women's Wear Daily, 187, 191, 201
WorldCom scandal, 213
World War I, 135, 142, 223
World War II, 152, 165, 177
Wright, John C., 71

Yellow Corp., 244, *244*, 245
Young, Kolbe and Company, 167
Young, Robert R., 166, 167, *167*, 169, 172, 173, 266
Yuma, Arizona, 65

Zeller's, 189

GPSR Authorized Representative: Easy Access System Europe, Mustamäe tee
50, 10621 Tallinn, Estonia, gpsr.requests@easproject.com

www.ingramcontent.com/pod-product-compliance
Lightning Source LLC
Chambersburg PA
CBHW030450210326
41597CB00013B/607